Moving to ASP.NET: Web Development with VB .NET

STEVE HARRIS AND ROB MACDONALD

Apress™

ISBN (pbk): 1-59059-009-0

Printed and bound in the United States of America 12345678910

Technical Reviewer: Scott Brown
Editorial Directors: Dan Appleman, Peter Blackburn, Gary Cornell, Jason Gilmore, Karen Watterson, John Zukowski
Managing Editor: Grace Wong
Project Manager and Production Editor: Laura Cheu
Copy Editors: Christina Vaughn and Kim Wimpsett
Compositor: Impressions Book and Journal Services, Inc.
Indexer: Rebecca Plunkett
Cover Designer: Tom Debolski
Marketing Manager: Stephanie Rodriguez

Distributed to the book trade in the United States by Springer-Verlag New York, Inc., 175 Fifth Avenue, New York, NY, 10010 and outside the United States by Springer-Verlag GmbH & Co. KG, Tiergartenstr. 17, 69112 Heidelberg, Germany.
In the United States, phone 1-800-SPRINGER, email orders@springer-ny.com, or visit http://www.springer-ny.com.
Outside the United States, fax +49 6221 345229, email orders@springer.de, or visit http://www.springer.de.

For information on translations, please contact Apress directly at 2560 9th Street, Suite 219, Berkeley, CA 94710.
Email info@apress.com or visit http://www.apress.com.

The source code for this book is available to readers at http://www.apress.com in the Downloads section. You will need to answer questions pertaining to this book in order to successfully download the code.

To my daughter, Rebecca Harris, on the day of her fifth birthday
—Steve Harris

To my parents, Barbara and Ken Macdonald
—Rob Macdonald

Contents at a Glance

Contents

Foreword

I REMEMBER ATTENDING A LUNCHEON ONCE where Alan Cooper (the "father of Visual Basic") discussed that nobody likes to feel like a beginner, at least not for long. This has been in my thoughts frequently during the past year, because if there is one thing that .NET has certainly done, it has made all of us feel like beginners again.

And as fun as it is to study all of this new material, we can't help but look forward to the time when we can feel confident—if not in being an expert, at least in no longer being a beginner.

Books can play a crucial role in this process.

You see, Microsoft's documentation excels in two areas: It provides a comprehensive reference to .NET, and it provides introductory material to help you get started. However, where it consistently falls flat is in its ability to help programmers bridge that gap from beginner to expert. It's that crucial intermediate area where books play such a key role. They can bring you from a place where you sort of know how things work and are able to perform basic tasks, to where you have a solid understanding of the technology and the confidence to recognize trouble spots—and how to avoid them.

That is what I was looking for when I started reading this book. I already had a basic understanding of ASP.NET and had created some simple applications, not really understanding exactly what was going on. I sort of knew what "code-behind" and "postback" meant, and I could use them. But I really didn't understand as well as I wanted to. I had this nagging feeling that I might be making mistakes due to this lack of understanding, and that there might be features in ASP.NET I should be using, but of which I was not aware (a common predicament in .NET). I also wanted a good book that I could share with the rest of Desaware's developers, since we are looking at doing more work in the ASP.NET arena. Above all, I did not want yet another manual rehash or generic introduction to ASP.NET where you have to read most of the way through the book before you see anything new.

Well, my hat's off to Steve Harris and Rob Macdonald; they wrote the book I was looking for.

Having read this book, I still won't claim to be an expert—I think I'd like to have a few Web applications under my belt before I go that far. But I get it. Now, ASP.NET really makes sense.

- I wasn't a big ASP developer, but I had used IIS applications. Now, I understand how the HTML templates (from Web classes) have been replaced by both controls and data binding (and who would have imagined that data binding was really that easy?).

- Security doesn't scare me any more. I now understand the different approaches available, and I know enough to choose among them.

- I finally understand why datasets have never made that much sense to me. As useful as they are in some cases, I now see that there are many cases where simpler approaches are much more effective.

Teaching a subject is more than just sharing facts and procedures. Steve and Rob take the time to explain how ASP.NET works and why it works. Equally important, they provide a context on which you can base your own design decisions. Take scalability, for example: Microsoft's documentation focuses heavily on how important it is to design for scalability. But Steve and Rob make it clear that designing for scalability has a cost, and it's stupid to focus on scalability if you won't actually have large numbers of concurrent users, or if your business infrastructure couldn't handle them anyway. At the same time, they explain how to make a site scalable (if that's what you need), as well as how to design scalability in from the start rather than trying to graft it in later.

I'm a firm believer that technology should only be deployed to solve a problem—not for its own sake. What I wanted was a book that would teach me enough to decide how to use ASP.NET to solve my problems, not some generic problem, and certainly not the boilerplate problems that Microsoft uses in their examples (sorry, my company isn't named Northwind).

This book nailed it.

Every book is ultimately judged by the person who counts most—the reader—and by how well it meets their expectations. Some of you may find this book too simple (though I find that unlikely), some may find it too advanced (because the authors kindly don't endlessly repeat material that most VB and Web developers already know, assigning that material to appendices that I could safely ignore). But I think most of you will find it a good and useful read. More importantly, I think you'll find yourself in the same situation as I find myself now.

I'm not a beginner anymore.

Dan Appleman
March 2002

Acknowledgments

There are many people who have helped make this book happen, and all of them are due my unreserved thanks and respect. In particular, I'd like to thank Karen Watterson and Gary Cornell at Apress for giving me the opportunity, and Rob Macdonald and Dan Remenyi for persuading me to take it. The team at Apress—including Grace Wong, Laura Cheu, Kim Wimpsett, and Chrissy Vaughn—have performed miracles in transforming my jottings and scribbles into the finished item you now see before you. I'm indebted to our technical editor, Scott Brown, from Microsoft Global Learning Services, who shared his boundless knowledge and enthusiasm throughout the project.

Over the last 18 months there have been many others who have contributed indirectly to this book, by way of their ideas, comments, and experiences. I'd especially like to thank Fraser Mackie, who was willing to trust me when I persuaded him to roll out our first public ASP.NET application with the phrase, "Don't worry—it'll be fine." And it was.

But the greatest acknowledgments must go to my wife, Karen, and my daughter, Rebecca. For the last six months, they've put up with long days and late nights, with weekends when I was glued to the keyboard, and with a vacation where I spent more time with the laptop than I did with them. Without their patience, support, and understanding, I could have never succeeded. To both of them I give my greatest thanks and all my love.

—Steve Harris

Many thanks to Russ Lewis, whose idea this book was. I'd also like to thank Karen Watterson and Gary Cornell at Apress for so enthusiastically embracing the project. I can't offer enough thanks to the wonderful team at Apress, including Laura Cheu, Kim Wimpsett, Chrissy Vaughn, Doris Wong, and Grace Wong and everyone else at Apress who knows how to turn words into a book. I'd also like to thank Steve Harris for allowing me to pretend I wrote half this book.

I've had the pleasure of working alongside some fine people in Microsoft's Global Learning Services team over the past 18 months, most notably Debra Kelly, Parker Lindner, and Katie McGrath; they all deserve thanks, and that's just for putting up with me. Nowhere have I met anyone who can match the sheer knowledge of ASP.NET and grasp of how people learn it than Scott Brown, our wonderful technical editor (also from Microsoft Global Learning Services and also a fine person). Thank you, Scott, the benefits of having a genuine Microsoft expert as technical editor cannot be over-emphasized. Steve and I take full blame for any errors left in the text.

I must also thank Caroline and Graham Parker at VBUG (UK) for giving me the opportunity to train many people in all aspects of .NET whose questions and comments have shaped the contents of this book.

Finally, my everlasting love and thanks to Margaret Feetham, my lifelong partner, for being there.

—*Rob Macdonald*

How to Use This Book

Readers have very different backgrounds. We've tried to organize *Moving to ASP.NET* to accommodate readers with different levels of knowledge about .NET or Web development by placing prerequisite information in appendices at the back of the book, instead of filling up the first few chapters with stuff that many readers will already know.

We expect readers of *Moving to ASP.NET* to come mostly from one of three backgrounds:

- **You're already an ASP programmer, familiar with the pre-.NET technology for Web development on Windows.** You'll know a fair bit about Web development with ASP, VBScript, and Visual Basic and really want to get into ASP.NET quickly. You probably don't have much background knowledge in the .NET platform. We ask you to familiarize yourself with Appendices B, C, D, and E before delving into Chapter 1. You'll find that these appendices provide a useful .NET orientation background for making sense of ASP.NET.

- **You're an experienced Visual Basic developer, familiar with desktop and client/server development, and maybe, n-tier as well.** You've heard that ASP.NET makes Web development more accessible, and are keen to break into the growing community of Internet developers. You are either completely new to .NET or have seen some basic programs—but nothing in depth. You should start with Appendix A and read through to Appendix E.

- **You've already read several .NET books and have some hands-on experience with VB .NET or C#.** You are fed up with wading through three chapters on .NET basics before getting to the stuff you really want to read. You may or may not have Web experience. If you have limited Web knowledge, you should read Appendix A before getting into Chapter 1. If you already understand basic Web stuff, skip the appendices and get started!

Please note that this book is called *Moving to ASP.NET.* Like Dan Appleman's *Moving to VB .NET,* it's aimed at developers who already know how to program in Visual Basic or VBScript, and need a book that talks about ASP.NET and not introductory programming topics. So please don't buy this book if you are new to programming.

HiFlyers

The examples used in this book are based around the IT needs of a fictitious flying club and private airfield called HiFlyers. Since much of the book refers to issues relating to reserving aircraft and flight instructors or processing membership applications and changes, it's worth spending a few moments to familiarize yourself with the basic entities involved in HiFlyers. While it's useful to have a "real-world" scenario at hand, our task is to write about ASP.NET and not flying; so, the organizational needs described in these pages are far simpler than those of any genuine business. Figure 1 (produced using Visual Studio .NET) introduces all the tables in the HiFlyers database.

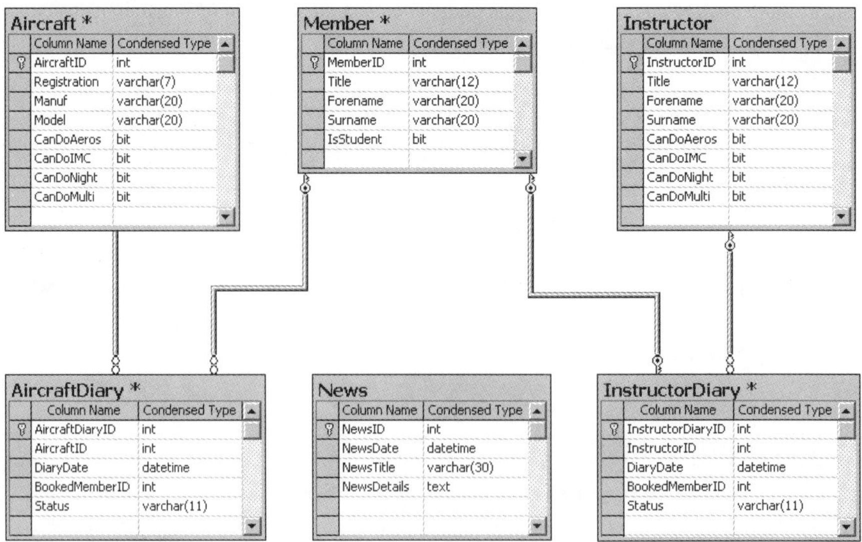

Figure 1. The HiFlyers database

The main entities are aircraft, members, and instructors. The Aircraft table holds identification information about each aircraft and information about its capabilities, which is needed when booking a member for a particular training lesson. Members hold basic name information, plus a flag to identify student members. Student members need to book an instructor for their lessons, and the

Instructor table identifies which instructor can train which skills. Member reservations are stored in the aircraft diary and in the instructor diary when an instructor is needed. Finally, a News table allows mobile phone users to access the HiFlyers system to get relevant news items. You can get SQLServer scripts to create and populate these tables from `www.apress.com`.

Sample Programs, Downloads, and Further Information

We've made all the main code samples used in this book accessible online for download. We have also created working versions of the programs so that you can try them out while reading about them. You can access working versions and downloadable code from `http://www.hiflyers.org`.

Moving to ASP.NET is not a beta book. The samples and techniques presented in these pages were developed and tested on the final RTM version of Microsoft .NET Framework 1.0 and Microsoft Development Environment 2002, running on Windows 2000 Professional and Server versions. Windows 2000 has been updated using the Component Update required before installing .NET. Information about compatibility with released versions of systems not yet released at the time of writing will be published on the Web site.

If you have questions resulting from anything you read in *Moving to ASP.NET* or have comments (good or bad), please e-mail them to us: Steve Harris `steve@hcs-solutions.co.uk` or Rob Macdonald `robm@salterton.com`.

Thank you for buying our book. We hope you find it useful.

CHAPTER 1

Introducing ASP.NET

ASP.NET: The Five-Minute Guide

ASP.NET vs. Classic ASP

Developing Web Applications

Key Concepts for ASP.NET

Understanding Web Applications

Understanding Web Services

Introducing ASP.NET Intrinsic Objects

BY NOW, MOST DEVELOPERS will have heard of ASP.NET and will have seen it in action. In fact, it's a pretty sure bet that if you've bought this book then you already have it installed, maybe with Visual Studio .NET, and there's a good chance you've tried a few things out. You probably already know that ASP.NET brings an object-oriented and event-driven programming model to the world of Web development and that it can dramatically simplify the structure and creation of Web applications. You might, like us, be *really* excited about the possibilities and improvements it brings, or you might just see it as a tool you can use to save a bit of time so you can get to the game earlier or spend more time with your kids. Either way, you can't afford to ignore it—ASP.NET is big news and plays a key role in Microsoft's .NET strategy.

ASP.NET solves many of the problems that currently face Web developers, and it greatly simplifies the tasks of creating, debugging, and deploying Web applications. It's radically different from its predecessors in many ways, but it shares a common heritage and background to some. It requires that you learn new skills and forget about some you already have. It'll take time to master, but that investment will be repaid many times over once you start working with it in earnest. In short, it's what many Web developers have been asking for over the past few years.

ASP.NET: The Five-Minute Guide

Okay, let's start by going (very briefly) back to basics. ASP.NET is the next stage in the evolution of Microsoft's server-side technologies for dynamically creating Web pages. It's a successor to ASP 1.0, 2.0, and 3.0 (now collectively referred to as *classic ASP*) and enables you to do everything that these older technologies could do, plus a whole lot more. Although it's different from its predecessors, it does share many classic ASP language features and supports much of the old object model, thus providing a reasonable amount of backward compatibility.

Classic ASP

Over the past few years, classic ASP has provided a convenient and effective way for developers to build dynamic and interactive Web applications. It's widely used in Internet and intranet applications, and it has found favor with developers who already have experience with other Microsoft technologies. Like every development tool, classic ASP isn't perfect, and the different versions suffer from a variety of limitations:

- VBScript, the language of choice for most ASP developers, is loosely typed, is late bound, and is interpreted rather than compiled. It offers less functionality than its "big-brother" versions of Visual Basic for Applications (VBA) and Visual Basic (VB), even in terms of fundamental requirements such as error trapping and management.

- The design and architecture of ASP applications are different from desktop applications. If we're honest, they're primitive when compared to the object-oriented designs that you can achieve with tools such as VB, Visual C++, and Visual J++.

- Continuing on the theme of architecture, one of the greatest limitations in ASP is the way it requires you to combine interface elements and code into a single ASP file. This is awkward when creating more sophisticated applications and limits code reuse and sharing.

- ASP is largely procedural, with the code within an ASP page being executed from top to bottom on each request. Modern developers are more familiar with object-oriented or event-driven models, both of which offer greater flexibility and savings in development and maintenance time.

- State management techniques in ASP are rather basic, and although they're satisfactory if you're deploying to a single server, they're completely inappropriate if you're hosting the application on a Web farm. *Web farms* consist of multiple servers, each running a copy of your Web application. With the limited state management in classic ASP, each server in the Web farm maintains its own state and is unable to share it with other servers.

- Configuration and deployment of medium- to large-scale ASP applications is cumbersome. You can copy basic content files to target servers with minimum effort, but there remains a variety of manual tasks for configuring virtual directory settings and permissions, as well as the need to register COM components and install Microsoft Transaction Server (MTS) packages and COM+ applications. The situation is further worsened because the Internet Information Server (IIS) Metabase holds IIS and ASP settings, with relatively few tools available to manage them.

- The development tools are rather immature (although usable). Visual InterDev helps developers who are prepared to accommodate its quirks and foibles, but it has the capacity to surprise the unwary user of server components, design-time controls, and so on. Some third-party tools offer improvements in a few areas, but none are perfect.

- Finally, ASP is all about server-side features. Client-side control and interaction is possible but requires manual coding from the developer. This means that pure ASP applications often require frequent server roundtrips, and this in turn often compromises performance.

ASP.NET

ASP.NET is full of new features and improvements, and throughout this book we'll look at all the important ones. It might be useful to start with a checklist of what to look for, though, so you can start planning your approach to learning the tools and techniques. The following list summarizes what we think are the most significant changes and additions; however, once you've spent some time working on your own projects, you may well want to extend this list with some of your favorites:

- ASP.NET is fully integrated with the .NET Framework and with the Visual Studio .NET development environment. It's not a bolt-on addition or afterthought, and ASP.NET applications have full and unrestricted access to all of the .NET classes and features.

- ASP.NET applications are built on top of the common language runtime (CLR) and can be written in VB .NET, C#, or any other .NET-compliant language.

- ASP.NET applications are largely component-based and modularized, and almost every object, page, and HTML element can be a runtime component that can be programmed through properties, methods, and events. The currently supported languages offer full support for object-oriented development, and third-party companies deliver additional languages.•

- ASP.NET applications typically involve less code than classic ASP through the use of Web Forms, server controls, components, and other intrinsic features. Also, the architecture and structure of ASP.NET applications emphasize the separation of code from content, with interface elements held in ASPX files while programming logic is compiled into a .dll.

- ASP.NET provides browser independence, with a base level of HTML 3.2 for older browsers while taking advantage of client-side features in later browsers. ASP.NET causes the same source code to be rendered in the most appropriate form for the browser in use.•

- Powerful server-side controls provide additional functionality and rich content. Validation controls allow for automatic validating and checking of user-entered data, and data-binding features enable the display and updating of compatible data sources, including database and XML information.

- Microsoft has also made available an additional library of server controls (the Internet Explorer Web Controls) that generate rich *client-side* content for clients using Internet Explorer 5.5 or later. This content takes the form of DHTML, JavaScript, and DHTML behaviors to provide an interactive interface including tab strips, tree views, and toolbars, with much of the processing performed in client-side scripts. For clients using other browsers, these server controls render to HTML 3.2 to present a similar look and feel—though in this case any processing will be performed server-side.

- ASP.NET supports numerous caching technologies to allow efficient storage and retrieval of any kind of object or data, including XML, database query results, partial or complete pages, any part of the browser stream, images, and much more. You can associate cached items with a priority that ASP.NET uses as a guide when clearing cached items if space is a premium, so you can preserve items that are costly to rebuild at the expense of simpler items.

- ASP.NET is more crash tolerant than classic ASP, with better and tighter security management. Much of the improvement is because of the .NET environment and CLR, which provides reliable garbage collection, application isolation, thread management, resource pooling, and more. If a Web application crashes, ASP.NET restarts it when the next browser request is received.

- There are major improvements to debugging and error handling, including page- and application-level tracing. Error information can be reliably passed between pages, so that common, centralized error logging and reporting systems can be built. VB .NET supports structured error handling, with consistent reporting of errors and error information regardless of the source or cause of the error.

- ASP.NET supports easy deployment, updates and component management, and text-based configuration through XML documents. You can roll out changes to live Web servers, even while the application is running. .NET objects have no direct dependency on the registry in terms of their location and configuration, dramatically simplifying the tasks of initial deployment and updates.

- The Microsoft development team made sure that Web farms and Web gardens were supported by giving ASP.NET powerful and flexible state management, server independence across page calls and postbacks, and free-threaded components.

- ASP.NET supports creating and managing Web Services, replacing DCOM technology with a solution that is platform neutral and firewall friendly, plus incredibly easy to build, test, and deploy.

As you might imagine, we could continue this list even further, but these details should give you a good idea of what ASP.NET offers. Hopefully these points have also started to make you aware of just how different ASP.NET is from desktop development and from classic ASP Web development. If you want to make the most of these new tools and techniques, then you'll need to invest some time and effort into learning them; it's unrealistic to expect to simply "pick things up as you go." What we aim to do in this book is to give your ASP.NET career a real kick-start, not just by showing what ASP.NET offers but more importantly by showing how you'll likely use it to create real-world Web applications.

ASP.NET vs. Classic ASP

As the previous section highlighted, there are many differences between classic ASP and ASP.NET. They both seek to solve the same problems—the need to deliver flexible and efficient architectures for Web applications, but the way they achieve that goal is vastly different.

Although there are clearly differences in the implementation details, the real difference lies at the heart of ASP.NET, which delivers a truly event-driven and object-oriented development experience. What this means for you and other real-world developers is that you should be able to write less code to achieve the same objectives, which in turn should generate fewer errors and less maintenance. Organizations that have begun developing ASP.NET applications are reporting remarkable improvements in code efficiency and volume compared to older technologies. Compare some well-known sample applications such as IBuySpy (`www.ibuyspystore.com`) and Fitch and Mather (`www.fmstocks.com`), and it becomes clear that the ASP.NET solution can have as little as 25 percent of the code of its classic ASP sibling. Additionally, that code is better organized and structured and is much easier to test, debug, deploy, and maintain.

All this is great news for new developments, but what about existing classic ASP applications; how can they benefit? Well, we've found that the migration process is far from painless, and because of the new programming model, many classic ASP applications would best be rewritten from scratch rather than simply converted. As a result, classic ASP remains a necessary technology for existing installations. As time moves on, we recommend you seriously consider ASP.NET for new projects and for any significant redevelopment or enhancement of current ones, but in many cases it won't be financially viable to convert existing applications.

Fortunately, there's a simple solution; to ease the pressure of migrating from ASP to ASP.NET, both technologies can coexist on the same Web server, and even in the same application. When IIS receives a request, it uses the extension of the requested filename to determine how a request is processed; Filename.asp would be processed using ASP technologies, and Filename.aspx would be passed to ASP.NET. Chapter 10 discusses exactly how this differentiation is achieved. If you've been through previous upgrades of Microsoft's developer tools, you might feel a little suspicious, though—after all, can you *really* run two different versions of ASP on a single Web server? Well, from our experience so far, we would say that you can. It really does seem that there are no serious technical problems or difficulties, although there will be design issues arising from the differences in state management, component management, and so on.

Where we recommend caution is if you try to install Visual Studio .NET alongside Visual Studio 6. In theory this should work fine, as the two environments share few files and should have no conflicting settings. However, where you may notice changes is in terms of the supporting components and technologies, rather than the development tools themselves. For example, Visual Studio .NET installs ADO 2.7 alongside any existing versions and upgrades your browser to Internet Explorer 6.0. Depending on how you've written your code and the features you've used, you may find these newer versions change the way your existing Visual Basic 6 applications behave. On the whole, though, the ability to have Visual Studio 6 and Visual Studio .NET installed alongside each other is positive, giving you the opportunity to build new projects in .NET while continuing to support existing ones with the original development tools.

Developing Web Applications

Many of you reading this book will have strong desktop development skills, and you'll have experience coding Windows Forms, .dll files, and .exe files. You'll be used to the idea that if you put a value into a class-level variable, that value stays there and won't be changed or destroyed except under the control of your code. You'll have used components and controls within your application because you know they can be deployed to client machines with the rest of the application. More importantly, though, you'll be familiar with the way in which events are raised and handled, allowing your code to instantaneously react to almost every user action.

Web development is different. A Web application could be comprised of many different elements, some of which are compiled into .dll files and others are deployed to the server in plain-text form. Web applications don't automatically maintain state for you, requiring that you add code to manage the persistence of values, objects, and any other data you want to keep "alive." Web applications run in a diverse and unpredictable environment, and although you have a certain degree of control over the configuration of the Web server, you have no influence over the client browser's type, version, or configuration.

Also, Web applications have traditionally been procedural rather than event driven, but this is one of the big changes for ASP.NET as it now supports a rich and powerful event model. However, ASP.NET events are generally handled on the server, so actions in the client browser are passed across the network for handling, and the result passed back to the browser. Too many round-trips can cause performance problems, and although ASP.NET provides some facilities for you to minimize and control the number of round-trips, it's up to you to write the code to do so.

Web vs. Desktop Development

To summarize the differences between these development styles, consider the following list of key Web application features:

- **Thin-client**: The Internet is a large and varied environment, and robust Web applications must be accessible from as many different client platforms and browsers as possible. For many developers the solution is to adopt a thin-client design, whereby the application returns browser-neutral HTML to the client, but this approach results in static applications that require round-trips to the server to perform any processing or updates. Contrast this with desktop development where it's usual to have thick-client technology, interactive controls and code, and the ability to access workstation features and software.

- **Rich versus reach**: An Internet developer needs to make a conscious decision to either target specific browsers (and provide a rich and interactive application) or support the widest possible set of browsers (and reach a broader audience). Desktop developers have this decision made for them—the interactive nature of a typical desktop application means that it has specific software and hardware requirements.

- **Round-trips**: Because of the thin-client nature of typical Web applications it's necessary to make a server round-trip to perform any processing, validation, or data retrieval. Each of these round-trips is expensive, however, involving measurable delays as well as the possibility of network errors because of poor Internet connections, routers, and so on. In a desktop environment, the number of server hits can be kept to a minimum through client-side caching, validation, and processing.

- **State and scalability**: You can design desktop applications using a variety of architectures, from monolithic through client-server to n-tier. However, from the point of view of building the client-side code, the developer can be sure that they can store data in memory, save values to disk files if needed, and generally write the code such that it will be used by a single user. The Web environment is different—many users will call a single Web page, often simultaneously, and therefore the code behind the page must allow this level of concurrency while still maintaining each user's information in a suitable way. Failure to design the application correctly leads to a non-scalable architecture, where the performance and reliability degrade quickly as the number of users increases.

In the ASP.NET environment, some of the new features address these problems:

- **Thin-client**: You can configure ASP.NET to generate browser-neutral HTML 3.2, with a minimal dependence on client-side features such as JavaScript support. You achieve this through Web Forms, although their default property settings mean that they're optimized for more modern browsers, in particular Microsoft Internet Explorer 5.5. It's up to you to change the properties to the settings required for your chosen audience.

- **Rich versus reach**: Certain ASP.NET features are able to adapt their behavior according to the browser in use. For example, validation controls are special server controls you add to your Web page to check that the user has entered data correctly. If a JavaScript-enabled browser (such as Internet Explorer 5.5) is detected, the validation controls will be rendered using some client-side code, but if a non-JavaScript browser is identified then the client-side code will not be generated. This adaptive behavior allows developers to take advantage of new browser technologies without compromising support for older standards.

- **Round-trips**: ASP.NET is by definition a server-side technology, so the majority of event handling and processing is on the server. However, there are times when a small amount of client-side code would prevent a server hit, such as in the previous validation control example. In many cases such as this, ASP.NET generates client-side code that minimizes or negates the need for server round-trips.

- **State and scalability**: ASP.NET eases the management of state in Web applications through numerous mechanisms. A special hidden control on each Web Form now stores page state, which is sent to and from the server transparently. This eases the creation of *postback* pages and means that such page state need not be held on the server, thus increasing scalability. Session state, which relates to a single user of the application, can now be stored in a service that is distinct from the Web server or in a SQL Server database. In both cases, you can specify a remote server to ease deployment of the application to a Web farm. You can also control caching options at page or application level, enhancing performance with increasing numbers of users.

The Visual Studio .NET development environment makes it easy for you to build these features into your project, and it makes the process of building Web applications easier than ever. In many cases it does an excellent job of hiding the underlying detail, providing developers with a set of tools similar to the traditional Windows Forms/toolbox combination present in Visual Basic.

In fact, in some ways it's almost too good at hiding these specifics and can lead unwary developers into producing Web Forms that are fully featured but incredibly inefficient. For example, ASP.NET server controls support a property called AutoPostback that causes the page containing the control to be submitted to the Web server if the control is changed or clicked. As you can imagine, incorrect use of this property is likely to result in many server round-trips, and across the Internet this will almost certainly render the application unusable.

Key Concepts for ASP.NET

By now you should have a broad idea of what ASP.NET is about, and you're probably itching to get started. Well, before we jump in and start building, there are just a few concepts to introduce. These really are important, and with a grasp of these ideas you'll find creating and understanding ASP.NET Web Applications to be a whole lot easier.

Web Application

The first concept we'll investigate is a *Web Application*. As you might imagine, a Web Application is pretty central to ASP.NET and Web development in general, so it makes a good start point. There are a number of ways of defining a Web Application, but one that works well for ASP.NET is as follows:

> A Web Application consists of all the files, pages, handlers, modules, and executable code that can be invoked or run in the scope of a given virtual directory (and its subdirectories) on a Web Application server.

If you're familiar with classic ASP then you should recognize this definition, and it's true to say that at first sight, little appears to have changed in the way that ASP.NET Web Applications run. In reality there are big differences, most of which are buried deep in the .NET Framework and supporting technologies. As a developer, you need to make sure the files and content you create are placed into the correct folder, but even that is largely automated by Visual Studio .NET.

It's important to realize a Web Application is different from a traditional desktop application. In particular, Web Applications do not have to be comprised of a specific .exe or .dll file, and they're likely to be made up of many individual files of varying types. In fact, as you shall see later, there's no need to have a compiled .exe or .dll at all—you can create all Web Application functionality with plain-text files.

We'll return to investigate Web Applications later in this chapter in "Understanding Web Applications," but for now let's look at some other important ideas that make up ASP.NET.

Web Form

Web Forms are the most common components in Web Applications. They're the combination of the user interface and the associated logic that gets rendered as a page in the user's browser, and they're implemented in ASP.NET as .aspx files, in a similar way to the use of .asp files in classic ASP. However, where ASP.NET differs is that the associated logic for a Web Form can be written in a powerful and full-featured language such as VB .NET or C# and stored in a compiled .dll. In contrast, classic ASP relies on interpreting scripts embedded in the ASP file itself.

Each Web Form represents a separate page within an application and contains an HTML `<form>` element. Any additional tags, elements, or controls you add using Visual Studio .NET go within the `<form>`, which means that all of the content of a Web Form passes back to the Web server when the form is submitted. To make the creation of Web Forms as easy as possible, Visual Studio .NET provides you with a convenient designer that supports drag-and-drop editing and a What-You-See-Is-What-You-Get (WYSIWYG) viewer. For example, Figure 1-1 shows a simple page in the designer, consisting of labels, text boxes, an image, and a button.

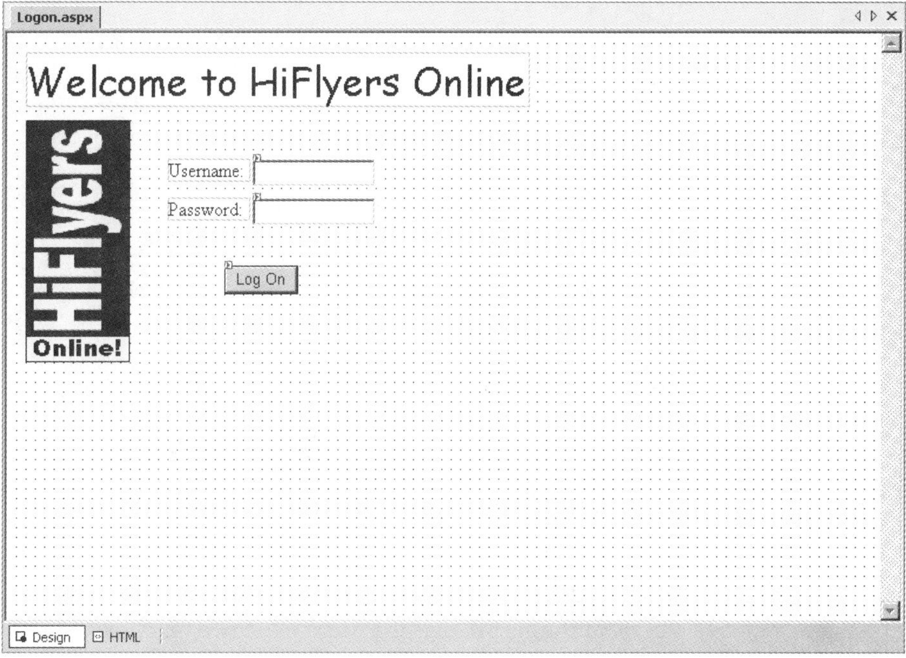

Figure 1-1. The Logon.aspx file

Some of the content added in this example is static HTML, much as you might create using Microsoft FrontPage, Macromedia Dreamweaver, or even Notepad. However, the two text boxes and the button are *server controls* that, as you'll soon see, are intelligent server-side interface objects that allow for easy interaction between your code and the Web Form. If you look closely at Figure 1-1, you'll see that the server controls have a small icon in their top-left corner; static content is not annotated in this way.

It's worth emphasizing that the designer is just a convenient tool for creating a Web Form's content. Anything added to the designer is actually converted and stored as HTML elements, and you can see this representation of the Web Form by clicking the HTML tab at the bottom of the designer. Figure 1-2 shows the HTML View of the Web Form shown in Figure 1-1.

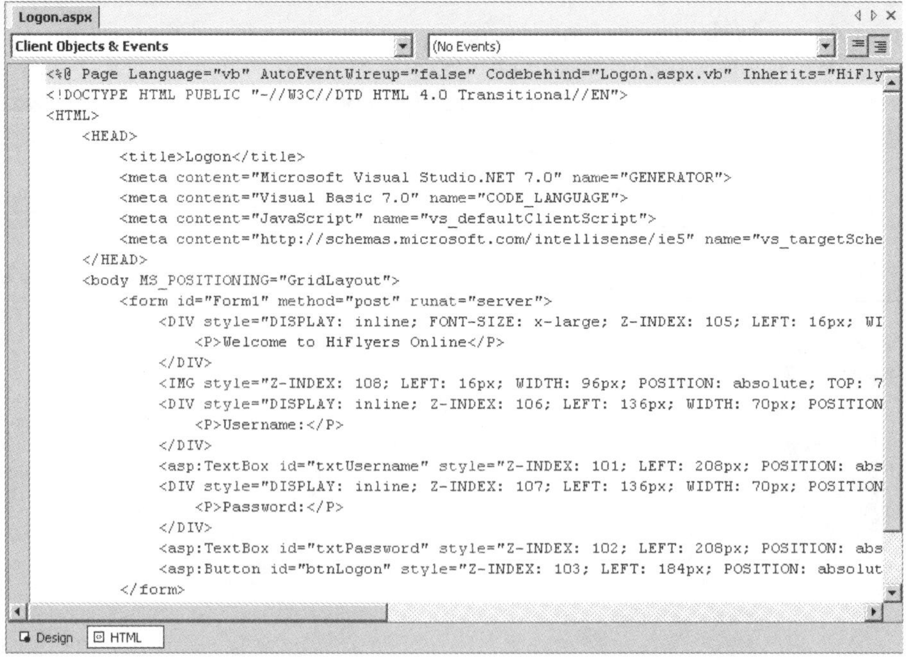

Figure 1-2. HTML View of Logon.aspx

If you're familiar with HTML then you should recognize much of this content. However, look closely at the HTML tags that define the two text boxes and button, and you'll see they have a rather non-standard format, consisting of <asp:TextBox> and <asp:Button> tags as well as a variety of non-standard attributes. Remember that these three controls are server controls—what you're seeing are the server control tags; the HTML sent to the browser by this Web

Form will be quite different, and these server control tags will be replaced with standard HTML elements.

As well as the visual content added in the designer, Web Forms will usually contain code. This may be stored within the Web Form's file itself (<filename>.aspx) or may be placed into a *code-behind* module associated with the Web Form. These modules typically have names that end in .aspx.vb for Visual Basic .NET and .aspx.cs for C# code. We'll return to the topic of code and modules in the "Understanding Web Applications" section later in this chapter.

If you're not familiar with HTML notation, or just want to brush up on your knowledge, refer to Appendix A, which provides an overview of HTML syntax and behavior. Chapter 2 returns to the topic of Web Forms in far more detail, showing how they can be created, customized, and used throughout Web Applications.

Server Control

Server controls are intelligent user interface objects you add to your Web Forms. Some server controls represent simple objects, such as text boxes, buttons, and lists, and others represent more complex structures such as grids, tables, and calendars. Server controls are able to change the way they render their output according to the client browser's capabilities. On modern browsers, they can take advantage of features such as client-side scripts and DHTML to provide a richer and more responsive interface while at the same time maintaining base-level HTML 3.2 support for older browsers. They're also interactive elements, both with the user and with your code. This enables you to manipulate a server control by setting or reading its properties and invoking its methods; at the same time, the user sees it on their screen and can use it in the same way as a regular HTML element.

Server controls can have quite different design-time and runtime appearances. For example, Figures 1-1 and 1-2 showed the Design and HTML Views for a Web Form containing text box and button server controls, but if you view the page in a Web browser and display the HTML source, it appears similar to Figure 1-3.

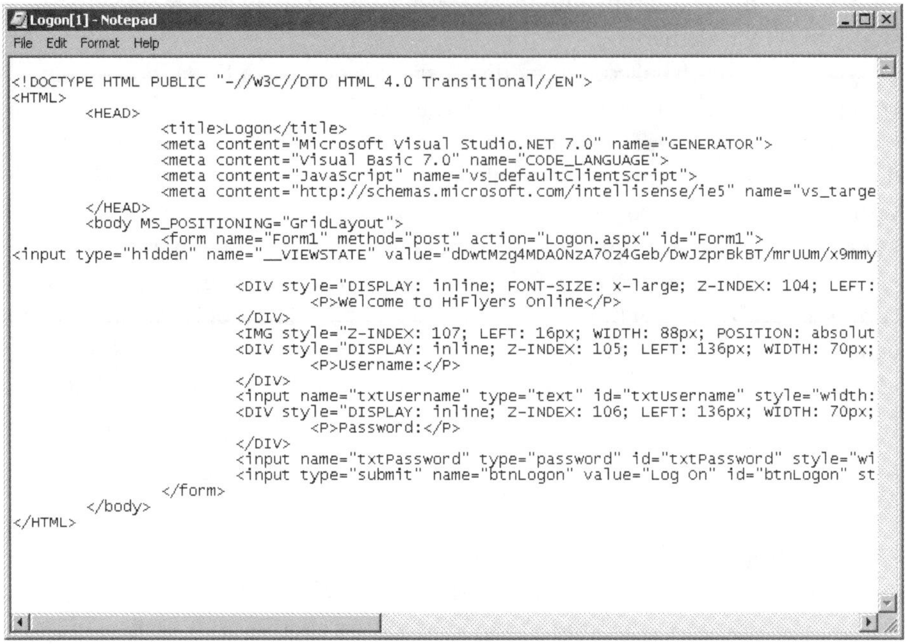

Logon[1] - Notepad

File Edit Format Help

```
<!DOCTYPE HTML PUBLIC "-//W3C//DTD HTML 4.0 Transitional//EN">
<HTML>
	<HEAD>
		<title>Logon</title>
		<meta content="Microsoft Visual Studio.NET 7.0" name="GENERATOR">
		<meta content="Visual Basic 7.0" name="CODE_LANGUAGE">
		<meta content="JavaScript" name="vs_defaultClientScript">
		<meta content="http://schemas.microsoft.com/intellisense/ie5" name="vs_targe
	</HEAD>
	<body MS_POSITIONING="GridLayout">
		<form name="Form1" method="post" action="Logon.aspx" id="Form1">
<input type="hidden" name="__VIEWSTATE" value="dDwtMzg4MDA0NzA7Oz4Geb/DwJzprBkBT/mrUUm/x9mmy

			<DIV style="DISPLAY: inline; FONT-SIZE: x-large; Z-INDEX: 104; LEFT:
				<P>Welcome to HiFlyers Online</P>
			</DIV>
			<IMG style="Z-INDEX: 107; LEFT: 16px; WIDTH: 88px; POSITION: absolut
			<DIV style="DISPLAY: inline; Z-INDEX: 105; LEFT: 136px; WIDTH: 70px;
				<P>Username:</P>
			</DIV>
			<input name="txtUsername" type="text" id="txtUsername" style="width:
			<DIV style="DISPLAY: inline; Z-INDEX: 106; LEFT: 136px; WIDTH: 70px;
				<P>Password:</P>
			</DIV>
			<input name="txtPassword" type="password" id="txtPassword" style="wi
			<input type="submit" name="btnLogon" value="Log On" id="btnLogon" st
		</form>
	</body>
</HTML>
```

Figure 1-3. Browser-side HTML for Logon.aspx

You can see that the `<asp:TextBox>` and `<asp:Button>` tags have been translated to regular HTML `<input>` tags and that the `runat="server"` attribute has gone. Also, although the *id* attribute has been maintained, a matching *name* attribute has been added in the HTML sent to the browser. These changes were made within ASP.NET and were controlled by the logic within the controls themselves. There are other differences, too, including that the second textbox has been rendered to an input element of type `password` as this had a `TextMode="password"` setting in the source file.

However, the really interesting thing about server controls is that, from the point of view of code on the server, the controls are simply programmable objects with rich sets of properties, methods, and events. They're not HTML tags nor elements, and they're not textual definitions that have to be generated by "cookie-cutter" code. They're objects. This enables you to take a completely new approach to Web development and lifts the barrier on structured coding, code reuse, and many other often-requested features.

Postback

Postback is the term given to the process that occurs when a Web Form is submitted. Submission occurs when the user clicks one of the buttons on a Web Form or when some other action causes a request to be sent to the Web server.

The definitive thing about postbacks—that is, the thing that makes them different from other submissions and requests—is that the Web Form is *submitted to itself.* In other words, the code used to process the request and create the next Web page is the same code used to create the current Web page.

The use of postbacks in this way enables ASP.NET to simplify page processing because it ensures that all the logic for handling the Web Form request (which is used when the postback occurs) has direct access to the objects that define its interface. This is the same approach used for Visual Basic desktop development, where each Windows Form contains the user interface objects and the associated code that is executed when events occur for those objects. In fact, as you'll see in the next section, ASP.NET also adopts the concept of events (known as *server events*) that are raised during the postback process.

Postbacks are the default mechanism used by Web Forms in ASP.NET and occur because the `<form>` element within the Web Form has no `action` attribute defined for it. For example, look back at the HTML View of the Web Form in Figure 1-2 and notice that the only attributes are `id`, `method`, and `runat`. Now, look back at Figure 1-3 and examine the `<form>` element sent to the browser. When ASP.NET processed the Web Form, it replaced the design-time attributes with valid HTML settings including an `action="Logon.aspx"` attribute to cause the postback.

If for some reason we didn't want a postback to occur, but instead wanted to submit the content of the Logon form to another page for processing, then at design-time we could define an action attribute that referred to the required page. At runtime ASP.NET will simply pass this through to the browser unmodified.

Server Event

The final concept we'll introduce at this stage is the *server event.* Server events are closely allied to Web Forms and server controls, and indeed these two types of object are the source for many server events. As the term implies, server events are notifications sent to your server-side code from ASP.NET objects, and these events correspond to phases in the page-processing cycle or to actions initiated by the user. Irrespective of the event's cause, when it triggers on the server, your code can respond to it by way of event procedures.

For example, if you return to Visual Studio .NET and double-click the button on Logon.aspx, you're presented with an empty event procedure for the button's click event. Any code you add to this procedure will be executed when the user clicks the button in the browser. Figure 1-4 shows an extract of code to perform simple verification of the details entered into the username and password text boxes.

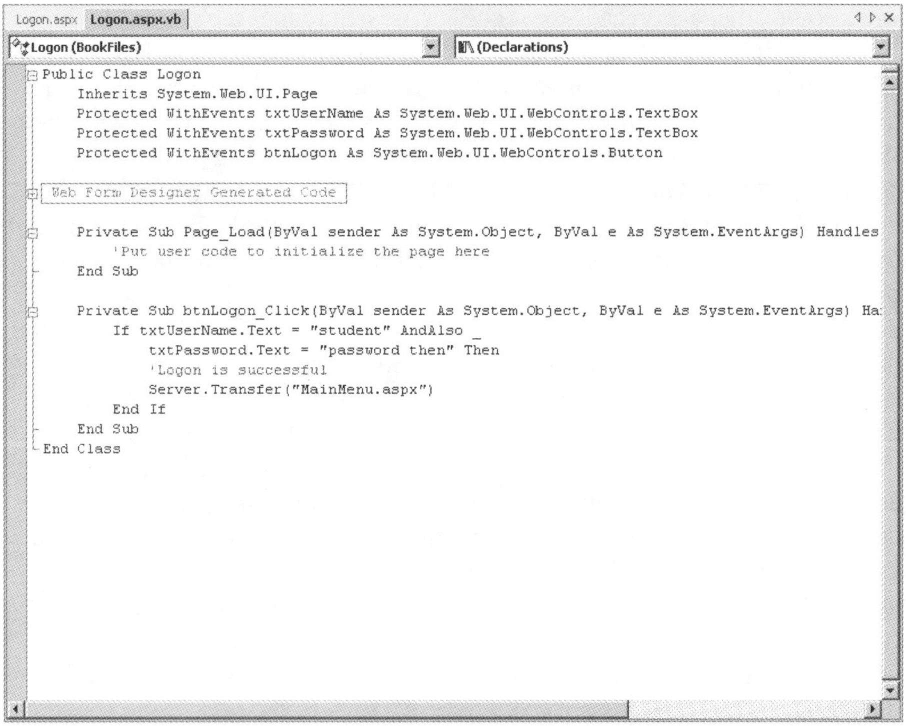

```
Logon.aspx  Logon.aspx.vb
Logon (BookFiles)                    (Declarations)

Public Class Logon
    Inherits System.Web.UI.Page
    Protected WithEvents txtUserName As System.Web.UI.WebControls.TextBox
    Protected WithEvents txtPassword As System.Web.UI.WebControls.TextBox
    Protected WithEvents btnLogon As System.Web.UI.WebControls.Button

 Web Form Designer Generated Code

    Private Sub Page_Load(ByVal sender As System.Object, ByVal e As System.EventArgs) Handles
        'Put user code to initialize the page here
    End Sub

    Private Sub btnLogon_Click(ByVal sender As System.Object, ByVal e As System.EventArgs) Ha
        If txtUserName.Text = "student" AndAlso _
            txtPassword.Text = "password then" Then
            'Logon is successful
            Server.Transfer("MainMenu.aspx")
        End If
    End Sub
End Class
```

Figure 1-4. Code for the click event

You can see that the controls are referenced as objects, and that the code simply reads the Text property of each. In this respect it's similar to code you may write for desktop applications, but compared to classic ASP it's a revolutionary change.

We'll examine how these events are raised in much more detail in later chapters, but for now you should remember that although the source of the event was an action in the browser, the effect of the event is to run code on the server.

Understanding Web Applications

It's worth spending a little more time investigating Web Applications at this stage, but rather than just letting us describe what a Web Application looks like and where it's stored, why don't you go ahead and create one?

Start by loading Visual Studio .NET. Unless you've configured it otherwise, you should see a Start Page similar to that shown in Figure 1-5.

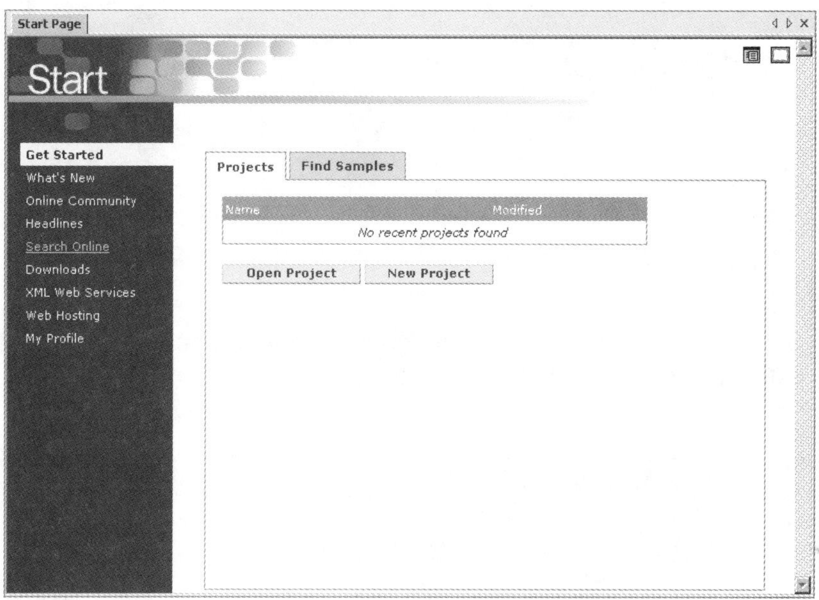

Figure 1-5. Visual Studio .NET Start Page

Click **New Project**, select **Visual Basic Projects** for the project type, and then select the **ASP.NET Web Application** icon in the Templates pane. Finally, enter the Location of the application as `http://localhost/FirstApplication`, at which point the dialog box looks like Figure 1-6, and then click **OK**.

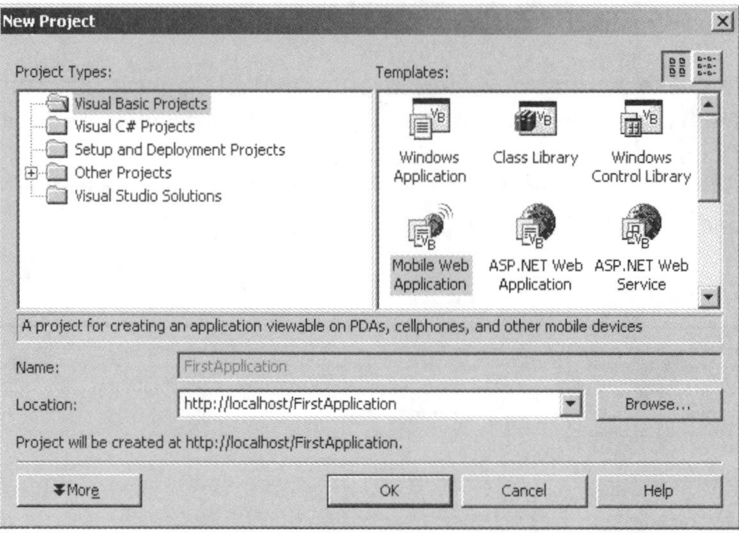

Figure 1-6. Creating your first Web Application

Once the project has been created, Visual Studio .NET shows a summary of its content in the Solution Explorer. At the moment you should see that it contains the following files:

- AssemblyInfo.vb
- FirstApplication.vsdisco
- Global.asax
- Styles.css
- Web.config
- WebForm1.aspx

It should also contain a References folder containing the .NET assemblies currently referenced from the project, much as the References dialog box in Visual Basic 6.0 lists the COM components currently referenced.

This is merely a summary of the project's content because the default configuration of Visual Studio .NET hides many files from you. If you want to see all of the files in the project, select **Project ➢ Show All Files** from the menu, and you'll see additional elements, mostly child elements of the existing files. Figure 1-7 shows the Solution Explorer with all of the files displayed.

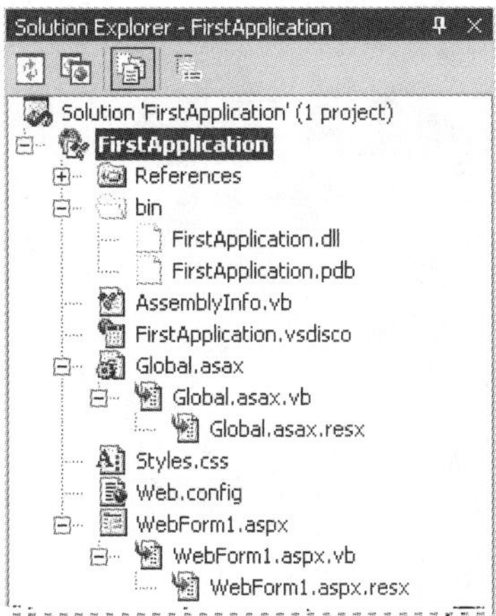

Figure 1-7. Complete project contents

Okay, so this is the Visual Studio .NET view; what about when you run it? Well, if you try and run the application right now (by selecting **Debug ➢ Start**), then it'll look pretty plain. In fact, it'll look empty because you've not created anything on the Web Form to be displayed in the browser. Although there's not much to see at this stage, it's actually quite useful to go and have a look at the project files from the point of view of IIS because this is ultimately the software that hosts the Web Application.

Load Windows Explorer and navigate to the main IIS root folder. This is usually C:\Inetpub\wwwroot but could be different on your PC. You'll see a **FirstApplication** folder, which in turn contains the files shown in Figure 1-8.

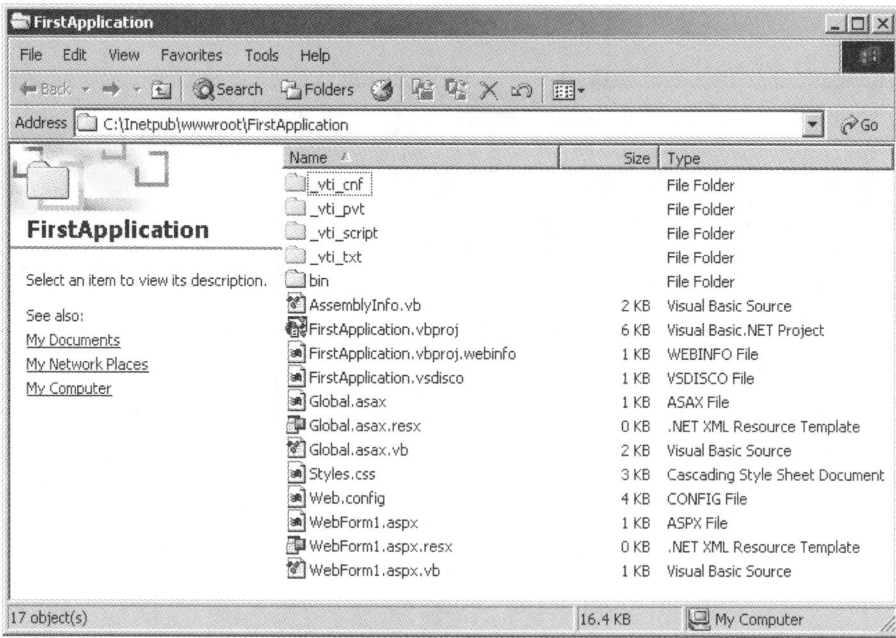

Figure 1-8. Project contents through Windows Explorer

You can see that all of the files shown in the Solution Explorer are present, plus some additional folders (which are flagged with a hidden attribute) and the project file itself. Any files added to the Web project in Visual Studio .NET will be copied to this folder as well.

NOTE *This is the only copy of your project and its content that is maintained by Visual Studio .NET. Make regular backups of this folder.*

Additional Content

The files that Visual Studio .NET creates within a Web Application are only a starting point. You'll most likely need to create additional Web Forms, classes, controls, and Web Services at some stage (although not necessarily in the same application), and you'll probably want to bring in existing content files such as HTML and XML documents. In truth, the list of possible content files is endless because your Web Application can contain any valid file type that the operating system supports. However, most applications use a small subset of the possible file types, with the following being the most common:

- **.asp files**: Classic ASP files, which can be run side by side with ASP.NET applications, even within the same virtual directory. This eases migration and upgrades by allowing conversion to be performed gradually. However, classic ASP files will not have access to any of the new .NET features and will be handled by the standard asp.dll handler.

- **.aspx files**: ASP.NET Web Forms, which form the user interface of a Web Application. They're often associated with .aspx.vb and .aspx.resx files, which are used within the development environment to hold code and resource information respectively.

- **.asmx files**: ASP.NET Web Services, which are components that can be called over the network by other applications to perform specific functions. Web Services are one of the replacement technologies for DCOM, and they're designed to be Internet and firewall friendly. As with Web Forms, they're usually associated with .asmx.vb and .asmx.resx files.

- **Global.asax**: ASP.NET version of global.asa, which contains application-level event handlers, definitions, and objects.

- **.htm, .html, .css**: Traditional HTML files and style sheets.

- **.xml**: XML documents, which can be processed by .NET applications (see Chapter 9) or passed straight to the browser for client-side manipulation.

- **.gif, .jpeg**: Image files and graphics, often maintained in their own \Images directory, although this is a preference rather than a requirement.

- **.config**: XML documents that manage .NET specific settings. The project will contain a Web.config file in the virtual root, but each subdirectory can have its own Web.config file to override specific settings. There's also a global Machine.config file that maintains machine-wide settings; you can find this file under the folder
  C:\WINNT\Microsoft.NET\Framework\v1.0.XXXX\CONFIG
  rather than within any single application.

- **\bin directory**: Contains .NET assemblies and compiled code required by the Web Application. If you use Visual Studio .NET to build Web Applications, there will be a .dll file with the same name as the project that contains the compiled code for the application.

To add any of these files types to an application, you need only to place them into the Web Application's virtual directory. Subject to permissions and configuration settings (see Chapters 10 and 11 for a full discussion of these issues), the files will then be accessible from the client browser.

However, content added in this way will *not* automatically become a part of the Visual Studio .NET project. To add a file to the project you can select **Project ➢ Add Existing Item** and then browse for the names of the files to be added. If necessary, Visual Studio .NET will copy them to the virtual directory and then add them to the list of files shown in the Solution Explorer.

The benefit of adding files to the project becomes clear when you need to deploy the application because a Web Setup Project can be used to automatically deploy *all* of the project content. Web Setup Projects are the .NET equivalent of tools such as the Package and Deployment Wizard and the Visual Studio Installer; you'll see how to create them in Chapter 10, which discusses the processes of packaging and deploying Web Applications. You may also find that other management and development tasks are also eased, as you will have the full capabilities of the Visual Studio .NET development environment available to you.

Virtual Directories and ASP.NET

IIS configures the FirstApplication folder that contains the Web Application as a virtual directory (see Appendix A for more information if you're not sure what this means). This happens when the Web Application is first created and enables IIS to apply a variety of configuration parameters to the application independently of any other sites or applications running on the same server. To see the virtual directory configuration, load the Internet Services Manager utility, found in Administrative Tools, and then expand the **ComputerName** and **Default Web Site** nodes to display the list of folders, virtual directories, and applications. Click on **FirstDirectory** to display the content. Figure 1-9 shows how this may appear, although the list of virtual directories on your computer will contain different entries.

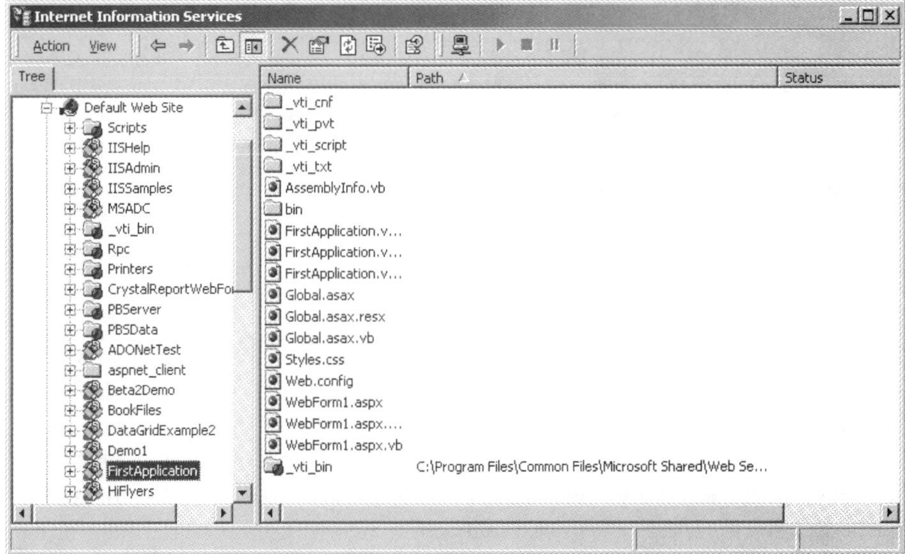

Figure 1-9. Project contents shown through Internet Services Manager

As you can see, the content of the virtual directory matches that shown in Windows Explorer, but Internet Services Manager also allows you to view the properties of the virtual Web directory. Right-click the **FirstApplication** entry, select **Properties** from the context menu, and you'll see the dialog box shown in Figure 1-10.

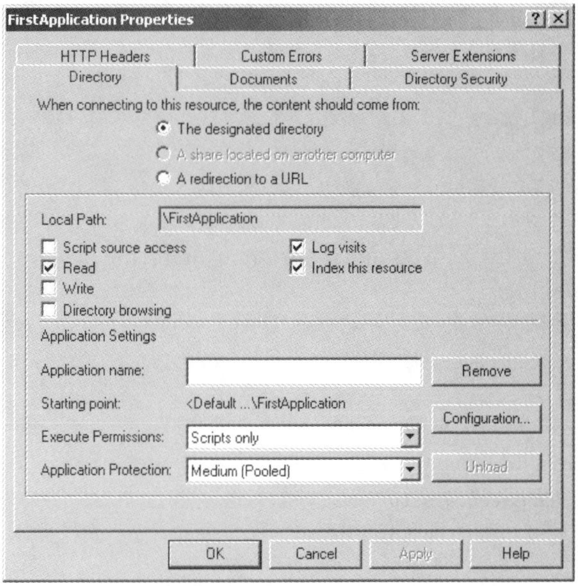

Figure 1-10. Properties for the FirstApplication virtual directory

Clearly, you can define many settings, some of which we'll return to later. For now, notice that the Directory tab contains basic permissions and application settings. If you switch to the Documents tab, you'll see that it defines the names of the default files that IIS will search for when a user browses to this application. Visual Studio .NET defined all of these settings when it created the virtual directory, during the initial creation of the project.

Web Application Content

In our previous definition of a Web Application we stated, "a Web Application consists of all the files, pages, handlers, modules, and executable code that can..." How does this compare with the Visual Studio .NET view of a Web Application? Well, you can clearly see that all the content added to the application was placed in a single virtual directory, and when we delve further into the architecture of .NET you'll see that ASP.NET functionality contained within HTTP Handlers and HTTP Modules are also executed within the scope of the application.

However, this does not mean you *must* create all content within Visual Studio .NET. To illustrate this, we'll use Notepad to create an additional file in our virtual directory:

1. If Visual Studio .NET is open, close it completely, so you can be sure it doesn't play any role in what follows.

2. Load Notepad, and open the Webform1.aspx file in the FirstApplication directory. Add a heading to identify the page between the `<form>` and `</form>` tags:

   ```
   <form id="Form1" method="post" runat="server">
        <h1>This is WebForm1.aspx</h1>
   </form>
   ```

3. Save Webform1.aspx, then create a new blank file in Notepad, and enter the following:

   ```
   <%@ Page Language="vb" %>
   <html>
     <body>
       <form id="Form1" method="post" runat="server">
           <h1>Welcome to FirstApplication</h1>
           <asp:button id="btnNavigate" runat="server" text="Navigate"/>
       </form>
     </body>
   </html>
   ```

4. Save this file as Default.aspx in the FirstApplication directory. Make sure that Notepad doesn't add its own .txt file extension.

5. Load your browser, and navigate to `http://LocalHost/FirstApplication`. You should see the Default.aspx page because this name is configured as one of the default documents that IIS recognizes. However, although the button is displayed, it doesn't do anything yet.

6. Return to the source code of Default.aspx in Notepad, and add the following at the bottom of the file:

```
<script runat="server">
    Protected Sub btnNavigate_Click(Sender as Object, E as EventArgs)
        Server.Transfer("webform1.aspx")
    End Sub
</script>
```

   This code defines an event-handling routine, the purpose of which is to transfer control to another Web Form (Webform1.aspx) when a user clicks the Navigate button. We've chosen to do this with the `Server.Transfer` method, although we could also have used `Response.Redirect`. Chapter 12 examines navigation techniques and methods, and describes the relative merits and disadvantages of each approach. The signature of this procedure is important, as all .NET event handlers are expected to accept two parameters.

   The first parameter (**Sender**) is a reference to the object that raised the event. You might think this is redundant because we've already decided that this handler will be associated with events from the Navigate button; however, as we shall see in Chapter 4, you can define event-handling routines to be associated with multiple controls, and so the Sender parameter provides an easy way to identify which of these controls has raised the event.

   The second parameter (**E**) is a reference to an object that provides additional information about the event. In the case of a click event there's no useful additional information, but for events such as ItemClick (in a ListBox) or ItemCommand (in a DataGrid) the E parameter includes details of which item or row has been selected or activated.

7. Modify the tag for the `<asp:button>` by adding a definition of the `OnClick` handler. This will read as follows:

```
<asp:button id="btnNavigate" runat="server" text="Navigate"
                    onclick="btnNavigate_Click"/>
```

We need to add this additional attribute to ensure that ASP.NET associates our server-side event procedure with the control.

8. In the Web browser, navigate to `http://LocalHost/FirstApplication` once again. Click the button on the page, and you'll be redirected to the WebForm1.aspx page. Return to the Default.aspx page and view its source—you'll see that there's no client-side script, demonstrating that the event handler we added is executed only on the server.

Although you can create content using Notepad or other text editors, in most cases it would be inappropriate to do so. In this example, the Default.aspx file contains both the visual elements for the page as well as the code that handles the events. This approach can be problematic in the long term, increasing maintenance requirements and minimizing the chance of reusing code. One of the key features of ASP.NET is its ability to separate code from content, and this is emphasized when you build applications using the Visual Studio .NET tools.

Another point worth noting is that if you return to Visual Studio .NET and view the content of the project in the Solution Explorer, the Default.aspx file will either be gray (if Show All Files is selected) or be hidden (if the option is off). This is because you have not added the Default.aspx file to the ASP.NET project, even though you added it to the application's virtual directory. Figure 1-11 shows the view when Show All Files has been selected.

Figure 1-11. Solution Explorer showing all files

As mentioned earlier, you may find it easier to manage Web Applications if *all* of the content is included in the Visual Studio .NET project. Because Default.aspx is already present in the application's virtual directory, the easiest way to add it to the project is to right-click on the name in the Solution Explorer and select **Include In Project**. You'll be warned that no class file exists for the Web Form, but you should specify No when asked if one should be created. Our Web Form contains code embedded in the .aspx file, whereas Visual Studio .NET expects it to be in a code-behind module. There's nothing wrong with this approach, it's just not what the development environment is expecting.

Understanding Web Services

The type of application you've seen up until this point is perhaps more accurately described as a *Web Forms application* because it uses Web Forms to create a visible user interface that can be displayed in a browser. However, Web Applications can contain other types of component as well, and one of these is a *Web Service.*

Web Services present a programmatic interface rather than a visible one, and users usually access them from other applications (including Web Applications and desktop applications) rather than from a browser. You build Web Services using .asmx files rather than .aspx files, but the two types of file can freely coexist within the same project. Web Services and Web Forms share many features, and you'll find that their coding structures and style are similar.

We'll discuss Web Services in much more detail in Chapter 14, and you'll get plenty of opportunities to try creating your own. For now, let's add a simple Web Service to the FirstApplication project created previously:

1. If necessary, load Visual Studio .NET and open the FirstApplication project.
2. Select **Project ➢ Add Web Service** and set the Name for the new component to `Forecast.asmx`.
3. You'll be presented with a blank designer, which you can close as this Web Service will be entirely code-based.
4. Select Forecast.aspx in the Solution Explorer, then display the code for the component by selecting **View ➢ Code** or pressing the F7 function key. It'll appear as shown in Figure 1-12.

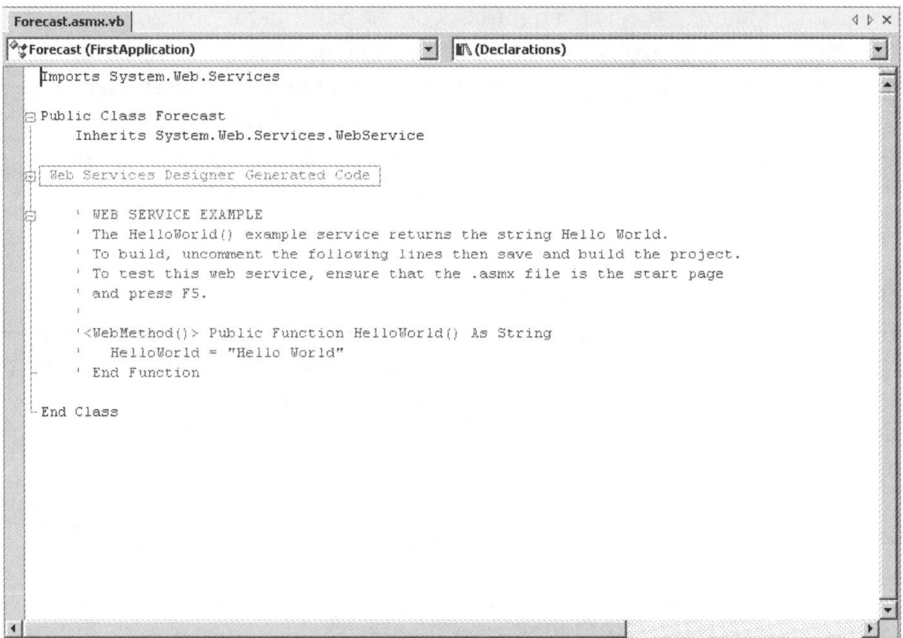

Figure 1-12. Default content of a Web Service file

5. Delete all of the commented (green) code, and replace it with the following:

```
<WebMethod()> Public Function GetUKWeather() As String
    Dim intRandom As New Random()
    Select Case intRandom.Next(3)
        Case 0
            Return "It is cloudy"
        Case 1
            Return "It is raining"
        Case 2
            Return "It is raining hard"
        Case 3
            Return "It is raining very hard"
    End Select
End Function
```

6. Save the file, then right-click in the Solution Explorer and choose **Build And Browse**. Ordinarily you would use a separate client application to call the Web Service, but in this case you don't yet have one. Fortunately,

ASP.NET helps out by creating a browser-based interface that you can use for testing. Figure 1-13 shows how this appears in the browser window.

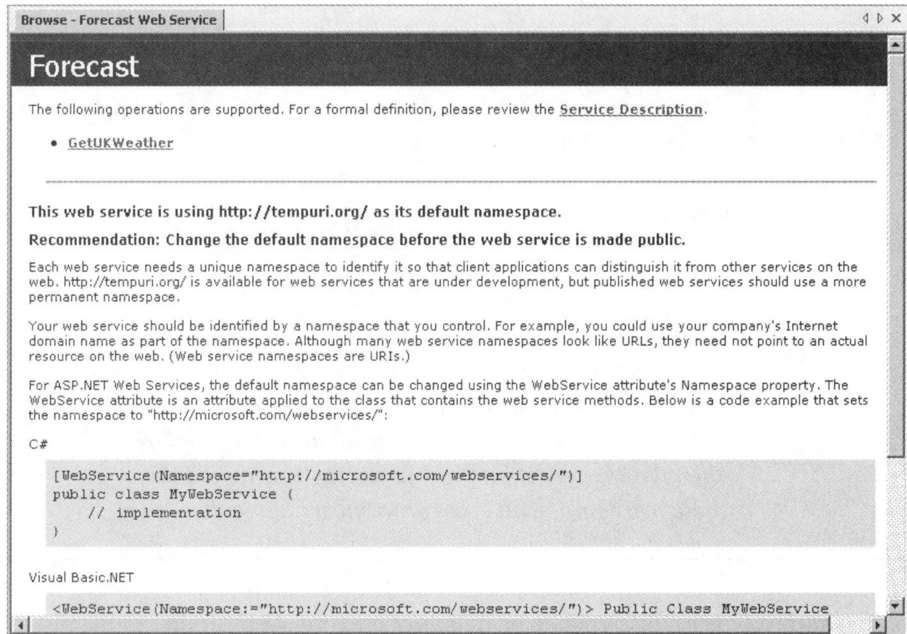

Figure 1-13. Testing the Web Service

7. Click the **GetUKWeather** hyperlink to display the next page, and then click the **Invoke** button to test the Web Service. A separate browser window opens to show the result, as shown in Figure 1-14.

Browse - Forecast Web Service | **http://localh.../GetUKWeather?**

```
<?xml version="1.0" encoding="utf-8" ?>
<string xmlns="http://tempuri.org/">It is raining hard</string>
```

Figure 1-14. Results from the Web Service

Notice that the results display in XML notation, which is the format in which all Web Service information is transferred. The reason Web Services return information in the form of XML is that XML is a completely language- and platform-independent way of representing data that can be passed across the Internet, so virtually every developer in the world can call your Web Service. Typically, developers will use client tools to call Web Services, which completely hide the fact that the Web Service uses XML at all. For example, a .NET client program can create a *Web reference* to your Web Service, after which it can call the `GetUKWeather` method simply using code such as the following:

```
Dim objSvc As New MyServerName.Forecast()
lblWeather.Text = objSvc.GetUKWeather
```

This example assumes that the machine hosting the Web Service is called `MyServerName`.

NOTE *You should remember that Web Services are simply components that can be placed into a Web Application and that they're created, executed, and managed in a similar way to Web Forms. There are some major differences in terms of their design and planning, but the features available to these two component types are almost identical.*

Chapter 14 examines the specific details of creating Web Service applications and Web Service clients. However, remember that there's a lot of shared technology between Web Form applications and Web Service applications, so the content of most other chapters in the book is equally applicable.

Introducing ASP.NET Intrinsic Objects

Visual elements and components, such as Web Forms and server controls, provide many powerful features, and you'll use at least some of them in almost every application. They play a similar role to that of Windows Forms and controls in desktop applications, but as with desktop applications it's also often necessary to get "under the surface" of Web Applications.

In the case of ASP.NET, *under the surface* means using the classes provided within the .NET Framework, most of which are common to all .NET application types. However, ASP.NET has a set of specialized objects you use for interacting with a Web server, as well as manipulating the information received from and sent to the client browser. These are known as ASP.NET *intrinsic objects* and are available to every Web Form and Web Service element in a project.

Strictly speaking, the intrinsic objects are exposed as properties of a number of classes, including the System.Web.UI.Page and the System.Web.Services.WebService classes, which are the base classes for Web

Forms and Web Services, respectively. Because your Web Form or Web Service derives from one of these classes, it inherits all of the class properties, methods, and events. We'll see more about this inheritance relationship in Chapter 2. (If the concept of inheritance is new to you, you may find it useful to review Appendix C first.)

There are many intrinsic objects, of which the following sections describe only the most commonly used. We've included these objects in this introductory chapter to make you aware of their presence, as we'll be using some of them in examples and code fragments throughout the book. In fact, you've already used the Server object when you called the `Server.Transfer` method in the earlier exercise. This emphasizes the fact that even for the most trivial of ASP.NET applications, there's a good chance you'll need to use some of this functionality.

Application

The `Application` object is an instance of the HTTPApplicationState class, and its main purpose is to allow you to store *state* (information) in a Web Application such that it:

- Is persistent across page requests and user sessions
- Is shared between all concurrent users of a Web Application

Chapter 12 discusses state management in detail, including a thorough coverage of how you use and control the Application object.

Cache

The `Cache` object is an instance of the Cache class. It's also provided to allow state management; however, it works differently than the Application object:

- Cache state is persistent across page requests and user sessions but can be associated with dependencies that cause the data to become invalidated under certain circumstances, such as when a time period elapses or a file on disk changes.
- The Cache object is automatically thread-safe, whereas the Application object requires that your code make explicit calls to the `Lock` and `Unlock` methods.

We'll leave further discussion of the Cache object to Chapter 12, where we'll compare and contrast the different options available for state management.

`Error`

The `Error` object is an instance of the Exception class, and it represents the *first* error that occurred (if any) during the processing of the current request. As we will see in Chapter 10, there are multiple phases to the request processing cycle, many of which occur before any of your code can run. The Error object provides a way for you to determine if those phases were error-free, or if some problem occurred that you now have to handle.

The Error object is not exposed directly as a property of the Page or WebService classes, but instead must be referenced through the page's Context property. For example:

```
strFirstExcep = "Exception caused by " + Context.Error.Source
```

`Request`

The `Request` object is an instance of the HTTPRequest class and is created by ASP.NET to enable your code to read information passed from the client browser to the server when the page request was made. This enables you to do a number of key things:

- Read data entered by the user into an HTML form on the page that generated the request.

- Read data from the *querystring* defined for the request. The querystring is the sequence of characters that is appended to the URL part of the requested page address, and the querystring and URL are separated with a *?* character.

- Read cookie values from the information passed by the browser. Note that if the browser does not pass the cookie values to the server, your code cannot read them; you have access only to the information sent from the browser.

- Read the value of *server variables* sent with the request or generated from it. Server variables provide additional information about a request, such as what browser is in use, what the user's IP and hostname are.

Note that ASP.NET performs some of these tasks automatically. For example, the browser type and version is automatically identified and used to determine what client features are rendered, and the content of form data is read automatically during the postback process. However, the Request object is still extremely important.

Response

The `Response` object is an instance of the HTTPResponse class, and it performs a complementary process to the Request object. Where Request enables your code to obtain information from the client browser, Response enables you to send information back. There are many tasks where the Response object will be used, including the following:

- Sending textual and binary data to the browser
- Controlling how page content is transmitted and defining whether buffering is enabled to prevent pages being drawn piecemeal in the browser
- Controlling page caching, at the server and browser levels
- Specifying additional HTTP headers
- Controlling navigation

The Response object is used extensively in most ASP.NET applications, as it allows fine control as well as dynamic content generation.

Server

The `Server` object is an instance of the HttpServerUtility class. This class provides properties and methods that assist in processing page requests. Typical tasks the Server object can perform include:

- Application-wide exception handling.
- Encoding of strings into valid HTML and URL notations. This includes substitution of special characters with their HTML equivalents.

- Controlling page execution, processing, and navigation.
- Mapping logical file names to physical locations.

Although not used as much as Request and Response, Server is still an important object and allows code to interact more readily with Web clients without the need for custom translations and mappings.

Session

The `Session` object is an instance of the HTTPSessionState class, and it's used for session and state management. If Session state is enabled (see Chapter 12), each user is allocated a session ID when they first access the application. This session ID is usually stored in a transient cookie and passed to the server with each request. The server uses the session ID to track each individual user and to allow storage of user-specific state. ASP.NET also uses the session ID to track which users are continuing to use the application and therefore to timeout or expire the sessions of inactive users.

Transient cookies are typically stored in-memory within the browser process, so when the browser is closed the session ID is lost. If the user subsequently opens another browser and views the same application, they'll receive a different session ID. Also, if a user opens two browsers on the same computer and navigates to the same application in each, each browser will be allocated a different session ID, and so the application believes there are two distinct users.

If cookies are disabled on the client browser, ASP.NET instead inserts the session ID into the URL of the response sent to the browser—this is known as *munging* the URL. When subsequent requests are made from this page, the munged URL is passed back to the server and the session ID retrieved. In this way, ASP.NET is not dependent on cookies for session support, although the cookie-based approach is neater.

As with the Application object, the main purpose of Session is to allow you to store state in a Web Application such that it:

- Is persistent across page requests
- Is correctly released and destroyed when the session terminates
- Is unique to a single user session within a Web Application

Chapter 12 discusses state management in detail, including a thorough coverage of how the Session object is used and controlled.

Trace

The `Trace` object is an instance of the TraceContext class, and it provides methods and properties that enable you to write custom entries to the trace log that ASP.NET can generate for your application.

As you'll see in Chapter 10, you can enable tracing for the entire application or for specific pages, and by default it'll record details relating to request details, server events, form and query string content, cookies, and much more. By using the Trace object you're able to supplement this default output with your own messages, including details of any exceptions that have occurred in your code.

User

The `User` object is an instance of either a GenericPrincipal or WindowsPrincipal class, depending on the current security configuration of the Web Application. The main purpose of the User object is to provide a mechanism for determining the security permissions and privileges of the user making the request.

If you make use of the User object for checking security, you're said to be implementing a *programmatic security* policy; it's a technique that provides great flexibility and control, as you can perform security checks at any level in the application—when displaying a page, when rendering a control, or when responding to a server event.

The alternative to programmatic security is to implement *declarative security*, where the security settings are defined in the Web.config file. This approach is more granular, or coarse, because declarative security settings can be applied only at the folder or file level, rather than on a method-specific basis.

Chapter 11 deals with the topic of security and examines how declarative and programmatic techniques can be applied to ASP.NET applications.

Summary

Right now, ASP.NET has to be *the* reason for switching to the .NET environment. ASP.NET applications are by definition centralized onto a single Web server or Web farm, and if you plan it properly, you can install the .NET Framework and components with minimal disruption and interruption.

Developers of ASP.NET applications have the most to gain, with a much simplified event-driven programming model, powerful server controls, practical data binding, and comprehensive full-featured languages such as VB .NET and C#. System administrators and tech-support personnel are catered to with easy text-based configuration and management, no-touch deployment and upgrades, and an independence from the registry and COM.

CHAPTER 2

Web Forms

WEB FORMS ARE CORE components in the ASP.NET environment, providing the basis for the visual interface of your Web Application. Each Web Form is a combination of user interface and programming logic that gets rendered as a page in the user's browser. In the development environment you will see and manipulate Web Forms as programmable classes with properties, methods, and events, but at runtime their visual results take the form of HTML documents. This enormous difference between their runtime and design-time appearance is the real magic of Web Forms technology; but, it can be confusing at first, so let's begin this chapter by looking at precisely what a Web Form is and how it is used.

What Is a Web Form?

As far as a user is concerned, a Web Form is simply what displays in a Web browser. A Web Form won't really look any different from any other Web page, although the extra productivity that ASP.NET gives you may encourage you to design more attractive Web pages.

As a developer, you will treat Web Forms as design-time objects that you can create and modify. They usually have both a visual interface and some associated code, and they can be built and edited using development tools such as Visual Studio .NET, or simple editors such as Notepad or ASPEdit. We'll go into much more detail on this topic very soon, but let's first see what a Web Form looks like to .NET.

From the perspective of the .NET Framework, a Web Form is a class that can be compiled and executed at runtime in much the same way as any other class. This class will expose methods and properties, which the ASP.NET Framework will call during the process of responding to a request from a browser.

From these definitions, you might think that a Web Form is a pretty vague term; after all, how could something be structured so that it supports these different views and behaviors. In practice, however, Web Forms are very well defined in .NET, with a single base class that provides the core functionality, and a library of supporting classes to add a level of flexibility. Because Web Forms play such a key role in ASP.NET (and underpin almost everything else we will discuss in this book), it's worth taking a moment to build on this description and look in greater depth at just how they are structured.

Web Form Structure

There are two different approaches to the structure and creation of Web Forms:

- A Web Form can be created as a single .aspx file that contains both the visual elements and the code.
- A Web Form can be created as two distinct files: an .aspx file that defines the visual elements and a separate file for the class that contains the code. The class can be represented in source-code form, in which case it will be within a .vb file (for Visual Basic .NET classes) or a .cs file (for C# classes), or it can be implemented in compiled form, in which case it will most likely be within a .dll file.

The first approach is very similar to the one used with classic ASP and was illustrated by the simple Default.aspx that we created in Chapter 1. You might also remember from the discussion in Chapter 1 that there are some serious drawbacks from the viewpoint of application planning, design, and management; so, for these reasons, this first approach is not one we would recommend for most Web applications.

We prefer the second approach, which also happens to be the architecture favored by Visual Studio .NET. Every Web Form that you create and build in Visual Studio .NET will consist of an .aspx and a .vb file (assuming you're using VB .NET), as well as a .resx file that stores some additional information. When you build the project (the Visual Studio .NET term for compiling) the code from all of the individual .vb files is compiled into the application's .dll, which .NET then uses at runtime.

As we mentioned above, you can also leave the .vb files in source-code form rather than compiling them to a .dll. This may be a useful technique in situations where the code must be regularly modified since you can make the changes with a simple text editor rather than with a full-blown development tool. Making such "on-the-fly" changes is something we'd recommend you do as little as possible because such changes lead to a greater chance of errors and bugs creeping in—but there are times when it's unavoidable. Configuring your Web Forms to use source-code files is a straight-forward process, but there is no obvious configuration option in Visual Studio .NET to do so. We'll look at this technique again in the Page Directive Attributes section later in this chapter.

Web Form Classes

The code in the .vb file is a class that derives from a base class called System.Web.UI.Page. As you'd expect, this base class provides the majority of behaviors required by the Web Form; and, as a developer, you have only to add the aspects that are specific to your application. This class is often known as a *code-behind class*, as it is distinct from the visual elements of the Web Form (in the .aspx file) but still associated with them.

The association between the .vb class and the .aspx file is not governed by filenames, locations, or any other "loose" relationship. Instead, the .aspx file itself is actually a class that derives from the class defined in the .vb file; therefore, it inherits all of the member properties and methods that you define plus all of those from the base System.Web.UI.Page class.

The inheritance relationship between these two elements—namely, the .vb class and the .aspx file—is defined by a special `Inherits` attribute entered in the Page directive at the top of the file. For example, in a newly created Web Application you will find a Web Form named WebForm1.aspx. Within the associated .vb file you will find the following definition:

```
Public Class WebForm1
    Inherits System.Web.UI.Page
    .
    .
    .
End Class
```

If you examine the content of the .aspx file in HTML View, you will see that the Page directive at the top of the file contains an *Inherits* attribute that refers to this class:

```
<%@ Page Language="vb" ..... Inherits="FirstApplication.WebForm1"%>
```

NOTE *The Page directive contains several other attributes as well—one of which is* `Codebehind`. *As we will see later in this chapter,* `Codebehind` *is used by Visual Studio .NET at design-time, but has no effect on the runtime behavior of the Web Form.*

So why are Web Forms structured this way? Well, there are many reasons, but two of the most important are:

- **This structure matches the .NET approach used in other application and component types, and indeed, throughout the .NET Framework.** It would be inappropriate for the majority of the .NET classes and namespaces to be designed with inheritance in mind, only for this aspect to be different.

- **The use of two distinct but associated classes allows you to keep code separate from a Web Form's visual content.** If you're an existing desktop developer, then you've almost certainly been working this way for years and would never question the fact that the interface and logic are kept quite separate. However, for many Web developers, this is a brand new approach since classic ASP and other Web development technologies have largely relied on intermixing code and HTML.

At this stage, the point to remember is that an inheritance relationship exists between the .aspx and the .vb file; the content of the .aspx file itself defines this relationship (see Figure 2-1).

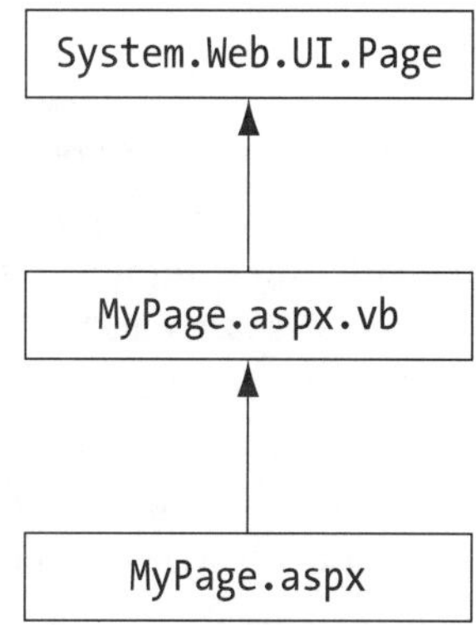

Figure 2-1. Inheritance relationship for Web Forms.

You might be wondering whether this inheritance is limited to being a one-to-one association as in Figure 2-1. Well, although it is the default approach taken by Visual Studio, it is quite possible to specify a different class from which to inherit in the .aspx file. This leads to the possibility of having several distinct interfaces, all of which share common implementation code, as shown in Figure 2-2.

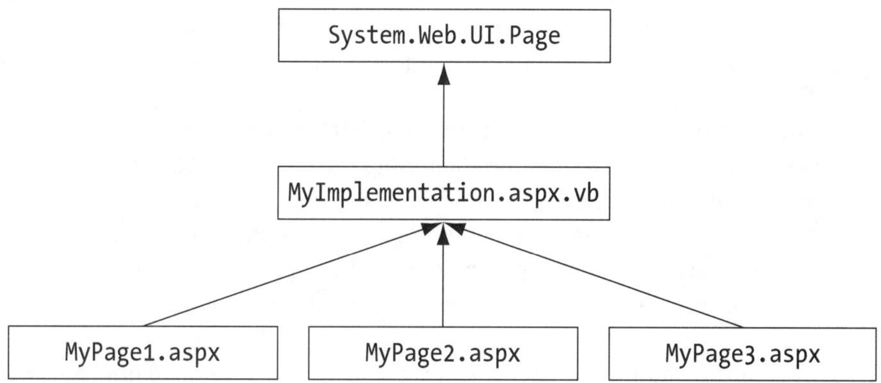

Figure 2-2. Defining a common code-behind class

This technique can be useful when it is necessary to have multiple pages with similar functionality but quite different appearances. However, don't be fooled into thinking this is the best approach for handling multiple browser types and versions. As you'll see later in the book, ASP.NET addresses this problem head-on with some powerful features of its own. In reality, you will rarely have multiple .aspx pages inheriting from one Visual Basic class; but don't dismiss it as a design possibility.

Browsing Web Forms

Each Web Form represents one page in a Web Application and is referenced from the browser (or from hyperlinks, URLs, etc.) via the associated .aspx file. As discussed in Chapter 1, ASP.NET loads and compiles Web Forms on demand; so, the first time the page is requested, the .aspx and its associated class are loaded by the runtime and compiled to native code. The compiled results are cached to speed up subsequent access and then executed to generate the HTML that is returned to the client. As with classic ASP, it is not the Web Form itself that is returned to the browser, but rather the results of executing the code that the Web Form contains.

There are two special points to note here:

- The .aspx and the class both have to be compiled on the first reference at runtime, but we said previously that Visual Studio .NET compiles the classes into a .dll when the project is built. Does this mean that compilation happens twice? Well, yes, in .NET that's exactly what happens. When Visual Studio .NET compiles the classes, it performs only a "partial" compilation since the design-time compiler generates Intermediate Language (IL) code rather than native code. The runtime compiler takes the IL from the .dll and compiles to processor-specific code for execution. If this doesn't make too much sense, we suggest you take a look at Appendix E.

- Although the compiled results are cached, .NET keeps track of the files that were used during compilation (including the .aspx, the .dll, and any associated .config files) and will automatically recompile if it detects any changes to them. This mechanism allows you to deploy updated files without having to restart or reset the application; ASP.NET automatically recompiles after the changes and uses the new code for all subsequent requests.

This all means that when using Visual Studio, the .vb files need not be deployed to the live Web server because the combination of the .aspx and .dll provide all that is required.

Creating Web Forms

Your Web application will no doubt have many different pages, just as a desktop application has many different forms or dialogs. You will usually create a distinct Web Form for each page the user will see. After you have created a Web application project in Visual Studio .NET, you can add a Web Form either by selecting **Project ➢ Add Web Form** or by right-clicking the project in the Solution Explorer window and selecting **Add ➢ Add Web Form**. Both of these commands produce the Add New Item dialog as shown in Figure 2-3.

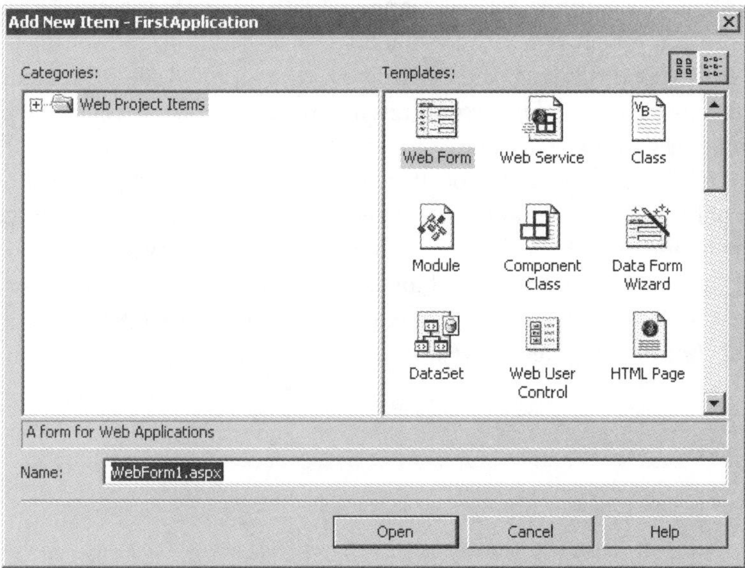

Figure 2-3. Adding a Web Form

Choose the name of the Web Form carefully. It is possible to rename Web Forms at any stage, but Visual Studio does not automatically rename the associated class in the .vb file; so, it is best to get the name correct from the start.

Also, try to choose a name for the .aspx that is not a reserved word and that does not conflict with an existing class. While you won't always be able to do this, you will probably find the project is easier to build and manage if you stick to this rule. If you choose a name for a Web Form that *is* the same as a reserved word, Visual Studio .NET will prefix the name of the class in the .vb file with an underscore. For example, if you name a Web Form Default.aspx, it becomes the "default document" and is automatically returned to the browser when you navigate to the application using only the application or directory name. As you'd expect, this is a very useful facility, but Default is a reserved word in VB .NET and so .NET would generate an error if you named a class Default. Visual Studio .NET solves the problem by naming the class `_Default` and by setting the `Inherits` attribute in the .aspx file accordingly.

Web Form Designer

Once you've added a Web Form to the project, Visual Studio will display the Web Form designer. As with the Form designer in VB 6.0, you use the Web Form designer to graphically create the visual interface by adding, and setting properties for, HTML Controls and Web Controls. Of course, you'll see some significant differences in the detail of the properties and the code you write, but the principles should be extremely familiar.

The Web Form designer supports two different views. *Design View* shows the content of the Web Form graphically, while *HTML View* shows the underlying elements, tags, and attributes. Figure 2-4 shows the Design View, which you will probably find easiest to use most of the time. However, there will be times when you might prefer HTML View (shown in Figure 2-5) because it provides a greater degree of control, often necessary for fine adjustments.

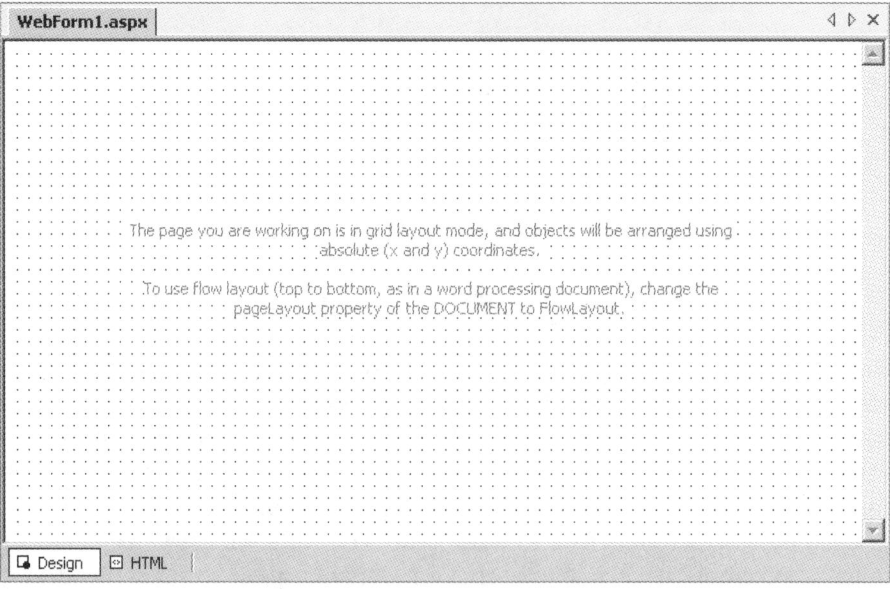

Figure 2-4. WebForm1.aspx in Design View

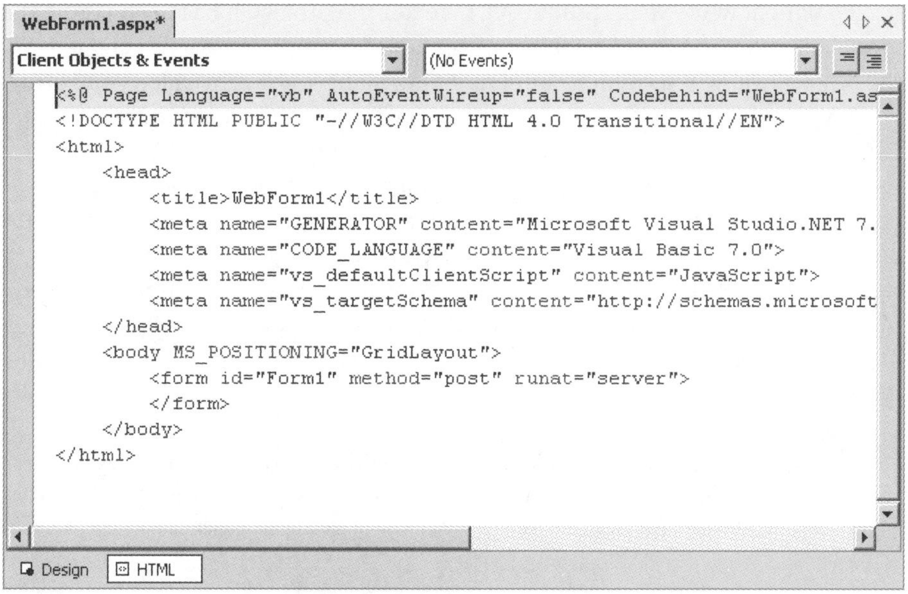

WebForm1.aspx*

Client Objects & Events | (No Events)

```
<%@ Page Language="vb" AutoEventWireup="false" Codebehind="WebForm1.as
<!DOCTYPE HTML PUBLIC "-//W3C//DTD HTML 4.0 Transitional//EN">
<html>
    <head>
        <title>WebForm1</title>
        <meta name="GENERATOR" content="Microsoft Visual Studio.NET 7.
        <meta name="CODE_LANGUAGE" content="Visual Basic 7.0">
        <meta name="vs_defaultClientScript" content="JavaScript">
        <meta name="vs_targetSchema" content="http://schemas.microsoft
    </head>
    <body MS_POSITIONING="GridLayout">
        <form id="Form1" method="post" runat="server">
        </form>
    </body>
</html>
```

Design | HTML

Figure 2-5. WebForm1.aspx in HTML View

Notice the grid displayed in Figure 2-4. Web Forms support two layout modes for visual content. *Grid Layout* (which displays the grid) allows absolute positioning of content, much the same as a regular VB 6.0 Form. *Flow Layout* supports relative positioning of content in the same way as many HTML editors. The default setting is GridLayout, but you can change the mode through the Web Form's pageLayout property as we shall soon see.

Your First Web Application

We've discussed enough of the theory and structure behind Web Forms for now. As with any programming task, the best way to really learn ASP.NET is to start using it.

1. Start Visual Studio .NET, if you need to.

2. **Select File ➢ New ➢ Project.**

3. Select the **Visual Basic Projects** folder, then select the **ASP.NET Web Application** template.

4. Set the **Location** to `http://localhost/HiFlyers`.

Be patient while Visual Studio .NET creates the project; it has to configure the virtual directory in IIS and establish a number of settings. Once it has created the project, you will see that it contains a new, blank Web Form called WebForm1.

If you've followed these steps above, you will have just created a Visual Studio .NET *Solution*, and within it, a Visual Studio .NET *Project*. Within VB 6.0 it was possible to create project groups (sets of projects that could be loaded, saved, compiled, and managed together). A solution is a Visual Studio .NET device to achieve the same goal, although in a more flexible way. Within the solution you can have multiple projects, each of which typically represents an application—in our case, a Web application. It is worth knowing where the project files get created so that you can manage them, deploy them, and back them up. The default locations are:

- Solution files are stored in a directory within Visual Studio Projects within your My Documents folder. For example, if you are logged in as "Developer" this would be:

```
C:\Documents and Settings\Developer\My Documents\Visual Studio
Projects\HiFlyers
```

- The project and content files are stored in a directory within the www root directory used by IIS. For our HiFlyers project this will be:

```
C:\Inetpub\wwwroot\HiFlyers
```

Of course you may have your PC configured differently so that these locations may not match exactly, but you should take a moment to determine where your newly created project files are located.

We mentioned before that if you rename a Web Form, Visual Studio .NET doesn't automatically rename the associated class in the .vb file. To see this in practice, close the designer for WebForm1 and then rename it to RegionPicker.aspx. Now view the code for the Web Form (select **View ➢ Code**) and you will see that the class is still called WebForm1. You *could* rename the class, but then you would have to also modify the Page directive in the .aspx file as well. Now you start to see why we recommend you get the name right from the start.

When you get into situations like this, we have found the best solution is to delete the unwanted files and create new ones. Just right-click on the Web Form in the Solution Explorer window and select **Delete** from the context menu. You can now add a new Web Form and call it RegionPicker.aspx. If you check the code you'll see that the class is now also called RegionPicker.

Adding Controls

Now we have the Web Form in place, we'll build a simple user interface for our application. The purpose of this Web Form is to allow the user to select any number of different regions from one list and add them to a second list. To do this, ensure that the **Web Forms** tab is selected in the toolbox and then add two list boxes and one button, positioned as shown in Figure 2-6:

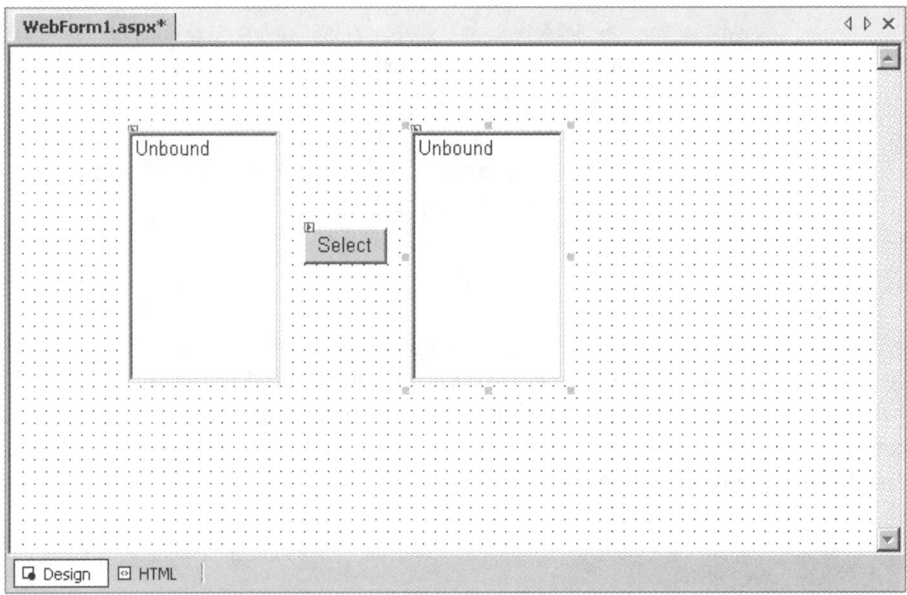

Figure 2-6. Controls for RegionPicker.aspx

Use the Properties window to set the ID of the left list box to `SourceList`, the ID of the button to `btnSelect`, and the ID of the right list box to `SelectedList`. Set the Text property of the button to `Select`. Once you have added these controls and set their properties, click the **HTML** button at the bottom of the Web Form designer and you'll see the textual representation of the controls:

```
<%@ Page Language="vb" AutoEventWireup="false" Codebehind="WebForm1.aspx.vb"
            Inherits="FirstApplication.WebForm11"%>
<!DOCTYPE HTML PUBLIC "-//W3C//DTD HTML 4.0 Transitional//EN">
<HTML>
    <HEAD>
        <title>WebForm1</title>
        <meta name="GENERATOR" content="Microsoft Visual Studio.NET 7.0">
        <meta name="CODE_LANGUAGE" content="Visual Basic 7.0">
```

```
        <meta name="vs_defaultClientScript" content="JavaScript">
        <meta name="vs_targetSchema"
                        content="http://schemas.microsoft.com/intellisense/ie5">
    </HEAD>
    <body MS_POSITIONING="GridLayout">
        <form id="Form1" method="post" runat="server">
            <asp:ListBox id="SourceList" style="Z-INDEX: 101; LEFT: 80px;
                        POSITION: absolute; TOP: 56px" runat="server" Width="104px"
                        Height="168px"></asp:ListBox>
            <asp:ListBox id="SelectedList" style="Z-INDEX: 102; LEFT: 272px;
                        POSITION: absolute; TOP: 56px" runat="server" Width="104px"
                        Height="168px"></asp:ListBox>
            <asp:Button id="btnSelect" style="Z-INDEX: 103; LEFT: 200px;
                        POSITION: absolute; TOP: 120px" runat="server" Width="56px"
                        Text="Select"></asp:Button>
        </form>
    </body>
</HTML>
```

Notice that each of the Web Form controls you added is represented by an `<asp:. . .>` tag with attributes that define its position and size, as well as a `runat="server"` attribute that specifies it is a server-side control. We will examine these attributes in more detail in Chapter 3.

Adding Code

Code within a Web Form is event-driven, much the same as the code behind a form in a traditional desktop VB application. In our simple example, we want to add code to perform two tasks:

- Initialize the list boxes when the Web Form is loaded.
- Transfer from SourceList to SelectedList when the button is clicked.

We will initialize the list boxes in the Load event; double-clicking the Web Form in the designer will display the skeleton for the event-handling procedure:

```
Private Sub Page_Load(ByVal sender As System.Object, ByVal e As System.EventArgs)_
                                    Handles MyBase.Load
    'Put user code to initialize the page here
End Sub
```

Notice the additional `Handles MyBase.Load` suffix to the procedure definition. It is this part of the statement that indicates to the compiler that this procedure will run when the Load event occurs. `MyBase` is a reference to the *base class*, which for a standard Web Form is System.Web.UI.Page. Unlike VB 6.0, your event-handling procedures are not restricted to the *object_event* naming syntax and you can give them any valid name because the association with the event is explicitly specified in this way.

Replace the existing comment with the following code:

```
With SourceList
    .Items.Add("North")
    .Items.Add("West")
    .Items.Add("Central")
    .Items.Add("East")
    .Items.Add("South")
End With
```

As you can see, `SourceList` is an object with a property called Items. You add entries to the list by calling the `Add` method on this property, passing the text of the entry you want added as a parameter. As you'd expect, there are many other properties and methods exposed by the list box, some of which we will shortly use. Before we look at these, ask yourself, "How does the .vb class know that SourceList is a list box?" After all, the .aspx class inherits from the .vb class, and with the inheritance relationship established in this direction, there's no way that the .vb class should know anything about the content of the .aspx.

The answer to this is wrapped up in the way that Visual Studio .NET creates controls on Web Forms. When you added the list boxes and the button earlier, Visual Studio .NET did two things:

1. It added the `<asp. . .>` tags to the .aspx file in order to define the visual element for each of the controls.

2. It added three class-level protected variable declarations to the .vb file—one per control. The variable names match the control IDs, and the variable data types match the control types:

   ```
   Protected WithEvents SourceList As System.Web.UI.WebControls.ListBox
   Protected WithEvents SelectedList As System.Web.UI.WebControls.ListBox
   Protected WithEvents btnSelect As System.Web.UI.WebControls.Button
   ```

Since these variables are declared using the `WithEvents` keyword they are able to receive events raised by the control objects in ASP.NET. When the Web

Form is compiled and executed at runtime, ASP.NET seamlessly combines the controls defined in the .aspx with the variables declared in the .vb file to provide the appearance, behavior, and functionality that is required.

As well as initializing the Web Form, we also need code to respond to the click-event of the Select button. As before, double-click the button on the designer to produce the skeleton procedure and add the following code:

```
Private Sub btnSelect_Click(ByVal sender As System.Object, _
                ByVal e As System.EventArgs) Handles btnSelect.Click
    If SourceList.SelectedIndex >= 0 Then
        SelectedList.ClearSelection()
        SelectedList.Items.Add(SourceList.SelectedItem)
        SourceList.Items.Remove(SourceList.SelectedItem)
    End If
End Sub
```

The purpose of this code should be fairly obvious. It first checks to see that an entry was selected in the SourceList list box, and if so, it clears the current selection in SelectedList, adds the selected item to the SelectedList and then removes it from SourceList. This process has the effect of moving the selected item from the left-hand to the right-hand list box.

Running the Application

Now we're in a position to run and test the application. Before we can do this, however, we must set the Web Form as the *Initial Page* by right-clicking RegionPicker.aspx in the Solution Explorer Window and selecting **Set as Start Page**. You can now start the application either with (**Debug ➢ Start**) or without debugging (**Debug ➢ Start Without Debugging**). Alternatively, if you want to test only a single page, then you can right-click the page in the Solution Explorer and choose **Build and Browse**. Whichever method you use, the Web Form should be processed and displayed in a browser window. Select one of the entries in the left-hand list and click the button to transfer to the right-hand list. Congratulations, it works! But look again. Something has gone wrong: The source list box now has some of the entries duplicated. If you try selecting another region and clicking the button, you'll find even more are added.

What's happening here is that the `Page_Load` event handler is running every time the page is processed—in other words, on every *postback*—whereas we want it to run only when the page is loaded for the first time. The solution to this problem is to add a check into the `Page_Load` event handler to identify whether the page request was caused by an initial loading of the page or by a subsequent postback. ASP.NET makes this really easy by providing a property of the Page object called IsPostback. All we need to do is check the value and only perform the initialization of the list box if `IsPostback = False`:

```
If Page.IsPostBack = False Then
    With SourceList
        .Items.Add("North")
        .Items.Add("West")
        .Items.Add("Central")
        .Items.Add("East")
        .Items.Add("South")
    End With
End If
```

Test the application again and you'll see that the list is populated only once—when the page is first displayed. If you've had experience of creating postback pages using classic ASP, you might now wonder how the Listbox controls retain their content between postbacks. Once again this is an automatic feature in ASP.NET, implemented using a facility known as *ViewState*. ViewState will be discussed in more detail in Chapter 3.

Positioning Controls

Web Forms themselves are really just containers, and it is unlikely that you will work with many Web Forms that do not contain some additional controls. Positioning and sizing these controls is an important task. You've seen in the above example how easy this process appears to be. However, in the real world it's rarely this simple. One of the challenges facing Web developers is how to create user interfaces that look good in all the different browsers, versions, screen sizes, and resolutions that users have.

If our simple RegionPicker Web Form is displayed in a small browser window, the browser is expected to automatically display scroll bars to allow you to see the entire content. The controls will retain their original position and size, even though that means they may not always be visible. Whilst this approach is fine in many situations, the design of your Web application may call for a different approach where the content of the Web Form automatically flows and wraps to fit the browser. How can you achieve this alternate view?

The solution to this is to use the *PageLayout* property of the Web Form to select either *grid layout* or *flow layout* mode.

Grid Layout

By default, the Web Form will be in grid layout mode, which allows absolute positioning of all content. This means that you place controls on a Web Form in exactly the same way that a Visual Basic desktop programmer places controls on a Windows Form—in other words, they stay where you want them to stay.

Grid layout mode was used in the RegionPicker Web Form. If you go back and examine the HTML view of the .aspx file, you'll see that `Style` attributes are used to define position and size for each control. For example:

```
<asp:ListBox id="SourceList" style="Z-INDEX: 101; LEFT: 16px;
        POSITION: absolute; TOP: 16px" runat="server" Width="128px"
        Height="160px"></asp:ListBox>
```

Flow Layout

You can set the PageLayout property to FlowLayout, which causes the designer to arrange the objects relative to one another with no absolute positioning. Flow layout is what most classic ASP programmers will be most used to. Even though grid layout always sounds the best choice, flow layout can actually be easier to work with for complex or very dynamic pages.

Any changes you make to the PageLayout property are **not** applied retrospectively. For example, if you return to RegionPicker.aspx and set its PageLayout property to FlowLayout, you will see that the existing controls remain unchanged; only the controls added after the property is changed are affected.

To really see the effect of flow layout, create another Web Form called RegionPickerFlow and set its PageLayout property to FlowLayout. Add two list boxes and a button, but notice that the controls are positioned relative to one another and you cannot relocate them just by dragging. If you view the HTML source for this Web Form, the section representing the controls will appear similar to the following:

```
<form id="Form1" method="post" runat="server">
    <asp:ListBox id="SourceList" runat="server"></asp:ListBox>
    <asp:Button id="btnSelect" runat="server" Text="Select"></asp:Button>
    <asp:ListBox id="SelectedList" runat="server"></asp:ListBox>
</form>
```

If you want better control over the location of the controls in flow layout mode, then you must insert line breaks, whitespace, and other HTML elements to position the controls as required—or use tables.

Browser Rendering

The PageLayout property determines how controls are positioned and sized both at design-time and runtime. As you've already seen, the PageLayout property uses `Style` attributes for absolute positioning when you set the grid layout mode. Unfortunately, not all browsers support the `Style` attribute, as it was only introduced with HTML 4.0. Trying to render such a tag in an older browser will obviously fail, with the most likely outcome being that the position and size information will be completely ignored.

If you are building an ASP.NET application with a target audience that includes users with older browsers, then you will also need to consider another property: TargetSchema. The TargetSchema property can be set to any of the following values:

- Internet Explorer 3.02 / Navigator 3.0
- Internet Explorer 5.0 (this is the default)
- Navigator 4.0

The chosen setting determines how the page is rendered to the browser, including what tags and attributes are used. All of the examples shown so far have used a TargetSchema setting of *Internet Explorer 5.0*, which generates `Style` attributes to control positioning and sizing. The following shows an extract of the HTML rendered to an Internet Explorer 6.0 browser with this setting:

```
<form name="Form1" method="post" action="RegionPicker.aspx" id="Form1">
    <input type="hidden" name="__VIEWSTATE" value="dD . . ... 4=" />
    <select name="SourceList" id="SourceList" size="4"
            style="height:160px;width:128px;Z-INDEX: 101; LEFT: 16px;
            POSITION: absolute; TOP: 16px">
        <option value="North">North</option>
        <option value="West">West</option>
        <option value="Central">Central</option>
        <option value="East">East</option>
        <option value="South">South</option>
    </select>
    <select name="SelectedList" id="SelectedList" size="4"
            style="height:160px;width:128px;Z-INDEX: 102; LEFT: 224px;
            POSITION: absolute; TOP: 16px">
    </select>
    <input type="submit" name="btnSelect" value="Select" id="btnSelect"
            style="width:64px;Z-INDEX: 103; LEFT: 152px;
```

```
            POSITION: absolute; TOP: 72px" />
</form>
```

Conversely, setting the TargetSchema to *Navigator 4*.0 produces the following output for the same Web Form:

```
<TABLE height="366" cellSpacing="0" cellPadding="0"
            width="194" border="0" ms_2d_layout="TRUE">
    <TR vAlign="top">
        <TD width="194" height="366">
            <form name="Form1" method="post" action="RegionPicker.aspx" id="Form1">
                <input type="hidden" name="__VIEWSTATE" value="dD . . . . . 4=" />
                <TABLE height="177" cellSpacing="0" cellPadding="0" width="354"
                            border="0" ms_2d_layout="TRUE">
                    <TR vAlign="top">
                        <TD width="16" height="16">
                        </TD>
                        <TD width="136">
                        </TD>
                        <TD width="72" rowSpan="2">
                        </TD>
                        <TD width="130">
                        </TD>
                    </TR>
                    <TR vAlign="top">
                        <TD height="56">
                        </TD>
                        <TD rowSpan="2">
                            <select name="SourceList" id="SourceList" size="4"
                                        style="height:160px;width:128px;">
                                <option value="North">North</option>
                                <option value="West">West</option>
                                <option value="Central">Central</option>
                                <option value="East">East</option>
                                <option value="South">South</option>
                             </select>
                        </TD>
                        <TD rowSpan="2">
                           <select name="SelectedList" id="SelectedList" size="4"
                                        style="height:160px;width:128px;">
                            </select>
                        </TD>
                    </TR>
```

```
                    <TR vAlign="top">
                        <TD height="105">
                        </TD>
                        <TD>
                            <input type="submit" name="btnSelect" value="Select"
                                     id="btnSelect" style="width:64px;" />
                        </TD>
                    </TR>
                </TABLE>
            </form>
        </TD>
    </TR>
</TABLE>
```

This time the rendered output is quite different, being comprised of two nested tables. Also the `<input>` tag for the text box has no `Style` attribute defined, as the browser is assumed not to support it. From the user's perspective, both pages appear the same in the browser, so ASP.NET has provided us with a way to render similar output despite possible technological differences in the browser.

So which setting should you use? Ultimately this depends on your target audience. If you can guarantee that your target audience will be using Microsoft Internet Explorer 5.0 or later, then use the default setting (it minimizes the amount of data that needs to be sent to the browser). In our simple example, the *Internet Explorer 5.0* setting generated an HTML file of 1439 bytes, compared to 2149 bytes when using the *Navigator 4.0* setting. On a more realistic page with many controls and a sophisticated layout, this difference will be much more pronounced.

If you need to support older browsers, then you will need to use the *Navigator 4.0* or *Internet Explorer 3.02 / Navigator 3.0* settings, depending on the mix of browser types and versions that you expect to find. The bottom line is that for public Web applications, you cannot afford to turn users away. Using the baseline *Internet Explorer 3.02 / Navigator 3.0* setting guarantees that anyone with an HTML 3.2-compliant browser will be able to view the page.

Defining Web Form Properties and Methods

As previously mentioned, Web Forms are programmable objects and so have a rich and varied set of properties and methods. Some properties represent standard HTML tags, elements, and attributes—such as `background`, `bgColor`, `link`, `title`, etc.—while others are specific to the ASP.NET environment.

It would be possible (although rather tedious) for us to list each of these members, summarize the key points, and provide a thorough listing of all the details, however, you've already got such a reference in the form of the Visual Studio .NET online documentation. This documentation has the added advantages of thorough cross-referencing and powerful search capabilities. Instead, we've decided to pick on some of the really important members—the ones that are going to make a big difference in the way your applications work—and to show what they're about and how best they're used.

`ClientTarget`

As we saw in Chapter 1, ASP.NET can generate browser-specific HTML from a single, standard Web Form. It does this by detecting and identifying the browser type for each request and then passing this information to the Web Form, which in turn passes it to each constituent control. However, the process of identifying the browser type adds an overhead to each page request and introduces the possibility that certain browsers (including future versions) could be misidentified.

You can disable this detection process by explicitly setting the Web Form's ClientTarget property. The value for ClientTarget can be any valid string, although only specific values will be effective. In particular, the following can be entered:

- `Auto`
- `DownLevel`
- `UpLevel`
- Any valid User-Agent string for a browser

Auto,the default value, causes ASP.NET to detect and identify browser strings from each request. **DownLevel** forces ASP.NET to treat the browser as a generic HTML 3.2-compliant browser with no support for features such as scripting and DHTML. **UpLevel** forces ASP.NET to assume that the browser does provide support for HTML 4.0 and the more advanced features found in many modern browsers. Finally, browser User-Agent strings can also be entered, and these will force ASP.NET to target a specific browser.

For example, some Web Controls are able to generate client-side script to minimize the number of server round-trips required to process an event, but the script is generated only if the browser is identified as supporting it. To ensure that all processing is performed server-side (and hence no script is created), ClientTarget would be set to *DownLevel.* Conversely, to force client script to be generated, the property could be set to *UpLevel.*

EnableViewState and EnableViewStateMac

ViewState is the term given to the maintenance of page- and control-specific content and data between postbacks. In simple language, each control on the page stores and retrieves all of its property values whenever there is a server round-trip; and it all happens without you needing to write a single line of code. In classic ASP you would need to code this type of behavior manually, but ASP.NET does it automatically. However, you don't get this functionality for free because the ViewState information is passed to and from the browser in a hidden control on each Web Form. The content of this hidden control can be quite significant, and the time required to pass the data over a slow Internet link can be noticeable. The only way to see the detail of the control is to view the source of the page from the browser. Figure 2-7 shows how this could appear, with the ViewState shown in the middle of the image.

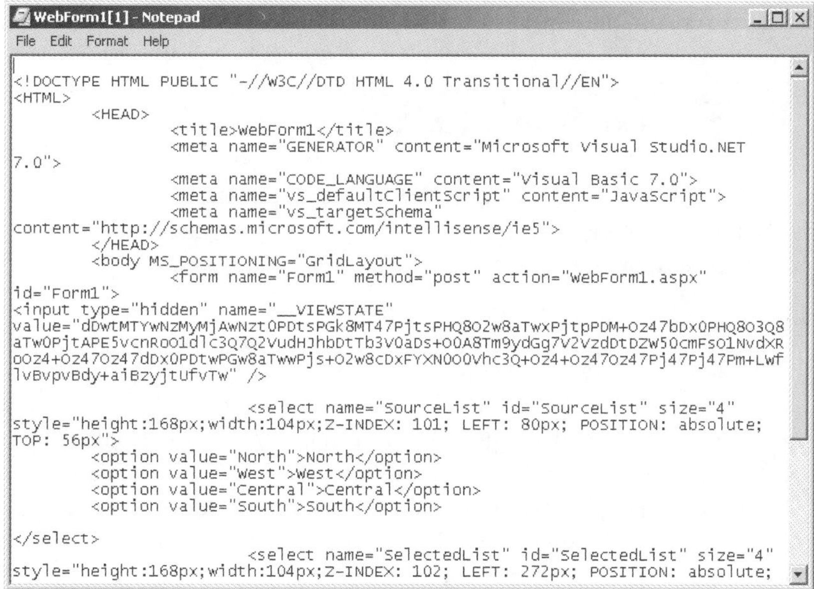

```
WebForm1[1] - Notepad
File Edit Format Help

<!DOCTYPE HTML PUBLIC "-//W3C//DTD HTML 4.0 Transitional//EN">
<HTML>
        <HEAD>
                <title>WebForm1</title>
                <meta name="GENERATOR" content="Microsoft Visual Studio.NET
7.0">
                <meta name="CODE_LANGUAGE" content="Visual Basic 7.0">
                <meta name="vs_defaultClientScript" content="JavaScript">
                <meta name="vs_targetSchema"
content="http://schemas.microsoft.com/intellisense/ie5">
        </HEAD>
        <body MS_POSITIONING="GridLayout">
                <form name="Form1" method="post" action="WebForm1.aspx"
id="Form1">
<input type="hidden" name="__VIEWSTATE"
value="dDwtMTYwNzMyMjAwNzt0PDtsPGk8MT47PjtsPHQ8O2w8aTwxPjtpPDM+Oz47bDx0PHQ8O3Q8
aTw0PjtAPE5vcnRoO1dlc3Q7Q2VudHJhbDtTb3V0aDs+O0A8Tm9ydGg7V2VzdDtDZW50cmFsO1NvdXR
oOz4+Oz47Oz47dDx0PDtwPGw8aTwwPjs+O2w8cDxFYXN0O0Vhc3Q+Oz4+Oz47Oz47Pj47Pj47Pm+LWf
lvBvpvBdy+aiBzyjtUfvTw" />

                        <select name="SourceList" id="SourceList" size="4"
style="height:168px;width:104px;Z-INDEX: 101; LEFT: 80px; POSITION: absolute;
TOP: 56px">
        <option value="North">North</option>
        <option value="West">West</option>
        <option value="Central">Central</option>
        <option value="South">South</option>

</select>
                        <select name="SelectedList" id="SelectedList" size="4"
style="height:168px;width:104px;Z-INDEX: 102; LEFT: 272px; POSITION: absolute;
```

Figure 2-7. HTML source showing the ViewState control

The EnableViewState property allows you to control whether ViewState is maintained for a Web Form or not. Setting EnableViewState to False disables the process completely and so can speed up transfer of data. However, since most postback forms depend on ViewState (as we will see in Chapter 3), completely disabling ViewState for the entire Web Form in this way is likely to cause problems. Instead, you should consider setting the EnableViewState property for each control independently.

Generally, ViewState should only be used for non-sensitive, non-critical information, and so needs no special validation or verification when it is used. However, in some applications it may be necessary to ensure that the ViewState data has not been tampered with; you can do this by setting EnableViewStateMac to True. This causes ASP.NET to encrypt and decrypt the ViewState on each page processing cycle so that the data cannot be tampered with outside of the application. As you may expect, these additional tasks cause ASP.NET to slow down when processing page requests, so they should only be used if specifically required.

IsPostback

IsPostback is a read-only, runtime-only property, and is used to detect whether a page-processing request is an initial request (in which case the value is False) or whether it is the result of a postback request from a browser (the value is True).

As discussed previously, this property is often used in the `Load` event for the Web Form to ensure that initialization is performed only on the initial request.

PageLayout and TargetSchema

PageLayout and TargetSchema collectively control how the Web Form is rendered to HTML for positioning and sizing controls. These properties should be considered together, as changes to one can impact the other.

Understanding Web Form Events

One of the greatest conceptual changes in the move from classic ASP is that ASP.NET has become event-driven rather than procedural. If you, like most people who buy this book, have experience with building desktop applications, then this should seem like familiar ground. If, on the other hand, you're from a classic ASP background, then the idea of event-driven Web applications may take a little getting used to.

The way that events are implemented and supported in ASP.NET is quite straightforward. For example, a Web Form has events such as `Init`, `Load`, and `Unload`, and these are fired in a logical and predictable sequence. However, there is one major difference between events in an ASP.NET application and events in a desktop application. In desktop applications, events are triggered by actions on the client and are handled by event procedures on the client. In ASP.NET applications, events are triggered in the client browser but are handled in server-side code.

So how does ASP.NET handle this separation? The complete answer to this question is a little involved and requires that you understand the role and usage of HTML Controls and Web Controls. These are covered in Chapters 3 and 4, and so we will defer a full discussion of event handling until later in the book.

At this stage you need to realize that ASP.NET automatically generates server-side events during the process of responding to a page request. For example, if you were to navigate to a page called ListAvailability.aspx, then the class for that Web Form would be executed (after being compiled if necessary). As a part of the sequence of steps that occur during the execution of a Web Form class, the following events will be fired:

1. `Init`, which occurs when the class is initialized. This is automatically coded by the Web Form designer.

2. `Load`, which occurs as the next step in the lifecycle. Load is typically used for initializing controls, variables, and structures.

3. `PreRender`, which occurs when the page is ready to be rendered to the browser.

4. `Unload`, which occurs when page processing has completed and the class is about to be terminated.

5. `Disposed`, which occurs when the class has been destroyed and removed from memory by the garbage collector.

Notice that since this is the initial call to the page, no control-specific events occur. However, if you change something on the page (such as selecting from a list or entering text into a text box) and then click a button, a postback will occur. The sequence of events is quite similar for the Web Form, but numerous control-specific events may also occur:

1. `Init` for the Web Form.

2. `Load` for the Web Form.

3. **Control Change events** occur next for the controls. These include SelectedIndexChanged for list boxes and TextChanged for text boxes. These events are discussed in more detail in Chapter 4.

4. **Control Passing events** occur for the button (or other control) that caused the postback. For a button control these include the `Click` and `Command` events, both of which are discussed in Chapter 4.

5. **PreRender**, which occurs when the page is ready to be rendered to the browser.

6. **Unload**, which occurs when page processing has completed and the class is about to be terminated.

7. **Disposed**, which occurs when the class has been destroyed and removed from memory by the garbage collector.

There are two things that you should remember about the event sequence:

- ASP.NET determines which events should occur based on the page request that caused the page to be processed. The client does not actually raise or cause an event directly; instead, the client simply generates a page request.

- The `Init`, `Load`, `PreRender`, `Unload`, `Disposed` events occur for every page request because the page objects are not retained between calls. Time-consuming initialization and cleanup code in the `Load` and `Unload` events are likely to cause poor performance.

Additional Events

As well as the "core" events described above, Web Forms support a number of additional events for particular tasks:

- **AbortTransaction** and **CommitTransaction** occur when a transaction within a transactional Web Form either fails or succeeds. These events provide a simple method for you to return information to the user about the outcome of any updates. Transactional behavior in Web Forms is governed by directives, and is discussed in Chapter 13.

- **DataBinding** occurs when controls are bound to a datasource. Data binding is discussed in Chapter 8.

- **Error** occurs when any unhandled exception is thrown in the Web Form, either by code or by controls.

These events are often important when building Web Forms that manipulate data through bound controls and ADO.NET; this will be discussed in more detail in Chapter 8.

Handling Events

The events described above are inherited from the System.Web.UI.Page class from which all Web Forms derive. They are handled by event procedures in your class; the event procedure is "hooked up" to the base class event with the statement

```
Handles MyBase.<Event Name>
```

The name of the procedure is irrelevant, although Visual Studio .NET retains the familiar object_Event notation from VB 6.0. All of the event-handling procedures accept two parameters: the first is a reference to the object generating the event and the second represents additional event arguments. Putting this together, we get:

```
Private Sub Page_Load(ByVal sender As System.Object, _
                ByVal e As System.EventArgs) Handles MyBase.Load
```

or

```
Private Sub Page_Error(ByVal sender As Object, _
                ByVal e As System.EventArgs) Handles MyBase.Error
```

Exploring Navigation

Navigation is a general term for the process of moving between pages or requesting updates for the current page. The simple application shown earlier in the chapter illustrates one form of navigation—the postback—but two other forms are also widely used, namely direct navigation and code-based navigation.

Each of these techniques is worthy of some further discussion, as you will be using them extensively within your Web applications. Since direct navigation is the simplest, we will deal with it first.

Direct Navigation

Direct navigation refers to the use of standard HTML techniques, elements, and tags to move through the application. Direct navigation techniques work with Web Forms, classic ASP pages, as well as regular HTML and DHTML Web pages. The process is largely controlled by the browser.

The most common HTML elements used with direct navigation are:

- **Hyperlinks**, where the address of the target page is embedded in the <A> tag. Navigation occurs when the user clicks the hyperlink.

```
Click for <A href="Details.aspx">Further Details</A>
```

- **Forms**, where the address of the target page is embedded in the <Form> tag. Navigation occurs when the user submits the form, which usually happens when they click a Submit button in the form.

```
<FORM action="ProcessLogin.aspx" method="post">
```

- **Client-side code**, where the address of the target page is embedded in the script. Navigation occurs when the script runs, which is usually aided by attaching it to an event on a control or hyperlink.

```
window.open("MoreInfo.htm","_top");
```

The target page for these techniques can be anything at all, including Web pages, text files, Microsoft Office documents, XML documents, and so on. All that happens is that when the navigation occurs, the browser requests the indicated document from the specified location. This is a useful technique for simple navigation because it places no load on the server and requires no specific processing.

Postbacks

Postbacks are a special case of direct navigation. What is special is that the target page for navigation is the same page that is currently being viewed. In other words, the page request is "posted back" to itself. Postbacks still have to be triggered in some way. In ASP.NET the most common causes are that the user clicks a button in a Web Form or they perform an action (such as changing the content of a control) that runs some client-side JavaScript to submit the form. As we will see in Chapter 4, you don't have to perform any special coding to achieve this since ASP.NET's Web Controls automatically provide this functionality.

When working with postbacks in classic ASP it is often necessary to write additional code to manage the process since there are a number of tasks that you usually need to perform:

- You would need to check whether the page request was an initial one, in which case the form was displayed with blank values, or whether it was a postback, in which case the code took a different course of action by validating and processing the form content.

- You would need to perform validation on the content of the form.
- You would need to ensure that any content entered by the user (e.g. page state) would also be redisplayed. There is nothing that annoys a user more than getting a page sent back because they forgot to type in their e-mail address, only to find that they need to reenter all the other information all over again.

ASP.NET has made the process of creating such postback forms easier than ever by automating the following features:

- **Every Web Form supports the IsPostback property.** This property is automatically set to True if the source of the current request was the page itself, and False if the page was requested by another source. IsPostback dramatically simplifies the task of initializing the content on the first call only.
- **ASP.NET provides Web Controls to simplify client-side and server-side validation.** Special-purpose validation controls can be configured to perform checks on required fields, permissible values, or ranges of values. Server-side validation is made easier because HTML Controls and Web Controls can be referenced as objects in server-side code.
- **ASP.NET can automatically maintain page state through the ViewState facility.** ViewState is used by ASP.NET to do two things. Firstly, it records the original property values of any control marked as a server-side control on a Web Form. By comparing the current properties of a control to their original values, ViewState allows ASP.NET to determine which controls have been changed by a user. ViewState is actually stored in the page that is sent to the user (in the hidden control), so it requires no server-side state in order to work. Secondly, ViewState allows developers to persist custom values—such as variables or objects—between postback calls to the page. Once again, this minimizes the need for such values to be held in server-side state. ViewState is discussed in more detail in Chapter 3.

A good example of how you can use the `Page_Load` event and the IsPostback property to perform once-only initialization was shown in the earlier example:

```
Private Sub Page_Load(ByVal sender As System.Object,
                ByVal e As System.EventArgs) Handles MyBase.Load
    If Page.IsPostBack = False Then
        With SourceList
            .Items.Add("North")
```

```
                .Items.Add("West")
                .Items.Add("Central")
                .Items.Add("East")
                .Items.Add("South")
            End With
        End If
    End Sub
```

The code that initializes the list box runs only on the first call to the page (`IsPostBack = False`). On subsequent postback requests to the page, the ViewState automatically ensures that the content of the list is maintained.

Code-Based Navigation

Code-based navigation is managed by server-side code and allows your application to determine its navigation path independently of the browser. ASP.NET provides two techniques for code-based navigation: *Response.Redirect* and *Server.Transfer*.

Response.Redirect

`Response.Redirect` has been the traditional technique for code-based navigation and was supported in all versions of classic ASP. It works by generating an HTTP Redirect header and sending it to the browser, complete with the URL you specify for the redirection. This causes the browser to make another request against the new URL, so the server effectively gets hit twice.

The following example shows how `Response.Redirect` can be used to navigate to a Web Form called FailedLogon.aspx:

```
Response.Redirect("FailedLogon.aspx")
```

The problem with `Response.Redirect` is that it requires two server roundtrips to perform the navigation—the first to process the page containing the redirection, and then another to obtain the redirected page. You can avoid this unnecessary overhead by using `Server.Transfer`, as discussed below.

`Response.Redirect` does have an important use though, and that is when you want to redirect a user to a completely different Web application or Web site. For example, you may support paid advertising on your Web site, in which case you almost certainly want to measure the number of click-throughs for billing purposes. A simple way to do this is to have a `ProcessAdvert` function which accepts the ID of the advert clicked as a parameter and calls it from the click-event procedure of each of the advert buttons or links. In this function you can run some code to increment the click-through count and read the URL of the advertiser's site (both of these would usually be held in a database table, XML document, or similar). Having retrieved the URL, your code can then perform a `Response.Redirect` to take the user to that site.

Server.Transfer

`Server.Transfer` was introduced in ASP 3.0 as a more efficient replacement for `Response.Redirect`. It continues to be supported in ASP.NET and is the preferred code-based method in most cases. Rather than generating an HTTP header to perform the redirection, `Server.Transfer` handles the navigation internally and so bypasses the need for an additional server round-trip.

When you call `Server.Transfer`, ASP.NET stops processing the code in the current page and instead loads and executes the class for the page specified in the URL. This page is processed in its entirety, including the Init and Load events that may perform initialization (remember, this request is an initial request rather than a postback). When control is transferred to this new page. ASP.NET also transfers all of the information in the in-built objects (Server, Application, Session, Request, Response, and Context).

The final point worth noting is that `Server.Transfer` is transparent to the browser. This means that if the browser requests a page called Login.aspx, but your code calls `Server.Transfer("LoginFailed.aspx")`, then the page URL displayed in the browser is still Login.aspx, even though the processing has been performed by LoginFailed.aspx. This is a useful technique when you want to hide the fact that a redirection has occurred.

Understanding Web Form File Structure

As you've already seen, every Web Form is based on an .aspx file, much as classic ASP used ASP files. However, the source-code implementation of a Web Form typically consists of more than the .aspx alone and often includes three files:

- <Filename>.aspx
- <Filename>.aspx.resx
- <Filename>.aspx.vb or <Filename>.aspx.cs

<Filename>.aspx

The .aspx file contains the definition of the interface elements, including the HTML tags and elements, server controls, Web Form properties, etc. The .aspx is the navigation target for users' browsers and is rendered to a regular HTML page according to the Web Form's properties, content, and code.

The .aspx file remains in text form in the final application, even after compilation. This allows the developer to make changes to the visual interface without having to return to the development environment and recompile. Optionally, the .aspx file can contain embedded code (see below). This code will be compiled on first access and thereafter will function much like the compiled code in a .dll.

<Filename>.aspx.resx

The .resx file is a reference file for binary and other resources required by the Web Form. The file is formatted as an XML document, and is used during the compilation process to determine which additional resources or components should be compiled into the .dll.

The .resx for a Web Form will initially be empty and will remain so until a reference to a resource or component is required; but, when necessary, Visual Studio .NET will update and extend the .resx file to include appropriate information.

In most cases you will have no need to view or edit the .resx file directly, just like you had little reason to ever consider the .frx files created in VB 6.0. If the need does arise though, simply double-click the .resx file in the Solution Explorer window and it will open in Visual Studio .NET's XML editor.

<Filename>.aspx.vb

The .vb file contains the source code written by the developer in the *code-behind* module. The file extension denotes the language being used—Visual Basic—and the code within the file is compiled into the application's .dll by Visual Studio .NET. This .dll must be placed in the \bin directory beneath the application's virtual root. In addition to VB .NET, you can create ASP.NET applications using C#; support for additional languages such as COBOL, SmallTalk, and Python has been provided by third-party organizations.

The relationship and association between the .aspx and the associated .vb file is governed by a *Page directive* in the .aspx. For example, consider the Page directive used in the RegionPicker.aspx file:

```
<%@ Page Language="vb" AutoEventWireup="false" Codebehind="RegionPicker.aspx.vb"
          Inherits="HiFlyers.RegionPicker"%>
```

The AutoEventWireup attribute determines how event handlers are associated with events. If set to False, you need to use the Handles statement in the procedure definition to define which events each routine will handle. This is the preferred setting in Visual Studio .NET; it allows you to choose any valid names for your event-handling routines. If AutoEventWireup is set to True, ASP.NET will associate handlers with events according to their names, in the same way as VB 6.0. This means that a handler for the load event of the page would have to be called Page_Load, while a handler for the click event of btnSubmit would need to be called btnSubmit_Click. There's no clear advantage to using the second approach; in fact, it could cause conflicts with any code produced by Visual Studio .NET (which always uses the Handles keyword).

The Codebehind attribute is used only by development environments such as Visual Studio .NET. This attribute specifies the source code file that should be associated with the .aspx when the file is loaded into the development tool. The Inherits attribute is used at runtime to define the code-behind class for the page; this will usually be found in the application's .dll. One other attribute that may be used is *Src*, which specifies a source code file that contains the code for the Web Form. Unlike the Codebehind attribute, which is used only by development tools, Src is used by the runtime compiler to identify, load, and compile a code-behind module when the .aspx is first accessed. Src isn't needed when your code is compiled into a .dll and placed in the \bin directory of the Web application—which is exactly what Visual Studio does for you.

Note that you don't actually need a code-behind module or class for an .aspx file because you can embed all source code into the .aspx itself. This approach may be suitable during the migration of classic ASP applications to ASP.NET, but as a long-term development strategy we don't recommend it. There are many benefits to be gained from separation of code from content, and although it may take you time to adopt the new style, the time spent learning the new approach will pay off several times over.

Content of a Web Form

So far, we haven't seen the full range of things that can appear in an .aspx file. In fact, we've only scratched the surface. Web Forms can comprise a combination of HTML, Web Controls, server-side code, client-side script, directives, comments, and various other elements.

HTML

Just as a classic ASP page could contain static HTML alongside its server-side script, so can a Web Form. Visual Studio automatically builds many of the static elements, such as the definition of the document type, `<html>`, `<head>`, and `<body>` elements, `<meta>` tags, and other boring bits you really don't want to type yourself. You can manually add other elements as well, such as text, forms, form elements including `<input>` and `<select>` tags, plus tables, spans, divs, and any other valid HTML content.

You can create this content using the Web Form designer or the HTML textual view; it can also be imported into the solution from prebuilt HTML files by selecting **Project ➢ Add Existing Item**. Be careful with this last approach though since Visual Studio .NET copies the specified file into the application, rather than referencing it in its original location. If the original file is updated, it must be brought into the project again.

Figures 2-8 to 2-10 show three different views of a Web Form. Figures 2-8 and 2-9 show the visual designer and HTML View, while Figure 2-10 shows the results rendered to the browser:

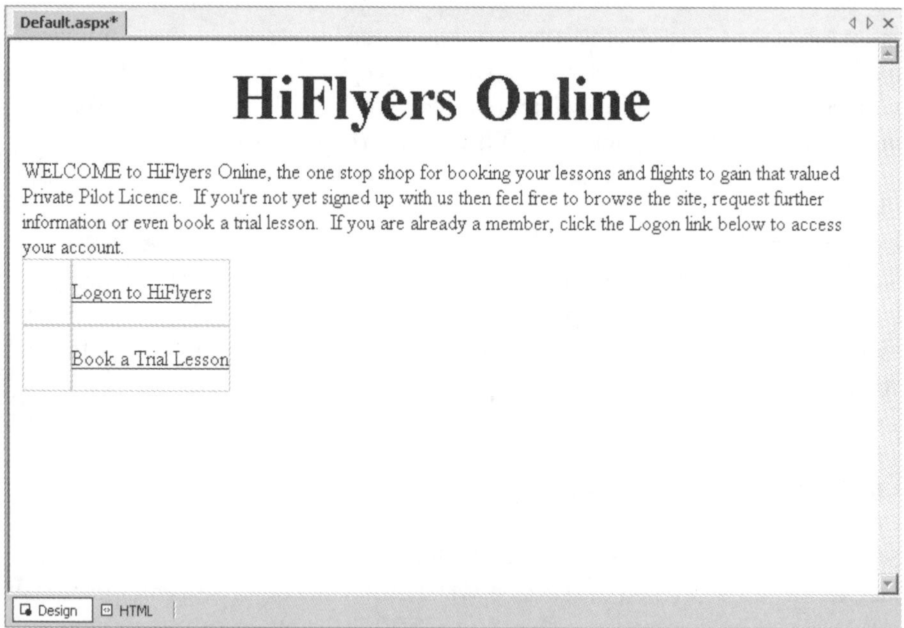

Figure 2-8. Web Form Design View for Default.aspx

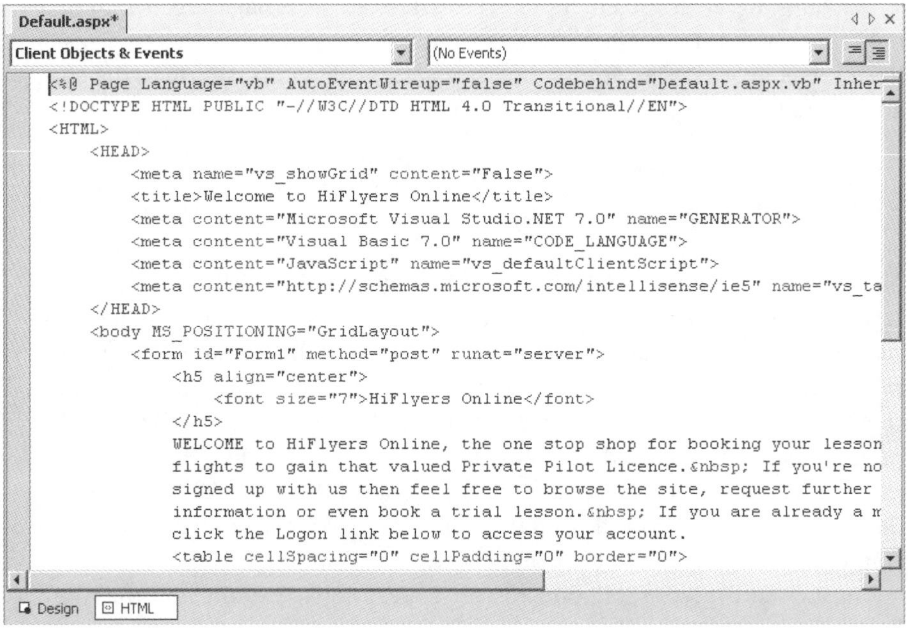

```
Default.aspx*
Client Objects & Events          (No Events)
<%@ Page Language="vb" AutoEventWireup="false" Codebehind="Default.aspx.vb" Inher
<!DOCTYPE HTML PUBLIC "-//W3C//DTD HTML 4.0 Transitional//EN">
<HTML>
    <HEAD>
        <meta name="vs_showGrid" content="False">
        <title>Welcome to HiFlyers Online</title>
        <meta content="Microsoft Visual Studio.NET 7.0" name="GENERATOR">
        <meta content="Visual Basic 7.0" name="CODE_LANGUAGE">
        <meta content="JavaScript" name="vs_defaultClientScript">
        <meta content="http://schemas.microsoft.com/intellisense/ie5" name="vs_ta
    </HEAD>
    <body MS_POSITIONING="GridLayout">
        <form id="Form1" method="post" runat="server">
            <h5 align="center">
                <font size="7">HiFlyers Online</font>
            </h5>
            WELCOME to HiFlyers Online, the one stop shop for booking your lesson
            flights to gain that valued Private Pilot Licence.  If you're no
            signed up with us then feel free to browse the site, request further
            information or even book a trial lesson.  If you are already a m
            click the Logon link below to access your account.
            <table cellSpacing="0" cellPadding="0" border="0">
Design  HTML
```

Figure 2-9. HTML View of Default.aspx

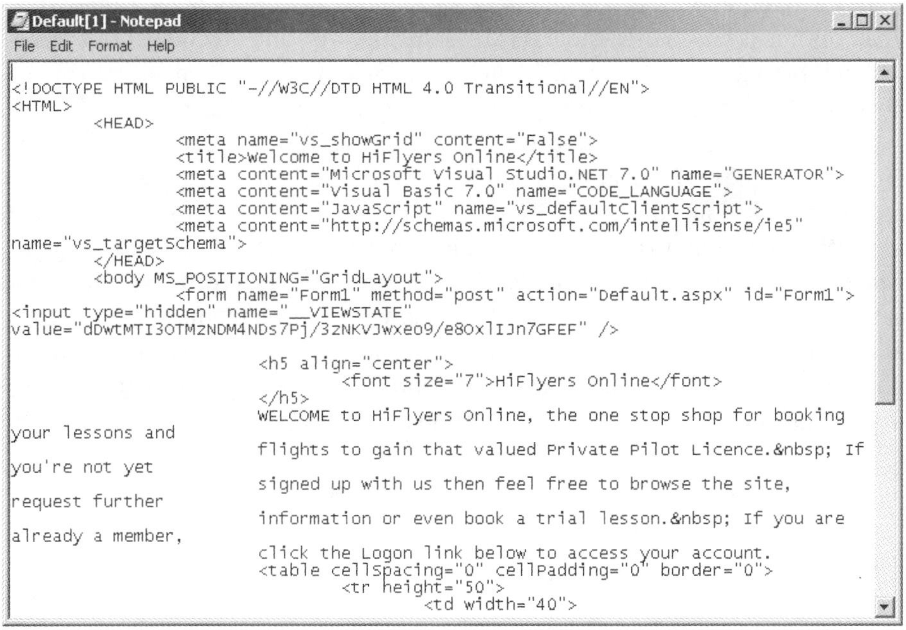

```
Default[1] - Notepad
File  Edit  Format  Help

<!DOCTYPE HTML PUBLIC "-//W3C//DTD HTML 4.0 Transitional//EN">
<HTML>
        <HEAD>
                <meta name="vs_showGrid" content="False">
                <title>Welcome to HiFlyers Online</title>
                <meta content="Microsoft Visual Studio.NET 7.0" name="GENERATOR">
                <meta content="Visual Basic 7.0" name="CODE_LANGUAGE">
                <meta content="JavaScript" name="vs_defaultClientScript">
                <meta content="http://schemas.microsoft.com/intellisense/ie5"
name="vs_targetSchema">
        </HEAD>
        <body MS_POSITIONING="GridLayout">
                <form name="Form1" method="post" action="Default.aspx" id="Form1">
<input type="hidden" name="__VIEWSTATE"
value="dDwtMTI3OTMzNDM4NDs7Pj/3zNKVJwxeo9/e8OxlIJn7GFEF" />

                        <h5 align="center">
                                <font size="7">HiFlyers Online</font>
                        </h5>
                        WELCOME to HiFlyers Online, the one stop shop for booking
your lessons and
                        flights to gain that valued Private Pilot Licence.  If
you're not yet
                        signed up with us then feel free to browse the site,
request further
                        information or even book a trial lesson.  If you are
already a member,
                        click the Logon link below to access your account.
                        <table cellSpacing="0" cellPadding="0" border="0">
                                <tr height="50">
                                        <td width="40">
```

Figure 2-10. HTML rendered to the browser from Default.aspx

As you can see, if you enter pure HTML into an .aspx page, it gets sent to the browser as pure HTML. ASP.NET adds additional tags and elements (such as the hidden `__ViewState` control), but the tags and elements we add to the page are sent to the browser in the unchanged form.

HTML Controls

An interesting extension to the inclusion of static HTML is the introduction of server-side HTML. ASP.NET allows almost all HTML elements to support a new `runat="server"` attribute. HTML elements marked in this way are known as HTML Controls, and while not making any fundamental change to the client-side rendering or behavior of the element, the attribute allows the HTML to be programmatically accessed and controlled by server-side code. HTML Controls exist primarily to ease the migration from classic ASP to ASP.NET, and allow developers to begin taking advantage of the new .NET features without having to completely restructure their existing pages.

At the same time, HTML Controls are a great way to explore how the Web Forms model simplifies programming. Classic ASP programmers have to wrestle with HTML text to create Web page output, while ASP.NET programmers work with objects to generate Web pages. Notice the word "object." You can read and write properties of the control, call its methods, and handle its events just as you can for other objects. The difference is that HTML Control objects present their output as browser-friendly HTML elements, tags, and attributes. This translation is performed automatically when the page is processed, leaving you to focus on the things that are really important in the application.

We'll see much more about HTML Controls in Chapter 3, but its worth introducing a simple example at this point to show the fundamental difference between the classic ASP and ASP.NET approaches. Let's assume we have a page in the Web Application to display information about members of the flying school and that allows updates to be made. The member data has already been read into a number of variables; now we want to use some HTML elements in a form to display the details. Two of these items are the member's name and whether or not they are a student; so, we'll use a text field and a check box to represent them. In classic ASP the page content would be similar to:

```
<P>Member Name:  <INPUT type="text" id="txtName" value="<%=strName%>"></P>
<P>Student? <INPUT type="checkbox" id="chkStudent"
                <% =IIF(blnIsStudent,"CHECKED","")%></P>
```

Here, you can see code (contained inside `<% %>` delimiters) entwined with pure HTML markup. The code for the text field is just a simple reference to the variable holding the data, but to generate the `CHECKED` attribute for the check box we need a rather messy IIF (Immediate If Function). We could have used a standard `If . . . Then. . . Else. . .` instead, but it would still be an excessive amount of code for such a simple requirement as ticking a box. It's also messy and error prone, with simple errors—such as missing quote marks or mismatched brackets—creeping in all the time.

At runtime, the results would be rendered to the browser as:

```
<P>Member Name:  <INPUT type="text" id="txtName" value="Steve"></P>
<P>Student? <INPUT type="checkbox" id="chkStudent" CHECKED></P>
```

This style of integrating code and content dominates in classic ASP because there is no real generally applied alternative. It doesn't look so bad in such a simple example, but for anything less trivial, the result soon becomes so much spaghetti.

However, in an ASP.NET Web Form, similar results can be achieved by changing the HTML to:

```
<P>Member Name:  <INPUT type="text" id="txtName" runat="server"></P>
<P>Student? <INPUT type="checkbox" id="chkStudent" runat="server"></P>
```

Notice that the assignments to the `value` and `checked` attributes have been removed, and that `runat="server"` attributes have been added. As well as the changes to the .aspx, two entries need to be made to the associated code-behind module. The first is to declare object variables that represent the controls so that the code in the module can refer to them:

```
Protected WithEvents txtName As System.Web.UI.HtmlControls.HtmlInputText
Protected WithEvents chkStudent As System.Web.UI.HtmlControls.HtmlInputCheckBox
```

The second change is to add code to the `Page_Load` event of the Web Form to set the property values:

```
Private Sub Page_Load(ByVal sender As System.Object,
                ByVal e As System.EventArgs) Handles MyBase.Load
    txtName.Value = strName
    chkStudent.Checked = blnIsStudent
End Sub
```

Do we *really* have to manually make these changes? Fortunately, no you don't. In Chapter 3 you'll see how you can tell ASP.NET to automatically convert standard HTML elements into server-side HTML Controls; but right now it's useful to perform the task manually so you can see what's involved in the process.

When viewed in the browser, the rendered result is slightly different, but why? When we define the element as a server-side HTML Control we ask ASP.NET to do a bit more work for us. To do this, ASP.NET needs to manage the HTML that is sent to the browser:

```
<P>Member Name:  <input name="txtName" id="txtName" type="text"
                value="Steve" /></P>
<P>Student?  <input name="chkStudent" id="chkStudent" type="checkbox"
                checked="checked" /></P>
```

What ASP.NET has actually done is to turn our "short-cut" HTML into well-formed, XHTML-compliant HTML. Notice that it has converted the tag and attributes to lower case and has added an `id` attribute. If we had omitted the quotation marks around the values, it would have put these in as well. Finally, and for no real reason, it has changed the order of the attributes. Despite these changes, the element is still defined using pure HTML.

As a first step toward separating code from content, this is a big improvement; no longer do developers have to create lengthy code to dynamically build HTML tags and attributes. The controls can now be treated as programmable objects, with all of their attributes exposed as properties. However, marking HTML elements with the `runat="server"` attribute also provides more very powerful features.

In particular, form-based controls—such as the textbox and checkbox used above—can generate server-side events. Server-side events allow us to handle events in much the same way a Visual Basic desktop programmer handles events for the controls they use. This huge step forward in Web programming requires no special browser capability. Exactly how it works will be explored more fully in Chapters 4 and 10.

One of the most important server events for an HTML Control is the `ServerChange` event. This event fires on the server when the user changes the content of the control and then submits the form. Server-side events allow easier validation and processing since it is now a simple matter to check only the controls that have changed.

Certain HTML Controls have additional special features. For example, if you make a `<select>` element into an HTML Control (by adding `runat="server"`) you can program it using an Items collection (just as we did with the Web Form Listbox control we added to the designer in our earlier example). The Items collection exposed by an HTML Control is exactly the same as the Items collection exposed by the Web Form control, providing the same methods for adding, removing, and clearing entries.

For example, the following `<Select>` could be defined in the .aspx file:

```
<SELECT id="Select1" name="Select1" size="1" runat="server">
```

In the code-behind module the following code could be added to the page's load event:

```
Select1.Items.Add("North")
Select1.Items.Add("South")
Select1.Items.Add("East")
Select1.Items.Add("West")
```

It is worth remembering that, in both of these examples, the controls being used are standard HTML, with the only addition being the `runat="server"` attribute.

This section has provided only a brief discussion of HTML Controls and their capabilities. Chapter 3 revisits this topic in much greater depth, and expands on all of the key points for using and managing HTML Controls.

Web Controls

While HTML Controls are undoubtedly powerful, they do have a number of drawbacks:

- There is no flexibility or intelligence in the rendering of HTML Controls. The elements you place on the Web Form are exactly what the user gets in the browser.

- Element names and tags "overlap." For example, a button and a text field are both created from `<input>` tags. If you have an HTML background, then you'll already be familiar with these tags, but to a VB programmer it is rather illogical because Buttons and Text controls do very different things.

- Property and attribute names are not consistent with standard naming of other objects and components. For example, the content of an HTML textbox is accessed through the value property, rather than text.

- All HTML Control properties are of type string. This is not always convenient and can lead to problems with data type conversion and validation.

- You, as the developer, must ensure that the elements, tags, and attributes being used will be supported by the target browsers. In the diverse Internet environment, this is a difficult guarantee to make.

ASP.NET provides a solution to these problems in the form of Web Controls. Web Controls are server-side objects that you add to the Web Form's designer in much the same way as HTML elements—and can be programmed just as easily.

Web Controls have rich sets of properties, methods, and events, all of which have standardized names, data types, and argument lists. Some Web Controls are adaptive, that is, they identify the current browser's capabilities and limitations and render their output in a compatible form. You should note that this feature is *not* provided by the ASP.NET Framework, but instead by each control. Simple controls—such as the TextBox and Button—often don't justify the additional development work that adaptive behavior requires, so they render themselves the same way for every browser. Also, adaptive behaviors work only for identified and supported browsers; clients running unsupported browsers may get unexpected results. For older browsers there may be no fix for the problem, but newer browsers can often be supported by reconfiguring ASP.NET, as we will see in later chapters.

You will see lots of Web Controls used throughout this book. The standard Web Controls supplied with Visual Studio .NET are addressed in more detail in Chapter 4, while Chapter 5 looks at the topic of building Custom Web Controls. A special type of Web Control is the Mobile Web Control, and these are discussed in Chapter 6.

Server-side Code

As you have already seen through previous examples, Web Forms can be associated with code that will be executed on the server and the results returned in the HTML stream to the browser. This code can be embedded directly in the .aspx file of the Web Form or it can be placed in a code-behind module. If using embedded code, it is enclosed in standard ASP delimiters within the file using either of the following formats:

- `<%. . . . .%>`
- `<script runat=server>. . . . . .</script>`

In classic ASP there was little difference between the uses of these two notations, but in ASP.NET the latter approach *must* be used when creating Subs or Functions. The `<%. . .%>` notation can only be used for "inline" code, as we saw earlier.

Client-side Code

Despite the power of ASP.NET, client-side code is still required for some tasks and thus remains an important part of the Web Form. Just as standard HTML elements are ignored by ASP.NET, any script code that is not marked as server code is simply sent to the browser with no interference from ASP.NET. ASP.NET will even generate client-side code in some cases, such as when using validation controls.

The following extract from a Web Form shows how a client-side JavaScript function can be associated with an HTML Button even though that HTML button has been marked as a server control:

```
<script language="javascript">
    function openNewWindow(windowURL)
    {
        window.open(windowURL,"_New");
    }
</script>
.
.
.
<INPUT type="button" value="Details" id="btnDetails" runat="server"
               onclick="javascript:openNewWindow('Details.htm')">
```

CAUTION *The above example works fine as long as you* ***do not*** *write an event handler for the button. When an event handler is present, ASP.NET often writes its own client-side code to perform a postback and to trigger the server-side routine. This code would conflict with our function since ASP.NET would attempt (and fail) to associate both with the* `onclick` *attribute.*

Directives

We can't finish describing the contents of a Web Form without describing directives. These are declarations added to the .aspx file that define how the page should be processed and managed by ASP.NET. Every Web Form you create must have a Page directive, but there are other types of directives available for managing special behaviors.

Directives are entries in the Web Form that specify settings to be used by the compiler when the file is processed. With ASP.NET, the directives can be located anywhere in the file, although standard practice is to include them at the beginning. classic ASP requires that the directives are all enclosed in a single delimited block, but ASP.NET removes this restriction.

There are a number of different directives supported and used in ASP.NET, some of which relate to Web Forms, while others are applicable to Web Controls or Web Services. Of the available directives, there are really only three that you are likely to use on a regular basis:

- `@ Page,` which defines page-specific attributes used by the parser and compiler. The different attributes for the Page directive are discussed below.
- `@ Register`, which associates aliases with namespaces and class names. As we will see in Chapter 5, you will use the @Register directive when you want to add a custom Web Control to a Web Form. In many cases, ASP.NET automatically generates this directive for you.
- `@ OutputCache`, which controls the output caching policies of the Web Form. Caching techniques are covered in Chapter 12, including use of the OutputCache directive.

The remaining directives are likely only to be used if you choose to embed your ASP.NET server-side code in the .aspx file itself, rather than using a code-behind class. These additional directives perform the same tasks that VB .NET handles for code-behind modules, including referencing assemblies, importing namespaces, and implementing interfaces.

- `@ Import,` which imports a namespace into a Web Form. This is the equivalent of the VB .NET `Imports` statement.
- `@ Implements,` which indicates that the Web Form implements a specified interface. This is the equivalent of the VB .NET `Implements` statement.
- `@ Assembly`, which links an assembly to the current Web Form. This is the equivalent of setting a reference to an assembly from within your project.
- `@ Reference`, which links a specified page or control to the current Web Form. This allows you to create instances of the page or control in code using early binding techniques.

Remember, if you build Web Forms using code-behind modules you do not need these four directives; they are relevant only if the code is embedded in the .aspx file.

Page Directive Attributes

Each directive that you specify can contain one or more attributes, which in turn may be paired with values. These attribute-value pairs provide additional guidance to the compiler to control how the page is compiled and processed.

For example, the following Page directive specifies the language for a page and that implementation code is to be inherited from an associated class. It also specifies the Codebehind attribute that Visual Studio .NET uses to load the associated source code at design-time:

```
<%@ Page Language="vb" Codebehind="Default.aspx.vb" Inherits="HiFlyers.CDefault"%>
```

Alternatively, the following Page directive could be used to specify that the implementation code is to be read from a source-code file deployed on the server rather than a compiled .dll:

```
<%@ Page Language="vb" Src="Default.aspx.vb" Inherits="HiFlyers.CDefault"%>
```

Many attributes can be applied to the Page directive, although a number of them duplicate properties of the Web Form and so can be more easily set using the property browser. The Visual Studio .NET Help system provides a comprehensive listing of all the attributes and their possible values, but the following are the most important:

AspCompat—Default: False

Setting this attribute to True causes the page to be executed on a single-threaded apartment (STA) thread. This is important when the code calls other STA components, such as those developed with VB 6.0. Setting this attribute to True also allows the page to call COM+ 1.0 components that require access to the unmanaged ASP built-in objects, such as Request or Response.

AutoEventWireup—Default: True

Indicates whether the page's events are autowired (i.e. the page events are automatically enabled). This is not the way that Visual Studio .NET handles events. Even though the ASP.NET default is True, Visual Studio .NET sets this attribute to False and adds explicit code to handle the events.

Buffer—Default: True

Determines whether page buffering is enabled. If so, the entire page's output is composed on the server and then sent to the browser in one chunk. If Buffer is set to False, page output is sent to the browser in a constant stream as the page is processed.

CodeBehind

Specifies the name of the associated code-behind module to be loaded into Visual Studio .NET. This attribute has no effect at runtime and is ignored by the compiler.

ErrorPage

Allows you to define the URL of a page which will be displayed if an unhandled exception occurs during the processing of a request for the current page.

EnableSessionState—Default: True

This attribute value determines how session state is managed for the page. A value of True means that session state is enabled; False means that it is disabled; and ReadOnly allows the page to read—but not change, create, or delete—session state values. For further discussion of session state, see Chapter 12.

EnableViewState—Default: True

Determines whether ViewState is maintained for the page between postbacks. This attribute is the same as the EnableViewState property for the Web Form discussed earlier in the Defining Web Form Properties and Methods section earlier in this chapter.

Inherits

Defines a code-behind class for the page to inherit. The code-behind class can be any class that derives from the System.Web.UI.Page class. See the Web Form Classes section earlier in this chapter for further information.

Language

Specifies the language used when compiling all inline rendering (<% %> and <%=%>) and code declaration blocks within the page. Values can represent any .NET-supported language, including VB, C#, or JScript.

Src

Specifies the source file name of the code-behind class to dynamically compile when the page is requested. If the `Src` attribute is not found in a Web Form, ASP.NET automatically looks for a compiled assembly that contains the code-behind class.

NOTE *RAD designers—such as Visual Studio .NET—do not use this attribute. Instead, they precompile code-behind classes and then use the* `Inherits` *attribute.*

Trace

Determines whether page-level tracing is enabled or disabled. The default value is blank, which allows the Web.config setting to define whether tracing takes place. You can set this attribute value to True or False to explicitly control trace behavior. See Chapter 10 for a thorough discussion of tracing.

Transaction—Default: NotSupported

Indicates whether COM+ automatic transactions are supported on the page. Possible values are NotSupported, Supported, Required, and RequiresNew.

Comments

Comments can be included as HTML comments, delimited with <!--> and <-->, or they can be placed in server-side code blocks and identified with a single apostrophe. HTML comments will, of course, be rendered to the browser, whereas server-side code comments will not.

Where to Locate Code?

ASP.NET strongly emphasizes the separation of code and content; many of the features discussed in this chapter contribute directly to this goal by allowing you to place code in code-behind modules. While this is very much the preferred style, there may be times when it is still appropriate to take the classic ASP approach of embedding code within the .aspx:

- **If code needs to be changed frequently.** .aspx files can be edited with a text editor and will be compiled automatically the first time they are referenced after being edited. Code-behind modules implemented in Visual Studio .NET are compiled into the application .dll, so any changes made to the code-behind module would have to be made back in the development environment. As will be seen in Chapter 10, the Page directive allows the use of a `Src` attribute, which specifies the name of a code-behind module that will be maintained in source-code form, thereby providing separation of code and content but still allowing on-the-fly changes.

- **If you want to use client-side code.** The most convenient way to send script code for the browser to process is to type it directly into the .aspx page.

- **If client-side code is interacting with content that is dynamically created, or if client-side code is dynamically created by server-side code.** ASP.NET provides no direct support for managing client-side code in the same way it provides support for forms and controls. So, you will probably find it easier to manage client-side code generation from within the .aspx file itself.

Code placed into a code-behind module and compiled to a .dll offers advantages in terms of performance (when first referenced), security (more difficult to hack), and management and maintainability (more structured approach to coding), and so should be used when possible.

The Shift from Procedural to Object-Oriented

As you've realized by now, there has been a fundamental shift in ASP.NET from the old procedural way of coding in classic ASP, to a fully object-oriented approach under .NET. If you're an old-timer—a programmer from the era of million-dollar mainframes and thousand-dollar disk drives—then you'll have been through this process with other languages and development tools. If you're a more recent addition to the developer community then you may have wondered why ASP was always so clunky and cumbersome compared to VB.

Either way, ASP.NET requires that you take a different perspective on future Web development. You need to think in object-oriented (OO) terms, and you'll benefit from adopting OO designs and methodologies. In short, you need to think .NET, and that could require some significant changes to the way you plan your coding.

One of the tricks to coding efficient and effective ASP.NET applications is to make use of the available .NET classes. There are literally thousands available that manage everything from file I/O to string handling, and dates and times to databases. These classes are going to save you a lot of work, providing an enormous amount of in-built functionality yet generally being very easy to work with. But you do have to invest the time up front to learn your way through the namespaces and classes.

Whilst this change of style and architecture has introduced new requirements, it has also delivered many improvements. One of the most welcome improvements has been the introduction of event-driven Web Forms and Web Controls. As you have started to see in this chapter, they provide a far more structured and logical way to build interactive Web Applications, allowing you to apply existing skills and abilities to this type of development. An immediate benefit of this is that development times can be reduced when compared to classic ASP development; subsequent maintenance should also be reduced.

In the longer term, the OO approach now used for Web Application development should fit more cleanly into the OO architectures used for other tiers of larger scale applications. This should make it easier to build enterprise-scale projects that take advantage of many of the powerful .NET features and abilities to deliver robust, high-performance applications without the tears.

Summary

In this chapter we have explored Web Forms and how they are used in .NET all the way from the development environment to the browser. You have seen that Web Forms—like almost everything in .NET—are classes and that they inherit many powerful behaviors from the Page base class. You have begun to investigate their key properties and methods, and examined the Web Form lifecycle in terms of the events that can be raised.

You've also had a first look under the hood, and seen how Web Forms can render browser-neutral HTML under your control, as well as how you can make use of more advanced browser features if you are willing to forego a little portability. This is certainly a key area—one that you need to explore in depth if you are building broad-reach Internet applications.

The chapter also gave us a chance to look at Web Applications in a broader sense, and to begin to make decisions about their architecture, structure, and code locations. These are topics that we will cover in more detail in later chapters.

In conclusion, Web Forms may look just like simple Web pages, but in reality they are active, customizable classes that provide the fundamental building blocks for .NET Web Applications. They give Web developers a powerful object-oriented model that has been available to desktop developers for years. Yet, when Web Forms run they can generate flat-file, browser-neutral HTML that can be viewed and manipulated by almost any browser, on almost any platform. As a launch pad for further development, they're an impressive starting point.

CHAPTER 3

HTML Controls

As you saw in Chapter 2, Visual Studio .NET's Web Form designer enables you to add, position, and configure a variety of different visual components when you create the user interface. In this chapter we'll look at the use of standard HTML tags and elements and the use of server-side HTML controls. If you're new to HTML, or if your knowledge is a little rusty, you'll probably want to check out our ten-minute primer in Appendix A because we'll be dealing with HTML at a fairly low level.

Introducing HTML Tags, Elements, and Controls

So what, briefly, do we mean by HTML tags, elements, and controls?

HTML tags are the directives entered in a Web Form that tell the browser how to render the page. Tags are enclosed in pointy brackets and are defined in the various HTML specifications. Examples of tags include `<body>`, `<br>`, `<font>`, and `<h1>`.

Tags often have *attributes* associated with them to provide more information. Attributes take the form of name/value pairs, with multiple pairs separated by spaces. For example, `<body scroll="no">` or `<font size="10" color="blue">`. Current HTML standards specify that attribute values should be enclosed in quotes, although some browsers (including Microsoft Internet Explorer) do not enforce this rule and will usually process unquoted values without problems.

HTML elements are structural parts of the Web Form and are defined using HTML tags. Although there are some elements that consist of a single tag, such as <br> or <hr>, it's quite likely that two separate tags will be needed, in the form of beginning and ending tags. For example, the section of a Web Form enclosed within the <body> and </body> tags is an element, as is any <font>...</font> section. The body element shows an important feature of HTML elements—they can act as containers for other elements. In other words, you can expect to see further HTML tags and elements within the <body>...</body> section.

HTML tags and elements are client-side features, so ASP.NET does not process or modify them in any way. However, the client's browser uses the tags and elements to render the page, so it must understand and recognize the names of the tags used in the Web Form. If the page contains unrecognized tags, then the browser may choose to either ignore them completely or display the tag in its raw form to the user.

HTML Controls are a special type of HTML element. ASP.NET processes HTML Controls on the server-side, which means they can be accessed as programmable objects by server-side code and can raise server-side events. You define an element as an HTML Control by including a special `runat="server"` attribute in the opening tag. In addition, the opening tag must also have a valid `id` attribute, which defines the name you'll use to refer to the control. For example:

```
<INPUT id="Button1" type="submit" value="Button" name="Button1" runat="server">
```

Some documentation refers to HTML Controls as *HTML Server Controls* to emphasize their server-side capabilities. In this book we'll stick with calling them *HTML Controls.*

Using HTML Controls

Given that we've already said that Web Controls are more powerful than HTML Controls, we forgive you for wondering whether you should skip directly onto Chapter 4. This would be a mistake, though, for two reasons:

- HTML Controls have a number of valid purposes in ASP.NET and some surprisingly powerful features. At the end of the chapter, we'll discuss some of the reasons for using HTML Controls over Web Controls in more depth, but for now, trust us when we say you should spend a little time getting to know them.

- Some of the most powerful features of ASP.NET apply to both Web Controls and HTML Controls. Because HTML Controls are easier to understand than Web Controls, they're ideal for exploring some of these powerful features, and so we're using this chapter to address some core ASP.NET topics such as server-side events and ViewState.

You create HTML Controls by adding them to a Web Form. At design-time, you do this in two steps by first adding an HTML element to the page and then converting it to run as a server-side control. You can also create HTML Controls dynamically at runtime by using code.

Design-Time Creation

As mentioned previously, there are two stages to creating HTML Controls at design-time. The first stage is to add an HTML element to the page, and for many developers the easiest way to do this is to use the tools on the HTML tab of the Toolbox. Figure 3-1 shows the HTML tools (the icons in your Toolbox may appear in a different sequence).

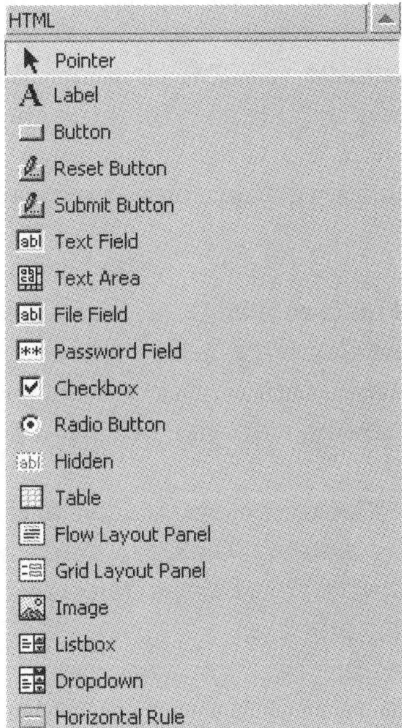

Figure 3-1. The HTML Controls in the Toolbox

You can add any of these to the Web Form by double-clicking or by dragging and drawing. You may find that when the Web Form's PageLayout property is set to FlowLayout, the drag-and-draw method is unsuccessful. If so, double-click the tool to add the element and then reposition or size it afterward.

NOTE *Remember that at this stage you're creating a regular client-side HTML element, not a control. The element will not be accessible to server-side code (yet) and will be rendered directly to the client browser.*

As well as the elements supported by the tools shown in Figure 3-1, there are additional elements supported in HTML. You can create some of these (including Bookmark and Hyperlink elements) using commands on the **Insert** menu, while the **Table** menu provides further commands for creating and configuring HTML tables, rows, and cells. If none of these tools or commands supports the element you need, then you must manually enter the tags into the HTML View of the Web Form designer.

The HTML tools map directly to HTML elements, although the name of the tool is not necessarily the same as the name of the element it'll create. For example, a Text Field control generates an `<input>` tag with a `type="text"` attribute. However, there are five controls that are a little less obvious and worthy of special mention:

- The Label control renders to an HTML `<div>` element. The text of the label renders as the content of the element and goes between the `<div>` and `</div>` tags. Also, an attribute is associated with the `<div>` to indicate its content should be treated with FlowLayout positioning.

- The Flow Layout Panel control also renders to an HTML `<div>` element with FlowLayout positioning. The real difference between this and the Label control is that the Flow Layout Panel is likely to be used as a container for more than just text.

- The Grid Layout Panel renders to an HTML `<div>` tag with GridLayout positioning.

The Flow Layout Panel and Grid Layout Panel enable you to create sections and areas of Web Forms that have different layout properties to the rest of the page. For example, you may need to use FlowLayout as the PageLayout setting for a Web Form, but you want an area within the page organized in grid layout mode. You can easily achieve this by adding a Grid Layout Panel control.

- The Listbox control renders to an HTML `<select>` element with a size attribute of 2 or more. The default Listbox control contains a single `<option>` element, but this can be modified as discussed next.

- The Dropdown control renders to an HTML `<select>` element with a size attribute of 1. It also contains a single `<option>` element by default.

The Listbox and Dropdown controls can contain a number of `<option>` elements, each defining a list entry. You can enter these `<option>` elements manually into the HTML View for the Web Form, or you can use the Property Pages dialog box. Open this dialog box by right-clicking the control and selecting **Properties**, or by choosing **View ➢ Property Pages** when the control is selected. Figure 3-2 shows an example of these settings.

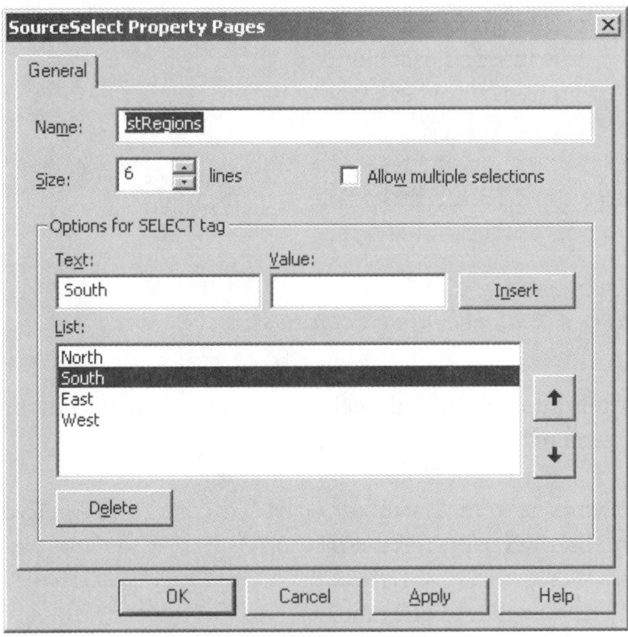

Figure 3-2. The Property Pages dialog box for a Listbox control

Server-Side or Client-Side

What we've achieved so far is only the first stage of creating an HTML Control, and although the Visual Studio .NET tools have helped us define elements and their attributes in a relatively friendly way, the result is still limited to producing client-side HTML. If we want these elements to be server-side programmable objects, then we need to make an additional change by converting them to HTML Controls.

Defining Server-Side Elements

As you've already seen, you define a server-side HTML Control with a "runat=server" attribute in the opening tag. In addition, the code for the Web Form must also contain a declaration for a corresponding object variable in the code-behind module. Fortunately, Visual Studio .NET can make both of these changes automatically; all you need to do is right-click the element and select **Run As Server Control** from the context menu.

Having marked an element as a server control, it displays on the designer with a small green arrow icon in its top-left corner. Figure 3-3 shows examples of a label, button, and text field marked as server-side.

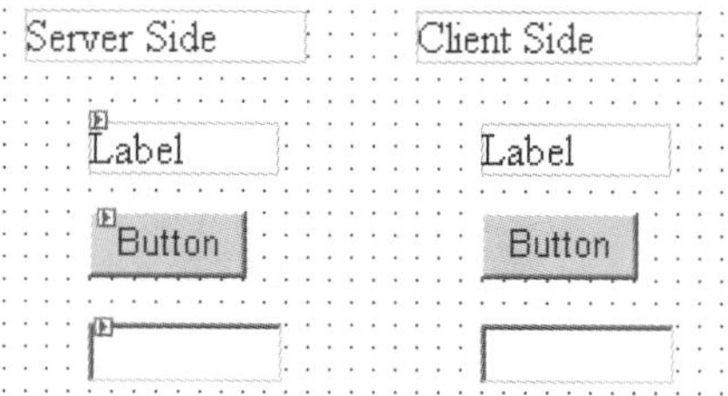

Figure 3-3. Server-side and client-side controls

The class definition in the code-behind module will now contain three variables, one for each of the server controls:

```
Protected WithEvents DIV1 As System.Web.UI.HtmlControls.HtmlGenericControl
Protected WithEvents Text1 As System.Web.UI.HtmlControls.HtmlInputText
Protected WithEvents Button1 As System.Web.UI.HtmlControls.HtmlInputButton
```

You can see from these declarations what the full class reference for the HTML Controls can be. Fortunately, you won't need to type this long-winded declaration yourself. We'll return to this subject when we discuss dynamically adding controls to a Web Form in the "Runtime Creation."

Defining Client-Side Elements

Generally, when you mark an element as a server control it should have no negative effects other than a slight impact on performance. The additional time required to process a single element is unlikely to be noticed, but if you were to mark many elements of a Web Form as server controls, then the effects would be more pronounced. We recommend you only mark elements as server-side controls if you want to work with their properties, methods, or events in code. Otherwise, it is inappropriate and wasteful to flag them as such; they should be left as client-side HTML.

If you've already marked an element as a server control and want to change it back to being a client-side element, then right-click the control again and select **Run As Server Control** from the context menu. Repeating the process in this way will "unmark" the control by removing the `runat="server"` attribute and the variable declaration in the code-behind class. The control will lose its server-side functionality and return to being simple, client-side HTML.

Runtime Creation

One of the most common requirements in any Web Application is to have the visual content generated dynamically, possibly from information in a database. In classic ASP it's necessary to dynamically generate tags, attributes, and values and to slot them together so that the page renders and formats correctly. ASP.NET makes this a whole lot easier by allowing dynamic creation of HTML elements and controls through code.

The easiest way to understand the techniques is to see them in action, so we'll use a simple example to illustrate. Our requirement is for a Web page that lists the aircraft in the HiFlyers training school fleet. There are many different ways of doing this, including:

- Data binding with a DataGrid control
- Data binding with a Repeater control
- Using code to dynamically build the table rows and cells

If you're a desktop developer, the phrase *data binding* may fill you with terror, as it is widely agreed that VB 6.0–style data binding is not an option in most professional applications. Remarkably, in ASP.NET quite the reverse is true, and data binding is likely to be the most efficient way to meet this requirement. However, data binding works only with Web Controls, not HTML Controls, so we'll leave its discussion until Chapter 8. For this example we'll adopt the third approach and use code to build the rows and cells needed to show the list.

We'll begin by creating a Web page containing a simple HTML table. The table is called tblAircraft and appears as shown in Figures 3-4 and 3-5.

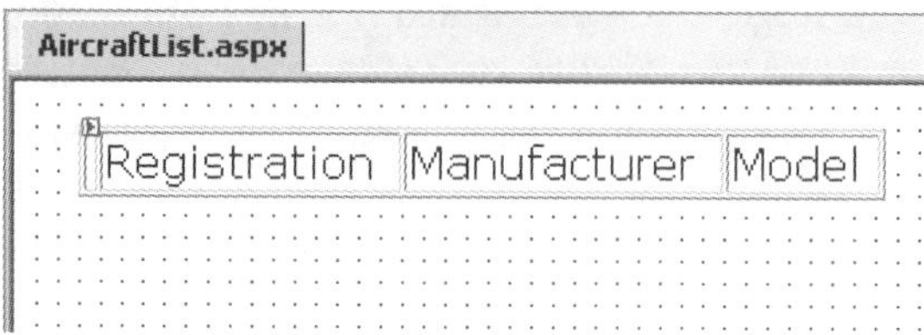

Figure 3-4. Graphical view of an HTML table

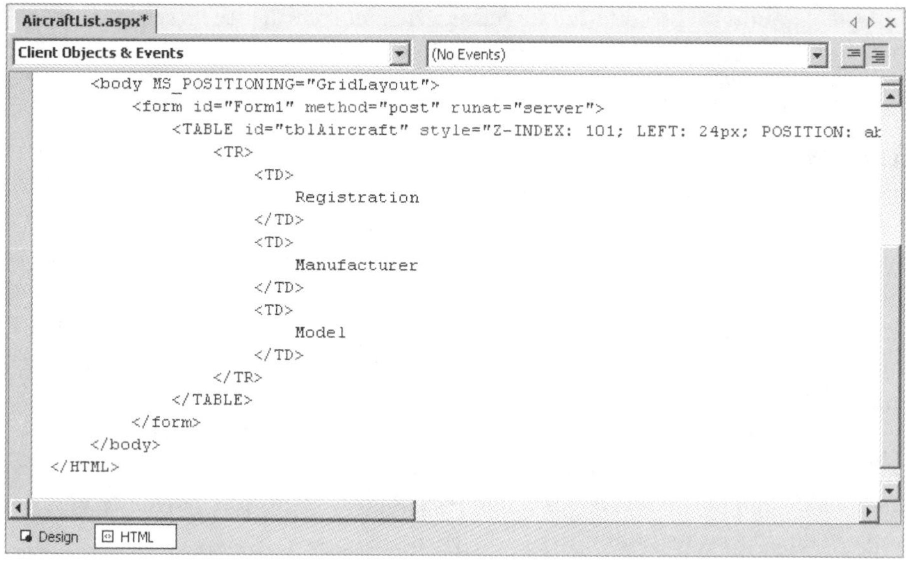

Figure 3-5. HTML View of the table

Remember that this is an HTML table rather than a Web Control table. If you want to try this example out you'll need to ensure you choose the tool from the HTML tab in the Toolbox. Also, the table has been flagged as a server control, as you can see from the green arrow in the graphical designer.

In the `Page_Load` event handler on the Web Form, we'll add code that reads from the database and populates the table. The first thing we need to do is open a connection to the database and retrieve the data for the table. This is comprised of the aircraft ID, registration, manufacturer, and model. In Chapters 7 and 8 we'll cover some more advanced techniques for working with databases. However, there are times when the simple approach used here will suit you best. If you're completely new to ADO.NET, Appendix D provides a brief overview, including the coverage of the objects used in this example. In this example we'll create a DataReader to retrieve the data because we're performing a simple, read-only operation:

```
Dim CN As New OleDbConnection("Provider=SQLOLEDB.1;Data Source=(local);" +
        "_Initial Catalog=HiFlyer;User ID=sa;")
CN.Open()
Dim CM As New OleDbCommand( _
        "SELECT AircraftID, Registration, Manuf, Model FROM Aircraft", CN)
Dim DR As OleDbDataReader

DR = CM.ExecuteReader()
```

NOTE *If you have problems logging on to SQL Server or MSDE, see the notes in Appendix D relating to how ASP.NET manages SQL Server Logons.*

We can now loop through the data in the DataReader and construct the controls. We can start with a `While...End While` structure, plus the definition of the new table row object:

```
While DR.Read()
    Dim TR As New HtmlTableRow()
```

Now, we can create the three cells for the table. Each is built using an individual object variable, and the InnerText property of each cell is set to the text from the corresponding database field:

```
    Dim TCReg As New HtmlTableCell()
    TCReg.InnerText = DR(1)

    Dim TCManuf As New HtmlTableCell()
    TCManuf.InnerText = DR(2)

    Dim TCModel As New HtmlTableCell()
    TCModel.InnerText = DR(3)
```

The cells are added to the row, and the row is added to the table:

```
    TR.Cells.Add(TCReg)
    TR.Cells.Add(TCManuf)
    TR.Cells.Add(TCModel)
    tblAircraft.Rows.Add(TR)
```

Finally we can complete the loop and then close the DataReader and Connection objects before we exit the routine:

```
    End While

    DR.Close()
    CN.Close()
End If
```

When tested, this Web Form retrieves the data from the table, generating one TableRow control per record. For each field, it generates a TableCell control. Figure 3-6 shows the results rendered to a browser.

Registration	Manufacturer	Model
G-29572	Cessna	C172
G-10593	Cessna	C152
G-48201	Cessna	C152

Figure 3-6. Dynamically generated table

If you view the Web page source, you'll see that even though the content is dynamically generated from runtime objects, it's still rendered to the browser as plain HTML:

```
<table id="tblAircraft" style="Z-INDEX: 101; LEFT: 24px; TOP: 16px"
            cellspacing="1" cellpadding="1" width="300" border="1">
    <tr>
        <TD>
                            Registration
                        </TD>
        <TD>
                            Manufacturer
                        </TD>
        <TD>
                            Model
                        </TD>
    </tr>
    <tr>
        <td>G-29572</td>
        <td>Cessna</td>
        <td>C172</td>
    </tr>
```

```
    <tr>
        <td>G-10593</td>
        <td>Cessna</td>
        <td>C152</td>
    </tr>
    <tr>
        <td>G-48201</td>
        <td>Cessna</td>
        <td>C152</td>
    </tr>
</table>
```

Handling Dynamic Events

The previous example's controls were non-interactive and did not respond to, or raise, events no matter what the user did. Although many dynamically created controls will be non-interactive, there will also be some that need to support event handling. Fortunately, ASP.NET makes this quite straightforward.

Once again it's easiest to illustrate the technique by example. What we'll do is to extend our aircraft list Web Form so that it also shows a Details button in the first column, which can delete further information on an aircraft. To start, we'll add an additional column to the left side of the table. You can do this by clicking in the first column, then selecting **Table ➢Insert ➢ Column To The Left**.

You can then modify the `Page_Load` event handler to include some code before the TCReg cell is instantiated. This additional code will need to first create an additional cell and then create an HTML button within the cell:

```
Dim TCDetails As New HtmlTableCell()
Dim btnDetails As New HtmlButton()
```

You can set the properties for the button next. We'll set the `InnerText` to `Details` as this will be shown as the caption of the button. We'll also set the `ID` of the button to the aircraft's ID from the database. This will be made accessible to the event-handling routine:

```
btnDetails.InnerText = "Details"
btnDetails.ID = DR(0)
```

Next, we want to wire up the button's `ServerClick` event to an event handler. You're probably familiar with the new `Handles` keyword in VB .NET (see Appendix C for an explanation), and this is a great way to specify event handlers statically, at design-time. The `AddHandler` statement does a similar thing, except that it enables us to wire up events dynamically, at runtime. We need to specify the event to be handled, which is `btnDetails.ServerClick`, and the *delegate* for the event handling procedure, which will be called `ShowDetails`. Fortunately the `AddressOf` operator is an easy way to provide a delegate:

```
AddHandler btnDetails.ServerClick, AddressOf ShowDetails
```

To display the button in the table, it must be added to the `Controls` collection of the table cell. Like many HTML Controls, a table cell is a container and supports the Controls collection for this purpose:

```
TCDetails.Controls.Add(btnDetails)
```

At the bottom of the `Load` event handler, the new TCDetails cell must be added to the cells collection of the table row along with the other cells. To ensure that everything still lines up, this should be the first cell that you add:

```
TR.Cells.Add(TCDetails)
TR.Cells.Add(TCReg)
TR.Cells.Add(TCManuf)
TR.Cells.Add(TCModel)
```

The modified `Load` event handler now appears as follows:

```
Private Sub Page_Load(ByVal sender As System.Object, _
                ByVal e As System.EventArgs) Handles MyBase.Load
    Dim CN As New OleDbConnection("Provider=SQLOLEDB.1;Data Source=(local);" &
            "_Initial Catalog=HiFlyer;User ID=sa;")
    CN.Open()
    Dim CM As New OleDbCommand( _
            "SELECT AircraftID, Registration, Manuf, Model FROM Aircraft", CN)
    Dim DR As OleDbDataReader

    DR = CM.ExecuteReader()
    While DR.Read
        Dim TR As New HtmlTableRow()

        Dim TCDetails As New HtmlTableCell()
        Dim btnDetails As New HtmlButton()
        btnDetails.InnerText = "Details"
        btnDetails.ID = DR(0)
        AddHandler btnDetails.ServerClick, AddressOf ShowDetails
        TCDetails.Controls.Add(btnDetails)
```

```
        Dim TCReg As New HtmlTableCell()
        TCReg.InnerText = DR(1)

        Dim TCManuf As New HtmlTableCell()
        TCManuf.InnerText = DR(2)

        Dim TCModel As New HtmlTableCell()
        TCModel.InnerText = DR(3)

        TR.Cells.Add(TCDetails)
        TR.Cells.Add(TCReg)
        TR.Cells.Add(TCManuf)
        TR.Cells.Add(TCModel)

        tblAircraft.Rows.Add(TR)
    End While

    DR.Close()
    CN.Close()
End Sub
```

Finally, we must create the ShowDetails routine and ensure that it accepts two parameters—the first will represent the control that raised the event and must be of type Object, and the second must be of type System.EventArgs:

```
Private Sub ShowDetails(ByVal Sender As Object, ByVal e As System.EventArgs)
    'Show the aircraft details - Sender.ID provides the AircraftID
End Sub
```

NOTE *As mentioned at the start of this section, this approach to generating tables dynamically is quite inefficient but extremely flexible and controllable. In Chapter 4 you'll learn more about Web Controls, and in Chapter 8 we'll investigate the automatic data-binding features that can be used to achieve the same results with less effort.*

This example has illustrated how you can dynamically create controls and add them to a table. You can use the same techniques to add controls to other elements as well, including the underlying <form> element in the Web Form itself. In fact, any HTML element that supports a Controls property can have controls created in it in this way.

Formatting and Style

Visual Studio .NET provides a number of methods for you to control the formatting, appearance, and layout of controls on a Web Form. You can position and size controls using:

- **Format ➢ Align**
- **Format ➢ Make Same Size**
- **Format ➢ Horizontal Spacing**
- **Format ➢ Vertical Spacing**

If you need fine control of position and size, then you can manually edit the setting for the Style property or use the Style Builder dialog box discussed in the next section. You can also display or hide the grid by selecting **Format ➢ Show Grid**, and you can turn Snap To Grid feature on or off by clicking **Format ➢ Snap To Grid**.

The Style Builder

The properties exposed by HTML Controls can be a little inconsistent. For example, an HTML Table supports a BackColor property, but an HTML Label does not. This inconsistency is not because of .NET, but instead lies within the HTML standards. The properties that we see exposed by HTML Controls are really just a convenient mechanism to assign values to HTML attributes from server-side code; any inconsistencies within HTML will therefore also appear within the HTML Control behaviors. Such inconsistencies can mean it's sometimes difficult to define the required appearance using properties alone. Instead, Visual Studio .NET provides the Style Builder dialog box. You can display this in two ways:

- Right-click an HTML Control and select **Build Style** from the context menu.
- Select the control and then click the **Builder** button for the Style property in the Properties window.

When displayed, the Build Style dialog box allows the control's Style property setting to be modified by way of friendly settings and options. Figure 3-7 shows how you can use the dialog box to define position and size information to individual pixel accuracy.

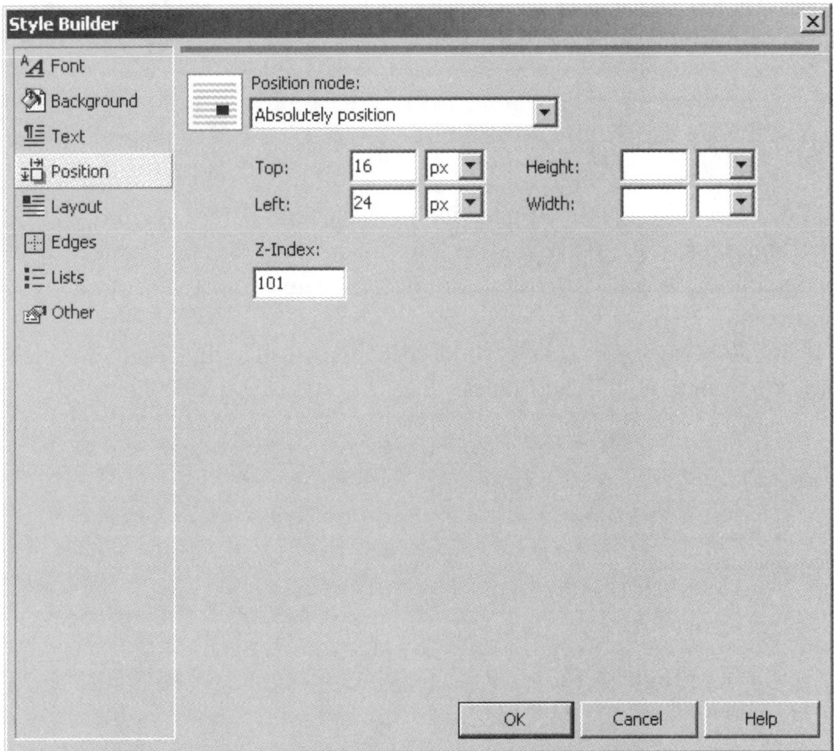

Figure 3-7. The Style Builder dialog box

Using Cascading Style Sheets

The final technique for formatting that we'll cover is the use of Cascading Style Sheets (CSS). CSS is a standardized technique for applying page-wide or application-wide styles and works on the basis of having separate files (.css files) that store the definition of the styles. You can create these styles in two main ways:

- You can define styles for any HTML element.
- You can define styles and give them a unique name.

You link the .css file to each Web page with a `<link>` tag in the `<head>` section of the document. Styles defined for HTML elements are then automatically applied to the content of the Web page, whilst you can individually apply named styles to particular elements, tags, or controls.

CSS is a client-side technology, and not all browsers support the same CSS features. Therefore, if you choose to use CSS, be aware that the results may not be quite as planned on some older browsers.

Creating CSS Styles

When you created your Web Application in Visual Studio .NET, an initial .css file (called Styles.css) was created for you. You can create additional .css files by selecting **Project ➢ Add New Item**, although to begin with, Styles.css will be sufficient.

If you open the Styles.css file, you'll see it displayed in the designer, which allows you to view, edit, or add styles. Figure 3-8 shows the Style View.

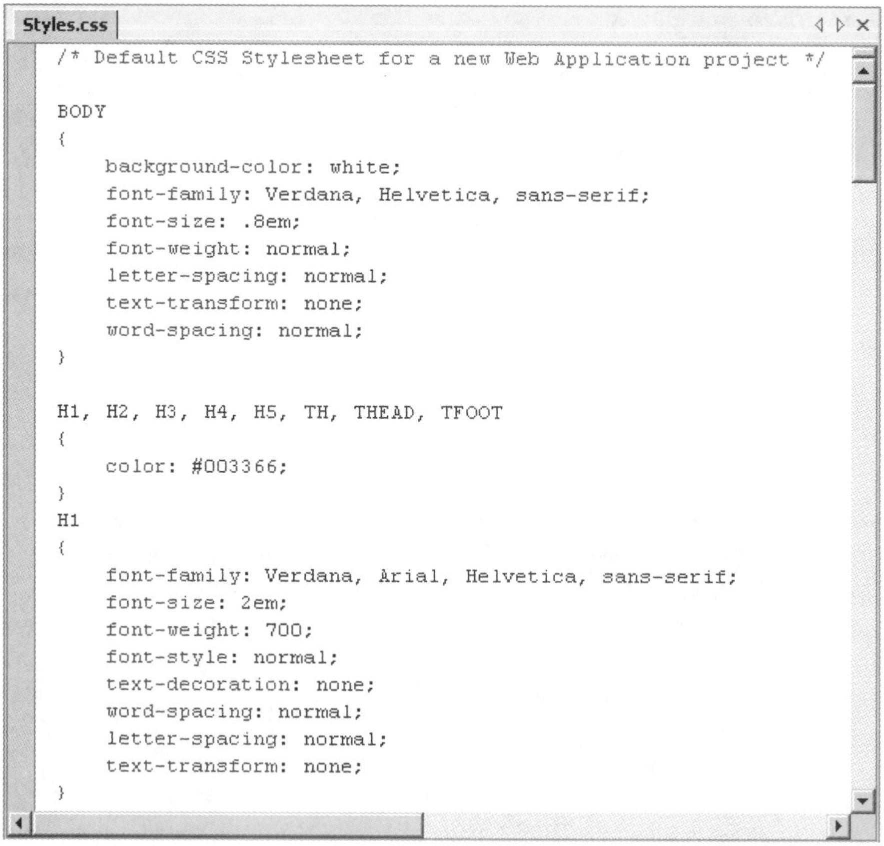

```
/* Default CSS Stylesheet for a new Web Application project */

BODY
{
    background-color: white;
    font-family: Verdana, Helvetica, sans-serif;
    font-size: .8em;
    font-weight: normal;
    letter-spacing: normal;
    text-transform: none;
    word-spacing: normal;
}

H1, H2, H3, H4, H5, TH, THEAD, TFOOT
{
    color: #003366;
}
H1
{
    font-family: Verdana, Arial, Helvetica, sans-serif;
    font-size: 2em;
    font-weight: 700;
    font-style: normal;
    text-decoration: none;
    word-spacing: normal;
    letter-spacing: normal;
    text-transform: none;
}
```

Figure 3-8. Style View

If you're not familiar with the definition of styles within style sheets, the easiest way to modify them is to right-click on the element name and select **Build Style**. This displays the Style Builder dialog box, which you can use to modify the style you had selected.

If you want to define a style for an element not listed, or define a named style that can be individually applied, right-click in the style sheet and select **Add Style Rule** from the context menu, or select **Styles ➢ Add Style Rule**. Figure 3-9 shows the Add Style Rule dialog box that appears.

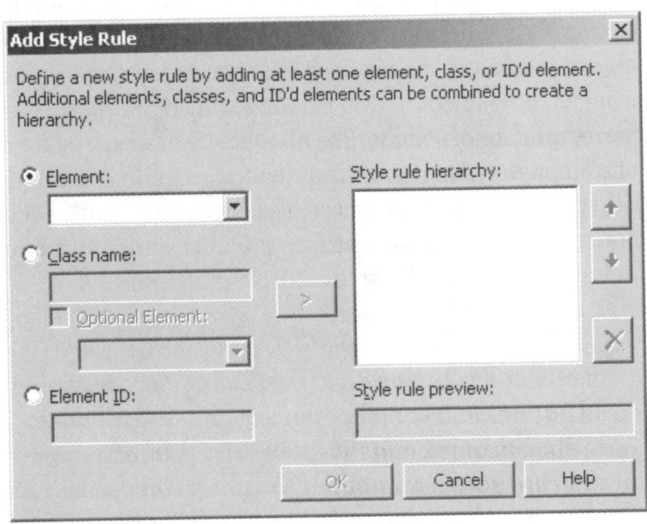

Figure 3-9. Add Style Rule dialog box

To define a style for a new element, select the name in the Element drop-down list. To create a new named style, enter the name into the Class Name box. If you want to define a style that will be applied to an element with a specific ID (remember, in HTML terms the ID is the name of the element), then enter the ID into the Element ID box. Clicking OK in this box adds the element, name, or ID to the style sheet so that you can then define its style attributes using the Style Builder.

Applying CSS Styles

Having created and saved the style sheet, open the Web page you want to format and drag the .css file from the Solution Explorer onto the body of the page. Visual Studio .NET creates a link to the style sheet in the `<head>` section of the document:

```
<HEAD>
    .
    .
    .
    <LINK href="Styles.css" type="text/css" rel="stylesheet">
</HEAD>
```

The Element and ID styles defined in the .css file will automatically be applied to the elements in the Web Form, unless they've already been formatted with specific styles (in which case the specific style overrides the settings in the .css file). To apply a named style to a control, select its Class property in the Properties window and enter the name of the style as it was defined in the .css.

This has been a brief introduction to using and creating CSS, but if you're going to make regular use of style sheets (they're the easiest way to control the formatting of Web pages), then we recommend you get hold of a good HTML reference book that covers CSS. Because CSS is a client-side feature, ASP.NET has little impact on its use and behavior, so any guidance and information in a standard HTML reference will be valid in the .NET environment.

NOTE *You may want to read* Doing Web Development: Client-Side Techniques *by Deborah Kurata (Apress, 2001). This book targets application developers and covers the key client-side techniques you can use to complement your server-side development with Visual Studio .NET.*

Properties, Methods, and Events

HTML Controls do not offer as rich a set of properties, methods, and events as the Web Controls you'll see in Chapter 4. Instead, the properties supported by HTML Controls largely represent the attributes and values that would normally be used in HTML tags, and the methods tend to be general-purpose methods used for managing controls from server-side code, rather than generating any specific output. Likewise, the events are rather limited, being constrained in most cases to either `ServerChange` or `ServerClick` events, depending on the type of control.

Nevertheless, the basic model by which ASP.NET supports properties, methods, and events is identical for both HTML Controls and Web Controls. Because HTML Controls are significantly simpler than Web Controls, it makes sense to learn how these essential ASP.NET features apply to HTML Controls, as you'll get a clearer picture of what is actually going on.

It's extremely important to realize that the properties, methods, and events discussed next exist only while a Web Form is being processed in the Web server—they're not available to the browser, nor do they impose any browser technology requirements. However, because all of the processing takes place server-side, it *is* necessary for the browser to generate a request to the Web server, either in the form of an initial page request or as a postback. This is especially true of the `ServerChange` and `ServerClick` events, which will only be raised during a postback.

However, before we look at the specific details of some of the HTML Controls, it's worth taking a step backward to view the class hierarchy from which these controls derive.

HTML Control Classes in ASP.NET

ASP.NET supports all HTML Controls and elements through a set of classes derived from System.Web.UI.HtmlControl. Figure 3-10 shows the class hierarchy.

```
Object
       Control
              LiteralControl
              HtmlControl
                     HtmlContainerControl
                            HtmlAnchor
                            HtmlButton
                            HtmlForm
                            HtmlGenericControl
                            HtmlSelect
                            HtmlTable
                            HtmlTableCell
                            HtmlTableRow
                            HtmlTextArea
                     HtmlImage
                     HtmlInputControl
                            HtmlInputButton
                            HtmlInputCheckBox
                            HtmlInputFile
                            HtmlInputHidden
                            HtmlInputImage
                            HtmlInputRadioButton
                            HtmlInputText
```

Figure 3-10. HTML control class hierarchy

When ASP.NET processes a Web Form, it does so by converting *all* of the visual content into executable classes. Although this may seem laborious, it only performs this compilation when the page is first referenced. Thereafter, as long as the page is not modified, it uses the previously compiled version of the page and its classes to respond to requests.

In the class hierarchy shown in Figure 3-10, each class has its own set of supported properties, methods, and events. Clearly, it's quite important to know which class represents each element if you're to make the most of these members. You can't begin to do this until you're aware of the following:

- All HTML elements and tags that are *not* marked with `runat="server"` are compiled into instances of the LiteralControl class. This is a limited class with relatively few members but is more efficient than the richer classes used for server-side elements.

- All HTML elements marked `with runat="server"` are compiled into instances of classes based on the element type. HtmlControl is the common base class, but there is a further split so that some classes derive from HtmlContainerControl, one from HtmlImage and the remader from HtmlInputControl.

The reason this point is so important is that many of the useful properties, methods, and events are common to the base classes. Any classes that derive from these inherit their fundamental behaviors.

Members Derived from HtmlControl

All server-side HTML control classes derive from HtmlControl, and so they share certain properties, methods, and events. The list is quite lengthy, and as with the previous chapter we've decided not to provide exhaustive coverage of every member. Instead, we'll focus on those that are relevant and useful to real-world Web development (see Table 3-1).

Table 3-1. Common Members Shared by All HTML Control Classes

MEMBER NAME	DESCRIPTION
`Attributes`	The Attributes property returns the attribute name and value pairs used on the control tag. This can be useful when you want to examine or edit an attribute that is not exposed as a property, or when you want to generate an attribute that ASP.NET knows nothing about (such as a browser-specific rendering instructions).
`Disabled`	This property returns or assigns the value that indicates whether the disabled attribute is included in the rendered output for the control. If it is set to True, the control will be read-only and incapable of receiving the focus.
`Style`	The Style property returns all the CSS properties that are applied to the control.
`TagName`	The TagName property returns the element name of the tag. This is useful because in some cases different elements are instantiated from the same class. For example, `<span>`, `<body>`, `<div>`, and `<font>` all map to HtmlGenericControl, but your code may need to decipher between them. It can do this with the TagName property.
`Visible`	This property returns or assigns a boolean value to determine the control's visibility. If the control is not visible, it won't be rendered to the HTML output stream at all.

Members Derived from HtmlInputControl

Those classes derived from HtmlInputControl represent elements that render to an `<input>` tag. Table 3-2 shows the members they share.

Table 3-2. Common Properties for Controls Derived from HTMLInputControl

MEMBER NAME	DESCRIPTION
`Value`	This is a key property that returns or assigns the value or content of the control and is the property you'll work with most often.
`Name`	This returns or assigns the unique identifier for the control.
`Type`	This is a string value that indicates the type of the HTMLInputControl. Possible values include `text`, `password`, `radio`, `checkbox`, and others.

In addition to the members derived from these base classes, some controls have specific features worthy of special note:

- HtmlInputButton defines a CausesValidation property. If set to True, this causes the button to trigger any client-side and server-side validation defined for the Web Form, whereas setting it to False prevents these validation checks from taking place. The False setting is especially useful when placing a Cancel button on a Web Form, which may need to submit the form (to continue processing) but would not require that the validation be performed. We'll examine client-side and server-side validation in some detail in Chapter 4.

- HtmlInputText defines Size and MaxLength properties, corresponding to standard HTML attributes but accessible through code.

- HtmlInputFile defines PostedFile, which represents the file uploaded to the server via the control.

Members Derived from HtmlContainerControl

Classes derived from HtmlContainerControl map to HTML elements that require an opening and closing tag such as `<select>`, `<span>`, and `<form>`. Table 3-3 shows the properties they share.

Table 3-3. Common Properties for Controls Derived from HTMLContainerControl

MEMBER NAME	DESCRIPTION
InnerHTML	This returns or assigns the content found between the opening and closing tags of the HTML control.
InnerText	This returns or assigns all text between the opening and closing tags of the HTML control. Unlike the InnerHTML property, InnerText provides automatic HTML encoding and decoding.

The HtmlSelect and HtmlTable classes are worth mentioning in more detail. In classic ASP, one of the more common requirements is to get the content of a Recordset or other structure into a list, drop-down box, or table. Various methods and schemes were adopted to achieve this goal, but once again ASP.NET provides a simpler and more direct solution:

- HtmlSelect defines an Items property, which in turn is a collection of ListItem objects. This collection supports methods such as Add, Clear, Remove, and RemoveAt for controlling the content of the list and an Item method for retrieving items. Collectively these features make it easy for you to write code that programmatically fills, empties, or clears a Listbox or Dropdown control. For example, the RegionPicker Web Form built in Chapter 2 could as easily have been coded to use HTML Controls rather than Web Controls. If so, the following code would have been used to initialize the lists:

```
If Page.IsPostBack = False Then
    With SourceSelect
        .Items.Add("North")
        .Items.Add("West")
        .Items.Add("Central")
        .Items.Add("East")
        .Items.Add("South")
    End With

    TargetSelect.Items.Clear()
End If
```

HtmlTable defines a Rows property, which is a collection of HtmlTableRow objects. Each row has a Cells property, representing a collection of HtmlTableCell objects for the columns. Each collection supports Add,

Clear, Item, Remove, and RemoveAt methods, and so again this makes it a simple matter to programmatically control the content and size of any table, as you saw earlier in the "Runtime Creation" section.

HtmlImage

The HtmlImage class represents only the HTML `<img>` tag. You can use it for programmatic manipulation of image source, type, size, and other attributes. It supports numerous properties that map to standard HTML attributes for the tag, such as `alt`, `src`, `height`, and `width`.

HTML Control Events

HTML Controls support a common set of events inherited from the Control class:

- `DataBinding`
- `Disposed`
- `Init`
- `Load`
- `PreRender`
- `Unload`

However, these events are *internal* events, so it's unlikely you'll provide handlers for them in most applications. Instead, the events we're more interested in are those raised by changes made to the content of the Web Form and events raised by the user clicking buttons on the Web Form. For HTML Controls, these are the `ServerChange` and `ServerClick` events.

ServerChange

The `ServerChange` event occurs during postback processing when ASP.NET detects that the data in the Web Form has been changed. When a Web Form is processed, ASP.NET uses the ViewState feature (described in "Maintaining Page State") to store the original content of every server-side control in a hidden field on the form. During the postback process it compares the current content of the control with the value from the ViewState and raises the ServerChange event for any controls where there is a difference.

To illustrate how ServerChange works, create a new Web Form containing three HTML Text Fields, one HTML Label, and one HTML Submit Button. Ensure they're marked as server controls by selecting them, then right-clicking and choosing **Run As Server Control**. Position and size them as shown in Figure 3-11.

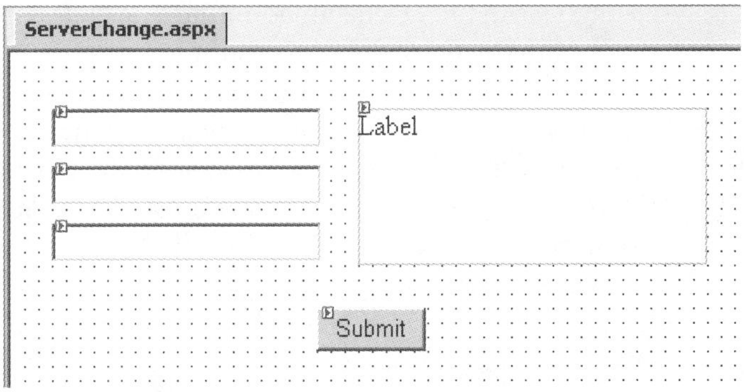

Figure 3-11. Layout of the ServerChange Web Form

Create a new procedure called TextBoxChange as follows. Notice the definition of the Handles statement; this specifies that this one procedure will handle events from all three text boxes:

```
Private Sub TextBoxChange(ByVal sender As System.Object, _
                ByVal e As system.EventArgs) _
                Handles Text1.ServerChange, Text2.ServerChange,
                Text3.ServerChange
    DIV1.InnerHtml += sender.id + " changed<br>"
End Sub
```

In the Page_Load event handler, clear the label's content:

```
Private Sub Page_Load(ByVal sender As System.Object, _
                ByVal e As System.EventArgs) Handles MyBase.Load
    DIV1.InnerHtml = ""
End Sub
```

View the page in the browser, enter something into one of the text boxes, and then click the Submit button to perform the postback. The Label should display a message indicating which text box was modified. Now change the text in two of the boxes and click the button. You should see two separate messages. In other words, during the postback process a separate `ServerChange` event is being raised for each control that has been modified.

ServerClick

`ServerClick` occurs for Button, Reset Button, and Submit Button controls. Unlike the `ServerChange` event that can fire several times during a postback, there can be only one `ServerClick` event, which will fire for the button that was clicked to perform the postback.

For example, return to the code for the previous demonstration and add an HTML Button and an HTML Reset Button to the Web Form. Mark them as server-side controls and then create the following procedure to handle the `ServerClick` event from all three buttons now on the Web Form:

```
Private Sub ButtonClicked(ByVal sender As System.Object, _
                ByVal e As System.EventArgs) _
                Handles Submit1.ServerClick, Reset1.ServerClick,
                Button1.ServerClick
    DIV1.InnerHtml += sender.id + " clicked<br>"
End Sub
```

View the page in the browser and click either the Submit Button or the regular Button control. You'll see that a corresponding message is generated in the Label. Modify one or more of the text fields and click either button again, and you'll see the `ServerChange` events and the `ServerClick` events are fired. Notice that the `ServerChange` events always fire first, though. This is the only guarantee you get about event ordering. You can't rely on the order in which `ServerChange` events fire, but you do know that all the `ServerChange` events will fire before the `ServerClick` event.

Now click the Reset Button. Notice that nothing happens—there is no message shown in the label and no appreciable change on the form. In fact, if you watch the browser window carefully you'll see that it doesn't even seem to generate a postback. The purpose of the Reset Button control is to reset any changes made in the controls on the Web page, and this is handled client-side by the browser. To see this in action, modify the entries in one or more of the text fields and click the Reset Button—the controls return to their original content. It may seem a little confusing that the Reset Button control supports a `ServerClick` event, but it doesn't actually fire in the Web Form. Remember that you're dealing with HTML elements here, and in HTML the behavior of a Reset Button control is that it does *not* cause a postback or page submission, but instead performs only a client-side reset of the form. No matter what .NET tries, if you tell it to create a Reset Button, then that's exactly what you'll get. If you want an event and a post-back, then you must use either a Button or a Submit Button control.

Maintaining Page State

Because of the way HyperText Transfer Protocol (HTTP) functions, Web Applications (and hence Web Forms) are both connectionless and stateless. In practice this means that once a Web server has responded to a request for a Web page, it forgets all about that request and moves onto the next request. This basic feature of how HTTP works requires that Web Forms are re-created from scratch with each round-trip to the server, and ordinarily this would cause all information associated with the form to be lost each time.

If you've worked with classic ASP you may have come across this problem. The typical solution is to manually produce code that manages and maintains page state, possibly by reading and writing the `Request.Form()` collection or by using Session state (see Chapter 12). Whilst these solutions are successful, they're far from elegant and often introduce unwanted side effects, problems, and possible security holes, as well as requiring significant coding effort.

In ASP.NET, the Web Forms framework can save the state of the page and its controls in what is known as the *ViewState*. A ViewState object is created automatically each time a page is instantiated. During the process of rendering the page to the client browser, each Web Control is able to save its content to the ViewState. The values within the ViewState are automatically converted to a string and rendered to a hidden control (called __VIEWSTATE) on the Web Form. This hidden control is then submitted with the other page content during any post-backs, and ASP.NET transparently extracts the values that it contains and re-creates the ViewState. Thus the entire page state can be passed to and from the browser with no developer input required.

Using the ViewState

ViewState is crucial to the operation of server-side events because ASP.NET depends on comparing each control's original value (which is held in ViewState) with its current value (read from the control itself) to determine whether a `ServerChange` event should be fired. Fortunately, for most ordinary form processing there is no need to worry about explicitly saving and restoring values with each round-trip—the ViewState is used automatically, as you've seen in the previous event processing examples. The only steps needed are to ensure that the Web Form contains a server-side HTML form and that each control is marked with `runat="server"` if its content is to be maintained.

As well as maintaining state for the server controls, the ViewState can be accessed in code to allow storage of custom values and data items. The object supports all the normal methods and properties for collection management—Add, Clear, Count, Item, and Remove—and can also be used directly to store and retrieve values. When working with custom values in the ViewState, remember that they're referenced as key/value pairs. For example, to place and read a value in the ViewState, you can use the following code:

```
ViewState("UserName") = strUserName
strUserName = ViewState("UserName")
```

ViewState: Important Guidelines

ViewState is a powerful and useful feature if used in the right way. Used wrongly, ViewState can lead to unmanageable designs and poor performance. Keep the following guidelines in mind when you're deciding how best to use ViewState:

- ViewState is designed for persisting form data on a single page across round-trips or postbacks. It's not intended for use between pages and should not be used in that way.

- ViewState is not suitable for storing information such as personalization settings, page navigation histories, shopping carts, and file paths that would probably need to be persistent. If such items are to be stored, it would be more appropriate to use Session state, or possibly Application state. Chapters 12 and 13 address these topics.

- ViewState content is insecure and can be intercepted in the same way as any other unencrypted HTML content. For these reasons it's inappropriate to store any confidential data such as passwords or connection strings in ViewState.

- The content of the ViewState is passed to and from the server with every request and response. If a large amount of data is stored in ViewState (such as objects, files, or XML documents), then you may experience serious performance problems. In principle, any primitive type, and any object derived from a class that is serializable, can be stored in the ViewState. In practice, it should be limited to compact items of data that can be efficiently passed.

- If ViewState is not required for a page, or for any Web Control, it can be disabled by setting the EnableViewState property for the object to False.

Used wisely, ViewState can greatly contribute to enhancing the scalability of your Web Applications by minimizing the amount of data that must be stored in Session state. However, even on the fastest links, excessive use of ViewState will lead to network performance problems that could be difficult to identify, diagnose, and fix.

CAUTION *You can disable ViewState for a Web Form by setting the EnableViewState property to False. However, doing so prevents ASP.NET from firing server-side events correctly, and therefore it must only be disabled at the Web Form level if no* `ServerChange` *events have been coded. In Chapter 4 you'll see how ViewState can be selectively enabled or disabled for individual Web Controls, but this facility does not exist for HTML Controls.*

Why Use HTML Controls?

As you've seen in this chapter, HTML Controls provide a structured object library for building interfaces to Web Applications. However, as you may also be aware, ASP.NET supports Web Controls that do much the same thing, so why should you consider using HTML Controls?

In practice, there are three reasons for using HTML Controls over Web Controls:

- If your knowledge and background of ASP and Web development is stronger than your experience of desktop programming, then you may find the object model offered by HTML Controls more familiar because it maintains the names and classes you already know.

- If you need to generate specific HTML to be sent to the browser, then HTML Controls should be more predictable than Web Controls. As you'll see in Chapter 4, Web Controls can adjust their output to suit the browser they detect. This means that if you were to compare the HTML rendered for two different browsers from a single Web Form, it could be very different indeed. You may be creating features, especially in client-side script, that rely on particular elements, tags, and attributes being present. HTML Controls give you this consistency.

- You have existing HTML and ASP files that you want to convert the ASP.NET with a minimum of effort. In reality this is why most people will use HTML Controls, as regular HTML tags and elements can be converted to server controls with a couple of mouse clicks. This is one of the quickest upgrade paths to take existing Web content into the .NET environment.

Remember though that you only need to have server controls for those objects that you'll code to or handle events from. A proportion of any Web page will be static content such as text, images, and tables. It would be wholly inappropriate to mark such content as server-side as it would most likely slow down the processing of the entire page. In such situations you should be using HTML elements.

Summary

HTML Controls provide a relatively quick and easy migration path that enables existing Web pages and content to be brought into the .NET environment. Simply marking an HTML element with `runat="server"` is sufficient to allow it to be treated as a fully programmable server-side object with properties, methods and events. In the case of certain controls, especially tables, list boxes, and drop-downs, the change is revolutionary, allowing you to replace vast amounts of "cookie-cutter" code with a few structured routines.

However, HTML controls are only one part of the Web Form story. As Chapter 4 shows, Web Controls provide all the features and functions of HTML controls and more. Further, you can use them for new developments to further reduce the amount of manual coding and HTML creation that you're required to do.

CHAPTER 4

Web Controls

Using Web Controls

Introducing Web Control Classes and Categories

Understanding Intrinsic Controls

Exploring List Controls

Using Rich Controls

Using Validation Controls

Implementing Formatting and Style

Understanding Event Processing and AutoPostBack

WEB CONTROLS ARE ONE of the real "wow" features of ASP.NET, providing you with a rich and powerful set of user interface elements. Some of them appear similar to HTML Controls (discussed in Chapter 3), while others offer unparalleled features and functions for server-side developers.

In the last two chapters we introduced Web Forms and HTML Controls, two very important types of component for building user interfaces. Where do Web Controls fit then? In reality, they sit alongside the HTML Controls, and there is little, if anything, you can do with HTML Controls that you can't do with Web Controls. However, Web Controls go much farther, allowing you to create lists, tables, calendars, and many other visual components with greater ease. Web Controls can also be intelligently rendered to the browser, taking advantage of browser-specific features as and when they are detected, but falling back to safe base-level functions if not. We say they *can* be intelligently rendered, because this is determined by the developer of the control, rather than by you or the ASP.NET environment. If the developer of a control chose to generate rendered output in

HTML 3.2 compliant format, there's probably little you can do to change that, even if you know the browser supports DHTML, XML, and client-side script.

As well as providing powerful functionality, Web Controls offer you other advantages as well:

- They have richer sets of properties, methods, and events.
- They are named and organized into intuitive and logical groupings.
- They have strongly typed properties.
- Some, such as the DataGrid, support the use of templates to help organize content.

What this means for you as a developer is that you are likely to write less code to achieve any given result with Web Controls than you would with HTML Controls, and the code that you do write should be clearer and less buggy.

So is there a downside? Well that depends on whether you are creating new Web Forms or converting existing HTML pages into ASP.NET. If you're building from scratch, Web Controls are the way to go; you'll get all the benefits with no obvious disadvantages. If you're converting existing pages, especially if they contain many controls, you may find HTML Controls easier and quicker to use during migration. Remember, all you have to do to convert an HTML element into an HTML Control is to right-click on the element and select **Run as Server Control**.

TIP *Web Controls and HTML Controls both require server-side processing and so consume more processor time than standard HTML elements. For a complex Web Form with many Web Controls, the time required to process and render the page can be quite significant. To maximize performance you should use standard HTML for static content and use Web Controls or HTML Controls only if you need their specific features.*

Web Control Concepts

In many ways, Web Controls and HTML Controls are similar. Both can be thought of as programmable interface elements, with properties, methods, and events. Both are processed server-side and are rendered to HTML that is sent to the browser. Where they differ is that any single HTML Control renders to a single HTML element, whereas the HTML rendered from a Web Control can be quite different from the object model the developer sees, and may well consist of many separate HTML tags and elements.

For example, you might add a RadioButtonList control to a Web Form:

```
<asp:RadioButtonList id="RadioButtonList1" runat="server">
</asp:RadioButtonList>
```

You can then manipulate the control as a single programmable object with a comprehensive set of properties and methods. You might add the following code to the `Page.Load` event handler to populate the list of radio buttons:

```
With RadioButtonList1.Items
    .Add("North")
    .Add("South")
    .Add("East")
    .Add("West")
End With
```

This shouldn't look too different from the code used in Chapter 2 to populate the Items collection of the ListBox controls. However, the RadioButtonList is a Web Control and renders to a set of HTML elements comprising a table containing `<span>`, `<input>`, and `<label>` tags:

```
<table id="RadioButtonList1" border="0">
    <tr>
        <td>
            <span value="North"><input id="RadioButtonList1_0" type="radio"
                name="RadioButtonList1" value="North" />
                <label for="RadioButtonList1_0">North</label></span>
        </td>
    </tr><tr>
        <td>
            <span value="South"><input id="RadioButtonList1_1" type="radio"
                name="RadioButtonList1" value="South" />
                <label for="RadioButtonList1_1">South</label></span>
        </td>
    </tr><tr>
        <td>
            <span value="East"><input id="RadioButtonList1_2" type="radio"
                name="RadioButtonList1" value="East" />
                <label for="RadioButtonList1_2">East</label></span>
```

```
        </td>
    </tr><tr>
        <td>
            <span value="West"><input id="RadioButtonList1_3" type="radio"
                name="RadioButtonList1" value="West" />
                <label for="RadioButtonList1_3">West</label></span>
        </td>
    </tr>3
</table>
```

Fortunately, as developers, we mainly see the design-time view with just a single element. As long as we're prepared to trust the control to render itself to suitable HTML, we need not be concerned with the complex structures that it produces.

Web Control Features

Web Controls include traditional form elements such as buttons and text boxes, as well as complex controls such as tables. They also include controls that provide commonly used form functionality such as displaying data in a grid, choosing dates, and so on. We'll see more about the specific controls later on, but to begin with we'll review some of the common features that all the controls provide.

Many of the standard features duplicate those offered by HTML Controls, but as you'll see, Web Controls have a lot more to offer as well. The following are among the more important of these additional features:

- Web Controls support a rich set of properties and methods, providing some great functionality in an easy-to-use fashion. Properties are consistent and intuitively-named across the different controls, making it simpler to learn their features and capabilities.

- Web Controls are able to raise a greater variety of server-side events. You should remember that these are *server-side* events, so there will be a server round-trip every time an event needs to be handled. Using Web Control events inappropriately can lead to serious performance problems, but when used well, the server-side events make the creation of powerful Web applications much easier, as you've begun to see in previous chapters.

- Most input-oriented controls—such as the TextBox and RadioButton—support an AutoPostback property. AutoPostback allows you to specify whether changes to the content of the control cause an immediate post-back, or whether the postback is delayed until the form is submitted. This provides an easy way for you to perform automatic control-by-control validation, checks, and updates, as long as you are aware of the performance penalties of constant round-tripping.

- Properties are strictly typed, as opposed to the String data type used for properties of HTML Controls. Strict typing helps minimize errors and bugs by ensuring that only appropriate values are assigned to properties.

- Some controls—such as the DataGrid—support the use of templates to allow you to define a custom look and style for the control. Different templates are used for headers, footers, alternating rows, and editable rows. We'll be exploring this in detail in Chapter 8.

- Web Controls can render themselves intelligently to the client using a format appropriate for whatever browser is detected or specified. You don't need to worry about how a grid, table, or calendar can be created—the controls take care of it themselves.

- Some Web Controls—such as the Table and Repeater controls—can function as containers. Containers host other controls and are often used when you want to dynamically create child controls. Most containers also support the idea of event bubbling; that is, the ability of the container to handle events triggered for any of the contained controls.

- Web Controls have consistent and logical names for their classes, properties, methods, and events. If you have a background in VB, you should find that Web Controls offer a more familiar programming model than HTML Controls.

This chapter will illustrate all of these points and more, demonstrating how much easier it is to build Web Applications with ASP.NET and Web Controls.

Extensibility

One of the reasons that Microsoft Visual Basic became so successful was its extensibility. It began with the earlier versions of VB, which supported VBX files, and continued to the support of OCX files by later versions. This support, in turn, created a whole new sector of the software industry. Custom control—the term used to refer to these add-on components—founds its origins in VB 4.0, 5.0, and 6.0, and continues to exist in VB .NET. Of course the implementation has changed over the years, but the ability of VB to support add-on visual components from third-parties is still one of its most important attributes.

In the Web environment there have been attempts to do much the same—such as the Design Time Controls (DTCs) that could be used in FrontPage and Visual InterDev, and client-side OCXs that could be embedded in Web pages and sent to the browser. These technologies were never as popular as their desktop equivalents though, typically requiring specific support on the server or the browser. It was also more challenging to build DTCs than it was to build regular custom controls, and not all development environments properly supported them.

ASP.NET doesn't use VBX, OCX, or DTC components, but instead introduces the concept of a *custom web control*. As you'd expect, these are pre-built visual components that you add to Web Forms to build the user interface. They typically offer rich sets of properties, methods, and events to provide programmatic control. An example of a custom web control is the CrystalReportViewer control that ships with Visual Studio .NET, which you use to render CrystalReport objects as a part of a Web Form. It is also expected that the third-party market will adopt this new technology just as they did VBX and OCX controls; so, in the near future it is likely that a rich and varied set of controls will be available.

There are two specific types of custom web controls:

- You can create Web User Controls using similar techniques to those used for Web Forms. A visual designer is provided for creating the interface. Code can be placed in the Web User Control file or in a code-behind module. Web User Controls are saved and used as .ascx files. Because these files contain source code, they are likely to be used only for in-house control development.

- You will find various terms used to describe the alternate approach, but perhaps the best is Web Custom Control. This category includes composite controls and derived controls. These are built programmatically, usually without the aid of a designer. More work is involved, but the feature set is richer and the capabilities are wider. Web Custom Controls are compiled to DLLs and can appear in the toolbox. This is the model that will be used by component developers (including commercial software houses) who want to build and distribute their controls to other developers.

Chapter 5 provides a thorough look at how you can build Custom Web Controls using either of these approaches, including a discussion of the relative merits and disadvantages of each approach.

Using Web Controls

Web Controls are used in the same way as HTML controls. You add them from the toolbox or manually enter their tags in HTML view, and you write code that references their properties, methods, and events.

Web Control tags are prefixed with `asp:` and flagged with a `runat="server"` attribute, which causes the control to be processed server-side (the browser would be unable to render the element). In addition, all Web Controls must have an `ID` attribute specified. If you add the control to the Web Form from the toolbox, then these settings will be made automatically. If you choose to manually enter the tag into the HTML source, then you must ensure the correct entries are made. Visual Studio .NET doesn't always make it clear when you leave any of them out.

The following shows the HTML source view of one of the simplest (but most often used) Web Controls: the TextBox. Notice that both the opening and closing tags are included:

```
<asp:TextBox runat="server" id="TextBox1"></asp:TextBox>
```

This would be rendered to an HTML text field by ASP.NET:

```
<input name="TextBox1" type="text" id="TextBox1" />
```

Clearly in this example there is a one-to-one mapping between the Web Control and the rendered output. In many other cases—as illustrated previously with the RadioButtonList control—the mapping may be far more involved.

Limitations

While Web Controls are generally very powerful, there are some limitations to how they can be used. If you add controls using the toolbox (rather than directly entering their tags into the HTML source), then the development environment will automatically enforce these limitations. If you manually change the HTML source and break the following rules, then you are likely to generate runtime errors when the page is processed.

- Most Web Controls cannot function as containers; therefore, you cannot overlap or nest their tags. The controls that can act as containers include the Panel, the Table, and the Repeater control.

- The way in which you manage style and layout is different to the approach used with HTML Controls. Web Controls generally support a rich set of individual properties—such as `BackColor`, `ForeColor`, and `Font`—but do not support the Style Builder dialog discussed in Chapter 3. Also, Visual Studio .NET does not allow you to set the Style property through the Properties window, although you can hand-code the `Style` attribute in HTML View or set it through code. Fortunately, you can use cascading style sheets (CSS) with Web Controls because each supports a CssClass property. Refer to Chapter 3 and Appendix A for more information on CSS.

- It may prove difficult or impossible to use complex Web Controls—such as Tables, DataGrids, and Repeaters—with client-side scripts since you have no direct control over how the control is rendered. If client-side scripting is an important part of your application you'll probably find it easier to use HTML Controls instead, as discussed in Chapter 3.

Other than these points, you will find that almost anything is possible with Web Controls. Even if you think there is nothing available that does exactly what you want, ASP.NET provides you with an extensible framework; you can either buy or build a control with the features you require.

Introducing Web Control Classes and Categories

With the exception of the Repeater control, Web Control classes are derived from the WebControl class. The Repeater control is derived from the Control class and has some obvious differences from other Web Controls (for example, unless you add constituent HTML elements or controls to the Repeater, it will not render a visible user interface). All Web Controls are found in the System.Web.UI.WebControls namespace and are made accessible in Visual Studio .NET through the Web Forms tab in the toolbox.

There are four categories of Web Controls, each of which have particular features and functions:

- **Intrinsic controls** are rendered to simple HTML elements, but provide additional server-side functionality for the developer.

- **List controls** are data-aware and provide data flow across a page. They may be rendered to `<select>` or `<table>` elements or to a combination of HTML elements that provide the required functionality.

- **Rich controls** provide a rich user interface for particular tasks. For example, the Calendar control provides a developer- and browser-friendly calendar feature that is typically rendered as a combination of HTML and client-side script. Dropping the Rich control onto a Web Form automatically provides all of this.

- **Validation controls** perform a variety of data validation tasks, most of which can be implemented in client-side script and so reduce the number of server round-trips.

Understanding Intrinsic Controls

Intrinsic controls are designed to replace and supplement the standard set of HTML controls. As we've already said, they also provide a richer and more consistent set of properties, methods, and events than those offered by HTML Controls.

Figure 4-1 shows the intrinsic controls in the Web Forms tab of the toolbox.

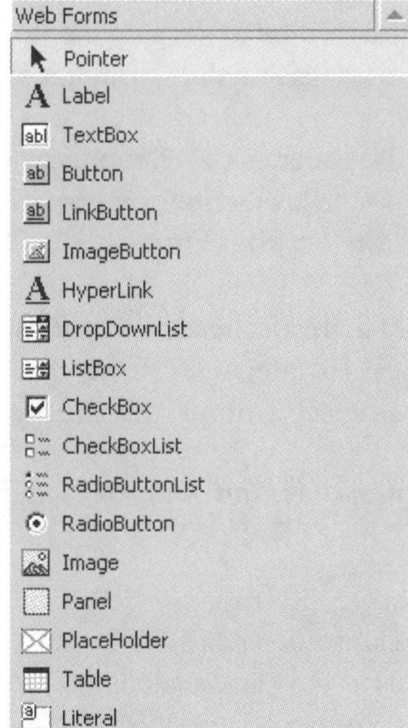

Figure 4-1. Web Controls in the toolbox

When discussing these controls, it is perhaps easiest to think of them in terms of their behavior and offered functionality. As with Chapter 3, we're not going to list every property, method, and event for each control; instead, we'll show the most important ones and focus on how they can best be used.

Control-Passing

There are four controls that allow passing of control back to the server. Three of them generate postbacks and one performs direct navigation:

Button, ImageButton and LinkButton

When clicked, these three controls all cause a postback to occur and raise server-side events. The difference between them is one of visual style:

- **Button** controls render as `<input>` elements with a type of `submit`. Button controls have text on the button face.
- **ImageButton** controls render as `<input>` elements with a type of `image`. They have graphical images on the button face.
- **LinkButton** controls render as `<a>` elements, with their `href` attribute set to reference a client-side JavaScript function. The client-side function is automatically generated by the control.

The three controls share many properties, methods, and events and most are quite straightforward, being associated with sizing, positioning, or appearance. However, Table 4-1 lists three specific properties worthy of special note:

Table 4-1. Common Properties for Button, ImageButton, and LinkButton Controls

PROPERTY	DESCRIPTION
`CausesValidation`	This property determines whether validation controls are checked and enforced when the button is clicked. It works in the same way as the CausesValidation property for HTMLInputButton controls discussed in Chapter 3. See below for an example of how and when this property would be used.
`CommandArgument`	String value that will be returned as the CommandArgument value when the button's Command event is triggered.
`CommandName`	String value that will be returned as the CommandName value when the button's Command event is triggered.

The three button controls share two important events: Click and Command. Both events are triggered when the user clicks the button. Unlike the Click event, the Command event is provided with more information about the source of the event—information that is especially useful if you have coded an event handler shared by multiple controls.

For example, Figure 4-2 shows a section of a Web Form with four Button controls.

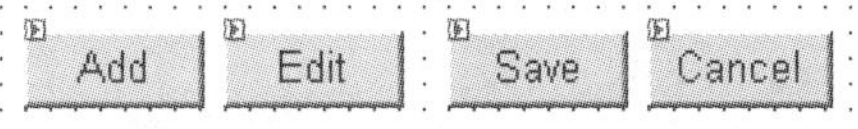

Figure 4-2. Web Form Button controls

All of these buttons share a common event-handling procedure, but rather than coding the Click event, we can code the Command event and determine which button has been clicked by way of the CommandName property of the EventArgs parameter:

```
Private Sub ButtonCommand(ByVal sender As Object, _
        ByVal e As System.Web.UI.WebControls.CommandEventArgs) _
        Handles cmdAdd.Command, cmdCancel.Command, _
            cmdEdit.Command, cmdSave.Command
    Select Case e.CommandName
        Case "Add"
            'Add code here
        Case "Edit"
            'Edit code here
        Case "Save"
            'Save code here
        Case "Cancel"
            'Cancel code here
    End Select
End Sub
```

At design-time, each button would have its CommandName property set to the appropriate string value: `Add`, `Edit`, `Cancel` or `Save`. The Cancel button would also have its CausesValidation property set to False. If CausesValidation were set to True, it would only be possible to click the Cancel button if all of the entries in the Web Form's controls were valid – in other words you would have to complete the Web Form before you could cancel it!

Another important use of the CommandArgument and CommandName properties occurs when you make use of event "bubbling." As we mentioned earlier, event bubbling is the term used to refer to the way in which a container control can handle events raised by its child controls. Event bubbling is supported by the DataGrid, DataList, and Repeater controls; in practice, these may be populated with an unknown number of child controls through data binding. It would be awkward to manually assign event-handling routines to each child control, so bubbling provides a convenient solution. By bubbling the Command event (rather than Click) the additional information in CommandName and CommandArgument can be used to determine which button was clicked. You'll see examples of event bubbling in Chapter 8 when we discuss the use of Button Columns and Template Columns in DataGrids.

HyperLink

The HyperLink Web Control renders to a standard HTML hyperlink. It does NOT submit the Web Form, nor does it raise server-side Click or Command events. Hyperlink controls are the most efficient way of performing simple page navigation, but they lack the server-side functionality that the Button, ImageButton, and LinkButton offer.

Three of the more important properties for the HyperLink control are listed in Table 4-2:

Table 4-2. HyperLink Control Properties

PROPERTY	DESCRIPTION
`ImageUrl`	String value that specifies a URL for the image to be used as the visual representation of the HyperLink. If you do not specify the ImageUrl, the HyperLink will be shown as text.
`NavigateUrl`	String value that specifies the target page for navigation when the HyperLink is clicked.
`Target`	String value that specifies the name of a frame or browser window that will be used to display the page indicated by NavigateUrl.

Although HyperLink controls appear rather simple and limited compared to the other control-passing components, they may prove more efficient because they cause no postback, but instead navigate directly to the required page. Compared with using an HTML element, you will find the HyperLink control is more flexible; its properties can be determined programmatically, rather than having your code generate HTML tags and attributes on the fly.

AutoPostBack from Input Controls

Another way of passing control and causing a postback is to set the AutoPostBack property of an input control to True. When set this way, a client-side JavaScript routine is added to the Web page to generate a postback whenever the content of the control is changed (the script is usually associated with the `onChange` event). Not all controls support AutoPostBack, but many do. We'll provide a more thorough discussion of the uses and abuses of the AutoPostBack property later in the chapter.

Text Entry

There is only one text entry control: the TextBox. This single control replaces the distinct TextField, TextArea, and Password type `<input>` controls used by HTML. Through its properties, you can configure the TextBox control to perform functions just like those of the three controls it replaces. This added functionality provides you with a simpler and more consistent way of getting any form of textual input from the user. This is one of the reasons that generally makes Web Controls more appealing than HTML Controls—just tell the TextBox control what you want to do and it will take care of generating the required HTML.

As Table 4-3 lists, the TextBox control has a number of important properties that control the way it is used:

Table 4-3. TextBox Control Properties

PROPERTY	**DESCRIPTION**
`Columns`	Determines how wide the control is, measured in characters. This is different from the Width property, which is measured in pixels. Note that if a value is provided for the Width property, the Columns entry is ignored.
`Rows`	Determines how tall the control is, measured in characters. This is different from Height, which is measured in pixels. This property is effective only if TextMode is set to MultiLine. Also, if a value is provided for the Height property, the Rows value is ignored.
`MaxLength`	Determines the maximum number of characters that can be entered. If the textbox is not big enough to show all of the text, it will be scrolled as you type.
`ReadOnly`	Determines whether the data in the TextBox can be edited.
`Text`	The text entered by the user or displayed to them.
`TextMode`	Determines how text is entered and viewed in the control. Possible values are SingleLine, MultiLine and Password.
`AutoPostBack`	Determines whether the Web Form is automatically submitted when the content of the control is changed.

The most important event for the TextBox is `TextChanged`. This event is triggered on the server whenever the Web Form is submitted after the data in the TextBox has been changed. ASP.NET uses the information held in the ViewState to determine whether the data has been modified and raises the event accordingly. We'll examine the whole issue of event processing and ViewState in more detail after we've looked at the other controls.

Selections

There are a variety of different controls that allow selection. Starting with individual controls, we have the CheckBox and RadioButton, and then we have compound versions of these same controls: the CheckBoxList and RadioButtonList. There's also the DropDownList and ListBox controls. Many of the features of these controls are common to all, though (of course) each offers a slightly different look or feel in some way.

CheckBox

The CheckBox allows Boolean selection by the user. It automatically displays a configurable label. As Table 4-4 shows, its properties are very simple:

Table 4-4. CheckBox Control Properties

PROPERTY	DESCRIPTION
`AutoPostBack`	See description of AutoPostBack for the TextBox control above (in Table 4-3).
`Checked`	Main "value" property that specifies or returns a Boolean value relating to whether the box is checked or not. Note that unlike VB 6.0, the CheckBox control returns True or False, rather than the vbChecked and vbUnchecked constants used in VB 6.0 and earlier. Also note that there is no "indeterminate" value; the box is either ticked or clear.
`Text`	Text of the label that is automatically generated for the CheckBox.
`TextAlign`	Determines whether the textual label is displayed to the right or left of the CheckBox.

The most important event is `CheckedChanged`. As with the TextBox control, ASP.NET uses the information held in the ViewState to determine whether the value of the control has changed; if the value has changed, then the `CheckedChanged` event is raised.

RadioButton

RadioButton controls operate in groups and are mutually exclusive within each group. They support the same properties and events as CheckBox controls, plus one additional important property (Table 4-5):

Table 4-5: RadioButton Control Properties

PROPERTY	DESCRIPTION
GroupName	String value that determines of which group the control is a member. This can be any string value that you want, but all buttons in the same logical group must have the same GroupName. If you don't set the GroupName consistently, you won't get the behavior you expect from RadioButtons.

CheckBoxList and RadioButtonList

The CheckBoxList and RadioButtonList controls are list-oriented, data-aware versions of the CheckBox and RadioButton. As you'd expect, the controls in the CheckBoxList can be selected in any combination, while those in the RadioButtonList are mutually exclusive.

There two controls share the same properties, methods, and events listed in Tables 4-6 and 4-7:

Table 4-6. CheckBoxList and RadioButtonList Properties

PROPERTY	DESCRIPTION
AutoPostBack	See previous controls (Table 4-3).
CellPadding CellSpacing	These two properties determine the amount of padding and spacing between items when the control is rendered to the browser. CellPadding is the amount of space between the cell's content and its border, while CellSpacing is the amount of space between adjacent cells.
DataMember DataSource	These two properties are used when the control is data-bound. They determine the source of data used to generate the entries in the list.
DataTextField DataValueField	If the control is data-bound, these properties determine which field in the datasource is displayed and which field is returned as the value of any selected entries.

(continued)

Table 4-6. CheckBoxList and RadioButtonList Properties (continued)

PROPERTY	DESCRIPTION
`Items`	The Items collection contains one ListItem object for every entry in the list. The Items collection supports its own properties and methods, including Add, Clear, Remove, and RemoveAt. Each ListItem object also has properties including Select, Text, and Value. Items can be added programmatically, they can be added at design-time via the Properties window or they can be generated by data binding the control.

`RepeatColumns`
`RepeatDirection`
`RepeatLayout`
	Ordinarily, the entries in the control will be displayed in a single vertical list. These three properties allow you to change the layout to be split between multiple columns.

`SelectedIndex`	The position of the currently selected entry. In the case of the CheckBoxList, this is the most recently selected entry.
`SelectedItem`	Object reference to the ListItem representing the current or most recently selected entry.

Table 4-7. CheckBoxList and RadioButtonList Methods

METHOD	DESCRIPTION
`ClearSelection`	De-selects all entries and resets the Selected property of all ListItem objects in the Items collection to False.
`DataBind`	Causes the control to try and bind to the object specified by DataSource and DataMember. If successful, the control is populated from the data and the Items are generated.

As with most of the controls we've seen so far, there is only one important event: `SelectedIndexChanged`. This event is raised during the postback process if ASP.NET determines that the currently selected item has been modified. Note that in the case of a CheckBoxList, it is quite possible that several entries (not just the current one) have been modified, although the event will still fire only once. To determine the entries that have been checked or unchecked, your code will need to iterate through the Items collection and check the Selected property of each in turn.

Populating a CheckBoxList or RadioButtonList

There are three ways in which these controls can be populated:

- At design-time, by manually entering values into the Items collection
- At runtime, by adding entries to the Items collection programmatically
- At runtime, by using data binding

It's worth taking a moment out to look at these techniques because you'll find that they are common to other Web Controls as well.

The first approach is to enter the values manually. You can do this by adding the control to a Web Form, then selecting the Items property in the Properties window, and clicking its builder button. Figure 4-3 shows the ListItem editor dialog that will be displayed:

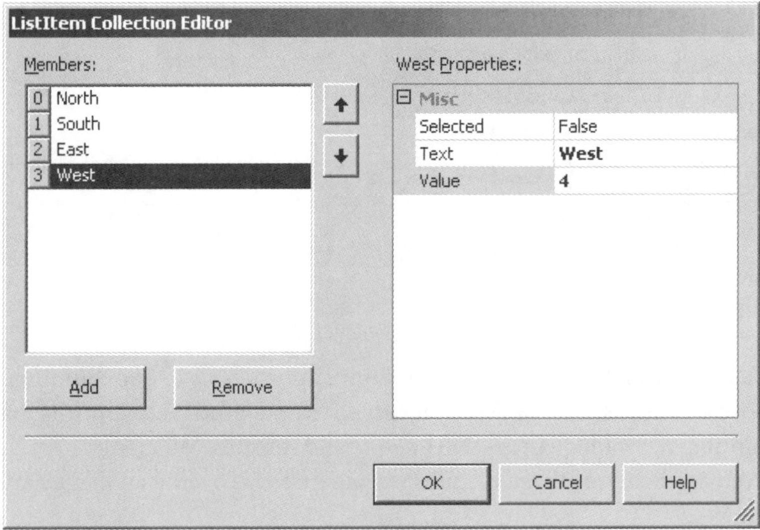

Figure 4-3. The ListItem Editor

Manual entries made in this way can form the entire list, although there is nothing to stop you from dynamically adding or modifying entries at runtime as well. The most direct way of modifying the list from code is to manipulate the Items collection. Previous examples have shown how the `Add` method can be called on Items property to create new entries. The following code fragment shows how selected entries can be copied from a CheckBoxList to a ListBox:

```
Dim objItm As ListItem

For Each objItm In CheckBoxList1.Items
    If objItm.Selected Then
        ListBox1.Items.Add(objItm)
    End If
Next
```

The final technique populates the control with data from a suitable source. This can be a DataSet, DataView, Array, ArrayList, etc. For example, the following code populates a RadioButtonList control from an ADO.NET DataReader:

```
Dim CN As New OleDbConnection("Provider=SQLOLEDB;. . .")
Dim CM As New OleDbCommand("SELECT AircraftID, Registration FROM Aircraft", CN)
Dim DR As OleDbDataReader

CN.Open()
DR = CM.ExecuteReader

With RadioButtonList1
    .DataSource = DR
    .DataTextField = "Registration"
    .DataValueField = "AircraftID"
    .DataBind()
End With
DR.Close
CN.Close
```

Chapter 8 will be discussing the different approaches to data binding, but the above example shows how easy it can be to data bind Web Controls. Also, the data-binding technology in ASP.NET is fast and resource-efficient, so for large-scale Web Applications these techniques can improve overall efficiency and performance.

DropdownList

The DropDownList control displays a single item at a time and allows only single selection. It shares many of the properties of a RadioButtonList and is very similar in its behavior—it just looks different.

ListBox

The ListBox control displays multiple items and can allow single or multiple selection. It shares many of the properties and behaviors of the CheckBoxList, although visually, it is rendered differently.

As Table 4-8 lists, the ListBox has two important properties not found in the CheckBoxList:

Table 4-8. ListBox Control Properties

PROPERTY	DESCRIPTION
Rows	Determines the height of the control, measured in characters. Note that this value is ignored if a value is specified for the Height property. If the ListBox contains more entries than can be displayed in the control, then a scrollbar is automatically displayed and activated.
SelectionMode	Can be set to Single or Multiple to determine how items can be selected.

Images

The Image control renders to the HTML `<img>` element. It is not interactive and raises no events to the server. To create an interactive image, you should use an ImageButton control instead. The image has three significant properties—AlternateText, ImageAlign, and ImageUrl—all of which map to standard HTML attributes for the `<img>` element.

Text Display

Two text display controls are provided: the Label and the Literal control.

Label

The Label control renders to a `<span>` element, and is usually restricted to containing text. As with labels in desktop development tools, this text can be changed programmatically by setting the Text property. There are no other significant properties or methods, and the Label control raises no events to the server because it is non-interactive.

TIP *As we mentioned earlier in the chapter, server-side controls consume more processor time than static HTML. To maximize performance, you should avoid using Web Control Labels if you don't need to access them programmatically; use standard HTML or a Literal control instead.*

Literal

You can use a Literal control to represent any string, text, or HTML element that requires no special server-side processing. It supports only one significant property—Text—which gets displayed in place of the Literal when rendered. This control contains no important methods or events.

Visually, Literal controls are very similar to Labels, although they differ in two respects:

- Labels render to `<span>` elements. Literal controls render to their content only.
- You can use a Label control's properties to determine formatting and layout. To format a Literal, you must include the required HTML tags and attributes in the Text property setting.

Whilst you can use Literal controls in your Web Forms, ASP.NET generally uses them automatically when rendering static HTML content.

Containers

Containers are designed to be parent controls, with other controls or content held within them.

Panel

The Panel control is a generic container and can encapsulate other controls for easier management. For example, if several controls need to have their visibility controlled together, placing them into a panel makes it much easier. At runtime the Panel renders to a `<div>` element.

The Panel supports three important properties—BackImageUrl, HorizontalAlign, and Wrap—all of which affect the visual appearance of the control rather than its behavior. The Panel itself is non-interactive, but of course the controls that it contains can raise events, perform submissions and navigation, and provide any functionality that you need.

You may find using the graphical designer to add controls to the Panel a little cumbersome. The simplest way is to first draw the controls on the Web Form itself; then drag the controls into the Panel. Alternatively, add the controls through HTML source view.

PlaceHolder

The PlaceHolder control renders no visual output of its own (not even an empty element!) and serves only as a container for other controls that may be created and managed by code. The PlaceHolder supports the Controls property, which returns a collection of Control objects that can be added, removed, or retrieved. For example, to add a TextBox control to a PlaceHolder:

```
Dim Ctl As New TextBox()
Ctl.Text = "Dynamic Control"
PlaceHolder1.Controls.Add(Ctl)
```

You cannot add the TextBox (or any other Web Form controls) directly to the Page.Controls collection, since all Web Form controls must be placed within a Form or other container rather than directly on the Page. The PlaceHolder provides a simple way around this limitation, as well as allowing you to choose where in the Page's control hierarchy the new controls will be inserted. This may be important when considering event sequences because certain events (such as TextChanged, Click, and Command) are triggered according to the order of controls in the hierarchy—with those at the top of the hierarchy triggering before those at the bottom.

For example, Figure 4-4 shows a simple control hierarchy, including a PlaceHolder (called `PlaceHolder1`) and a dynamically created TextBox control (called `ctl0`). The TextBox has been added to the `PlaceHolder1.Controls` collection using the code shown previously.

Control Tree			
Control Id	Type	Render Size Bytes (including children)	Viewstate Size Bytes (excluding children)
__PAGE	ASP.PlaceHolder_aspx	818	20
_ctl1	System.Web.UI.ResourceBasedLiteralControl	439	0
Form1	System.Web.UI.HtmlControls.HtmlForm	358	0
_ctl2	System.Web.UI.LiteralControl	5	0
PlaceHolder1	System.Web.UI.WebControls.PlaceHolder	34	0
_ctl0	System.Web.UI.WebControls.TextBox	34	0
_ctl3	System.Web.UI.LiteralControl	5	0
Button1	System.Web.UI.WebControls.Button	130	0
_ctl4	System.Web.UI.LiteralControl	4	0
_ctl5	System.Web.UI.LiteralControl	21	0

Figure 4-4. TextBox Control added to a PlaceHolder

If the TextBox had instead been added to `Form1.Controls`, the hierarchy would appear as shown in Figure 4-5. Note that to reference Form1 (the `<Form>` element defined in the .aspx file) it was necessary to declare a class-level reference in the code-behind:

```
Protected WithEvents Form1 As System.Web.UI.HtmlControls.HtmlForm
```

Control Tree			
Control Id	Type	Render Size Bytes (including children)	Viewstate Size Bytes (excluding children)
__PAGE	ASP.PlaceHolder_aspx	818	20
_ctl1	System.Web.UI.ResourceBasedLiteralControl	439	0
Form1	System.Web.UI.HtmlControls.HtmlForm	358	0
_ctl2	System.Web.UI.LiteralControl	5	0
PlaceHolder1	System.Web.UI.WebControls.PlaceHolder	0	0
_ctl3	System.Web.UI.LiteralControl	5	0
Button1	System.Web.UI.WebControls.Button	130	0
_ctl4	System.Web.UI.LiteralControl	4	0
_ctl0	System.Web.UI.WebControls.TextBox	34	0
_ctl5	System.Web.UI.LiteralControl	21	0

Figure 4-5. TextBox control added directly to the Form

These images were generated by enabling the Trace feature for the Web Form. This will be discussed in detail in Chapter 10.

Table, TableRow, TableCell

The Table, TableRow, and TableCell controls allow the creation and management of tables. They are valid container controls, although, as with the Panel control, you may find the graphical Web Form designer to be a little inconsistent when creating child controls. Once again, it is probably easiest to use HTML source view at design-time; or you can create the table in code.

When you start working with tables it is important to realize that they work within a rigid hierarchy. The Table contains a collection of TableRow objects, each of which contains a collection of TableCell objects. It is not possible to navigate directly from the Table to a TableCell—the reference must be made through a TableRow.

The properties supported by Table, TableRow, and TableCell controls are largely related to the HTML attributes that will be rendered to the browser in the tags and elements. As you would expect, most of these will relate to the appearance, format, and layout of the table. The Rows and Cells collections support a number of methods for adding, removing, and retrieving objects—much the same as the Items collection discussed above for the selection controls.

Note that the Table is not directly data-aware. The DataGrid can be bound directly to a datasource and rendered to an HTML table. However, the Table provides far more control and precision in terms of style, content, and layout.

Exploring List Controls

List controls are data-aware and can be bound to a variety of datasources including DataSet, DataReader, and ArrayList objects. As with traditional desktop data binding, data-aware controls can automatically display the content of a data object and some can offer additional features such as sorting and paging.

Figure 4-6 shows the three controls that fall into this category:

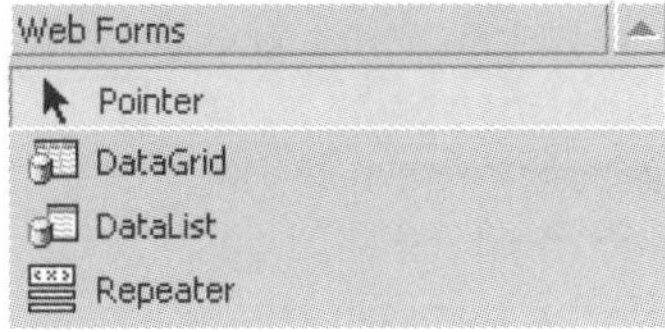

Figure 4-6. List controls

We've already discussed the disconnected and stateless nature of Web applications in Chapter 1, but it's worth reviewing this concept when considering how and when to use data binding. In a desktop application, when users make changes to data-aware controls, they are interacting with a real control. In ASP.NET Web Applications, users are interacting with relatively dumb HTML; the controls that generated the data only ever exist on the server and are destroyed before the user even gets their requested page. This makes handling updates to a user interface generated with data binding rather more complicated than you might imagine; we will be dedicating a large part of Chapter 8 to this topic.

However, display-only data binding in ASP.NET is straightforward and has some real advantages. For example, a DataGrid control can be added to a Web Form and bound to a DataReader with a minimum of code:

```
Dim CN As New OleDbConnection("Provider=SQLOLEDB.1;....")
CN.Open()
Dim CM As New OleDbCommand("SELECT AircraftID, Registration, Manuf, Model " & _
                 FROM Aircraft", CN)
Dim DR As OleDbDataReader

DR = CM.ExecuteReader()

DataGrid1.DataSource = DR
DataGrid1.DataBind()

DR.Close()
CN.Close()
```

This code results in the DataGrid being rendered to a table in the user's browser; the content of the DataReader is shown automatically, as illustrated in Figure 4-7:

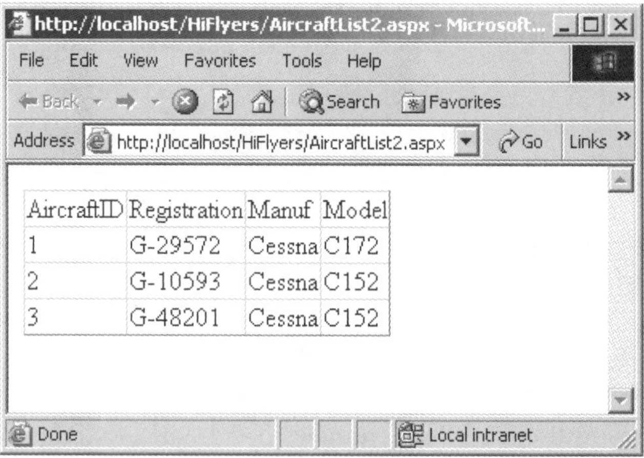

Figure 4-7. Rendered output from the DataGrid

Although it displays the data, the grid has not been rendered very attractively. You can improve its appearance in a number of ways, such as through the definition of TemplateColumns, styles, properties, and code. For example, the previous example can be rendered in a more attractive style by defining the following attributes for the tag:

```
<asp:DataGrid id="DataGrid1" runat="server"
              HeaderStyle-BackColor="blue"
              HeaderStyle-ForeColor="white"
              AlternatingItemStyle-BackColor="#ccffff"
              Font-Name="Arial">
</asp:DataGrid>
```

The rendered output will then appear as shown in Figure 4-8:

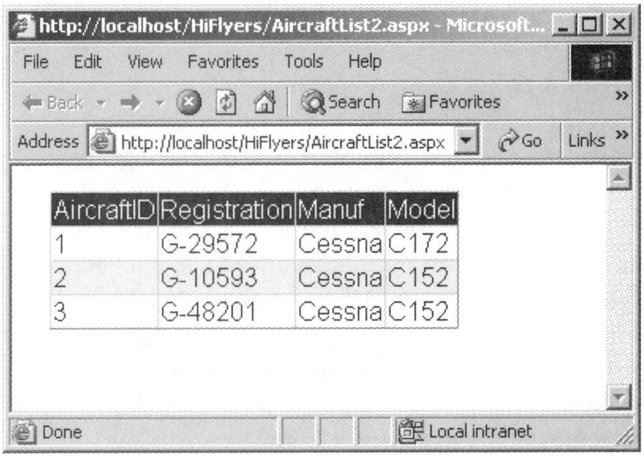
http://localhost/HiFlyers/AircraftList2.aspx - Microsoft...
File Edit View Favorites Tools Help
Back
Search
Favorites
Address
http://localhost/HiFlyers/AircraftList2.aspx
Go
Links
AircraftID Registration Manuf Model
1 G-29572 Cessna C172
2 G-10593 Cessna C152
3 G-48201 Cessna C152
Done
Local intranet

Figure 4-8 DataGrid with style settings

Clearly there is still work to do to improve the presentation of the grid. For example, we may want to change the column headings, provide wider columns for the manufacturer and model, and add columns with buttons to allow further details on the aircraft to be checked. We can also allow rows or columns to be edited (if appropriate) and provide drill-down capabilities, all of which are techniques that have long been available in desktop applications, but were previously quite awkward to implement with Web technologies.

Rather than cover the specifics of the List controls in this chapter, we will defer further discussion until Chapter 8, where we will provide a full and thorough coverage of all the relevant database and data-binding techniques.

Using Rich Controls

We've included the category of Rich controls as a convenient way to describe two of the more complex Web Controls packaged with ASP.NET. Broadly speaking, Rich controls offer sophisticated features and functions, and can be expected to render to a combination of controls and elements when sent to the client browser. Figure 4-9 shows the toolbox icons for the two standard Rich controls, although many third-party controls will fall into this category as well.

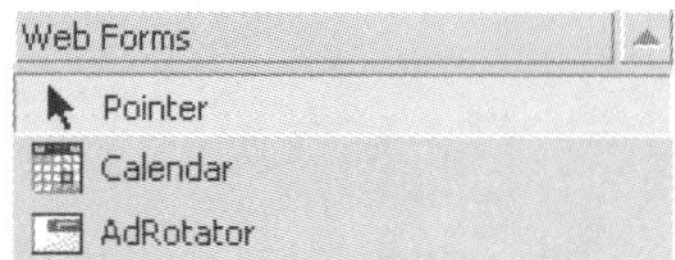

Figure 4-9. Rich controls in the Toolbox

AdRotator

The AdRotator control provides a simple way of displaying adverts and graphics in a pseudo-random sequence. It is an updated version of the AdRotator component provided with classic ASP, but is somewhat easier to use and configure.

To use the AdRotator control you must have a list of the items to be displayed; this can be specified in an XML file or generated programmatically. Each time the Web Form is processed, the AdRotator randomly selects one of the items to be displayed and renders it to the browser. Each item must have an image, but can also have alternate text, a hyperlink, a keyword, and a weighting that influences how often the item is displayed.

The AdRotator supports the important properties listed in Table 4-9:

Table 4-9. AdRotator Control Properties

PROPERTY	DESCRIPTION
`AdvertisementFile`	Specifies the URL of the XML document file containing the list of items to be displayed. This file must conform to a specific structure, which is described below in the next section.
`KeywordFilter`	Keywords can be defined in the item list; the KeywordFilter property can then be used to restrict which adverts are displayed. For example, if you determine that the current Web user is a middle-aged office worker, then you can choose to display different adverts than if they were identified as a college student.
`Target`	Specifies the name of the frame or browser window that will be used for navigation if the user clicks the advert to follow a hyperlink defined for the current item.

Advertisement List

If you use an XML document for the list of advertisements, then it must conform to a specific structure. An example of such a document is as follows:

```
<Advertisements>
    <Ad>
        <ImageUrl>images/hiflyers.gif</ImageUrl>
        <NavigateUrl>http://www.hiflyers.org</NavigateUrl>
        <AlternateText>Hi Flyers</AlternateText>
        <Impressions>80</Impressions>
        <Keyword>Training</Keyword>
    </Ad>
    <Ad>
        <ImageUrl>images/faa_logo.gif</ImageUrl>
        <NavigateUrl>http://www.faa.gov </NavigateUrl>
        <AlternateText>Federal Aviation Administration</AlternateText>
        <Impressions>80</Impressions>
        <Keyword>Regulation</Keyword>
    </Ad>
</Advertisements>
```

You must define an `ImageUrl` for each entry, but other attributes are optional. The `Impressions` attribute is a weighting that the AdRotator uses when determining which item to display; the higher the weighting, the more often the item is displayed.

AdCreated Event

The `AdCreated` event is important if the displayed item is to be controlled programmatically. The event fires with every round-trip to the server—after the control is created, but before the page is rendered. If you have specified an AdvertisementFile, the AdRotator will select its chosen advert before the event is triggered. If you have not specified an AdvertisementFile, the code you write in the event handler is responsible for generating the required details that the AdRotator will need to display the advert.

The event handler is passed two arguments: The first is the object that raised the event and the second is derived from AdCreatedEventArgs. This argument passes information relating to the advert about to be displayed, including the properties in Table 4-10:

Table 4-10. Properties of the AdCreatedEventArgs Class

PROPERTY	DESCRIPTION
`AdProperties`	Returns a Dictionary object containing all of the properties for the advert that has been selected.
`AlternateText`	Returns or assigns the alternate text that will be rendered to the browser by the AdRotator.
`ImageUrl`	Returns or assigns the URL of the image that will be displayed in the browser.
`NavigateUrl`	Returns or assigns the URL of the Web site or page linked to the image.

These values can be read from or written to within the event handler, allowing you to synchronize the behavior and appearance of other controls on the Web page to the displayed event. For example, if you had a hyperlink control displayed at the foot of a Web Form containing an AdRotator, it could be directed to the same URL as the advert with:

```
HyperLink1.NavigateUrl = e.NavigateUrl
```

Calendar

The Calendar control provides a customizable one-month view calendar and allows selection of days, weeks, or months according to property settings. When rendered, the Calendar is most likely to be represented as a table containing hyperlinks to JavaScript routines that perform the postback. The calendar is always fully displayed, rather than being of the drop-down or pop-up style favored by many Web developers.

The Calendar has many different properties that control its appearance and determine what features it offers the user. We won't try and list them all here since they are well-defined and documented in Visual Studio .NET. However, Table 4-11 lists the most important properties for the Calendar control.

Table 4-11. Calendar Control Properties

PROPERTY	DESCRIPTION
SelectedDate	Returns the day selected in the calendar. This is most useful when the SelectionMode is set to Day.
SelectedDates	Returns a collection of DateTime objects that represent the day or days selected in the calendar. This property is used when the SelectionMode is set to Week or Month.
SelectionMode	Determines whether the user can select single days, weeks, or months.
VisibleDate	Determines which month's calendar is displayed.

The Calendar control supports one significant event: SelectionChanged. This event triggers on the server when either the SelectedDate or SelectedDates property values change. For example, the following code illustrates how the SelectionChanged event could be used to retrieve the date or dates that have been chosen:

```
Private Sub Calendar1_SelectionChanged(ByVal sender As System.Object,
    ByVal e As System.EventArgs) Handles Calendar1.SelectionChanged
    Dim objSelDat As DateTime
    Label1.Text = Calendar1.SelectedDate

    Label2.Text = ""
    For Each objSelDat In Calendar1.SelectedDates
        Label2.Text &= objSelDat.ToShortDateString & ", "
    Next
End Sub
```

When the Calendar control is set to allow selection of weeks or months, it will display additional active hyperlinks to allow the required dates to be highlighted. Figure 4-10 shows how such a Calendar control may appear. This example has also been formatted using styles.

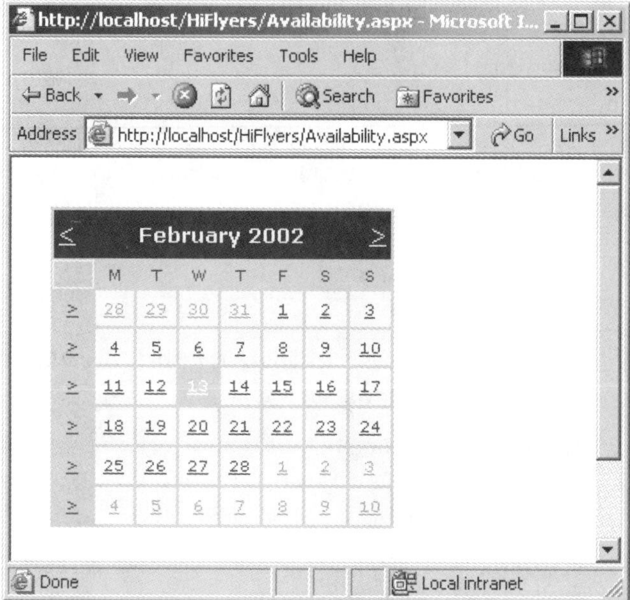

Figure 4-10. Calendar control offering week and day selection

Using Validation Controls

The task of validating user-entered data is an essential one in every application; ASP.NET Web Applications are no exception. One of the key decisions to be taken when building Web Applications is where this validation will take place:

- **Client-side validation** can be performed using client-side script before the page is submitted to the server. This approach prevents unnecessary round-trips and reduces the load on the server. However, client-side validation relies on the browser supporting script. It also has limited functionality because validation can only be performed against rules and data passed to the client.

- **Server-side validation** can be performed within the Web Form, usually by code in event procedures. Any level or type of validation is possible (including checks against databases and other resources), but this approach requires a round-trip. On a slow link, users can quickly become dissatisfied with the delays that they encounter.

The choice of approach is therefore a tradeoff between the functionality that you expect the client to have and the need to perform round-trips for server-side checks.

ASP.NET simplifies this choice by providing Validation controls that can automatically detect the capabilities of the client browser and perform client-side validation when appropriate. The minimum requirements are that the browser supports ECMAScript 1.2 or later and a Document Object Model (DOM) that is compatible with Microsoft Internet Explorer 4.0 or later.

With a suitable browser, Validation controls render script to the client that is executed as the user makes changes to the controls in the form. You choose the checks that are performed by selecting appropriate Validation controls and setting their properties. You also decide what input controls are to be validated. ASP.NET generates the necessary script and attaches it to the events of the chosen input controls. ASP.NET also intercepts the normal client-side actions that would cause a page to be submitted. When the page is in the browser and the user is editing the data, checks are performed as the focus leaves each control; if the check fails (that is, the validation rule you defined is breached) then a message can be immediately displayed. When the user tries to submit the form, all of the Validation controls on the page are again checked; if any of them fail, the submission is blocked until the user corrects the offending entries.

The client-side functionality is great if the browser supports it, but what if it doesn't? Validation controls handle this situation by also performing server-side checks during the postback process. These checks are performed before your event procedures run. If the validation is successful, the Page.IsValid property is set to True; if validation is not successful, the property is set to False. Within your code you need only check the current value of Page.IsValid to determine whether you should process the information or simply return the page to the browser for the user to correct.

There are six controls that fall into this category, five of which perform different types of checks and a final one that summarizes the results of the others. Figure 4-11 shows the Toolbox icons for these controls:

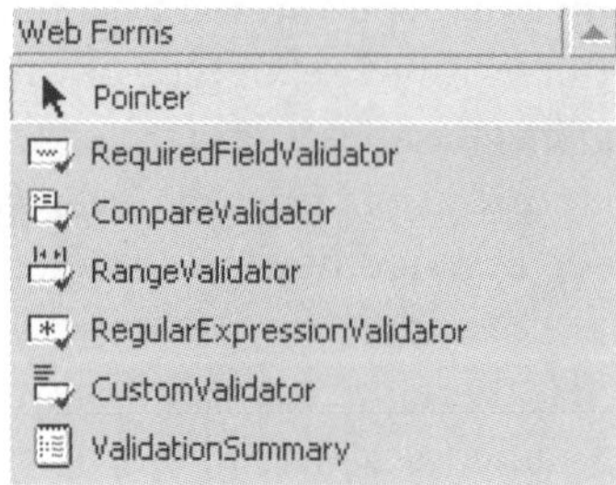

Figure 4-11. Validation controls

Using Validation Controls

Validation controls are "paired" with other Web Controls by setting their ControlToValidate property. For example, if you have a TextBox control called txtUserName and wanted to ensure that the user had entered a value, you would add a RequiredFieldValidator to the Web Form and set its ControlToValidate property to `txtUserName`. Each Validation control can be set to validate only one Web Control, although you can use any number of Validation controls to check the content of a single Web Control.

If validation fails, the Validation control will display the message defined by the control's ErrorMessage property. You will probably want to keep the messages quite brief (but still make them sufficiently descriptive) and you'll want to position the Validation controls adjacent to their associated input controls so that the message is positioned accordingly. As we'll see later, you can also choose to display the messages in a separate location by using a ValidationSummary control.

For example, the Web Form shown in Figure 4-12 is used to allow HiFlyers' customers to check the availability of aircraft and instructors for a particular date. It contains two ListBox controls and a single TextBox:

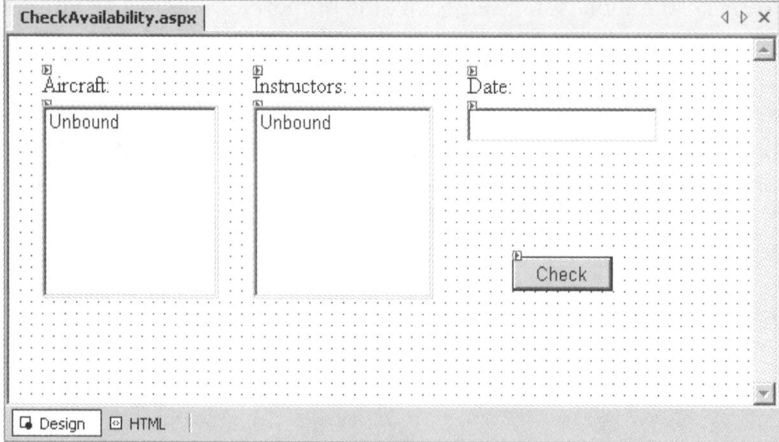

Figure 4-12. "Check Availability" Web Form

To ensure that the user has chosen an Aircraft and an Instructor, we can add two RequiredFieldValidator controls. Each would have its ControlToValidate property set to the name of the appropriate ListBox. We could also add a RequiredFieldValidator for the date field, plus a CompareValidator to ensure that the value entered is indeed a valid date; both of these controls have `txtDate` set as their ControlToValidate. Figure 4-13 shows the RequiredFieldValidator and CompareValidator controls in place.

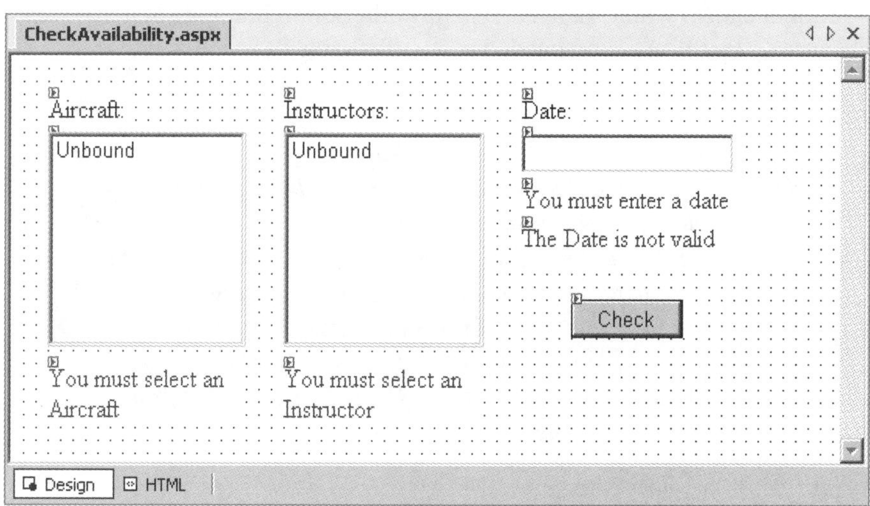

Figure 4-13. Validation Controls in place

If client-side scripting is supported in the user's browser, the Validation controls are automatically checked when focus is lost from the associated input control. If the validation fails, the ErrorMessage is displayed to the user and the postback process is then blocked. This means that the user cannot submit the form until all of the validation checks have succeeded.

However, if client-side scripting is not supported, the checks have to be performed server-side; this means that the form *will* be posted back to the server. ASP.NET ensures that all of the appropriate checks are carried out automatically, but it then allows all the normal events that occur during a postback to fire—including `Page.Load`, `DataChanged`, `Click`, and `Command` events. Any code you write for these events must check to see whether validation succeeded or not, and then take appropriate action depending on the result. Do this by testing the Page.IsValid property, which returns True or False. ASP.NET sets the Page.IsValid property by logically ANDing all of the IsValid properties for the individual validation controls.

For example, the code behind the Check button in Figure 4-13 would be similar to the following:

```
Private Sub cmdCheck_Click(ByVal sender As System.Object, _
                ByVal e As System.EventArgs) Handles cmdCheck.Click
    If Page.IsValid Then
        'Perform the check on availability

    End If
End Sub
```

Similar checks would be needed in any other event handlers that used the data entered by the user and needed to ensure that it was valid.

NOTE *Don't be fooled into thinking that you only need to do this check if you are targeting down-level browsers (ones that do not support client script). It is good practice to always implement these checks because they block malformed and malicious requests against the Web Application. Also, performing the server-side check allows for the situation in which a user has disabled client-side JavaScript in their browser, so preventing the client-side validation from being performed.*

If you need to know more about the cause of validation failure, you can interrogate each of the Validation controls through the Page.Validators property. This collection contains references to each of the validation controls on the form and allows you to access their individual IsValid and ErrorMessage properties, as well as their `Validate` event. These members are exposed through the IValidator interface of each control. The following code shows how we could extend the check on Page.IsValid so that it sets the foreground color of each invalid control to Red:

```
If Page.IsValid Then
    'Perform the check on availability

Else
    Dim ctlValidator As BaseValidator
    Dim ctlValidatee As WebControl

    For Each ctlValidator In Page.Validators
        If ctlValidator.IsValid = False Then
            'Identify the control to validate and set its foreground to Red
            ctlValidatee = CType(Me.FindControl(ctlValidator.ControlToValidate), _
                    WebControl)
```

```
            ctlValidatee.ForeColor = System.Drawing.Color.Red
        End If
    Next
End If
```

A similar approach could be used to display graphics in place of the standard textual validation errors, though you should remember that this would work only when the validation was performed on the server.

Common Properties and Methods

Now that you've seen some of the validation controls in action, we'll summarize the properties, methods, and events that you'll want to use when configuring these controls. The RequiredFieldValidator, CompareValidator, RangeValidator, RegularExpressionValidator, and CustomValidator all derive from System.Web.UI.WebControls.BaseValidator, and so share a common set of properties and methods. Table 4-12 lists those that rank among the more important:

Table 4-12. Common Validation Control Properties

PROPERTY	DESCRIPTION
`ControlToValidate`	Specifies which control will be validated
`Display`	Determines how the message from the validator is displayed. `Static` causes space to be allocated in the rendered output whether there is a message or not; `Dynamic` causes space to be allocated only if needed; and `None` prevents the message from being displayed at all. This last setting is often used when you are using a ValidationSummary control (see later) to display all the validation messages in one place.
`EnableClientScript`	Determines whether client-side script is generated (should the browser allow it) to perform client-side validation. Setting this property to False causes all validation to be performed server-side only.
`ErrorMessage`	Specifies the text of the message to be displayed if validation fails.
`IsValid`	Returns a Boolean value indicating whether the content of the control is valid. Can be quite useful if validation is being performed server-side.
`Text`	Specifies the text of the message to be displayed if validation succeeds.

Note that the Display property is quite different from the Visible property. Display determines how the message from the Validation control is displayed, whereas Visible determines whether the entire control, including the client-side script, is rendered to the browser. Setting Visible to False prevents any validation from being performed, while setting Display to None simply prevents the display of the resulting message.

Table 4-13 lists the two significant methods shared by all Validation controls:

Table 4-13. Validation Control Methods

METHOD	DESCRIPTION
`GetValidationProperty`	This method is primarily of interest if you are building your own custom Web Controls. It returns the property of the associated control that should be validated.
`Validate`	This method forces the validation to be performed in code. You may want to do this if you programmatically change the properties of the validator or its associated control. Calling Validate sets the IsValid property.

NOTE *With the exception of the RequiredFieldValidator, all of the other controls pass validation if the control they are validating is empty. If a control is required to have a value, then a RequiredFieldValidator should be used as well.*

RequiredFieldValidator

You use the RequiredFieldValidator control to ensure that a value has been entered into a control. It performs no additional type or range checking beyond this. This control supports only one relevant property in addition to those discussed above: InitialValue.

InitialValue is not as simple as it may at first appear. The property has two effects:

- It specifies the initial value of the input control.
- It determines the way in which validation is performed. The validation check fails if, and only if, the value of the associated input control matches this InitialValue upon losing focus.

In other words, the InitialValue property allows you to use a RequiredFieldValidator to not only check for empty fields, but also for fields that have specific values. This allows you to populate the input control with a default descriptive value which the user is forced to change.

NOTE *The strings in the InitialValue property and the input control are both trimmed of leading and trailing spaces before validation is performed. Also, the comparison is case-sensitive.*

CompareValidator

The CompareValidator checks a control against a specific value or checks it with the contents of another control. You can use a CompareValidator to check that values are equal to, not equal to, less than, or more than a particular value. You can also use them to perform data type checks on the input values.

Table 4-14 summarizes the more important properties of the CompareValidator control:

Table 4-14. CompareValidator Control Properties

PROPERTY	DESCRIPTION
`ControlToCompare`	Determines what the input control will be validated against. This can be left blank if ValueToCompare is specified instead.
`Operator`	Determines how the comparison will be performed. Possible values are Equal, NotEqual, GreaterThan, GreaterThanEqual, LessThan, LessThanEqual, and DataTypeCheck. DataTypeCheck is very useful, since it performs a check on the type of data in the input control rather than its actual value. The check is performed against the value specified for the Type property.
`Type`	Specifies the data type that will be used for comparisons. Note that the default setting of this property is String, which causes all comparisons to be performed textually. If you want to compare numeric values, ensure that Type is set to Integer, Double, or Currency as appropriate.
`ValueToCompare`	Specifies a value against which the input control will be compared. If both ControlToCompare and ValueToCompare are specified, then ControlToCompare takes precedence.

It is interesting that the Type property can be set to Currency, since .NET doesn't support a distinct currency data type. The Currency setting validates the entry made by the user to determine whether it is a valid number with a maximum of two decimal places. It accepts commas to separate the thousands, but does *not* permit any currency symbols.

TIP *Ensure that the Type property is set correctly for the data types in use. For example, with Type set to String, ValueToCompare set to 100, and Operator set to LessThan, the validator will fail the check on an input value of 24, since the value 24 is alphabetically* greater *than 100.*

RangeValidator

You can use RangeValidator controls to ensure that the data entered falls within a certain range of values. Effectively, this is a slightly more sophisticated version of the CompareValidator. See Table 4-15 for descriptions of the important RangeValidator properties.

Table 4-15. RangeValidator Control Properties

PROPERTY	DESCRIPTION
MaximumValue	Maximum value of permissible range.
MinimumValue	Minimum value of permissible range.
Type	Data type to be used when comparing the input value. See the discussion on the CompareValidator's Type property above.

RegularExpressionValidator

The RegularExpressionValidator checks that the value entered matches a specific *regular expression*. Regular expressions have been a part of many languages for some time, but have had very little support in Visual Basic until now. Regular expressions allow you to perform powerful pattern-matching, extraction, and replacement operations; they are likely to make extensive string handling much easier.

The RegularExpressionValidator control may be used for many purposes, although the most common is for ensuring that entered data matches required formats—such as telephone numbers, zip codes, product codes, to name but a few.

The key property for this control is ValidationExpression, which specifies the regular expression that will be used for the check. Microsoft has developed their own language and notation for regular expressions, bringing together the best aspects of regular expression support found in other languages and environments. For example, the following value for ValidationExpression would check a control for a 16-digit number, such as may be found on some credit cards:

```
\d{16}
```

The `\d` indicates that a digit is required, and the `{16}` indicates that the previous pattern (that is, the digit) is to be repeated 16 times. We don't have the space in this book to provide a comprehensive discussion of the creation and use of regular expressions, but Chapter 6 includes a further example that uses a Mobile RegularExpressionValidator control to illustrate how regular expressions can be used to pattern match a code entered by the user. Also, the Visual Studio .NET documentation includes thorough coverage and many examples.

CustomValidator

You will find that the four Validation controls we've already discussed are extremely useful and very easy to implement. However, there will be situations where the standard controls don't perform quite the right checks. In this case you can use a CustomValidator to help you run your own customized validation routines.

CustomValidator controls provide a developer-defined validation function for an input control. You write the code for this function in the form of a server-side event handler, and optionally a client-side scripting function. It is your responsibility to perform the check server-side; the control simply provides a convenient event in which you can do it.

Server-Side Validation Using a CustomValidator

To perform server-side validation, add code to the `ServerValidate` event. The event handler is passed a ServerValidateEventArgs that includes the data from the input control. The routine should perform its check on this value and then store the result (either True or False) in the IsValid property of the ServerValidateEventArgs object. All of this is performed using standard server-side code, but obviously requires a server round-trip to perform the check.

For example, HiFlyers have a host of special deals for customers who want to book flying lessons during weekdays, so they need a Validation control that can perform this check on the date that the user selects when making their inquiry. The following code could be used in the ServerValidate event:

```
Private Sub CustomValidator1_ServerValidate(ByVal source As System.Object, _
                ByVal args As System.Web.UI.WebControls.ServerValidateEventArgs) _
                Handles CustomValidator1.ServerValidate
    If IsDate(args.Value) = False Then
        args.IsValid = False
    ElseIf Weekday(args.Value) = 1 Or Weekday(args.Value) = 7 Then
        args.IsValid = False
    Else
        args.IsValid = True
    End If
End Sub
```

Notice that this code sets the IsValid property to True or False to indicate success or failure. ASP.NET checks this value, along with all other Validation controls, when it determines the value for Page.IsValid. If you do not explicitly set a value for IsValid, it will default to True.

Client-Side Validation Using a CustomValidator

Client-side validation is managed separately from the server-side validation function described above. The code to perform client-side validation is created as a script function in the .aspx page, using any scripting language that the browser will support. The function must be in the form:

```
function ValidationFunctionName(source, arguments)
```

You must write this function yourself, and you must ensure that the language you choose will be supported by any browsers that are used. In public-access situations, this means that you must use JavaScript, although VBScript can be used if you are targeting only modern Microsoft browsers. The arguments parameter passed to the function is an object and has two important properties:

- Value, which is the content of the control to be validated
- IsValid, which is set to True or False to indicate validation success or failure

Once you have written the client-side code, set the CustomValidator control's ClientValidationFunction property to the name of the function. When the page is rendered to the browser, ASP.NET will generate the additional code needed to ensure the function is called on the client side.

The following example shows a VBScript function that performs the client-side validation that matches the server-side routine described above:

```
<script language="vbscript">
    Sub ValidWeekDay(source, arguments)
        If IsDate(arguments.Value) = False Then
            arguments.IsValid = False
        ElseIf WeekDay(arguments.Value) = 1 or WeekDay(arguments.Value) = 7 Then
            arguments.IsValid = False
        Else
            arguments.IsValid=True
        End If
    End Sub
</script>
```

ValidationSummary

All of the controls we have so far discussed perform some type of validation and then display a suitable message if validation fails. The position of the message is defined by the position of the Validation control when it was added to the Web Form. Although this can work well for simple Web Forms, it is likely that you'll want more command over how and where the messages are displayed for more complex layouts.

The ValidationSummary gives you this additional control, allowing you to determine position and style of all validation messages, plus whether or not a popup alert should be generated if any validation fails. Table 4-16 lists those properties which the ValidationSummary supports:

Table 4-16. ValidationSummary Control Properties

PROPERTY	DESCRIPTION
DisplayMode	Determines whether the messages are displayed in the form of a list, bulleted list, or a single paragraph.
HeaderText	Specifies the string value that will be displayed at the top or start of the message summary.
ShowMessageBox	If True, causes the message summary to be displayed in a popup alert box.
ShowSummary	If True, causes the message summary to be displayed on the Web Form.

One of the most interesting things about the ValidationSummary control is that the developer does not need to specify which Validation controls will be summarized. Instead, the ValidationSummary is automatically populated with the ErrorMessage text from every control on the Web Form that derives from System.Web.UI.WebControls.BaseValidator.

TIP *When using the ValidationSummary it is likely that you will want the standard error messages to be suppressed. You can do this by setting each control's Display property to None.*

For example, if we take the CheckAvailability Web Form shown in Figure 4-13, we can add a ValidationSummary to group the validation error messages just above the Check button. Along with adding the new control, we must also set the Display property of each existing validation control to None to prevent the messages from being displayed twice. After we've made these changes, the Web Form will appear as shown in Figure 4-14. Note that the validators for the Date text box have been moved to improve clarity.

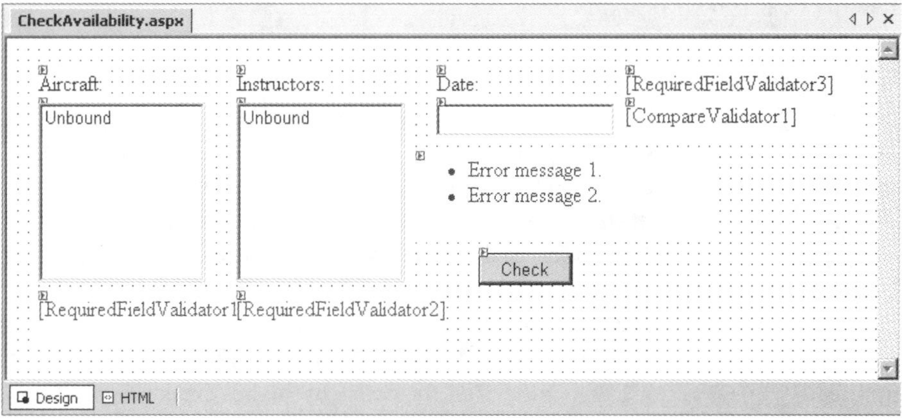

Figure 4-14. Adding a ValidationSummary

Notice that VisualStudio .NET has hidden the ErrorMessages that would normally be displayed at design-time, replacing each with just the name of the Validation control. This happens when the control's Display properties are set to None.

If the user attempts to click the **Check** button, submitting the page without making any selections or entries, the validation errors will be displayed in the summary control, as shown in Figure 4-15.

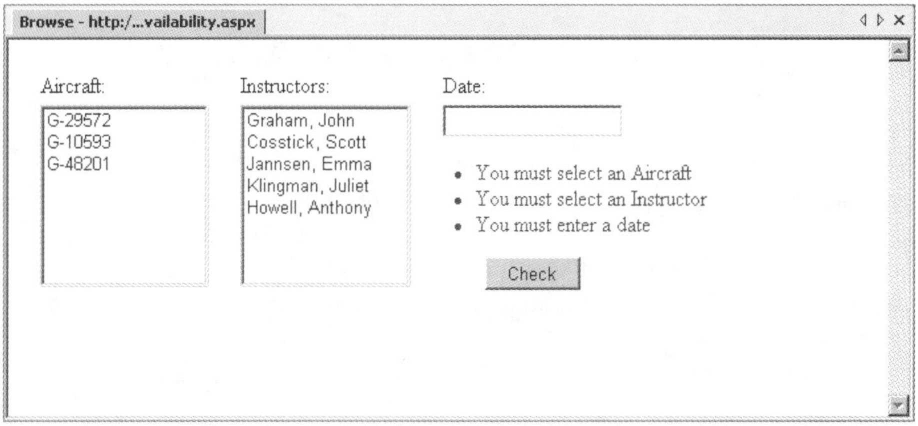

Figure 4-15. Summary of validation errors

Canceling Validation

When present on a Web Form, Validation Controls are active for almost every postback generated from the browser (see Limitations of Validation Controls below). There may be some cases where you do not want to perform validation though, such as when a user clicks a Cancel or Logout button, or maybe if they perform some other action which nullifies the changes they were making.

If you want to inhibit validation for a specific button, you need to set that button's CausesValidation property to False. This prevents the client-side validation function from being associated with the button, allowing a normal (unvalidated) postback to occur. On the server, the validation events will also be ignored because ASP.NET will detect that the cause of the postback was a button configured to skip validation.

Limitations of Validation Controls

On the whole, Validation controls are extremely powerful and effective, but there are some instances where validation can be bypassed. In particular:

- If you have used additional customized client-side script to perform postbacks.
- If you have hyperlinks that point to the current page.
- Some controls, especially rich and third-party controls, may bypass validation.

It is fair to say that the first two instances are uncommon situations. Also, if you have defined your own postback mechanisms (either client-side code or hyperlinks) that duplicate the features provided by ASP.NET, then it's unrealistic to expect ASP.NET to apply all of its normal checks and features. The third point is more serious; the Calendar is an example of a rich control that performs non-validated postbacks.

To illustrate this, try the following:

1. Create a new, blank Web Form.
2. Add a TextBox, a Calendar, and a Button. Add a RequiredField validator and set its ControlToValidate property to the name of the TextBox.

3. Build and browse the page and test that validation is performed by leaving the TextBox blank and clicking the Button. You should see the validation error message.

4. Now click one of the links in the Calendar (either one of the days or weeks, or one of the navigation links). Notice that client-side validation is not performed.

Now the good news. This should not be a problem. In fact, it's a required feature of the Calendar control's behavior. If validation *was* performed when the calendar generated postbacks, it would have to occur while the user moved from month-to-month when selecting dates. If the calendar itself had a validator associated with it, the validation would most likely prevent the user from selecting a date. In other words, you could end up with a "circular" validation problem where the user couldn't select a date without already having a valid date selected!

You need to know about this type of behavior so that you can accommodate it within your design. For example, if you are performing any processing in the `Load` event for the Page, or the `SelectionChanged` event for the Calendar, then you may first want to check that validation has succeeded. If you just try testing Page.IsValid, you'll receive an error because the validation routines haven't yet been triggered. Instead, you must first call Page.Validate, as the following illustrates:

```
Private Sub Calendar1_SelectionChanged(ByVal sender As System.Object, _
            ByVal e As System.EventArgs) Handles Calendar1.SelectionChanged
    Page.Validate()
    If Page.IsValid Then
        'Perform processing
    Else
        'Do nothing - just let the page be returned to the browser
    End If
End Sub
```

You will rarely run into problems such as these, since the designs that you'll be implementing will almost certainly perform processing when a button is clicked, rather than when changing individual controls. However, problems are always a possibility, and we'd suggest that you remember that validation can be skipped in some situations.

Implementing Formatting and Style

In Chapter 3 we looked at how you can use styles and style sheets to control the formatting and appearance of HTML Controls. If you look at HTML Controls, you'll find that nearly all of them support a Style property to allow individual element-by-element formatting. You can also use CSS (as a reminder, CSS means cascading style sheets) to define styles for each element type that will be automatically applied by the browser when the page is displayed.

Web Controls don't work this way though. Firstly, Visual Studio .NET makes the Style property less accessible by not displaying it in the Properties window; and secondly, you don't know exactly how a Web Control will be rendered, so how can you define element styles using CSS?

You can solve these problems in one of three ways:

- Using individual properties on each control
- Defining `Style` attribute values through HTML or through code
- Using CSS classes to define styles

Style Properties

Most Web Controls support a range of properties that determine how the control is rendered. Typical examples include the following:

- BackColor
- ForeColor
- Font
- Height
- Width

Also, some controls, including the Calendar, DataGrid, and DataList, support compound properties for defining various attributes of the appearance. The Calendar supports DayHeaderStyle, DayStyle, NextPrevStyle, and more, and the DataGrid supports AlternatingItemStyle, EditItemStyle, and so on.

To make it easier for you to set these compound properties, the controls support an AutoFormat facility, which you access by right-clicking the control and selecting **AutoFormat**. Figure 4-16 illustrates the Calendar Auto Format dialog box:

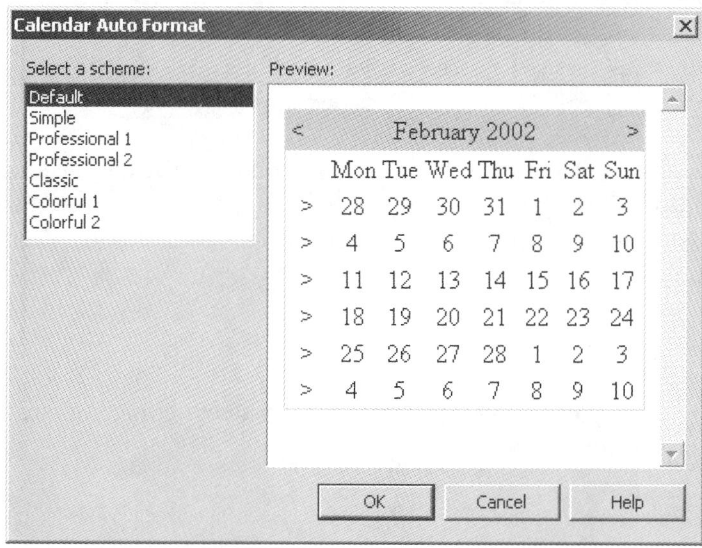

Figure 4-16. Calendar Auto Format dialog

The main problem with these approaches is one of consistency. Since every control is formatted individually, modifications that are required for the overall style or layout could involve changes to hundreds or possibly thousands of separate objects.

Style Attribute Values

Web Controls support a Style property, but you won't see it in the Properties window because Visual Studio .NET emphasizes the individual properties (BorderColor, Font-Size, ForeColor, etc.). Despite this, you can manually set `Style` attribute values in HTML View. For example, a Web Form in flow layout may contain the following TextBox element:

```
<asp:TextBox id="TextBox1" runat="server">Text</asp:TextBox>
```

To apply style values that format text to 14pt in blue, you can modify the tag by adding a `Style` attribute as follows:

```
<asp:TextBox style="FONT-SIZE: 14pt; COLOR: blue" id="TextBox1"
                runat="server">Text</asp:TextBox>
```

Of course, you can achieve similar results by setting the ForeColor and Font-Size properties individually:

```
<asp:TextBox id="TextBox1" runat="server" ForeColor="Blue"
                Font-Size="14pt">Text</asp:TextBox>
```

You can also define style values through code because the Page exposes a Style property, which is a collection of individual style attributes. You can add, remove, and change attributes at will. For example, the following will make the text within the TextBox bold:

```
TextBox1.Style.Add("Font-Weight", "Bold")
```

Once again, you could achieve the same result by setting a dedicated property of the TextBox object:

```
TextBox1.Font.Bold = True
```

So, it seems that there are two ways of applying formatting to Web Form controls, with the control-based properties being favored because they are usually easier to set. However, the significant advantage of using the `Style` attribute is that you can define *any* attribute values, even those that ASP.NET knows nothing about. Simple examples include the `Text-Transform` value, which allows for capitalizing and changing case of text, and `Cursor` for changing cursor types.

CSS Classes

Individual formatting of controls is hard work; as soon as you've laid everything out and formatted it in line with the specification, someone changes the requirements. Now all that text in Arial 14pt has to be changed to Verdana 12pt. This is why style sheets are favored in Web development. They allow you to define a single set of attributes that can be applied to multiple controls; any needed changes are made just to the definition in the style sheet, not manually to *every* instance of the incorrect items.

In classic ASP and HTML development it has become common to use Element styles within style sheets. These styles are automatically applied to all elements of a specific type. Web Controls don't lend themselves to formatting via CSS Element styles because you don't know *exactly* how the control will be rendered, but Web Controls *do* all support a property called CssClass. You can use this property to specify the name of a CSS class, and, when rendered to the browser, the style attributes defined for the class will be automatically applied to the control.

The creation and use of CSS was discussed in Chapter 3, so we won't go back over the topic. All you need to do for Web Controls is to create CSS classes in the style sheet using the Add Style Rule dialog, as shown in Figure 4-17:

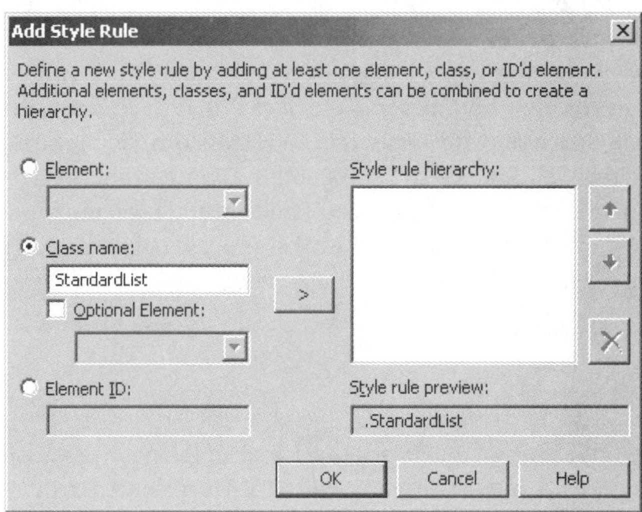

Figure 4-17. Defining a CSS class

You can then use the Style Builder discussed in Chapter 3 to set the attributes for the style, link the style sheet to the current Web Form, and then set the CssClass property of each control to the appropriate class name. For example, to apply the style defined in the dialog above, set CssClass to StandardList.

CSS classes offer you the chance to define consistent, application-wide styles. They can be applied to Web Controls and HTML Controls, as well as to static HTML. They can also be applied to Web Forms, classic ASP pages, and static HTML pages, providing a simple route to standardization. If you're planning a large Web application, it would pay to invest some time into identifying and designing a set of styles that you and other developers can then apply when the project is being built.

Understanding Event Processing and AutoPostback

To conclude this chapter we'll take a more in-depth look at events. So far in the book, we've discussed and demonstrated a number of events that can be raised for Web Forms, HTML Controls, and Web Controls. We've seen specific details and shown examples of how they can be used, but we haven't really attempted to show the big picture. From your existing experience as a developer you should already know that the big picture can be *very* important.

Events are at the heart of the revolutionary change in the way that ASP.NET allows us, as developers, to build interactive Web Applications. They play a key role in the overall process of managing page requests and generating HTML responses, a process which we will see in more detail in Chapter 10. If you have experience with Web development, or knowledge of the way that HTTP requests work, you might be wondering just how events actually work. After all, the browser knows nothing about events—all it can do is make a request to a Web Server, possibly including the content of an HTML form on the current page. Like the browser, the Web Server also knows nothing about events—all it can do is to receive a request from a client and pass it on to a suitable companion program, such as a CGI process or the ASP.NET worker process (see Chapter 10). So how does ASP.NET generate events?

Page Processing

To understand this we need to take a quick look at the page processing model—or at least part of the model—used by ASP.NET. The part we are interested in now is what happens when ASP.NET receives a request for a Web Form and how it generates a set of events that can be handled by our code. We'll return to the process of executing the code and generating the output in Chapter 10, but right now it's not that important.

Figure 4-18 shows a much-simplified view of the page processing model; it hides many of the technologies and processes that are involved. At this stage in our investigation though, this is all the detail we need.

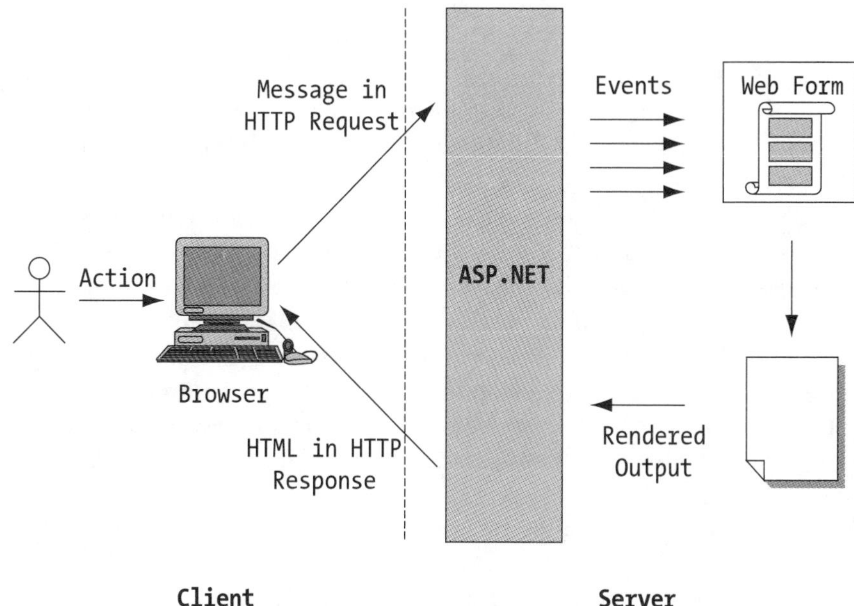

Figure 4-18. Simplified Page Processing Model

As you can see from Figure 4-18, the page processing model is circular. That is, the browser makes a request, the request is processed, and the results are returned to the browser. The browser can then use this information to make another request. Clearly the process has to start somewhere; thus, we have the *initial page request.* Subsequent requests for the same page are *postback requests.*

Initial Page Requests

An initial page request can be made in a number of different ways:

- The user types the URL for the page into the address bar of the browser
- The user selects a bookmark or favorites entry for the page
- The user clicks a hyperlink to the page
- Another page performs a redirection to this page

When ASP.NET receives any of these requests it locates and loads the requested Web Form and, if necessary, compiles its code. Once a Web Form has been compiled, it's stored in a location called the Temporary Assembly Cache; all subsequent requests will use the precompiled version from this cache. This is discussed in more detail in Chapter 10. During the compilation process, ASP.NET converts all of the content from the Web Form into executable classes—even literals, tags, and elements. All of the classes are organized into a class hierarchy representing their nesting and containment. The root of the hierarchy is the Page object itself.

Next, ASP.NET calls methods on the Page object, most of which are hidden from Web developers. These methods cause the page to begin the process of handling the request and generating the response. While executing these methods, the page may call methods of the classes it contains—in other words, the controls. Some of these methods are what we see as events; so, from our "developer" perspective the page is raising the events on the constituent controls. As you can imagine, there are many such events that occur during this process; but broadly speaking, they fall into the following sequence:

1. The `Init` event occurs for the Page.
2. The `Init` event occurs for each control on the Page.
3. The `Load` event occurs for the Page (this is where your `Page_Load` event handler code is executed).
4. The `Load` event occurs for each control on the Page.
5. The `PreRender` event occurs for the Page.
6. The `PreRender` event occurs for each control on the Page.
7. The `SaveViewState` event occurs for the Page.
8. The `Render` event occurs for the Page.

Note that by the end of stage four, the page and its constituent controls should have been initialized, loaded, and configured; by the end of stage six they should have been ready to render to the browser. Stage seven is an important (and automatic) one, in which ASP.NET allows each server control to store its properties—and any other values—in the ViewState. The page then generates the HTML that will form the hidden ViewState control, ready to be sent to the browser in stage eight.

It is also worth noting that the sequence in which events occur for different controls within a single stage may not be well defined. For example, in stage four, each control receives a `Load` event, but which control receives its event first? The sequence is largely influenced by the order in which the tags and elements appear in the HTML source view of the .aspx file. However, the easiest way to identify the sequence is to enable tracing for a page (see Chapter 10) and then examine the Control Tree in the resulting trace log. For example, Figure 4-19 shows the RegionPicker.aspx Web Form developed in Chapter 2; Figure 4-20 shows the control hierarchy for this Page.

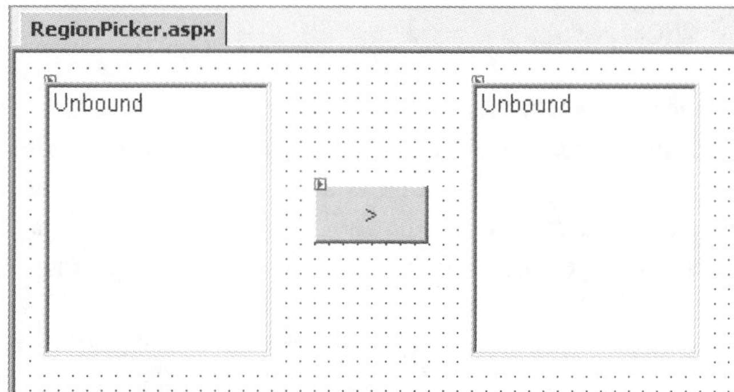

Figure 4-19. RegionPicker.aspx Web Form

Control Tree

Control Id	Type	Render Size Bytes (including children)	Viewstate Size Bytes (excluding children)
__PAGE	ASP.RegionPicker_aspx	1597	24
_ctl0	System.Web.UI.ResourceBasedLiteralControl	428	0
Form1	System.Web.UI.HtmlControls.HtmlForm	1148	0
_ctl1	System.Web.UI.LiteralControl	86	0
SourceList	System.Web.UI.WebControls.ListBox	348	156
_ctl2	System.Web.UI.LiteralControl	5	0
SelectedList	System.Web.UI.WebControls.ListBox	158	0
_ctl3	System.Web.UI.LiteralControl	5	0
btnSelect	System.Web.UI.WebControls.Button	153	0
_ctl4	System.Web.UI.LiteralControl	4	0
_ctl5	System.Web.UI.LiteralControl	21	0

Figure 4-20. Control Tree for the RegionPicker Web Form

Figure 4-20 clearly shows how the HTML tags, elements, and literals in the .aspx file have been converted to classes, either of type resourceBasedLiteralControl or LiteralControl. As their names imply, these really are controls and were generated for every HTML element in the Web Form when it was compiled. The Control Tree also clearly shows the size of each control and the amount of data that it has placed into ViewState. This can be useful when estimating performance and download times.

As we've seen in this section, ASP.NET generates events for initial page requests in a simple and consistent way. Although the browser generates an HTTP request and receives an HTTP response, the ASP.NET Framework treats our Web Form as a set of executable classes; it can call whichever methods and raise whichever events are appropriate.

Postback Requests

While initial page requests are relatively simple and consistent, the same cannot really be said for postback requests. A postback request occurs when a page is submitted to itself, which is the default behavior for ASP.NET Web Forms.

There are several significant details about postback requests that help us understand how ASP.NET processes the request and raises the correct events:

- The postback request contains the current value of every control on the Web Form, including any changes the user has made to the content of editable HTML elements. This is known as the Post Data.
- The Post Data also includes the content of the hidden ViewState control, which contains the *original* property values of each control on the Web Form, before the user made any changes.
- If the user clicked a button to generate the postback request, the corresponding button control will have a value that is also included in the Post Data. ASP.NET uses this value during the event sequence to deter mine which button was pressed.

When ASP.NET receives a postback request, it follows a very similar process to the one described for initial page requests. There are, however, additional stages in the event processing sequence, as shown in **bold** below:

1. The `Init` event occurs for the Page.
2. The `Init` event occurs for each control on the Page.
3. **The `LoadViewState` method is called for the Page.**
4. **The `ProcessPostData` method is called for the Page. This process reads the Post Data from the request and applies the values to the controls initialized in stage two.**
5. The `Load` event occurs for the Page.

6. The `Load` event occurs for each control on the Page.

7. **The current content of each control is compared to the original value loaded from the ViewState in stage three. Where there is a difference, the appropriate Changed event is raised for that control (`CheckedChanged`, `SelectedIndexChanged`, `TextChanged`, etc.).**

8. **Server-side events are raised and processed for any validation controls, including the `ServerValidate` event for any CustomValidator controls.**

9. **The `Click` event occurs for the button that generated the postback, if any.**

10. **The `Command` event occurs for the button that generated the postback, if any.**

11. The `PreRender` event occurs for the Page.

12. The `PreRender` event occurs for each control on the Page.

13. The `SaveViewState` event occurs for the Page.

14. The `Render` event occurs for the Page.

This is a more involved sequence of events and method calls than was encountered with an initial page request, but it's still quite clear how ASP.NET is able to use the information in the ViewState and the Post Data to generate the required events and method calls. Fortunately, as developers, we rarely need to consider how the events are triggered—we can just trust ASP.NET to trigger the correct event at the correct time. If things aren't quite working as you expected though, you may find it useful to refer back to this sequence to get a better understanding of where the cause of any problems may lie.

The above sequence has assumed that the postback was directly generated by a button click, but it's also possible that client-side script (such as that used for a LinkButton control) could be the cause. If that's the case, the script will have stored the name of the control that ran the script in additional hidden fields on the form. These hidden fields are a part of the Post Data and so are processed along with the rest of the Web Form controls in stage four. When the sequence reaches stage nine it uses the information in the hidden controls to raise the event on the LinkButton instead.

A Final Note on Page Requests

OK, it's time for us to own up: What we told you about initial page requests was a lie. It was a convenient lie though, because it allowed you to focus on the simple `Init`, `Load`, `PreRender`, and `Render` events that occur for the first request.

What actually happens is that ASP.NET always follows the described event sequence for postback requests, including the processing of ViewState, Post Data, Changed events, and so on. The difference is that for an initial request, there's no Post Data and there's no ViewState; thus, there are no control-related Changed, Click, or Command events to raise. ASP.NET still has to call the methods to perform the checks though; so, if you enable tracing for a page and then view the trace log, you should expect to see these events for every request that is processed.

Event Handlers

Now that you understand how and when events occur, let's look at how you can write code to handle them. All Web and HTML Controls adhere to the .NET standard in which all events pass two arguments to the handling method.

- The first argument is a reference to the Page or Web Control that raised the event. This is declared as type Object.

- The second argument is an instance of the class that contains any specific event information. This argument can vary by control type, but will always be present. If there is no event information, then an instance of the class EventArgs type can be used.

When developing applications using Visual Studio .NET, the easiest way to create the skeleton code for a control's event handler is to double-click the control in the designer, or to select the required control and event from the **Class Name** and **Method Name** dropdown lists at the top of the code window. The following examples show the code that is produced for a Button control's Click and Command events:

```
Private Sub Button1_Click(ByVal sender As System.Object, _
                ByVal e As System.EventArgs) Handles Button1.Click
    'Code for the event handler
End Sub

Private Sub Button1_Command(ByVal sender As Object,
                ByVal e As _    System.Web.UI.WebControls.CommandEventArgs) _
                Handles Button1.Command
```

```
    'Code for the event handler
End Sub
```

Notice that the second argument—the event information—is of a different class in the two handlers. The Click event provides no additional information, and so its second argument is of type System.EventArgs. The Command event provides information on the CommandName and CommandArgument; the System.Web.UI.WebControls.CommandEventArgs class provides this detail.

Also, remember that the association between the event procedure and the event that it handles is not simply based on the name of the procedure (as is the case in Visual Basic 6.0). Instead, the procedure explicitly defines the events it will handle with the `Handles` statement. This was introduced in Chapter 3 with regard to HTML Controls and is discussed in more detail in Appendix C. The `Handles` statement is used in exactly the same way for Web Controls, and in fact, also works the same way for Windows controls in desktop applications.

AutoPostBack

Clearly the event handling process is rather more complex in the Web Form environment than it is in a desktop application. The need to perform a round-trip from the client to the server for processing introduces a real concern regarding performance. In the Internet, round-trip times are likely to be measured in seconds, or at best, tenths of seconds; so, it would be foolish to design an application that makes server requests on each change to a control. This is one of the reasons that ASP.NET supports such a sophisticated and powerful event-handling model: It allows the generation and handling of events to be deferred until the user manually submits the data.

While powerful, you may not want this approach in every situation. For example, you may need to perform control-by-control validation on a Web Form, or you may have a number of linked controls that need to be refreshed or repopulated when any of them are modified. In these cases, you cannot rely on the user submitting the form at the correct time—it could lead to problems or failures in the application. What we need is the ability to automatically submit the Web Form, an ability which is provided by the AutoPostBack property supported by many Web Controls.

Enabling AutoPostBack

When a control has its AutoPostBack property set to True, any changes made by the user to the data in the control cause the Web Form to be submitted, just as if they had manually clicked a submit button. The submission is achieved using a client-side function that is generated during the render process and attached to the control, usually through its `OnChange` event. Remember, all you have to do to enable this is to set the property to True; ASP.NET does the rest.

If several controls have their AutoPostBack set to True, ASP.NET generates only one client-side function but associates it with each control. It uses two hidden fields on the Web Form to identify the control and the event that caused the postback. This information can be obtained during the event processing sequence discussed previously.

TIP *As a general rule it is wise to set AutoPostBack to False. This is the default for Web Controls, so you need make no specific changes to adopt this approach. Where necessary, set AutoPostBack to True for individual controls, but remember the impact this will have on the Web Form and how it will appear to the user.*

Summary

Web Controls are truly revolutionary, providing the sort of rich component-based model that Web developers have dreamt about for years. Web Controls allow you to change your focus from thinking about how to use code to render specific content, style, and layout, to being able to concentrate on manipulating and processing data, leaving ASP.NET to render the output in the most appropriate format for the client browser.

Support for server-side properties, methods, and code has also caused a real change in the way that Web applications can be built. Far from the linear, embedded code approach of classic ASP, the ASP.NET approach moves firmly towards an OO architecture, with code neatly housed within event handlers that are called as and when needed.

Not only are these controls functional and flexible, they're also attractive. They make the creation of interactive Web pages a breeze, with automatic client-side features used where possible to minimize the number of round-trips. They support standard formatting techniques through CSS, plus their own unique property-based formatting, with some controls also having styles and auto formats.

All of these improvements come at a cost of course; there is the need to learn new skills, techniques, and tools, as well as the fact that the enormity of the ASP.NET toolset itself will take some time to fully master. Also, and perhaps of more concern to some developers, ASP.NET takes more control than classic ASP ever did. When things work as planned this is fine, but when they go wrong it could be more difficult to identify the cause of a problem and resolve it. When you come up against such problems you'll find the new tracing facility to be a real time-saver, showing you a whole range of information about the request, the controls, and the events.

None of this information is of much use unless you have an understanding of how ASP.NET works. In this chapter we have started to look at page processing and event handling, but these topics have only scratched the surface of the ASP.NET architecture. Chapter 10 will continue this investigation, and take us much deeper into the workings of the .NET Framework.

CHAPTER 5

Building Custom Web Controls

Implementing Web User Controls

Using Active Web User Controls

Developing Web Custom Controls

AS AN EXPERIENCED DEVELOPER you'll already be familiar with the concepts of component-based design and code reuse, and of the benefits that these approaches can bring. As you might expect .NET promotes these techniques for desktop and Web Application projects, and one of the technologies it supports is the creation of custom controls for Web Applications.

ASP.NET supports two models of control creation:

- You build Web User Controls in a similar way to Web Forms and include them in a Web Application in source-code form. Web User Controls support visual inheritance—that is, you create their interface using existing controls and elements from the Toolbox. Web User Controls are sometimes referred to as *composite controls.*

- You build Web Custom Controls differently; they consist only of code rather than visual components. You include them in a Web Application by setting a reference to their .dll and they're available through the Toolbox. Web Custom Controls are sometimes referred to as *rendered controls.*

It's highly likely the current market for supplying controls and components to Visual Basic developers will expand to provide controls and components for .NET, including a whole range of custom Web controls. These will be packaged almost exclusively as Web Custom Controls (rather than Web User Controls) because they're easier to deploy and offer greater functionality. However, don't be fooled into thinking one approach is better than the other; each has its strengths and weaknesses, and you'll probably find both to be useful in real applications.

It's fair to say that Web User Controls are simpler to create, so it's with this type of control that we'll begin our discussion.

Implementing Web User Controls

Web User Controls enable you to quickly and easily build reusable interface components for Web Applications. At the simplest level, you can think of a Web User Control as a type of Include file that you can use to easily manage common content such as contact details or copyright messages. At their most powerful, they provide a comprehensive and powerful framework for building server-side components. You determine this difference in power by the content you add to the control when you create it.

To create a Web User Control, you need to start by adding a Web User Control component to a Web Application. You then define the control's visual interface by adding other Web Controls and HTML elements to the User Control's designer, positioning and sizing them as required. You implement functionality for the control by adding appropriate properties and methods and by handling and raising events. This approach parallels the way in which you create Web Forms, and indeed Web User Controls and Web Form share many common features and behaviors.

There are two key issues associated with Web User Controls, and depending on how you develop and use your control, they may become significant disadvantages:

- When compared to Web Custom Controls, the performance of Web User Controls can be poor. This is because of the overhead of instancing the constituent child controls each time, plus the corresponding event-handling code that would be triggered. With complex controls, or on pages using many Web User Controls, the impact can be significant.

- The functionality of Web User Controls is largely limited to that provided by the constituent controls. They are best used where existing controls offer nearly, but not quite, the required behavior. If you need to develop a control that is completely different to anything that currently exists, you may find it easier to create a Web Custom Control.

In many situations, these issues are not serious and will not prevent you from building controls, but it's worth emphasizing that this approach does have some limitations.

Creating a Web User Control

One of the simplest uses of a Web User Control is to represent unchanging content that appears on multiple Web pages, such as copyright information or contact details. As you would expect, the static nature of such information makes this the simplest type of control to create, so it's an ideal introduction to the techniques that are required.

Let's start by adding a Web User Control to the HiFlyers project. Load Visual Studio .NET and open the HiFlyers solution, then select **Project ➢ Add Web User Control** and call the new control Copyright. Copyright.ascx will be added to the project, together with Copyright.ascx.vb and Copyright.ascx.resx. These are much the same as the files used for Web Forms, with the .ascx file representing the visual content, the .ascx.vb file containing the code, and the .ascx.resx file holding additional resource information. An inheritance relationship is established so that the Web User Control derives from System.Web.UI.UserControl, as illustrated in Figure 5-1.

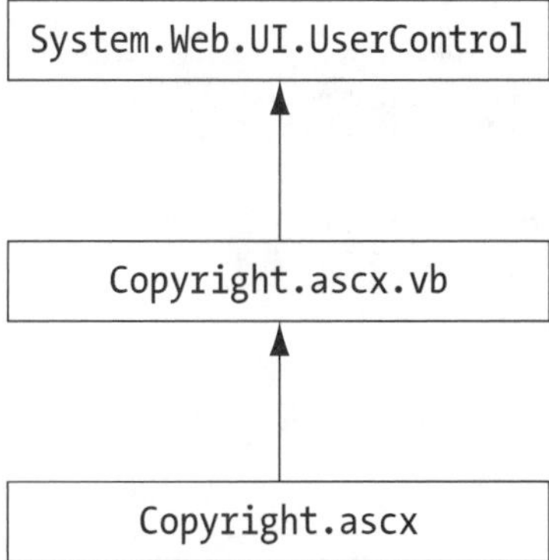

Figure 5-1. Inheritance relationship for Web User Controls

Currently, the designer for Copyright.ascx will be completely empty, and viewing its HTML source reveals only the `@Control` directive. You'll also notice that FlowLayout is used, as this is most often the preferred way of positioning constituent elements. If you want to use GridLayout, you'll need to add a Grid Layout Panel from the HTML tab in the Toolbox.

If you examine the Properties window for the User Control, you'll see it offers relatively few settings. All of these properties exist for Web Forms, and Chapter 4 introduced most of them, so we won't cover them again here.

Adding Content

We'll keep our Copyright control simple, with it containing only static HTML and client-side hyperlinks. This is contained within an HTML table, as shown in Figure 5-2.

Figure 5-2. Content of the Copyright control

The position of the elements and the size of the table and its cells are defined within the HTML using `width` and `align` attributes. The `border`, `cellpadding`, and `cellspacing` of the table have all been set to 0, as shown in the HTML View in Figure 5-3.

```
Copyright.ascx | Default.aspx*
Client Objects & Events          (No Events)

<%@ Control Language="vb" AutoEventWireup="false" Codebehind="Copyright.ascx.vb"
<table width="100%" cellspacing="0" cellpadding="0" border="0">
    <TR>
        <TD align="left" width="40%">
            Copyright HiFlyers © 2001-2002
        </TD>
        <TD align="middle" width="20%">
            Contact <A href="info@HiFlyers.org">HiFlyers</A>
        </TD>
        <TD align="right" width="40%">
            <A href="Terms.aspx">Terms and Conditions</A>
        </TD>
    </TR>
</table>
```

Figure 5-3. HTML View of the content

So, what's significant about what you've created so far? Nothing—everything you've done has used the same techniques and content that you could have used directly on a Web Form. All you've done is to encapsulate that content into a separate component so that it can be applied more easily.

You could continue with the layout and formatting of the content to improve its appearance, but by now you get the idea. What's more important is to see how the control is used, so make sure you save everything and then read on.

Applying Web User Controls

You can add Web User Controls to Web Forms in much the same way as other Web controls, by adding their tags and defining any attributes in the .aspx file. You can do this in two ways:

- By dragging the control from the Solution Explorer onto the designer for a Web Form
- By manually entering the required tags

You'll use the first approach in this example as it'll automatically generate the required tags and attribute values. Start by creating a new blank Web Form called ContactDetails.aspx. Make sure its designer is open, and then drag Copyright.ascx from the Solution Explorer onto the Web Form. If you were using flow layout mode, the new control will be positioned in the top left of the Web Form; if you were using grid layout, the control will be positioned wherever it was dropped. Figure 5-4 shows the view in grid layout mode.

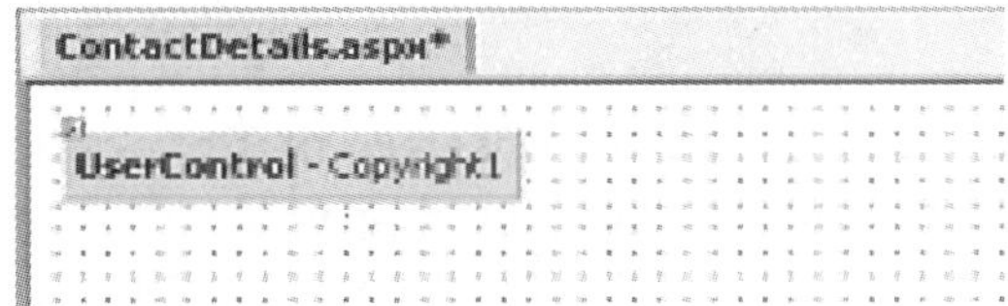

Figure 5-4. Adding the control to a Web Form

Notice that the design-time appearance bears no relationship to the content placed on the control; this can be confusing at times and may make it more difficult to plan the layout and positioning of other content on the Web Form. Fortunately, when you view the page in a browser window, the control renders as expected, as shown in Figure 5-5.

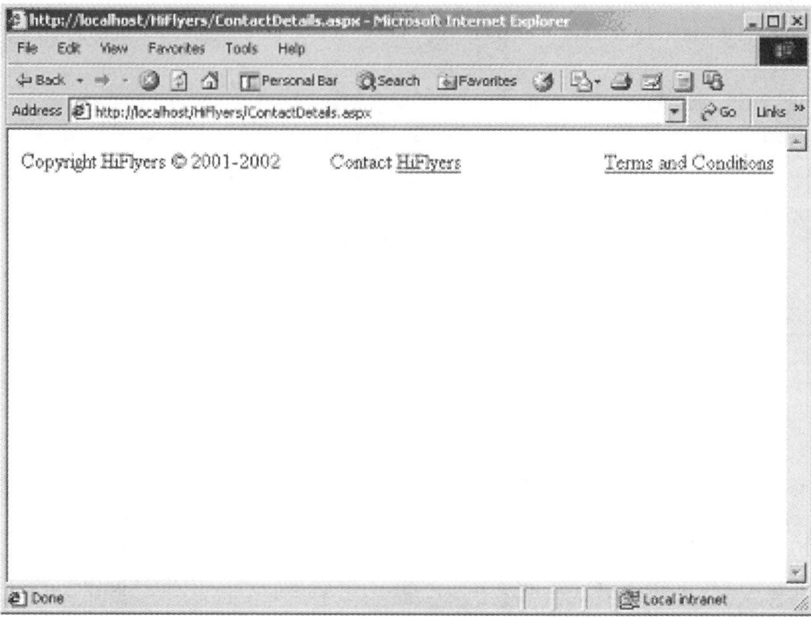

Figure 5-5. Web User Control viewed in a browser

The drag-and-drop approach is quick and easy, but it hides the detail of how ASP.NET embeds our User Control in the Web Form. This detail is important because you'll need that information if you want to manually enter the tags or modify the Web Form's HTML content. Return to Visual Studio .NET and view ContactDetails.aspx in HTML View. It should appear similar to the following (note that some lines have been removed or abbreviated for clarity):

```
<%@ Register TagPrefix="uc1" TagName="Copyright" Src="Copyright.ascx" %>
<%@ Page Language="vb"....Inherits="HiFlyers.ContactDetails" %>
<HTML>
    <HEAD>
        <title></title>
        .
        .
        .
    </HEAD>
    <body MS_POSITIONING="GridLayout">
        <form id="Form1" method="post" runat="server">
            <uc1:Copyright id="Copyright1" runat="server">
            </uc1:Copyright>
        </form>
    </body>
</HTML>
```

The first line in the file is the `@ Register` directive. This associates an arbitrary `TagPrefix` and `TagName` with the User Control held in the file specified by the `Src` attribute. The TagPrefix and TagName are then used to insert the control into the Web Form, as shown within the `<form>` section of the file. In our example, Visual Studio .NET has allocated `uc1` as the TagPrefix (a simple abbreviation for User Control 1) and `Copyright` for the TagName (derived from the name given to the .ascx file). You're free to change these, and we recommend adopting a more meaningful TagPrefix, either relating to the author (such as the organization name) of the control or its purpose. For example:

```
<%@ Register TagPrefix="pageUtil" TagName="Copyright" Src="Copyright.ascx" %>
        .
        .
        .
    <pageUtil:Copyright id="Copyright1" runat="server"></ pageUtil:Copyright>
```

Creating Active Web User Controls

The Web Control you built in the previous example was extremely simple and completely passive. By *passive* we mean it has no server-side functionality or behavior, other than that automatically provided by ASP.NET for controls that derive from `System.Web.UI.UserControl`. Such controls are useful, solving real problems that developers come up against time and time again. For example:

- They allow centralization of standard content, making it easier to update and manage.
- You can use them in conjunction with the `@ OutputCache` directive to allow caching of partial Web pages. This is a powerful technique that can substantially reduce the loading on Web servers when processing pages with a large proportion of static content (for more information, see Chapter 12).

These are great reasons for creating Web User Controls because any .ascx that you create and use can deliver these benefits. However, many controls you create will not be this simple, and they'll need to expose properties and methods of their own, as well as responding to and raising events. To illustrate how you can do these things, you'll now build a more substantial Web User Control—a custom navigation bar.

Building a Custom Navigation Bar

Our navigation bar will present itself as a set of HyperLinks or Buttons and will be configurable so that they can display vertically or horizontally. Each HyperLink or Button has a Caption and a URL, and the User Control will be responsible for performing any necessary redirection.

Let's start by adding a new Web User Control called NavBar.ascx. Add a Table control from the Web Forms tab, and configure it to have a single row but no cells. Figure 5-6 shows what it looks like in the HTML View.

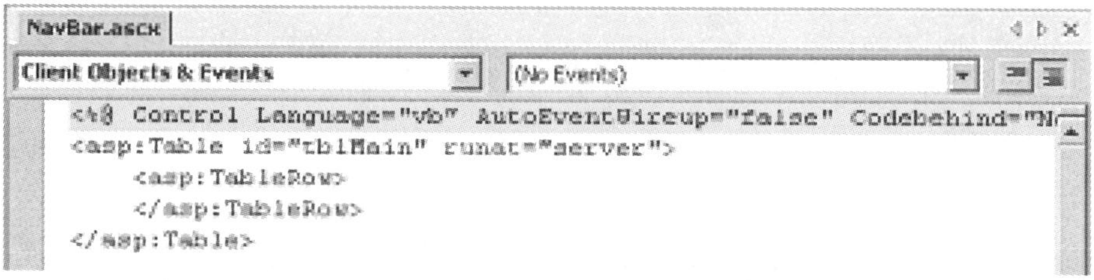

NavBar.ascx

Client Objects & Events | (No Events)

```
<%@ Control Language="vb" AutoEventWireup="false" Codebehind="N
<asp:Table id="tblMain" runat="server">
    <asp:TableRow>
    </asp:TableRow>
</asp:Table>
```

Figure 5-6. HTML content for NavBar.ascx

That's all the static content that you'll need because everything else will depend on how the control is used within a page. For example, we want the control to support any number of links or buttons (within reason) and to be able to show itself either horizontally or vertically. To achieve this, you'll have to dynamically create the additional Buttons, HyperLinks, and Cells through code, and that means you also need to provide a set of properties and methods that can be called to configure the control. Once you've done this, you'll have a flexible navigation bar control that can meet a whole range of different requirements.

Exposing Properties and Methods

Like all .NET components, Web User Controls are implemented using classes. This means you define custom properties and methods just as you would for any class, by using Property Procedures, Subs, and Functions.

Properties

We'll begin by defining an Orientation property. We want to constrain this to two values—Horizontal and Vertical—so let's create an enumeration with these members. Open the NavBar.ascx.vb file and enter the following at the top of the module, before the definition of the Class:

```
Public Enum NavBarOrientation
    Horizontal
    Vertical
End Enum
```

Within the Class, you can now define a variable to store the orientation value locally:

```
Private m_intOrientation As NavBarOrientation
```

Notice that this is a private variable. You *can* create properties using public variables, but it's a technique of limited use because your code can't automatically respond to changes in the property value. Instead, Property Procedures define specific methods for reading and writing the property value:

```
Public Property Orientation() As NavBarOrientation
    Get
        Return m_intOrientation
    End Get
    Set(ByVal Value As NavBarOrientation)
        m_intOrientation = Value
    End Set
End Property
```

If you're new to VB.NET then this syntax may look a little different than what you're expecting. In VB 6.0, one, two, or three distinct procedures would be defined for Property Get, Property Let, and Property Set, but in VB .NET, these are merged into a single block. The absence of a Property Let and Property Set in VB 6.0 automatically made the property read-only, but in VB .NET this would need to be defined with a `ReadOnly` attribute in the property definition. For example:

```
Public ReadOnly Property NumControls() As Integer
    Get
        If m_intOrientation = NavBarOrientation.Horizontal Then
            Return tblMain.Rows(0).Cells.Count
        Else
            Return tblMain.Rows.Count
        End If
    End Get
End Property
```

So, aside from the ability to create read-only properties, what's the advantage of using Property Procedures over public variables? To answer this you need to think about what happens when a property value is assigned. Quite often, when a property is set, some action needs to take place based on the property value. In other words, you want some code to run when a property value is assigned, and the Property Procedure enables you to do just that—write code that will be triggered when a property value is altered.

To illustrate this, you'll enhance the Orientation property so that it only allows the orientation to be changed if no links or buttons have yet been defined for the control. You'll use another class-level variable to track this, so add the following definition at the top of the class:

```
Private m_blnAddedControls As Boolean
```

The value of this variable will be set to True if any Links or Buttons are added to the NavBar, but you'll come back to writing this code shortly. You can now modify the `Orientation` Property Procedure as follows:

```
Public Property Orientation() As NavBarOrientation
    Get
        Return m_intOrientation
    End Get
    Set(ByVal Value As NavBarOrientation)
        If m_blnAddedControls Then
            Throw New System.Exception( _
                        "Cannot set Orientation after adding Links")
        Else
            m_intOrientation = Value
        End If
    End Set
End Property
```

Methods

You now need to create the methods to add the HyperLinks and Buttons. Each of these will be held within the table that you originally added to the designer, but the code needs to create a cell for each additional control. The position of this new cell will be determined by the Orientation property—Horizontal keeps all the cells on one row, and Vertical causes them to be placed on separate rows. Because the code to do this will be the same for both HyperLinks and Buttons, let's create a common routine to perform the task:

```
Private Function AddCell() As TableCell
    Dim celTemp As New TableCell()
    Dim rowTemp As TableRow

    If m_intOrientation = NavBarOrientation.Horizontal Then
        rowTemp = tblMain.Rows(0)'Horizontal uses the current row
    ElseIf m_blnAddedControls = False Then
        rowTemp = tblMain.Rows(0)'First vertical cell uses the current row
    Else
        rowTemp = New TableRow()'Create a new row
        tblMain.Rows.Add(rowTemp)
    End If

    rowTemp.Cells.Add(celTemp)
    m_blnAddedControls = True    'Indicate we've now created a control

    Return celTemp
End Function
```

You can now create the two methods that add Buttons and HyperLinks. Each starts by creating one object to represent the new control, and one TableCell object, which you obtain from the `AddCell` function. You then set the properties of the control and add it to the cell. The methods are as follows:

```
Public Sub AddLink(ByVal Caption As String, ByVal URL As String)
    Dim lnkTemp As New HyperLink()
    Dim celTemp As TableCell = AddCell()

    lnkTemp.Text = Caption
    lnkTemp.NavigateUrl = URL

    celTemp.Controls.Add(lnkTemp)
End Sub

Public Sub AddButton(ByVal Caption As String, ByVal URL As String)
    Dim btnTemp As New Button()
    Dim celTemp As TableCell = AddCell()

    btnTemp.Text = Caption
    btnTemp.CommandName = URL

    celTemp.Controls.Add(btnTemp)
End Sub
```

Using the NavBar Control

You now have a control that can be tested, so save the Web User Control and open a Web Form. Embed the NavBar into the Web Form either by dragging and dropping it or by entering the tags. On its own, the NavBar renders no obvious interface, so some code will be needed in the Page_Load event of the Web Form to create some links:

```
Private Sub Page_Load(ByVal sender As System.Object, _
                 ByVal e As System.EventArgs) Handles MyBase.Load
    With NavBar1
        .Orientation = NavBarOrientation.Vertical
        .AddLink("Page 1", "Page1.aspx")
        .AddLink("Page 2", "Page2.aspx")
        .AddLink("Page 3", "Page3.aspx")
        .AddLink("Page 4", "Page4.aspx")
    End With
End Sub
```

As you enter this text you may notice that you get no Intellisense information within the `With NavBar1` block. The reason is that Visual Studio .NET has added the control to the Web Form designer, but it has not added a corresponding variable definition to the code-behind module. To remedy this, add the following class-level definition:

```
Protected WithEvents NavBar1 As NavBar
```

Why don't you need to declare the variable as `New`? Well, remember that the class in the code-behind module combines with a class derived from the .aspx file, and it's in the .aspx that the NavBar control is actually created. What you're doing here is creating an object variable that enables us to manipulate that NavBar in code. As long as the ID of the NavBar control is the same as the name of the variable that you define in the code-behind module, ASP.NET automatically ties the two together for you.

You can now test the Web Form. Ensure that the project is built, and then view the page in a browser. The NavBar control should be rendered as four HyperLinks, one above another, as shown in Figure 5-7.

Browse - http:/...actDetails.aspx

Page 1
Page 2
Page 3
Page 4

Figure 5-7. NavBar control in action

Click any of the links and the browser should navigate to the specified URL. If these pages don't exist, then you'll receive an error, but you should at least see a response. Return to the Web Form code and modify the statements in the `With` block to call the AddButton method rather than `AddLink`, and then test the page again. Figure 5-8 shows the revised view.

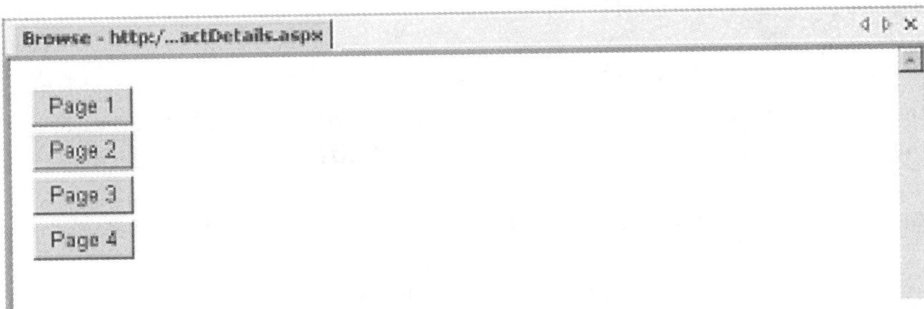

Figure 5-8. NavBar showing Button controls

Test the page by clicking the buttons, and you'll find that nothing happens. Although the HyperLink controls automatically navigate to the specified URL, Button controls must be handled in code if they're to perform the same task.

Handling and Raising Events

The HyperLink controls have client-side functionality; in other words, the `NavigateUrl` property becomes the value for the `href` in the `<a>` tag rendered to the client browser. There's no postback required, and no server-side code. The Button controls are different, though, as they *do* require server-side code and the corresponding postback if they're to be active.

Up to now, the event handlers you've used have been associated with the controls at design-time, using the `Handles` keyword in the procedure definition. In the NavBar control you can't use this technique because the instances of the controls are created at runtime rather than design-time. In VB 6.0 you could use a control array in this situation, but .NET offers no support for these, even for Windows applications. So how do you define an event handler for the button?

The solution is a simple, yet elegant, mechanism for adding event-handling routines at runtime: the AddHandler statement. The first thing you need to do is to write the procedure that will handle the events, remembering that it needs to be defined with the correct arguments for the event you want to handle. You'll handle the Command event, which passes additional information in the form of the Button's CommandName and CommandArgument properties and requires us to handle an event argument of type CommandEventArgs. You'll use this argument to determine which button was clicked. You should add the procedure to the class as follows:

```
Private Sub ButtonClicked(ByVal sender As System.Object, _
                ByVal e As System.web.UI.webcontrols.CommandEventArgs)
    Response.Redirect(e.CommandName)
End Sub
```

When you wrote the code for the AddButton method, you stored the URL in the CommandName property of the Button that was created. All the handler does is pass the URL from CommandName to the Response.Redirect method.

To associate the handler with the event, you need to add the following line toward the bottom of the AddButton routine:

```
AddHandler btnTemp.Command, AddressOf ButtonClicked
```

As you can see, you use the AddHandler statement by passing two parameters:

- The first parameter is the event to be handled.
- The second parameter is an expression that evaluates to a *delegate class*. Delegate classes are key to event handling in .NET, although often their presence is completely hidden. The AddressOf operator conveniently provides a reference to a delegate class for the method that you specify. In this case, the delegate will be an object capable of calling the ButtonClicked procedure.

Build the project and view the page in a browser window again. Click the buttons and notice that they now cause postbacks and that the events are indeed processed, although you'll once again receive errors if the specified pages don't exist.

AddHandler is an important statement in situations such as this and is perhaps more powerful than it at first appears. For example, AddHandler enables you to associate many events with one handler and many handlers with one event, and by creating your own Delegate classes, you have great control over this association. Also, you can use RemoveHandler to disassociate handlers from events at runtime. We don't have time to explore the finer points of dynamically adding and removing event handlers in this book, but it's something you may want to investigate further if you find that your applications need to create controls at runtime.

Raising Events

To complete the picture, let's examine how you might go about raising an event from the control. For example, instead of automatically performing a redirection when the button is clicked, you'll simply raise a Command event back from our NavBar with the appropriate CommandName and CommandArgument parameters. This will make the control more flexible because it allows the control's user to determine the outcome of a user event.

There are three steps involved in the process:

1. The event must be defined within the class. For example, the following could be placed inside the class definition for NavBar (note that it must appear *after* the Inherits statement):

   ```
   Public Event Command(ByVal Sender As System.Object, _
                        ByVal e As System.web.ui.WebControls.CommandEventArgs)
   ```

2. The event must be raised in code. In this example you'll do this instead of the Response.Redirect in the event handler, so replace the code in the ButtonClicked procedure with this:

   ```
   RaiseEvent Command(sender, e)
   ```

3. The event must be handled within the Web Form. To do this return to the page where you tested the control and ensure that the class-level variable for the NavBar is declared using the WithEvents keyword. All that's then needed is a regular event handler for NavBar1.Command:

   ```
   Private Sub NavBar1_Command(ByVal Sender As System.Object, _
                    ByVal E As System.Web.UI.WebControls.CommandEventArgs) _
                    Handles NavBar1.Command
       Response.Redirect(E.CommandName")
   End Sub
   ```

If you've created and handled custom events using VB 6.0, then you should be on familiar ground. In fact, the only appreciable difference is that you define control-based event handlers using two arguments, and even this is only by convention. Technically, you can define as many or as few arguments for your event handlers as you want, and they can be of any data types. For example:

```
Public Event Command(ByVal CommandName As String)
.
.
.
Private Sub ButtonClicked(ByVal sender As System.Object, _
                ByVal e As System.web.UI.webcontrols.CommandEventArgs)
    RaiseEvent Command(e.CommandName)
End Sub
```

Dynamically Loading User Controls

So far you've only added User Controls to a Web Form at design-time, but in live applications you may find you need to add them at runtime, as well. If you try and create objects from User Control classes using the New keyword, you'll receive an error because User Control classes are flagged with a `MustInherit` attribute. To solve this problem, ASP.NET provides the `LoadControl` method.

For example, to dynamically load an instance of our NavBar, provide it with three buttons, and then display it within a panel, you would do the following:

```
Dim NavBar2 As NavBar
NavBar2 = CType(LoadControl("NavBar.ascx"), NavBar)

NavBar2.AddButton("Page1", "Page1.aspx")
NavBar2.AddButton("Page2", "Page2.aspx ")
NavBar2.AddButton("Page3", "Page3.aspx ")

Panel1.Controls.Add(NavBar2)
```

Having loaded a control in this way, you can then treat it the same as any other class. For example, you can set its properties, call its methods, and use the `AddHandler` statement to associate an event handler. In short, the only thing that's different about dynamically creating user controls is that they must be instantiated using `LoadControl`.

Developing Web Custom Controls

The Web User Controls you've built so far are extremely useful, while remaining easy to build. For many tasks you'll find that Web User Controls offer a perfect model for creating controls, especially if the control is unique to a specific project. However, sooner or later you'll want to build controls that exhibit some of the following features:

- You want the control to provide functionality that is unavailable through any of the intrinsic controls.
- You want to build a control in the most performance-efficient way.
- You want to use the control in several projects but don't want the maintenance overhead of having several copies of the source code around.
- You want to be able to deploy the control to other developers without giving them your source code. These may be other developers within your organization, or you may want to distribute the control commercially.
- You want the professional touch of seeing your control on the Toolbox.

Web User Controls don't really achieve these objectives. Firstly, they're largely limited to the features offered by intrinsic controls because this is what they're comprised of. Secondly, they use *containment* to create their interface, which means that ASP.NET first has to individually generate the contained controls before it can generate the completed element. Finally, the problem for the third and fourth points is that Web User Controls are included in projects as ASCX files, containing viewable (and editable) source code and HTML.

You can solve these problems (and many others) by using Web Custom Controls. These are fully compiled components that take the form of .dll files and are referenced and used within Web Applications in much the same way as Web Form controls. You can add Web Custom Controls to the Visual Studio .NET Toolbox and then draw them on Web Form designers as you would with any other visual element.

Benefits of Web Custom Controls

As well as solving the problems outlined in the previous section, you'll find many other good reasons for developing Web Custom Controls. One of the greatest overall advantages is that you have complete control over the features and functionality provided because you start with a "clean slate" in the form of a basic class. It's up to you to add properties, methods, and events and to override the base class's methods to provide the behavior you want.

This is both a blessing and a curse; it's a blessing because you know exactly what's happening in the control, so you can make it as simple or sophisticated as you need. It's a curse because .NET provides relatively little assistance when compared with creating Web User Controls. It *does* provide numerous base classes and interfaces to help you hook up with the .NET Framework and the HTTP Runtime, but you still have to write the code to do all of this.

You'll also find that Web Custom Controls can potentially provide greater performance, too, because you're free to use any supported languages, data types, algorithms, or other techniques you want. You'll certainly find they're more flexible, enabling you to create almost any visual interface that can be generated through a Web page.

Creating a Web Custom Control

You'll build a Web Custom Control that illustrates the majority of the techniques you're likely to need. The control's purpose is to provide a pop-up style calendar for use in Web pages, and it'll initially be rendered to the browser as a text field (to contain the date) and a button (to allow a date to be selected). When a user clicks the button, a calendar displays within the browser window using some client-side JavaScript. When the user selects from the calendar, the date is placed into the text box and the calendar is once again hidden. To minimize ambiguity, let's display the date in international format, for example, 05/Mar/2002.

NOTE *This control depends on the client-side JavaScript for its functionality. The script comprises a number of separate functions that collectively draw a pop-up calendar, complete with month-by-month navigation and day selection. We haven't reproduced the script in the book as it's rather long, but you can download the complete file. The file is named Calendar.js and is available in the Downloads area of www.apress.com.*

Web Custom Controls are created in separate projects from the applications that use them so that the controls can be more easily maintained, deployed, and shared. Let's begin by creating a Web Control Library project in Visual Studio .NET, calling it `HiFlyerControls`. Figure 5-9 shows the Add New Project dialog box with the template selected.

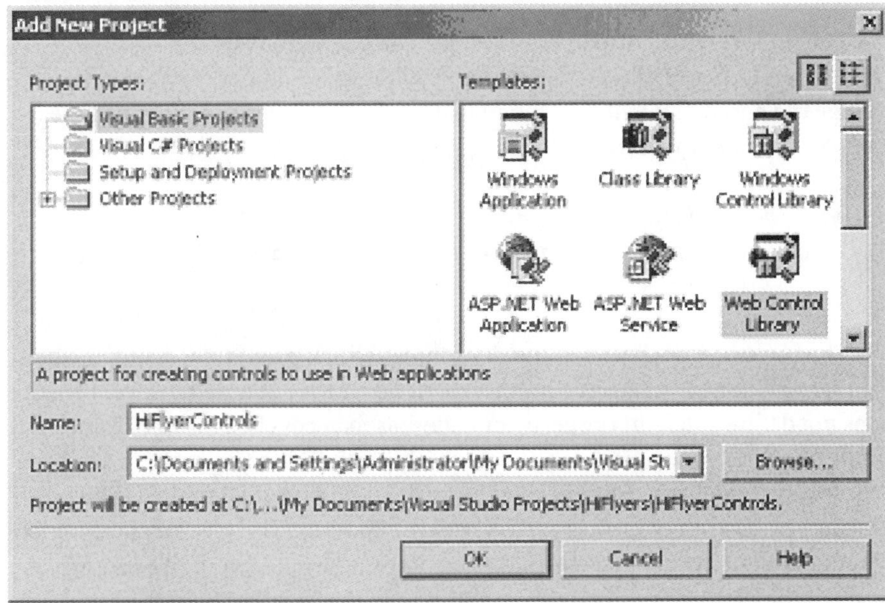

Figure 5-9. Creating the Web Control Library project

We've chosen to add the project to the HiFlyers solution, as this can ease testing while you're building the controls. Alternatively, you can create Web control libraries in their own solution—it makes no difference to how they run. Figure 5-10 shows the Solution Explorer and the default files contained in the HiFlyerControls project.

Figure 5-10. Content of the Web Control Library project

NOTE *When you have multiple dependent projects in a solution, ensure that you define the correct build order by selecting **Project ➢ Project Build Order** and establishing the correct dependencies.*

The project currently contains a single control defined by the WebCustomControl1 class. The first thing you need to do is rename this, so change the name of the file to Calendar.vb and edit the code that defines the name of the class to read as follows:

```
<DefaultProperty("Text"), _
    ToolboxData("<{0}:Calendar runat=server></{0}:Calendar>")> _
    Public Class Calendar
```

The `DefaultProperty` attribute determines which property will initially be highlighted in the Properties window when the control is added to a Web Form. It does *not* define a default property for code-based access because .NET doesn't support the traditional concept of default properties. The `ToolboxData` attribute enables you to define additional attributes that will be added to the HTML designer when your control is added from the Toolbox. The `{0}` is a placeholder that the designer will replace with the tag prefix associated with the control through the `@Register` directive. Currently, only the `runat=server` attribute is defined.

The `Inherits` statement within the class currently specifies that the control will inherit from `System.Web.UI.WebControls.WebControl`. For our purposes this is ideal because the base class provides not only the core functionality you need for a control, but also routine properties and behaviors such as color settings and styles. If you wanted to develop a control that rendered no visual interface then it would be more efficient to inherit from `System.Web.UI.Control` because none of the visual features would be required.

The class also contains some sample code, illustrating how a simple `Text` property can be exposed and its value rendered to the browser. For now you'll leave it in place; however, you'll shortly be replacing it with your own routines to manage the content and appearance of the calendar.

Key Events in the Control Lifecycle

Before getting into the details of how controls are coded, you need to understand the key phases of their lifecycle, with special emphasis on the events that occur. As you might expect, many of these are similar to the events that occur for a Web

Form, including initialization, loading, rendering, and finalization. However, with controls it's much more likely that you'll need to provide implementation for these events, in the form of either event handlers or methods that override base class members.

One of the concerns when building controls is what your code can do in each lifecycle phase. For example, code running in the Initialize phase is unable to reliably access other controls on the page as they may not have been loaded. Similarly, code running in the Render phase is unable to save changes to ViewState because the ViewState content that will be sent to the browser is already determined by this point. The following list identifies the key phases, together with their major purposes and limitations. It also highlights some of the key points at which code added to the page that contains your control will be executed:

- **Initialize**: During this phase, the control will initialize values that will be needed during the lifetime of the control (the lifetime parallels the time during which the inbound request is processed, after which the control is destroyed). During this phase your code can reliably access internal values (such as variables and properties) but not external values (such as other controls, the Page object, or ViewState).

- **Page Initialize**: Once the contained controls have been initialized, the `Page_Init` event is raised, and any code defined in the handler is executed.

- **Load ViewState**: Each control has a ViewState property, which is populated during this phase. The population is automatic, but if required it can be overridden to perform customized state management.

- **Process Postback Data**: This phase is not implemented by default for controls. Instead, the phase is activated only for controls that implement the `IPostBackDataHandler` interface. Such controls will need to implement the `LoadPostData` method, during which they can read data posted from the client and update internal variables and properties as required.

- **Page Load:** The `Page_Load` event is raised before the `Load` event for each control. This allows the developer using your control to set properties that will then be read and used by any code that you add to the control's `Load` event handler.

- **Load**: The Load phase enables your code to perform generic actions based on the property values and postback data, both of which are by now available. All of the other controls on the Web Form should by now be created and initialized, so they can be referenced if required.

- **Send Postback Change Notifications**: Any controls that handle postback data (by implementing `IPostBackDataHandler`) are able to raise change events in this phase in response to differences between the current and previous state values.

- **Page Handlers**: Handlers associated with the events raised by Postback Change Notifications are triggered in this phase. ASP.NET determines the precise sequence of events, though it's usually governed by the order of the controls in the text of the .aspx file.

- **Handle Postback Events**: Just as controls can handle postback data, they can be coded to implement the `IPostBackEventHandler` interface to handle postback events as well. These events are typically generated by buttons, links, and other "non-value" controls, and they can be raised to the client code in this phase.

- **Page Handlers**: The handler associated with the postback event is triggered in this phase. There should be only one such event, as there can be only one cause of a postback.

- **Prerender**: During the Prerender phase, controls can perform any final updates to properties or state values before the control is rendered. This is the last phase in which ViewState information can be written if it's to be preserved across the next postback.

- **Save ViewState**: In this phase, the ViewState property of the control is serialized and converted to a string. ASP.NET performs this phase for each control, then accumulates the strings and writes them to the hidden `__VIEWSTATE` control on the page. The process of saving ViewState is automatic, but you may want to override it to manage state in a customized way.

- **Render**: The Render phase generates output that will be sent to the client. Your code will need to override the `Render` method in most cases to achieve this. No changes to ViewState can be made at this stage, and changes made to property values from this phase on won't be persisted.

- **Dispose**: The standard .NET dispose phase enables your code to perform any final cleanup before the control is destroyed. This phase is automatically performed and the events will be called, but it's your responsibility to add code to respond to them. Typical tasks include releasing expensive resources such as file handles or database connections.

Most controls will implement some, but not all, of these phases. Some of the implementation code takes the form of event handlers, such as for Init, Load, PreRender, and Dispose, and other phases are coded by overriding methods of the base WebControl class. You'll see more examples of these techniques throughout this chapter.

Rendering HTML

You can start adding code to your control in many different ways, but you'll probably find it easiest if you start by defining the code to render the user interface. This way, you can immediately test the control in a container, and as you continue by defining properties and methods you have a simple way to check they're working as expected.

You must also decide *how* you'll render the control. You have two real options, and which you choose will depend on how unique the rendered appearance of your control will be:

- Base your control on an existing HTML element but add additional tags, attributes, and behaviors to obtain the functionality you require. This sounds much the same as the approach used for Web User Controls, but here you're using code-based inheritance for the derived class. Web User Controls depend on visual inheritance.

- Generate HTML directly from code, providing all of the tags and elements manually.

The first approach is preferable when you want to add or change functionality within a control, and the second is better when you need a completely different look and feel. Although our control will look rather different to anything that ASP.NET already offers, it'll share certain common features. Specifically, our control will be encased in a `<span>` that handles the sizing, positioning, and style for us, so it makes sense to allow ASP.NET to take care of this by using the first approach. What you'll need to generate is the HTML that represents the real content of the control, for which you'll require a visible text field, a hidden element, a button, and some client-side JavaScript. Figure 5-11 shows how you want the control to appear in the browser; the left-hand control shows the effect when the button has been clicked, and the right-hand control shows its normal appearance.

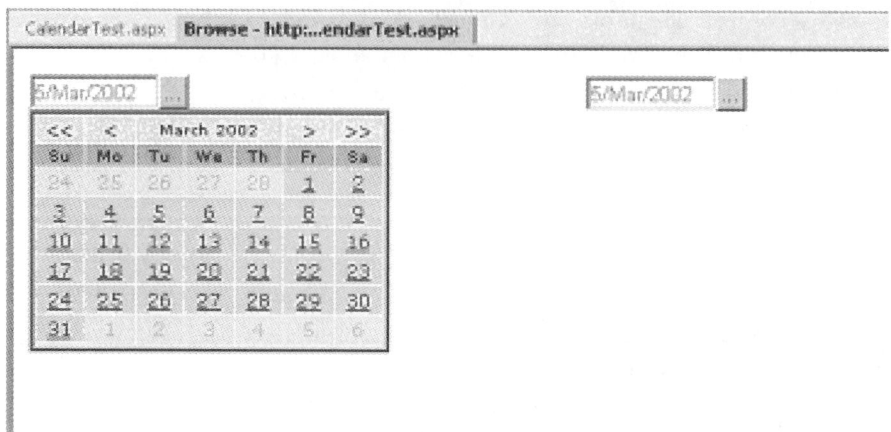

Figure 5-11. The pop-up Calendar control in action

You need two distinct methods in our class to achieve this; the first will generate the `<span>`, and the second will create the control-specific content.

Creating the Container Element

Creation of the `<span>` is performed by the constructor, which is implemented in all VB .NET classes through a public method called `New()`. You should add this to the class as follows:

```
Public Sub New()
    MyBase.New(HtmlTextWriterTag.Span)
End Sub
```

In this code you're calling the `New` method on the base class (referenced as `MyBase`). The base class is the class that our control inherits from, `System.Web.UI.WebControls.WebControl`, and its constructor allows us to create a *container* element for our control. As well as creating `<span>` elements, you can also create `<div>`, `<h1>`, `<h2>`, and so on. You'll find that nearly all HTML elements can be created in this way, and ASP.NET automatically handles styles, formatting, and other standard visual features for such controls. This is one of the advantages of deriving from the `System.Web.UI.WebControls.WebControl` class rather than `System.Web.UI.Control`.

As it happens, this method is redundant because the default behavior of the WebControl class constructor is to create a `<span>`, and so you could omit the code completely. However, you may initially find it easier to understand what's happening if you explicitly create the span, so leave the constructor code in place for now.

Creating the Content

Now you've got the container element, you can go ahead and create the content. You need to initially render three separate elements:

- An `<input>` of type `text` to display the selected date
- An `<input>` of type `hidden` to hold the selected date for calculations
- An `<input>` of type `button` that you'll later link to a JavaScript function

If you examine the ASP.NET documentation relating to Custom Web Controls, it appears you have several different methods that can be overridden to perform these tasks, including `Render`, `RenderBeginTag`, `RenderEndTag`, and `RenderContents`. Examine the sample code that was added when you created the initial class for the control, and you'll see that it uses the `Render` method, but this isn't quite what you need. The `Render` method ignores the container element you defined in the constructor, so this would cause the content elements to be added directly to the page. Although this would generate some output, it wouldn't be ideal as you wouldn't be able to control position and style without writing even more code yourself. `Render` *is* useful when creating controls from scratch, but when you're using a container element (as we are) you should use the `RenderContents` method instead.

When the `RenderContents` method is invoked, it performs three tasks:

- It causes the opening tag of the container element to be generated.
- It runs the code within the method to generate the content.
- It generates the closing tag for the container element.

The method is invoked automatically as a part of the control lifecycle; all you need to do is add code to the method to render the required tags. For example:

```
Protected Overrides Sub RenderContents(ByVal output As _
                System.Web.UI.HtmlTextWriter)
    Dim strOutput As String

    strOutput = "<INPUT type=text disabled style=""WIDTH: 83px; HEIGHT: 22px"">"
```

```
    strOutput += "<INPUT type=hidden>"
    strOutput += "<INPUT type=button style=""WIDTH: 22px; HEIGHT: 22px"" " & _
                 "value="". . ."">"

    output.Write(strOutput)
End Sub
```

RenderContents is a method of the base class, so you must override it to provide our own functionality. The method is passed a single parameter of type System.Web.UI.HtmlTextWriter, and this allows us to write directly to the HTML stream. Our code creates three <input> elements and then writes them to the HtmlTextWriter in one go. Other methods are available to assist with the generation of the tags and elements.

Before going any further, there's an important task to perform—you must delete the original Render method from the class. If you don't, ASP.NET will not trigger the RenderContents method and so our control will not be generated. While clearing this up, also remove the Text property procedure and associated local variable, plus the DefaultProperty attribute from the Class. This now leaves us with the bare-bones of the control containing the New and RenderContents methods, which should read as follows:

```
Imports System.ComponentModel
Imports System.Web.UI

<ToolboxData("<{0}:Calendar runat=server></{0}:Calendar>")> _
  Public Class Calendar
  Inherits System.Web.UI.WebControls.WebControl

  Public Sub New()
    MyBase.New(HtmlTextWriterTag.Span)
  End Sub

  Protected Overrides Sub RenderContents(ByVal output As _
                System.Web.UI.HtmlTextWriter)
    Dim strOutput As String
```

```
    strOutput += "<INPUT type=text disabled style=""WIDTH: 83px; HEIGHT:
22px"">"
    strOutput += "<INPUT type=hidden>"
    strOutput += "<INPUT type=button style=""WIDTH: 22px; HEIGHT: 22px"" " & _
                 "value="". . ."">"

    output.Write(strOutput)
  End Sub

End Class
```

Testing the Control

It's worthwhile testing the control at this stage to ensure it works as expected. Because you added the Web Control Library project to the HiFlyers solution, you can just add a test Web Form to the HiFlyers project and add the Calendar to it:

1. Ensure the control is saved and compiled by selecting **Build ➢ Build HiFlyer Controls**.
2. Click on the **HiFlyers** project and add a new Web Form.
3. With the Web Form designer open, right-click the Toolbox and select **Add Tab** from the context menu. Name the new tab **Custom**.
4. Select the Custom tab (which will currently be empty) and then right-click and choose **Customize Toolbox** from the context menu. The Customize Toolbox dialog box will appear, as shown in Figure 5-12. Select the **.NET Framework Components** tab.

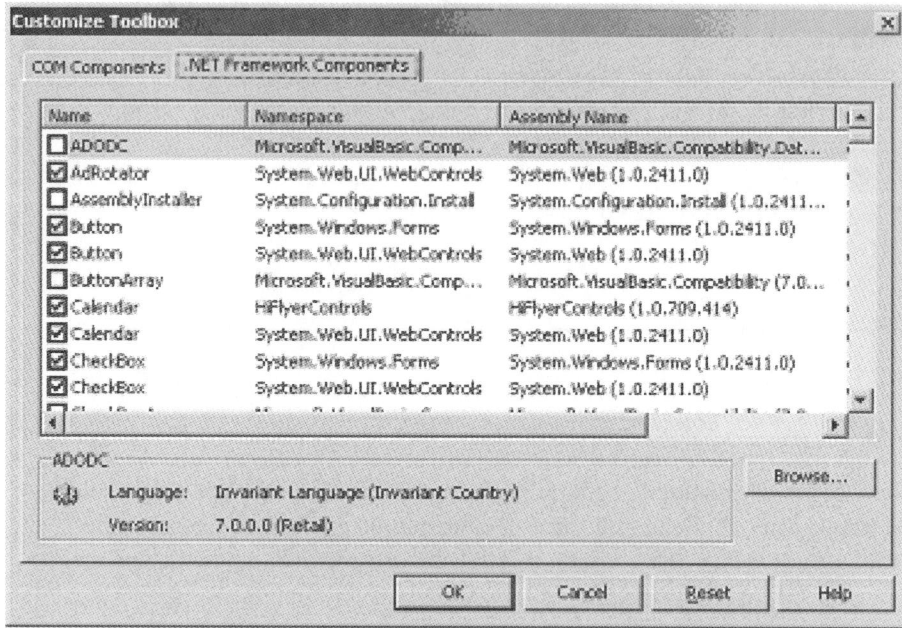

Figure 5-12. Adding the control to the Toolbox

5. Click the **Browse** button, then locate and select the HiFlyerControls.dll file that was created when the control project was compiled. This is most likely to be under `My Documents\Visual Studio Projects`.

6. The Calendar control will be added to the list of available .NET Framework Components. To add it to the Toolbox, tick the checkbox beside its name and then click **OK** to close the dialog box.

7. Drag the Calendar control onto the Web Form designer, and then build and browse the page to see the results in the browser. It should display a textbox and a button, and if you view the page's source you should see the hidden control and the span.

Exposing Properties and Methods

You now have a simple framework for the class, but it doesn't do anything. If you want to add programmatic features, then you can define properties and methods in exactly the same way as you did with the Web User Control.

For example, you'll add a `SelectedDate` property to the control. Rather than just using a local variable, you'll make this property persistent by using the `ViewState` object to store the value:

```
<Category("Appearance")> Property SelectedDate() As Date
    Get
        Try
            Return Date.Parse(Viewstate("Date").ToString)
        Catch
            Return Date.Today
        End Try
    End Get

    Set(ByVal Value As Date)
        ViewState("Date") = Value
    End Set
End Property
```

The structure is similar to the one you created for the `Orientation` property, so we won't cover the obvious features again. There are some specific techniques worthy of note, though:

- You've used a method attribute to specify this property that should be seen in the Appearance category of the property browser.
- You're storing the date in the ViewState object, which contains a collection of key/value pairs that you can create and use. You've created an entry called Date, but the chosen name can be anything at all.
- Because there's no guarantee that the ViewState contains a valid value for Date, you've used a simple `Try. . .Catch` block to handle reading from ViewState. In the event of an exception, the property procedure simply returns the current system date. This effectively sets a default as well as handling bad data.

Methods could be added by defining public subs or functions, though in this control you won't actually define any.

Rendering Property Values

Having added the SelectedDate property, you'll find no obvious difference in the way the control works. This is to be expected because all you've done is to define the property—you haven't actually used it yet.

What you'll now do is take a *big* jump forward by modifying the code used to render the output of the control so that it shows the selected date, and you'll also make reference to the JavaScript function that creates the calendar when the button is clicked. For simplicity this JavaScript code is in a separate file, which you would have to copy to the directory containing the pages that use the Calendar control. We've made this file available in the Downloads area of www.apress.com.

We won't try and describe the detail of what the JavaScript code does because it's largely irrelevant and hidden from you as an ASP.NET developer. What you do need to know is that there is a function called CreateCalendar that expects two parameters:

- A reference to a control on the page that will show the formatted date
- A reference to a control on the page that will store the numeric date

We've chosen to use two controls because it's easier to manipulate dates in JavaScript when in U.S. format (mm/dd/yyyy), but many users, especially non-U.S. users, prefer to see dates in a different format such as dd/mmm/yyyy. By using two controls, you can display the date in one format, but manipulate it in another. An example of the syntax of the function call is the following:

```
javascript:CreateCalendar(Form1.Calendar1_Date, Form1.Calendar1)
```

Where Form1 is the name of the HTML form, Calendar1_Date is the text field that will show the formatted date and Calendar1 is the text field that will store the numeric date. In practice you cannot hard-code these names because they're determined by the Web page hosting our control. Therefore, in this control you must look up the names and generate the function call dynamically.

The complete code for the RenderContents method now appears as follows:

```
Protected Overrides Sub RenderContents(ByVal output As _
              System.Web.UI.HtmlTextWriter)
  Dim strFormName As String = Me.Parent.UniqueID
  Dim strControlName As String = Me.UniqueID
  Dim strOutput As String

  strOutput = "<script language=""JavaScript"" src=""Calendar.js""></script>"
  strOutput += "<INPUT type=text disabled align=top id=" & strControlName & _
```

```
                "_Date name=" & strControlName & "_Date style=""WIDTH: 83px; " & _
                "HEIGHT: 22px"" value=""" & Format(SelectedDate, "dd/MMM/yyyy") & _
                """>"
    strOutput += "<INPUT type=hidden align=top id=" & strControlName & " name=" & _
                strControlName & " value=""" & SelectedDate.ToShortDateString & _
                """>"
    strOutput += "<INPUT type=button id=" & strControlName & "_Button onclick=" & _
                """javascript:CreateCalendar(" & strFormName & "." & _
                strControlName & "_Date, " & strFormName & "." & _
                strControlName & ");"" name=cmdDisplayCal style=""WIDTH: 22px;" & _
                " HEIGHT: 22px"" value="". . ."">"

    output.Write(strOutput)
End Sub
```

This may seem like a big change from what you had before, but although there's a lot more detail, the core purpose of the code is unchanged. The routine now begins by obtaining the name of the form and the `UniqueID` assigned to the control by the container. This `UniqueID` must be assigned to the control used for handling postback data, so it plays a vital role.

You then write a `<script>` tag to define the JavaScript source file, followed by the three tags you had previously. This time, the tags are properly qualified with `name` and `id` attributes, and the `SelectedDate` value is written into the two text fields. Also, the button is now associated with the JavaScript routine by way of its `onclick` attribute.

Having made these changes (and copied the JavaScript source file into the appropriate directory), you can test the page. When you now click the button the calendar should be displayed, and when you select a date it should be shown in the text field.

Rendering Pages Efficiently

One of the problems to be wary of when building controls is unnecessary duplication and redundant content. In this example, you can do several things to minimize duplication, but you'll focus on just one for now—the `<script>` tag.

Currently, this tag renders separately for each control on the page, so if you had a page containing four of the Calendar controls, it would render with four copies of the `<script>` tag. As well as being wasteful, this may lead to errors when interpreting the JavaScript and so cause the page to fail. You'll modify the control so that it renders the tag only once, when the first Calendar is generated on the page.

To achieve this, you'll use two methods of the Page class:

- `RegisterClientScriptBlock`
- `IsClientScriptBlockRegistered`.

The `RegisterClientScriptBlock` method enables a control to generate a script block at the top of the page, and the `IsClientScriptBlockRegistered` method enables you to determine whether such a script block has already been created (by another control on the page, for example). These two methods make use of a keyname to identify and track the script block; the keyname can be any valid string of your choice. The following changes are needed in our code:

1. Create a handler for the `PreRender` event for the control. In this event, you'll check to see if the script block has already been created and, if not, call the `RegisterClientScriptBlock` method to do so:

```
Private Sub Calendar_PreRender(ByVal sender As Object, _
                ByVal e As System.EventArgs) Handles MyBase.PreRender
    If Not Page.IsClientScriptBlockRegistered("CalendarJS") Then
        Page.RegisterClientScriptBlock("CalendarJS", _
        "<script language=""JavaScript"" src=""Calendar.js""></script>")
    End If
End Sub
```

2. Modify the `RenderContents` method and remove the first assignment to `strOutput` so that the routine no longer generates the `<script>` tag, but instead produces only the three `<input>` elements:

```
Protected Overrides Sub RenderContents(ByVal output As _
                System.Web.UI.HtmlTextWriter)
  Dim strFormName As String = Me.Parent.UniqueID
  Dim strControlName As String = Me.UniqueID
  Dim strOutput As String

  strOutput = "<INPUT type=text disabled align=top id=" & strControlName & _
      "_Date name=" & strControlName & "_Date style=""WIDTH: 83px; " & _
      "HEIGHT: 22px"" value=""" & Format(SelectedDate, "dd/MMM/yyyy") & _
        """>"
 strOutput += "<INPUT type=hidden align=top id=" & strControlName & " name=" & _
      strControlName & " value=""" & SelectedDate.ToShortDateString & _
      """>"
 strOutput += "<INPUT type=button id=" & strControlName & "_Button onclick=" & _
```

```
            """javascript:CreateCalendar(" & strFormName & "." & _
            strControlName & "_Date, " & strFormName & "." & _
            strControlName & ");"" name=cmdDisplayCal style=""WIDTH: 22px;" & _
             " HEIGHT: 22px"" value="". . ."">"

    output.Write(strOutput)
End Sub
```

Test the control after these modifications and you'll see that the `<script>` tag is rendered only once in the page. This example shows how important it is for you to learn the capabilities and features of the .NET classes you use. By using the `RegisterClientScriptBlock` and `IsClientScriptBlockRegistered` methods, we made this task simple; without them we would need to have created our own tracking system that ensured the controls did not produce duplicate output.

Detecting Browser Capabilities

We've made a bold assumption in our control—we've assumed the client browser supports JavaScript, and although it's likely that client browsers will support JavaScript, it's far from guaranteed. You should design the control to fallback to *downlevel* features if a non-JavaScript browser is being used, but the question is, how do you know what the browser supports? The answer is provided through the `Browser` object, which is available to your control through its container.

Within the control you can refer to the properties of the `Page.Request.Browser` object. These include the following:

- **ActiveXControls**: Does the browser support ActiveX controls?
- **AOL**: Is the browser an America Online (AOL) browser?
- **Beta**: Is the browser a beta release?
- **Browser**: Returns the User-Agent string that provides information to identify the browser.
- **ClrVersion**: What version of the .NET CLR is installed on the client?
- **Cookies**: Does the browser support cookies?
- **Crawler**: Is the client a Web crawler search engine?

- **EcmaScriptVersion**: What version of ECMA script does the browser support?
- **Frames**: Does the browser support HTML frames?
- **JavaApplets**: Does the browser support Java applets?
- **JavaScript**: Does the browser support JavaScript?
- **MajorVersion**: Returns the major version number of the browser.
- **MinorVersion**: Returns the minor version number of the browser.
- **Platform**: Returns the name of the client platform.
- **Tables**: Does the browser support HTML tables?
- **Type**: Returns the name and major version number of the browser.
- **VBScript**: Does the browser support VBScript?
- **Version**: Returns the full version number of the browser.
- **Win16**: Is the client a Win16-based machine?
- **Win32**: Is the client a Win32-based machine?

Note that all of these properties return values based on whether the browser could support the specific feature, rather than whether it's actually enabled. For example, if the user is working with Internet Explorer 6.0, then ActiveX controls and JavaApplets will both be supported, although they may have disabled these features because of security concerns. Despite this, `Browser.ActiveXControls` and `Browser.JavaScript` will both return `True`.

With this limitation in mind, if you want to change the behavior of the control according to JavaScript support, you'll need to change the `RenderContents` and the `PreRender` event handlers by performing an additional test:

```
Protected Overrides Sub RenderContents(ByVal output As _
                System.Web.UI.HtmlTextWriter)
    Dim strFormName As String = Me.Parent.UniqueID
    Dim strControlName As String = Me.UniqueID
    Dim strOutput As String
```

```
    If Page.Request.Browser.JavaScript Then
        'Previous code to render the UI
        strOutput = . . .
    Else
        'Render a simple text box
        strOutput += "<INPUT type=text align=top id=" & strControlName & _
                        " name=" & strControlName & " style=""VISIBILITY: " & _
                        " visible; WIDTH: 83px; HEIGHT: 22px"" value=""" & _
                        SelectedDate.ToShortDateString & """>"
    End If

    output.Write(strOutput)
End Sub

Private Sub HFCalendar_PreRender(ByVal sender As Object, _
                ByVal e As System.EventArgs) Handles MyBase.PreRender
    If Page.Request.Browser.JavaScript AndAlso _
                Not Page.IsClientScriptBlockRegistered("CalendarJS") Then
        Page.RegisterClientScriptBlock("CalendarJS", _
                "<script language=""JavaScript"" src=""Calendar.js""></script>")
    End If
End Sub
```

Our modified event handlers now render the original user interface if JavaScript is supported, or a simple text box if not. This text box has the same name and ID as the hidden control in the original interface, so the supporting code, properties, and methods will continue to work.

Receiving and Raising Events

The final technique you'll examine is how you can detect changes in the control's data between postbacks and raise corresponding events to the container. This is standard behavior for most standard controls (for example, it's how intrinsic controls such as TextBoxes process ViewState data to determine whether to raise events) and is something you'll almost certainly want to implement for every control you create.

To handle postback information your control needs to implement the `IPostBackDataHandler` interface. This has two methods:

- `LoadPostData` is called during the control lifecycle by ASP.NET. It passes two parameters that enable your code to retrieve the content of the control as it was entered by the user. You implement code in this method to compare the posted data with the previous content and return True if there's a change.

- RaisePostDataChangedEvent is called only if LoadPostData returned True. You typically implement code in this method to raise an event back to the container to indicate that a change has occurred.

Posted data is the term given to the information passed from the browser to the server as a part of the HTTP request, and it represents the current content of the controls on the Web Form, including any changes made by the user before they generated the postback. ASP.NET identifies which elements of the posted data are relevant to each control and passes them to the LoadPostData method in the form of a NameValueCollection class (similar to a Dictionary class under classic ASP or VB 6.0).

You'll begin by specifying the interface and declaring an event for the Calendar control's class by adding the following lines just below the Inherits statement:

```
Implements IPostBackDataHandler
Public Event DateChanged As EventHandler
```

You can now provide an implementation of the LoadPostData method:

```
Public Function LoadPostData(ByVal postDataKey As String, ByVal postCollection As _
        System.Collections.Specialized.NameValueCollection) As Boolean _
        Implements System.Web.UI.IPostBackDataHandler.LoadPostData

    Dim strPostedDate As String = postCollection(postDataKey)

    If Not SelectedDate = Date.Parse(strPostedDate) Then
        SelectedDate = Date.Parse(strPostedDate)
        Return True
    Else
        Return False
    End If
End Function
```

This routine first retrieves the posted data from the postCollection and then compares it against the current value of SelectedDate, which has been read from ViewState. If the posted data is different to the ViewState value, then the user must have selected a different date during the last postback cycle, so you store the posted date and return True.

You can now implement the method to raise the event back to the container as follows:

```
Public Sub RaisePostDataChangedEvent() _
        Implements System.Web.UI.IPostBackDataHandler.RaisePostDataChangedEvent
    RaiseEvent DateChanged(Me, EventArgs.Empty)
End Sub
```

Earlier in this chapter we mentioned about the importance of the UniqueID assigned to the control by the container. The postback data received in these events is obtained from the control that has the specified UniqueID; if you had named the hidden `<input>` element with a different name, then the data it contained would *not* have been made available to the `LoadPostData` method.

Summary

Creating controls is an important part of ASP.NET, enabling you to produce reusable components that can be distributed between members of a development team. Web User Controls cater to simple control requirements, and Web Custom Controls cater to more sophisticated requirements.

Both approaches take time to master, and in this chapter we've only begun to illustrate the many different facilities that ASP.NET provides to help you. You may find it useful to more thoroughly investigate the properties and methods of the WebControl class because this is used as the base class of many Web Custom Controls, and you may also want to take a look at other techniques for rendering output.

As long as you continue to reuse your controls, this investment in time and effort will be paid off in the long term. However, for the controls to remain useful over an extended period of time you'll need to get their design and functionality right from the start, so don't skip over the design and planning phases—they apply as much to control creation as they do to any other development discipline.

An added benefit of building your own controls is that you'll gain a much deeper understanding of how Web Controls work in general. If you subsequently encounter problems or limitations with standard or third-party controls, you then have a better chance of finding a satisfactory solution or work-around.

CHAPTER 6

Building Mobile Web Applications

What Is a Mobile Web Application?

Creating a Mobile Web Application

Using Mobile Controls

Limitations, Problems, and Challenges

In recent years there has been a well-documented explosion in the telecommunications industry; and, with the help of some fancy marketing, the situation has now reached the point where almost everyone is mobile in some way. In this case, *mobile* means being in contact while on the move. The technologies and devices for making mobility possible are now here to stay—like it or not.

The broad definition of mobile encompasses many different technologies—everything from simple voice and text devices to complex interactive graphical computers. For our purposes, however, we're really only interested in the standardized ones that can browse the Web, which currently limits us to two categories:

- Wireless Application Protocol (WAP) Phones
- Personal Digital Assistants (PDAs)—including Handspring, Pocket PC, and Palm™ handheld devices

Devices and products from many different manufacturers fall within these two categories, with even more reaching the market every day. As we'll soon see, this diversity is one of the biggest challenges you'll face when creating mobile Web applications since there are just so many variations.

What Is a Mobile Web Application?

Before we get into the detail of creating mobile Web applications, it's important to have a clear idea of just what we're talking about here. We would suggest the following definition as a good starting point:

> A *mobile Web application* consists of all the files, pages, handlers, modules, and executable code that can be invoked or run in the scope of a given virtual directory (and its subdirectories) on a Web application server. Mobile Web applications render output in a format suitable for viewing on mobile devices such as WAP phones, PDAs, and PocketPCs.

If you refer back to Chapter 1 and review the definition of a regular Web application, you'll find it to be very similar. In fact, the first part of the definition is exactly the same; the difference lies in the fact that mobile Web applications generate output targeted at mobile devices, while regular Web applications generate output targeted at desktop browsers. This is an important point because much of the design and development effort of any project will be put into the data elements and the business logic, both of which are largely independent of the user interface features. If you have an existing application and want to extend it to target mobile devices, you can use much of the current functionality by simply adding a new presentation layer in the form of Mobile Pages and Mobile Controls.

A common question that gets asked at this point is: "Can I build a single application to target both mobile and non-mobile browsers?" Well, yes you can, but it will involve a lot of hard work because of the real differences between the browser technologies. We'll come onto some of the technical differences a little later, but one of the most obvious practical ones is screen size. Even the most advanced WAP phones rarely have screens larger than 320 pixels by 160 pixels, while the more common ones are limited to around 100 pixels by 160 pixels. Compare these sizes with desktop browsers where even 800 pixels by 600 pixels is considered low resolution. It's very difficult to design a page that renders well on such varying screen sizes, so it would be much easier to design two distinct pages—that is, one for desktop browsers and one for mobile devices. Since we will need to do this for every page in the application, you'll almost certainly find it easier to partition this content into two separate projects, and so create two distinct applications.

Keep in mind that we are only talking about having separate presentation tiers; if you build your business logic into .NET assemblies that can be called from the pages, then both applications will still be able to share a common set of components.

Architecture

ASP.NET provides support for Mobile Web Applications through the Microsoft Mobile Internet Toolkit (MMIT) add-on. This is not distributed as a standard part of the .NET Framework, nor does it come with Visual Studio .NET (at least not yet). Instead, you must download the MMIT from the Microsoft Web site and install it separately. The precise location of the MMIT may vary, but at the time of writing it can be obtained from the following URL:

```
http://msdn.microsoft.com/mobileinternettoolkit.
```

You may need to use the search facility if you cannot find the download at this location.

MMIT contains the necessary design-time and runtime files to make it easy for you to build and deploy mobile Web applications. It's not a large download (approximately 4 MB), but it contains the following:

- Mobile Internet Controls runtime
- Device adapters for HTML 3.2, cHTML, and WML
- Mobile Internet Designer
- Developer documentation and reference

The Mobile Internet Controls runtime is a set of classes that extends the capabilities of the regular Web Forms and Web Form Controls libraries by providing dedicated support for mobile devices. These mobile controls provide much the same functionality as the intrinsic Web controls (including Label, TextBox, Button, Link, and Image controls), but also provide mobile-specific features such as a PhoneCall control. Figure 6-1 shows how these controls are integrated into the .NET Framework. Chapter 10 and Appendix E discuss the .NET Framework in more detail.

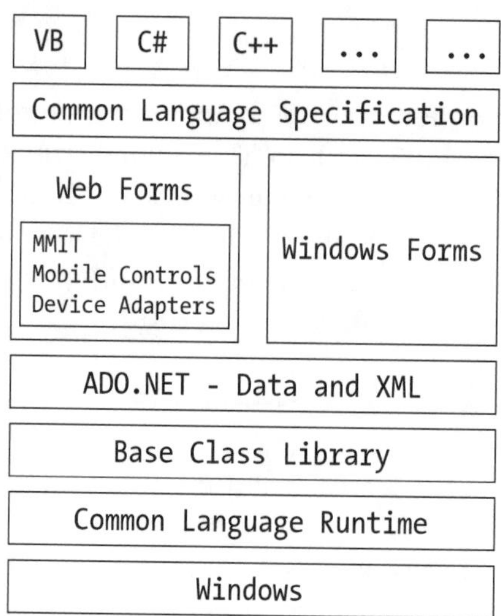

Figure 6-1. Integration of MMIT and the .NET Framework

When you build a mobile Web application that uses mobile controls, you can still use all the other facilities provided by the .NET Framework, and you can use any ASP.NET-supported language. The only difference lies in the way that the Web Forms are themselves created and the components you add to them.

Adaptive Behavior

In Chapter 4 you learned that Web Form controls are able to render their own HTML to the browser, and it is this capability that allows them to be adaptive. Mobile Internet controls are quite different in this respect, and are, in fact, device-agnostic. What we mean by this is that a mobile TextBox does not change its behavior according to whether the client is a WAP phone or PDA. The generation of rendered output in a device-specific format is delegated to a set of classes called *device adapters*. Every mobile control has a set of device adapters associated with it, one for each target markup language. For example, MMIT provides the following adapters for the mobile TextBox:

- cHTMLTextBoxAdapter
- HTMLTextBoxAdapter
- WMLTextBoxAdapter

Each device adapter is implemented as a class and is compiled into a common assembly. Configuration details for the device adapters are placed into Machine.config, and this information will be examined by ASP.NET when it processes a request for a mobile page within an application. As we will see in Chapter 10, Machine.config is an XML document that stores system-wide configuration settings for .NET, including information on recognized browser types, versions, and capabilities; it makes sense for the complementary MMIT settings to be stored here too.

The reason for the separation of the rendering code from the control is quite simple: New classes of devices will become available and new standards will evolve for the existing markup languages (you can expect these changes to occur with startling frequency). If the markup-specific rendering code was embedded into the control itself, Microsoft would have to distribute an updated version of MMIT every time the markup standards were changed or added to. By extracting the code responsible for rendering the control into a separate device adapter class, anyone can produce a new assembly containing customized device adapters to support a new type of device or standard. The assembly can be copied to any development or production system and enabled by just adding configuration details into the `<mobileControls>` section of Machine.config.

MMIT is supplied with the source code for the standard device adapters to allow you to customize them or to build your own device adapters based on the existing ones. This source code is written in C# rather than VB .NET, although you can use any language if you wish to build your own classes. By default, the location of the source code files is `C:\Program Files\Microsoft Mobile Internet Toolkit\Adapter Source`.

Creating a Mobile Web Application

Now that we know what we're dealing with, let's get started on creating a mobile Web application. We will create an application that allows HiFlyers to distribute up-to-the-minute information to their customers. This will include current weather, breaking news relating to aircraft failure or instructor sickness, and a list of aircraft that are currently available for hire that day. There are two benefits to be gained from this service:

- Customers are kept happy by allowing them to check whether there are any factors that may prevent them from flying before they leave for the airfield. They can use any supported mobile device for this, so they can check from the office, while they're in the car, and so on.

- By listing the available aircraft, HiFlyers may be able to tempt customers to make last minute bookings that may not otherwise occur. To make this as easy as possible, we'll include the facility to make a call direct from the Web page.

We will build our mobile Web application using ASP.NET and Visual Studio .NET, but as we mentioned previously, additional software will be needed to enable this functionality.

Requirements

The first thing you'll need to do is to ensure that you have downloaded and installed the current version of MMIT. This provides the runtime support and documentation that you'll need, as well as a mobile page designer that integrates with the Visual Studio .NET development environment. You'll also want the ability to test your mobile application on the development machine; the easiest way to do this is using an emulator. There are many desktop emulators available, but for our purposes we will use the following:

- Microsoft Mobile Emulator, available from `www.microsoft.com`
- Microsoft PocketPC Emulator, available from `www.microsoft.com`
- Nokia SimApp Emulator, available from `www.nokia.com`

There is also a simulator available from Openwave (`www.openwave.com`). This is a particularly useful simulator to have since Openwave doesn't create devices of their own, but instead develops the firmware that is embedded in many other manufacturers' devices. When you test your application with the Openwave simulator, you are effectively testing its behavior in a number of devices rather than just one.

NOTE *Emulators do not exactly replicate the behavior and features of the real-world devices they represent, but instead provide you with an impression of how your application may operate. Emulators are useful and convenient during development, but it is essential to perform full testing with real devices in a live environment to really see how the application runs. See the Limitations, Problems, and Challenges section for more information.*

Getting Started

Having installed MMIT and one or more emulators, you are ready to begin creating your first Mobile Web Application. Launch Visual Studio .NET and create a new project based on the **Mobile Web Application** template. Set the Location to `http://localhost/HiFlyersMobile`, as shown in Figure 6-2.

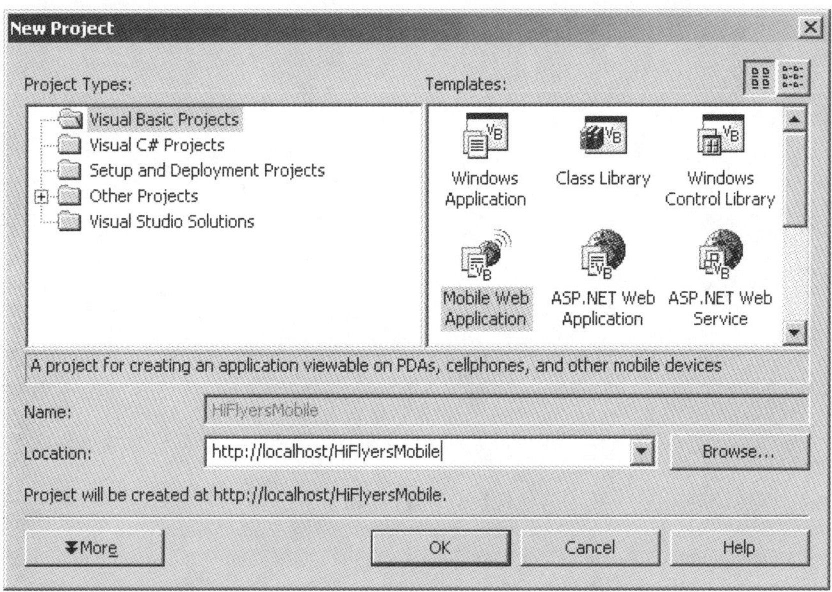

Figure 6-2. Creating a Mobile Web Application

Visual Studio .NET will create the project in the same way that it would create a regular Web application, but when the designer loads and shows the visual content, you will notice some clear differences—as shown in Figure 6-3.

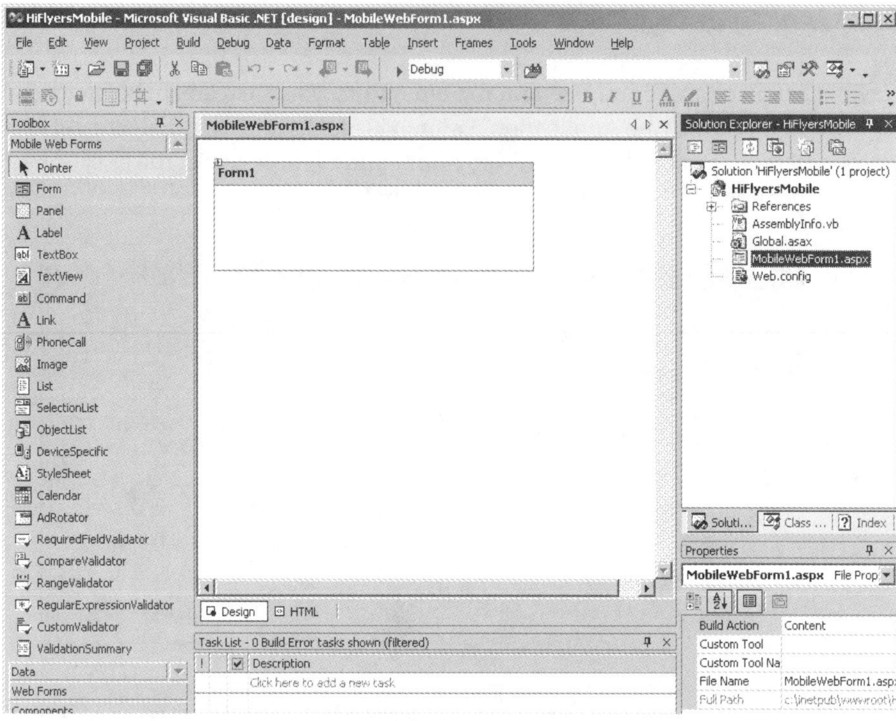

Figure 6-3. Content of a Mobile Web Application project

The most obvious difference lies with the designer for MobileWebForm1.aspx, which looks quite unlike the standard Web Form designer. As we will soon see, each mobile Web page can support multiple forms of data, allowing you to better partition the visual content to fit the small screens that most mobile devices have. In Figure 6-3 you can see that the page contains a single form, but you are able to add as many additional forms as you need.

You will also notice that the Toolbox contains a new tab—Mobile Web Forms—which holds the controls that you will use on mobile pages. Most of these controls match their equivalents on the Web Forms tab, although some (such as the Form and PhoneCall) are unique.

The other difference lies in the content of the project shown in the Solution Explorer window. A Mobile Web Application does not use CSS files, nor does it support the exposure of Web Services, so both the Styles.css and HiFlyersMobile.vsdisco files are omitted.

Creating Forms

Mobile Web pages are subdivided into forms, with each form *usually* representing an individual screen of information on the client device. We say "usually," because the final rendering and appearance is ultimately controlled by .NET and the device itself; so, if you try to create an excessively large form, then it will be further subdivided anyway. When you first start building mobile Web applications you may be worried by this lack of definitive control, but as you'll quickly learn, it's just one of the many limitations currently imposed on developers in the mobile world—and there are other limitations that are somewhat more significant.

We will initially need four separate forms in our application: one default screen with links to the others, then one each for weather, news, and aircraft availability. We will start by adding three additional Form controls (from the Mobile Web Forms tab in the Toolbox); then, we'll define the Name and Title for each (as listed in Table 6-1).

Table 6-1. Mobile Web Form Names and Titles

NAME	TITLE
frmMain	HiFlyers Now!
frmWeather	Weather
frmNews	News
frmAvailability	Availability

Having defined the forms, we can then add a label and three links to frmMain to create its content. The label will represent the visual title of the page on devices that choose not to define the form's title, while the links will allow users to navigate to the other forms. Set their properties and methods to the settings listed in Table 6-2.

Table 6-2. Mobile Controls for the Main Form

CONTROL	NAME	TEXT	NAVIGATEURL
Label	lblHeading	HiFlyers Now!	N/A
Link	lnkWeather	Weather	#frmWeather
Link	lnkNews	News	#frmNews
Link	lnkAvailability	Availability	#frmAvailability

Having created these controls, the page will appear as shown in Figure 6-4.

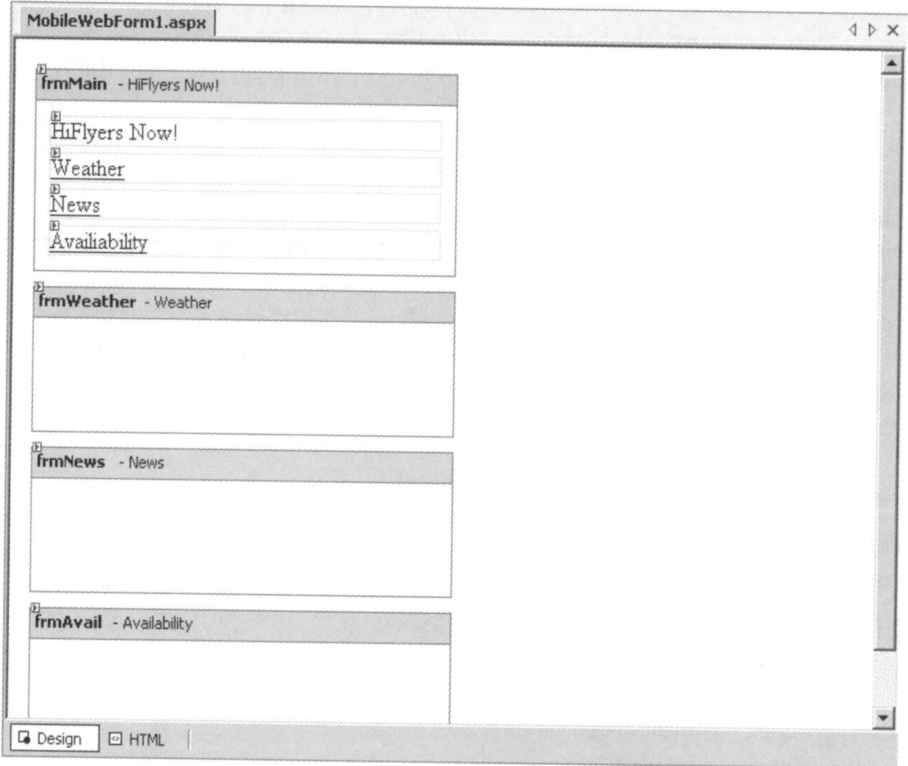

Figure 6-4. Mobile Page Designer

Pages or Forms?

In the above example we built a single page containing four separate forms, but we could have also generated the same look and feel by creating four separate pages, each with one form. Which approach is best then, and which should you use in your applications?

The approach you choose will have an impact at both a design and an implementation level. For example, if you separate your forms into distinct pages, then they more closely mirror the structure and design that would be used for a regular ASP.NET application. Conceptually, each form is a separate object, so why not represent them in the same way physically?

On a more practical level, if the forms are placed into a single page, then they can reference each other's controls directly, reducing the need to pass or preserve state between page requests. However, the real difference lies in the way that the forms are rendered to the client device:

- If you place each form in a separate page, only one form will be passed to the client device when a request is processed. This minimizes the amount of data passed with each round-trip.

- If you place several forms in a single page, they will *all* be passed to the client when a request is received for any one of them. If navigation is performed within the forms (using simple Link controls) then there is no need for the device to perform a server round-trip to service the requests—it already has everything it needs and will display the new form immediately. This minimizes the number of server hits and round-trips.

The latter approach is usually preferred for mobile applications, because a lot of the delays inherent in mobile applications come from the negotiation that takes place at the start of every request. Although mobile communication is often slower than LAN or WAN based communication, it is usually fast enough for most purposes. However, you do have to be realistic about what you will render to the client—trying to display a 1000 row list in a WAP phone clearly won't work, no matter what technique you try.

So, to summarize: If your mobile forms require server-side processing on each user action (for example, you place code in the click events of Command controls), then you'll probably find better performance from the one-page-per-form approach, since there would be less to render to the device for each request. On the other hand, if you make use of Links to perform client-side navigation, you'll probably benefit by combining several forms onto each page. In most applications, chances are that you'll be using both techniques, so you'll probably end up with a mix of single- and multi-form pages.

Testing with the Emulator

Before we go much further, it's worth testing the application at this point to make sure that everything compiles and that the emulators work as expected. To make the testing process easier, we'll rename MobileWebForm1.aspx to **Default.aspx** so that we need only specify the virtual directory name rather than the entire URL.

Select **Build ➢ Build Solution** to build the application and ensure that everything is saved and compiled. Now you're ready to test. If you have installed the Microsoft Mobile Explorer (MME) Emulator, then you can just right-click the **Default.aspx** file in the Solution Explorer and select **Browse With . . .** from the context menu. This displays the dialog shown in Figure 6-5.

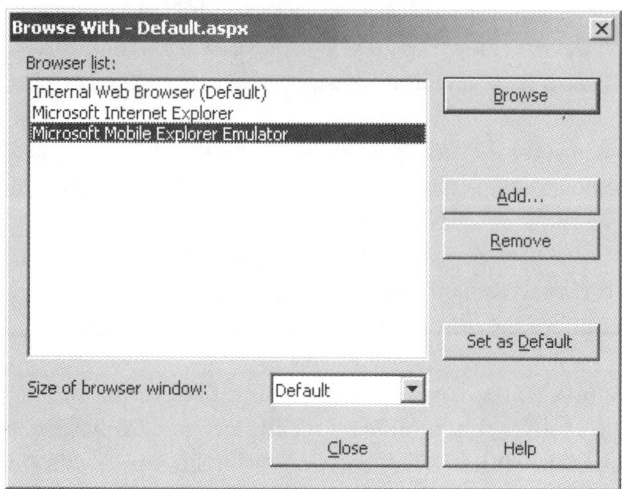

Figure 6-5. Selecting a browser

Select the **Microsoft Mobile Explorer Emulator** entry and click **Browse**. The emulator will load and display your page; you can activate the hyperlinks to navigate to the other forms. Figure 6-6 shows how the initial form will appear.

Figure 6-6. Browsing using the MME Emulator

NOTE *When using the MME Emulator, it is recommended that you use the keypad buttons for navigation and selection, just as you would with a normal WAP phone. Try to avoid clicking the links on the emulator's screen.*

If you have loaded other emulators, then you can try them now too. Some may need to be launched from the Start menu, while others may integrate more cleanly with Visual Studio. If you want to add your own entry to the Browse With dialog then follow these steps:

1. Right-click a mobile page in Visual Studio .NET and select **Browse With . . .**

2. Click **Add** in the resulting dialog.

3. In the **Add Program** dialog, click the **Browse** button and locate the executable for the browser you want to add. For example, the Nokia SimApp executable will install to **C:\Program Files\Nokia\Mobile Internet\bin\simapp.exe** by default.

4. Choose a friendly name for the browser to be identified by when displayed in the Browser List.

You can repeat this process to add any number of additional browsers and emulators to the list, making it easier to launch them when testing your application. Figure 6-7 shows how our Web application will currently appear when displayed in the Nokia SimApp, when the SimApp is set to emulate a Nokia Mobile Browser.

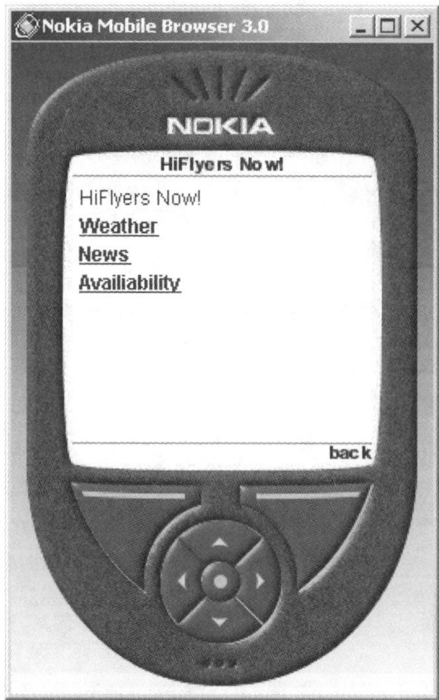

Figure 6-7. Browsing using Nokia SimApp

Notice that the Nokia Mobile Browser has displayed the form title, as well as the label, whereas the MME Emulator displayed only the label. This is one trivial example of how the rendered results can differ between devices; we'll see even more such discrepancies later.

Testing with Other Browsers

Testing your application against an emulator is important, but you'll often find that it takes longer to load a page into the emulator than it would to load the page into either Visual Studio .NET's internal browser or Microsoft Internet Explorer. Fortunately, if you just want to test functionality of the application rather than appearance, you can still use standard desktop browsers because MMIT will detect them and render the output of the mobile Web application to standard HTML 3.2 format.

For example, right-click **Default.aspx** in the Solution Explorer and select **Build and Browse** from the context menu. The page is processed and displayed in the internal browser—as shown in Figure 6-8.

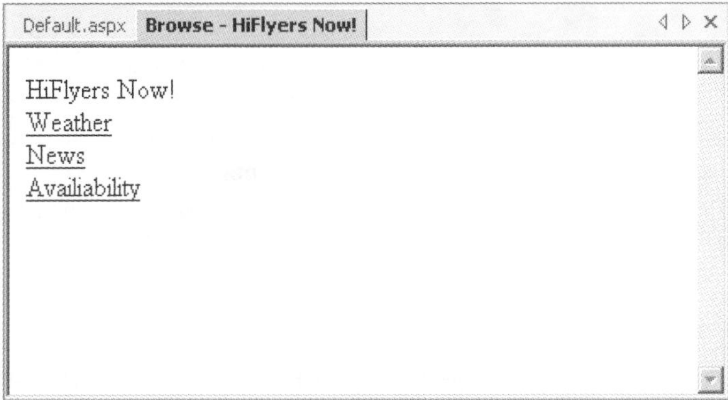

Figure 6-8. Browsing using the internal browser

Using Mobile Controls

So far, we've built a basic framework for our mobile application, which uses Link controls to allow navigation through the forms on the page. We've tested the application framework within the emulators, and are now ready to continue building the content for the other forms. We'll build one form at a time, as they are functionally independent from one another.

Implementing the Weather Form

The Weather form lets customers look up current weather details for any recognized airfield by entering its four-letter International Civil Aviation Organization (ICAO) code. For example, the New York JFK airport is KJFK, Chicago O'Hare is KORD, and London Heathrow is EGLL.

We'll begin by adding the controls listed in Table 6-3.

Table 6-3. Mobile Controls for the Weather Form

CONTROL	NAME	TEXT	NAVIGATEURL
Label	lblHeading1	Weather	N/A
Label	lblEnterCode	Enter airfield code	N/A
TextBox	txtICAOCode	(Blank)	N/A
Label	lblWeather	(Blank)	N/A
Command	btnCheckWeather	Check	N/A
Link	lnkBack1	Back	#frmMain

We will also set the Size and MaxLength properties of txtICAOCode to **4**, as this should always be the amount of text entered by the user. However, we also want to ensure that the user enters something into the TextBox, and that the code they enter consists only of four alphabetic characters. The easiest way to do this is to add a RequiredField validator and a RegularExpression validator—as listed in Table 6-4.

Table 6-4. Mobile Validation Controls for the Weather Form

CONTROL	NAME	CONTROLTOVALIDATE	ERRORMESSAGE	VALIDATIONEXPRESSION
RequiredField Validator	valCodeReq	txtICAOCode	Code is required	N/A
RegularExpression Validator	valCodeExp	txtICAOCode	Must be 4 characters	(?i:[a-z]{4})

The ValidationExpression shows the use of a grouping construct containing a regular expression option. The expression ensures that txtICAOCode contains exactly four alphabetic characters. The expression is comprised of the following three sections:

- The group and options are represented by the **(?i: . . .)** characters. The **?i** option specifies that the expression should be case-insensitive.

- The matching range is specified by the **[a-z]** section, indicating that only alphabetic characters are permissible.

- The quantifier is specified by {4} and indicates that there should be exactly four instances of the preceding section—that is, four characters, each between a and z.

Figure 6-9 shows how the Weather Form will appear at this point.

frmWeather - Weather

Weather

Enter airfield code

Code is required

Must be 4 characters

[lblWeather]

Check

Back

Figure 6-9. The Weather form

We can now place some code behind the Check button to retrieve the current weather at the chosen airfield, based on the code entered by the user. In a live application this would be a great place to use a Web Service, since all we are interested in is getting the information. Using a Web Service means we can leave the detail of how the data is collected and analyzed to an organization with meteorological expertise; as long as they expose suitable methods in the form of a Web Service, we can call them from our application.

Although it would be interesting to use a Web Service, it's a bit of a distraction from our core topic—mobile Web applications—so we'll code this example with a dummy routine that simply returns random data when called. Chapter 14 includes a thorough discussion of the creation and use of Web Services, illustrated with a weather-oriented example that you could incorporate if you prefer.

Begin by adding a function called `GetWeather` to the class. This will return the random weather information:

```
Private Function GetWeather(ByVal ICAOCode As String) As String
    Dim rnd As New Random()
    Select Case CInt(rnd.Next(3))
        Case 0
            Return "Sky is Clear"
        Case 1
```

```
            Return "It is Raining"
        Case 2
            Return "It is Stormy"
        Case Else
            Return "Unavailable"
    End Select
End Function
```

The event handler for `btnCheckWeather.Click` can then make a call to this routine:

```
Private Sub btnCheckWeather_Click(ByVal sender As System.Object, _
                ByVal e As System.EventArgs) Handles btnCheckWeather.Click
    If Page.IsValid Then
        lblWeather.Text = GetWeather(txtICAOCode.Text)
    Else
        lblWeather.Text = ""
    End If
End Sub
```

The routine first performs a check on `Page.IsValid`, to ensure that all of the validation rules have been obeyed. If so, we call the function to generate the weather information and display the result in the label; otherwise, the weather label is cleared.

After you have completed the application to this stage, you should build it and then test it in a browser or emulator. Once it is running, navigate to the Weather page and enter any four-letter code into the TextBox and then click the Check button to display a random weather forecast in the browser. Test that the validation controls are working by entering an incorrect code (for example, one that contains numbers) and by leaving the TextBox blank. Remember that you will need to click the Check button each time.

Improving Validation

Our application currently performs only basic validation on the code entered by the user, and while there are many airfields in the world represented by these codes, there are obviously certain ones which are invalid. Just as we could use a Web Service to retrieve weather information, we could also use a Web Service for validating codes. For our example though, we'll keep it simple and simulate this approach using local code in the application to perform the checks. The function we'll use is as follows and should be entered into the class:

```
Private Function CheckICAOCode(ByVal ICAOCode As String) As Boolean
    Dim reg As Regex
    Dim m As Match

    reg = New Regex("[ek][a-z]{3}", RegexOptions.IgnoreCase)

    m = reg.Match(ICAOCode)
    If m.Success Then
        Return True
    Else
        Return False
    End If
End Function
```

This function uses a regular expression to validate the ICAO code passed as a parameter. In our sample code the actual validation rule is fictitious and checks only that the code contains four letters beginning with either E (for U.K. airfields) or K (for airfields in the U.S.). The regular expression pattern represents this check with three sections: `[ek]` matches only letters 'e' or 'k', `[a-z]` matches any alphabetic character, and the `{3}` signifies that the previous section (any alphabetic character) should be repeated three times. The additional parameter passed to the constructor indicates that the pattern match should be case-insensitive. Real-world checks would not be so simple and would probably require a lookup against a known list of codes.

Before accepting that the code entered by the user is valid and running the routine to retrieve the weather, we need to make a call to this function. We could do this within the `btnCheckWeather_Click` routine, but a better way is to add a CustomValidator control. Position the control below the existing validators and set its properties as indicated in Table 6-5:

Table 6-5. Mobile CustomValidator Properties

CONTROL	NAME	CONTROLTOVALIDATE	ERRORMESSAGE
CustomValidator	valCodeRecognized	txtICAOCode	Code not recognized

Add code to the `ServerValidate` event handler for the control as follows:

```
Private Sub valCodeRecognized_ServerValidate(ByVal source As System.Object, _
                ByVal args As System.Web.UI.WebControls.ServerValidateEventArgs) _
                Handles valCodeRecognized.ServerValidate
    If CheckICAOCode(txtICAOCode.Text) Then
```

```
        args.IsValid = True
    Else
        args.IsValid = False
    End If
End Sub
```

This routine calls the `CheckICAOCode` function and sets the `IsValid` property of the event argument accordingly. ASP.NET checks this value when it determines the value for `Page.IsValid`, and so the code that we have added will be automatically called during the page processing cycle.

If we build the solution and then browse using the Nokia SimApp (this time configured to emulate a Nokia 6210) it will appear as shown in Figure 6-10 once a code has been entered and checked.

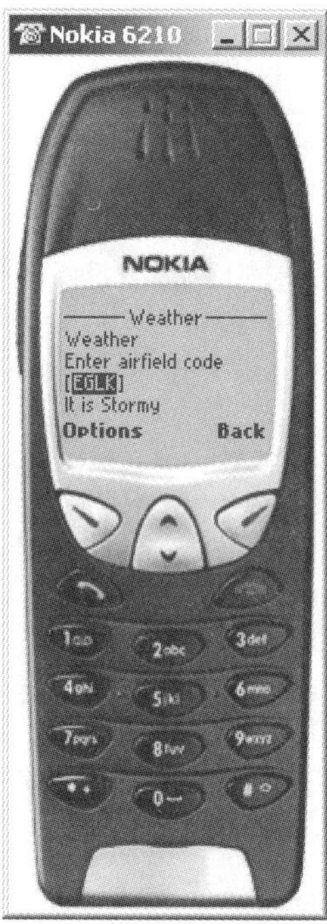

Figure 6-10. Retrieving weather information

If we enter an invalid ICAO code (such as **E2**) the validation controls do their job and display the validation error messages, as shown in Figure 6-11.

Figure 6-11. Validation failure

Although this is effective, it's not very pretty. The validation error messages are displayed alongside the other content, making it necessary to scroll down to see the cause of the failure. This type of display problem is very common on small-screen mobile devices, so much so that MMIT provides a simple way for you to display validation error messages in their own form.

To use this technique, add a new Mobile Form control to the bottom of the page and name it **frmICAOError**. Set its title to **ICAO Code Problem** and add a label with the same text. Add a ValidationSummary control below the label, and set its properties as indicated in Table 6-6:

Table 6-6. Mobile ValidationSummary Properties

CONTROL	NAME	FORMTOVALIDATE
ValidationSummary	valICAOCodeErrors	frmWeather

The validation summary will automatically display the error messages from each validator on frmWeather, and it will also display a Back link to allow the user to navigate back to the original page after the error messages have been displayed. However, it won't *automatically* display the validation summary in the event of an error; we must change the code in the btnCheckWeather_Click routine by setting Me.ActiveForm if the validation fails:

```
If Page.IsValid Then
    .
    .    'Original code here
    .
Else
    lblWeather.Text = ""
    Me.ActiveForm = frmICAOError   'Display the summary
End If
```

ActiveForm determines which form is displayed on a page and is the *only* code-based technique available for moving between forms. Note that you cannot use Response.Redirect or Server.Transfer for this purpose; they allow you to move to a different page, but *not* a different form within the same page.

The final change required for the Weather form is to set the Display property for each of the original validation controls to **None** to prevent the validation messages from being displayed in the original form. At this point you should test the application to ensure that the validation rules are still enforced, and that validation error messages are now displayed in a separate summary screen.

Implementing the News Form

The Weather form has illustrated a number of the different mobile controls and techniques available for mobile Web applications. We will build on this with the News form by looking at how we can use lists and data binding to easily retrieve information from a database and present it to the user.

The purpose of the News form is to allow customers to see up-to-the-minute news from the flying school. This could be used to inform customers of staff sickness, problems at the airfield, even traffic problems on nearby roads—anything, in fact, as long as its short enough to be read on a mobile device.

We'll use an interesting control called an ObjectList for this task. ObjectLists are data aware, which means they can be easily populated with database information and can represent multiple fields of data. The neat thing about the ObjectList, though, is that it renders itself with a drill-down capability, allowing your form to show a summary list of entries with each being a hyperlink to an automatically generated page containing the detail for the selected item. We'll see much more about database access, data-aware controls, and data binding in Chapters 7 and 8.

Start by adding the controls listed in Table 6-7 to the News form on the Default.aspx page, positioning them as shown in Figure 6-12.

Table 6-7. Mobile Controls for the News Form

CONTROL	NAME	TEXT	NAVIGATEURL	AUTOGENERATEFIELDS
Label	lblHeading2	News	N/A	N/A
ObjectList	objlstNews	N/A	N/A	False
Link	lnkBack2	Back	#frmMain	N/A

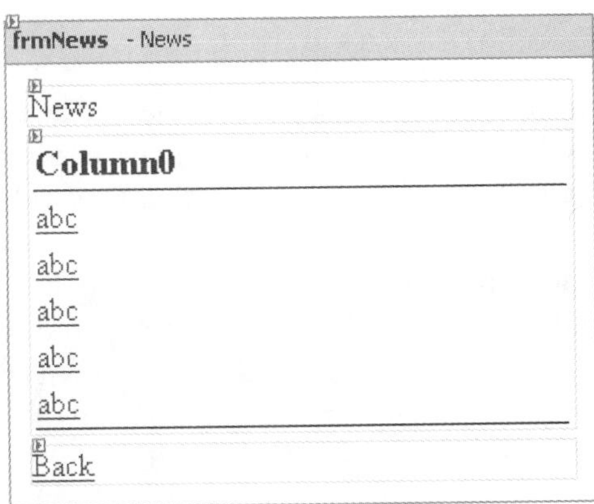

Figure 6-12. The News form

To populate the ObjectList, add the following code to the Page_Load event handler. Note that this code uses data access techniques that we will discuss more fully in Chapter 7:

```
If Page.IsPostBack = False Then
    Dim cn As New SqlClient.SqlConnection("Data Source=(local); " _
            + "Initial Catalog=HiFlyer;User ID=sa;Password=;")
    Dim cdNews As New SqlClient.SqlCommand("SELECT NewsTitle, NewsDetails " _
            + "FROM News WHERE NewsDate='" + DateTime.Today.ToShortDateString _
            + "'", cn)
    Dim dr As SqlClient.SqlDataReader
    Dim fld1 As New MobileControls.ObjectListField()
    Dim fld2 As New MobileControls.ObjectListField()

    fld1.DataField = "NewsTitle"
    fld2.DataField = "NewsDetails"
    With objlstNews
        .Fields.Add(fld1)
```

```
            .Fields.Add(fld2)
        End With

        cn.Open()
        dr = cdNews.ExecuteReader
        objlstNews.DataSource = dr
        objlstNews.DataBind()
        dr.Close()
        cn.Close()
    End If
```

This code starts by opening an SQLConnection to an SQL Server database and then creates an SQLCommand that retrieves news information relevant to the current day. The remainder of the prcoedure is concerned with using data binding to populate the ObjectList with this data. It creates two ObjectListField objects to represent the displayed data and adds them to the Fields collection of the ObjectList. We could have defined the fields through the Properties window, but you'll often find it clearer to establish such properties in code alongside the statements that retrieve the data. Having created the fields, the SQLCommand is executed and the results returned into an SQLDataReader. This is then bound to the ObjectList, which causes it to display the relevant data.

At runtime the ObjectList initially shows a summary of the database information, displaying only the first field (NewsTitle) in a single column list. Each entry in the list is a hyperlink that the user can select to display the full details for that entry. For example, Figure 6-13 shows how the form will appear when first viewed in the Microsoft Pocket PC Emulator.

Figure 6-13. Initial view of the News form

If we select the first link and choose **OK**, the browser displays the details for that entry—as shown in Figure 6-14.

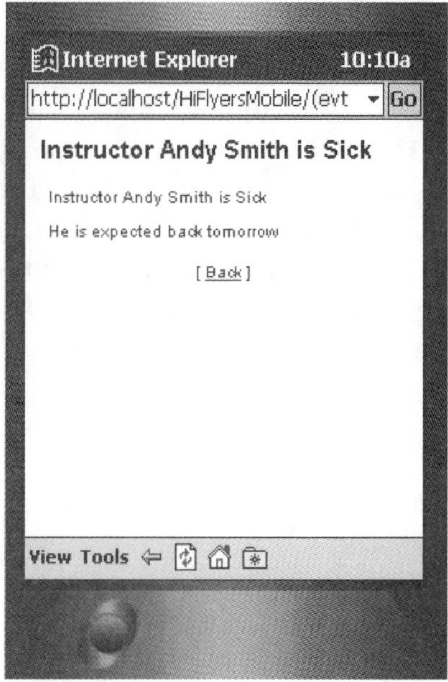

Figure 6-14. Drill-down view from the News form

The **Back** link returns us to the News form, from where we can select another News item or return to the main screen.

Implementing the Availability Form

The ObjectList control is useful when there is a sizeable amount of data to be displayed, but for smaller amounts you may want to use the simpler List control. We'll combine the List control with a PhoneCall control on the Availability form, so that we can allow users to check the availability of aircraft and then immediately call the flying school to make a booking.

To begin, add a Label, a List, a PhoneCall, and a Link to the form with the properties listed in Table 6-8.

Table 6-8. Mobile Controls for the Availability Form

CONTROL	NAME	TEXT	NAVIGATEURL
Label	lblHeading3	Availability	N/A
List	lstAvail	N/A	N/A
PhoneCall	calBookIt	Want to Book?	N/A
Link	lnkBack3	Back	#frmMain

Also, for the List control, set the DataTextField to **Registration**, and for the PhoneCall control, set **PhoneNumber** to your own phone number. You can also provide support for devices that do not have call capabilities by setting the AlternateFormat to **{0} Call {1}** and setting AlternateUrl to **http://www.hiflyers.org**. The AlternateFormat property defines the text used in place of the call control for devices that cannot make voice calls; the {0} is a placeholder for the Text property value, and the {1} is a placeholder for the PhoneNumber. These will be displayed as the text of a link that takes the user to the address specified by AlternateUrl. Having added and configured the controls, the page will appear as shown in Figure 6-15.

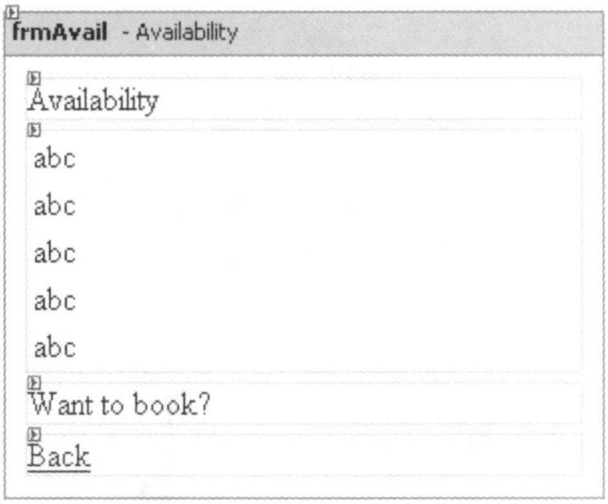

frmAvail - Availability

Availability

abc

abc

abc

abc

abc

Want to book?

Back

Figure 6-15. The Availability form

To populate the list, display the code for the `Page_Load` event handler and add the following declaration just after the existing SQLCommand object is declared:

```
Dim cdAvail As New SqlClient.SqlCommand("SELECT Registration FROM Aircraft " _
            + "WHERE AircraftID NOT IN (SELECT AircraftID FROM AircraftDiary " _
            + "WHERE DiaryDate='" + DateTime.Today.ToShortDateString + "')", cn)
```

Add the following code immediately before the existing `cn.Close` statement:

```
dr = cdAvail.ExecuteReader
lstAvail.DataSource = dr
lstAvail.DataBind()
dr.Close()
```

Build the project and browse to the form using an emulator for a call-capable device (such as the Microsoft Mobile Emulator). The text of the PhoneCall control acts as a hyperlink (as shown in Figure 6-16) which allows a simulated voice call to be initiated.

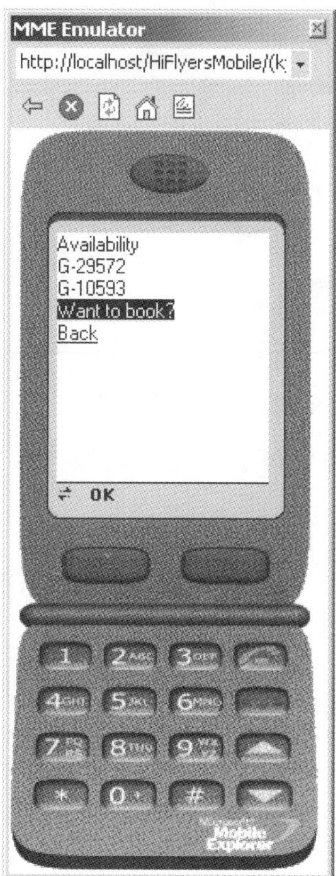

Figure 6-16. Viewing availability

If we browse the page using a device that is not call-capable—such as the Nokia SimApp configured as the Nokia Mobile Browser—the PhoneCall is rendered with its alternate format and acts as a hyperlink to the address specified in the AlternateUrl. Figure 6-17 shows this view.

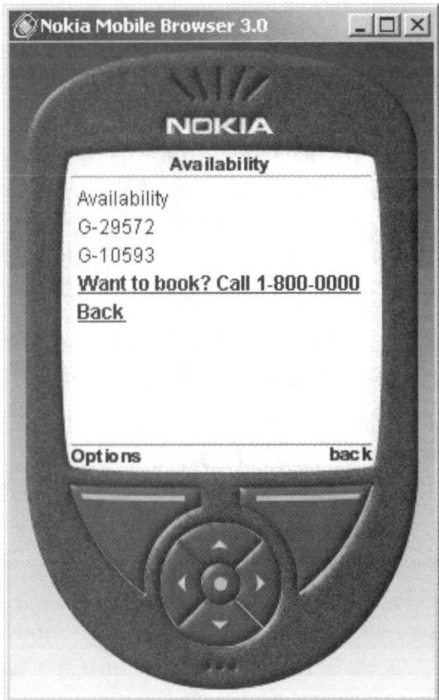

Figure 6-17. Availability view on a device with no call capability

Adding a Style Sheet

The final addition we'll make to our application is the definition of a style sheet. With mobile Web Forms, you cannot apply style sheets through traditional CSS files and Style elements, but instead you must add a *StyleSheet* control to the page. StyleSheet controls can be used in two ways:

- All of the styles can be defined within the StyleSheet control.
- The StyleSheet control can act as a reference to an external .ascx file containing the definition of the styles.

The second approach is much better suited to most applications because you will define the styles just once, but be able to use them on every mobile page. This really is the closest you'll get to using traditional CSS within mobile Web applications.

NOTE *We discussed .ascx files in Chapter 5 when we looked at creating and using Web User Controls and mentioned that, in some ways, .ascx files are similar to include files. This application of .ascx files reinforces this view, because we are using the .ascx to hold styles that can be included in multiple pages.*

To create a .ascx file to contain the style definitions, add a new Web User Control called MyStyles.ascx to the project. Select the HTML View tab from its designer and replace *all* of the current content with the following:

```
<%@ Control Inherits="System.Web.UI.MobileControls.MobileUserControl" %>
<%@ Register TagPrefix="mobile" Namespace="System.Web.UI.MobileControls"
                Assembly="System.Web.Mobile" %>
<mobile:StyleSheet id="StyleSheet1" runat="server">
  <mobile:Style Name="GenText" Font-Size="Small" Font-Name="Arial"></mobile:Style>
  <mobile:Style Name="PageHead" StyleReference="GenText" Font-Size="Large"
                Font-Bold="True"></mobile:Style>
</mobile:StyleSheet>
```

You should recognize the two directives at the top of the file from Chapter 5. The `@Control` directive specifies that this user control inherits from the *MobileUserControl* class as opposed to the normal *UserControl* class. The `@Register` directive defines the prefix used for referencing controls in the MobileControls namespace. Next comes the main `<mobile:StyleSheet>`element, which in turn contains `<mobile:Style>` elements that define each style.

The first style defined is called *GenText*, which simply specifies a font size of Small and a font name of Arial. The second style—*PageHead*—has a `StyleReference` attribute set so that it receives all of the attribute values of the named style (GenText). PageHead then provides an over-riding font size of Large and a font bold attribute.

Return to the Default.aspx page and add a StyleSheet control to the very bottom of the page, below the last Form control. StyleSheets are shared between all forms on a page, so cannot be placed within any single form. Set the control's ReferencePath property to MyStyles.ascx. You can now apply either of the defined styles to any of the controls on the page. For example, select each form in turn and set its StyleReference to GenText, and select each of the heading labels and set their StyleReference to PageHead.

NOTE *When you use a Web User Control to define an external style sheet, the development environment will not display the style names in the Properties window when you try to apply them to the page's controls. Instead, you must manually type in the style name, exactly as it was defined in the original* `<mobile:StyleSheet>` *element.*

Having taken great care to fine-tune the appearance of the application, you may be rather disappointed to find that many browsers and emulators completely ignore your styles and revert to their default formatting. Styles and StyleSheets are always treated as recommendations in the mobile world, and there is no way for you to guarantee that output is rendered in a particular format. For example, Figure 6-18 shows the Nokia SimApp configured to emulate a Nokia 7110 phone. You can see that it has ignored the formatting we defined and is showing both the headings and the link text in exactly the same font size and weight.

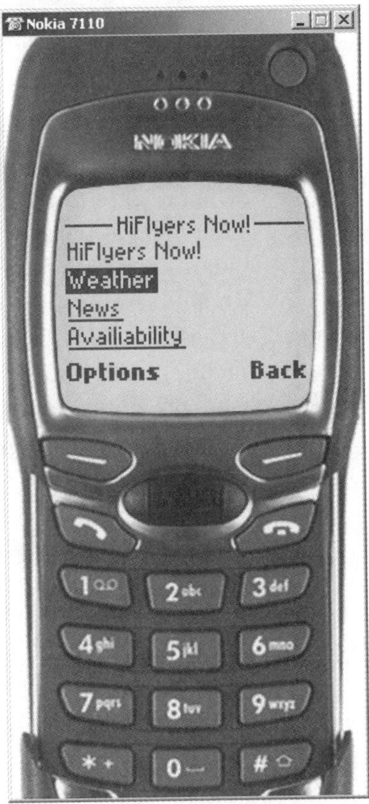

Figure 6-18. Ineffective styles in the Nokia SimApp

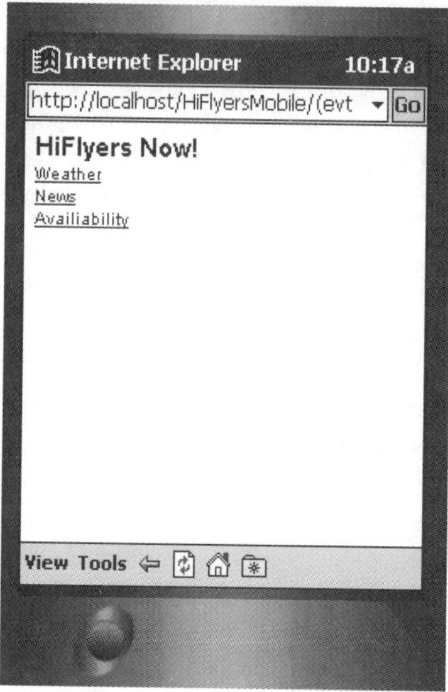

Figure 6-19. Effective styles rendered in Microsoft Pocket PC Emulator

If you browse the same application using Microsoft Pocket PC Emulator, you will see that the styles *are* used by the browser and so the headings and link items are formatted differently. Figure 6-19 shows how this will appear.

You should not think of these differences as being errors or faults in the emulators or devices. Mobile device standards don't call for every device to support styles and formatting, and so many manufacturers have chosen to focus on other aspects of their products instead. In the future, it is likely that more devices will support these features as the demand for rich user interfaces increases and begins to filter back to the research and development teams.

Default Styles

As well as any custom styles that you define, MMIT also provides three predefined styles that are always available: Error, Subcommand, and Title. They are automatically applied to certain controls (for example, validation controls automatically use the Error style), but you can also apply them to other elements by setting the control's StyleReference property to the name of the style.

Limitations, Problems, and Challenges

Throughout this chapter you've seen how a simple, but functional, user interface can be developed to target mobile devices. You've also seen some of the limitations facing mobile developers. Perhaps you've started to grasp the idea that although mobile development is conceptually similar to traditional Web application development, there's a whole new set of problems just waiting to trip you up. To conclude this chapter we will highlight some of the most significant challenges and provide some suggested solutions and alternatives. Some of the points raised here refer to ASP.NET capabilities that haven't been discussed yet, but are introduced in later chapters. We've decided to keep all of the mobile information together, however, so you may need to skip ahead if you want to dig into some of the specific details mentioned in the remainder of this chapter.

Standards

Standards for mobile devices are under constant review and development. At the time of writing, the MMIT supports the following standards:

- **HTML 3.2**, primarily for PDAs
- **WML 1.0/1.1**, for WAP phones and other devices
- **cHTML**, primarily for I-Mode phones that are popular in parts of Asia

As standards are revised and enhanced, MMIT can be updated by replacing or extending the device adapters discussed at the beginning of this chapter. Writing your own device adapters is no trivial task, but unless you're in a specialized environment or are working for a Telco or device manufacturer, the chances are that someone else will write them first.

Performance

Mobile communication performance is likely to be poor—even compared to the performance offered by modems to dial-up users. Many mobile devices are still constrained to transferring information at no more than 9.6 kbps, or at best 14.4 kbps, which means that you need to think long and hard about how much information you will move to the browser at any one time.

It really does make sense to move an absolute minimum of data around and rely on the browser making additional requests to obtain more information. Conversely, you probably don't want to send just one form at a time to the client because this would cause too many round-trips. So, the solution lies somewhere between these two extremes.

Among the many performance-related guidelines, the following are the more important:

- **Use multi-form pages intelligently.** They are most powerful when the browser is able to perform navigation without returning to the server—such as when you provide Link controls to navigate to other forms on the same page.
- **Graphics are performance-sapping.** If you must use graphics, choose the most compact form available, bearing in mind that the format may need to vary for different devices. The device capabilities section below discusses this in more depth.
- **Don't populate bound controls with large amounts of data.** There's no way a mobile user needs to see 1000 records at a time; 10 is probably all they need before they make another request against the server.
- **ViewState is used and supported in mobile Web applications in the same way as for regular Web applications.** With the limited bandwidth available for mobile devices, it is more important than ever to limit use of ViewState to essential controls only. This means you must set `EnableViewState` to **False** for controls that don't need to preserve their content across postbacks.
- **Don't rely on validation controls to help you out.** Mobile validation controls are always processed server-side, guaranteeing that a round-trip will be required.
- **If possible, use Links rather than server-side code for navigation.**

Device Capabilities

This is one of the most frustrating areas, since devices vary in almost every capability from whether they can support cookies to their screen sizes. MMIT allows you to detect device capabilities and adapt the behavior of your application accordingly, but you still have to do quite a lot of work to achieve this.

Among the key features for creating adaptive applications are the DeviceSpecific control, as well as the DeviceFilters and PropertyOverrides properties. This topic is an immense one and worthy of a book in its own right, so we won't even start to get into the detail of how to do this. However, you should remember that it's possible to customize output to suit specific devices and capabilities and that the MMIT contains a number of samples and much documentation on the topic.

Script Support

It might seem obvious to many readers, but there's no consistent support for scripting technologies among mobile devices. The safest option is to assume that client devices do not support script, but this may lead you to build applications that potentially make more round-trips than they need to.

Cookie Support

Cookie support is also inconsistent across devices and is further complicated by two external factors:

- Some national governments have banned the use of cookies within their country.
- Some gateway services, service providers, and telephone companies strip cookies or block communication containing cookies.

Of course, there is varying cookie support from browsers for regular Web applications, but it seems to be more of a problem in the mobile environment. The best solution is probably the one used by MMIT itself: Don't use cookies. If you examine the address bar of a mobile device or emulator while you are browsing, you will see that it contains an odd-looking string of characters, similar to the following:

```
http://localhost/HiFlyersMobile/(yuosuv55jk1f5urmrrhj52bl)/Default.aspx
```

The strange sequence is inserted by MMIT to represent the user's session ID so that it can track session state for them. Usually, this would be stored in a cookie, but MMIT makes the assumption that cookies are unavailable and so combines the ID into the URL. We'll see more about the use of cookieless session state for regular Web applications in Chapter 12.

Tracing

Tracing is the process of recording information about the progress and path taken during the processing of a Web request. In regular Web applications, trace information can be written to the Web page itself and viewed in the browser along with the normal page content. In mobile Web applications, you *must not* do this because it may cause the client browser to fail, or even freeze.

The solution is to use application-level tracing, where the trace data is accessed through a separate URL from the rest of the application. When tracing a mobile application, you would use a regular desktop browser to view the trace logs. Chapter 10 discusses page- and application-level tracing.

Navigation

There are some interesting problems that arise on the topic of navigation:

Response.Redirect

Not all mobile devices support the use of relative URLs for navigation and redirection; however, you'll find it is unrealistic to manually code all URLs in absolute notation because it makes the application very difficult to build and manage. Fortunately, MMIT can perform the relative to absolute translation for you, but you must configure Web.config by adding the `useFullyQualifiedRedirectUrl` attribute with a value of **true**, as shown below:

```
<configuration>
    <system.web>
        <httpRuntime useFullyQualifiedRedirectUrl="true" />
    </system.web>
</configuration>
```

Without this setting, devices which do not support relative URLs will be unable to maintain session state and will have difficulties when navigating.

Server.Transfer

If you're a classic ASP developer, you may prefer the Server.Transfer method over Response.Redirect anyway. Server.Transfer performs a server-side redirection so that the browser is unaware of the fact that the URL has changed. Unfortunately, this causes problems for some mobile applications; for example, if you have a form on Page1.aspx containing code that performs a Server.Transfer to Page2.aspx, when the user submits the form on Page2, the data is actually sent back to Page1!

If you encounter this problem you may want to revert back to using Response.Redirect.

Linking to a Non-Default Form

When you navigate to a mobile Web page, it will always display the first form on the page in the client device. If you want to be able to navigate directly to a different form, you'll need to code your own mechanism to do so.

A simple way to do this is to add some code to the `Page_Load` event handler that checks a querystring value:

```
Select Case Request.QueryString("FormName")
    Case "Main"
        ActiveForm = frmMain
    Case "Weather"
        ActiveForm = frmWeather
    Case "News"
        ActiveForm = frmNews
    Case "Avail"
        ActiveForm = frmAvail
End Select
```

Anytime you need to navigate to this page and display a specific form, the navigation URL will be similar to:

```
Default.aspx?FormName=Weather
```

Summary

In this chapter we have shown you how to start building mobile Web applications using the Microsoft Mobile Internet Toolkit. In principle, it is a very similar process to building regular Web applications; however, on a detailed level, there are some real differences and you will encounter some serious challenges.

Many of these difficulties stem from the devices themselves, and just as regular Web developers often have to make a decision to support only specific browsers, developers of mobile Web applications may need to limit support to a specific set of known devices. As it is shipped, the MMIT Framework does offer good support for quite a variety of devices, and it also allows you to define device-specific behaviors within your application. If you do decide to build public-access mobile Web applications, this is certainly a topic you will need to research further.

CHAPTER 7

Working with Databases

Reading a Single Row

Reading Multiple Rows

Performing Updates

Using Stored Procedures

Working with DataSets

Updating DataSets

DATABASES ARE THE WORKHORSES that power almost every commercial Web site. They can also become a bottleneck on Web-based applications unless the databases are well designed and the programs that use them are carefully written. It's not our purpose to address database design issues in this book. Our focus is how best to write the code for Web Applications that use databases and how to approach the design of data-driven Web pages. If you're completely new to ADO.NET, then we strongly recommend you temporarily part company from this chapter, and read Appendix D. This appendix explains the key features of ADO.NET and presents "starter" code that shows and explains some of the basic ADO.NET tasks. It also explains some important concepts, such as the difference between connected and disconnected data manipulation. If you already know your DataReaders from your DataTables, then read on. We'll be working exclusively with the HiFlyers database, an overview of which was presented in the Introduction. It's not a complex database, but it helps if you're familiar with its tables and relationships.

Although ADO.NET is similar in name to the "classic" ADO used in Visual Basic 6.0 and VBScript programs (and as Appendix D explains, the ideas behind ADO.NET are actually not that different from some of the more advanced ideas in classic ADO), you'll immediately notice that ADO.NET code looks different from classic ADO code in a number of ways. There are new objects and methods to learn about, and some features that you may have relied on in the past have been removed. You may be tempted to ask if you should continue to use classic

ADO for data access within your ASP.NET Web Forms, and thereby avoid learning new stuff for the sake of it. You can indeed use familiar ADO programming techniques, simply by setting a reference to the existing COM libraries that contain the classic ADO objects. However, there are two reasons why we advise against doing this. Firstly, although it's easy to make calls between .NET code and COM code (which includes calling classic ADO objects), there is a performance overhead involved. Your programs will never be as efficient as they would be if you used pure .NET classes. Secondly, Microsoft hasn't removed features from ADO.NET out of spite. In fact, one of the most impressive aspects of ADO.NET is that its designers have been bold enough to remove features that may be popular but don't work well in applications designed to support a large number of users. Therefore, you can console yourself that most of the changes in ADO.NET actually make it easier to apply best practice for database programming. There may be some pain, but there will also be some gain.

ADO.NET splits into two distinct sets of functionality, these being the DataSet and its related objects, which provide a rich set of features for disconnected data access, and the .NET Data Providers, designed for use while connected to a data source. Although the DataSet object model has received most of the attention, it so happens that its role in Web Forms is fairly specialized, so we'll begin by discussing *connected* data access using the .NET Data Provider objects, and return to DataSets later.

Figure 7-1 shows a simple Web Form that we'll construct to explore connected data programming using ADO.NET. This is a purely functional user interface, which might be used by an employee of HiFlyer's Flying Club to call up and manipulate information about a particular member. We're concentrating entirely on the programming aspects of working with databases in this chapter, so don't expect any pretty user interfaces until Chapter 8!

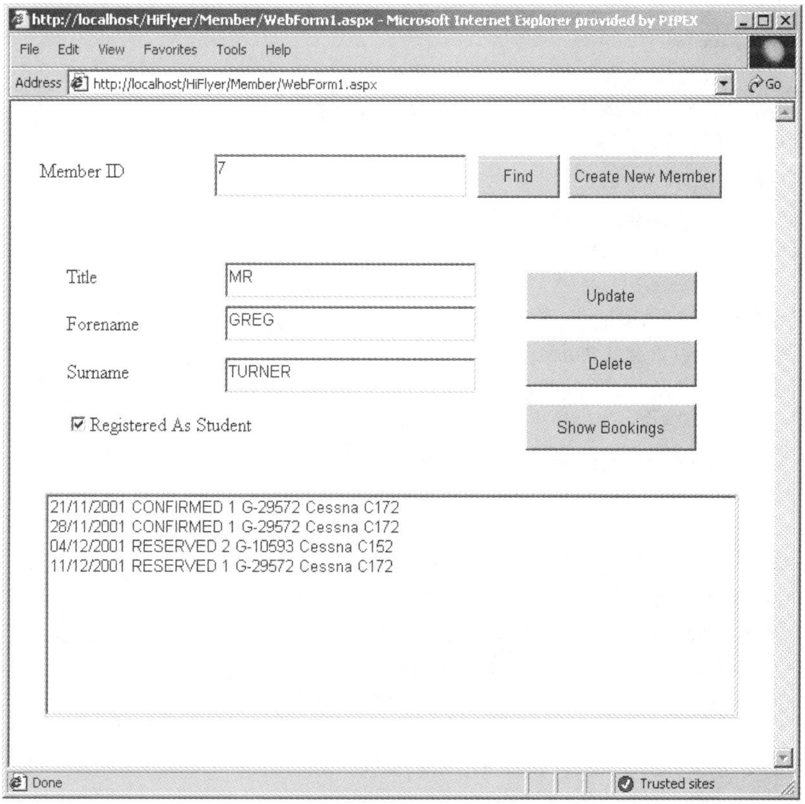

Figure 7-1. A simple member admin form

Reading a Single Row

A user of the Web Form shown in Figure 7-1 enters a Member ID, and hits the Find button to retrieve the Title, Forename, Surname, and IsStudent values for the specified member. This is about as simple a data retrieval task as anyone could be asked to do, so let's take a look at how to perform it. We'll be using the SQL .NET Data Provider in this chapter, which is the recommended provider for SQL Server 7.0 or later. For other databases, the ODBC .NET Data Provider will typically be the best choice, unless you have access to a specific provider for your database. Regardless of which .NET Data Provider you choose to use, you'll need to get used to importing the appropriate namespace for your provider. All the code samples in this chapter will assume you imported the SqlClient namespace (which refers to the SQL .NET Data Provider) by adding the following statement at the top of each code window:

```
Imports System.Data.SqlClient
```

Listing 7-1 shows some code you could place in the event handler for the Find button's click event.

Listing 7-1. Retrieving the Details for a Specific Member

```
Dim MemberID As String = txtID.Text
Dim dr As SqlDataReader
Dim cn As New SqlConnection()
Dim cd As New SqlCommand()
Try
    cn.ConnectionString = "Data Source=localhost;" + _
        "Integrated Security=SSPI;Initial Catalog=HiFlyer;"
    cd.Connection = cn
    cd.CommandText = "select Title, ForeName, Surname,IsStudent " + _
        "from Member where MemberID = " + MemberID
    cn.Open()
    dr = cd.ExecuteReader()
    dr.Read()
    txtTitle.Text = dr("Title").ToString
    txtForeName.Text = dr("ForeName").ToString
    txtSurName.Text = dr("Surname").ToString
    chkStudent.Checked = CType(dr("IsStudent"), Boolean)
Catch
    lblError.Text = "Unable to find details for Member " + MemberID
    lblError.Visible = True
Finally
   If Not dr Is Nothing Then dr.Close()
   cn.Close()
End Try
```

Note that Listing 7-1 uses integrated security instead of including a user ID and password in the connection string. Appendix D explains how to configure either SQL Server or ASP.NET to make integrated security work.

Listing 7-1 shows an SqlCommand object called `cd` being executed to return an SqlDataReader called `dr`. The SqlCommand searches for a row based on a MemberID that has been typed into a TextBox called `txtID`, whose text is assigned to a string called `MemberID` in the first line of code. If the command executes successfully, the SqlDataReader assigns data to various Web Form controls. Notice that `dr.Read` is called to get access to the first (and only) row returned by the query. If you're a classic ADO programmer, this is a change you'll have to get used to because a DataReader does not automatically refer to the first row; you need to remember to call `Read` first.

If an exception occurs, the `Catch` block provides belt-and-braces error handling by writing a simple text message to the Web Form via a Label control.

Whether or not an exception occurs, the `Finally` block makes sure that no external resources created for the operation are left hanging around.

It's impossible to overemphasize the importance of explicitly closing unwanted DataReader and Connection objects as soon as you've finished with them. This is another big difference from classic ADO. In ADO.NET, you have no idea when the garbage collector will get around to tidying up unwanted objects, so you have no option but to take control and close each DataReader and Connection object you open. Bear in mind that there is usually no cost in repeatedly opening and closing connections because (as explained in Appendix D) connection pooling works automatically with ADO.NET.

A convenient way to correctly release all unwanted resources is to use a `Finally` block, as shown in Listing 7-1. You won't get an error if you call `Close` on an already closed (or an unopened) DataReader or Connection, so the code in the `Finally` block does not need to test whether these objects are open. The only test required is to make sure that the DataReader object actually exists before attempting to call a method on it.

What you've seen so far is perfectly decent code for retrieving one row from a database, but it's worth exploring a couple of alternatives. The `ExecuteReader` method on Command objects is overloaded and can be called either with no argument (as previously), or with one argument, which must be a value from the CommandBehavior enumeration. You can use CommandBehavior values to control how the `ExecuteReader` method behaves. There are several options available, but for our purposes, two in particular are worth exploring.

When you know you're requesting a single row, you can use the `SingleRow` option when executing the Command:

```
dr = cd.ExecuteReader(CommandBehavior.SingleRow)
```

.NET Data Providers can use this information to optimize the way they request the data. Don't expect earth-shattering improvements, but at the same time, performance enhancements that are easily achieved are worth having.

An alternative option to using SingleRow is the `CloseConnection` option:

```
dr = cd.ExecuteReader(CommandBehavior.CloseConnection)
```

Using CloseConnection ensures that the Connection used by the Command that generated the DataReader will automatically be closed when the DataReader is closed. On first sight, this sounds like a neat way to make sure you don't forget to close the Connection after closing the DataReader, while at the same time, saving a line of code. However, it makes no sense to use this option if you handle exceptions in the manner of Listing 7-1. Because an exception might occur before the DataReader object is created, this code cannot rely on calling the DataReader's `Close` method, and therefore the Connection's `Close` must also be called explicitly. There is therefore no benefit to be gained from using the CloseConnection option. Of course, if you use a different scheme for handling exceptions, then this particular option may be of use to you.

Using Visual Programming

One of the most interesting new features of Visual Studio is the approach it has taken to providing graphical tools to make data programming easier. In the past, "visual" data programming techniques (whether in the form of Data Controls or the Visual Basic 6.0 DataEnvironment) have always presented developers with something of a dilemma. Although such features can definitely reduce the lines of code needed to create certain types of functionality, they do so at the expense of taking control away from the developer, making it hard to achieve specific results or difficult to intervene when things go wrong.

Visual Studio .NET provides easy-to-use, drag-and-drop tools for building data access functionality, but it does so by generating code that you're then free to use, analyze, and edit to your heart's content. The net result of this code-generation approach is simplified development with no loss of control.

To see what these features look like, let's redevelop the functionality of the member Find button, using the visual approach.

In Figure 7-2 you can see the Design View of the Members Form, with the Data section of the Toolbox also showing. Two objects have been dragged onto the Web Form designer. These are an SqlConnection that has been renamed `cn` and an SqlCommand object that has been renamed `cdGetMember`. Using the Properties box to edit `cn`'s `ConnectionString` displays the Data Link Properties window familiar from pre-.NET days, as shown in Figure 7-3.

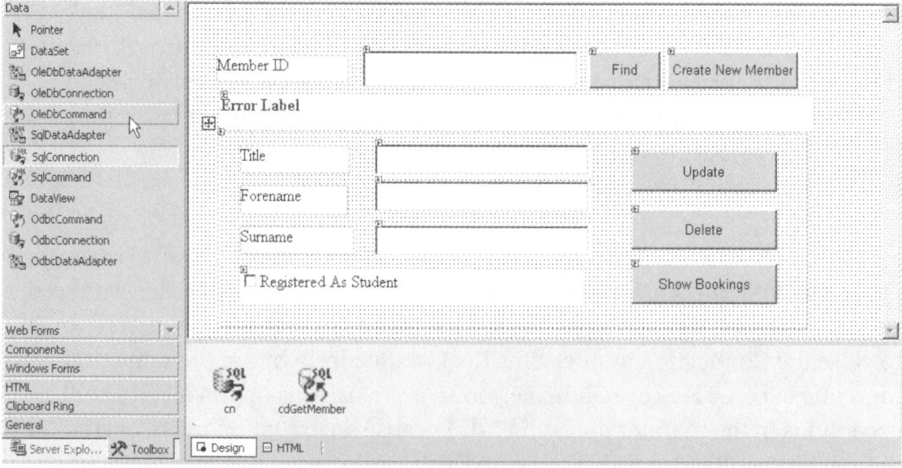

Figure 7-2. Using Visual Studio .NET's data features

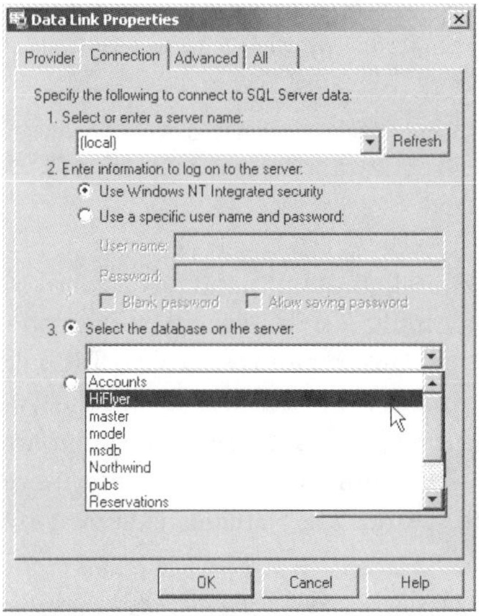

Figure 7-3. Building a Connection string

The interesting part of all this is what Visual Studio .NET does when you click the OK button. You can see exactly what it does when you open the code window. In the declarations section at the top of the code window, Visual Studio .NET has added this:

```
Protected WithEvents cn As System.Data.SqlClient.SqlConnection
```

If you then expand the region in the code window called Web Form Designer Generated Code you'll also see that the following code has been automatically generated:

```
Me.cn = New System.Data.SqlClient.SqlConnection()
Me.cn.ConnectionString = "data source=(local);initial catalog=HiFlyer; " & _
    " integrated security=SSPI;persist security info=False;workstation " & _
    " id=ERMINE;packet size=4096"
```

In other words, all the fiddly connection string code has been built for you. At this point you could choose to go no further with visual programming. You could just start using the `cn` variable in your otherwise normal .NET code, and you would find it hard to admit that visual programming wasn't of some use. Let's be brave, however, and see what happens when we start working with the `cdGetMember` object that we also dragged onto the designer. This enables us to explore visual programming with Command objects. Using the Properties box, the first step is to set cd.GetMember's connection to be cn. At this point, the following code will have been automatically added to the code window:

```
Protected WithEvents cdGetMember As System.Data.SqlClient.SqlCommand
Me.cdGetMember = New System.Data.SqlClient.SqlCommand()
Me.cdGetMember.Connection = Me.cn
```

We still need to generate the command text for the cdGetMember Command object. Once again, you could decide just to type this code in, but alternatively, you might like to get the SQL built for you as well. If so, click on the CommandText property in the Properties box and use it to display the Query Builder. A dialog box opens that enables you to select one or more tables from your database that will be used to create the command text. In our case, we've selected the Member table, which gets added to the Query Builder, as shown in Figure 7-4.

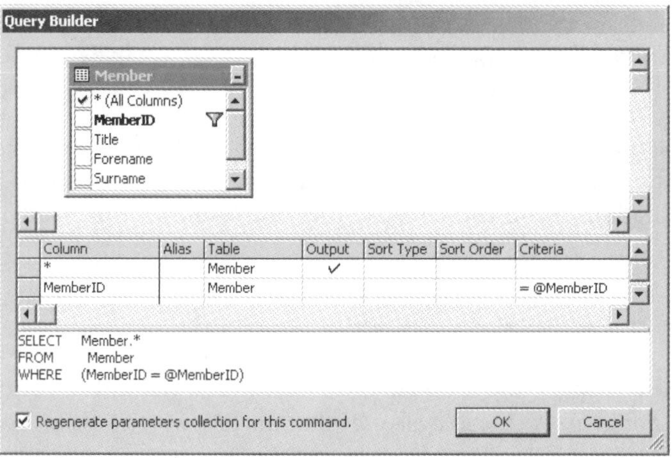

Figure 7-4. Building a Command string

Here you can see the use of the Query Builder to specify a query that returns all columns from the Member table, subject to the criterion that the MemberID must match the value of a Parameter called @MemberID. It is likely you've seen the Query Builder in action before, but it's less likely you've seen it used to generate .NET code. Here's what Visual Studio generates when you click **OK**:

```
Me.cdGetMember.CommandText = "SELECT Member.* FROM Member WHERE " & _
    " (MemberID = @MemberID)"
Me.cdGetMember.Parameters.Add( _
    New System.Data.SqlClient.SqlParameter("@MemberID", _
        System.Data.SqlDbType.Int, 4, "MemberID"))
```

If you want to know what every part of this code does, you'll need to read up on ADO.NET Parameters. For our purposes, it's enough to know that Visual Studio .NET has generated the `CommandText` property for `cdGetMember`, based on an input parameter called `@MemberID`. Visual Studio.NET has also generated code that adds a parameter to `cdGetMember`'s Parameter collection. You can see that this is a parameter called `@MemberID` whose data type is Integer (or, specifically, SqlDbType.Int).

Remember that all of this code (apart from the variable declarations) is stored in a usually hidden region with your code window. More often than not, you don't even need to know about it. So let's forget about the generated code for a moment and take a look at the code we need to write in order to program the Find button's functionality (see Listing 7-2).

Listing 7-2. Retrieving Details for a Specific Member Using Visually Generated Objects

```
Dim MemberID As String = txtID.Text
Dim dr As SqlDataReader
Try
    cdGetMember.Parameters("@MemberID").Value = CInt(MemberID)
    cn.Open()
    dr = cdGetMember.ExecuteReader(CommandBehavior.SingleResult)
    dr.Read()
    txtTitle.Text = dr("Title").ToString
    txtForeName.Text = dr("ForeName").ToString
    txtSurName.Text = dr("Surname").ToString
    chkStudent.Checked = CType(dr("IsStudent"), Boolean)
Catch
    lblError.Text = "Unable to find details for Member " + MemberID
    lblError.Visible = True
Finally
    If Not dr Is Nothing Then dr.Close()
    cn.Close()
End Try
```

There's no need to declare or initialize Connection or Command objects. The only initialization task is to set the value of the `@MemberID` parameter. The result of using visual programming is cleaner code that is easier to put together. Because you can see the source behind the objects if you want, there's no need to worry about "behind-the-scenes" tricks that might affect performance because you can go look and see what the code does. And if you don't like what you see, you can copy it out of the designer-managed code region and edit it your way.

We'll continue to use the visual approach in the following sections, but we're not saying this is the only way to use ADO.NET. If you prefer typing in your own connection and SQL strings, don't be switched off from reading on because most of what follows applies regardless of which approach you favor.

Reading Multiple Rows

Reading multiple rows returned by a database is not so different from reading a single row. The main differences are the need to loop through the result set and some extra performance issues that become worth considering when reading a large set of results. In this section, we'll load data into a ListBox. This is a good way of exploring ADO.NET functionality, but in most cases you're more likely to use data binding techniques to create a display that is more appropriate for a Web page. You'll see how to do this in Chapter 8.

We'll explore multiple row processing by adding functionality that displays the bookings for the selected member. A Command object called `cdShowBookings` has been created to retrieve this data, and Figure 7-5 shows how this Command has been set up using the Query Builder.

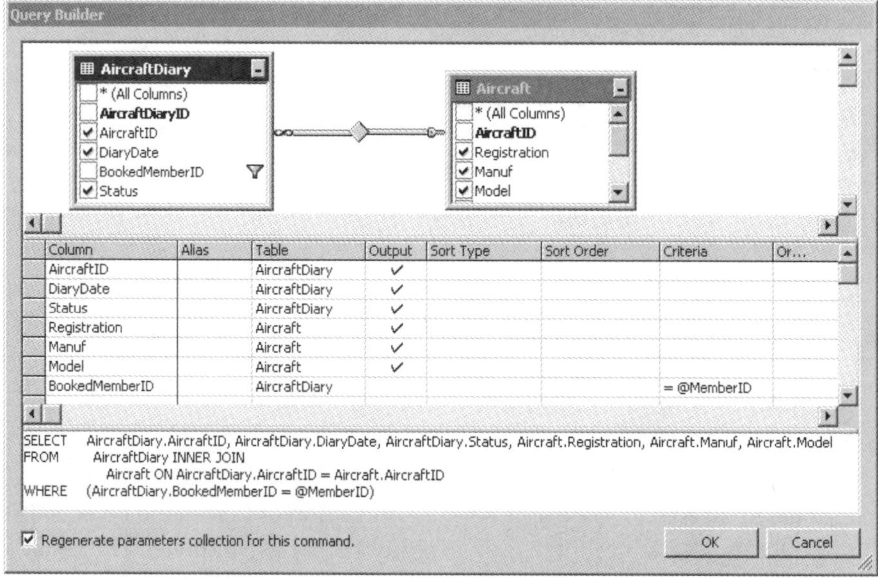

Figure 7-5. Building a Command string based on a two-table join

This query is a two-table join, based on the AircraftDiary and Aircraft tables. The AircraftDiary table contains a column called BookedMemberID that is used as an input parameter to select only those rows that match a specified

MemberID. Once this Command has been constructed, using it is a straightforward process. Listing 7-3 shows the code for the ShowBookings button.

Listing 7-3. Retrieving Multiple Rows of Member Details

```
Dim MemberID As String = txtID.Text
Dim dr As SqlDataReader
Dim Booking As String
Const AIRCRAFTID_COL As Integer = 0
Const DIARYDATE_COL As Integer = 1
Const STATUS_COL As Integer = 2
Const REGISTRATION_COL As Integer = 3
Const MANUF_COL As Integer = 4
Const MODEL_COL As Integer = 5
Try
    cdShowBookings.Parameters("@MemberID").Value = CInt(MemberID)
    cn.Open()
    dr = cdShowBookings.ExecuteReader()
    lstBookings.Items.Clear()
    While dr.Read()
        Booking = dr.GetDateTime(DIARYDATE_COL).ToShortDateString + " "
        Booking += dr.GetString(STATUS_COL) + " "
        Booking += dr.GetInt32(AIRCRAFTID_COL).ToString() + " "
        Booking += dr.GetString(REGISTRATION_COL) + " "
        Booking += dr.GetString(MANUF_COL) + " "
        Booking += dr.GetString(MODEL_COL) + " "
        lstBookings.Items.Add(Booking)
    End While
Catch ex As Exception
    lblError.Text = "Unable to find details for Member " + MemberID
    lblError.Visible = True
Finally
    If Not dr Is Nothing Then dr.Close()
    cn.Close()
End Try
```

Listing 7-3 uses a `While` loop to read each row returned by executing the `cdShowBookings` command. For each row, a string called `Booking` is constructed, which is then added to the `lstBookings` ListBox. The exception handling and `Finally` code are just as before.

What is different is the way you access the individual columns from the DataReader. Of course, it would be perfectly legal to access the Status column using code such as this:

```
Booking += dr("Status") + " "
```

However, this is less efficient than the technique actually used, where each value is accessed by a strongly typed method and the columns are identified by ordinal position rather than by name. You're not going to notice the difference when accessing a few dozen rows from a lightly used Web site, so don't feel that this more code-intensive approach is always justified. However, where performance is tight, the extra effort makes sense, and we often use the strongly typed access methods when writing code that loops through multiple rows. When doing so, it also makes sense to create constants for each column, just to keep the readability of the code high. In fact, the strongly typed access methods are also an aid to readability, as they communicate clearly the data type of the column being accessed.

Figure 7-6 shows the output of the code. It was never intended to be pretty!

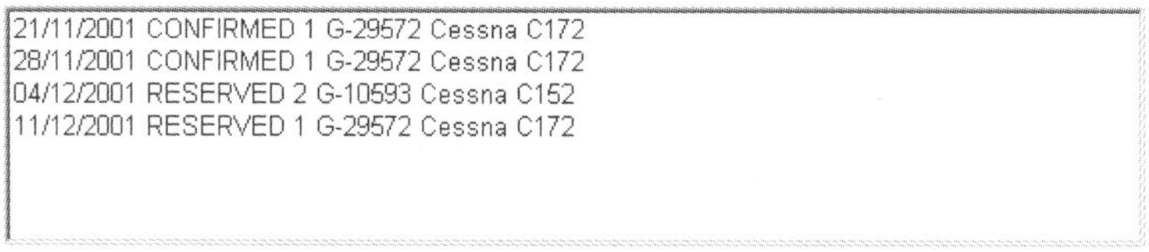

```
21/11/2001 CONFIRMED 1 G-29572 Cessna C172
28/11/2001 CONFIRMED 1 G-29572 Cessna C172
04/12/2001 RESERVED 2 G-10593 Cessna C152
11/12/2001 RESERVED 1 G-29572 Cessna C172
```

Figure 7-6. A ListBox showing multiple rows

We've now said most of what needs to be said about processing multiple rows. This may come as a shock if you were expecting to learn about scrolling, cursor and lock types, and how to perform updates when using a DataReader. The reason there is nothing to say on these topics is that these concepts don't make sense in ADO.NET. When working with a DataReader, the only way of moving between rows is by calling `Read`, which always gives you the next row if there is one, or returns `False` otherwise. As you'll see later, DataSets provide random access to rows, but only after all the data has been read into the DataSet and the database connection has been released.

Providing full scrolling functionality through methods such as `MoveLast` and `MovePrevious` makes sense in some classic ADO programs where the user has the opportunity to interact directly with objects that represent the data. However, in Web Applications, the user is interacting with a browser and HTML, and the data objects that created the HTML will have been destroyed before the user even gets to see the data. When most of your code is about processing data to generate HTML, the need for features such as `MoveLast` and `MovePrevious` is much reduced, and because such features can be inefficient and complex to support, .NET Data Providers don't offer them.

There's also no way to write changes to a database using a DataReader. Does this mean that ADO.NET is read-only? No, it just means the only way of changing a database is by using Command objects that execute update SQL or stored procedures. You'll see how to do this in the next section.

Performing Updates

As you've seen, retrieving data from a database is largely a matter of building Command objects, supplying parameter values, and processing the results. Writing changes back to a database is a surprisingly similar process. We'll begin with the simplest situation—where you don't care too much if some other user is working with the same data at the same time.

The Members Web Form has an update button that will take any changes made by the user and write those changes back to the database. The process is made easier by using a Command object called `cdUpdateMember` created using the Query Builder, as shown in Figure 7-7.

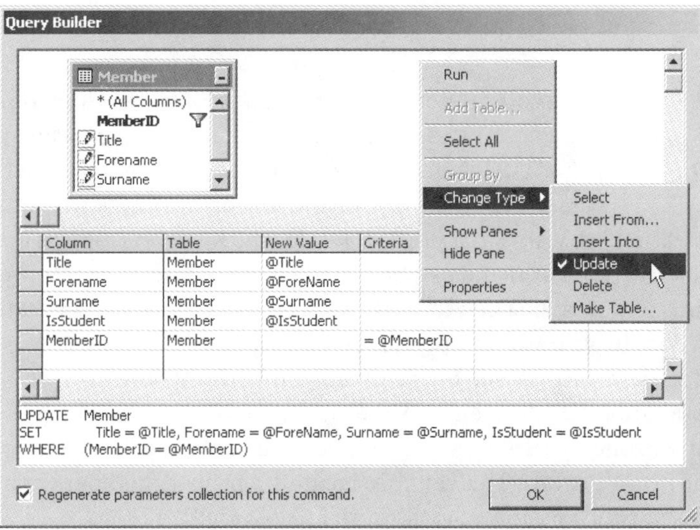

Figure 7-7. Building a Command to update the Members table

Note that you use the Change Type menu option to specify that this should be an update command. The Query Builder then automatically generates update SQL logic. (It will behave appropriately for insert and delete logic too). `cdUpdateMember` uses parameters to control not just the `WHERE` clause, but also to supply the new values that the command will write to the database for the specified row.

Because so much of the code for the Update button is auto-generated, the actual code required behind the button is amazingly simple (see Listing 7-4).

Listing 7-4. A Database Update

```
Dim MemberID As String = txtID.Text
Try
    With cdUpdateMember.Parameters
        .Item("@MemberID").Value = MemberID
        .Item("@Title").Value = txtTitle.Text
        .Item("@ForeName").Value = txtForeName.Text
        .Item("@SurName").Value = txtSurName.Text
        .Item("@IsStudent").Value = CInt(chkStudent.Checked)
    End With
    cn.Open()
    cdUpdateMember.ExecuteNonQuery()
Catch
    lblError.Text = "Unable to perform update for Member " + MemberID
    lblError.Visible = True
Finally
    cn.Close()
End Try
```

The whole process requires nothing more than setting the required parameter values, opening the connection, executing the command, and closing the connection. There is no DataReader required, and therefore it makes sense to use the `ExecuteNonQuery` method on the Command object to execute the command.

In this particular design, the primary key for the Members table is actually displayed on the Web Form and can be edited by the user to select new rows. Although this removes the need to store the primary key in some separate location, it does leave the door open for certain types of error. For example, the user could retrieve a row based on a certain MemberID. If they then change the MemberID and then click the Update button, this has the effect of updating the wrong row. To overcome this, we can easily use the `TextChanged` event of the `txtID` TextBox. This requires creating a private member variable for this Web Form, which we may choose to call `IDModified`:

```
Private IDModified As Boolean = False
```

We can then code the `TextChanged` event of `txtID` as follows:

```
Private Sub txtID_TextChanged(. . .) Handles txtID.TextChanged
    IDModified = True
End Sub
```

You can then add the following code to the Update button's handler, before the existing code:

```
If IDModified Then
    lblError.Text = "Unable to perform update when MemberID has been modified"
    lblError.Visible = True
    Exit Sub
End If
```

Of course, it would make sense to ensure the user can't click Update again until they've clicked the Find button to retrieve the correct details for whichever MemberID happens to be in the `txtID` TextBox, which you could achieve by hiding the Update button.

It's easy to think that the stateless nature of Web Forms makes them more difficult to program than the "rich-client" forms traditionally developed by Visual Basic programmers. Sometimes, the stateless approach is actually easier, and the previous example illustrates this nicely—we can rely on the fact that a new Web Form object will be created for each round-trip from the browser, and therefore `IDModified` will always be `False` unless the `txtID.TextChanged` event fires.

Dealing with Concurrency

We've added fully functioning update capability to our Web Form, but we've made one huge assumption. We've assumed either that our application only ever has one user or that we don't care if some other user makes changes to the data we're using.

Imagine our application was dealing with member's accounts with the Flying Club and two separate users happen to be inputting changes for the same member (called Jill). As Figure 7-8 shows, both users read the current balance for the member. User 2 has just received a big check from Jill and so updates her account to $1,100 and clicks the Save button. User 1 is adding a $50 refund to Jill's balance. He adds $50 to the balance he sees and clicks the Save button, which writes $150 to the database, overwriting User 2's update. Sometime soon, Jill will have a bad day.

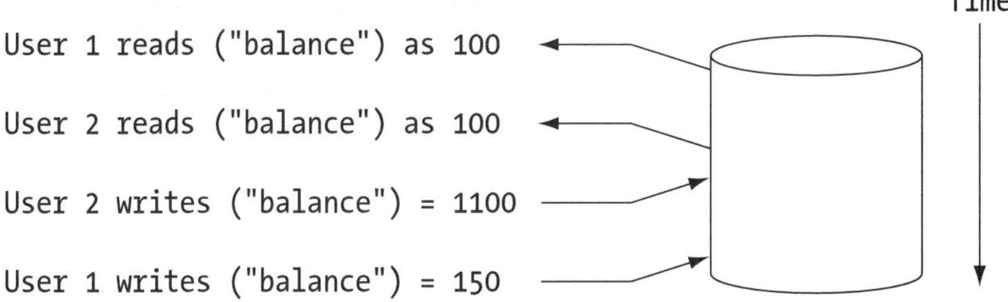

Figure 7-8. The need for concurrency management

Clearly, there are times when you need to make sure that the data you're changing has not itself been changed since you last retrieved it from the database. One approach is to reread the data. This won't necessarily solve the problem (unless you use a transaction) because there will still be a gap between this second read operation and any update you perform. It's also an expensive approach because it always requires reading the database twice.

An alternative approach is to make sure the database update uses a more selective WHERE clause. For example, in the previous member's account scenario, a pseudo-SQL update statement for User 1 would have been something like this:

```
UPDATE Accounts
    SET balance = 150
    WHERE member = 'Jill'
```

Now, if instead, the SQL was more like this:

```
UPDATE Accounts
    SET balance = 150
    WHERE member = 'Jill'
    AND balance = 100
```

then the problem of overwriting User 2's update would never have occurred because there would be no row in the database matching this WHERE clause after User 2 changed the member's balance. The update would fail, and all you would need to do is to report to User 1 that the update failed and that they must refetch the data.

You'll see later that ADO.NET actually generates SQL rather like this when performing updates using DataSets. Even when you're not using DataSets, you can borrow the same approach to provide concurrency control in the Update button on the Members Web Form.

There are two parts to the task of adding concurrency management to a query using the WHERE clause model. First, you need to add criteria to the query that enables you to supply all the original values (those that were read from the database) to the WHERE clause when performing the update. Figure 7-9 shows what this looks like in the Query Builder for the update behind the Update button. It helps to use a standard naming convention when creating these parameter names.

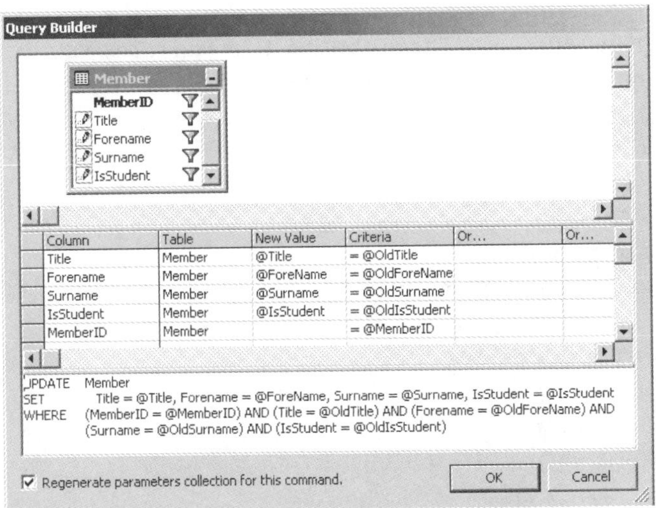

Figure 7-9. Adding concurrency management to a query

The second task is to supply the old/original values when calling the update. This is slightly more complex because you need somewhere to store the old values. Here is a situation where the stateless nature of Web Forms acts against you because you can't simply store the old values in private member variables of the form. You need to store them such that their values are preserved between requests from the user—in other words, you need to use a state management service. We'll talk about state management in some detail in Chapters 12 and 13, at which time we'll discuss the factors you should consider when selecting a state management service for a particular task. For our current purposes we'll simply use a state model that you learned about in Chapter 3, the ViewState model. Please bear in mind that although ViewState is often appropriate for the sort of task we're performing here, there are situations where other state management services may be better.

The Members Web Form uses the Find button to read data from the database, so it's in this button's event handler that you need to add code that stores the original values in the ViewState. Here's the code that does this, which uses the values that have previously been written into the form's controls:

```
ViewState("Title") = txtTitle.Text
ViewState("ForeName") = txtForeName.Text
ViewState("SurName") = txtSurName.Text
ViewState("IsStudent") = chkStudent.Checked
```

This code ensures that the original values are safely stored in ViewState. Tedious it may be. Rocket science it ain't.

The next step is to use the ViewState values to supply the old values for the command in the code for the Update button. Here you can see the `With` block inside the Update button's event handler, modified to perform this extra task:

```
With cdUpdateMember.Parameters
    'set the old values
    .Item("@OldTitle").Value = ViewState("Title")
    .Item("@OldForeName").Value = ViewState("ForeName")
    .Item("@OldSurName").Value = ViewState("SurName")
    .Item("@OldIsStudent").Value = ViewState("IsStudent")
    'set the current values
    .Item("@MemberID").Value = MemberID
    .Item("@Title").Value = txtTitle.Text
    .Item("@ForeName").Value = txtForeName.Text
    .Item("@SurName").Value = txtSurName.Text
    .Item("@IsStudent").Value = CInt(chkStudent.Checked)
End With
```

This extension is enough to make sure that any changes made by other users since you read the data will not be overwritten. However, although the command may fail to update the database if any value has been changed by another user, it is a perfectly valid SQL statement, and it will not raise any errors, even if it fails to change any data.

It's likely that you'll want to inform the user that the update has failed. You can do this by checking the value returned by calling `ExecuteNonQuery`. This method returns an integer whose value is the number of rows affected by executing the command. You can expect this value to be 1 for a successful update and 0 for an unsuccessful update. Therefore, you can replace the call to `ExecuteNonQuery` with the following:

```
If cdUpdateMember.ExecuteNonQuery() = 0 Then
    lblError.Text = "Update failed because another user has modified your data"
    lblError.Visible = True
End If
```

With this code in place, not only will you avoid the danger of using out-of-date data when deciding to update the database, but you've also informed the user when an update fails because of a concurrency violation.

There is one final touch you may think is helpful. Assuming the update is successful, the data stored in ViewState will become out-of-date after the update takes place. This means that if the user attempts to update the data again (without first clicking the Find button) the update will always fail because the data in ViewState has not been updated to reflect the new values in the database (if you're not sure why this is so, it might be worth going over the past couple of pages again). To resolve this problem, you could simply update the ViewState if the `ExecuteNonQuery` method returns 1.

You may be wondering why we didn't simply use some form of database lock to make sure the data used by one user isn't updated by another user. Holding locks open limits the ability for the database to support multiple users. In desktop applications a common (although not necessarily wise) approach is to hold a pessimistic lock while the user edits data. Pessimistic locks are easy to create in classic ADO (via the `LockType` property of a Recordset), and they ensure that no other user can modify data that you have locked. The problem is that it isn't easy to control how long a user will take to edit data, and so the pessimistic lock approach can easily make whole sections of the database out of bounds to other users for long periods of time. This kind of approach would never work in a Web Application.

An alternative locking approach is to use an optimistic lock. An optimistic lock is also easy to create using classic ADO. It enables other users to make changes to data you're using, but if they do make changes to the data, your update will fail and you'll receive an error message. If you think this sounds similar in principle to the approach taken earlier using an extended `WHERE` clause, you're correct. The extended `WHERE` clause approach *simulates* an optimistic lock without actually locking any database records. To physically lock database records, you'd need to keep the same connection open between user requests. This is hard to manage properly in a stateless Web Application, and instead it makes a great deal more sense to use connection pooling to deliver a connection quickly whenever you need one, without the need to hold on to the same connection. Holding locks open doesn't work when you use connection pooling because there's no guarantee you'll get the same connection each time. It's also worth noting that maintaining locks is an expensive task for a database to perform, and simulating locks in the manner described in this section results in a more scalable solution.

If you're still not convinced, then you need to consider that the designers of ADO.NET agree with this argument, and for this reason provide no direct way of creating either pessimistic or optimistic locks, other than by using extended `WHERE` clauses. Of course there are times when some form of row locking is essential, and it's possible to use ADO.NET's transaction features to lock rows for short periods of time.

Using Transactions

A *transaction* is a computer technique for simulating the real world. When you go to a bar and order a drink, what you really want is a drink in a glass. A drink with no container to hold it is hard work. An empty glass won't quench your thirst. So, really, you're asking the bartender to give you two things (a glass and a drink) in return for your money. You won't accept just a glass even for half your money; it has to be all or nothing.

Real life is like that, one *logical* operation often involves two or more *physical* operations, and it makes no sense (and can be dangerous) to perform only part of the logical operation. The same is true of computer programs, and for this reason you need the ability to perform logical units of work in an all-or-nothing fashion. Such operations are called *transactions*.

ADO.NET provides a Transaction object to enable you to write transactions. You can use the same Transaction object to perform a set of database operations. When you've finished the operations you can ask the Transaction object to "commit" all the changes made by the operations, in which case all the operations will be permanently saved in the database. If anything goes wrong, you can ask the Transaction to "roll back," in which case any changes made since the transaction started will be erased.

When using an ADO.NET transaction, it's necessary to perform all operations using the same Connection object. This is one of the few occasions where you need to keep a Connection open between operations. This doesn't mean you can keep the Connection open at your leisure, however. During transactions, physical database locks are maintained on all the rows affected by the transaction (and often, other rows as well), and it's very much your responsibility to keep transactions as short as possible.

In this section, you'll see how to control a transaction using ADO.NET's Transaction object. There is another way to control a transaction, which enables you to perform a single transaction involving multiple databases. This approach requires you to use .NET's Enterprise Services and is discussed in Chapter 13.

The Members Web Form has a Delete button. If you delete a member, you should also delete any bookings the member may have in the AircraftDiary and InstructorDiary tables. In other words, one logical operation actually requires three physical operations (one on the Member table and one on each of the diary tables), and so a transaction is needed.

To perform this transaction, three Command objects are required, which we've called `cdDeleteMember`, `cdDeleteAircraftBookings`, and `cdDeleteInstructorBookings`. All of these are similar, so there's no need to see how each is created. Figure 7-10 shows the Query Builder display for the `cdDeleteInstructorBookings` command.

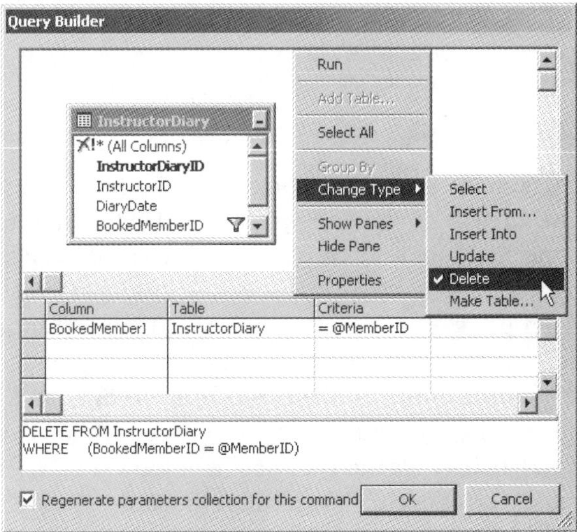

Figure 7-10. The cdDeleteInstructorBookings command

Listing 7-5 shows the code that uses a Transaction object to control the execution of these three commands.

Listing 7-5. Controlling Multiple Operations Using a Transaction

```
Dim MemberID As String = txtID.Text
Dim tx As SqlTransaction
Try

    cdDeleteMember.Parameters("@MemberID").Value = CInt(MemberID)
    cdDeleteAircraftBookings.Parameters("@MemberID").Value = CInt(MemberID)
    cdDeleteInstructorBookings.Parameters("@MemberID").Value = CInt(MemberID)
    cn.Open()
    tx = cn.BeginTransaction

    cdDeleteMember.Transaction = tx
    cdDeleteAircraftBookings.Transaction = tx
    cdDeleteInstructorBookings.Transaction = tx

    cdDeleteMember.ExecuteNonQuery()
    cdDeleteAircraftBookings.ExecuteNonQuery()
    cdDeleteInstructorBookings.ExecuteNonQuery()
    tx.Commit()
Catch
    If Not tx Is Nothing Then tx.Rollback()
    lblError.Text = "Unable to delete Member " + MemberID
```

```
    lblError.Visible = True
Finally
    cn.Close()
End Try
```

The Delete functionality shown in Listing 7-5 begins by setting the parameter value for each of the three Command objects involved in the transaction. After opening the `cn` connection, the Transaction object is created by calling the `BeginTransaction` method on `cn`. The Transaction object must then be assigned to the `Transaction` property of each Command object (once a transaction is open, all commands executed using the transaction's connection must be executed as part of that transaction). You then execute each command. If all goes well, the transaction can be committed and then the connection closed. If an error occurs, the `Catch` block calls the Transaction object's `RollBack` method. Regardless of where the error occurs, the result is the same. The `RollBack` makes sure none of the changes made during the transaction are saved to the database, thereby maintaining the all-or-nothing guarantee of transaction processing.

Using Stored Procedures

There is still one piece of functionality required to complete the Member Web Form, which is the ability to add new members. We could of course use exactly the same approach as we've taken for all the other functionality, but instead, we'll use this as an opportunity to explore how stored procedures work in .NET.

At its simplest, a *stored procedure* is an SQL command stored and compiled in the database. Each stored procedure has a name, and when a stored procedure is executed (using a Command object), you can pass arguments to it (by using Parameter objects). Stored procedure arguments can be output arguments as well as input arguments, creating the opportunity to get data back from a database without needing to use a DataReader.

The most common reason for using stored procedures is for performance. When you use a Command object that executes an SQL statement, the database must interpret the SQL before it can actually execute it. When you call a stored procedure, the SQL is already compiled, and so the time taken to interpret the SQL is saved. The performance gain that using stored procedures delivers can be substantial, especially for complex SQL.

There are other performance gains to be made from using stored procedures. A stored procedure can contain more than just SQL statements; it can contain program logic. A stored procedure might execute several SQL statements and use program logic to calculate a single value that is returned to your Web Application. Without stored procedures, you would need to fetch the results for each SQL statement into the Web Application just to calculate the single value you desire. This approach involves a great deal more traffic between the Web Application and the database than the stored procedure approach, which can therefore be many times faster.

Traditionally, developers have been aware of two major objections to using stored procedures. The first is that stored procedures written for SQL Server can't necessarily be ported to a different database server such as Oracle, or vice versa. When you choose to use stored procedures, you make a significant commitment to a specific database server. In many organizations, this is not really an issue, because the organization has made a strategic decision about what database server to use for all its applications. However, if portability between database servers is important to you, you need to think carefully about whether to use stored procedures.

The second objection to stored procedures is that they're more difficult to write. They can't be developed in a nice, friendly development environment such as Visual Studio, and so they require significantly more time to write and debug. Visual Studio .NET goes a long way to removing this objection, as it has integrated support for working with stored procedures with either SQL Server or Oracle databases.

To create a new stored procedure using Visual Studio .NET, start by locating your database in the Server Explorer (use the View menu to locate the Server Explorer if it isn't visible). Within the Server Explorer, right-click on the `Stored Procedures` node for your database and select the option for creating a new stored procedure. A stored procedure editor appears within which you can start coding. Figure 7-11 shows what this looks like.

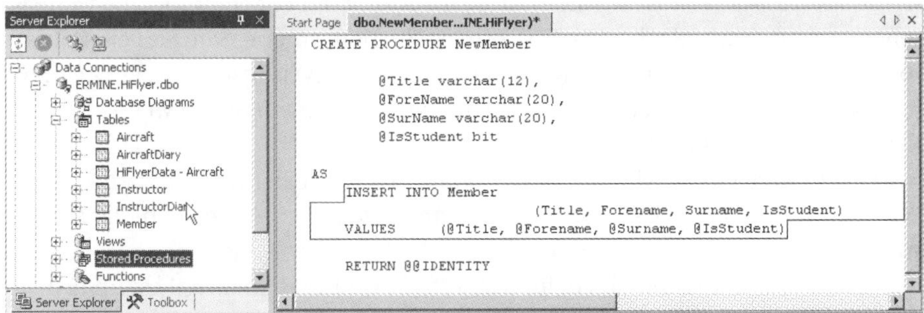

Figure 7-11. Building the NewMember stored procedure

To define this stored procedure, we had to type in the argument list and use the Server Explorer to find out about the data types for each argument. However, we didn't need to type in the INSERT SQL statement because we can use the Query Builder from inside the stored procedure editor. A right-click in the editor window shows a menu containing the Insert SQL option, which displays the

Query Builder. Figure 7-12 shows the Query Builder being used to create this INSERT statement.

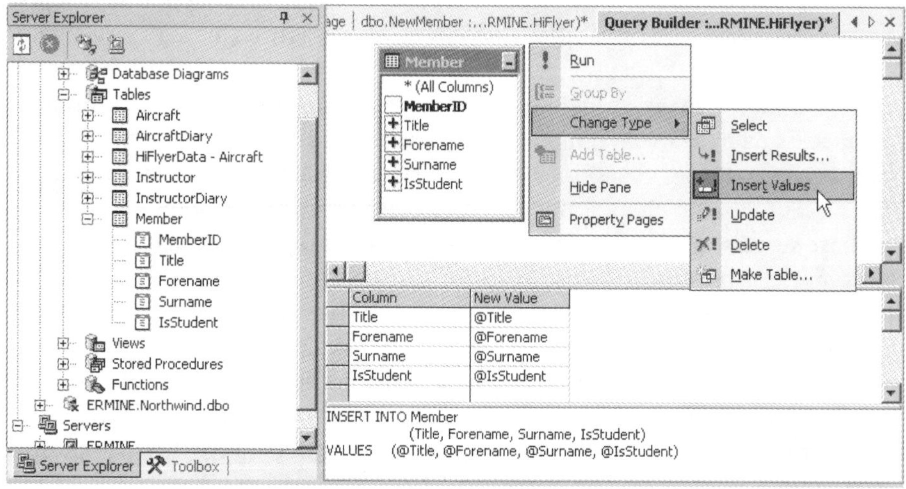

Figure 7-12. Editing a stored procedure graphically

Closing the Query Builder causes the SQL to be written into the stored procedure editor. It's worth exploring the other features of this editor, which enable you to run and debug stored procedures from within Visual Studio .NET.

You may have noticed that this stored procedure doesn't have a @MemberID argument. This is because MemberID is an auto-increment column—the value is generated automatically by SQL Server to ensure it is unique. SQL Server enables you to access the value that it allocated when a new row is inserted via the global @@IDENTITY variable, which you can see in Figure 7-11 is the return value of the NewMember stored procedure.

Once you're happy with the stored procedure, you can save it. Visual Studio .NET will automatically ask SQL Server to create it, and you'll be warned if there are any errors.

Creating a Command object for a stored procedure is amazingly simple. Just drag the stored procedure you require from the stored procedures listed in the Server Explorer, and Visual Studio .NET will automatically generate a Command object, and any Parameter objects required. The code generated by Visual Studio .NET for the NewMember stored procedure (with some details suppressed) is as follows:

```
Me.cdNewMember.CommandText = "dbo.[NewMember]"
Me.cdNewMember.CommandType = System.Data.CommandType.StoredProcedure
```

```
Me.cdNewMember.Connection = Me.cn
Me.cdNewMember.Parameters.Add(New SqlParameter("@RETURN_VALUE", _
    SqlDbType.Int, 4, ParameterDirection.ReturnValue,. . .))
Me.cdNewMember.Parameters.Add(New SqlParameter("@Title", SqlDbType.VarChar, 12))
Me.cdNewMember.Parameters.Add(New SqlParameter("@Forename", _
    SqlDbType.VarChar, 20))
Me.cdNewMember.Parameters.Add(New SqlParameter("@Surname", _
    SqlDbType.VarChar, 20))
Me.cdNewMember.Parameters.Add(New SqlParameter("@IsStudent", SqlDbType.Bit, 1))
```

You can then immediately write code that uses this Command object (which we've called `cdNewMember`). Because our user interface is purely functional, the Create New Member button simply takes the values from Web Form controls (ignoring the `txtID` TextBox) and calls the `cdNewMember` command. The return value is then written into the `txtID` TextBox in case the user wants to see the MemberID value generated by the database when the Web Form is posted back (in reality, you'd probably want to create a more helpful user interface than this). Let's see what this bare-bones Create New Member function looks like:

```
Try
    With cdNewMember.Parameters
        .Item("@Title").Value = txtTitle.Text
        .Item("@ForeName").Value = txtForeName.Text
        .Item("@SurName").Value = txtSurName.Text
        .Item("@IsStudent").Value = CInt(chkStudent.Checked)

        cn.Open()
        cdNewMember.ExecuteNonQuery()
        txtID.Text = .Item("@RETURN_VALUE").Value.ToString
    End With
Catch
    lblError.Text = "Unable to create new Member"
    lblError.Text = ex.Message
    lblError.Visible = True
Finally
    cn.Close()
End Try
```

As with all these examples, the code follows a straightforward pattern. First set parameter values, then execute, then tidy up. The only real difference is that this code reads the `RETURN_VALUE` parameter after the stored procedure has been executed.

We've now explored most of the functionality provided by .NET Data Providers and seen how you can use them to read data, perform updates, execute transactions, and work with stored procedures.

ADO.NET does not provide all the features for working with databases that you may have come to expect from classic ADO. The primary reason for removing some features is to avoid functionality that is traditionally expensive or that may affect scalability. Another benefit of the ADO.NET approach is that it provides a straightforward programming model. Whatever type of operation you're performing, coding is basically a process of opening a connection, executing a command, maybe looping rapidly through a DataReader, and then closing the connection (returning it back to the connection pool). Although this simple approach may seem limiting, it covers much of what you need to do with databases in Web Applications. There are great benefits from having a simple, regular pattern like this, and the more we program the ADO.NET way, the more we come to like it. There's actually much less to learn, and support and maintenance become easier, so if you follow the kind of approach we have seen so far in this chapter, you're almost bound to write efficient and effective database access code.

The only major object provided by .NET Data Providers that hasn't been discussed yet is the DataAdapter. The reason for this is that DataAdapters are only ever used in conjunction with the DataSet object model, which is the focus of the next few sections.

Working with DataSets

As you've already seen in this chapter, you can go a long way with ADO.NET without ever touching a DataSet, particularly in Web Applications. It's easy to believe the hype that DataSets are the centerpiece of ADO.NET, but to do so is to make a mistake. In Web Applications, DataSets have only limited utility. Don't get us wrong, we like DataSets and acknowledge they're powerful features for data manipulation and when used appropriately they're important items in the ASP.NET developers' toolbag. It's just that they're not one you're likely to reach for every day.

In Web Applications, DataSets are tied up closely with the concept of *state*. As you know, the default ASP.NET processing model is to create some objects in response to a user request, build a new page, and throw the objects away. This model raises some issues about any data that you want to reuse between multiple requests (the sort of data you'd hold in global variables in a desktop application). You've already seen one way of storing state in ASP.NET, by making use of ViewState (also known as *page state*) as discussed in Chapter 3. Cast your mind back to the ShowBookings functionality we investigated earlier on in this chapter. The only time this data was retrieved from the database was when the ShowBookings button was clicked. However, after clicking another button (such as the Update button), any existing bookings are still shown. This is because the content of the ListBox used to display Bookings is saved in View State (that is, it is compacted and stored in the hidden `__VIEWSTATE` HTML element that is part of the Web page sent to the user). Although this is often an acceptable solution, there are a number of reasons why it is not always ideal. These include:

- If the current member has hundreds of bookings, the ViewState can become very large. It's often advisable to disable ViewState for controls that display large amounts of data.

- The data stored in View State is not always made available in a format suitable for further processing. For example, it would be quite hard to sort this data if the user wanted to see the same data presented in a different order.

- The ListBox contains only some of the required data. For example, you would typically choose not to display an artificial primary key to a user. Therefore, this information will not automatically be stored in View State.

If you decide not to store this data in View State, but you still want to use the data when building the next page, you're forced to choose between two options:

- Refetch the data from the database each time you need it.

- Store the data somewhere else.

This is hardly an earth-shattering insight, but it does raise a key point—you need to make stark decisions about where to store information. In many cases, refetching the data is going to be the best choice. It means that you always get the latest view of the data, and it saves clogging up your servers with copies of data that are already stored in the database. But there are times when storing the data elsewhere makes sense. In these situations, it can be appropriate to hold the data in a DataSet object. In our view, this is the only situation where it's appropriate to create a DataSet to hold relational data, and in some cases, there will be better alternatives to a DataSet. As you can see, DataSets have a very specific role to play in ASP.NET applications.

We'll discuss the whole issue of state management in great detail in Chapters 12 and 13. In this chapter, we'll use a built-in mechanism provided by ASP.NET that enables you to store state information in memory on your Web server. This mechanism is called Session state and will be familiar to any reader who has previously worked with classic ASP. Before continuing, we need to issue a warning.

CAUTION *There are some serious issues to consider when using Session state (or any other state management mechanism, for that matter). We urge you to read about state management in Chapters 12 and 13 before using Session state in production systems. We'll ignore these issues in this chapter and simply treat Session state as a convenient, harmless way to store DataSets in Web server memory (you have been warned!).*

So what, then, is a DataSet? The easiest way to think of a DataSet is as an object that can store the results of one or more SQL queries, without needing to maintain a live database connection. Classic ADO provides exactly the same capability through the use of disconnected, hierarchical Recordsets. DataSets makes this functionality more visible in the hope that more people will use it. Appendix D presents an outline of ADO.NET, and if you're not familiar with the roles played by DataSets, DataTables, and DataAdapters, you should take some time out to read it.

As you can see in Figure 7-13, a DataSet is filled with data using a DataAdapter object. To perform this task, the DataAdapter executes a Command object and uses a DataReader to build a DataTable object that is then inserted into a DataSet object. In other words, just creating a DataSet always involves creating a DataReader and reading each row of data once. If you only intend to process this data once, it makes little sense to create a DataSet. You may as well just create a DataReader and use it directly, instead of wasting time copying the data into a DataTable before you even start using it.

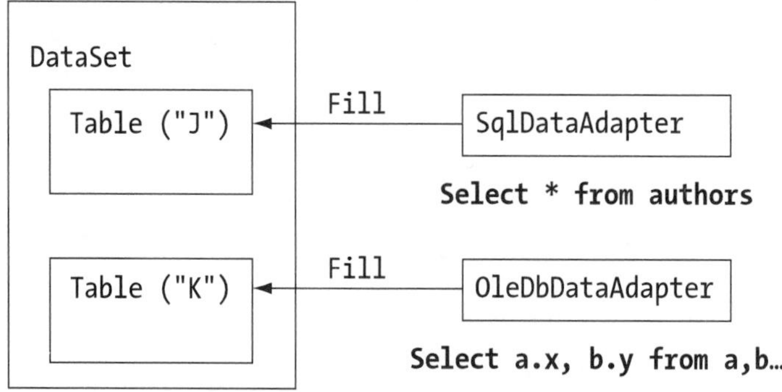

Figure 7-13. DataSets, DataTables, and DataAdapters

Where DataSets become useful is where you intend to use this data multiple times, or over a long period of time. In this case, the additional cost of reading all the data once even before you start using it can be offset against the benefit of having ready access to data in the DataSet without needing to go back to the database to get it (remember, a DataSet is never connected to a database. It is a stand-alone cache of data).

A Read-Only DataTable

Let's say you want to allow a user to browse through all the bookings that a member has made. Maybe you want them to be able to sort the data in various ways or filter it to see only certain bookings. This is one scenario where it can make sense to use a DataSet. The functionality built into a DataSet makes it possible to provide this kind of browse behavior without needing to trouble the database for each new presentation of data.

In Figure 7-14, you can see the Design View of the first version of a Web Form for this task.

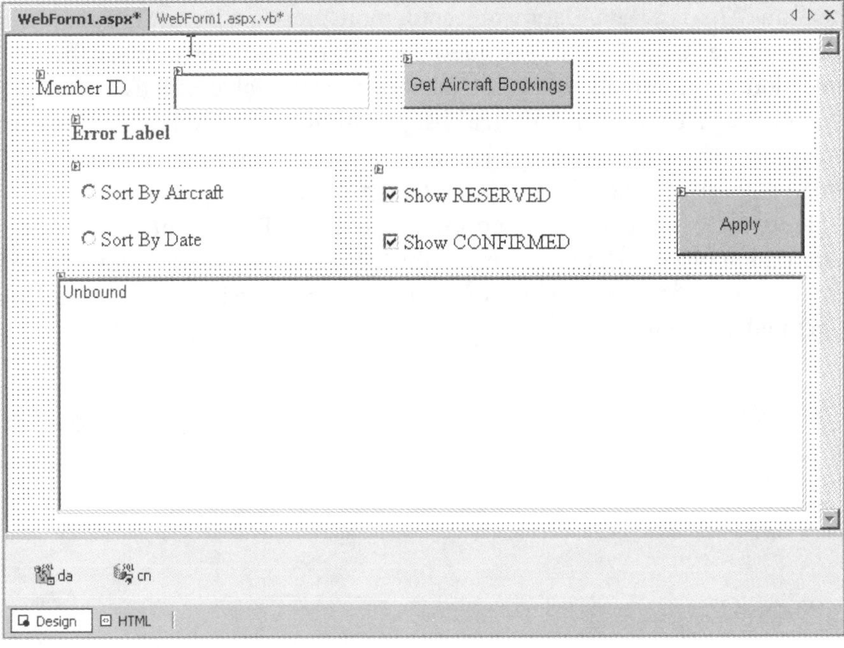

Figure 7-14 Designing a data browsing page

A user of this Web Form can type in a Member ID to display the bookings for that member. Unlike the earlier Web Form we created, this one displays only data from the AircraftDiary table, so it's only suitable for members who are qualified pilots and therefore don't need an instructor. Once the data has been loaded, the user can apply sort and filter operations to the data without needing to execute any further database queries. This is because all the data will be cached in Session state. Once again, the output is a fairly ugly ListBox—we'll look at data binding in Chapter 8 and see how to make more attractive Web pages. You'll learn there how to use the DataGrid control (and other related controls) to create the kinds of user interfaces your users expect—but you need to know the data programming principles first.

We're going to use the DataSet *approach*, but to begin with, we won't actually use a DataSet *object*. This may sound strange, but remember that a DataSet is designed to hold a set of DataTable objects. Remember also that a DataTable is part of the DataSet object model and is actually its central object. As we only need one database query at this stage in the application, we don't actually need to go through the extra step of creating a DataSet—a single DataTable object will meet all our needs. Later, we'll extend the application to require the results of more than one query, at which stage we'll use a DataSet object as well.

Take a final look at Figure 7-14 and notice a component called `da` in the component tray. This is a DataAdapter object (or more precisely, it's an SqlDataAdapter object from the SQL .NET Data Provider). Its job is to create and manage the Connection and Command objects needed to fill a DataTable with data.

If you drag a DataAdapter onto a designer from the Data tab of the Toolbox, a tool called the DataAdapter Configuration Wizard is displayed. It takes you through the task of building a DataAdapter graphically.

Figure 7-15 shows the most important page in the DataAdapter Configuration Wizard. Here you can see the SQL query required for the new Web Form. You can either type the query into the wizard or use the Query Builder button to build it graphically.

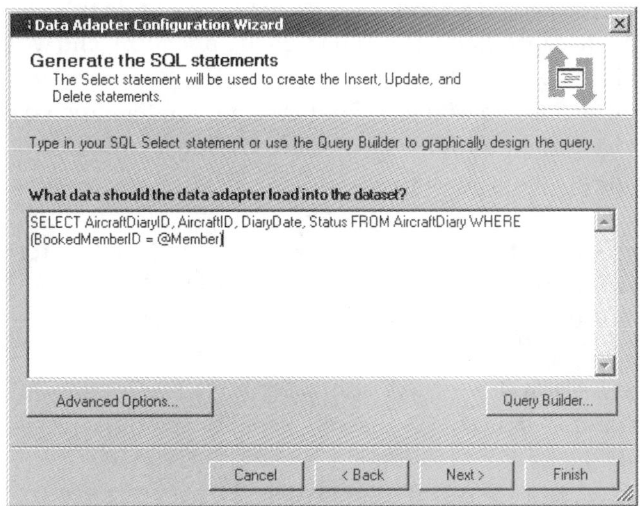

Figure 7-15. The DataAdapter Configuration Wizard

There is another important button shown in Figure 7-15 called the Advanced Options button. It should be called the Fundamental Options button because you should review it every time you create a DataAdapter using the wizard. It displays the set of options shown in Figure 7-16.

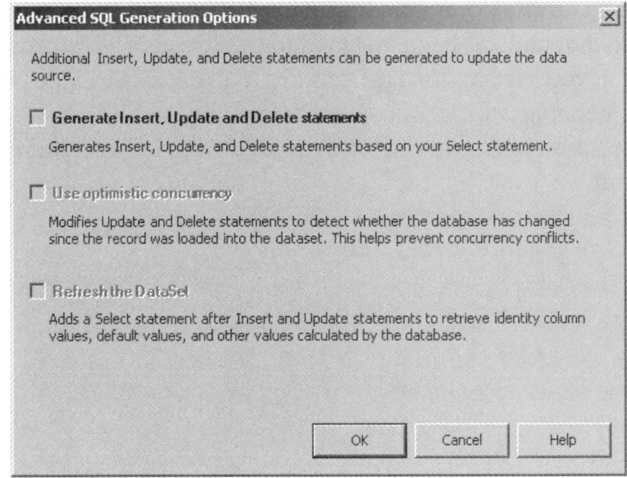

Figure 7-16. Fundamental options

This dialog box specifies options that control how the DataAdapter will perform updates. At present, our Web Form is read-only. For read-only

DataAdapters, you should always uncheck all the options in this dialog box. We'll add some update capability to the Web Form in Appendix F, and we'll review what the other options do at that time.

When you've finished with it, the DataAdapter Configuration Wizard generates code and adds it into your code window. The most important parts of the generated code are the following:

```
Protected WithEvents da As System.Data.SqlClient.SqlDataAdapter
Protected WithEvents cn As System.Data.SqlClient.SqlConnection
Protected WithEvents SqlSelectCommand1 As System.Data.SqlClient.SqlCommand

Me.cn.ConnectionString = "data source=ERMINE;initial catalog=HiFlyer; " & _
    "integrated security=SSPI;persist security info=False;workstation " & _
    "id=ERMINE;packet size=4096"
Me.da.SelectCommand = Me.SqlSelectCommand1
Me.SqlSelectCommand1.CommandText = "SELECT AircraftDiaryID, " & _
    "AircraftID, DiaryDate, Status FROM AircraftDiary WHERE (" & _
    " BookedMemberID = @Member)"
 Me.SqlSelectCommand1.Connection = Me.cn
 Me.SqlSelectCommand1.Parameters.Add(New  SqlParameter( _
     "@Member", SqlDbType.Int, 4, "BookedMemberID")))
```

Notice that the wizard has generated a Connection, DataAdapter, and a Command object. The Command object has been initialized with the SQL captured by the wizard and has been assigned to the `SelectCommand` property of the DataAdapter. (If you prefer stored procedures to dynamic SQL, the wizard will automatically generate stored procedures for you instead.)

Listing 7-6 shows the code you have to write for the Get Aircraft Bookings button.

Listing 7-6. Retrieving Data Using a DataTable

```
Dim dt As New DataTable()
Dim dr As DataRow
Dim Booking As String
Dim MemberID As String = txtID.Text
Try
    da.SelectCommand.Parameters("@Member").Value = MemberID
    da.Fill(dt)
    Session("Bookings") = dt

    lstBookings.Items.Clear()
    For Each dr In dt.Rows
        Booking = dr("AircraftID").ToString + " "
```

```
        Booking += dr("DiaryDate").ToString + " "
        Booking += dr("Status").ToString
        lstBookings.Items.Add(Booking)
    Next
Catch
    lblError.Text = "Unable to find details for Member " + MemberID
    lblError.Visible = True
End Try
```

What you see in Listing 7-6 is the entirety of this code. It breaks down into two main sections. We'll begin with the first three lines:

```
da.SelectCommand.Parameters("@Member").Value = MemberID
da.Fill(dt)
Session("Bookings") = dt
```

The first task is to assign a value to the parameter on the DataAdapter's `SelectCommand` (the one created by the wizard). You then call the `Fill` method. The `Fill` method takes care of opening and closing a connection, so you should have no worries about the effect of garbage collection on your database connection—it's all handled for you. The `Fill` method uses a DataReader to add each row in the `SelectCommand` into the DataTable object (note that although it does so much for you, the `Fill` method won't actually create the DataTable object for you. `dt` was created "As New" to be sure that a live DataTable object is passed to `Fill`).

So that you can use the same DataTable for future requests, assign it to the Session object with a key name of `Bookings`. As you can see, the programming model for using Session state is simple. Behind the scenes, though, a lot is going on. For one thing, Session state is stored on a per-user basis. Each user will have their own data stored in `Session("Bookings")`, and to make this possible, ASP.NET generates a unique session ID and stores it in a cookie passed between the user's browser and the Web server on each request. This *session cookie* makes sure that the correct Bookings DataTable is used for each user.

The remainder of the code uses a simple processing loop to build up a string for each row of data before adding each string to the ListBox. This looks fairly similar to the way we processed the DataReader earlier in the chapter. However, there are some subtle differences. Each DataTable contains a collection of DataRow objects, and the code in Listing 7-6 uses standard collection processing techniques to access these DataRow objects. This means that you need to declare a DataRow variable for use inside the `For...Each` loop. Also, there are no strongly typed data access methods for DataRows (remember that for the DataReader, you could use `GetString`, `GetInt32`, and so on). The DataSet processing model forces you to treat each piece of data as being of the generic Object type in .NET, so you need to manually convert each datum to the data type you require (unless you turn Option Strict Off, which we do not recommend).

The next task is to code the Apply button. This button enables the user to view only those bookings they're interested in and to see them sorted in an order of their choice. Because the data for every booking for the current member is being held on the Web server in Session state, there is no need to go back to the database to fetch this data. DataTables contain functionality that makes it easy to simply extract and sort the rows of data you want.

Before exploring the code for this functionality, take a look at the following code from the ASPX page containing the definition of the RadioButtonList and CheckBoxList controls used in this example and note the Value property used in each one:

```
<asp:RadioButtonList id="rdlSort" style=. . .">
    <asp:ListItem Value="AircraftID">Sort By Aircraft</asp:ListItem>
    <asp:ListItem Value="DiaryDate">Sort By Date</asp:ListItem>
</asp:RadioButtonList>
<asp:CheckBoxList id="chlFilter" style=. . .">
    <asp:ListItem Value="RESERVED" Selected="True">Show RESERVED</asp:ListItem>
    <asp:ListItem Value="CONFIRMED" Selected="True">Show CONFIRMED</asp:ListItem>
</asp:CheckBoxList>
```

We're going to use a method on the DataTable called Select. You can use the Select method to filter and sort data contained in a DataTable, without needing to revisit the database. To do this, you need to create two strings that represent the filter and sort criteria. This code does this:

```
Private Sub getCriteria(ByRef Filter As String, ByVal Sort As String)
    If chlFilter.Items(0).Selected Xor chlFilter.Items(1).Selected Then
        Filter = "Status = '" + chlFilter.SelectedItem.Value + "'"
    End If
    If Not (rdlSort.SelectedItem Is Nothing) Then
        Sort = rdlSort.SelectedItem.Value
    End If
End Sub
```

The first If statement makes sure that only one of the items in the chlFilter CheckBoxList is selected (using an Xor statement) and then uses the value from the selected item to construct a filter string. For example, if only the Show CONFIRMED CheckBox is selected, the filter string would be this:

```
Status = 'CONFIRMED'
```

If both CheckBoxes are selected, the filter string will be an empty string in which case no filter will be applied (and so all rows will be selected when the `Select` method is called). The filter looks rather like an SQL `WHERE` clause, and in fact the DataTable contains built-in processing capability that supports a wide range of `WHERE` clause-like behavior. You can find the full specification for a filter string in the online help.

The second `If` statement simply uses a column name from the data in the DataTable to specify a sort string. You can append `ASC` or `DESC` if you want to specify sorting in ascending or descending order.

Once these two strings are created, you can call the `Select` method to extract rows that meet these two criteria. Here's the code that does this:

```
Dim Filter, Sort As String
Dim dt As DataTable
Dim drs() As DataRow
dt = CType(Session("Bookings"), DataTable)
getCriteria(Filter, Sort)
drs = dt.Select(Filter, Sort)
```

This code looks simple enough, but it deserves a little attention. First, it extracts the DataTable from Session state and assigns it to a variable called `dt`. Now, the data stored in Session state could be anything, so (because `Option Strict` is `On`) you need to specify that this data can be safely treated as a DataTable by using the `CType` function. After this, you call `getCriteria`, which will assign the correct strings to the two variables passed in by reference. The final line of code calls the `Select` method on this DataTable, passing in the filter and sort strings just created. Once again this looks straightforward enough, but take a careful look at the return type of the `drs` variable to which the results of the `Select` method are assigned. This is an array! In fact, it is an array of DataRow objects. The nice thing about this array is that it only contains DataRows that meet the filter criterion, and those rows are sorted according to the sort criterion.

We're now clearly processing data in a way that's completely different from anything classic ADO made possible. Fortunately, although this processing model seems a little unusual, every programmer knows how to handle arrays. The following code loops through the array, adding data to the ListBox:

```
Dim dr As DataRow
Dim i As Integer
Dim Booking As String
lstBookings.Items.Clear()
For i = 0 To drs.Length - 1
    dr = drs(i)
    Booking = dr("AircraftID").ToString + " "
```

```
    Booking += dr("DiaryDate").ToString + " "
    Booking += dr("Status").ToString
    lstBookings.Items.Add(Booking)
Next
```

Now that we've explored all this code, let's see what it looks like. Figure 7-17 shows our Web Form listing all the bookings for a given member.

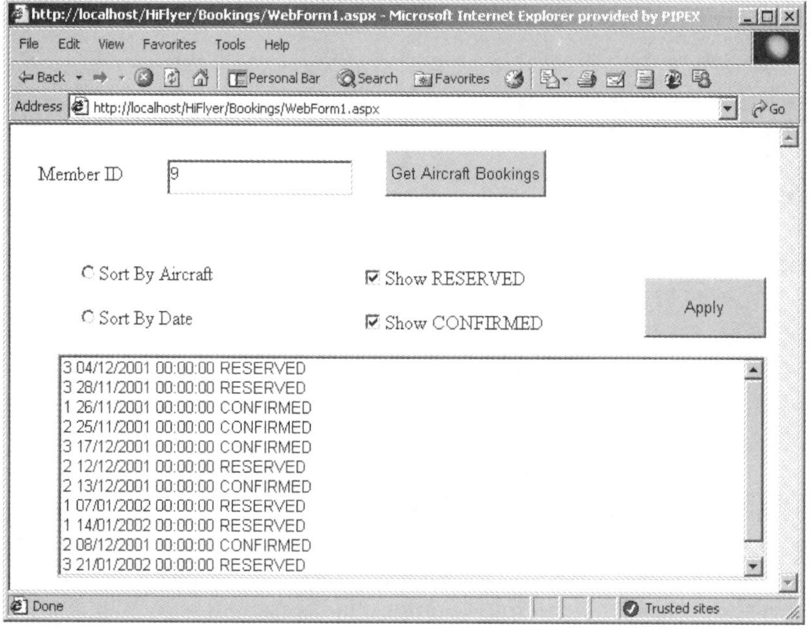

Figure 7-17. The Get Aircraft Bookings functionality

Figure 7-18 shows data from the same DataSet, sorted by date and filtered to display only confirmed bookings.

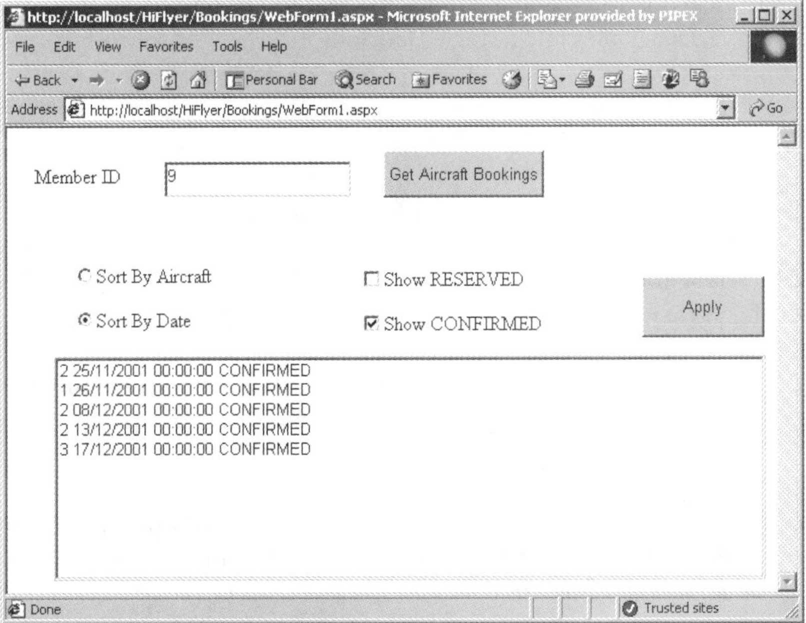

Figure 7-18. The Apply functionality

So far, you've seen how to populate a DataTable using a DataAdapter and how the data in a DataTable can be processed either as a collection of rows or as an array of rows. You've seen that by repeatedly applying the `Select` method, you can extract different subsets of data from a DataTable without needing to revisit the database.

Using DataTables cached in Session state can significantly improve an application's performance because accessing data in memory is so much faster than reading it from a database. In one sense, using DataTables like this can also be a great boost to an application's scalability. Although it's relatively easy to replicate a Web Application on multiple servers, replicating databases is a far less straightforward task (unless they're purely read-only) and therefore anytime you can take the load off a database you're potentially improving the scalability of your applications because databases can become an overall bottleneck on a growing application. Because DataTables contain some powerful data processing capabilities traditionally only found in databases, they can play a protective role in minimizing the demand you place on databases. At the same time, you need to bear in mind that holding large amounts of data in Web server local memory can easily become an overbearing burden. This is especially true of Session state, where the memory demand is multiplied by the number of users. We'll return to the trade-offs involved in balancing the performance and scalability of Web Applications in Chapter 13—they're trade-offs never to lose sight of.

We'll finish this section on the DataSet object model by looking at how to load multiple DataTables into a single DataSet.

A Read-Only DataSet

Our Bookings Browser Web Form currently only uses data from one database table. In real-life applications, this is often an unrealistic simplicity, and the need to retrieve data from multiple tables is extremely common. The DataSet object model offers two ways to do this:

1. Build an SQL join and execute it using a DataAdapter. The result will be a single DataTable containing data from more than one physical data base table.

2. Build separate SQL statements for the data required from each database table. Create a DataAdapter for each statement and use them to add multiple DataTables into a single DataSet object.

It's our guess that you won't find many books advocating Option 1. Is this because it is a bad option? No, in fact in many circumstances it is a sensible option to choose. The main reason it's not widely discussed is because the simple examples supplied by Microsoft in early versions of .NET were all based on Option 2. Option 2 involves more programming (at least for read-only scenarios) and involves executing multiple database queries instead of just one, so it's likely to be slower to execute. Is Option 2 a bad choice? No, it just depends on what you want to achieve.

The most important difference between the two options concerns what the data looks like when you have retrieved it. Let's say you have two tables of data in a physical database and you want to retrieve a subset of data from both tables. If you execute an SQL join, you'll end up flattening the original structure of the data (two tables) into a single tabular result set (one DataTable). If this is actually what you want (because it suits the purpose you have in mind for the data), then you should probably choose this option. If you build two separate SQL statements and store them in a DataSet as two separate DataTables (Option 2) you'll retain the original structure of the physical database. Sometimes this is exactly what you want, and sometimes it is precisely what you don't want. You should make your choice accordingly.

There is another difference between the two options that is worth mentioning at this point. If you use Option 2, you might be able to use the functionality built into DataAdapters that enables you to automate the process of writing changes back to the database. If you choose Option 1, the database update process can only ever be semi-automatic. We'll discuss this more in Appendix F, but it's worth bearing in mind that if you create DataTables based on SQL joins, you *may* end up writing more code to perform database updates than if you created a DataTable for each physical database table you use.

In our case, we don't really need to provide an example of Option 1. When we created the Members Web page we used an SQL join across two tables. You can easily use the same query with a DataAdapter to explore Option 1 yourself. So we'll explore Option 2. However, don't get into thinking that we're saying this is *the* way to use DataTables where multiple tables are concerned. It just happens to be the approach that suits our current purpose.

We're going to extend the Bookings Browser so that the user can click an entry in the ListBox to see more details of the aircraft that has been booked. To do this, we'll place the DataTable containing the bookings for a given member (the Bookings DataTable) and a DataTable containing details of each aircraft (the Aircraft DataTable) into a single DataSet. We'll then store this DataSet as a single object in Session state. When a user clicks on a booking, we'll locate the associated entry in the aircraft DataTable and display its details without needing to revisit the database. To make navigation between the DataTables easier, we'll add a DataRelation to the DataSet object before placing it in Session state. Figure 7-19 shows what the resulting structure will look like.

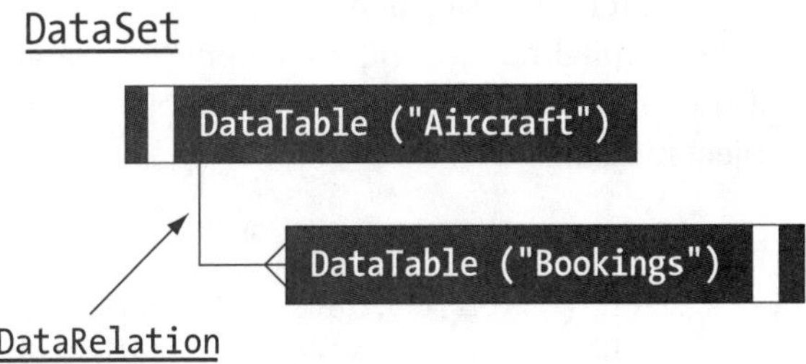

Figure 7-19. DataTables within a DataSet

Before going any further, ask yourself whether this sounds like a good idea. Essentially, you're loading all the data from the Aircraft table into memory so that you can save a bit of time when a user clicks on a booking to see the aircraft details. In many cases, this would not be a good idea at all. It would be better to load the details for a single aircraft directly from the database, each time the user clicks a booking. However, in this case, we never expect HiFlyers to have many aircraft, so we can justify "prefetching" all this data because there is not much of it.

Let's see the code that makes this possible. The first task is to build a new DataAdapter (called `daAircraft`) that returns the entire Aircraft table. Assuming this has been done, we can use this DataAdapter in the Get Aircraft Bookings button to build the DataSet. Here's how:

```
Dim ds As New DataSet()
da.SelectCommand.Parameters("@Member").Value = MemberID
da.Fill(ds, "Bookings")
daAircraft.Fill(ds, "Aircraft")
Session("Data") = ds
```

Once again, we've used the DataAdapter's `Fill` method, but this time, we've passed a DataSet instead of a DataTable as the first argument. In doing so we're exploiting .NET's ability (called *overloading*) for a class to have more than one method with the same name, but different types of argument. In this case, the DataAdapter will still build a DataTable, but it will automatically insert it into the DataSet (in a collection called `Tables`) with a key name as defined by the second argument. Having created a DataSet containing two tables, we add the DataSet into Session state, this time with a different key name from before.

We want to make it easy to navigate between the two DataTables so that if we know about a particular DataRow in the Bookings table, we can easily get hold of the associated DataRow in the Aircraft table and display its contents. We can achieve this objective by creating a relationship between the two tables, or more specifically, a relationship between the AircraftID column in the Aircraft table and the AircraftID column in the Bookings table. Once again, be aware that this relationship is being built into the in-memory DataSet object—it does not require or involve any similar relationship in the physical database. The relationship itself is established by creating a DataRelation object (DataRelations are part of the DataSet object model):

```
Dim rl As New DataRelation("Rel1", _
                ds.Tables("Aircraft").Columns("AircraftID"),  _
                ds.Tables("Bookings").Columns("AircraftID"))
ds.Relations.Add(rl)
```

Here we've created a DataRelation called '`Rel1`' between the two nominated columns. It may be that you have a situation where a relationship depends on more than one column in each DataTable. You can model this kind of relationship by supplying the DataRelation with arrays of columns, rather than individual columns.

To build the initial display of all bookings for the current member, you need to extract the Bookings table from the DataSet so that you can build the ListBox. The ListBox-building code will be the same as before, so here is just the code for extracting the Bookings table that should appear after the DataSet has been populated (you will need to remove the previous declaration of `dt`):

```
Dim dt As DataTable = ds.Tables("Bookings")
```

A similar approach can be taken for the Apply button, which will need to be modified now that you're storing a DataSet rather than a DataTable in Session state.

All that remains is to use the relationship stored in the DataSet to retrieve the appropriate aircraft details. To do this, the ListBox has had its `AutoPostback` property set to `True` so that selecting a row in the ListBox automatically posts back to the Web server and fires the `lstBookings.SelectedIndexChanged` event. The first part of the code for this event simply identifies the DataRow in the Bookings table associated with the row selected by the user:

```
Dim ds As DataSet = CType(Session("Data"), DataSet)
Dim Filter, Sort As String
Dim drs(), drChild As DataRow
Dim dt As DataTable
getCriteria(Filter, Sort)
dt = CType(Session("Data"), DataSet).Tables("Bookings")
drs = dt.Select(Filter, Sort)
drChild = drs(lstBookings.SelectedIndex)
```

This code works by rebuilding the array of DataRows that was used to create the ListBox. The index number of the row selected by the user is used to look up the correct row from the array. The end result is a DataRow variable called `drChild`. Here is a typical example of the trade-off between processor time and memory. It takes additional processing time to re-create the array of DataRows. The alternative would have been to create additional state to make it easier to map a selected ListBox item onto a DataRow in the DataSet. In this case, we've opted to create no additional state.

Having identified the Bookings row, we can use the DataRelation to locate the related row in the Aircraft DataTable. Each DataRow has a `GetParentRow` and a `GetChildRows` method, which can be used to navigate between one "end" of the relationship and another. There is also a `GetParentRows` in the case where a child row may have more than one parent row. In this case, we've identified a child row, and we want to find its parent row in the Aircraft table. Here's the code to do this:

```
Dim drParent As DataRow
drParent = drChild.GetParentRow("Rel1")
lblRegistration.Text = drParent("Registration").ToString
...
```

Here we've called `GetParentRow` on the `drChild` variable, specifying the name of the relationship to use. This returns the associated parent row in the Aircraft table. All that remains is to display the data from this row somewhere on the Web Form. You can see the first line of this code, which assigns the aircraft's registration string in a Label control, in the previous code snippet. The code that sets the remaining Label and Checkbox controls is not shown. Figure 7-20 shows the final result.

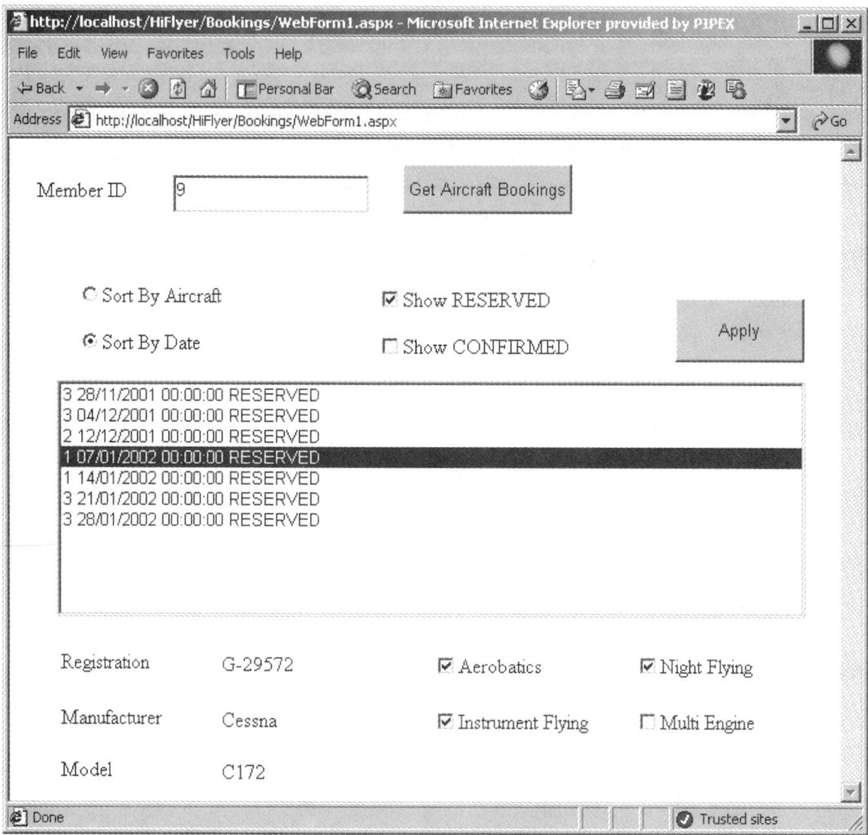

Figure 7-20. Navigating a DataRelation

Updating DataSets

You can use DataSets to write changes back to a database without needing to write your own SQL statements to perform this task. This fact alone is enough to make DataSets seem attractive to many developers—but be warned: DataSet updating is a complex process, and you need to understand a great deal about it to be able to use it safely.

Right now, you probably want to find out how to use what you've already learned about ADO.NET to start creating some attractive Web pages using ASP.NET's flexible data binding techniques. For this reason, instead of providing a detailed introduction to DataSet updating in this chapter, we cover the topic in Appendix F.

Summary

This chapter covered .NET Data Providers in reasonable detail and provided enough information to get started with the DataSet object model. Working with relational databases forms a significant part of most commercial Web Applications, and therefore knowledge of ADO.NET is an essential part of the ASP.NET developer's repertoire.

Don't believe anyone who tells you ADO.NET is all about using DataSets—it simply isn't true. There is no database-related operation that you can do with DataSets that you can't do simply using a .NET Data Provider. At the end of the day, .NET Data Providers are more efficient and easier to understand than DataSets. Furthermore, DataSets only really make sense for data that you intend to hold onto for some time because otherwise the cost of creating them can be hard to justify. Nevertheless, we can't deny that there is some great functionality in DataSets. Our closing message on the topic is to bear in mind that although DataSets are easy to program with, they're hard to understand, and you should really understand them pretty well before getting too heavily involved. This message applies in particular to updating databases the DataSet way.

So far, we've looked at the programming aspects of working with ADO.NET, and in doing so, we've created fairly mundane user interfaces. In the next chapter we'll explore the more visually exciting data binding features available for .NET Web Applications.

CHAPTER 8

Data Binding

Understanding Data Bound Lists

Binding Expressions

Implementing Data Bound Input Controls

Using Templates, Repeaters, DataLists, and DataGrids

Putting It Together

DataGrid Sorting and Paging

Editing and Updating

Using Templates with Datagrids

Event Bubbling

DATA BINDING—THE SIGHT OF those two words may cause many of you to think about skipping straight to the next chapter. After all, data binding has historically been one of those techniques that "real programmers" don't use. There have long been concerns that data binding can introduce unwanted side effects and can have an unpredictable impact on the way that applications run.

However, we urge you to forget all that's gone before; put aside any preconceptions you may have about data binding and read on. As you'll see in this chapter, data binding is a very powerful tool in ASP.NET and can help simplify your code and applications; yet, at the same time, it offers optimized performance. So, data binding in ASP.NET is quite unlike traditional data binding in VB 6.0; it performs a similar task, but it does so in a completely different way.

So, what's data binding all about? Data binding gives you a way to transfer information into the user interface of your application with a minimum amount of code. The techniques are efficient and have been optimized to work with specific types of data (such as ADO.NET DataReaders and DataTables), although they also support many other forms such as arrays, collections, properties, functions, expressions, and simple variables.

The previous chapter introduced a number of ADO.NET techniques for retrieving, updating, adding, and deleting data; it also showed how the techniques could be applied to Web Applications created with ASP.NET. In these examples (and many of your own applications if you follow this style) you will see that a fair proportion of the code deals with displaying the data; it's this code that can typically be reduced or eliminated by using ASP.NET data binding. So why is this different from historic data binding?

- ASP.NET data binding is **always** read-only. There's no way to automatically write changes back to the datasource—even if you wanted to. Instead, you must use the updating techniques that we covered in the previous chapter.

- ASP.NET data binding can be tightly controlled, allowing you to determine what information appears, where it appears, and what format is used.

- ASP.NET data binding is not limited to using ADO.NET sources, although these are probably the most likely to be used. In fact, ASP.NET data binding is not even limited to database information and can be performed against almost any type and source of data.

Before you dive in and start data binding all your controls, there are a couple of potential pitfalls of which you should be aware:

- **By using data binding in your application, you are relinquishing a (very small) degree of control.** ASP.NET will have the final say about what data appears where and when. While you have a lot of influence over the process, you don't have complete control.

- **Data binding often requires that you insert *binding expressions* into the content of your .aspx files.** We'll see more about binding expressions shortly, but for now you should think of them as being small extracts of code that determine what data is bound to a control. By inserting code in this way you are negating one of ASP.NET's real benefits: separation of code from visual content. While it may not seem to be a big problem at first, this can make maintenance more difficult and time consuming.

In most situations, the benefits offered by data binding outweigh the disadvantages, but as with all programming tasks, you need to consider all of the issues before implementing a data-binding solution.

Understanding Data Bound Lists

One of the simplest and most useful forms of data binding is the automatic population of controls, such as the ListBox, DropDownList, CheckBoxList, and RadioButtonList. Chapter 7 showed how DataReaders and DataSets can be used to retrieve the data, after which a loop is used to transfer the information to the control. Data binding makes much of this code unnecessary.

All of the controls that can be used in this way support a common set of members:

- The **DataBind** method is called to activate the binding after the data has been retrieved and after the control's properties have been set.

- **DataMember** and **DataSource** define the source of data for the control. DataSource is more frequently used and is assigned a DataReader, DataTable, or other suitable object. DataMember is used if DataSource represents a compound datasource (such as a DataSet) and defines which element should be used (such as the Table within the DataSet).

- The **DataTextField** property specifies the field that will be used for the visible content of the control. This corresponds to the Text property of the ListItem objects in the control.

- **DataValueField** specifies the field that will be used for the value of each ListItem in the control. When an entry is selected, it is the content of this field that is returned as the Value of the control.

- **DataTextFormatString** defines a .NET format string to control the appearance of the control's content. This is especially useful when specific numeric or date formats are required.

The most common way of using these members to bind a control is as follows:

1. Add the control to the Web Form.

2. Define the values for DataTextField and DataValueField. This can be done in the Property window at design-time, or in code.

3. Add code to retrieve the data that will be used to populate the control, ensuring that the fields named in step two are included. In ASP.NET, DataReaders are the most efficient technique.

4. Assign the DataReader to the control's DataSource property, and call the DataBind method.

For example, Figure 8-1 shows a Web Form that displays Aircraft Details for the HiFlyers application. In the top right of the page is a DropDownList control that will list all of the school-operated aircraft. Let's see what's involved in data binding this list.

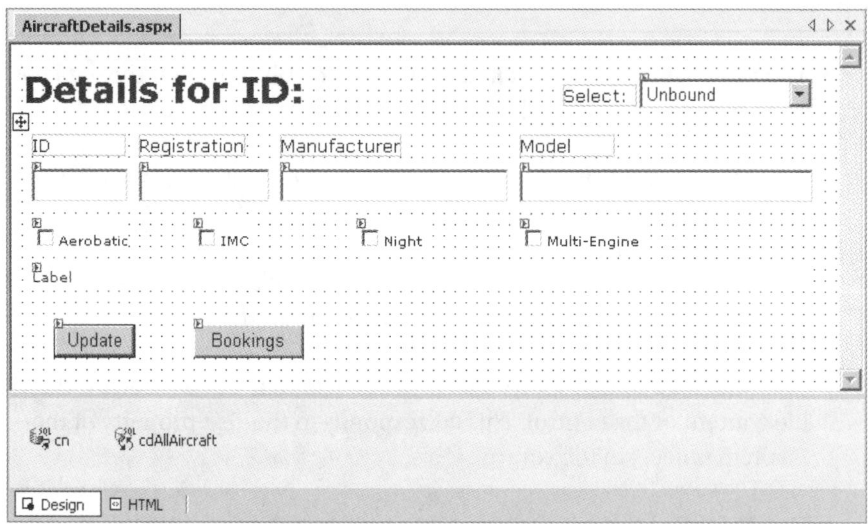

Figure 8-1. Aircraft Details page

The DropDownList control is named lstAircraft, and has its DataTextField property set to `Registration` and its DataValueField set to `AircraftID`. These two fields will be retrieved from the database in the form of a DataReader, which will be generated from two components that have also been added to the Web Form:

- An SQLClient.SQLConnection called cn to connect to the database.
- An SQLClient.SQLCommand called cdAllAircraft which returns the ID and registration of each aircraft in the fleet. The command text is `SELECT AircraftID, Registration FROM Aircraft` and the command's Connection property is set to `cn`.

In the `Page_Load` handler for the Web Form, the following code is used to data bind the list:

```
If IsPostBack = False Then
    Dim dr As SqlClient.SqlDataReader
    cn.Open()
    dr = cdAllAircraft.ExecuteReader
    lstAircraft.DataSource = dr
    lstAircraft.DataBind()
    dr.Close()
    cn.Close()
End If
```

By now you should recognize that this opens a DataReader from the command; but, rather than calling the `Read()` method to loop through the records, the DataReader is assigned to the `DataSource` of the DropDownList control. The control's `DataBind` method is then called to activate the binding and populate the control. As soon as this has completed, the DataReader and Connection can be closed (remember that the Connection will be pooled for efficient reuse).

Notice that we are doing all of this only when `Page.IsPostback=False`; in other words, on the initial page request. The DropDownList is automatically populated on subsequent postbacks from ViewState (see Chapter 3 for a refresher), making it unnecessary for us to run our code. Of course, if ViewState had been disabled for the control (by setting the DropDownList's EnableViewState property to `False`), then we *would* need to perform the data binding each time. Remember, when you're using data-binding techniques with controls, you either rely on ViewState to maintain the content across postbacks or you disable ViewState and run your own code each time.

NOTE *If your page uses ViewState to maintain the control, it is quite possible that the data shown to the user is rather out-of-date because the original query is run only once, irrespective of the number of postbacks. You may want to add a Refresh button to the Web Form to allow users to retrieve the most current data.*

You can use exactly the same techniques to data bind a ListBox, CheckBoxList, or RadioButtonList. While the control on the Web Form will be different, the code in the Page_Load handler will remain the same. You can also use a DataSet or DataTable object as the datasource, but there will be no benefit unless the object has already been created or it will be used again elsewhere in the code.

Binding Expressions

The approach to data binding that we've just covered is great for populating list-oriented controls, but what if we want to data bind other controls. Well, ASP.NET actually allows you to bind almost anything on a Web Form page to almost anything in the code-behind class—but only list-oriented controls tend to support properties such as DataTextField and DataValueField. How then do we perform data binding to TextBoxes, Tables, and even plain HTML? The key to this is the use of *binding expressions*. Binding expressions are links between visual elements and the data they display. The binding expression is entered into the .aspx file (usually using HTML View) and takes the following form:

```
<%# expression %>
```

The `expression` can refer to any valid source of data—such as a variable, constant, calculation, or function. Strictly speaking, any values must be exposed as properties or method calls of the Web Form's class, so they are defined as public or protected variables or functions. The actual data type is irrelevant because you can bind as easily to a simple Integer property as a complex DataSet—even if Option Strict has been turned on! Some examples of simple binding expressions are as follows (remember, these binding expressions are written directly into the .aspx file):

```
Details for Aircraft <%# intAircraftID %>
<td><%# strForename + " " + strSurname %></td>
<asp:TextBox id="txtDOB" Text="<%# dr.GetString(3) %>"...../>
```

These examples show that you can place binding expressions anywhere within the content of the .aspx—even within an attribute value inside a tag. To make these examples work, `intAircraftID`, `strForename`, `strSurname`, and `dr` need to be exposed as properties from the Web Form's class. For example, you can use any of the following definitions:

```
Public Property intAircraftID() As Integer
    Get
       .....
    End Get
End Property
Protected strForename, strSurname As String
Public dr As SqlClient.SqlDataReader
```

Alternatively, the datasource may be a public or protected function:

```
<%# CalcTotalCost() %>
```

Using Binding Expressions

Binding expressions are entered into the Web Form page and can be positioned almost anywhere. For example, a binding expression can be used in the opening tag of a TextBox server control to data bind the `Text` attribute:

```
<asp:TextBox id="txtID" runat="server" Text='<%# intAircraftID %>'>
```

Alternatively, a binding expression can be inserted into a standard `<h1>` tag to generate part of a heading:

```
<h1>Details for ID: <%# intAircraftID %></h1>
```

When creating binding expressions, it's important that you leave no scope for ambiguity because ASP.NET can easily misinterpret the content of a binding expression. For example, the following binding expression will generate a "server tag is not well formed" error when the page is processed:

```
<asp:TextBox id="TextBox1" runat="server"
        Text="<%# strForename + " " + strSurname %>"></asp:TextBox>
```

The cause of the error is the use of double quotes for both the `Text` attribute and the string literal in the binding expression. ASP.NET cannot resolve the delimiters and so reports an error with the tag. The solution is to replace the delimiters for the attribute with single quotes:

```
<asp:TextBox id="TextBox1" runat="server"
        Text='<%# strForename + " " + strSurname %>'></asp:TextBox>
```

Implementing Data Bound Input Controls

To better illustrate binding expressions, let's continue with our Aircraft Details Web Form and data bind the TextBox and CheckBox controls that were shown in Figure 8-1. We'll do this by creating a DataReader that represents the details for the aircraft selected in the DropDownList. Then we'll data bind the fields in the DataReader to the appropriate controls.

Retrieving the Data

To begin, we'll add a new SQLCommand component to the Web Form. We'll call it cdAircraftDetails, set its Connection to cn, and set its CommandText property to the following:

```
SELECT AircraftID, Registration, Manuf, Model, CanDoAeros,
CanDoIMC, CanDoNight, CanDoMulti FROM Aircraft
WHERE (AircraftID = @AircraftID)
```

This SQL statement selects the required fields from the table and is parameterized by AircraftID. The command will be executed from a routine in the Web Form's class, and the results retrieved into a DataReader. The declaration for the DataReader should be made at class-level using the `Protected` keyword:

```
Protected drDetails As SqlClient.SqlDataReader
```

By defining the DataReader as `Protected`, it can be accessed within the class, as well as by any derived classes. Remember that there is an inheritance relationship between the .aspx and the class defined in the .aspx.vb file; so, by declaring the variable as `Protected`, we are able to access it within the Web Form page.

Next, we'll create a procedure to call the command and place the results into the DataReader:

```
Private Sub ShowDetails(ByVal AircraftID As Long)
    cn.Open()
    cdAircraftDetails.Parameters(0).Value = AircraftID
    drDetails = cdAircraftDetails.ExecuteReader(CommandBehavior.SingleRow)
    drDetails.Read()
    Me.DataBind()
    cn.Close()
End Sub
```

Notice that once ExecuteReader has been called to retrieve the results into the DataReader, the `Read()` method is called to access the first (and only) row and then the `DataBind()` method is called for the class. You might wonder why we need to call `Read()` in this case, since we didn't when we were binding the ListBox and DropDownList controls in the earlier example. The reason is that we are now binding a single row using binding expressions, while in the earlier example we were binding multiple rows using the control's DataSource property. When using DataSource, ASP.NET automatically uses the appropriate technique (such as calling `Read()`) to iterate through the rows in the supplied data so that it can populate the control. Binding expressions don't do this and require that you ensure the data is correctly initialized.

Also in this example, we are calling the page-level `DataBind()` method to bind all the controls in one go, rather than calling `DataBind()` for each control in turn; this can be much more efficient. However, we haven't yet defined any data bindings on the Web Form for this DataReader, so the next step is to add the binding expressions.

Binding the Controls

The data in the DataReader will be bound to the TextBox and CheckBox controls, so we need to define binding expressions for the controls' properties as follows:

```
<asp:textbox id="txtID"...Text='<%# drDetails(0) %>'></asp:textbox>
<asp:textbox id="txtReg"...Text='<%# drDetails(1) %>'></asp:textbox>
<asp:textbox id="txtManuf"...Text='<%# drDetails(2) %>'></asp:textbox>
<asp:textbox id="txtModel" ...Text='<%# drDetails(3) %>'></asp:textbox>
<asp:checkbox id="chkAeros"...Checked='<%# drDetails(4) %>'></asp:checkbox>
<asp:checkbox id="chkIMC"...Checked='<%# drDetails(5) %>'></asp:checkbox>
<asp:checkbox id="chkNight"...Checked='<%# drDetails(6) %>'></asp:checkbox>
<asp:checkbox id="chkMulti"...Checked='<%# drDetails(7) %>'></asp:checkbox>
```

We've found it easiest and quickest to enter binding expressions directly into the HTML View of the Web Form page. In the above listing you can see that the binding expressions have been created within the `Text` and `Checked` properties.

As well as manually entering binding expressions, you can also use the **(DataBindings)** entry in the Property browser, as shown in Figure 8-2.

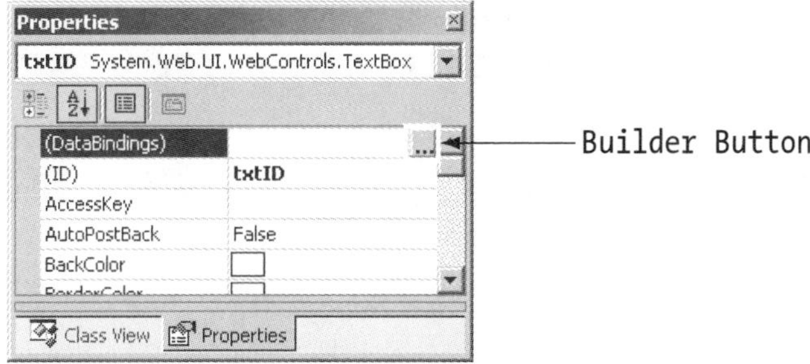

Figure 8-2. (DataBindings) in the Property browser

Clicking the builder button for the property displays the DataBindings Property Builder dialog, as shown in Figure 8-3. The **Text** property is shown with a different icon, indicating that it is data bound; and when selected, the right-hand side shows the binding expression.

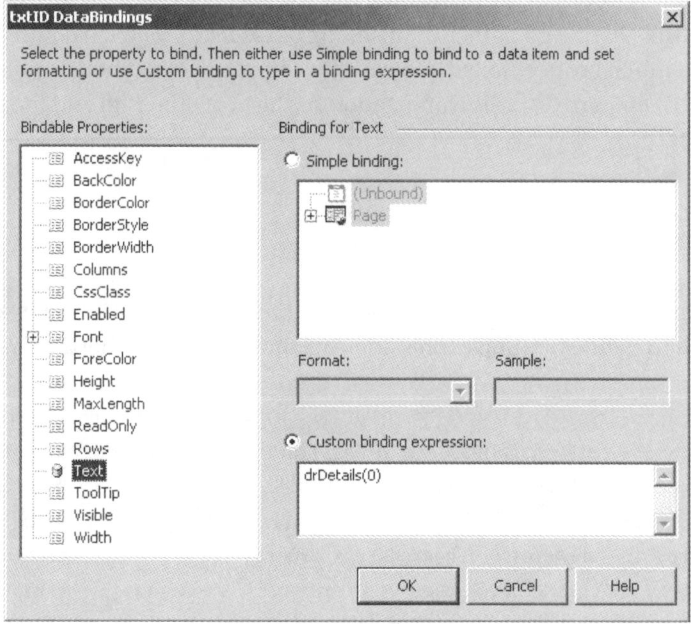

Figure 8-3. (DataBindings) Property Builder dialog

If you return to the Properties window and view the **Text** property, you'll see that it is also annotated with the same icon, as shown in Figure 8-4.

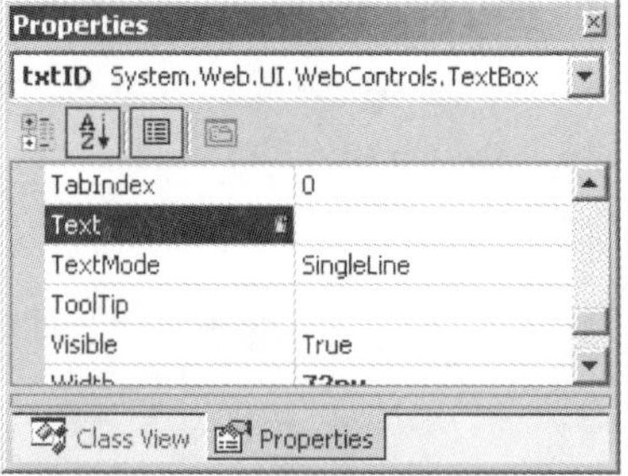

Figure 8-4. Data bound property annotation

Binding Static HTML

You may think that binding expressions are specific to Web Controls, but you'd be very wrong. Binding expressions can be placed almost anywhere in the Web Form, including within sections of static HTML.

For example, refer back to Figure 8-1 and you'll see that there's a heading at the top of the page that reads "Details for ID:". We can add a binding expression to this heading to show the aircraft ID by defining the HTML as follows:

```
<h1>
    Details for ID:
    <%# drDetails(0) %>
</h1>
```

Notice that the syntax of the binding expression is exactly the same—only its position is different. As you can imagine, this ability to place binding expressions anywhere provides great power and flexibility, allowing you to bind almost any property of Web and HTML Controls—as well as use binding expressions—with hyperlinks, client-side script, and more.

Activating the Binding

The final step is to ensure that the ShowDetails() routine is called when an aircraft is selected in the DropDownList. Not surprisingly, we'll use the SelectedIndexChanged event of lstAircraft to do this:

```
Private Sub lstAircraft_SelectedIndexChanged(ByVal sender As System.Object, _
         ByVal e As System.EventArgs) Handles lstAircraft.SelectedIndexChanged
   ShowDetails(lstAircraft.SelectedItem.Value)
   lblError.Visible = False
End Sub
```

The event handler simply calls ShowDetails() passing the value of the currently selected entry. It also makes the error label invisible; this label is used in the update routine as we'll soon see. As well as coding the routine, we must also set the AutoPostback property of the DropDownList to True, so that the request is submitted as soon as the user selects a different entry in the list. Without this setting, the user would need to click a submit button in order to generate the postback.

Test the page by selecting **Build and Browse** and select one of the aircraft from the list. The details should be displayed in the Web Form, similar to those shown in Figure 8-5.

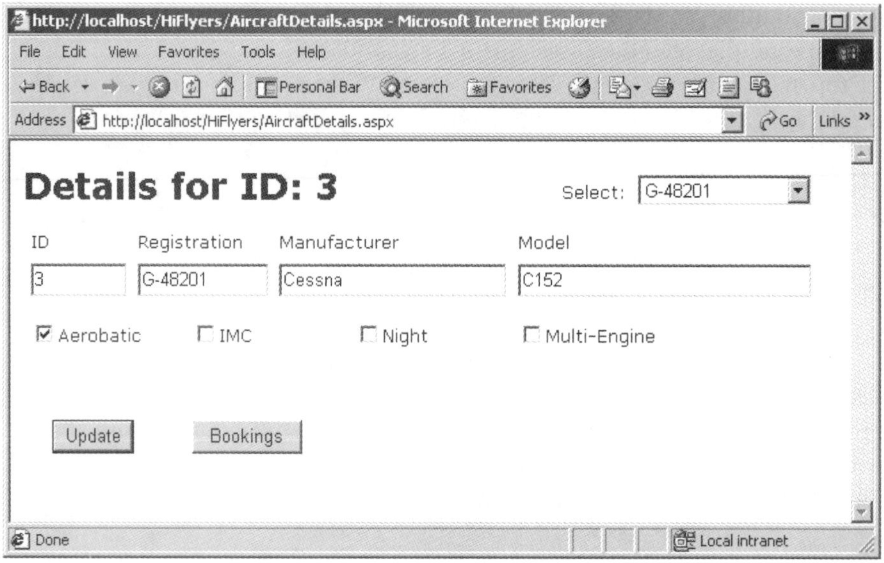

Figure 8-5. Viewing the Aircraft Details page

There's one slight anomaly with the Web Form as it currently stands. When first displayed, the selection list shows a registration (as if it had been selected), but its details are not displayed in the page. This is more of an aesthetic problem than a practical one, but it's still worth solving.

The reason for this behavior is quite obvious: In the `Page_Load` handler we are initializing the DropDownList, causing it to automatically display the first entry. But, the code to display the details is called only when the selection is changed. By now it should also be obvious that to solve this problem, we need only make a call to `ShowDetails()` from within `Page_Load`:

```
Private Sub Page_Load(ByVal sender As System.Object, _
            ByVal e As System.EventArgs) Handles MyBase.Load
    If IsPostBack = False Then
       ....
       ....

        ShowDetails(lstAircraft.SelectedItem.Value)
    End If
End Sub
```

Whilst this seems to be a perfectly workable solution, it actually causes the entire Web page to fail when the `ShowDetails()` routine is executed. Figure 8-6 shows the results.

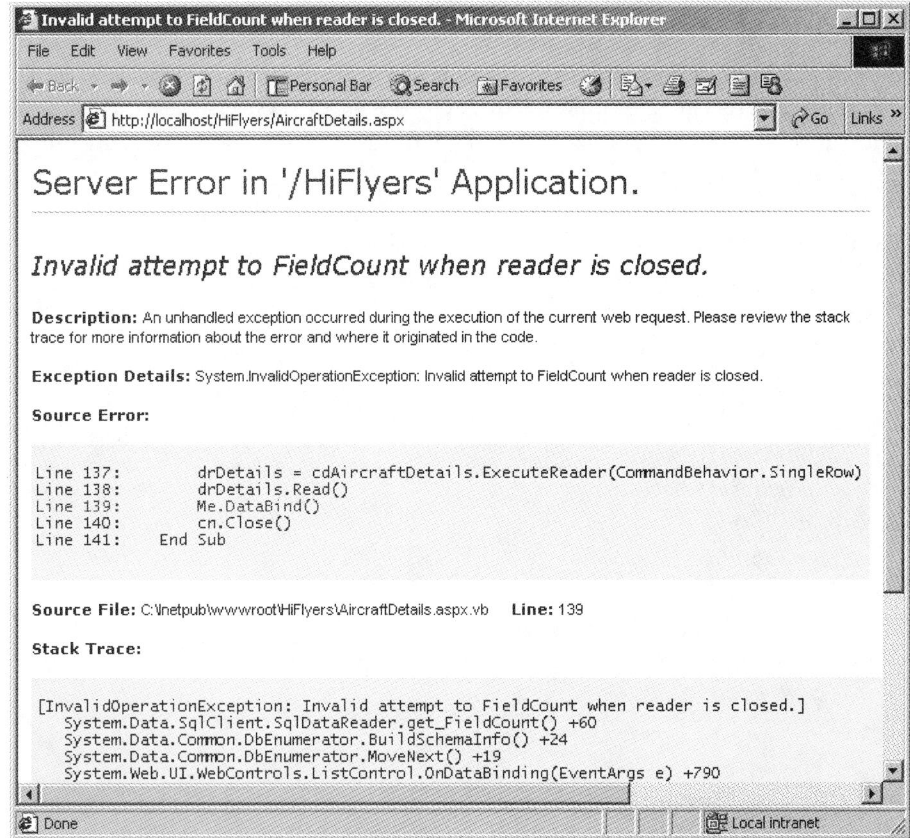

Figure 8-6. Failure during data binding

The true cause of this failure may not be immediately apparent because the error message appears to imply that `drDetails` is the closed DataReader. However, the real origin of the problem is in the `Page_Load` routine, when we created the dr DataReader to populate the DropDownList. The sequence is as follows:

1. `Page_Load` is triggered for the initial page request.

2. The dr DataReader is populated from the cdAllAircraft command, bound to lstAircraft, and then closed.

3. `ShowDetails()` is called to display the details for the first aircraft in the list. When the `Me.DataBind()` statement is executed, ASP.NET attempts to bind *all* of the controls on the Web Form, including lstAircraft. However, the DataReader that provided the DataSource for the list has been closed, hence the error.

The simplest solution to the problem is to set the DataSource of lstAircraft to `Nothing` after it has been populated, but before `ShowDetails()` is called. This prevents the `Me.DataBind()` statement from attempting to activate the binding for the DropDownList a second time:

```
Private Sub Page_Load(ByVal sender As System.Object, _
            ByVal e As System.EventArgs) Handles MyBase.Load
    If IsPostBack = False Then
        Dim dr As SqlClient.SqlDataReader
        cn.Open()
        dr = cdAllAircraft.ExecuteReader
        lstAircraft.DataSource = dr
        lstAircraft.DataBind()
        dr.Close()
        cn.Close()

        lstAircraft.DataSource = Nothing
        ShowDetails(lstAircraft.SelectedItem.Value)
    End If
End Sub
```

This is a good example of the unexpected side-effects that data binding can introduce. Once you understand them they can usually be remedied very quickly. The challenge is to understand why the problems occur in the first place and to design them out of the application from the start.

Issuing Updates

As we've already mentioned, data binding in ASP.NET is read-only, and the only way you'll issue any updates to the database is by using the techniques discussed in Chapter 7. For our Aircraft Details page we'll create a parameterized command that can be executed when the user clicks the Update button.

To start, we'll add another SQLCommand to the Web Form, with its Connection set to `cn` and its CommandText set to the following:

```
UPDATE Aircraft SET Registration = @Registration, Manuf = @Manuf,
Model = @Model, CanDoAeros = @CanDoAeros, CanDoIMC = @CanDoIMC,
CanDoNight = @CanDoNight, CanDoMulti = @CanDoMulti
WHERE (AircraftID = @AircraftID)
```

You could use any of the techniques discussed in Chapter 7 to manage conflicts and concurrency issues, but for our purposes we'll keep things simple. Having defined the components, the handler for the Update button can then be coded as follows:

```
Private Sub btnUpdate_Click(ByVal sender As System.Object, _
                ByVal e As System.EventArgs) Handles btnUpdate.Click
    Try
        With cdUpdateAircraft.Parameters
            .Item("@AircraftID").Value = CInt(txtID.Text)
            .Item("@Registration").Value = txtReg.Text
            .Item("@Manuf").Value = txtManuf.Text
            .Item("@Model").Value = txtModel.Text
            .Item("@CanDoAeros").Value = CInt(chkAeros.Checked)
            .Item("@CanDoIMC").Value = CInt(chkIMC.Checked)
            .Item("@CanDoNight").Value = CInt(chkNight.Checked)
            .Item("@CanDoMulti").Value = CInt(chkMulti.Checked)
        End With

        cn.Open()
        cdUpdateAircraft.ExecuteNonQuery()

    Catch ex As Exception
        lblError.Text = "Unable to perform update for Aircraft " + txtID.Text
        lblError.Visible = True
    Finally
        cn.Close()
    End Try
End Sub
```

This code uses exactly the same approach as the examples in Chapter 7, so you can see that the method you use to display the data has no impact on the method you use to update it. By now you should have sufficient skills to create similar routines for adding and deleting aircraft records, so we won't go into further detail on these topics.

Using Templates, Repeaters, DataLists, and DataGrids

So far, we've looked at two different approaches to binding—both of which will find potential uses in many Web applications. However, they both have certain limitations:

- The first approach allowed us to bind multiple rows of data, but was limited to working with specific controls. It also limited us to working with particular properties of those controls.
- The second approach allowed us to use any control or HTML element. We could create binding expressions for almost any property or attribute. However, we were only able to display data from a single row at a time.

What if we want to combine these techniques and display multiple rows of data, but retain the flexibility and control that binding expressions provide? That's where the Repeater, DataList, and DataGrid controls come in. They fall into the *List Controls* category of Web Controls and were introduced in Chapter 4. While they share certain common features, they also differ somewhat in terms of the functionality they offer.

Repeater

The *Repeater* is the most lightweight of the List controls, and when rendered to the browser, it offers no inherent visual interface of its own. Instead, you define *templates* that contain the tags, controls, and other content that you require in the different sections of the control. The Repeater supports five different templates:

- The **HeaderTemplate** defines how the content for the start of the control is rendered. For example, if you're using a list where each item is on a separate line, you can use the HeaderTemplate to define the heading row.
- The **ItemTemplate** determines how standard items are rendered in the list.
- The **AlternatingItemTemplate** allows you to define a different style and layout that will be applied to alternating items in the list.
- The **SeparatorTemplate** defines how items are separated from one another.

- The **FooterTemplate** defines how the content for the end of the control is rendered. For example, you could use this to display a summary, such as the total number of items in the list.

TIP *You don't have to define all of the templates for every Repeater control you use—just define the ones you need.*

When you think of generating a list, you may well focus on generating a vertical list, with each item on a separate line. In this case, the HeaderTemplate would be rendered at the top, the FooterTemplate at the bottom, and the other templates in between. However, you can as easily use the Repeater to generate a horizontal list (perhaps with entries separated by commas or semicolons), in which case the HeaderTemplate is rendered on the left, the FooterTemplate on the right, and the others in the middle.

For example, Figure 8-7 shows two different lists, both generated using Repeater controls.

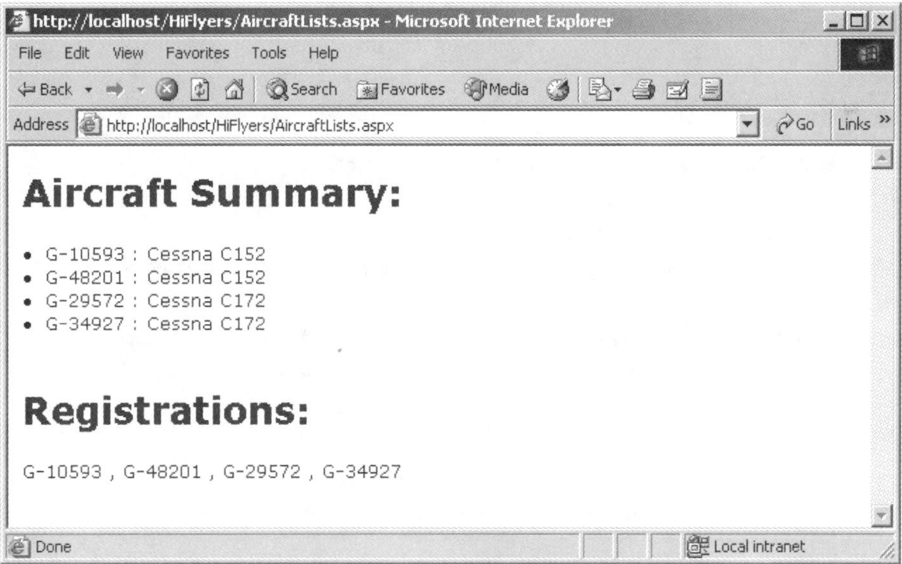

Figure 8-7. Repeater controls

The **Aircraft Summary** is presented as a bulleted list, and is defined using the following elements inside the .aspx file:

```
<asp:repeater id="Repeater1" runat="server">
    <ItemTemplate>
        <li>
            <%# dr("Registration") %>
            :
            <%# dr("Details") %>
        </li>
    </ItemTemplate>
</asp:repeater>
```

This example uses only an `<ItemTemplate>` section, which contains a `<li>` (ListItem) element. Browsers typically render `<li>` elements with a bullet point. Within the ListItem we've placed a binding expression to retrieve the Registration field from a DataReader, then a colon, then another binding expression to retrieve the Details field from the same DataReader. This example renders as a vertical list because the browser automatically inserts line breaks after each `<li> . . . </li>` element.

In addition to the HTML tags and elements in the .aspx file, we also need the following in the code-behind module to create the DataReader and bind it to the Repeater:

```
Protected dr As SqlClient.SqlDataReader

Private Sub Page_Load(ByVal sender As System.Object, _
                ByVal e As System.EventArgs) Handles MyBase.Load
    If Me.IsPostBack = False Then
        Dim strCon As String = "Data Source=(local);Initial Catalog=HiFlyer;" & _
                "Integrated Security=SSPI"
        Dim strSQL As String = "SELECT Registration, Manuf + ' ' + Model AS " & _
                "Details, AircraftID FROM Aircraft ORDER BY " & _
                "Manuf + ' ' + Model, Registration"

        Dim cn As New SqlClient.SqlConnection(strCon)
        Dim cd As New SqlClient.SqlCommand(strSQL, cn)

        cn.Open()
        dr = cd.ExecuteReader
        Repeater1.DataSource = dr
        Repeater1.DataBind()
        dr.Close()
```

```
        cn.Close()
    End If
End Sub
```

The dr variable is declared at the class level with the Protected keyword to make it available within both the code class and the .aspx page. On the initial page request, the Page_Load routine populates the Repeater by creating an SQLCommand that selects the required fields from the database and then fills the dr DataReader by calling the ExecuteReader method. The DataReader is assigned to the DataSource of the Repeater, and the DataBind method is called to activate the binding and populate the control. The control renders the ItemTemplate once for each record in the DataReader, and so generates the bulleted list shown in Figure 8-7.

The **Registrations** list in Figure 8-7 is also created with a Repeater control, but this time we have defined an <ItemTemplate> and a <SeparatorTemplate> to create a comma-separated list:

```
<asp:repeater id="Repeater2" runat="server">
    <ItemTemplate>
        <%# dr("Registration") %>
    </ItemTemplate>
    <SeparatorTemplate>
        ,
    </SeparatorTemplate>
</asp:repeater>
```

The <ItemTemplate> contains only a binding expression to obtain the Registration field from the dr DataReader, while the <SeparatorTemplate> contains just a single comma. The code in the Page_Load event would be much the same as for the Aircraft Summary list above, although the SQL statement would need to retrieve only the Registration field. When the page is viewed in the browser, the ItemTemplate is rendered for each record in the DataReader, with a SeparatorTemplate rendered between each pair. As you'd expect, the control *doesn't* render a SeparatorTemplate after the last item. The resulting list is displayed on a single line because we have not used any <br> or <p> tags, nor any other elements which would cause a line break to occur.

NOTE *At design-time, the templates within the Repeater control must be created in HTML View. Also, the Repeater control offers no support for Property Builders, AutoFormats, or predefined styles.*

You'll probably make frequent use of the Repeater because it gives you complete flexibility and control. It makes no assumption or supposition about how the output will look; instead, it allows you to generate any visual rendering you want. However, in some situations you may want additional functionality such as editing, sorting, or paging, or you may find that you end up defining templates containing many <tr> and <td> tags to create complex tables. In such cases, you may find that either the DataList or the DataGrid is a better alternative.

DataList

The *DataList control* offers a richer feature set than the Repeater, including automatic generation of <table>, <tr>, and <td> tags to hold each list item, as well as a degree of support for editing entries within the list. You still retain a great degree of flexibility with DataLists because they require that you create templates to define the content and layout of each item.

DataLists support a total of seven different templates: *HeaderTemplate, FooterTemplate, ItemTemplate, AlternatingItemTemplate,* and *SeparatorTemplate* are the same as those found in the Repeater. In addition, the *SelectedItemTemplate* defines the content and appearance of the selected row and *EditItemTemplate* defines the content and appearance for any row being edited. However, to use either of these additional features you will need to add code and controls to allow the user to trigger the selection or editing processes.

For example, the following DataList will display the summary statistics for the number of flights each aircraft has made, using color coding to highlight underutilized aircraft and applying an alternating item style.

```
<asp:datalist id="DataList1" runat="server" BorderColor="#DEDFDE"
                BorderStyle="None" BackColor="White" CellPadding="4"
                GridLines="Vertical" BorderWidth="1px" ForeColor="Black"
                Width="296px" Height="120px">
    <AlternatingItemStyle BackColor="White" />
    <ItemStyle BackColor="#F7F7DE" />
    <ItemTemplate>
        <%# dr("Registration") %>,
        <%# dr("Manuf") %>
        <%# dr("Model") %>,
        <font color='<%# dr("AlertColor") %>'>
            <%# dr("Flights") %> Flights
        </font>
    </ItemTemplate>
</asp:datalist>
```

Notice that we're using only the <ItemTemplate>, but we've applied styles to the list items using the <ItemStyle> and <AlternatingItemStyle> elements. When you're deciding whether to use templates or styles for alternating items, a good guideline is that if the content is to be the same, but it is to be formatted differently, then you should use styles. If the content needs to be different (for example, you use different controls), then you'll need to use templates.

The binding expressions in this example have been used for two tasks. In the body of the ItemTemplate are four binding expressions to retrieve and display values from the fields in the database, while the <font> element contains a binding expression applied to its color attribute. As you can see, binding expressions are not restricted to displaying data—they can also be used to provide values for attributes.

Figure 8-8 shows how this DataList will appear when viewed in a browser.

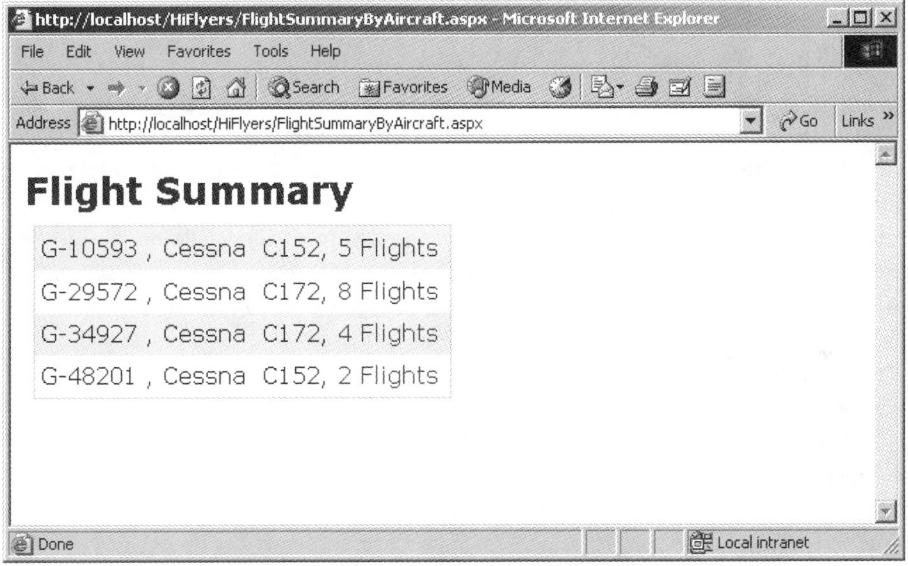

Figure 8-8. DataList with alternating row styles

In Chapter 4 we showed a brief example of a DataGrid, and in our next section we'll investigate DataGrids in much more detail. However, at this point you might be wondering why we didn't use a DataGrid for this last task, since the results look remarkably grid-like. The answer is, quite simply, that we didn't need to; the DataList provides all of the functionality that we need and allows us to render the content exactly as required. There's no need to use the more heavyweight DataGrid control.

Functionality

DataLists are quite different from Repeaters in terms of the features they offer and the way that they work. For example, in the Repeater examples that you saw previously, we were able to control the direction of the control (horizontal or vertical) by adding different tags to the ItemTemplate. The DataList is different though, with this behavior being controlled by the RepeatDirection property.

However, that doesn't mean that you can simply take a DataList and change its RepeatDirection from `Vertical` to `Horizontal`. In practice, you'll also need to make other changes, such as changing the content of the templates to suit the orientation that you've chosen. For example, let's take our previous DataList and convert it to render horizontally. As well as changing the RepeatDirection property to `Horizontal` (or `RepeatDirection.Horizontal` in code), we'll need to modify the ItemTemplate by inserting `<br>` tags between the binding expressions that make up each entry. The following shows the changes that would be required:

```
<ItemTemplate>
    <%# dr("Registration") %>
    <br>
    <%# dr("Manuf") %> <%# dr("Model") %>
    <br>
    <font color='<%# dr("AlertColor") %>'>
        <%# dr("Flights") %> Flights
    </font>
</ItemTemplate>
```

Figure 8-9 shows how this will appear when rendered to a browser.

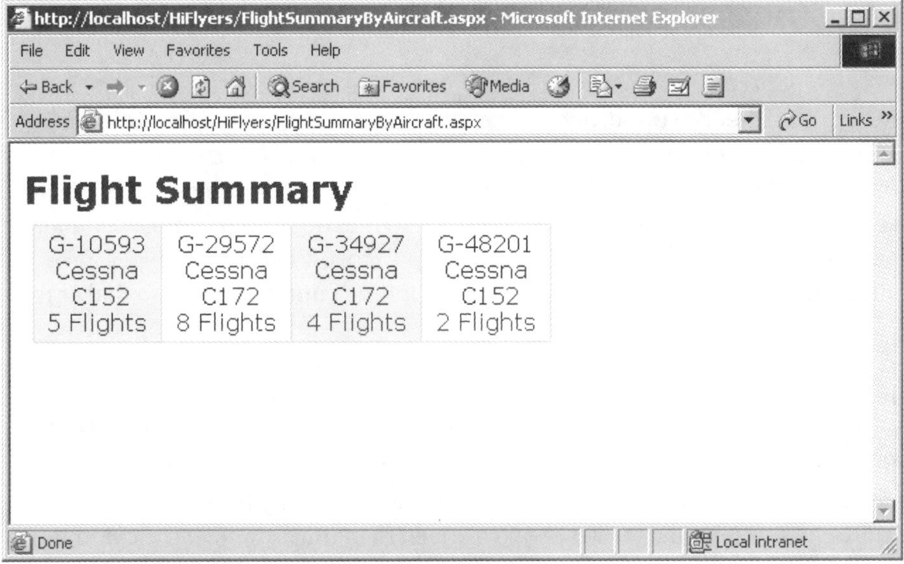

Figure 8-9. DataList rendered horizontally

Another option you have with a DataList is to "snake" the list over multiple columns. This is controlled by the RepeatColumns property, but you can only do this when RepeatDirection is set to `Vertical`. In fact, if you set RepeatColumns to a number greater than zero, the DataList ignores the value of RepeatDirection and always renders the list vertically.

The final appearance-related property we'll discuss is RepeatLayout. This can be set to `Table` (the default) or `Flow`, and determines what HTML is generated for the list when it is rendered to the browser. If you specify `Table`, the control will automatically generate a `<table>` element, together with all the necessary `<tr>` and `<td>` elements, to represent the list. If you specify `Flow`, none of these elements are generated; the list will be rendered using only the controls that you added to the templates. This may be useful when you want to use a DataList control, but don't want the tabular layout that it usually generates.

TIP *DataList controls also support editing and selection of individual list items. The techniques discussed in the DataGrid section below to perform these tasks can also be applied to DataLists.*

DataGrid

The *DataGrid control* extends the concepts behind the Repeater and DataList one stage further by supporting the definition of multiple columns within the control. Each column can be individually configured and tailored, and can either display a field of data (known as a *bound* column), buttons or hyperlinks (known as *button* or *hyperlink* columns), or you can define the content using a *template* column. As we'll see in this section, this support for varied column types gives you great flexibility in creating the interface for the control, but it also makes the DataGrid remarkably easy to use.

Visually, the DataGrid is displayed in a tabular layout and, by default, it's rendered as an HTML table with each item of data represented as HTML text. This automatic rendering of data items into columns is controlled by the DataGrid's AutoGenerateColumns property; when set to `True` (the default value), columns are automatically created to match the datasource, but if you set AutoGenerateColumns to `False` you will need to manually define the columns you want. We'll return to this topic shortly.

The DataGrid is capable of displaying text boxes and other controls that allow users to modify the displayed values, but you must add code to write these changes back to the underlying datasource. The DataGrid also supports row selection, sorting, and paging, although once again you will need to add code to activate these features. Figure 8-10 shows an example of a DataGrid that has been customized with these features.

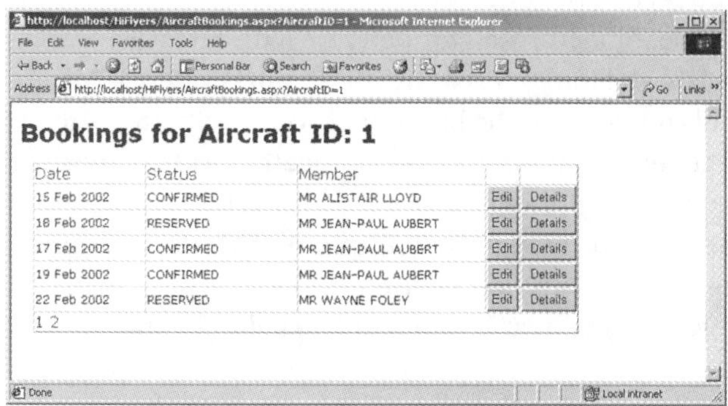

Figure 8-10. DataGrid with paging and sorting

At design-time, the DataGrid offers a friendly Property Builder dialog, and supports an AutoFormat capability with a number of predefined styles. The content of the DataGrid is defined using graphical (WYSIWYG) or text-based (HTML) editing, and it provides numerous styles and templates to define appearance.

The DataGrid provides a number of different column types for you to use. If you're using the AutoGenerateColumns feature, every column that is created will be a Bound column that represents a single item of data (such as a field from a DataReader). If you want the user to interact with the DataGrid, you can create Button columns and HyperLink columns. For example, in Figure 8-10 you can see two Button columns for the Edit and Details buttons. All of these column types are great, and you'll probably use them often, but there will always be times when you want the DataGrid to look different. For example, maybe you want to display a CheckBox instead of writing True or False as text, or maybe you want to combine several fields of data into one column in the DataGrid. In this situation you would use Template columns, which give you complete control over the content, positioning, and formatting of each column.

Template columns in DataGrid controls are like templates in Repeaters and DataLists; you define the content and layout of the column by adding tags, elements, and controls. DataGrids support four different types of template: ItemTemplates define appearance for regular rows in the grid, EditItemTemplates allow you to create a different look and feel for a row when it is being modified, and HeaderTemplates and FooterTemplates control the appearance for the first and last rows. Note that DataGrid controls do not support as AlternatingItemTemplate, although there is an `<AlternatingItemStyle>` element to control appearance.

You may not always want to use templates—after all they take more effort than using ordinary Bound columns, and you can freely mix template columns with ordinary bound columns within the same grid—however, you'll probably find that templates make it much easier to achieve the right results when you start using DataGrids in your applications. We'll have a more thorough look at using templates with DataGrids later in this chapter.

Multirow Binding

One of the reasons these three controls are so powerful is the fact that they provide good support for binding expressions. However, the use of binding expressions within List controls is a little different from their use when performing single-row binding to simple controls; this is because the data for the control may consist of multiple rows.

There are various classes that you can use to represent such data, including DataReaders, DataTables, DataViews, Collections, Arrays, and ArrayLists. You start by creating an object containing the data you require, and then assign this to the control's DataSource property. When you call the `DataBind()` method, ASP.NET enumerates the rows of data and renders one item in the control for each.

In our Repeater, DataList, and DataGrid examples above, we used DataReader objects that were exposed as protected variables (such as `dr`) from the code-behind class; we were able to refer directly to them in the binding expressions. This works fine for DataReaders, but not for DataSets, DataTables,

DataViews, or many of the other possible data sources. When working with any of these types, you need to refer to the data through the control rather than referring directly to the variable. The "through the control" reference is made by using `Container.DataItem`. When entered into a binding expression, `Container` refers to the parent object (in this case, the control containing the binding expression), and `DataItem` is a reference to the object bound to the `DataSource` for the control (more accurately, it refers to the current item in the `DataSource` object). `Container.DataItem` is too broad a reference to use on its own; after all, we want to retrieve the values from individual fields. To do this, we enclose the field name in parentheses. For example, if the data source was a DataReader that contained a field called Registration, the following binding expression could be used:

```
<%# Container.DataItem("Registration") %>
```

However, this is imperfect since we are relying on late binding to obtain the `Registration` field. You should already be aware that late binding impacts performance, but it can also introduce unwanted side-effects. For example, if we misspelled the field name, the expression would evaluate with no errors, but return a blank string as the result. A better approach is to explicitly convert the object within the binding expression:

```
<%# CType(Container.DataItem,DataReader)("Registration").ToString %>
```

This evaluates more efficiently at runtime and immediately reports any errors. Some of you may not want to undertake the process of explicit conversion yourself, or you may be writing code where the type of object assigned to the control's DataSource could vary. To assist in these situations, .NET provides another technique to resolve late-bound expressions: *reflection*. A discussion of reflection is beyond the scope of this book, but its implementation for binding expressions is fortunately very simple and uses one of the following notations:

```
DataBinder.Eval(DataObject, ReferenceString)
DataBinder.Eval(DataObject, ReferenceString, FormatString)
```

`DataObject` is the item containing the data, usually `Container.DataItem`. `ReferenceString` is the reference to be evaluated; this is usually a simple fieldname, but could potentially be a more complex multilevel reference. `FormatString` is a .NET formatting string that will control the appearance of the result of the evaluation. Examples of valid binding expressions using this syntax follow:

```
<%# DataBinder.Eval(Container.DataItem, "Registration") %>
<%# DataBinder.Eval(Container, "DataItem.Registration") %>
<%# DataBinder.Eval(Container.DataItem, "AccountBalance", "{0:c}") %>
```

The first two examples are equivalent; the difference is that the evaluation has more to do in the second case and so will take slightly longer. The third example illustrates a formatting expression being used to show account balances in currency format.

Unnecessary use of reflection is best avoided because the process of evaluating expressions in this way can be quite slow. We'd recommend that if performance is a major concern (as it will be for many Web developers), adopt the approach of explicitly converting `Container.DataItem` to an appropriate type, rather than using `DataBinder.Eval`.

Before we conclude this discussion, however, we'd like to discuss the application of one final technique. When using certain types of datasources, you can use the original approach of referring directly to a class-level protected or public variable. For example, if we had a DataReader as the datasource for a List control, we could use the following binding expression:

```
<%# dr("Registration").ToString %>
```

This technique only works when the datasource has one active row at a time—such as a DataReader—because it relies on the control to enumerate the rows when its `DataBind()` method is called. DataTables and DataViews could not be used in this way because they have multiple active rows; so, the binding expression would need to specify a row, as well as a field, to read from them. Of all the approaches, this appears the simplest and most efficient, but you must remember that it cannot be used with all types of data.

Putting It Together

To illustrate the different techniques used in conjunction with List controls, we'll examine the creation of the AircraftBookings Web Form shown in Figure 8-10. This page lists the bookings for a specific aircraft—showing the date, status, and member details. The page also allows the full Booking Details page to be displayed and allows the date and status of the booking to be modified. To make the facility easier to use, the list is paginated so that only five entries are shown at any time. The list also supports the ability to sort by any of the columns.

Before we begin creating the page, we'll make a change to the existing AircraftDetails page. If you refer back to Figure 8-1, you'll see a Bookings button that we will use to display the new page. The event handler for the button should be changed to read as follows:

```
Private Sub btnBookings_Click(ByVal sender As System.Object, _
                ByVal e As System.EventArgs) Handles btnBookings.Click
    Response.Redirect("AircraftBookings.aspx?AircraftID=" + _
                lstAircraft.SelectedItem.Value)
End Sub
```

Notice that the Response.Redirect passes control to the AircraftBookings.aspx page, but it also passes a querystring value for the AircraftID. We'll use this in the Load event for the page to ensure that only bookings for the selected aircraft are displayed.

Creating the Visual Interface

The page is quite simple, consisting only of some static HTML for the <h1> and a DataGrid control called grdBookings. The HTML heading can either be entered as static text or you can use an HTML label control; there's no reason to use a Web Form Label control since we have no need to subsequently access the control through server-side code.

We'll use a binding expression in the heading to display the ID of the aircraft whose bookings are being shown. The HTML for the heading will read as follows:

```
<h1>
    Bookings for Aircraft ID:
    <%# AircraftID %>
</h1>
```

Populating the Control

The next step is to add the components and code that will populate the grid. We use a DataSet for this because DataReader objects are not supported in DataGrid controls that allow paging (which was one of the requirements stated earlier). This is the only reason for using a DataSet; if there was no requirement for paging, we could use a DataReader as a replacement. In our code, we will recreate the DataSet with each postback, although we could improve efficiency by caching the DataSet between requests in Session state.

Drag an SQLDataAdapter onto the Web Form, establish its connection to the HiFlyer database, and set its command text to be the following SQL statement:

```
SELECT AircraftDiary.AircraftDiaryID, AircraftDiary.DiaryDate,
    AircraftDiary.Status, Member.Title + ' ' + Member.Forename +
    ' ' + Member.Surname AS MemberName FROM AircraftDiary INNER JOIN
    Member ON AircraftDiary.BookedMemberID = Member.MemberID WHERE
    (AircraftDiary.AircraftID = @AircraftID)
```

Having configured the SQLDataAdapter, rename it to daAircraftBookings. You will also see that an SQLConnection has been created, and this can be renamed to `cn`.

Display the code-behind module for the page and define a class-level protected variable called `AircraftID`. This will be used by the binding expression in the HTML heading, as well as by various other sections of code:

```
Protected AircraftID As Integer
```

Now create a routine called `ShowBookings()`, which retrieves the booking details into a DataSet, then binds the information to the DataGrid. This routine will be similar to the following:

```
Private Sub ShowBookings()
    Dim ds As New DataSet()

    daAircraftBookings.SelectCommand.Parameters("@AircraftID").Value = AircraftID
    daAircraftBookings.Fill(ds, "Bookings")

    grdBookings.DataSource = ds.Tables("Bookings")
    Me.DataBind()
End Sub
```

Finally, we need to add code to the `Page_Load` handler to do the following:

1. On the initial page request, retrieve the AircraftID from the querystring. The querystring is the term given to the set of parameters passed at the end of the URL when the page request was issued. Having obtained the ID, it should then be stored in ViewState (so that it can be retrieved on postBacks). Finally, the `ShowBookings()` routine is called to populate the grid.

2. On postback requests, the AircraftID should be read from ViewState. There's no need to populate the grid again because this will be managed by other event handlers.

The concept of ViewState was introduced in Chapter 3, and you may remember that it is a way of storing information so that it will remain available to a Web page across postback calls. We'll see more about ViewState (and other forms of state) in Chapter 12. The `QueryString` is read from the `Request` object, which is one of the intrinsic ASP objects introduced in Chapter 1. The code required in the `Page_Load` handler is as follows:

```
Private Sub Page_Load(ByVal sender As System.Object, _
                ByVal e As System.EventArgs) Handles MyBase.Load
    If IsPostBack = False Then
        AircraftID = CInt(Request.QueryString("AircraftID"))
        ViewState("AircraftID") = AircraftID

        ShowBookings()
    Else
        AircraftID = CInt(ViewState("AircraftID"))
    End If
End Sub
```

If you now build the project and display the AircraftDetails page, you can click the Bookings button to display the new page containing the booking information for the selected aircraft. The DataGrid is automatically populated because the default setting for the AutoGenerateColumns property is `True`. Figure 8-11 shows how the page may appear at this stage:

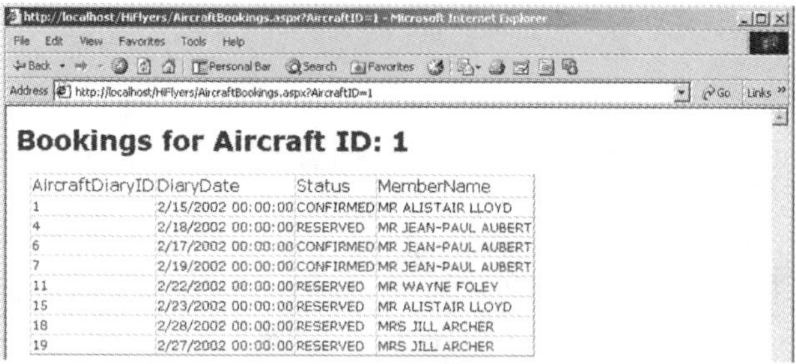

Figure 8-11. AircraftBookings page

Enhancing Appearance

If we're honest about the current appearance of our page, we've got to say it sucks. We need to make some changes to improve this, including the following:

- Hiding the AircraftDiaryID column
- Defining a more useful format for the DiaryDate column
- Controlling the width of the columns
- Selecting more appropriate headings for the columns

We could make these changes through the Properties window settings or even by manually editing the HTML View for the page. A more efficient way is to use the Property Builder dialog for the DataGrid. This provides a friendly interface to help you set properties of the control; it also makes the process a whole lot quicker and more simple than if you tried to make each change manually. The dialog is shown in Figure 8-12; to display it, right-click the DataGrid and select **Property Builder** from the context menu.

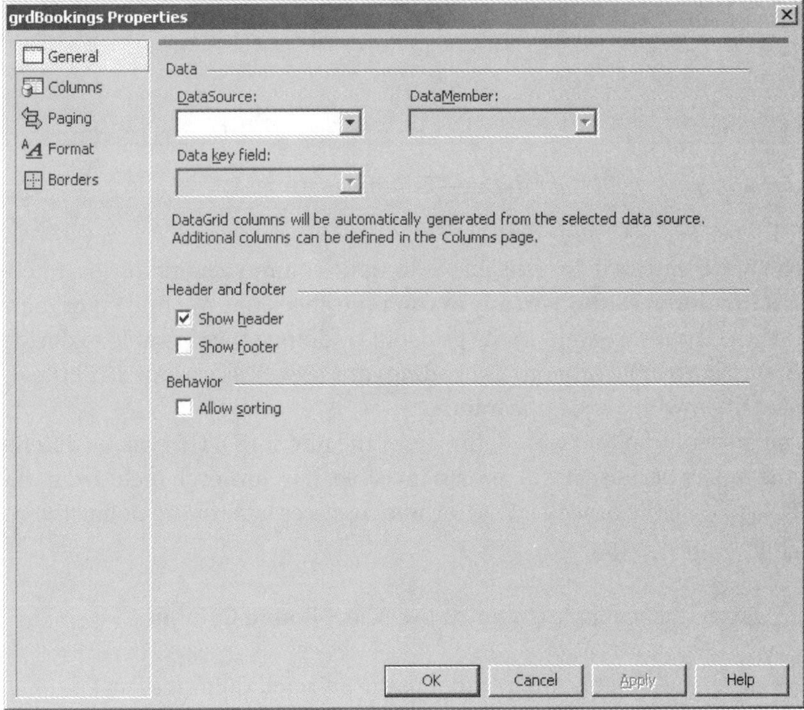

Figure 8-12. Property Builder dialog—General page settings

The General page contains little of interest to us at the moment, so click on the **Columns** entry to display the options shown in Figure 8-13.

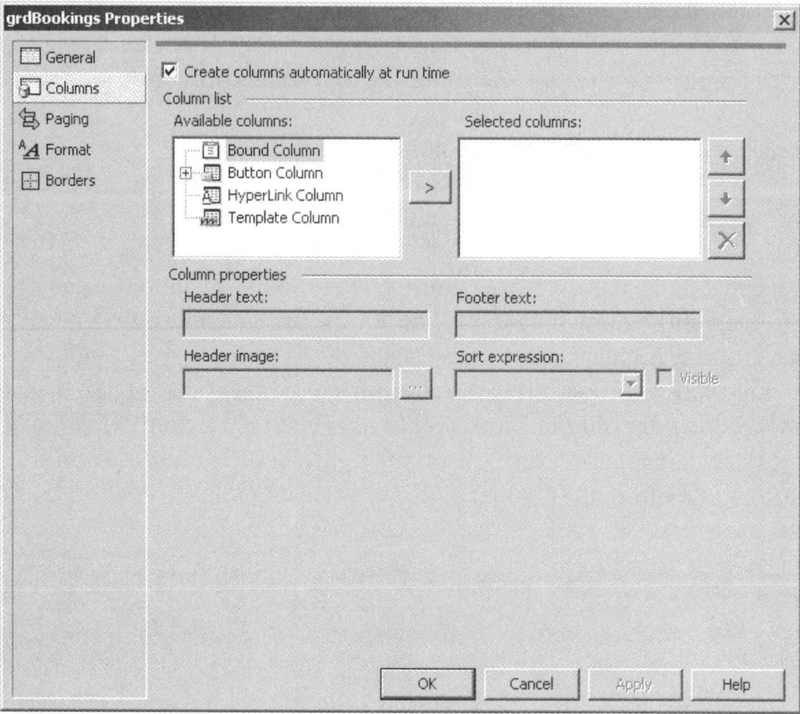

Figure 8-13. Property Builder dialog—Columns settings

The first thing we'll do is disable automatic column generation; so, uncheck the **Create columns automatically at run time** check box. We must now manually define the columns we want in the grid, but by doing so we are able to decide which ones are visible, what their headings are, as well as various attributes regarding their width and appearance.

The first column that we'll define is for the AircraftID. This will be different from the others because it will remain invisible. It is, however, included in the DataGrid to ease the process of performing updates later on. To define the column, follow these steps:

1. From the **Available Columns** list, select **Bound Column**.
2. Click the > button to add it to the **Selected Columns** list.
3. Set the **DataField** to `AircraftDiaryID`.
4. Uncheck the **Visible** checkbox.

A similar process is then used to add additional Bound Columns as follows in Table 8-1. Notice that all of these columns should remain visible:

Table 8-1. DataGrid Column Definitions

HEADERTEXT	VISIBLE	DATA FIELD	DATA FORMATTING EXPRESSION	READ-ONLY
Date	Yes	DiaryDate	{0:dd MMM yyyy}	No
Status	Yes	Status		No
Member	Yes	MemberName		Yes

The Data Formatting expression used for the DiaryDate field causes the date to be shown in the format "01 Mar 2002", rather than allowing .NET to use its default format (which also includes the time, as in "3/1/2002 00:00:00"). This is an example of a .NET formatting string, and must be specified exactly as shown in Table 8-1 (including the brace brackets and the `0:`). Many other formats are available for dates and numeric values, and all will use a similar syntax.

The options on the Format page can be used to control the appearance of the columns. We will change their widths, with the Date column having a width of `120px`, the Status column a width of `160px`, and the Member column a width of `200px`. We will also set the Font Size for each entry under the Items node to `X-Small`.

The changes we've made through the Properties dialog are written into the HTML of the Web Form. If you examine the elements that comprise the DataGrid, you can see tags and attributes that relate to each of the settings. After making these changes, the page will now appear as shown in Figure 8-14. While not perfect, it's certainly more readable than before.

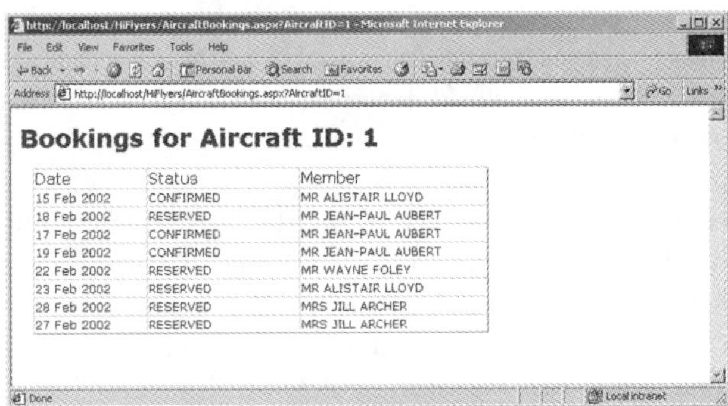

Figure 8-14. Customized AircraftBookings page

Now that we've got the appearance right, it's time to turn our attention to the functionality of the page; so, let's move on to looking at sorting and paging.

DataGrid Sorting and Paging

Sorting and Paging are two of the most often requested features for grid controls; and while they have been frequently implemented in desktop applications, Web applications have typically lagged behind. Fortunately for us, the trend is set to be reversed because ASP.NET makes it very easy for you to implement sorting and paging within DataGrid controls.

Sorting

To enable sorting in the DataGrid, we need to start by changing some of the property values:

1. Display the Property Builder dialog for the DataGrid.

2. On the **General** page, check the **Allow Sorting** check box.

3. Switch to the **Columns** page and select the existing **Date** column that you added previously.

4. In the **Sort Expression** box, enter `DiaryDate`; this is the name of the field that we will use for sorting if the user chooses to sort by date.

5. Select the **Status** column, and set its sort expression to `Status`, and set the sort expression for the **Member** column to `MemberName`.

Having made these changes, you'll see that the headings within the DataGrid are now shown as hyperlinks; you may be thinking that's all there is to do. Unfortunately, in this case you'd be wrong. We still have to write the code to handle the sorting of the data and then associate the code with the appropriate event handler.

Return to the code for the Web Form, and define an event handler for the `SortCommand` event in the DataGrid. This event is raised when the user clicks on one of the hyperlink headings and is passed the `SortExpression` of the appropriate column in the event parameters. Your code must read the sort expression, sort the data, and rebind the DataGrid. We'll do the first part of this in the `SortCommand` event handler, and the remainder in the `ShowBookings()` routine:

```
Private Sub grdBookings_SortCommand(ByVal source As Object, _
        ByVal e As System.Web.UI.WebControls.DataGridSortCommandEventArgs) _
        Handles grdBookings.SortCommand
```

```
    ViewState("SortOrder") = e.SortExpression
    ShowBookings()
End Sub
```

Notice that the event handler's second argument is of type `DataGridSortCommandEventArgs`. This passes the event handler the `SortExpression` for the column that the user clicked, allowing the handler to perform whatever processing is necessary to sort the data in the correct sequence.

The handler transfers the `SortExpression` into ViewState, so that it is maintained across postbacks. This is important because the user would expect the list to retain its sort order once they have set it. We could have used Session state to maintain the value, but this would have placed additional load onto the server, whereas ViewState is stored on the client and passed to and from the server with each postback. To sort the data, we need to modify the `ShowBookings()` routine as follows:

```
Private Sub ShowBookings()
    Dim ds As New DataSet()

    daAircraftBookings.SelectCommand.Parameters("@AircraftID").Value = AircraftID
    daAircraftBookings.Fill(ds, "Bookings")

    Dim dv As New DataView(ds.Tables("Bookings"))
    dv.Sort = ViewState("SortOrder")

    grdBookings.DataSource = dv
    Me.DataBind()
End Sub
```

The modified routine creates a sorted DataView from the DataSet, using the `SortExpression` in ViewState to determine the sort order. The routine then binds the DataView to the DataGrid, rather than the original DataSet. Having modified the code, test the page to ensure that the sorting works as expected.

Paging

With only a few records in the database, our page is quite usable; but, it would be a different matter if there were hundreds or thousands of records —the volume of data would be far too great. Paging helps overcome this problem by breaking the data into smaller sections for display and manipulation.

Paging is enabled through the Property Builder:

1. Display the dialog and select the **Paging** page.
2. Check the **Allow Paging** checkbox, and set the **Page Size** to 5 records.
3. Change the page navigation **Mode** from `Next, Previous Buttons` to `Page Numbers`.

If the page is now viewed in the browser it will appear as shown in Figure 8-15, with the paging controls displayed at the bottom and only five records displayed at a time.

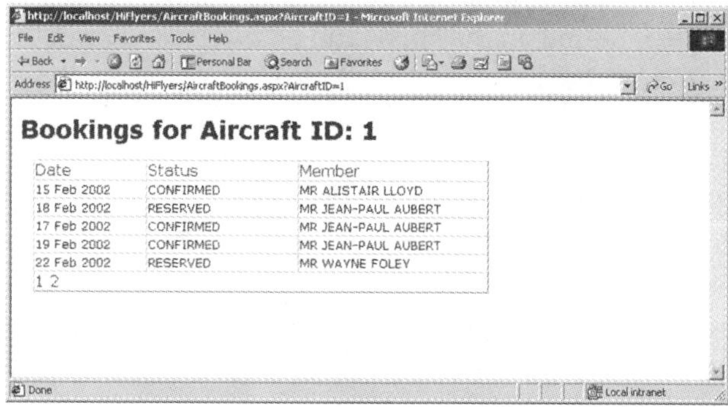

Figure 8-15. Sorting and paging controls

Although the page number links do perform postbacks, they don't actually cause the page to change. As with the sorting functionality, we must add code to handle a server-side event to manage the paging. Return to the Web Form's class and define a handler for the `PageIndexChanged` event:

```
Private Sub grdBookings_PageIndexChanged(ByVal source As Object, _
        ByVal e As System.Web.UI.WebControls.DataGridPageChangedEventArgs) _
        Handles grdBookings.PageIndexChanged
    grdBookings.CurrentPageIndex = e.NewPageIndex
    ShowBookings()
End Sub
```

The number of the page to be displayed is passed in the event parameters, so all the handler needs to do is to set this as the `CurrentPageIndex` for the control and then rebind the data. During the binding process, ASP.NET automatically renders only those records that appear on the specified page. Test the Web page now and you will find that the paging is fully operational, with the sort order maintained irrespective of which page is displayed.

Automatic and Custom Paging

The technique described above is known as *automatic paging*, since you're allowing ASP.NET to do the hard work; but, there is a potential drawback: Irrespective of the page size, the DataSet we assign to the DataSource in `ShowBookings()` is always populated with all of the records returned by the DataAdapter. Most of these records won't be displayed (because the page size is quite small), but they'll still be retrieved from the database and passed to the control. As you can imagine, this could introduce a significant performance penalty as the number of records increases.

To solve this problem, you can use *custom paging* by setting the AllowCustomPaging property of the DataGrid to `True`. You must then make the following changes to the code:

1. Modify the `ShowBookings()` routine to retrieve only those records that will be displayed in the current page of the DataGrid.

2. Within the `ShowBookings()` routine, set the DataGrid's VirtualItemCount property to the total number of items in the underlying data. ASP.NET uses this property value to calculate how many paging controls are needed.

When working with databases it is often difficult to retrieve a specific subset of records by position (which is what we would need to do) without resorting to complex stored procedures. Fortunately, .NET provides us with a good solution in the form of DataSets. While it's difficult to retrieve records by position from a database, it's actually very easy to do so from a DataSet. To benefit from the efficiency improvement that custom paging offers, we would need to cache the dataset between page requests so that it does not have to be regenerated every time.

Caching DataSets

If we want to cache the DataSet that we're using in this example, there are relatively few changes involved. Essentially, we want to create the DataSet on the initial page request and then place it into Session state; on subsequent requests, we retrieve it from Session state. The first change is to move the declaration of the `ds` variable from the `ShowBookings()` routine up to the class level:

```
Protected ds As New DataSet()
```

We must then modify the Page_Load handler so that on the initial request it creates the DataSet and places it into Session state, and that for subsequent requests it retrieves it from Session state:

```
Private Sub Page_Load(ByVal sender As System.Object, _
               ByVal e As System.EventArgs) Handles MyBase.Load
  If IsPostBack = False Then
     AircraftID = CInt(Request("AircraftID"))
     ViewState("AircraftID") = AircraftID

     daAircraftBookings.SelectCommand.Parameters("@AircraftID").Value = AircraftID
     daAircraftBookings.Fill(ds, "Bookings")
     Session("Bookings") = ds

     ShowBookings()
  Else
     AircraftID = CInt(ViewState("AircraftID"))
     ds = CType(Session("Bookings"), DataSet)
  End If
End Sub
```

Finally, the ShowBookings() routine is modified so that it no longer creates the DataSet, but instead, just creates the view to sort the data and then binds to the DataGrid:

```
Private Sub ShowBookings()
    Dim dv As New DataView(ds.Tables("Bookings"))
    dv.Sort = ViewState("SortOrder")
    grdBookings.DataSource = dv
    Me.DataBind()
End Sub
```

There are risks associated with caching data in this way, the main one being that any changes, additions, and deletions made by other users will be masked until we recreate the DataSet.

Editing and Updating

The next change we'll make to the page is to enable *editing* and *updating* for the DataGrid. We will allow the user to modify the date and status of a booking, but they will not be able to select a different member. To support editing, a number of steps must be taken:

1. Edit buttons must be displayed within the DataGrid.
2. Code must be added to the `EditCommand` handler. This event is raised when the Edit button is clicked by the user.
3. Code must be added to the `CancelCommand` handler, which is raised when the user clicks the Cancel button.
4. Code must be added to the `UpdateCommand` handler, which is raised when the Update button is clicked.
5. Optionally, you may want to define templates for specific columns if you want display controls other than the default text boxes.

If we were working with a Repeater or DataList control, things would be rather different. Repeaters have no in-built support for editing, updating, or canceling at all; DataLists support the EditCommand, CancelCommand, and UpdateCommand events, but require that you add your own controls to the ItemTemplate, AlternatingItemTemplate, and EditItemTemplate sections. Because of these requirements, you'll probably find that the DataGrid is by far the simplest control to use for these tasks.

Allowing Editing

Just as we did with sorting and paging, the first step is to configure the properties of the DataGrid to support editing:

1. Display the Property Builder dialog and select the **Columns** page.
2. Within the **Available Columns** list, expand the **Button Column** node.
3. Add an **Edit, Update, Cancel** button column and set the **Button Type** to **PushButton**.

NOTE *This is where the power of DataGrids over DataLists starts to become apparent. If we constructed this page using a DataList, we would need to manually add several* `asp:Button` *objects to the DataList's* `ItemTemplate`, *set their properties, position them, and so on. We would also need to ensure that the appropriate buttons were displayed depending on whether we were currently editing a row (when we would display Update and Cancel buttons) or just viewing it (when we would display an Edit button). The DataGrid's Button columns do all of this automatically.*

The code for the event handlers is also quite simple. DataGrids allow a maximum of one row at a time to be edited, and the location of this row is determined by the EditItemIndex property. All the `EditCommand` and `CancelCommand` handlers need to do is set (or reset) this property, then bind the data:

```
Private Sub grdBookings_EditCommand(ByVal source As Object, _
                ByVal e As System.Web.UI.WebControls.DataGridCommandEventArgs) _
                Handles grdBookings.EditCommand
    grdBookings.EditItemIndex = e.Item.ItemIndex
    ShowBookings()
End Sub

Private Sub grdBookings_CancelCommand(ByVal source As Object, _
                ByVal e As System.Web.UI.WebControls.DataGridCommandEventArgs) _
                Handles grdBookings.CancelCommand
    grdBookings.EditItemIndex = -1
    ShowBookings()
End Sub
```

In the `EditCommand` handler, you can see that the index of the row that the user wants to edit is passed within the event parameters. We assign this index value to the EditItemIndex property of the DataGrid. In the `CancelCommand` handler, we reset the editing by assigning a value of -1 to EditItemIndex. If EditItemIndex is set to a valid row number, the DataGrid switches that row to edit mode and displays its EditItemTemplate rather than its ItemTemplate. It also changes the appearance of other columns—for example, displaying bound columns as TextBox controls and ensuring that appropriate buttons are displayed in button columns.

NOTE *Along with the editing behavior that we are using in this example, DataGrids also support selection behavior by setting their SelectedIndex property.*

If you test the page and click one of the Edit buttons, it will appear as shown in Figure 8-16. Notice that the Date and Status columns are shown as text boxes, but the Member column is not. This is because when we first defined the columns, Member was flagged as read-only and so ASP.NET knows that it should not allow it to be edited.

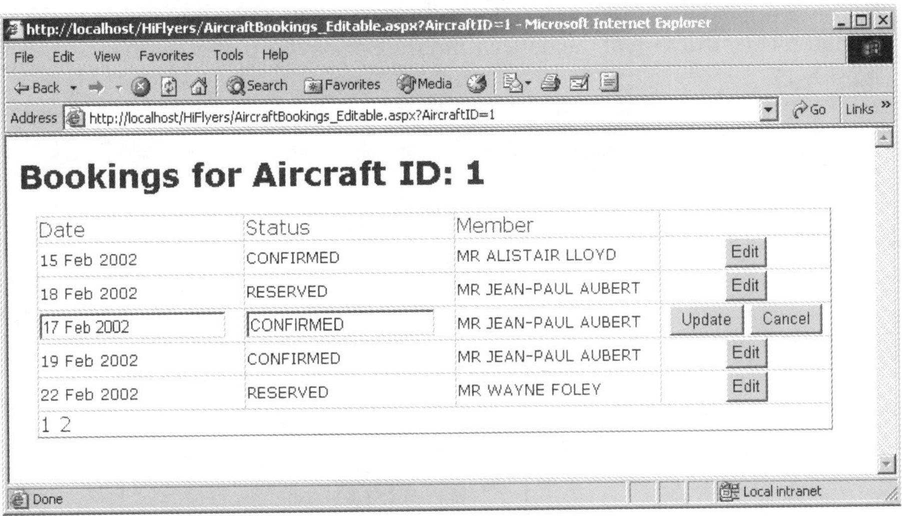

Figure 8-16. Editing within a DataGrid

If you experiment with the page, you may notice some odd behavior when you click an Edit button and then use either the sorting or paging features—the edited row remains in edit mode even though the data is reordered and redisplayed. This could become quite confusing for the users, so we'd suggest that you add the following at the start of the event-handling routines for SortCommand and PageIndexChanged:

```
grdBookings.EditItemIndex = -1
```

Handling Updates

The final handler that's required is for the UpdateCommand event, which is raised when the user clicks the Update button for the row currently being edited, allowing you to write code (using any technique you want) that will write the changed values back to the underlying database. The standard definition of the procedure stub is as follows:

```
Private Sub grdBookings_UpdateCommand(ByVal source As Object,
                 ByVal e As System.Web.UI.WebControls.DataGridCommandEventArgs)
                 Handles grdBookings.UpdateCommand
```

The information passed to the handler in the second parameter (e) is extremely important because it contains the newly edited values from the DataGrid. The structure of the data within the parameter is as shown in Figure 8-17.

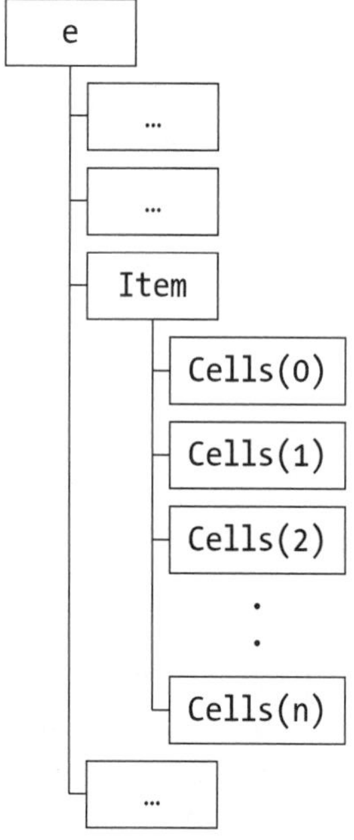

Figure 8-17. Structure of the DataGridCommandEventArgs

The parameter is named e, and has a property called Item, which represents the row in the DataGrid for which the event was raised (the row currently being edited). Within Item is a *Cells* collection, with one cell representing each column in the row currently being edited. Note that invisible cells are included in this collection, so our AircraftDiaryID column is made available to the code. Within each cell you can access the *Text* (that is, any static HTML) or a *Controls* collection (for columns being edited and template columns).

However, you need to be careful with the Controls collection because it will also contain controls that have been dynamically created by ASP.NET. In particular, any static HTML (including whitespace) that is found in the column is converted to an instance of an *HTMLLiteralControl* class when ASP.NET compiles the page. These literal controls become a part of the Controls collection within a cell, so this must be taken into account if you choose to access controls within the collection by their ordinal position.

So, if we want to read from the controls in the edited row of the grid, our handler just needs to know what column contains what piece of information:

```
Private Sub grdBookings_UpdateCommand(ByVal source As Object, _
                ByVal e As System.Web.UI.WebControls.DataGridCommandEventArgs) _
                Handles grdBookings.UpdateCommand
    Dim strACDiaryID As String = e.Item.Cells(0).Text
    Dim strDate As String = CType(e.Item.Cells(1).Controls(0), TextBox).Text
    Dim strStatus As String = CType(e.Item.Cells(2).Controls(0), TextBox).Text

    'Add code here to call a command to do the update
End Sub
```

The most efficient technique for writing these changes back to the database is usually by executing an SQLCommand. For example:

```
Private Sub grdBookings_UpdateCommand(ByVal source As Object, _
                ByVal e As System.Web.UI.WebControls.DataGridCommandEventArgs) _
                Handles grdBookings.UpdateCommand
    Dim strACDiaryID As String = e.Item.Cells(0).Text
    Dim strDate As String = CType(e.Item.Cells(1).Controls(0), TextBox).Text
    Dim strStatus As String = CType(e.Item.Cells(2).Controls(1), _
                DropDownList).SelectedItem.Value

    Try
        With cdUpdateBooking.Parameters
            .Item("@AircraftDiaryID").Value = CInt(strACDiaryID)
            .Item("@DiaryDate").Value = CDate(strDate)
            .Item("@Status").Value = strStatus
        End With
```

```
            cn.Open()
            cdUpdateAircraft.ExecuteNonQuery()

            grdBookings.EditItemIndex = -1
            ShowBookings()
        Catch ex As Exception
            lblError.Text = "Unable to update the booking."
            lblError.Visible = True
        Finally
            cn.Close()
        End Try
    End Sub
```

Using Templates with DataGrids

The techniques we've used within the DataGrid so far have relied on standard rendering and binding, and while these approaches work in many cases, they won't always be suitable. Templates provide additional control and flexibility, allowing you to define your own set of controls for each column as well as specifying custom-binding expressions. Templates are used in all three List controls—in fact they are crucially important when working with DataList and Repeater controls because these controls both depend on templates to produce the visual interface.

Within our DataGrid there's an immediate need for a template column for representing the status of a booking. At the moment, when a record is being edited, the user can enter any value for Status; the handler will then attempt to write it to the database. In reality, only the values `CONFIRMED` and `RESERVED` are valid. While database validation could prevent inappropriate entries, it would be much neater if the user was given a DropDownList containing only valid entries rather than a free-form text box.

Converting a Bound Column to a Template

To make this change, bring up the Property Builder dialog for the DataGrid and access the **Columns** page. Select the existing **Status** column, and click the link at the bottom of the dialog that reads **Convert this Column into a Template Column**. The icon for the Status column changes and some of its properties are hidden. Click **OK** to commit the changes, then view the HTML for the Web Form; the section for the DataGrid will now read as follows (some of the style-related tags have been removed to improve clarity):

```
<asp:datagrid id="grdBookings".....AllowPaging="True">
    <Columns>
        <asp:BoundColumn DataField="AircraftDiaryID".....></asp:BoundColumn>
        <asp:BoundColumn DataField="DiaryDate".....></asp:BoundColumn>
        <asp:TemplateColumn HeaderText="Status">
            <ItemTemplate>
                <asp:Label runat="server"
                    Text='<%# DataBinder.Eval(Container, "DataItem.Status") %>'>
                </asp:Label>
            </ItemTemplate>
            <EditItemTemplate>
                <asp:TextBox runat="server"
                    Text='<%# DataBinder.Eval(Container, "DataItem.Status") %>'>
                </asp:TextBox>
            </EditItemTemplate>
        </asp:TemplateColumn>
        <asp:BoundColumn DataField="MemberName".....></asp:BoundColumn>
        <asp:EditCommandColumn.....></asp:EditCommandColumn>
    </Columns>
</asp:datagrid>
```

The important section is the `<asp:TemplateColumn>` section, which has replaced the previous `<asp:BoundColumn>` definition for the Status column. You can see that there are currently two templates defined:

- **ItemTemplate** determines how standard read-only rows are rendered.
- **EditItemTemplate** determines how editable rows are rendered.

Other templates can also be defined if required:

- **HeaderTemplate** defines the appearance of the header row.
- **FooterTemplate** defines the appearance of the footer row.
- **SeparatorTemplate** is valid only in DataList and Repeater controls, and defines the visual rendering for the separator between adjacent rows.

Within the existing templates you can see that the Property Builder has created a label control (for the ItemTemplate) and a TextBox (for the EditItemTemplate). It has also created binding expressions to populate these controls with values from the DataGrid's datasource. If we want to replace the

TextBox with a DropDownList, all we need to do is edit the template and change the control:

```
<EditItemTemplate>
    <asp:DropDownList runat="server">
       <asp:ListItem Text="CONFIRMED"></asp:ListItem>
       <asp:ListItem Text="RESERVED"></asp:ListItem>
    </asp:DropDownList>
</EditItemTemplate>
```

But what about the binding expression? The previous expression was assigned to the Text property of the TextBox, but the DropDownList doesn't support Text, nor does it support Value. What we must do is to create a binding expression for the SelectedIndex property, but it needs to be a binding expression that generates a number (representing the position of the entry to be selected) rather than text (which is the title of the selected entry). A simple way to do this is with an `IIF` (Immediate If Function) in the binding expression:

```
<%# IIF(DataBinder.Eval(Container, "DataItem.Status")="CONFIRMED",0,1) %>
```

This is added to the tag for the DropDownList within the EditItemTemplate as follows:

```
<asp:DropDownList runat="server" SelectedIndex=
    '<%# IIF(DataBinder.Eval(Container, "DataItem.Status")="CONFIRMED",0,1) %>'>
     <asp:ListItem Text="CONFIRMED"></asp:ListItem>
     <asp:ListItem Text="RESERVED"></asp:ListItem>
</asp:DropDownList>
```

The binding expression in this section may need some careful study. Because we are displaying a DropDownList, we need to ensure that the current value for the field is selected. DropDownLists use a property called SelectedIndex to get or set the position of the selected item, with zero (0) being the first item in the list. We know our list contains `CONFIRMED` (at position 0) and `RESERVED` (at position 1), so we need to set SelectedIndex accordingly. The `IIF` within the binding expression checks the content of the Status field; if the field has a value of `CONFIRMED`, the `IIF` function returns 0 to the SelectedIndex property, otherwise it returns 1. As you can now see, the function call within the binding expression provides an easy way to select an entry by position, even though the data on which it depends is a string.

If the page is now tested and one of the rows edited, it will appear as shown in Figure 8-18. You can see that the Status column is now represented as a DropDownList with only two options. A similar technique could be used to replace the text box in the Date column.

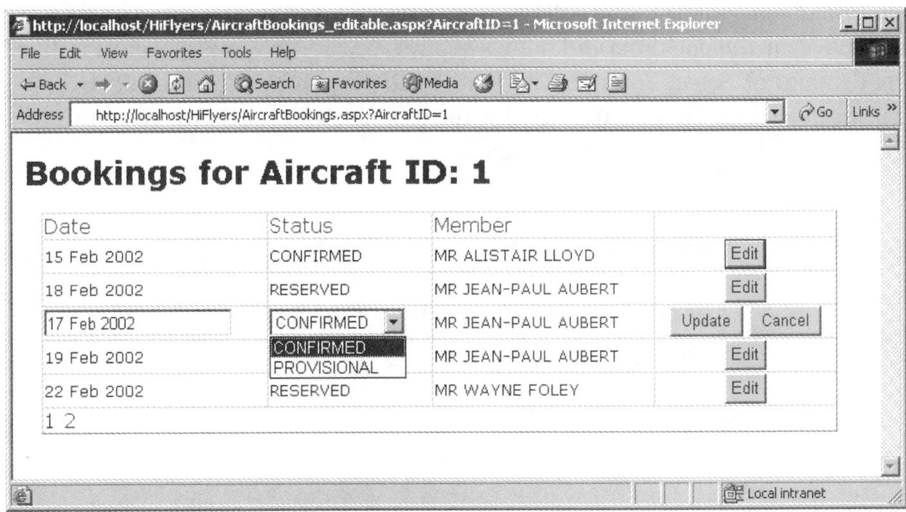

Figure 8-18. Editing within the Template column

Having changed the control used for editing, you must also modify the `UpdateCommand` event handler to take account of the fact that the DataGrid now displays a DropDownList rather than a TextBox. Currently, the routine retrieves the Status value from the DataGrid into a variable called `strStatus`; this must be modified to perform a type conversion to DropDownList rather than TextBox, and also to refer to `Controls(1)` within the cell rather than `Controls(0)`. The reason for this change is that ASP.NET automatically inserts some whitespace before the DropDownList; this gets converted to an HTMLLiteralControl that appears at position `(0)` within the controls collection. (Until you get used to working out which cell and control contains the data you want, you will probably make good use of trial and error!)

```
Dim strStatus As String = CType(e.Item.Cells(2).Controls(1), _
                  DropDownList).SelectedItem.Value
```

Graphical Template Creation

While you'll probably find it easiest to do most template creation and editing using HTML View, there will be occasions when it is useful to have a WYSIWYG view of the template content. Visual Studio .NET provides a graphical template editor for this task.

Return to the Web Form designer and right-click the DataGrid. Toward the bottom of the context menu will be the command **Edit Template**, and on its sub-menu will be the positions and names of any template columns currently defined for the control. Select **Columns[2] – Status** and the graphical editor will be displayed, allowing you to view or modify the templates for the Status column. Figure 8-19 shows how this will appear.

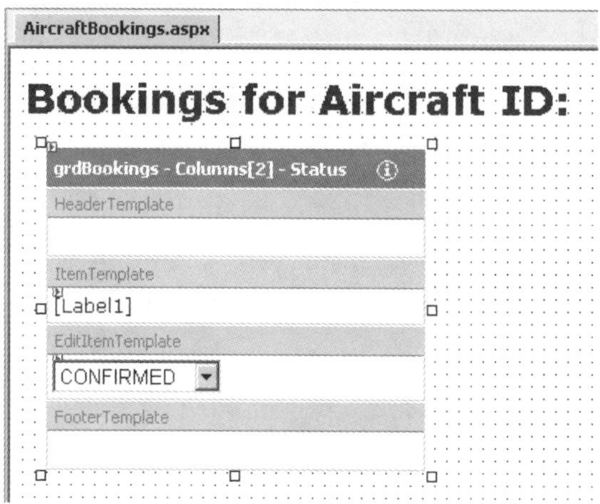

Figure 8-19. Graphical template editor

You can now drag in tools from the toolbox, position and size controls, use the Properties window, and generally make use of all the Visual Studio .NET design tools. Once you have made the changes, right-click the template and select **End Template Editing** from the context menu.

Event Bubbling

The term given to the use of a single container-level event handler is *event bubbling;* all of the events from contained controls are "bubbled up" to a common handler in the container, overcoming the need to create individual handlers for each control. We'll use event bubbling in the DataGrid by adding a button to each row to display the details for a booking.

1. Return to the Web Form designer, display the Property Builder for the DataGrid, and add a **Button Column** below all of the existing columns.

2. Set the **Text** of the button to Details; set the **Command Name** to Details; and set the **Button Type** to PushButton.

3. Click **OK** to commit the changes, at which point the DataGrid will appear as shown in Figure 8-20.

Figure 8-20. Adding a Button column

To handle the event raised when the button is clicked, we'll add code to the `ItemCommand` handler. This event is raised when *any* button with the DataGrid is clicked—even the intrinsic buttons such as Edit, Cancel, and Update. Therefore, we need to ensure that the code we add to the handler differentiates between the buttons; this is typically done by using the CommandName:

```
Private Sub grdBookings_ItemCommand(ByVal source As Object,
              ByVal e As System.Web.UI.WebControls.DataGridCommandEventArgs) _
              Handles grdBookings.ItemCommand
    If e.CommandName = "Details" Then
        Response.Redirect("BookingDetails.aspx?ACDiaryID=" + e.Item.Cells(0).Text)
    End If
End Sub
```

NOTE *You might think you could also use the* Source *parameter to identify which button was clicked, but this won't work. Source represents the container—in this case* **grdBookings**—*rather than the button within the container.*

If there were several different buttons used in each row, then a `Select Case` structure would be used to differentiate between them—again using the Command Name to identify which button was clicked.

Summary

Data binding is a powerful and important technology in ASP.NET. It has the capability to reduce the amount of code you need to write within an application. This reduction in code typically has two benefits:

- Programmer-generated code is usually slower than intrinsic features, so by reducing the amount of code there is often a corresponding performance gain.
- The number of errors in any given program is often related to the amount of programmer-generated code. Less code means fewer errors.

However, care needs to be taken to ensure that data binding is used in the most appropriate way. For example, while DataGrid controls are very powerful, they may well be overkill for simple requirements that could be better met by using Repeaters. Similarly, the fact that controls support in-place editing doesn't necessarily mean that they should be used; there may be good business reasons for not permitting editing of content within List-type controls.

Finally, it is worth remembering that data binding—and especially the use of binding expressions—can make Web Forms a little more difficult to understand due to the embedding of small chunks of code within the Web page. This need not be a problem with thorough documentation and organizational standards for the use and content of binding expressions; but, if the facility is abused, then the code may prove difficult to maintain.

CHAPTER 9

Working with XML

Learning XML Basics

Using DataSets and XML Schemas

As authors, we thought no one would buy this book unless we included a chapter on Extensible Markup Language (XML). Seriously, XML is a topic of such extreme importance that it seems impossible to write anything about programming these days without covering XML, and it's certainly true to say that XML is absolutely essential in many areas of .NET: Web Services, document management, client-side data manipulation, Biztalk, and so on. XML is also a mandatory feature of every ASP.NET project if only because .NET configuration files are XML documents. Later chapters examine the role of XML in project configuration and in Web Services.

But what of the role of XML in ASP.NET Web Applications? The popularity of XML has grown over the past few years, and in particular, it has made significant inroads into Web development. Almost all experienced ASP developers have developed at least a passing familiarity with XML, and many have exploited either its ability to be transformed into HTML or its ability to be manipulated by JavaScript and thus support some degree of browser-independent, client-side data manipulation.

It's actually rather hard to assess how much time a desktop developer moving to ASP.NET should invest in learning about XML in depth, especially at a time when .NET itself presents so much new to learn about. Many of the real strengths of XML are not as relevant to HTML-based browser applications as they are to other types of development. Let's just say that from our perspective, you should consider XML as *the* great alternative. Specifically:

- XML provides an alternative to relational databases with respect to the storage and manipulation of structured data. Both XML files and database servers provide good ways to store structured data, and in fact most relational database servers are rapidly evolving to be able to serve XML as well as more traditional tabular data structures so they can offer the best of both worlds. SQL has served the IT community well for about two decades as a powerful means to query and manipulate structured data, but, as you'll see, XML also comes with some powerful data searching and manipulation tools. It's fair to say that some of the more interesting developments in the standards arena today involve integrating the relative strengths and weaknesses of the relational and XML approaches to data. XML will continue to expand into new areas, but SQL and the relational model are not going away any time soon.

- XML provides an alternative to using Web Controls for generating HTML output. You'll shortly see how you can use XML data manipulation techniques to generate sophisticated HTML content—as an alternative to using templated controls, for example. This does *not* mean you should rush out and become an expert in XML transformations (described later)—Microsoft has invested a great deal of effort into Web Controls precisely so that you don't have to do this.

It may well be that your business logic absolutely requires you to use XML. However, you don't need XML skills to make an awful lot of progress with ASP.NET. We're not saying XML is not important. Far from it—every developer should have basic XML skills, just as every developer should have basic SQL and object-oriented skills. But at the risk of upsetting XML lovers, it remains a fact that although XML is at the heart of .NET, the .NET tool set goes a long way to concealing the role played by XML in day-to-day programming tasks.

So, you now have a choice. You could skip this chapter because it mainly discusses alternative ways to do tasks already covered. If you already know XML, you may choose to skip this chapter anyway, as it won't get into any advanced XML areas. However, we'll discuss some XML tools and techniques unique to .NET, so you may want to breeze past the first few pages until you find something new. If you're an XML virgin, this chapter will open your eyes to some technology you really ought to know.

Learning XML Basics

You're bound to have seen at least some XML. For example, Listing 9-1 shows a compound XML *element* representing an aircraft.

Listing 9-1. An Aircraft Represented As an XML Element

```
<Aircraft>
    <AircraftID>1</AircraftID>
    <Registration>G-29572</Registration>
    <Manuf>Cessna</Manuf>
    <Model>C172</Model>
    <CanDoAeros>true</CanDoAeros>
```

```
    <CanDoIMC>true</CanDoIMC>
    <CanDoNight>true</CanDoNight>
    <CanDoMulti>false</CanDoMulti>
  </Aircraft>
```

This compound XML element is itself made up of simple XML elements such as `Model` and `CanDoAeros`. XML can also contain *attributes*. Here is the same aircraft represented as a single XML element containing eight attributes:

```
<Aircraft AircraftID="1" Registration="G-29572" Manuf="Cessna" Model="C172"
  CanDoAeros="1" CanDoIMC="1" CanDoNight="1" CanDoMulti="0"/>
```

You can have long arguments about whether to use attributes or elements in XML if you've nothing better to do, but the bottom line is that you can use both techniques to represent much the same data.

There are various ways of processing XML documents. .NET provides two main techniques: You can use XmlReaders, or you can use an XML Document Object Model (XML DOM) processor. The two techniques are roughly equivalent to the two main processing techniques available in ADO.NET. Using an XmlReader is similar to using a DataReader. An XmlReader enables you to process one node of data at a time without needing to load the entire XML document in memory (although the comparison breaks down slightly because .NET offers XmlWriters as well as XmlReaders, whereas there's no DataWriter in ADO.NET.

An XML DOM works rather like an ADO.NET DataSet. When using a DOM, you load an entire document into memory. You can then navigate freely around the document. XML is fundamentally hierarchical in nature rather than tabular, and therefore navigation is a somewhat different task from DataSet navigation. That said, you often store tabular data in XML format (for example, an XML document may contain many Aircraft elements, one after the other, and each with the same structure). In fact, you can process XML documents containing tabular data either using XML classes or by using an ADO.NET DataSet, as you'll see later.

.NET's XML classes live in the System.Xml namespace. Let's begin by exploring the XmlReader class and its subclasses. You need to have a reference to the System.Xml assembly before using the XML classes.

It's possible to get XML directly from an SQL Server database by using the SqlCommand object's `ExecuteXmlReader` method, so before looking at processing a file containing XML, you'll see how to get XML from the HiFlyer database. Assuming you have a connection (`cn`) and a command (`cd`) containing the following SQL:

```
SELECT Aircraft.* FROM Aircraft FOR XML AUTO, ELEMENTS
```

you can execute the following code:

```
Dim xr As XmlReader
Dim NodeString As String
cd.Connection.Open()
xr = cd.ExecuteXmlReader

While (xr.Read)
    NodeString = New String("-"c, xr.Depth * 2)
    NodeString += xr.NodeType.ToString + ":" + xr.Name + ":" + xr.Value
    ListBox1.Items.Add(NodeString)
End While

xr.Close()
cd.Connection.Close()
```

Figure 9-1 shows the output of this code.

```
Element:Aircraft:
--Element:AircraftID:
----Text::1
--EndElement:AircraftID:
--Element:Registration:
----Text::G-29572
--EndElement:Registration:
--Element:Manuf:
----Text::Cessna
--EndElement:Manuf:
--Element:Model:
----Text::C172
--EndElement:Model:
--Element:CanDoAeros:
----Text::1
--EndElement:CanDoAeros:
--Element:CanDoIMC:
----Text::1
--EndElement:CanDoIMC:
--Element:CanDoNight:
----Text::1
--EndElement:CanDoNight:
--Element:CanDoMulti:
----Text::0
--EndElement:CanDoMulti:
EndElement:Aircraft:
Element:Aircraft:
```

Figure 9-1. XmlReader output

Calling ExecuteXmlReader on the SqlCommand object returns an XmlReader object. XmlReader provides forward-only, read-only access to a stream of XML data. Each time you call its Read method, it provides access to the next node in the stream of data, exactly like a DataReader's Read method provides access to the next row in an SQL resultset.

Once you're referring to a particular node, you can call methods on the XmlReader to get information about the current node. XML is a hierarchical system, and a node's *depth* relates to how deep it is in the XML stream being processed. We're using the node's depth to create an indent for each node before adding it to a ListBox. Each node also has a node type and/or a name and a value. You can see these properties being used to create Figure 9-1 (the first compound XML element returned by SQL Server is exactly the same as the XML fragment shown in Listing 9-1). There's also other information about a node, such as its attributes, that is available through the XmlReader.

When you've finished with an XmlReader, you need to close it.

It's been interesting comparing an XmlReader with an ADO.NET DataReader, but it's more usual to begin exploring XML by reading an XML document from a file. Here's the first part of a file, called data.xml:

```
<?xml version="1.0" standalone="yes"?>
<Fleet>
  <Aircraft>
    <AircraftID>1</AircraftID>
    <Registration>G-29572</Registration>
    <Manuf>Cessna</Manuf>
    <Model>C172</Model>
    . . .
```

An XML document always has a single root node, and in this case there's a root node called Fleet that contains a series of Aircraft elements (you've seen the first one before!). Let's see some code that processes this file:

```
Dim xr As XmlTextReader
Dim NodeString As String
xr = New XmlTextReader(Server.MapPath("data.xml"))
xr.WhitespaceHandling = WhitespaceHandling.None

While (xr.Read)
    If Not (xr.NodeType = XmlNodeType.XmlDeclaration _
            Or xr.Name = "Fleet") Then
        NodeString = New String("-"c, xr.Depth * 2)
        NodeString += xr.NodeType.ToString + ":" + xr.Name + ":" + xr.Value
        ListBox1.Items.Add(NodeString)
```

```
    End If
End While
```

Figure 9-2 shows the output of this code (can you spot the difference?).

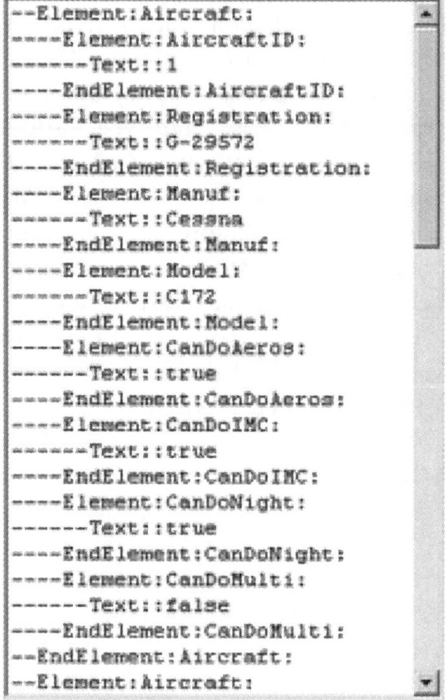

Figure 9-2. XmlTextReader output

The output is identical to Figure 9-1, except that the depth has increased by one for each node displayed. This is because the root node of an XML document now encloses the Aircraft elements. The code is fairly similar, too, but there are some important differences.

XmlReader is an abstract class (you can't actually create instances of it) that has a number of subclasses of which you *can* create instances. One of the most straightforward is XmlTextReader, which you can use to open a file of XML data, and this is the class that has generated Figure 9-2. In the previous code, you've used the reader's `Name` property to filter out the root node and the `NodeType` property to filter out the XML declaration node that appears at the top of the file. You've also asked the reader to ignore whitespace—otherwise, layout characters between the nodes would also be treated as nodes.

You've taken a basic look at how to use XmlReader classes, but you haven't yet generated any useful output. Take a look at Figure 9-3, which lists the registration, model, and ability to do aerobatics for the three aircraft whose details are stored in data.xml.

```
G-29572 C172 true
G-10593 C152 true
G-48201 C152 false
```

Figure 9-3. Simple data extraction

Writing basic XmlReader code to generate this simple output is quite fiddly, as you can see in this code:

```
Dim xr As XmlTextReader
Dim Description As String
xr = New XmlTextReader(Server.MapPath("data.xml"))
xr.WhitespaceHandling = WhitespaceHandling.None

While (xr.Read)
    If xr.NodeType = XmlNodeType.Element And xr.Name = "Aircraft" Then
        Description = ""
    End If
    Select Case xr.Name
        Case "Registration", "Model", "CanDoAeros"
            If xr.NodeType = XmlNodeType.Element Then
                xr.Read()
                Description += xr.Value.ToString + " "
            End If
    End Select
    If xr.NodeType = XmlNodeType.EndElement And xr.Name = "Aircraft" Then
        ListBox1.Items.Add(Description)
    End If
End While
```

This code is processing one node at a time, working out how to build up the required output strings. Note that inside the `Case` statement, you need to perform an extra `Read` to get hold of the data inside one of the selected elements. The structure of the data being processed is not easy to understand by looking at this code, even though the XML is extremely simple. At the same time, processing a document as a stream of data is often the most efficient and responsive approach. With a large document, it removes the need to wait until the entire document has been loaded into memory and keeps the amount of memory needed to process the document to a minimum.

Using Document Objects

XmlReaders are very efficient, especially for processing large documents. However, an easier approach is to load the entire document into an object that provides a navigational model for working with XML. .NET provides the XmlDocument object for this task (as discussed earlier, XmlDocument is the XML equivalent of the ADO.NET DataSet).

You'll begin exploring XmlDocument by re-creating the output shown in Figure 9-3. Listing 9-2 shows the code that'll do this using an XmlDocument.

Listing 9-2. Processing XML Using an XmlDocument Object

```
Dim doc As New XmlDocument()
Dim docNode, aircraftNode, dataNode As XmlNode
Dim i, j As Integer
Dim Description As String
doc.Load(Server.MapPath("data.xml"))
docNode = doc.DocumentElement
For i = 0 To docNode.ChildNodes.Count - 1
    aircraftNode = docNode.ChildNodes(i)
    Description = ""
    For j = 1 To aircraftNode.ChildNodes.Count
        dataNode = aircraftNode.ChildNodes(j - 1)
        Select Case dataNode.Name
            Case "Registration", "Model", "CanDoAeros"
                Description += dataNode.InnerText.ToString + " "
        End Select
    Next
    ListBox1.Items.Add(Description)
Next
```

Listing 9-2 begins by loading `data.xml` into an XmlDocument object. Once it's loaded, the XmlDocument data structure can be navigated to identify data of interest. In this case, you're using two nested loops. The outer loop (which uses `i` as its loop variable) goes through all the child nodes of the root node, each of which represents an aircraft element. The inner loop (which uses `j` as its loop variable) goes through all the child nodes of each aircraft node, giving access to the individual elements containing data about the current aircraft.

It's much easier to make sense of this code than the previous version based on the XmlReader. However, this code is still very procedural—it relies on processing logic to interpret the structure of the data. And there is still quite a lot of it for such a simple task.

Using XPath

There's a much easier way of extracting data from an XML document, which is to use a query language. Just as database programmers use WHERE clauses with SQL statements to retrieve only the records they require from a database, so XML programmers can use a query language, called XPath, to extract only the elements they require from an XML document object. XPath is the official replacement for an earlier query language for XML, which was called XSL Patterns. XSL Patterns has historically been the default query language used by Microsoft XML Document Objects, but .NET performs querying using XPath by default.

XPath is a sophisticated query language, supporting mathematical and boolean expressions and supplying a range of built-in functions. You'll need to use only the simplest types of XPath query to re-create Figure 9-3 (see Listing 9-3).

Listing 9-3. Processing XML Using XPath

```
Dim doc As New XmlDocument()
Dim Description As String
Dim aircraftList As XmlNodeList
Dim aircraftNode, dataNode As XmlNode

doc.Load(Server.MapPath("data.xml"))
aircraftList = doc.SelectNodes("/Fleet/Aircraft")
For Each aircraftNode In aircraftList
    Description = ""
    dataNode = aircraftNode.SelectSingleNode("Registration")
    Description += dataNode.InnerXml + " "
    dataNode = aircraftNode.SelectSingleNode("Model")
    Description += dataNode.InnerXml + " "
    dataNode = aircraftNode.SelectSingleNode("CanDoAeros")
    Description += dataNode.InnerXml + " "
    ListBox1.Items.Add(Description)
Next
```

You can use both the SelectNodes and the SelectSingleNode methods to execute XPath queries. You should use the SelectNodes method with a query that is expected to return multiple nodes. In Listing 9-3, SelectNodes returns an

XmlNodeList object representing all the `Aircraft` nodes within the root node of the document (the `Fleet` node). The XPath syntax for this expression is Fleet/Aircraft. You can process an XmlNodeList using a `For ... Each` loop, which makes it easy to process each aircraft. When an XPath query will return just one node, the `SelectSingleNode` method should be used, which returns an XmlNode object. Here, you've used `SelectSingleNode` to extract single values for each aircraft.

You can simplify this code even further by exploiting the fact that `SelectSingleNode` is the default member of XmlNode (VB .NET only allows default members if they're indexed):

```
Dim doc As New XmlDocument()
Dim aircraftNode As XmlNode
Dim Description As String
doc.Load(Server.MapPath("data.xml"))
For Each aircraftNode In doc.SelectNodes("/Fleet/Aircraft")
    Description = aircraftNode("Registration").InnerXml + " "
    Description += aircraftNode("Model").InnerXml + " "
    Description += aircraftNode("CanDoAeros").InnerXml + " "
    ListBox1.Items.Add(Description)
Next
```

All of a sudden, processing XML documents starts to look pretty easy. However, you've hardly scratched the surface of what can be achieved using XPath. It's well worth spending time learning about XPath—especially as you can use it to query SQL Server as an alternative to SQL. Let's go one step further and see how you can narrow the search to display only those aircraft that can perform aerobatics. Take a look at this next version of the code that passes a different XPath query to `SelectNodes`:

```
Dim doc As New XmlDocument()
Dim aircraftNode As XmlNode
Dim Description As String
doc.Load(Server.MapPath("data.xml"))
For Each aircraftNode In doc.SelectNodes("/Fleet/Aircraft[CanDoAeros='true']")
    Description = aircraftNode("Registration").InnerXml + " "
    Description += aircraftNode("Model").InnerXml + " "
    Description += aircraftNode("CanDoAeros").InnerXml + " "
    ListBox1.Items.Add(Description)
Next
```

By using the following query string:

```
"/Fleet/Aircraft[CanDoAeros='true']"
.
```

this code selects the two aircraft that contain a CanDoAeros element whose value is True.

A slightly more complex query might return only those aircraft whose registration contains the character `'2'`. The following query uses the XPath `contains` function to return the two nodes that meet this criteria:

```
"/Fleet/Aircraft[contains(./Registration,'2')]"
```

Transforming XML

Another powerful feature of the XML tool set is the ability to perform transforms—to turn an XML document with one particular structure into a document with a different structure. This capability is at the heart of major Microsoft technology such as Biztalk, but you can also use it to create HTML user interfaces. It's under the control of yet another XML standard, known as XSL Transformations (XSLT). The .NET XSLT functionality for XML transformations lives in the System.Xml.Xsl namespace.

The trick is to specify a transformation that turns an XML document into HTML, by merging HTML layout information with XML data. Listing 9-4 generates the output you see in Figure 9-4.

Listing 9-4. Transforming XML into HTML

```
Dim doc As New XmlDocument()
Dim tfm As New Xsl.XslTransform()
Dim output As New System.IO.StringWriter()
doc.Load(Server.MapPath("data.xml"))
tfm.Load(Server.MapPath("data.xslt"))
tfm.Transform(doc, Nothing, output)
'assign output to an HTML Label control
DIV1.InnerHtml = output.ToString
```

Cessna	G-29572
Cessna	G-10593
Cessna	G-48201

Figure 9-4. XML transformed into an HTML table

This code uses one magic resource (which you'll see shortly); otherwise, it's extremely straightforward. It loads `data.xml` into an XmlDocument object and loads a magic resource called `data.xslt` into an XmlTransform object. It then calls the `Transform` method on the XmlTransform object, which transforms the data loaded into the XmlDocument (`doc`) into HTML in the form of a .NET StringWriter object (`output`). Finally, the content of the StringWriter object is assigned to the `InnerHtml` property of an HTML Label control, set to `runat="server"`, and given an ID of `DIV1`. It's worth noting that although in this case the input to XMLTransform is an XML document and the output is a StringWriter object, the `XMLTransform` method itself is heavily overloaded. For example, you can specify both the input and output to be filenames, in which case you can use XMLTransform to transform one file of XML into another. Alternatively, the output could be an XMLReader object, in which case (having applied a transform to get into a suitable format) you could start processing it using the XMLReader techniques explored earlier in the chapter.

Now let's look at the magic, which is nothing more than another XML document specifying the appropriate transform. It contains the following:

```
<?xml version="1.0" encoding="UTF-8" ?>
<xsl:stylesheet version="1.0" xmlns:xsl="http://www.w3.org/1999/XSL/Transform">

  <xsl:template match="Fleet">
    <table border="1" width="400">
    <xsl:apply-templates select="Aircraft"/>
    </table>
  </xsl:template>
  <xsl:template match="Aircraft">
    <tr>
    <td><xsl:value-of select="Manuf"/></td>
    <td><xsl:value-of select="Registration"/></td>
    </tr>
  </xsl:template>
</xsl:stylesheet>
```

Without digging too deeply into this file you can see that it contains two templates. Whenever the transform process finds a `Fleet` node, it uses the `Fleet` template, which generates the beginning and end tags for an HTML table, and applies the `Aircraft` template to each `Aircraft` node. The `Aircraft` template generates an HTML table row for each aircraft it matches.

The XmlTransform object uses the XSLT document to transform the XML data document into HTML. It's easy to make the XSLT document generate far more elaborate output than this.

You can directly compare the work done by XML Transforms to the template-matching approach used by data-bound ASP.NET Web Controls such as the DataGrid and Repeater. Both techniques get the job done, and although there are strengths and weaknesses for each, the approach you choose will almost certainly be driven by personal preference. This last point takes us right back to the beginning of the chapter where we introduced XML as a great alternative. It's important to be aware of what you can achieve when working directly with XML and its supporting tools such as XPath and XSLT. Whether you work with them is up to you.

Using DataSets and XML Schemas

In addition to being able to process XML data using the classes in the System.Xml namespace, you can also load XML documents directly into an ADO.NET DataSet. The remainder of this chapter explores this capability of ADO.NET and also addresses the role of XML Schemas. We'll assume you're familiar with DataSets as these were discussed in detail in Chapter 7.

You can load data that fits into a regular, tabular structure (such as the data in `data.xml`) directly into a DataSet. The following code does this and also binds the DataSet to a DataGrid:

```
Dim ds As New DataSet()
ds.ReadXml(Server.MapPath("data.xml"))
DataGrid1.DataSource = ds
DataGrid1.DataBind()
```

Figure 9-5 shows this code in action.

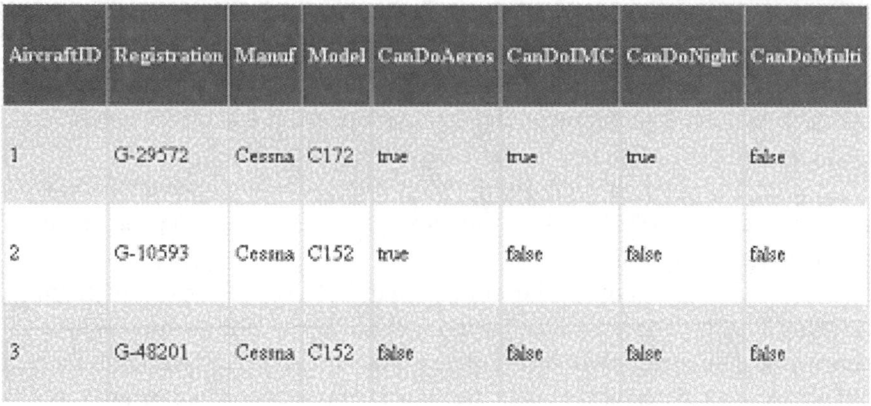

AircraftID	Registration	Manuf	Model	CanDoAeros	CanDoIMC	CanDoNight	CanDoMulti
1	G-29572	Cessna	C172	true	true	true	false
2	G-10593	Cessna	C152	true	false	false	false
3	G-48201	Cessna	C152	false	false	false	false

Figure 9-5. Binding XML data to a DataGrid

This is a simple way to get XML data into HTML format. You can apply everything you know about DataSets, data binding, and templates to create highly sophisticated presentations of XML data with little effort. You can also use the DataSet approach to modify data, saving it back to a file using the `WriteXml` method. It's worth adding that both `ReadXml` and `WriteXml` methods are heavily overloaded, and XML can be loaded and saved using a variety of sources, including XmlReaders and Streams.

If you're strong on DataSets and weak on XML, you're probably thinking that this is how you want to handle XML from now on. Before you get too excited, though, remember that you can only use DataSets in this way if the XML document has a tabular structure; if it's hierarchical, you'll have to use .NET's XML specific classes.

Understanding Schemas

Schemas define what data looks like. In the relational database world, schemas specify tables and columns, define relationships, and impose rules and restrictions on what data can be stored in a database. In the XML world, schemas perform very much the same task. Not so long ago, all schemas for XML documents were defined using Document Type Definitions (DTDs), but DTDs have certain limitations and are specified using a different syntax from standard XML syntax. The latest standard is called XML Schema Definition (XSD). XSD is more powerful than DTDs and uses XML syntax to specify the schema, and so it requires no additional parsing capability over and above that needed to process XML data. XSD is the preferred way to work with schemas in .NET.

A DataSet always requires a schema before it can process an XML document. This observation may surprise you because you didn't seem to create or load a schema in the previous simple code sample. What happened was that the DataSet automatically generated an XML schema by inspecting the data in `data.xml`. Although this behavior is convenient, you might want to provide your own schema instead for two reasons:

- To generate a schema, the DataSet must read through the data in the XML file twice—once to create the schema and once to load the data. It's obviously quicker to provide a schema, especially for large XML documents.

- The schema generated by the DataSet contains a minimal set of schema data; for example, all data types are treated as strings. You may want to create a more specific schema that more precisely matches the data you intend to read.

In many cases, a schema will be present at the top of an XML document. If this is the case, the `ReadXml` method will use this schema. Alternatively, you can load a schema separately using the `ReadXmlSchema` method. More often than not, XML developers have hand-coded their schemas, just as database designers hand-coded database schemas before the widespread availability of graphical tools that generate SQL Data Definition Language. Visual Studio .NET ships with a graphical designer for XML schemas. Let's take a quick look at this and other Visual Studio .NET tool for XSD.

A good starting point is to take an existing XML data document and add it to a Visual Studio .NET project. You can then immediately display the XML data in the Visual Studio .NET XML Editor. This enables you to view and edit the XML either as raw XML (XML View) or using a grid-like editor (Data View), as shown in Figure 9-6.

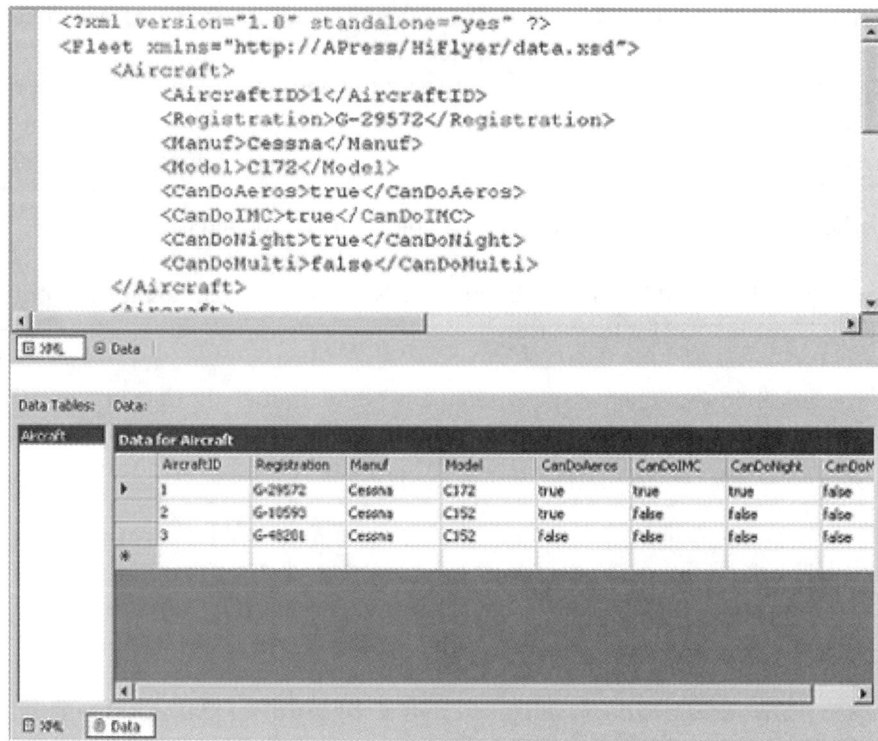

AircraftID	Registration	Manuf	Model	CanDoAeros	CanDoIMC	CanDoNight	CanDoM
1	G-29572	Cessna	C172	true	true	true	false
2	G-10593	Cessna	C152	true	false	false	false
3	G-48201	Cessna	C152	false	false	false	false

Figure 9-6. The Visual Studio .NET XML Editor showing XML and Data Views

While the XML Editor is open, Visual Studio .NET's main menu displays an XML menu item that you can use to generate a schema for the current XML file. The schema will be stored in a file with the same name as the XML document, but with an .xsd extension. Visual Studio .NET also provides a Schema Editor, which you can use to build XSD from scratch or to edit an auto-generated schema. Figure 9-7 shows this editor in action, editing the `data.xsd` file generated from `data.xml`.

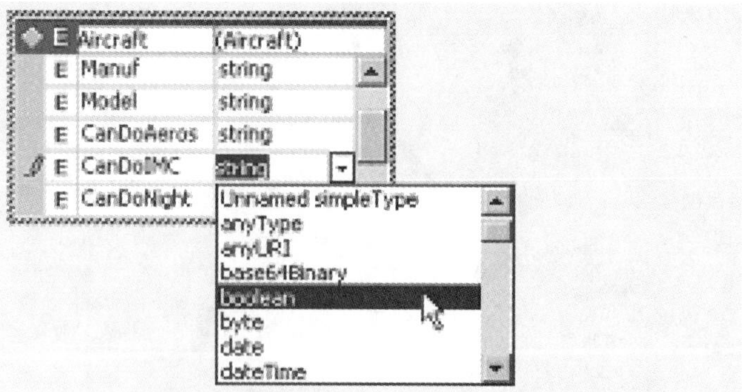

Figure 9-7. The Visual Studio .NET XML Schema Editor

The automatic schema generation process has correctly identified that `data.xml` contains `Aircraft` elements, which themselves contain a set of simple elements, although all of these have been defined as strings. Figure 9-7 shows the editor changing the data type of the `CanDoIMC` element from `string` to `boolean`. As with the XML Editor, the Schema editor also enables you to edit the raw schema if you want. Once you've edited all the boolean elements appropriately, the resulting XML Schema looks like Listing 9-5 (with some attributes of `xs:schema` and `xs:element` suppressed).

Listing 9-5. The XML Schema

```
<?xml version="1.0" ?>
<xs:schema id="Fleet" targetNamespace="http://APress/HiFlyer/data.xsd" . . . >
  <xs:element name="Fleet" msdata:IsDataSet="true" . . . >
    <xs:complexType>
      <xs:choice maxOccurs="unbounded">
        <xs:element name="Aircraft">
          <xs:complexType>
            <xs:sequence>
              <xs:element name="AircraftID" type="xs:string" minOccurs="0" />
              <xs:element name="Registration" type="xs:string" minOccurs="0" />
              <xs:element name="Manuf" type="xs:string" minOccurs="0" />
              <xs:element name="Model" type="xs:string" minOccurs="0" />
              <xs:element name="CanDoAeros" type="xs:bminOccurs="0" />
              <xs:element name="CanDoIMC" type="xs:boolean" minOccurs="0" />
              <xs:element name="CanDoNight" type="xs:boolean" minOccurs="0" />
              <xs:element name="CanDoMulti" type="xs:boolean" minOccurs="0" />
            </xs:sequence>
          </xs:complexType>
        </xs:element>
      </xs:choice>
    </xs:complexType>
  </xs:element>
</xs:schema>
```

This schema defines the elements that can appear within an `Aircraft` complex type. The data type of each element is specified but none of the elements are mandatory—because the minimum number of occurrences is 0.

Once a schema has been defined, you can modify the code that reads the XML to make use of it. Here is the code where the second line has been added to read the schema before reading the data:

```
Dim ds As New DataSet()
 ds.ReadXmlSchema(Server.MapPath("data.xsd"))
```

```
ds.ReadXml(Server.MapPath("data.xml"))
DataGrid1.DataSource = ds
DataGrid1.DataBind()
```

You can use XML Schemas for many purposes. One of the most common purposes is for validation. Because the schema defines the legal content of an XML document, the document can be validated against the schema when it's loaded. DataSets will automatically do this if provided with an XML Schema. For example, assume that one of the `CanDoAeros` elements had its value changed from True to `Green`. `Green` is clearly not a valid boolean value, and bad data such as this could mess up code further downstream or require extensive error handling. However, this code will raise the following exception if bad data appears in a boolean element anywhere in the XML document:

```
The string was not recognized as a valid Boolean value.
```

This automatic validation means that you can be sure that any XML document you load, regardless of its size, precisely matches the schema before you start doing any serious processing on it.

Schema validation is not a special feature of XML when used with DataSets. If you prefer processing XML using classes from the System.Xml namespace, .NET provides a subclass of XmlReader called XmlValidatingReader that you can use to validate XML documents against a schema. In fact, XmlValidatingReader gives you considerably more functionality when validating documents. For example, you may choose to ignore certain data errors because you know you can process them in your code. At the same time, the schema validation functionality built into DataSets is extremely easy to use.

Summary

This chapter's purpose has simply been to introduce some XML code and concepts for readers for whom XML is as new as .NET and to showcase some of the tools and techniques that you can use within ASP.NET when working with XML.

You've seen how tools such as XPath and XSLT provide powerful alternatives to techniques covered in earlier chapters. At the same time it's worth remembering that you haven't done anything in this chapter that can't be done in other, perhaps more familiar, ways. To re-state the message from the beginning of this chapter, XML has many applications and may well be essential for your business logic, but from the point of view of constructing ASP.NET Web Applications, it is an alternative, rather than a mandatory, skill set.

CHAPTER 10

Web Application Architecture

This chapter is about more than just ASP.NET architecture; it's about how that architecture supports your applications and how you can configure, deploy, cache, and trace those applications. Sure, we're going to start with some theory, and there are some real good reasons why you should spend some time absorbing and understanding this material—not least of which is that your entire application depends on these concepts. But you'll also see some of the practical, real-world issues, including how you can use this knowledge to your advantage when faced with challenging design, code, or maintenance tasks.

We'll begin with the big picture, looking at how ASP.NET and .NET in general work, and then delve into the detail as we start to home in on the more interesting aspects.

How ASP.NET Works

Up to now we've focused on the immediate hands-on aspects of ASP.NET, showing how you can build Web Forms, use controls, access data, and work with XML. However, to really master any technology you need to have a good understanding of how it works, so this section examines the core operation of ASP.NET, as well as how it interacts with other supporting technologies such as client browsers, Microsoft Internet Information Server (IIS), and the operating system. With this knowledge you'll be better prepared for troubleshooting and optimizing, as well as being able to design and implement solutions that take advantage of ASP.NET's more powerful features.

At a high level, ASP.NET appears to share much in common with classic ASP and other Web application architectures; it supports a request/response mechanism that enables browsers to obtain content, it provides for dynamic creation of page content through runtime code, it supports integration with database and data sources, and it provides infrastructure services such as security, caching, and state management. Figure 10-1 shows this high-level view, identifying some of the most important ASP.NET elements and services.

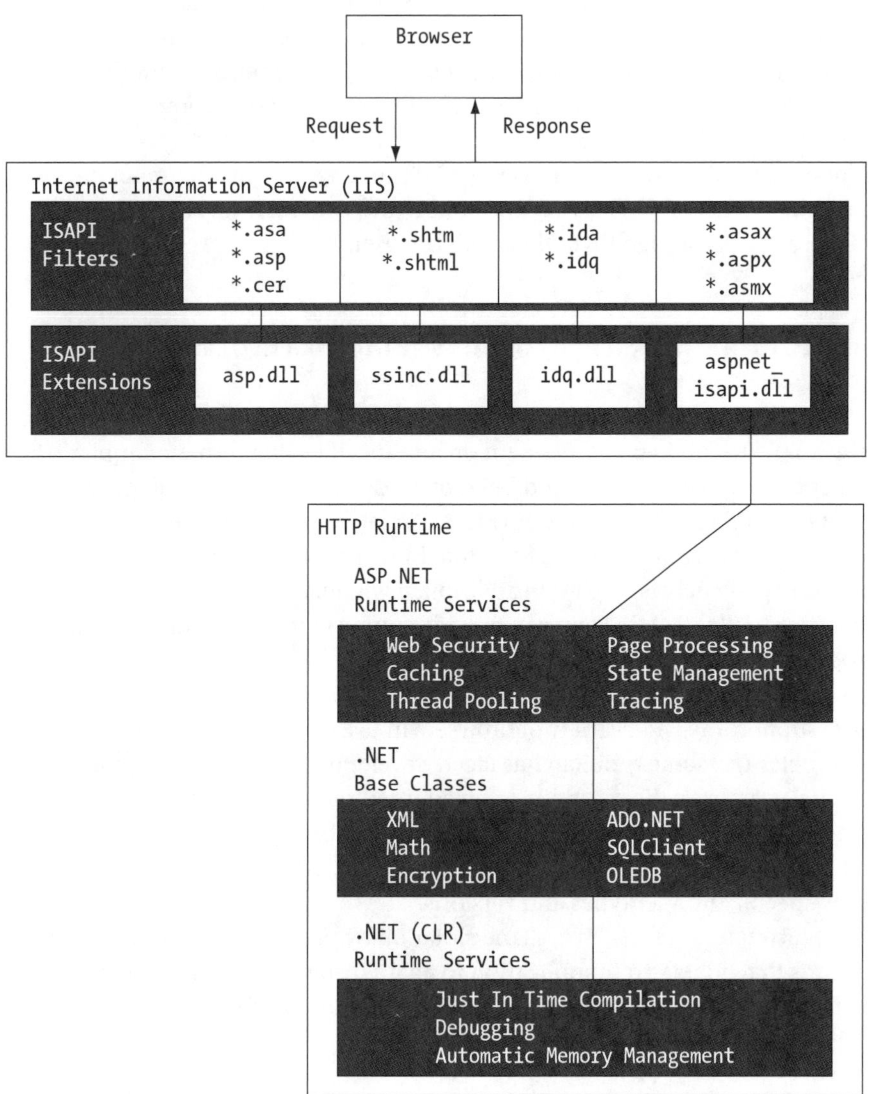

Figure 10-1. ASP.NET architecture

As Figure 10-1 shows, there are multiple technologies involved in processing a request for an ASP.NET Web Application, from the client browser to the underlying .NET Framework and runtime services. To put these technologies in perspective, let's run through the process and summarize the interactions. At this stage we'll keep things simple, but in the next few sections we'll introduce each of the key technologies and products in turn.

The process begins with an HTTP request issued by the browser, which is passed to the Web server. To run ASP.NET, the Web server must have IIS installed, and it's this software that initially processes the request. IIS examines the file extension of the URL requested by the user and passes the request to a processing component. Many of these processing components are implemented as in-process .dll files, but ASP.NET is different. Its processing component takes the form of an .exe file and is known as the *HTTP Runtime*. When it receives the request, the HTTP Runtime retrieves and processes the files, components, and resources necessary to service the request and generates an HTTP Response that it passes back through IIS to the client browser.

Exploring Client Browsers and Platforms

The first tier in Figure 10-1 is the client browser. ASP.NET is a server-side technology, so it's not in theory dependent on any specific client browser or platform. In practice, however, the standard build of ASP.NET requires that client systems support HTTP 1.0 or later and HTML 3.2 or later, which includes the vast majority of browsers running on PCs and Macintosh computers, as well as other technologies such as WebTV. In addition, if you install the Microsoft Mobile Internet Toolkit (MMIT) you can provide support for mobile devices such as PocketPCs and WAP phones.

This diversity of client systems leads to a potential concern: How can you best support the wide variety of browsers in use on the Internet and in corporate intranets? The same problem has faced developers of classic ASP applications for several years, and the solutions often adopted range from using only base HTML features, tags, and elements through creating hybrid Web sites with alternate pages that load according to browser type to deciding consciously to support only specific browser types and versions.

Fortunately, ASP.NET eases the situation by providing several different mechanisms that enable your application to adapt its behavior to suit the browser being used, the most significant of which is its support for adaptive controls.

Introducing Adaptive Controls

As you saw in Chapters 4, 5, and 6, some ASP.NET server controls automatically adapt themselves to suit the type and version of browser they detect. They get this information from the HTTP request received from the client in the form of a *User-Agent string*. For example, a request initiated from a PC running Internet Explorer 5.5 on Windows NT would generate the following:

```
GET /WebApp1/startup.aspx HTTP/1.1
Accept: image/gif, image/x-xbitmap, image/jpeg, image/pjpeg . . .
Accept-Language: en-us
```

```
Accept-Encoding: gzip, deflate
User-Agent: Mozilla/4.0 (compatible; MSIE 5.5; Windows NT 4.0)
Host: localhost
Connection: Keep-Alive
```

ASP.NET uses the information in the User-Agent entry to determine what the expected capabilities of the client's browser are, and then to select a suitable format to render the Web Form. For example, consider a Web Form containing validation controls:

- If the browser is identified as being capable of supporting scripting, the Web Form would be rendered to include client-side JavaScript. This enables the validation to be performed purely on the client, and so there's no need for a server round-trip.

- If the browser is not identified as supporting JavaScript, the Web Form would be rendered as a simple HTML page with the validation performed on the server.

This adaptive behavior applies to a variety of controls, and it may well be enhanced as newer browsers (and other devices) become available that have more powerful features. However, existing controls will not automatically recognize and use any new features; the only way this will happen is if the controls are updated by their authors and redistributed. (Refer to Chapter 5 for a more thorough discussion of how adaptive controls work.)

Using ClientTarget

Although this adaptive behavior is generally useful, there may be times when you need to ensure that your Web Form generates a particular type and format of HTML response. For example, security concerns may make it inappropriate for validation to be performed on the client, even though the browser is capable. The information gained from reading client-side validation code could potentially assist anyone launching a malicious attack, so it's important that you can control the generation of server-side code.

In these circumstances you can use the Web Form's ClientTarget property to determine what client-side features are used. Possible settings for ClientTarget include the following:

- Auto, which allows ASP.NET to detect browser type and make its own decision on whether to implement client-side functionality.

- Uplevel, which forces ASP.NET to implement features using client-side script, tags, and attributes. If the browser types and versions can be guaranteed, such as in an intranet environment, using Uplevel can enhance performance.

- Downlevel, which forces ASP.NET to use minimal client-side features and to perform validation on the server. When security and confidentiality of rules are more important than performance, Downlevel is more appropriate.

You can also specify any of the aliases or User-Agent strings defined in the `<clientTarget>` section of the Machine.config file. Machine.config is an XML document that contains server-wide configuration details and settings; it'll be discussed in detail later in this chapter. The following shows the standard `<clientTarget>` section that you'll find in the file:

```
<clientTarget>
    <add alias="ie5"
                userAgent="Mozilla/4.0 (compatible; MSIE 5.5; Windows NT 4.0)" />
    <add alias="ie4"
                userAgent="Mozilla/4.0 (compatible; MSIE 4.0; Windows NT 4.0)" />
    <add alias="uplevel"
                userAgent="Mozilla/4.0 (compatible; MSIE 4.0; Windows NT 4.0)" />
    <add alias="downlevel" userAgent="Unknown" />
</clientTarget>
```

As well as these aliases, there are pattern-matching sections that identify a range of User-Agent strings for common browsers. Each of the aliases and User-Agent matches has a number of attributes defined for it that describe the browser's capabilities. When you refer to the properties of the `Page.Request.Browser` object (as you did in Chapter 5 to determine support for JavaScript), ASP.NET looks up the corresponding attribute for the detected or specified browser and returns its value. Intrinsic controls (such as the validation controls) use this technique to determine how they should render their output. When you set a value for ClientTarget, you're overriding the default browser-detection mechanism and effectively forcing ASP.NET to always look in the specified section of Machine.config to read the capability values.

Working with IIS and ISAPI

ASP.NET applications need to be hosted by a suitable Web server, and at the time of writing the only option is IIS. IIS has been developed and enhanced over the past few years, and it has proven to be a largely reliable, robust, and developer-friendly Web server. It has been designed to be extensible and supports *plug-in* components through technologies such as Internet Server Application Programming Interface (ISAPI), which is the mechanism that both classic ASP and ASP.NET use.

When processing requests for ASP.NET applications, the majority of IIS features will remain unused. All IIS does is to examine the incoming request, perform its initial authentication and authorization checks, and then pass the request to the ASP.NET HTTP Runtime based on the extension of the file being requested. Referring back to Figure 10-1, you can see that IIS occupies a separate process to the HTTP Runtime used by ASP.NET; as you'll soon see, this separation is an advantage because it isolates failures and problems in one of these applications from affecting the other.

We'll return to the configuration of IIS later in this chapter, after we've dealt with the basic architecture and operation. However, one thing you should realize is that ASP.NET requires IIS 5.0 or later; it will not run with IIS 4.0 or earlier, and it won't run with Personal Web Server (PWS) or other Web server products. These requirements mean that your Web server must be running Windows 2000, Windows XP, or Windows .NET and that you can't run (or develop) ASP.NET applications on Windows NT, Windows ME, Windows 98, or similar.

Using ISAPI

ISAPI is a defined standard for writing components that you can add in to compliant Web servers such as IIS. ISAPI supports two types of components:

- ISAPI Filters process every request for the Web server and typically provide support services such as encryption, logging, or authentication. ISAPI filters actually process all inbound requests *and* outbound responses.

- ISAPI Extensions are mapped to specific file extensions that the client may request. ISAPI Extensions provide application-type functionality, such as enhanced page processing; classic ASP is implemented as an ISAPI Extension.

ISAPI components are typically created as DLLs and run in process with the Web server. In IIS, ISAPI Filters are loaded when the Web server starts and usually remain in memory to process incoming requests. ISAPI Extensions are loaded when they're first referenced but will also remain in memory. Figure 10-2 shows a schematic view of the process.

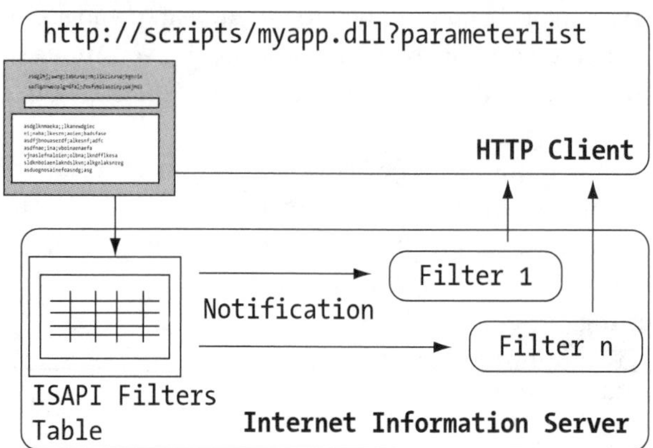

Figure 10-2. ISAPI processing model

IIS enables mapping of file extensions to ISAPI Extensions so that rather than requesting a specific ISAPI Extension by name (as in Figure 10-2), the browser simply requests a file (such as MyFile.asp) and IIS automatically invokes the corresponding Extension according to the defined settings. IIS's Application Configuration dialog box performs this mapping, as shown in Figure 10-3.

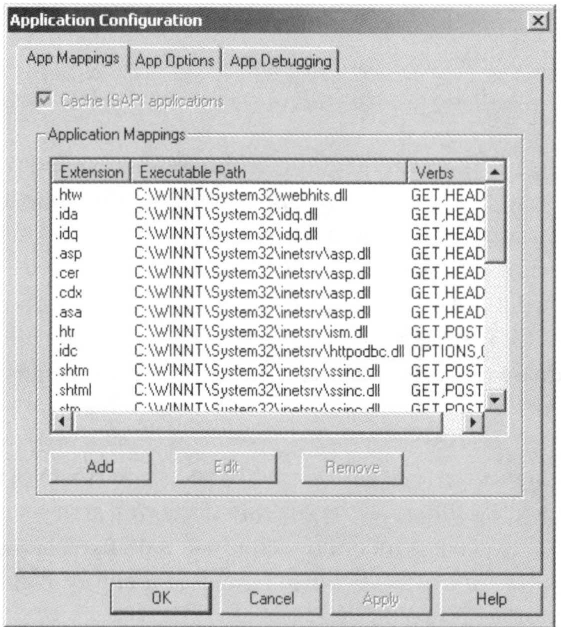

Figure 10-3. Mapping file extensions to ISAPI Extensions

Unfortunately for developers, creating custom ISAPI Extensions is not that straightforward. You can do it, but it requires careful planning and coding, and it requires knowledge of C++ and multithreaded programming. Also, debugging can be tricky because the DLLs run only within IIS. Finally, because ISAPI Filters and Extensions run within the IIS address space, a poorly written one can crash IIS and bring the entire Web server down.

It's therefore uncommon for developers to write their own Extensions, but instead most will typically use one of the existing components made available by Microsoft and third-party organizations. Although there's a variety of such components, two stand out, both of which were provided by Microsoft: HTTPODBC.DLL and ASP.DLL.

- HTTPODBC.DLL was known as the Internet Database Connector (IDC) and was an initial attempt at building an ISAPI Extension to provide dynamic output in Web pages. IDC focused on dynamic output from database queries and allowed developers to create .idc files containing queries and .htx files containing HTML templates. When run, the results of the query in the .idc file were merged into the .htx file and the results returned to the browser.

- ASP.DLL should need no introduction. This is the ISAPI Extension that underlies ASP processing and provides support for all the classic ASP features.

Classic ASP Web applications have made use of the ASP ISAPI Extension for some years, and although it offers quite good functionality, it does suffer from some limitations. One of the more serious concerns relates to security; because the ASP Extension ran within the IIS process, a malicious attack against the Web server could easily lead to a malicious attack on the ASP application, with disclosure or corruption of data, files, and programs. Despite Microsoft's continued efforts to safeguard IIS against attacks, it still remains a serious concern with successful attacks recorded and publicized almost every week.

Implementing ASP.NET ISAPI Extensions

As well as HTTPODBC.DLL and ASP.DLL, there's one other special ISAPI Extension: ASPNET_ISAPI.DLL. This is the ISAPI Extension responsible for passing requests to ASP.NET and for passing the responses from ASP.NET back to IIS to be sent to the browser. The Extension is automatically installed and configured when the .NET runtime files are installed onto the Web server (see the "Deploying Applications" section later in this chapter) and uses a set of application mappings similar to those shown in Figure 10-3. In particular, the mappings are configured to pass requests for the following file extensions across to the HTTP Runtime:

- .asax, .ascx, .ashx, .asmx, .aspx (Web Forms, Web controls, and Web Services)
- .axd (Trace requests)
- .rem, .soap, .vsdisco (Web Services and .NET Remoting)
- .config, .webinfo (Configuration files)
- .cs, .csproj, .vb, .vbproj, .licx, .resx, .resources (Code and development files)

It's worth emphasizing that the Extension does not process these requests itself; instead it passes them to the HTTP Runtime to enable .NET to process them using its full power and functionality. As you'll see in the next section, you can exert great control over the HTTP Runtime and customize its behavior using HTTP Modules and HTTP Handlers, but the ASPNET_ISAPI Extension really is just a thin transfer layer that lets IIS and .NET communicate. This contrasts with the classic ASP Extension, which gives developers the impression of being a magic black box that takes requests and generates responses but that can only be controlled or customized in specific ways (such as by creating .asp files).

Understanding the HTTP Runtime, Modules, and Handlers

A lot of effort has been put into the design of the .NET Framework to overcome problems such as those facing ISAPI Filters and Extensions. In modern enterprise-level applications, security, robustness, and efficiency are of paramount concern, and it's unacceptable for these measures to be compromised by weaknesses in third-party software.

.NET was founded on the principle of having a distinct process that manages all request, page, and response processing. Known as the *HTTP Runtime*, this process plays a controlling role in the ASP.NET architecture and processing model.

The HTTP Runtime

The HTTP Runtime is implemented as an .exe file named aspnet_wp.exe. As we've already said, the HTTP Runtime is a core component for ASP.NET because it's the HTTP Runtime that manages the page-processing cycle and ultimately coordinates the classes and components that constitute your Web Application. We'll be looking in detail at the responsibilities of the HTTP Runtime throughout much of this chapter, but there's one important fact you should keep in mind: The HTTP Runtime runs as a separate process, as shown in the Windows Task Manager dialog box in Figure 10-4.

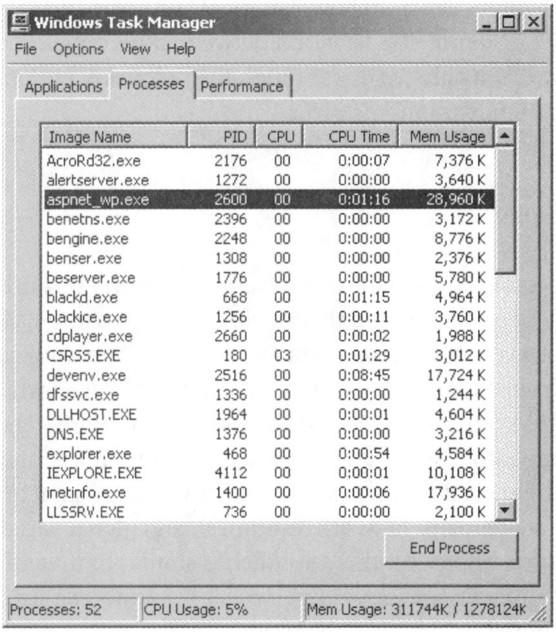

Figure 10-4. HTTP Runtime process in the Task Manager

Why is this so significant? Well, it shows the clear separation between the Web server process (inetinfo.exe) and the ASP.NET runtime process. Classic ASP is tightly coupled with inetinfo.exe, so any failures, locks, blocks, or restarts of one will usually affect the other. Also, this tight coupling makes it extremely difficult to implement ASP support on any other platform or Web server.

By keeping the HTTP Runtime as a separate process from IIS, ASP.NET and IIS are protected from each other, yet can still communicate through the ASP.NET ISAPI Extension. The benefits of this solution include:

- Any failures in the ASP.NET application are isolated from IIS; failures in IIS will affect ASP.NET, though, because it's IIS that has responsibility for receiving client requests and generating responses. If IIS fails, ASP.NET has no way to receive requests and so will effectively be inaccessible to clients.

- Any security breaches of IIS are isolated from the ASP.NET application.

- ASP.NET applications can take advantage of the full .NET Framework and are implemented as managed code, even though IIS itself is unmanaged.
- An architecture in which the Web application is distinct from the Web server is more easily ported to other platforms.

As well as providing isolation between the Web server and the HTTP Runtime, ASP.NET also provides isolation between different applications within the HTTP Runtime. You achieve this through the definition of application domains and HttpApplication instances.

Application Domains

On a single-processor, .NET-enabled Web server there will be only one instance of the HTTP Runtime process, and this single instance hosts all ASP.NET Web Applications. However, .NET ensures that all ASP.NET Web Applications are completely isolated from each other by executing each within its own unique *application domain*, a mechanism that partitions the memory and resources of the HTTP Runtime into distinct units. Application domains guarantee class isolation (no versioning or naming conflicts), security sandboxing (preventing access to certain machine or network resources), and global variable isolation. The level of isolation offered by this approach is similar to that offered by running classic ASP applications in separate processes. However, processes are expensive for Windows to create and maintain, so the .NET solution results in more efficient resource usage and hence more scalable applications.

At a practical level, the isolation offered by application domains means the following:

- If one Web Application fails, it shouldn't affect others.
- If you reconfigure a Web Application, the changes made should not affect others.
- Any hackers who successfully breach the security of IIS have several more hurdles to overcome before they can attack each Web Application.

Within each application domain, ASP.NET maintains a pool of *HttpApplication instances* throughout the application's lifetime. Each incoming HTTP request is automatically assigned one of these instances to process it; the HttpApplication instance is then responsible for managing the entire lifetime of the request and is reused only after the request has been completed. You can interact with the HttpApplication instance through the Global.asax file, which inherits from the class, and any events raised by the HttpApplication instance can be handled via procedures in Global.asax. The following events are raised at the start of the page processing cycle:

- BeginRequest
- AuthenticateRequest
- AuthorizeRequest
- ResolveRequestCache
- AcquireRequestState
- PreRequestHandlerExecute

At the end of the page processing cycle, a different set of events are raised:

- PostRequestHandlerExecute
- ReleaseRequestState
- UpdateRequestCache
- EndRequest

Finally, there are three *non-deterministic* events. Non-deterministic means that they may be raised at any point in the page processing cycle:

- Error
- PreSendRequestContent
- PreSendRequestHeaders

We won't endeavor to describe most of these events at this stage because you're unlikely to need to handle them in applications that you create. However, four events of special note are `BeginRequest` and `EndRequest`, which are raised at the start and end of the processing cycle, and `AuthenticateRequest` and `AuthorizeRequest`, which are raised by the security system. In Chapter 11 you'll see an example of an event handler for the `AuthenticateRequest` event that helps you manage security.

Note that the HttpApplication instance is different from the ASP.NET Application object. The intrinsic Application object also raises events handled in Global.asax, such as `Application_Start` and `Application_End`. However, the `Application_Start` event occurs only once in the application's lifetime, when the first HTTP request is received, whereas the `BeginRequest` event for the HttpApplication is raised on each and every request.

Web Gardens

The previous section said that on a single-processor server there will be only one instance of the HTTP Runtime process, but if you're using a multiprocessor machine then things may be different. By default, ASP.NET will run one instance of the HTTP Runtime on *each* processor, creating a configuration known as a *Web garden*. By having several distinct processes, ASP.NET applications typically suffer fewer problems with thread- and resource-blocking, and so are more scalable.

However, such configurations are not always the best; the use of multiple processors may introduce subtle problems because of timing and synchronization that just wouldn't occur with single-processor machines. Additionally, applications need special consideration during the design phase if they're to run on Web gardens because features such as Application state and Cache state are not Web garden–friendly.

If your server has multiple processors and you want to explicitly control Web garden behavior, you can do so through settings in the `<processmodel>` section of Web.config. The key attributes are `webGarden` and `cpuMask`.

Learning about HTTP Runtime Architecture

The HTTP Runtime is a high-performance, robust engine for processing HTTP requests. In conceptual design it's similar to the ISAPI architecture, in that the HTTP Runtime loads worker components (called *HTTP Modules* and *HTTP Handlers*) to perform the specific tasks necessary to service a request. However, its implementation is different; it runs as managed code within the .NET Framework. Figure 10-5 shows how HTTP requests are passed through IIS to be processed by the HTTP Modules and HTTP Handlers within the HTTP Runtime.

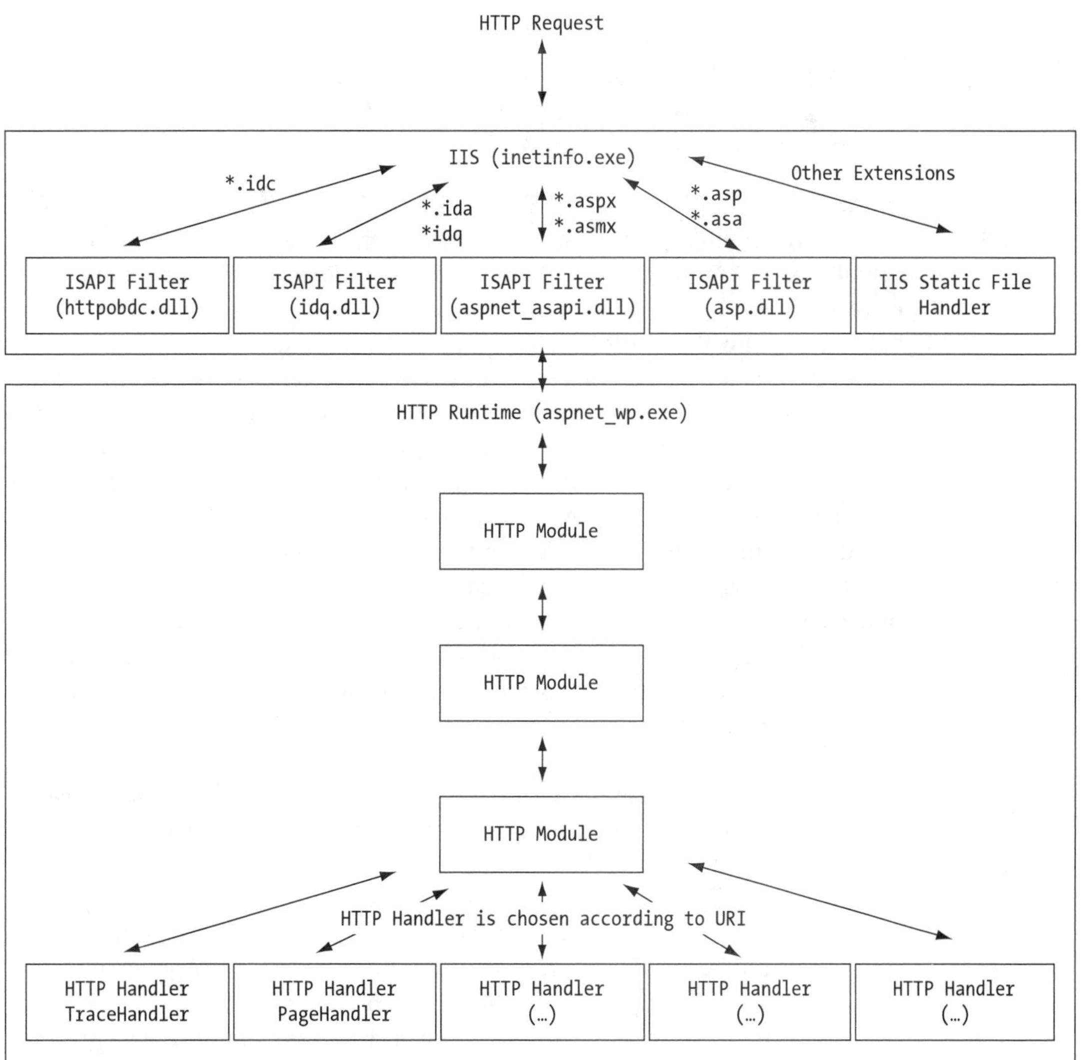

Figure 10-5. Interaction of IIS and the HTTP Runtime

Because the HTTP Runtime runs as a separate process, it's insulated from malicious attacks as well as inadvertent crashes and failures in IIS and other ISAPI Extensions. However, remember that if the IIS process crashes, clients will be unable to access ASP.NET applications until IIS restarts. Restarting IIS is usually a manual process performed by a system administrator, and more often than not it requires that the entire server be restarted. In this case, the ASP.NET Web Application will also be restarted.

TIP *One of the most common causes of IIS crashing was ill-behaved ASP application code; by keeping applications in a separate process (as ASP.NET does) the chances of crashes are greatly reduced.*

Failures in ASP.NET itself are much less severe. In fact, the HTTP Runtime actually assumes that failures will occur and is designed to automatically recover as best it can from access violations, memory leaks, deadlocks, and so on. Barring hardware failure, the runtime aims for 100-percent availability.

To provide the best possible performance and scalability, the HTTP Runtime is multithreaded and processes requests asynchronously, so it can't be blocked by bad application code from processing new requests. This does, of course, require that all assemblies and components used from within the runtime must either be completely thread-safe, or they must be managed in a way such that they're not called on multiple threads simultaneously. This might sound like a rather onerous task if you've been used to the free and easy world of classic ASP, but in practice you needn't worry too much. When your Web Forms are instantiated to service HTTP requests, ASP.NET ensures that they're not re-entrant, which minimizes the chances of threading problems. In fact, the only real causes of concern are the following:

- If you choose to use `Shared` (or `Static` in C#) methods, properties, or variables, you must add your own synchronization mechanisms to manage concurrent access.

- You need to take care with any code that accesses .NET classes that are not thread-safe. The most significant example is the intrinsic Application object, which supports Lock and Unlock methods; your code must call these methods to manage concurrent access. Note that the Cache object is automatically thread-safe and takes care of its own synchronization processes. Chapter 12 discusses the Application and Cache objects in more detail.

- If you access legacy COM components built on the Single Threaded Apartment (STA) model. STA components can be accessed only by the thread that created them, whereas .NET components have no thread affinity (that is, they can be called by any thread in the process). All components built using VB 4.0, 5.0, or 6.0 are STA components. ASP.NET provides support for STA components by way of the `AspCompat` attribute in the Page directive, as discussed in Chapter 2.

Using HTTP Modules

Within the runtime process, HTTP Modules are used to incrementally process a request. The modules are organized into a *pipeline* (as shown in Figure 10-5), which is followed in the same way for every request received by a Web Application. By default, ASP.NET provides seven HTTP modules, each of which focuses on a particular task that it will perform:

- The OutputCache module provides cache management for pages and Web User Controls. You'll see more about OutputCache in Chapter 12.
- The Session module is responsible for Session state and is also addressed in Chapter 12.
- The WindowsAuthentication, FormsAuthentication, and PassportAuthentication modules perform different types of security authentication. Chapter 11 discusses these techniques.
- The UrlAuthorization and FileAuthorization modules manage authorization of requests. Chapter 11 includes authorization within its discussion of security.

Modules are able to respond to events raised from HTTPApplication; these are the same events identified in the "Application Domains" section previously, including `BeginRequest`, `EndRequest`, `AuthenticateRequest`, and `AuthorizeRequest`. In addition, modules are able to raise their own events that you can respond to by adding code in Global.asax.

You can extend and customize these prebuilt modules if required, or you can build completely new modules to process requests received by an ASP.NET Web Application. For example, a custom authentication module may expose an `Authentication` event. Assuming the HTTP Module was given a "friendly" name of Security, the code within Global.asax to handle the events could look like this:

```
Sub Session_Start()
    'Session start-up code goes here.
End Sub
Sub Session_End()
    'Session clean-up code goes here.
End Sub
Sub Security_Authentication(Source As Object, _
             Details as AuthenticationEventArgs)
    'Authentication code goes here.
End Sub
```

The HTTP Modules in use can differ from one server to another and from one application to another, and so they need to be configured in some way. The Machine.config and Web.config files are used for this purpose (among many others), and you'll see more detail about these configuration files shortly. If you place the configuration settings into Machine.config, they'll be applied to all applications on the server. If you place the settings into an application's Web.config file, then they remain specific to that application. If conflicting settings exist in both files, the values in the application's Web.config dominate and will be used by the HTTP Runtime.

To see the default settings used by ASP.NET, load the Machine.config file into Notepad or some other text editor and search for `<httpModules>`. The section will be similar to the following:

```
<httpModules>
    <add name="OutputCache"
                type="System.Web.Caching.OutputCacheModule" />
    <add name="Session"
                type="System.Web.SessionState.SessionStateModule" />
    <add name="WindowsAuthentication"
                type="System.Web.Security.WindowsAuthenticationModule" />
    <add name="FormsAuthentication"
                type="System.Web.Security.FormsAuthenticationModule" />
    <add name="PassportAuthentication"
                type="System.Web.Security.PassportAuthenticationModule" />
    <add name="UrlAuthorization"
                type="System.Web.Security.UrlAuthorizationModule" />
    <add name="FileAuthorization"
                type="System.Web.Security.FileAuthorizationModule" />
</httpModules>
```

NOTE *You may want to disable unused HTTP Modules by removing their entries from the Machine.config file. This could potentially improve performance as there will be fewer modules processing each request.*

Using HTTP Handlers

HTTP Handlers are components that process HTTP requests, providing the functionality necessary to analyze an incoming request, perform whatever processing is necessary, and generate the appropriate output to be returned to the client.

ASP.NET provides a number of prebuilt HTTP Handlers, but you can also build custom handlers in Visual Studio .NET.

Each HTTPHandler is assigned to one or more combinations of path and verb in the configuration file settings. The path can either be a partial or fully defined URI; for example, `*.aspx` is a partial URI that matches any request for an .aspx file, and `Trace.axd` is a fully defined URI that includes both filename and extension. The verb can also be explicitly declared or can make use of wildcard matches. You can find these configuration settings in Machine.config, but you can also add them to Web.config to provide application-specific overrides of the central settings. To view the Machine.config entries, load the file into Notepad (or similar) and search for `<httpHandlers>`. The section will be similar to the following:

```
<httpHandlers>
    <add verb="*" path="trace.axd" type="System.Web.Handlers.TraceHandler"/>
    <add verb="*" path="*.aspx" type="System.Web.UI.PageHandlerFactory"/>
    <add verb="*" path="*.ashx" type="System.Web.UI.SimpleHandlerFactory"/>
    .
    .
    <add verb="*" path="*.licx" type="System.Web.HttpForbiddenHandler"/>
    <add verb="*" path="*.resx" type="System.Web.HttpForbiddenHandler"/>
    <add verb="*" path="*.resources" type="System.Web.HttpForbiddenHandler"/>
    <add verb="GET,HEAD" path="*" type="System.Web.StaticFileHandler"/>
    <add verb="*" path="*" type="System.Web.HttpMethodNotAllowedHandler"/>
</httpHandlers>
```

You'll notice that the list of defined handlers in Machine.config is quite lengthy (we've abbreviated it in this example) and includes handlers associated with obvious file extensions such as .aspx and .asmx, as well as less obvious ones such as .vb, .resx, and .config. You'll also notice that many of the file extensions are associated with the HTTPForbiddenHandler; this is .NET's way of protecting server-side code and configuration files from casual and malicious attempts to view their content. Put simply, a request for any of these file extensions will be processed by a handler that is unable to return the file and will instead return an HTTP status code and error message.

NOTE *Unlike HTTPModules, HTTPHandlers will only be used to process a request if they're mapped to the verb and URI in the configuration file. Also, only one HTTPHandler will be used (the first one found to match the request details, starting from the top), so there's no real need to disable unwanted handlers as you might do with HTTPModules.*

Introducing the ASP.NET Processing Model

Now that you've looked at the components and technologies in isolation, it's time to pull them all together and see how they work collectively to deliver the functionality and power behind ASP.NET. We'll do this by looking at the end-to-end processing model, from the request issued by a browser to the response it receives in reply. In fact, looking at one processing cycle isn't sufficient because there are many variations dependent on the exact nature of the request. Although we can't cover all permutations, we'll examine four different page processing scenarios: initial requests for pages that need to be compiled, requests for pages that have already been compiled, initial requests for pages that have code-behind classes, and requests for pages that have had their output cached by previous requests.

Before getting into these scenarios, though, let's recap what ASP.NET means to a Web Application and a Web Form page.

Web Application Behavior

In its simplest form, ASP.NET is a mechanism for building Web applications, albeit a richly featured and quite advanced one. Irrespective of the tools and technologies used, such Web applications have to conform to certain practical rules if they're to function well, including:

- Client browsers will make HTTP requests and will expect HTTP responses. The responses will usually contain HTML data that will be rendered by the browser, unless an error, redirection, or similar occurs. In these cases, the HTTP header will contain the appropriate status code and additional data.

- HTTP is connectionless. Once the browser has received its response, it's likely to disconnect from the server (or the server may forcibly disconnect it) and will need to reconnect to make its next request. Between the requests, the server has no contact with the browser at all.

- The application will need to support multiple concurrent users, sometimes thousands or more.

- Client-browsers come in many types and versions, although most offer support for at least HTML 3.2. Web applications will need to support as broad a range of browsers as possible by allowing output to be generated in this common format.

- Browsers are fundamentally simple. As far as interaction with the server goes, they're largely limited to issuing an HTTP request by way of a URL in an address bar, a hyperlink, a redirection from another page, a form on a Web page, or a chunk of client-side code. The server knows the details sent with the request, but that's about it.

ASP.NET doesn't magically sidestep these rules, but it does provide an effective way of building Web applications while obeying them. To do so, there are various key stages involved in processing a request from a browser and generating a response.

Web Form Structure

We've discussed Web Forms in many of the previous chapters, and by now you've probably realized that they're the most common ASP.NET component that will be processed in response to a page request. You should also remember that a Web Form consists of two components: the visual elements and the code. Either may be omitted, but in most cases they'll both be present. These two components can reside in the same file, as was the case with classic ASP, or they can be kept separate to ease development, testing, maintenance, and so on.

As you saw in Chapter 2, the visual elements are created in an .aspx file, which acts as a container for HTML elements and server controls. The code can be stored within the .aspx or in a separate .aspx.vb or .aspx.cs class file, with the code-behind approach being preferred. The .aspx file uses Page directives to specify details of the associated class file, if one exists.

Page Class

At runtime, the separate components that constitute a Web Form are combined to create a single unit. This unit takes the form of compiled code and will be generated when the first request for each Web Form is received. Notice that the compiled code is generated from *both* the visual and code components of the Web Form, with every server control and HTML element being converted to a corresponding .NET class. The class dynamically generated for the Web Form is derived either directly or indirectly from System.Web.UI.Page. If you have a code-behind class for the Web Form, then the inheritance will be indirect, as the class inherits from System.Web.UI.Page and the Web Form inherits from the class. If there is no code-behind class, the Web Form inherits directly from System.Web.UI.Page.

NOTE *When we say every server control and HTML element is converted to a corresponding .NET class, we really do mean it. Every single element, tag, and attribute is compiled to a class, no matter how simple it is. This allows the HTTP Runtime to execute all of the page content within the same framework, thus streamlining and optimizing the process.*

This new derived Page class executes on the server whenever the Web Form page is requested. At runtime, it processes incoming requests and responds by dynamically creating HTML and streaming it back to the browser. If the page contains Web Controls (as it typically would), the derived Page class acts as a container for the controls, and instances of the controls are created at runtime and likewise render HTML text to the stream.

Notice that this is quite different to classic ASP, where a page request is processed each time by retrieving the specified file, extracting and interpreting the code it contains and then fitting the results back into the static HTML before sending the entire response to the browser. Rather than combining the HTML and code results each time, an ASP.NET Web Form is really an executable program whose output is HTML, with the core of that program being a class derived from the ASP.NET Page class.

By treating a Web Form as a class, developers should find it easier to appreciate the processing stages through which it passes. Some of these are similar to other classes—initialize, process, and dispose—and some of them are quite different. One major difference is that the Page class performs these stages each time the page is called, so for every single request the page is initialized, processed, and disposed. As you can imagine, on an enterprise application this can place a heavy processing demand on the Web server, so there are some optimizations built into the .NET runtime to cache some of this detail and eliminate unnecessary processing. We'll return to the topic of caching in Chapter 12.

Code-Behind Classes and Visual Studio.NET

As discussed in the previous section, you can embed the code for a Web Form in the .aspx file, or you can place it into a code-behind class. Visual Studio .NET emphasizes the latter approach and by default creates a code-behind class and module for every Web Form added to a project.

A newly added Web Form will have a largely empty code-behind module, containing only the skeleton class definition:

```
Public Class WebForm1
    Inherits System.Web.UI.Page

#Region " Web Form Designer Generated Code "

    Private Sub Page_Load(ByVal sender As System.Object,
                ByVal e As System.EventArgs) Handles MyBase.Load
        'Put user code to initialize the page here
    End Sub

End Class
```

The name of the class is set to the name of the Web Form, as is the name of the code-behind module. You reference these names in the Page directive in the .aspx file:

```
<%@ Page Language="vb" Codebehind="WebForm1.aspx.vb" Inherits="WebApp1.WebForm1"%>
```

It's important to realize that you can (and probably will) change these names. However, when changing them, keep the following points in mind:

- The `Codebehind` attribute is used only in Visual Studio .NET to load an associated code-behind module into the development environment. This attribute is completely redundant at runtime.

- The `Inherits` attribute must match the name of a class derived from System.Web.UI.Page. At runtime, ASP.NET expects to find this class in the application's .dll file in the \bin directory.

Why make this point? Well, renaming things in Visual Studio .NET requires careful consideration, as the development environment makes some, but not all, the changes you may expect. For example, the previous code snippet used a page called WebForm1. Clearly this is an inappropriate name for a real site, so you would rename the page, perhaps to Login.aspx. Doing so would cause the following changes:

- Webform1.aspx becomes Login.aspx.

- Webform1.aspx.vb becomes Login.aspx.vb.

In the Login.aspx file, the Page directive now reads:

```
<%@ Page Language="vb" Codebehind="Login.aspx.vb" Inherits="WebApp1.WebForm1"%>
```

In the Login.aspx.vb source file, the content is now the following:

```
Public Class WebForm1
    Inherits System.Web.UI.Page

#Region " Web Form Designer Generated Code "

    Private Sub Page_Load(ByVal sender As System.Object,
                ByVal e As System.EventArgs) Handles MyBase.Load
        'Put user code to initialize the page here
    End Sub

End Class
```

So, the .aspx and the .aspx.vb files have been renamed, but the class within the code-behind module has retained its original name. The application still works and there are no errors, it's just that the Web Form inherits from a class with a different name. In reality it's probably best that the development environment doesn't automatically rename classes because it allows you to make whatever changes you want, but you do need to be aware of this behavior.

Compiled Code-Behind Classes

ASP.NET Web Applications built in Visual Studio .NET are created with the expectation that they'll be compiled prior to testing or deployment. The compilation involves taking the classes in the code-behind modules, together with any other .vb or .cs files, and compiling them into a single assembly or *application DLL*, which is then placed in the application's \bin directory. At this point, the content of the .aspx files is *not* compiled—this happens later.

This design-time compilation generates object files that contain Intermediate Language (IL) code rather than processor-specific native code. IL code is portable and language neutral, making it easier to achieve .NET's goals of cross-language inheritance and portability, but it can't be directly executed. Instead, the IL code must pass through another compiler to generate native code that the processor *can* execute, and this occurs at runtime when ASP.NET receives a request for the page containing the code. The timing of this secondary compilation lends the compiler its name—the Just In Time (JIT) compiler.

At runtime, when an .aspx file is requested from the application, ASP.NET reads the file and recognizes that a code-behind class is required from the Inherits attribute in the Page directive. It then attempts to locate the associated assembly, on the basis that it has the same name as the Web Application and a file extension of either DLL or EXE. It automatically checks the application's \bin directory, plus the Temporary ASP.NET Files directory. If it fails to find the assembly, or if the assembly does not contain the required class, it reports an error and aborts processing. If it finds the assembly, it passes it to the JIT compiler with the .aspx file, which is compiled into processor-specific code, ready for execution. Once the assembly has been loaded, it remains in memory; similarly, once a Web Form has been compiled, its object code is also cached. These two optimizations ensure that no unnecessary disk accesses and compilations take place.

When using compiled code-behind classes in this way, the .vb files are not needed at runtime as all code has already been compiled to IL. Therefore, you would not usually deploy them to the Web server; the only files needed on the target machine are the .aspx files and the application-specific assembly that must be placed in a \bin directory. Your application will probably also use a number of other ASP.NET support files such as Web.config and Global.asax.

Uncompiled Code-Behind Classes

The Visual Studio .NET approach is not the only option; it's also possible to use code-behind classes that *are* deployed to the Web server in source code form. To achieve this, you need to make the following changes to the Page directive in the .aspx file:

1. Add the `Src` attribute to specify the name of the code-behind file.

2. Change the `Inherits` attribute by removing the namespace part of the class name (unless you have added a `Namespace` declaration explicitly to your source code). The namespace is usually the same as the application's name.

For example, you may have the following Page directive in a regular Web Form created by Visual Studio .NET that uses a compiled code-behind class:

```
<%@ Page Language="vb" CodeBehind="Main.aspx.vb" Inherits="WebApp1.WebForm1"%>
```

To use an uncompiled code-behind class, it would need to be modified as follows:

```
<%@ Page Language="vb" CodeBehind="Main.aspx.vb"
              Src="Main.aspx.vb" Inherits="WebForm1"%>
```

Notice that both the `Codebehind` and `Src` attributes are used; Codebehind is used by the development environment to load the associated code module when the Web Form is being edited, and Src is used at runtime to control execution.

With this approach, the .vb files *will* be deployed to the server and will be compiled directly to native code by the JIT compiler when the Web Form is referenced. You may be concerned about the performance hit that this introduces, but it really isn't that significant as it occurs only for the first request for each page; once compiled, the object code is cached for use by subsequent requests. A bigger concern is security—if the Web server were breached it would be easy for a hacker to read the source code files, which could possibly further compromise the entire application's security.

Uncompiled code-behind classes provide a good solution to the problem of designing Web applications where the logic changes frequently. By leaving the logic in source-code form, you can modify it at any stage without requiring any development tools at all, just an editor such as Notepad. ASP.NET automatically recompiles when it detects a change in the file, so the next page request after the modification will trigger this process and thereafter the compiled content will be served from the temporary assembly cache.

However, this does lead to the question of whether Web applications *should* have their code modified on a regular basis. Sometimes it can't be avoided, but as a general rule an alternate approach (such as a data-driven application) would be preferred.

Processing Page Requests

Now that we've covered all the background technologies, let's take a look at how ASP.NET uses them to process page requests. As mentioned earlier, we'll do this by looking at a number of scenarios that illustrate the main differences you may encounter. Of course, we could cover many different variations, but to keep this section manageable we'll limit the discussion to four separate scenarios:

1. The first request for a page using an *uncompiled* code-behind module

2. Subsequent requests for the same page

3. An initial request for a page using a *compiled* code-behind module

4. Requests for pages that have cached their output

Scenario 1: First Request for a Page with Uncompiled Source Code

In this scenario a browser issues a request for an .aspx file containing uncompiled source code. This would be the case if a legacy ASP page had been converted to ASP.NET, but the code had been left as a part of the .aspx file, or if a .aspx had been created with a code-behind module in source-code form, rather than compiled using Visual Studio .NET. Figure 10-6 shows a schematic view of the page processing cycle for this scenario.

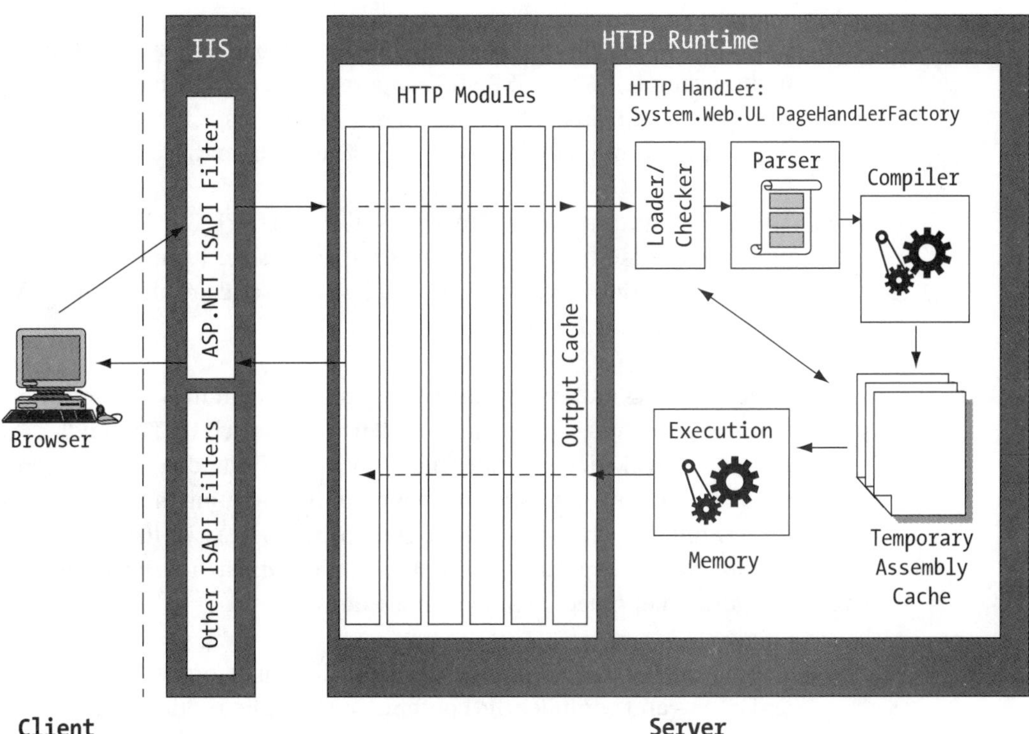

Figure 10-6. Page-processing cycle for an initial request

During this process there are a number of key stages:

1. The client browser makes the request to the Web server in this form:

```
HTTP://ServerName/AppName/MyPage.aspx
```

The request may include extra parameters, such as when the request is initiated by clicking a hyperlink or a submit button in a form. In the case of a POST request, the data will be hidden in the body of the HTTP request. For a GET request they'll be passed as a part of the URL in the querystring. For example:

```
HTTP://ServerName/AppName/MyPage.aspx?Name=xyz&ID=123
```

2. The request is received by the Web server, which for our purposes we'll assume to be Internet Information Server (IIS). IIS performs rudimentary checking on the request to ensure it's not malformed.

3. If OK, IIS checks the configuration for the specified application (`AppName` in this example). When ASP.NET support is added to IIS, it automatically configures each application to send requests for .aspx files (and some others, too) through the ASP.NET ISAPI Extension to the HTTP Runtime.

4. The HTTP Runtime passes the request through the HTTP Module pipeline. The modules perform tasks including security authentication and authorization, cache or state management, and are able to modify the request before it's processed further.

5. If the request is authorized, the HTTP Runtime examines the requested URI and checks its configuration to determine which HTTP Handler should be invoked. Remember that it's the HTTP Handler that is responsible for processing the specific request and generating the response. In this example, the request for MyPage.aspx will be passed to the System.Web.UI.PageHandlerFactory handler, which in turn will create a PageHandler object to process the request.

6. The PageHandler retrieves the requested file from storage (MyPage.aspx) and parses and compiles the content. The compiled code is then stored in the Temporary Assembly Cache (TAC) from where it will be loaded for subsequent requests.

7. The compiled class is instantiated by the HTTP Runtime. It also instantiates any contained classes that represent server controls and HTML elements. These classes support a range of events, including Init, Load, Dispose, and Finalize, as well as constructors and other methods that the Runtime will call.

8. As the classes are instantiated, their events are raised, and any code that you have defined within the event handlers will be executed. For example, consider the following code:

```
Public Class MyPage
    Inherits System.Web.UI.Page
    Protected WithEvents lstSource As System.Web.UI.WebControls.ListBox

    Private Sub Page_Load(ByVal sender As System.Object, _
                ByVal e As System.EventArgs) Handles MyBase.Load
            lstSource.Items.Add("North")
            lstSource.Items.Add("South")
            lstSource.Items.Add("East")
            lstSource.Items.Add("West")
    End Sub
End Class
```

   When the Load event is raised for the class, the code populates the list box with four entries. Note that the list box object will already have been created at this stage, as it's one of the server controls on the Web Form and so will have been instantiated during step 7.

9. When the Page's Load event has completed, ASP.NET triggers any other events that have been generated. (These are discussed later in the "Web Form Events" section.)

10. When all the developer-generated server-side code has been run, the page request is nearing completion. However, there are still some important tasks to perform, one of the most important being the rendering process. As you saw in Chapter 5, each of the server-side elements on a Web Form supports a Render method in which the element generates the appropriate HTML that it'll use to represent itself. For example, the ListBox control will generate `<select>` and `<option>` tags. Any static HTML elements on the Web Form will also have been instantiated as objects, and these too support a Render method to generate their content and send it to the browser stream.

11. The rendered HTML output is passed through the Output Cache and back to IIS, and then to the browser in the HTTP response. Pages can be selectively marked for caching (although by default they're not), which causes their rendered image to be retained in memory for use by subsequent requests, as you'll soon see.

12. Each server-side object has its Dispose event triggered, after which it's released and ultimately destroyed by the .NET Framework. Unless your code explicitly uses Application, Cache, Session, or View state then no information is retained.

In summary, the browser makes an HTTP request and receives an HTTP response, just as it would with any good Web server. However, ASP.NET has processed this request by instantiating a Page object and its constituent controls and running the code in the appropriate event handlers. The page object existed only for the brief duration of the request, and even though the rendered HTML output persists in the browser, the objects that generated that output will have been destroyed.

Scenario 2: Second Request for a Page

When the second request and subsequent requests are received for the same page, the process is slightly different, as shown in Figure 10-7.

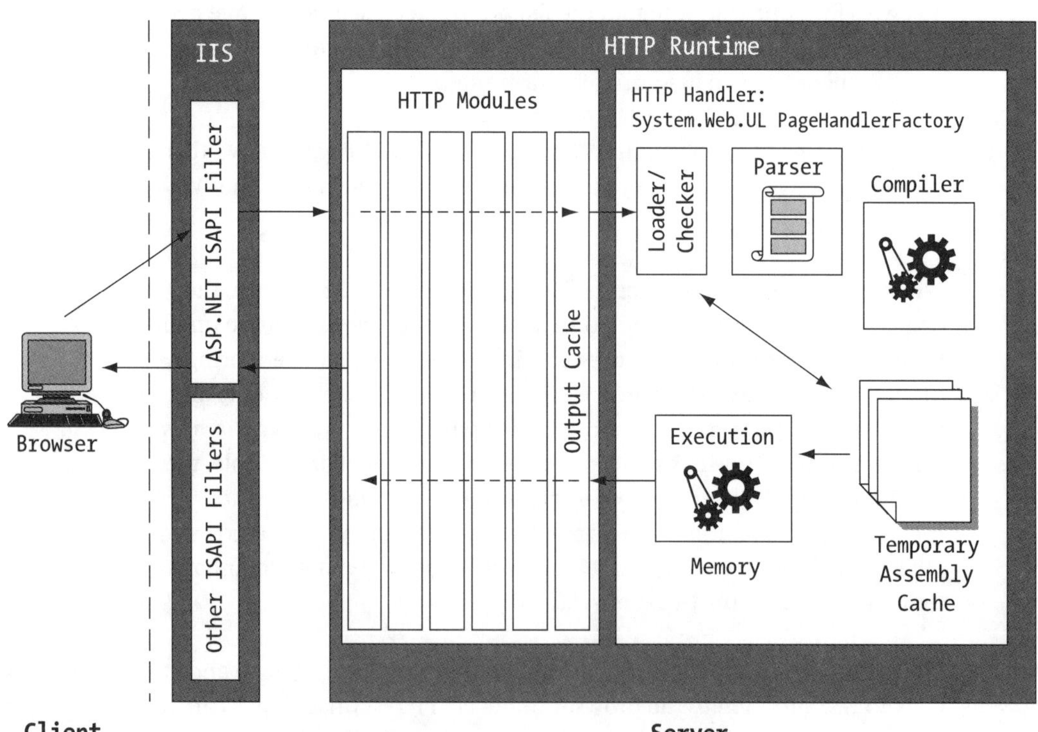

Figure 10-7. Page-processing cycle for subsequent requests

During this process, these are the key steps:

1. The browser issues the HTTP request for the .aspx file.

2. IIS receives and checks the request, examines the extension of the file being requested, and invokes the ASP.NET ISAPI Extension.

3. The Extension makes a cross-process call to the HTTP Runtime, passing in the information relating to the request.

4. The HTTP Runtime passes the request through the pipeline of HTTP Modules.

5. The HTTP Runtime invokes the HTTP Handler.

6. The Loader checks the TAC to see if the page has already been compiled. As long as the file has not been modified since it was compiled, the compiled code in the TAC will be used, removing the need to load, parse, and compile the file.

7. The compiled code is executed by the HTTP Runtime and passed back to the browser through the Output Cache as before.

8. From the Output Cache the results are returned back through IIS and viewed in the browser.

As you can see, the subsequent requests can be processed more quickly as the compiled code is readily available. However, remember that the process automatically reverts to that of Scenario 1 if the code or visual content in the .aspx file is modified in any way. This enables developers or administrators to change the code *on the fly* and have the next request for the modified page automatically compile and execute the new code. Any requests in progress when the change is made are unaffected, as they run from the compiled code in the TAC.

Scenario 3: Request for a Page with Compiled Code

When the browser requests an .aspx file that has associated compiled code, the process is slightly different once more, as shown in Figure 10-8. This would be the case when accessing a .aspx file that had been created and compiled using Visual Studio .NET (assuming the developer chose default options):

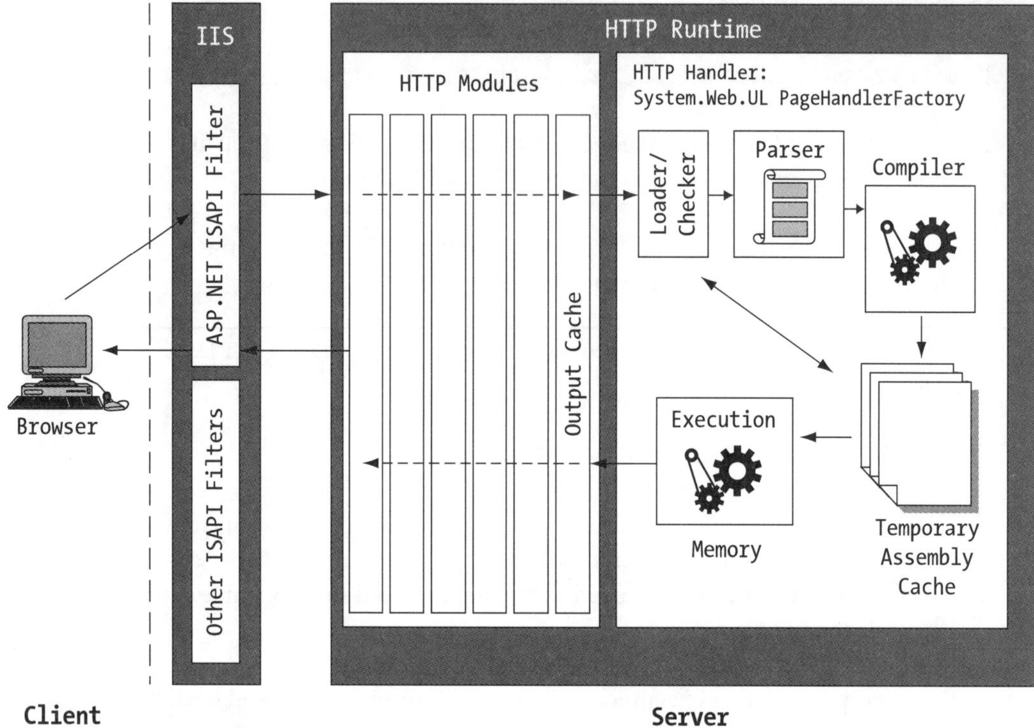

Figure 10-8. Initial request for a page with compiled code.

These are the main steps:

1. The browser issues the HTTP request for the .aspx file.

2. IIS receives and checks the request, examines the extension of the file being requested, and invokes the ASP.NET ISAPI Extension.

3. The Extension makes a cross-process call to the HTTP Runtime, passing in the information relating to the request.

4. The HTTP Runtime passes the request through the pipeline of HTTP Modules.

5. The HTTP Runtime invokes the HTTP Handler.

6. The Loader checks the Temporary Assembly Cache (TAC) to see if the page has already been compiled. As this is the first request for the page, it doesn't exist in the cache, so control passes to the Parser.

7. The .aspx file specified in the original request is loaded from a disk and processed by the Parser. During this process it will examine the Page directive and the Inherits attribute. Because the page derives from a class, but the Page directive contains no SRC attribute that specifies the name of a code-behind file, the loader will be invoked to locate and load the Web Application's DLL from its \bin directory.

8. The Compiler compiles the content of the .aspx file and the Intermediate Language (IL) code from the associated DLL. As before, this is compiled to processor-specific native code, which it then stores in the TAC.

9. The remainder of the process is then the same—the compiled code is read from the TAC and executed, the results are passed through the Output Cache to the browser.

Refer to Scenario 1, and you'll see that this process is similar. The only difference is that in Scenario 1 the code is compiled from source code to native code, whereas in this case it's compiled from IL code to native code. It's a little quicker to compile IL code as a lot of the validation, tokenization, and referencing will have been done, but in other respects there's relatively little difference at runtime between using source code and compiled code.

Subsequent requests for the same file are served from the Temporary Assembly Cache, as with Scenario 2.

Scenario 4: Request for a Cached Page

When the browser requests a .aspx that has already been processed and stored in the Output Cache, the process is quicker and more direct than any of the preceding scenarios. Figure 10-9 shows the schematic for this model.

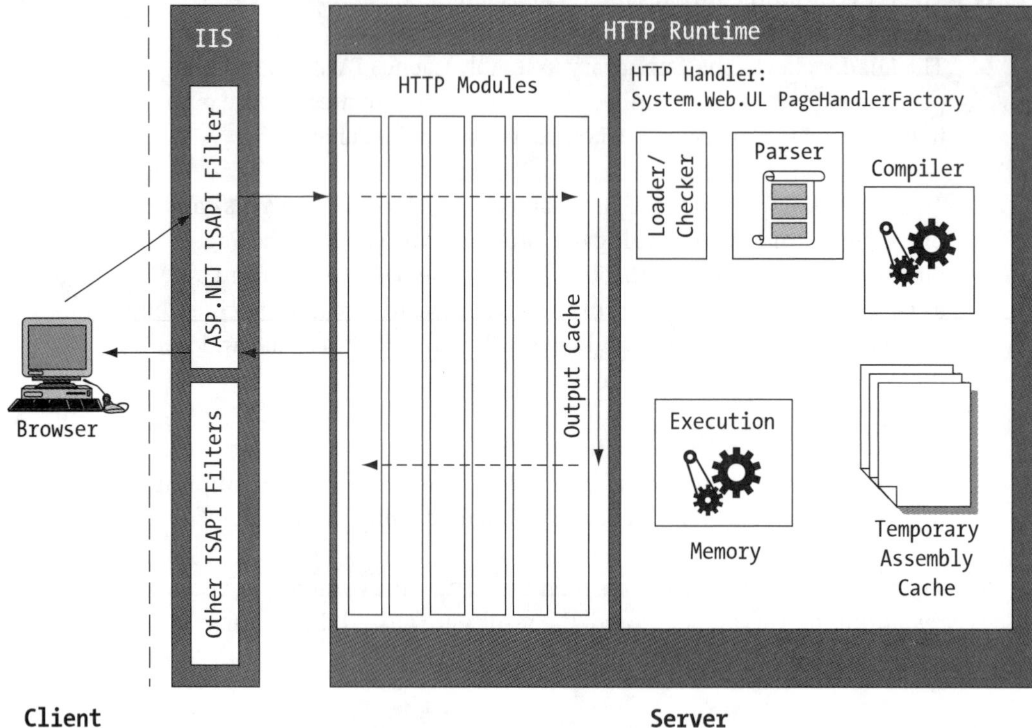

Figure 10-9. Request for a cached page

These are the main steps:

1. The browser issues the HTTP request for the .aspx file.

2. IIS receives and checks the request, examines the extension of the file being requested, and invokes the ASP.NET ISAPI Extension.

3. The Extension makes a cross-process call to the HTTP Runtime, passing in the information relating to the request.

4. The HTTP Runtime passes the request through the pipeline of HTTP Modules. When the request is processed by the Output Cache module, it identifies that the page has already been processed, and that it's still alive within the cache.

5. The cached results are read from the Output Cache and returned back through IIS and viewed in the browser.

Notice that the HTTP handler is not invoked, and the Web Form's class isn't loaded, compiled, or even executed. Instead, the rendered output generated by a previous request is returned directly to the browser, leading to a significant improvement in performance.

But wait a moment—what if the page had been modified, or was originally generated with different parameters, or had been rendered for a different browser? Well, all of these factors (and others, too) are under your control; you're able to cache different page images for different browsers, different parameter sets, different querystrings, and so on. The bottom line is that output caching is under your control, and it's your responsibility to use it in the most appropriate way for the type of pages with which you're working. Used correctly, caching can reduce the load on the Web server and can be a significant aid to scalability; used poorly, you'll end up delivering out-of-date and incorrect information to client browsers. You'll see more about the use and control of output caching in Chapter 12.

Web Form Events

The models we've presented so far are purposefully simplistic, hiding some of the detail of what happens when the code for the Web Form is actually executed. Think back to the control lifecycle events discussed in Chapter 5; all of these can occur during the page-processing cycle, mainly in steps 8 and 9 of Scenario 1. However, irrespective of what happens in the events, the other stages in the processing cycles still occur—the request is still received, processed, and a response generated.

When you're playing the role of Web developer, you *are* interested in these events, though, as they enable you to interact with the interface objects that you've defined for the page. You must remember that you can only write handlers for server-side events raised by server controls; in addition to the "standard" events such as Init, Load, Unload, and Disposed, there are two categories of "interaction" events, depending on the type of control:

- Most input controls support what are known as *DataChanged* events, such as `TextChanged`, `CheckedChanged`, and `SelectedIndexChanged`. ASP.NET determines which controls have been changed by comparing their original content (stored in the ViewState for each Web Form) with their current content (passed in the Post data in the HTTP header). ASP.NET then raises the appropriate events for these controls, enabling your code to run.

- Control-passing controls, such as Buttons, ImageButtons, and HyperLinks usually support a *Click* type event. ASP.NET identifies the cause of a server round-trip from the Post data in the HTTP header and once again raises the event.

Some controls support both categories of event. For example, the DataGrid supports events raised when a contained button is clicked (`CancelCommand`, `DeleteCommand`, `EditCommand`, `ItemCommand`, `SortCommand`, `UpdateCommand`) as well as events raised when different pages or rows are selected (`PageIndexChanged`, `SelectedIndexChanged`).

With such a rich and varied event model it can sometimes be difficult to know exactly which events are being raised and in what sequence. Desktop developers often make use of message boxes, event log entries, or the immediate window, but none of these are tremendously well-suited to Web development because of the multiuser, multithreaded nature of Web applications. Instead, ASP.NET supports a powerful tracing facility that you can use to trace as much or as little detail as you need. You'll see more on this facility later.

Creating Custom Modules and Handlers

The previous scenarios have shown how requests are processed using the standard HTTPModules and HTTPPageHandler, and you probably noticed there's a substantial amount of work involved in generating the response. Of course the advantage that this approach brings is flexibility; as developers we need only add controls to our Web Forms and add a few event handlers to the code-behind class, and we have a simple, yet fully functional application. The disadvantage is that it may be unduly complex and unnecessarily slow if our requirements are simple.

Where you have non-standard requirements for request processing, or when you need to perform server-side processing but don't need all the functionality that Web Forms offer, you might consider creating your own custom HTTPModules or HTTPHandlers.

Creating Custom HTTPModules

Creating a custom HTTPModule is quite straightforward in any .NET language. For example, you could create a custom HTTPModule to perform personalization services that could automatically retrieve and save user-specific preferences or permissions for your Web Application. The basic structure of such a module would be as follows:

```
Imports System
Imports System.Web
```

```
Public Class UserStateModule
    Implements IHttpModule

    Public ReadOnly Property ModuleName() As String
        Get
            Return "UserStateModule"
        End Get
    End Property

    Public Sub Init(ByVal application As HttpApplication) _
                        Implements IHttpModule.Init
        'Add our handlers for application events
        AddHandler application.BeginRequest, AddressOf Me. App_BeginRequest
        AddHandler application.EndRequest, AddressOf Me.App_EndRequest
    End Sub

    Private Sub App_BeginRequest(ByVal source As Object, ByVal e As EventArgs)
        Dim application As HttpApplication = CType(source, HttpApplication)
        Dim context As HttpContext = application.Context
        Dim request As HttpRequest = context.Request
        Dim response As HttpResponse = context.Response

        'Additional code that will run at the start of the processing cycle
    End Sub

    Private Sub App_EndRequest(ByVal source As Object, ByVal e As EventArgs)
        Dim application As HttpApplication = CType(source, HttpApplication)
        Dim context As HttpContext = application.Context
        Dim request As HttpRequest = context.Request
        Dim response As HttpResponse = context.Response

        'Additional code that will run at the end of the processing cycle
    End Sub

    Public Sub Dispose() Implements IHttpModule.Dispose
    End Sub
End Class
```

You would need to add the code that does the real work to the App_BeginRequest and App_EndRequest methods. There are relatively few limitations on the capabilities of such code because it's provided access to the intrinsic ASP.NET objects through the HTTPApplication class passed as the first parameter.

We'll assume that we've coded those events and created the class in a separate Class Library project (which we've called Personalization) and that it has been compiled into an assembly called Personalization.dll. To activate the module, you can add its definition to Web.config (in the host Web Application) as follows:

```
<httpModules>
    <add name="HiFlyers Personalization"
        type="Personalization.UserStateModule, Personalization" />
</httpModules>
```

Notice the additional `, Personalization` value in our custom declaration. This specifies the name of the assembly that contains the custom HTTPModule, and this assembly would need to be copied to the Web Application's `\bin` directory. If you had given the assembly a strong name and placed it in the global assembly cache, then this additional parameter would not be required. See Appendix E for more information on strong names and the global assembly cache.

You can also create the module in the main Web Application project itself. For example, if we had created our UserStateModule class within the HiFlyers project, the Web.config entry would read like this:

```
<httpModules>
    <add name="HiFlyers Personalization"
        type="HiFlyers.UserStateModule, HiFlyers" />
</httpModules>
```

NOTE *If you create custom modules for your Web Applications then you must take great care in their coding and design, as they'll process every request the Web Application receives. A poorly written HTTP Module will have a dramatic impact on scalability and possibly reliability.*

We don't have space within this book to look any further at the design and creation of custom HTTPModules, and it's fair to say that most Web developers would not need to call on these skills and techniques anyway. However, if you find yourself faced with a project where there's a requirement to perform some type of processing on each and every request, you may find that a custom HTTPModule is an elegant and relatively simple solution.

Creating Custom HTTPHandlers

Creating custom HTTPHandlers is no more difficult than creating custom HTTPModules. Every HTTP Handler must implement the IHttpHandler interface, which requires that they support two methods: IsReusable and ProcessRequest. IsReusable is called by ASP.NET to determine whether a specific handler can be recycled. ProcessRequest is called when the handler needs to respond to a request, and it's in this method that you'll find the main code.

For example, the following code shows a VB .NET framework for a simple handler that can process requests. You could replace the code in the `ProcessRequest` method so that it performed checks on the member account, aircraft and instructor availability, and the suitability of the aircraft based on the member's current skill and experience, and then it performed the necessary updates to the database. Finally, the method could generate a response or transfer the user to a status page:

```
Imports System
Imports System.Web

Public Class BookingHandler
    Implements IHttpHandler

    Public Sub ProcessRequest(ByVal context As System.Web.HttpContext) _
                Implements System.Web.IHttpHandler.ProcessRequest
        Dim request As HttpRequest = context.Request
        Dim response As HttpResponse = context.Response

        response.Write("<html>")
        response.Write("<body>")
        response.Write("<h1>Processed by the BookingHandler</h1>")
        response.Write("</body>")
        response.Write("</html>")

        'Code here to perform main processing of the request
    End Sub

    Public ReadOnly Property IsReusable() As Boolean _
                Implements System.Web.IHttpHandler.IsReusable
        Get
            'Return True if the handler can be pooled for reuse.  This
            'causes the handler to remain in memory between requests
            Return False
        End Get
```

```
    End Property
End Class
```

The ProcessRequest method is passed an HttpContext object as a parameter, which encapsulates all of the information associated with the specific HTTP request being handled. HttpContext also provides access to intrinsic ASP.NET objects such as Application, Cache, Request, Response, Server, and Session, plus many other essential properties and methods.

Once compiled into a .NET assembly, this class can be mapped to a Uniform Resource Identifier (URI) in the Web.config file for the HiFlyers Web Application:

```
<httpHandlers>
    <add verb="*" path="MakeBooking.aspx"
                type="HiFlyers.BookingHandler, HiFlyers" />
</httpHandlers>
```

Note that in this example the handler has been mapped to a specific page URI (MakeBooking.aspx), but it could as easily be a wildcard-based URI or any file extension or location. Also, we've placed the class defining the custom handler in the HiFlyers project so that it's compiled into the HiFlyers assembly.

You're probably wondering right now why you would use a custom handler rather than a Web Form and certainly in this example there's little reason to break the pattern of using Web Forms for user interaction. In practice, custom handlers are useful when Web Forms don't provide quite the right processing model, appearance, or format. For example, you may want to implement a custom handler if you need to return a dynamically generated Microsoft Word document to the user in response to a request, or if you wanted to stream live video to the browser. You'll probably find that there's little difference between the capabilities of a custom handler and the capabilities of a Web Form; instead, you should think more in terms of which is easier to implement in each situation.

Configuring ASP.NET

Throughout this chapter we've examined some of the configuration details for ASP.NET applications, showing how to add and modify modules and handlers and identify client browser support. This section continues that theme and addresses the broader topic of ASP.NET configuration, starting with the legacy settings maintained by IIS. As you'll see, configuration files play an important role in all ASP.NET applications because they let you enable many application-specific features such as tracing, state management, and error management. They also allow you to store your own application-specific configuration values, providing a structured and flexible replacement for the Windows Registry and INI files.

Configuring IIS and .NET

Configuration details for classic ASP applications are stored in the IIS Metabase, a proprietary store that can only be viewed and edited through selected tools such as Internet Service Manager and certain utilities provided with the IIS Resource Kit. Microsoft did publish the format and structure of the IIS Metabase, but there were relatively few third-parties that chose to build compatible tools or utilities.

This format made the process of application deployment and maintenance more awkward than it should have been. In particular, you were required to manually configure IIS Metabase settings on the deployment server, as it was not possible to copy or inherit them from the development server. Additionally, most maintenance and configuration had to be done from the server console, rather than being performed remotely.

ASP.NET has changed this approach somewhat, with the IIS Metabase being used for some settings while the XML-based Machine.config and Web.config files store the rest. This split configuration is required to support the use of ASP.NET on legacy Web servers (for example, IIS 5.0 and IIS 6.0); in the future the IIS Metabase may be replaced entirely, but for now it still has a role to play.

Although ASP.NET has not completely removed the need for the IIS Metabase, it has significantly reduced its dependencies on it. The new ASP.NET configuration system features an extensible infrastructure that defines configuration settings through a set of XML documents. These can be maintained with any editor, even Notepad, and can be copied between machines with ease. Anyone with permissions on the file can read and modify them, both locally and remotely, and a complete set of classes in the System.Configuration namespace have been provided to allow managed code to access configuration files programmatically.

IIS Metabase

The IIS Metabase is still used to manage core settings and parameters for the Site and/or Virtual Directory in which the ASP.NET application is located. These include name and location, access permissions, and default documents. A simple way to access these settings is to display the Properties dialog box for the virtual directory from within the Internet Services Manager utility, as shown in Figure 10-10.

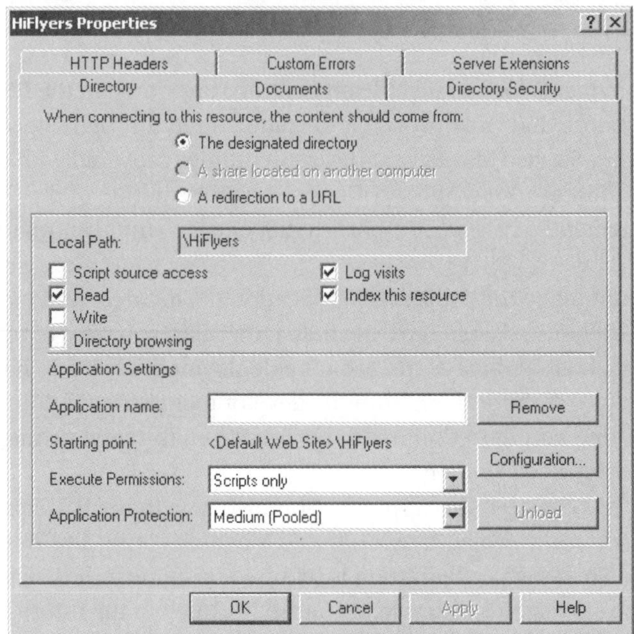

Figure 10-10. Virtual directory properties for HiFlyers

The existing Application Settings section shown in Figure 10-10 is now largely redundant, and most settings will be ignored for ASP.NET applications. In fact, the only settings in this section that affect ASP.NET are the ISAPI mappings, displayed by clicking the **Configuration** button. It's these mappings that determine which requests are passed through the ASPNET_ISAPI Extension to the HTTP Runtime, as discussed earlier in this chapter.

Manipulating ASP.NET Configuration Files

Configuration files are XML documents that store configuration parameters for applications. They can operate at a machine, application, or subdirectory level and can be changed as and when needed. ASP.NET automatically detects changed files and then parses and compiles them on the next request. As well as storing predefined values for Web Application parameters, configuration files can contain developer-defined content and thus allow applications to be reconfigured without having to be recompiled. One important note is that because configuration files use XML they *are* case sensitive.

There are three types of configuration files that play a role with ASP.NET:

- Machine configuration files, which specify settings for the entire machine
- Application configuration files, which define settings for an application or a child directory within an application
- Security configuration files, which define various security policies at enterprise, machine, and user level

Machine and application configuration file settings are evaluated in a hierarchical manner. First, the machine configuration file is read and compiled. Next, the Web Application's Web.config file is read and compiled. Where settings exist in both files, the values in Web.config override those in Machine.config. Finally, each child directory in a Web Application can also have its own Web.config, and its settings are dominant when processing requests for pages in that directory.

Security configuration files are also evaluated hierarchically, with the enterprise settings applied first, then the machine-specific settings. There are no application-specific or folder-specific security configuration files, although as you'll see in Chapter 11, the content of Web.config plays a key role in defining security policies for ASP.NET applications.

Having determined configuration settings for a specific URL, the settings are cached. ASP.NET monitors changes to configuration files at all levels, and the files are automatically recompiled if they are edited, even while a Web Application is running.

CAUTION *Editing configuration files on a live server with active connections is not recommended. If you modify the Web.config file for an application, ASP.NET automatically terminates the application and restarts it when it receives the next request. If you modify the Machine.config file, ASP.NET automatically terminates* ***all*** *Web Applications on the server, restarting each as it receives subsequent requests.*

ASP.NET needs to restart the applications as the settings in the configuration files are used during the JIT compilation process; if the settings are modified, the previously compiled code is no longer appropriate and so must be regenerated. Unfortunately, the process of terminating and restarting the application means that any state currently being maintained within the application is lost, so users could find themselves unceremoniously dumped from the application in the middle of a session.

ASP.NET protects configuration files from unauthorized client access by mapping the System.Web.HttpForbiddenHandler to the .config file extension.

This causes an HTTP access error 403 (forbidden) to be returned to any browser attempting to directly request a configuration file.

Machine Configuration File

The machine configuration file (Machine.config) contains settings that apply to the entire machine, such as HTTP Modules and Handlers, defaults for tracing and debugging, timeouts, and limits for request processing, and so on. The file is located here:

```
%runtime install path%\Config\Machine.config.
```

Machine.config is a large file, so it has not been reproduced here. It's also important to keep this file maintainable, and that means adding a minimum of new entries. For example, if a setting were to be required for every ASP.NET application on the server, then it would make sense to add it to Machine.config. However, if the setting is unique to two specific applications, it's probably better to add it to the individual Web.config files.

Application Configuration Files

Application configuration files are called Web.config, and they contain application-specific settings. The settings often overlap (and override) those in Machine.config, but there will generally be far fewer entries in Web.config.

This is an example of a simple Web.config (with comments removed):

```
<?xml version="1.0" encoding="utf-8" ?>
<configuration>
    <system.web>
        <compilation defaultLanguage="vb" debug="true" />
        <customErrors mode="RemoteOnly" />
        <authentication mode="Windows" />
        <authorization>
                <allow users="*" />
        </authorization>
        <trace enabled="false" requestLimit="10" pageOutput="false"
                traceMode="SortByTime" localOnly="true" />
        <sessionState mode="InProc"
                stateConnectionString="tcpip=127.0.0.1:42424"
                sqlConnectionString="data source=127.0.0.1;user
                id=sa;password=" cookieless="false" timeout="20" />
```

```
        <globalization requestEncoding="utf-8" responseEncoding="utf-8" />
    </system.web>
</configuration>
```

You'll be learning about many of the sections in Web.config in this and later chapters, as they control many of ASP.NET's more advanced features.

Security Configuration Files

Security configuration files exist at enterprise, server, and user levels. Their locations are as follows:

- Enterprise policy configuration file:

```
%CLR installDir%\Config\EnterpriseSec.config
```

- Machine policy configuration file:

```
%CLR InstallDir%\Config\Security.config
```

- User policy configuration file (non–Windows 95):

```
%USERPROFILE%\Application data\Microsoft\CLR security
config\version\Security.config
```

- User policy configuration file (Windows 95):

```
%WINDIR%\username\CLR security config\version\Security.config
```

User policy files are not generally relevant in an ASP.NET environment. The other two files are of more interest, as they store the current security configuration. However, it's crucial that no errors are introduced into these files as this could potentially cause *all* .NET applications on the machine to fail. We really don't recommend that you try changing these files unless you're prepared to invest a lot of time and effort in understanding their structure and purpose. Even then, Microsoft recommends that you make all changes using the Code Access Security Policy tool (caspol.exe) as this maintains the structure of the configuration files and minimizes the chance of corruption.

Configuration File Settings

There are clearly a lot of different settings contained in the configuration files, so rather than try and list them here what we'll do is introduce them as a part of the topic to which they're related. For example, we've already discussed HTTP Modules and HTTP Handlers earlier in the chapter, and we introduced the corresponding sections of Machine.config at that point. Similarly, when we discuss tracing, state management, and security, you'll see what settings in the configuration files need to be changed.

However, one example worth including at this point is to show how you can store and retrieve custom settings from within your application. Many developers will be familiar with the use of the registry or INI files for storing configuration details, and Web.config provides an ASP.NET equivalent to these techniques.

The simplest and most common technique is to store settings in a section of Web.config called `<appSettings>`. This section must be at the same level as the `<system.web>` section in the hierarchy in Web.config and can contain multiple `<add . . . />` elements that define the values to be stored. For example:

```
<?xml version="1.0" encoding="utf-8" ?>
<configuration>

  <appSettings>
     <add key="HiFlyerDSN" value="localhost;uid=HiFlyerUser;pwd=;" />
  </appSettings>

  <system.web>
    <compilation defaultLanguage="vb" debug="true" />
        .
        .
        .
  </system.web>

</configuration>
```

This extract from Web.config shows a custom entry named "HiFlyerDSN" defined with a string value. If you want to read this value in code (such as when establishing a connection to the database), then the following code is required:

```
Imports System.Configuration
    .
    .
    .
strDSN = ConfigurationSettings.AppSettings("HiFlyerDSN").ToString
```

`ConfigurationSettings` is a class within the System.Configuration namespace that supports a shared method called `AppSettings`. This method reads the specified key from the Web.config file and returns the value as a string. If the specified key is not found in the .config file, `AppSettings` will throw an exception.

As well as the `AppSettings` method, .NET provides other techniques that allow you to read from .config files. For example, `GetConfig` is another method of the ConfigurationSettings class that lets you read a section of data from Web.config, returning the settings as a collection of key/value pairs. Other classes that offer complementary features are the SingleTagSectionHandler class and the NameValueSectionHandler class, both of which are members of the System.Configuration namespace.

CAUTION *You can't simply define your own settings and sections in just any part of Web.config or Machine.config, as all settings must be supported by a valid configuration handler and held within a recognized section. If you incorrectly place additional content, or violate section rules (by incorrectly applying upper or lower case, for example) then the Web Application will not execute and will return errors to the browser. Therefore, you must consult the documentation for the configuration files before deciding how you'll modify them.*

Deploying Applications

Deploying classic ASP Web applications can actually be simple, straightforward, and predictable. That is, as long as the ASP application uses no components, doesn't talk to a database, and uses default settings for security, process isolation, and error pages, then there should be no problems. In reality, any significant Web application will need these things and more, and the deployment process can be a major headache.

The .NET developers have tried hard to implement a deployment mechanism that really is as easy as just copying files, and they've largely succeeded. If you're using Visual Studio .NET to build your applications, then you have two options for deployment: Xcopy deployment and Web Setup projects.

Using Xcopy Deployment

Xcopy deployment is the most basic method for deploying Web Applications onto other servers. In principle it requires only the following steps:

1. Create a directory on the target server. This will contain the Web Application and will be configured as a virtual directory, so it should be placed and named accordingly. Within this directory, create a further directory named `\bin`.

2. Copy the required content files to the newly created directory, using the same structure used on the development machine.

3. Copy the assemblies from the \bin directory on the development machine to the \bin directory created in step 1. This will include the application's own .dll, as well as any other assemblies needed by the project that are not otherwise present in the Global Assembly Cache. Note that unless you want to perform live, low-level debugging on the target server, you need not copy any .pbd files found in the development folder. These are symbol files used by certain debuggers and rarely (if ever) required on live servers.

4. Use IIS to create a virtual directory on the target machine that points to the newly created directory. Default settings are likely to be okay as further configuration settings are provided in Web.config.

5. Test it out with a browser.

This method works well for simple applications, but it still involves some manual work (creating directories and setting the virtual directory). There's also less ongoing support provided by Windows as it has no idea that an application has been installed. It also assumes that the target server already has the .NET runtime files installed and that they are the same version as the development machine.

In practice you'll find that Xcopy deployment works well for rolling out minor patches, bug fixes, and enhancements. In these scenarios it's fair to assume there will be few architectural changes to the application, and so the target server should already have the assemblies and support files required. For initial installs, we recommend you use the purpose-built mechanism that Microsoft provided: Web Setup projects.

Using Web Setup Projects

Web Setup projects provide a simple yet powerful way of deploying Web Applications to servers. This method offers advantages over the Xcopy technique in that the Web Setup project handles any issues with component installation and configuration automatically. It can also create the IIS virtual directory and provides a method for subsequent removal (if required) of the application.

You create and build Web Setup projects in Visual Studio .NET, and then copy the resulting .msi file to the target Web server computer to run there. The .msi file uses the settings that you defined to install and configure the application. For this to work, the user running the Web Setup project must have administrative access privileges for that computer.

Creating a Web Setup Project

To begin the creation of a Web Setup project, add a new project to the solution containing the Web Application based on the **Web Setup Project** template, as shown in Figure 10-11.

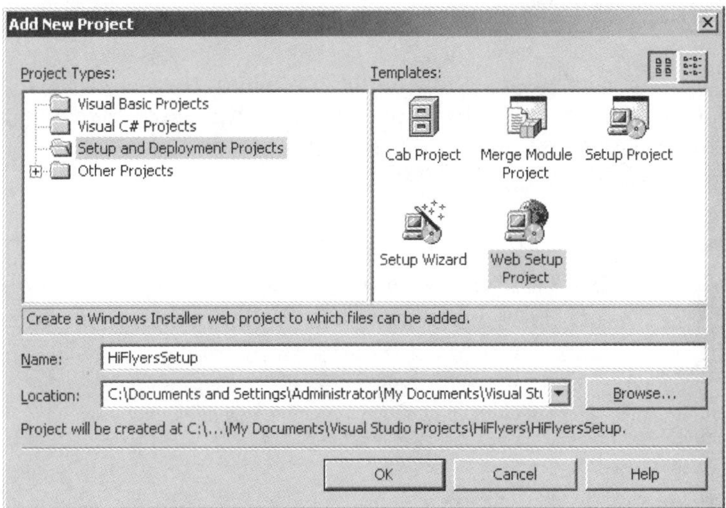

Figure 10-11. Creating a Web Setup project

Web Setup projects are quite different to Web Applications or Windows Applications; rather than depending on you to create an interface and write the code, the Web Setup project provides a number of dialog boxes that enable you to define its content and behavior. One of the most important is the File System editor, shown in Figure 10-12.

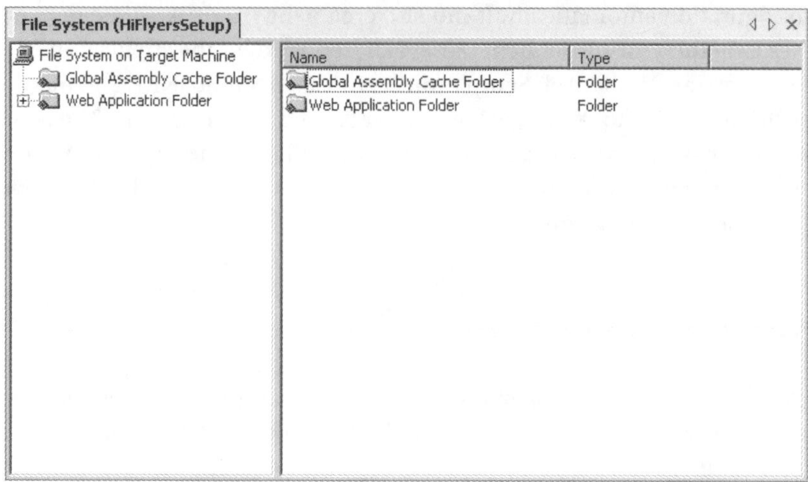

Figure 10-12. File System editor

Currently, the File System editor shows two folders: the Global Assembly Cache (GAC) Folder, which is where you place shared assemblies to be made available to all applications, and the Web Application Folder, which is where you place content specific to this application.

NOTE *There are specific requirements that an assembly must meet before you can place it in the GAC. Unless you're aware of these issues and know how to create strongly named assemblies, we suggest you don't try creating shared assemblies.*

Adding Content

Most of the content for the Web Application will be added to the Web Application Folder. You can do this by selecting the Web Application Folder and then either right-clicking and selecting **Add ➢Project Output**, or by selecting **Action ➢ Add ➢ Project Output** from the menu bar. These commands both display the Add Project Output Group dialog box, as shown in Figure 10-13.

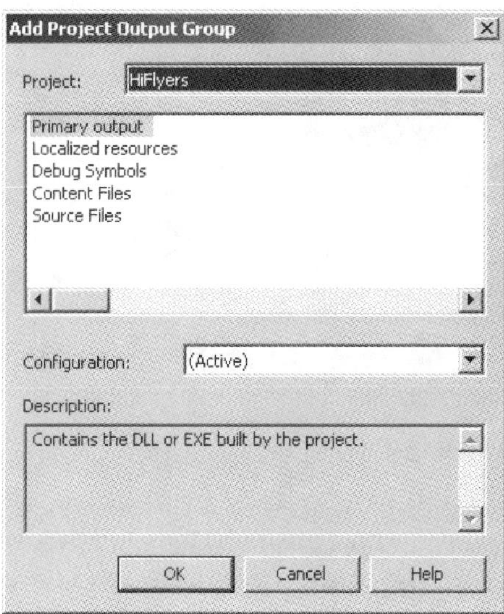

Figure 10-13. Adding project output

The Project list will show all the projects in the current solution. Once you've selected the appropriate Web Application, you can then choose which elements will be added to the setup project. For most deployments you will want to choose **Primary Output**, which causes the main .dll for the application to be included, and **Content Files**, which represents the .aspx, .html, .css, and other visual files. Care must be taken to include all relevant files, including the .aspx.vb or .aspx.cs for any Web Forms that have their code-behind modules implemented as source code rather than compiled code.

How does Visual Studio .NET know what you mean by Primary Output or Content File, though? After all, you may want to deploy source files, XML documents, and other resources in some projects but not in others. The answer can be found in the properties for each item in the main Web Application project. If you select one of the Web Forms in the Solution Explorer and view its properties, you will see a number of settings similar to those shown in Figure 10-14.

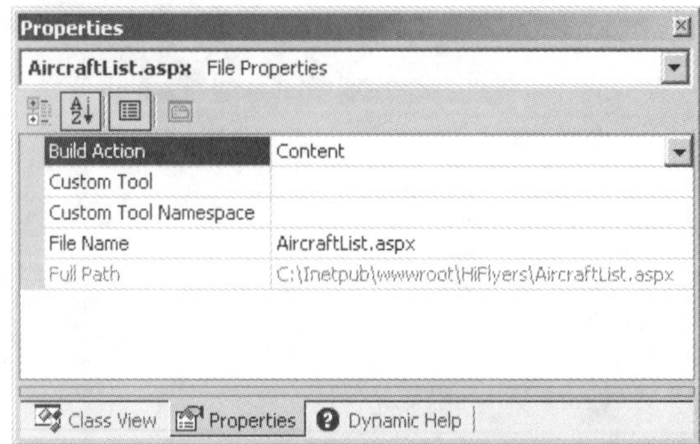

Figure 10-14. Properties of a project item

The property that controls how the item is treated for deployment is Build Action, and you can see from Figure 10-14 that it's set to Content for this .aspx file. The values that can be specified are as follows:

- **None** prevents the item from being deployed via the Add Project Output dialog box. You can manually add these items to the deployment (as you can with any file whatsoever) by selecting **Action ➢ Add ➢ File** from the File System editor.

- **Compile** causes the item to be sent to the compiler when the application is built. The result of the compilation process is then treated as Primary Output and placed into the application's \bin directory when it is installed.

- **Content** causes the item to be deployed to the target machine unchanged and is used for all page files (.aspx and .htm), style sheets, XML documents, and other items that do not need to be compiled.

- **Embedded Resource** is similar to Compile, although the compiler will treat the item as data rather than code. This is typically used with resource files that will be compiled into the project output.

The default values for Build Action will probably be correct for most project items that you create, although if you are deploying code-behind modules in source form, you'll need to change their Build Action setting from **Compile** to **Content**.

Setup Project Properties

As well as setting properties for individual items within the project, you'll also want to set some of the properties for the Web Setup project itself. Select the Web Setup project in the Solution Explorer and its properties should appear similar to those shown in Figure 10-15.

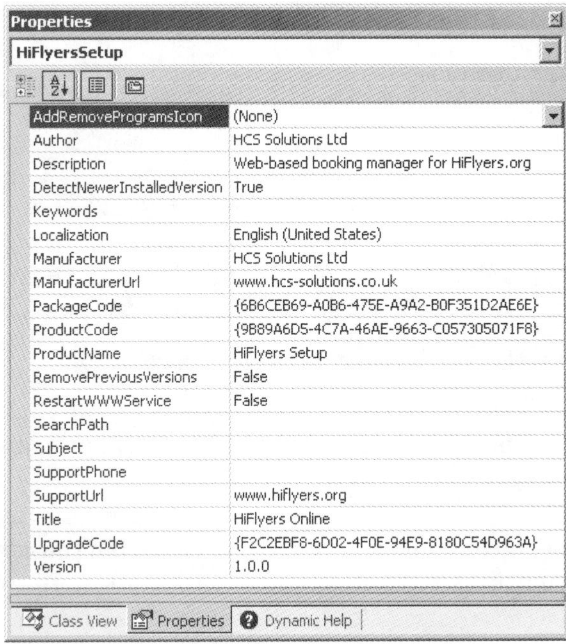

Figure 10-15. Properties of the Web Setup project

You'll want to provide values for the title, description and version as these will be shown during the installation process and subsequently used in the Add/Remove Programs facility in Windows. It also makes sense to provide support details in case the deployment or server management teams run into any problems.

In addition to setting the project properties, you'll also want to set properties for the application's virtual directory. To do this, first select the Web Application Folder in the File System editor and then view its properties. They'll appear similar to those shown in Figure 10-16.

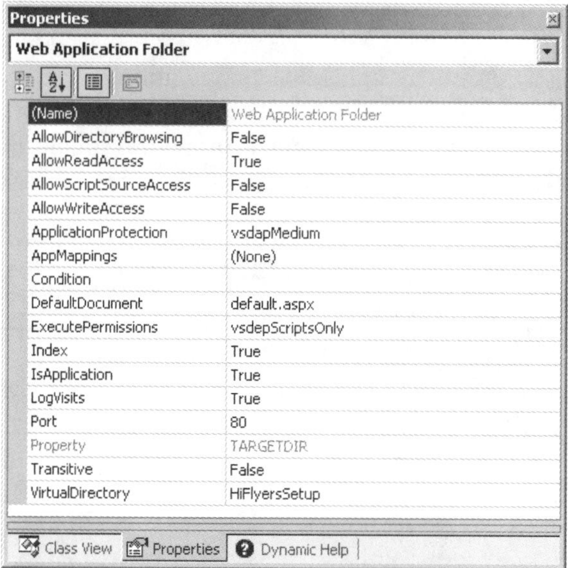

Figure 10-16. Properties of the Web Application Folder

The default settings for most properties will be OK, but you'll usually want to change the following:

- **DefaultDocument** is initially set to Default.aspx, but you can change this to any document you want.

- **Index** determines whether the content of the virtual directory will be managed by the full text indexer in IIS. If you don't plan to take advantage of indexing, you'll want to set this to False to prevent the unnecessary performance overhead the indexer introduces.

- **LogVisits** determines whether requests against this directory are logged by IIS. For better performance, you may want to set this to False.

- The default setting for **VirtualDirectory** will be the name of the setup project, rather than the name of the project you are deploying. Because this usually becomes a part of the URL for the application you'll probably want to change it to something more meaningful.

Building and Deployment

Once you've configured the project and added the content and output files, you're ready to go ahead and create the files for deployment. You do this by building the setup project, so select either **Build ➢ Build <ProjectName>** or **Build ➢ Build Solution**. During the build process Visual Studio .NET creates a Windows Installer file with a .msi file extension that contains all the relevant files, resources, and settings for your Web Application.

Before you can install the Web Application on the target server, you need to ensure that the server has suitable versions of the core operating system files and utilities and that it has Microsoft Internet Explorer 5.01 or later installed. For Windows 2000, you can do this by applying the Windows Component Update CD supplied with Visual Studio .NET (although you should first check the license agreement to see which files you're permitted to redistribute), while for Windows XP and Windows .NET you should ensure that the latest service packs are applied.

NOTE *You may need to restart the server during the installation of service pack files or other operating system updates, so it's not a great idea to try this in the middle of a busy day.*

You also need to install the .NET Framework to the target machine. This is provided in a file named Dotnetfx.exe, which can be found in the `dotNetFramework` folder on the Windows Component Update CD that came with Visual Studio .NET. To ensure you have the latest version, you can download the Microsoft .NET Framework Redistributable from the MSDN downloads site (`msdn.microsoft.com/downloads`). To install the framework, make sure you are logged in to the server with administrative permissions then run the Dotnetfx.exe program.

Finally, you need to copy the .msi file to the target server and install it by double-clicking or through the **Add/Remove Programs** facility in Control Panel. During installation it displays a standard Windows Installer type interface (which can be customized from within the Setup project) and will run through the installation and configuration of the Web Application. It should be completely automated (assuming the user is happy with the defaults provided) and should *not* require that the Web server be restarted.

TIP *Remember that you need to be logged in to the server with administrative permissions throughout the installation process.*

Ongoing Maintenance

As discussed in previous chapters, ASP.NET does not lock any content files, resources or assemblies in a Web application, even while it's running. Maintenance is therefore quite simple and straightforward:

- You can copy replacement files over the top of existing ones. ASP.NET detects the change and recompiles as necessary. Note that changes to Machine.config, Web.config and global.asax will cause the application to restart.
- You can edit files on the fly, with the changes becoming effective when they are saved. Again, ASP.NET recompiles the file as required with the same warnings applying about application restarts.
- .NET assemblies are treated the same way as any other .NET file, even after they're compiled to a DLL or EXE. Just replace the old file with the new and ASP.NET recompiles and executes the new content automatically.
- The only problem components are legacy COM ones, as the .NET Framework does not provide any special handling for them at all. If you want to replace a legacy COM component in use by a Web application, you'll have to shut the Web server down (NET STOP IISADMIN /Y), unregister the component (REGSVR32 –u component.dll) and then copy in the new one and register it.

Obviously there are strong reasons for not just changing things in a haphazard fashion; it's better to have specific periods of planned maintenance when user numbers are low (or the application is shut down) so that you can make and test changes before they affect hundreds or thousands of users. However, the point is that instant changes *can* be made if needed, such as when a simple but critical bug is found. Classic ASP never made it that easy.

Using Tracing

One of the core tasks associated with ongoing maintenance is bug fixing, but for Web developers this has historically proven to be one of the more difficult aspects of the project lifecycle. Bug fixing is difficult because of the lack of any decent debugging tools and, in particular, the lack of any tools that could perform tracing for Web applications. Without the ability to trace program execution, you have little chance of quickly working out where the code is going wrong.

In classic ASP, tracing was a tiresome and awkward process, usually involving the inclusion of `Response.Write` statements at key points in the code. Of course, prior to deployment, you had to remove these statements, and it was not uncommon for a few to "slip through the net." Although developers grudgingly accepted this approach to tracing, it was far from ideal. Fortunately the team at Microsoft took note of these problems and introduced a new, built-in trace facility as a part of ASP.NET.

This facility is capable of automatically tracing core page and code events as well as being accessed programmatically from your own routines. The trace data generated includes all sorts of useful information, from event-by-event timings to the size of each control's HTML when rendered to the browser. You shouldn't think of this as just a code tracing tool then, but rather a complete solution that addresses both the visual and programmatic aspects of any ASP.NET Web Application. The trace facility works at two levels:

- Page-level tracing, where ASP.NET automatically adds the trace output to the end of the rendered HTML
- Application-level tracing, where ASP.NET makes the trace outputs available through a special URI called `Trace.axd`

Page-Level Tracing

You control and enable page-level tracing on a per-page basis. Each Web Form has two properties that control this:

- **Trace**, which is set to True to allow tracing, False to disable it, or blank to allow it to be controlled at the application level. The default is that it's blank.
- **TraceMode**, which is set to SortByTime or SortByCategory and controls how the trace output is sequenced when sent to the browser. The default is SortByTime.

The values assigned to the properties are written as attribute values of the Page directive in the .aspx file:

```
<%@ Page Language="vb". . . . trace="True" traceMode="SortByTime"%>
```

When the page is viewed in the browser, the trace output displays on the page along with the content that you added to the designer. As you can see in Figure 10-17, ASP.NET does not always place it where you want it, and if you're using GridLayout on your Web Form, you'll probably find the trace output appears under the controls.

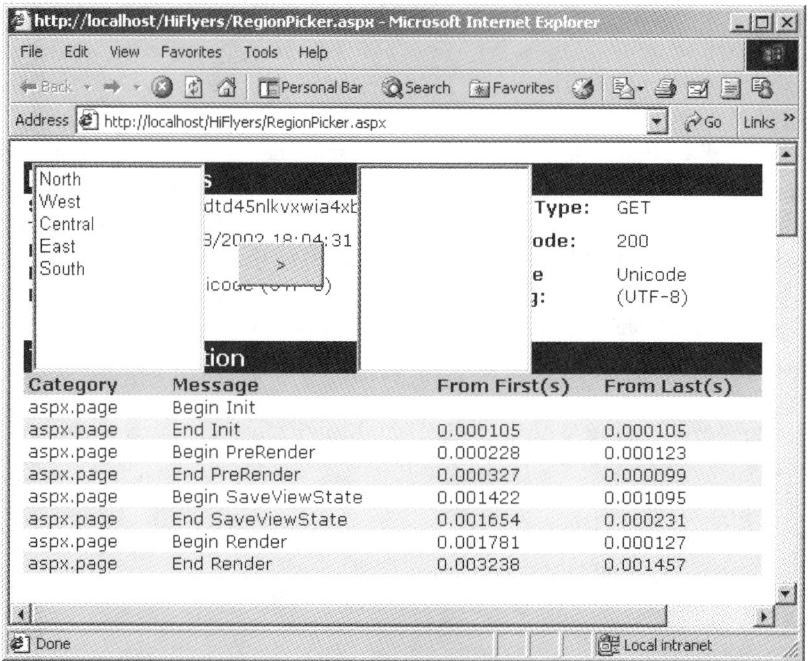

Figure 10-17. Default trace output, positioned under the Web Form content

If you add a number of <br> tags to the top of the page, you can move the output down the page without altering its appearance in any way, as shown in Figure 10-18.

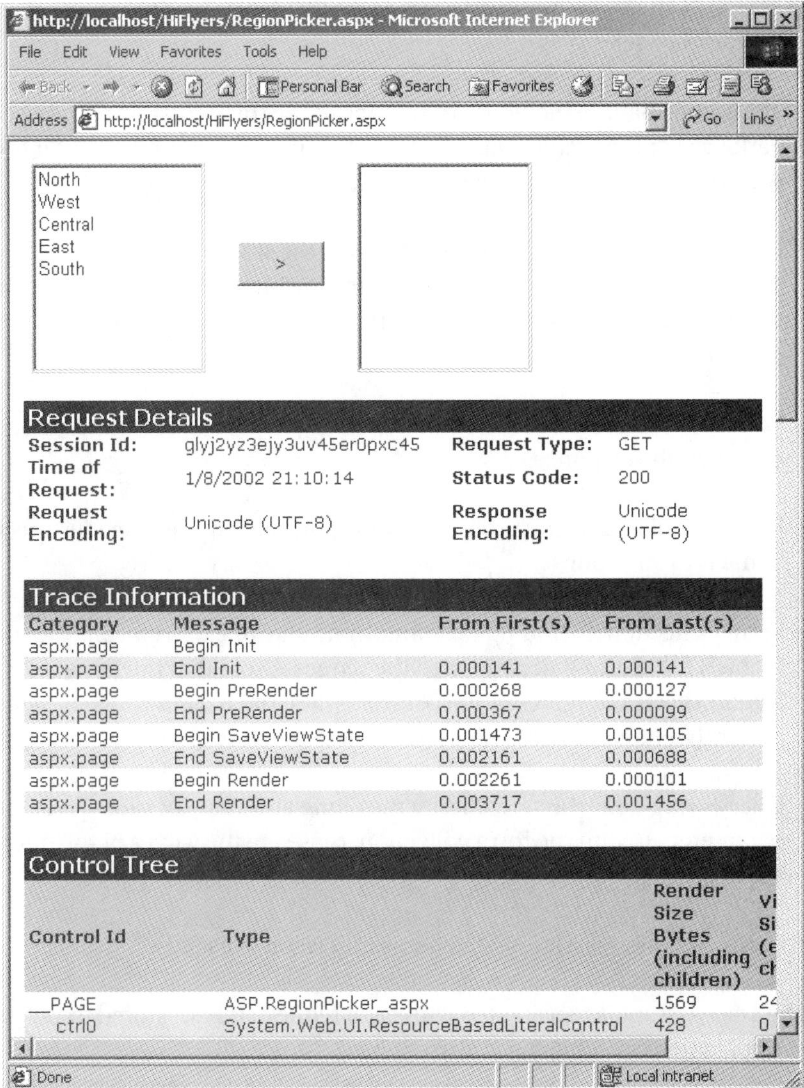

Figure 10-18. Expanded browser window showing repositioned trace output

A lot of information is displayed in the trace output, with the exact content depending on the exact request that was made when the trace was recorded. The different categories of information are shown in bands in the output, with the following sections being the most common:

- Request Details, including a summary of the data from the HTTP Request header.

- Trace Information, including the source of the trace entry and timing data. Various events are automatically traced in this section, and as you'll soon see, you can also add your own entries.

- Control Tree, including control IDs, types, the size of any rendered HTML, and the size of the associated view state. The hierarchical nature of this section makes it easy to see any containment relationships present in the page contents.

- Cookies Collection, including the name, content, and size of every cookie passed in the response.

- Headers Collection, including the name and value of each header specified in the HTTP Response.

- Form Collection, including the name and value of each non-blank control in the HTML form that generated the request. Note that the form collection shows the values of the controls when the *request* was generated, rather than their current values generated for the response.

- QueryString Collection, including the name and value of each query string parameter. As with the form collection, these are the values of the querystring passed with the request.

- Server Variables, including the name and value of each.

The Trace output is reevaluated with each request; it's not stored or persisted unless application-level tracing is also enabled.

Custom Tracing

As well as the standard content, developers can write their own custom content to the trace output using the TraceContext class. This is exposed from the Page object as the `Trace` property, and it supports two key methods for writing custom content to the trace output:

```
Trace.Write
Trace.Warn
```

These are both overloaded methods, the only difference between them being that `Write` generates text in black, and `Warn` generates text in red! Both methods are able to accept up to three parameters:

```
method(message As String)
method(category As String, message As String)
method(category As String, message As String, errorInfo As Exception )
```

The parameters are as follows:

- **Message** is any string value and will be written to the Message column.
- **Category** is any string value and will be written to the Category column.
- **ErrorInfo** is an Exception class. Its details will be written to an additional line in the Message column.

For example, the following writes to the Trace output when the `btnSelect_Click` handler starts, within the loop, and just before it terminates:

```
Private Sub btnSelect_Click(ByVal sender As System.Object, _
                ByVal e As System.EventArgs) Handles btnSelect.Click
    Dim itmSelected As ListItem

    Trace.Write("Entering the routine")
    For Each itmSelected In SourceList.Items
        Trace.Write("In the Loop")
        If itmSelected.Selected Then
            Trace.Write("Handling item: " & itmSelected.Text)
            SelectedList.Items.Add(itmSelected)
            itmSelected.Selected = False
        End If
    Next
    Trace.Write("Ending the loop")
End Sub
```

Figure 10-19 shows the results.

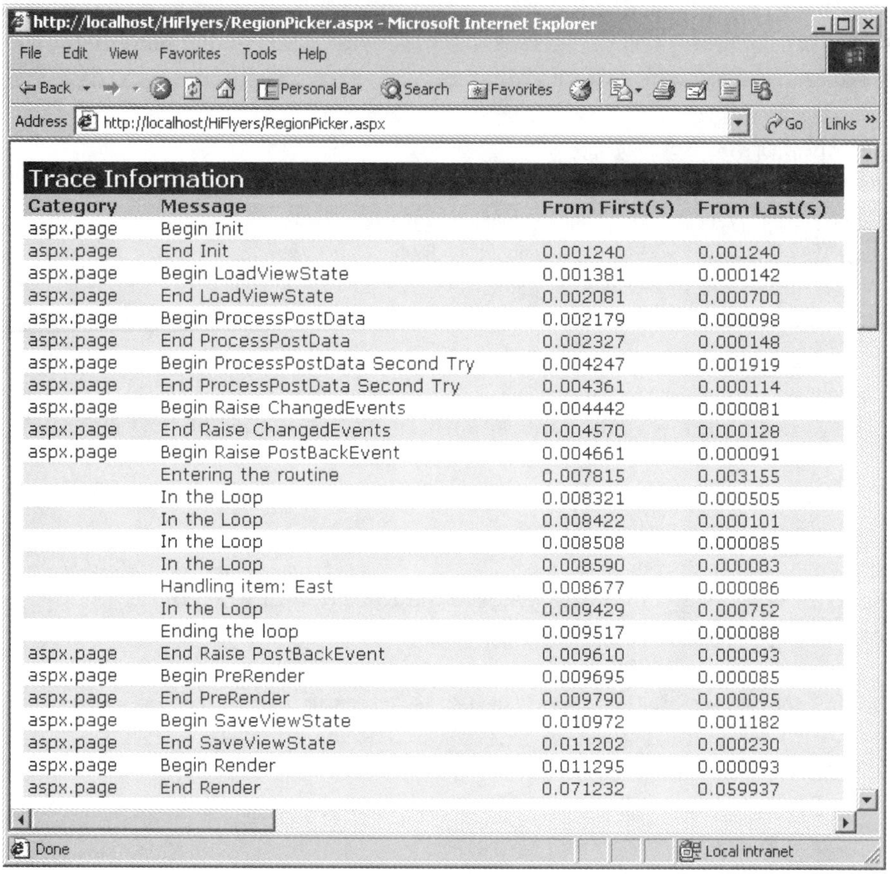
http://localhost/HiFlyers/RegionPicker.aspx - Microsoft Internet Explorer
File Edit View Favorites Tools Help
Back Personal Bar Search Favorites
Address http://localhost/HiFlyers/RegionPicker.aspx
Go Links
Done
Local intranet

Trace Information

Category	Message	From First(s)	From Last(s)
aspx.page	Begin Init		
aspx.page	End Init	0.001240	0.001240
aspx.page	Begin LoadViewState	0.001381	0.000142
aspx.page	End LoadViewState	0.002081	0.000700
aspx.page	Begin ProcessPostData	0.002179	0.000098
aspx.page	End ProcessPostData	0.002327	0.000148
aspx.page	Begin ProcessPostData Second Try	0.004247	0.001919
aspx.page	End ProcessPostData Second Try	0.004361	0.000114
aspx.page	Begin Raise ChangedEvents	0.004442	0.000081
aspx.page	End Raise ChangedEvents	0.004570	0.000128
aspx.page	Begin Raise PostBackEvent	0.004661	0.000091
	Entering the routine	0.007815	0.003155
	In the Loop	0.008321	0.000505
	In the Loop	0.008422	0.000101
	In the Loop	0.008508	0.000085
	In the Loop	0.008590	0.000083
	Handling item: East	0.008677	0.000086
	In the Loop	0.009429	0.000752
	Ending the loop	0.009517	0.000088
aspx.page	End Raise PostBackEvent	0.009610	0.000093
aspx.page	Begin PreRender	0.009695	0.000085
aspx.page	End PreRender	0.009790	0.000095
aspx.page	Begin SaveViewState	0.010972	0.001182
aspx.page	End SaveViewState	0.011202	0.000230
aspx.page	Begin Render	0.011295	0.000093
aspx.page	End Render	0.071232	0.059937

Figure 10-19. Custom entries in the trace output

You can leave `Trace.Write` and `Trace.Warn` methods in the code, even when you deploy the application to production systems. All that's needed to disable tracing is to set the Web Form's Trace property to False. You might think the presence of trace code could cause a performance overhead, but it won't—remember that the .NET JIT compiler converts the application's IL or source code into native code on first use. If the Web Form's Trace property is False, the runtime compiler simply ignores all references to the Trace object and therefore generates no additional code at all.

Application-Level Tracing

In many cases, the page-level tracing discussed in the previous section is insufficient. For example, when tracing pages that perform a `Response.Redirect`, you'll find that the trace output from the first page is immediately cleared as the browser performs the redirection to the new page. Also, the page-level trace output is transient, and it may be that the developer needs to preserve several traces to compare them.

Application-level tracing overcomes these problems by providing an application-wide mechanism for tracing all request/response processing models. Unlike page-level tracing, application-level trace output is usually viewed in a separate browser window and is accessed by navigating to a special URI. This URI is mapped to the System.Web.Handlers.TraceHandler HTTP Handler in Machine.config, and it's this class that presents and manages the output.

Application-level tracing is enabled through the Web.config file, by setting the `enabled` attribute for the `<trace>` section to `true`. For example:

```
<configuration>
    <system.web>
        <trace enabled="true" requestLimit="10" pageOutput="false"/>
    </system.web>
</configuration>
```

The `<trace>` section supports the attributes shown in Table 10-1.

Table 10-1. Attributes for the Trace Element

ATTRIBUTE	DESCRIPTION
enabled	`true` enables tracing for the application, `false` disables it. The default is false.
pageOutput	`true` causes trace information to be displayed both on the application's pages and in the .axd trace utility. `false` uses the Trace property of each page to determine whether it shows trace output. The default is false.
requestLimit	Determines the number of trace requests to store on the server. The default is 10, but you may want to change this to a higher number.
traceMode	Indicates whether trace information should be displayed in time order (`SortByTime`) or alphabetically by user-defined category (`SortByCategory`). SortByTime is the default.
localOnly	`true` limits the use of the trace viewer (trace.axd) to browsers running on the Web server itself. `false` allows browsers on remote workstations to access the trace viewer. The default is true.

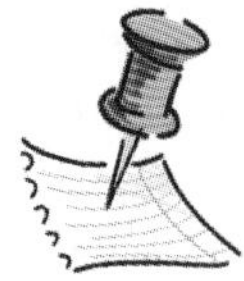

NOTE *Remember that the ASP.NET configuration system is case-sensitive. All single word configuration sections are lowercase, while any sections or attributes that are concatenations of two or more words must be camel-cased. For example,* `requestlimit` *and* `REQUESTLIMIT` *will cause a parser error, while* `requestLimit` *will not.*

Once you enable application-level tracing, tracing can begin. You load the application and test it with a regular browser window, and unless `pageOutput` has been set to `true`, there will be no trace information shown in this window at all. Instead, a separate browser window is opened and the following URI specified as the address:

```
http://server/appname/trace.axd
```

The browser will display a page similar to that shown in Figure 10-20.

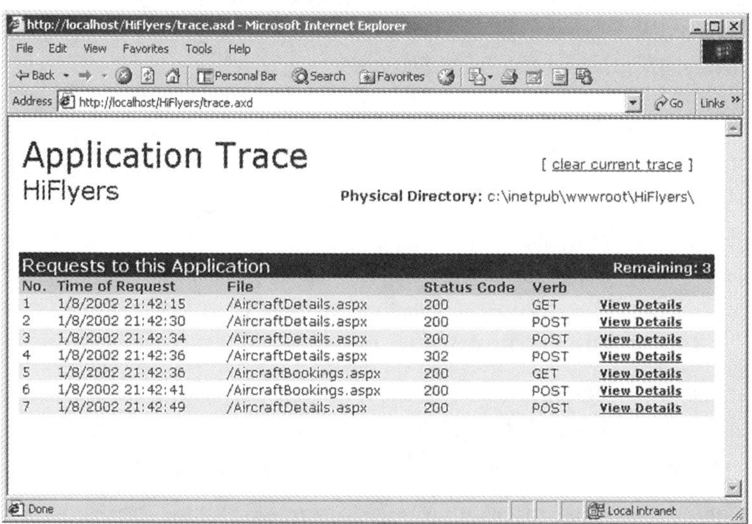

Figure 10-20. Application trace utility

This page shows that seven traces have so far been recorded; four for AircraftDetails.aspx, then two for AircraftBookings.aspx, then one more for AircraftDetails.aspx. If you click the **View Details** link on the right, the browser displays the content of the selected trace, as shown in Figure 10-21.

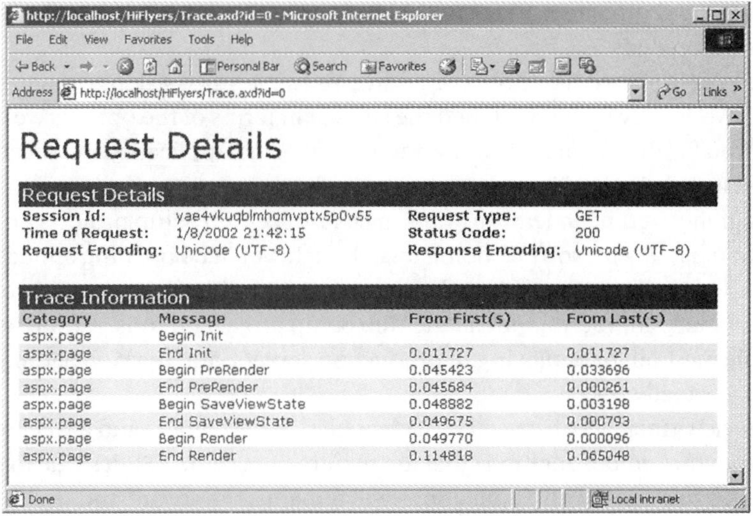

Figure 10-21. Details for the first recorded trace

Notice that this is just the trace log information; the page does *not* show the content of the page that generated the trace output. You'll probably find this to be a much neater and easier-to-use approach than using page-level tracing.

TIP *If the page contains* `Trace.Warn` *or* `Trace.Write` *statements, their output will still be shown in these trace logs.*

ASP.NET continues recording trace logs until it reaches the number specified by the `requestLimit` attribute in Web.config. At that point any new traces are simply ignored; it *won't* replace the older traces automatically. The trace.axd utility displays a hyperlink that allows you to **clear current trace**; by clicking this you can record additional trace logs without restarting the application.

Summary

This has been an important chapter, providing you with a good grounding in the architecture and operation of ASP.NET and showing how you can begin to configure it so it runs the way you want. Hopefully we've also shown you that the people in the .NET design team really have tried to overcome many of the limitations and problems associated with classic ASP, and so far it seems they've succeeded.

We've also shown how ASP.NET addresses two key tasks: deployment and tracing. We've only really scratched the surface in terms of the options we've shown you for deployment; if you want to create Web Applications that can be shipped worldwide and installed automatically, chances are you'll have to invest some significant time in learning how to customize Web Setup projects. In all honesty, most of you won't be doing this, though; you'll be building applications deployed to single servers (or maybe server farms) within your organization, and you won't need to worry about all the Web Setup project options. All you want is a reliable method for deploying to production servers, and the Web Setup projects do this really well.

The new tracing feature will be a great help to developers and a welcome relief from the tedious methods that are required in classic ASP. It's true to say that debugging large Web Applications will remain an awkward and tricky task, but with the built-in tracing capabilities, ASP.NET should make it achievable.

CHAPTER 11

Web Application Security

SECURITY IS A CONTENTIOUS ISSUE for Web applications, with developers and administrators sharing overall responsibility, while still focusing on their specialist abilities. As a developer, you need to consider tasks such as user authentication, authorization, and impersonation; you also need to produce a model that the administrators can use when the application goes live. Among other duties, administrators will be responsible for configuring Web server security, applying security patches and fixes, and assigning users to the different groups, roles, or access levels that you've defined. As you can imagine, these two sets of responsibilities are closely interwoven; so, it makes sense for both teams to work together when planning and designing security features, and subsequently, for them to maintain a good rapport as the application is developed and deployed.

In this chapter we'll tend to naturally focus on the developer responsibilities—after all, this is a book on ASP.NET, rather than IIS. However, we won't completely ignore the administrator-oriented requirements because you'll need to know at least a little about them before you can decide how your security features will work.

We will also focus in this chapter on Web Forms Applications; if you are building Web Service Applications, then the majority of these techniques can be used; although, as we'll see in Chapter 14, there are some additional options for controlling Web Service security.

Understanding Security

We all know what security is, right? Some would say that security is all about letting only the right people have access to your application; others might define it as protecting your data; a third definition could be that security is about protecting system integrity. These views represent what developers might think, but security also encompasses user concerns too. Users need to be confident that you aren't going to allow their details to be disclosed, they need to be sure that you won't abuse the information that they provide you, and they want to know that when they use your application—when placing an order, for example—they will get exactly what they expect. These concerns are often wrapped up into a very useful word: *trustworthy*. Trustworthiness is a topic that needs to be taken very seriously. If the users don't believe you're trustworthy, then they're unlikely to make use of your Web application.

Clearly these views are quite diverse, but they are all correct; security is a very broad topic encompassing different requirements and technologies, and it ultimately needs to address a broad range of threats.

As a Web developer, you probably won't have to deal with every aspect of security; but, instead, you can focus on a limited set of core topics, including the following:

- **Access control** is the process of defining who should be able to access specific parts of the application. This could be applied at a high-level (for example, power users can access individual member's account details but regular users cannot), or it could be applied in a more functional way (power users can edit and delete account details, regular users can view and add entries).

- **Transaction-based security** is about ensuring that our application really has done what it says it has done. For example, if the application says it has updated some item of data—or more likely, several items of data—then we need to be absolutely sure that it has done so. This task is complicated because of the use of external systems and software (such as databases) that could be hosted on remote systems, which may be subject to technical failure that the application cannot recognize.

- **Transmission-based security** deals with the problem of network snooping, where an intruder with the right hardware, software, and skills may be able to intercept, read, and even modify packets of data that your application sends over the wire.

- **Data privacy** refers to file snooping, where an intruder accesses a server or other file store and reads or modifies data directly. Data privacy also includes the task of ensuring that only appropriate users see secure information, irrespective of what they try to do.

- **Data integrity** is often associated with data privacy, but really has more of a focus on ensuring that data is consistent and accurate irrespective of physical, logical, hardware, or software failures.

- **Process security** is associated with ensuring that your application runs with an appropriate set of permissions for the operations it performs. This is important in the .NET world if we are to take advantage of the application isolation features that the .NET Framework provides.

You might argue in favor of adding more issues to this list, but in the interests of keeping the subject manageable, we'll restrict our discussions to those topics identified above.

Key Concepts

Before we get into the detail of security within Web applications, there are four important terms that need to be defined.

- **Authentication** is the process of checking whether a user actually is who they claim to be. Authentication has traditionally relied on a combination of username and password details, but more recently other techniques—such as the use of client certificates—have gained popularity. In principle, there are many other metrics that can be used to determine the validity of the user's claimed identity, although not all of them are appropriate in the Internet environment.

- **Authorization** is the process of determining a user's ability to access specific resources, usually based on their identity. Authorization can be applied at a file level by the operating system, or it can be applied by other layers—such as IIS and ASP.NET.

- **Impersonation** is the term given to the adoption of a different identity by a process. For example, ASP.NET applications usually run under the pre-configured **ASPNET** user account, but you may want your Web application to run with the permissions assigned to the user of the browser. Impersonation could be used to ensure that ASP.NET only accesses resources to which the end user has been granted permissions.

- **Delegation** extends the concept of impersonation to interaction between the Web server and other servers. In many Web applications it is common for the Web server to call another server to perform some task—such as retrieving data from a SQL Server database. If the Web server uses the client's identity and credentials during this process, then this is known as delegation. Delegation is a term that you'll find used by other products (such as SQL Server) rather than ASP.NET

So, to put it simply, *authentication* is all about knowing who the user is, *authorization* is about knowing what they can do, while *impersonation* is who they pretend to be while they're doing it.

The ASP.NET Security Model

Now that we've got these background concepts out of the way, let's see what ASP.NET can do to address potential security threats. There are, in fact, three distinct facets to the approach taken:

- ASP.NET has its own intrinsic security system that handles access control and process security.

- ASP.NET supports encryption technologies that allow you to implement transmission-based security and data privacy measures.

- ASP.NET works in conjunction with external systems to provide transaction-based security and data integrity.

External systems can also help enforce the access control, process security, transmission security, and data privacy measures that ASP.NET will apply. For example, we can implement SSL (Secure Sockets Layer) transmission to protect data sent over the network; and we can use database security to control access to database information. As you can see, it's not really possible to consider ASP.NET independently from these external systems; instead, you should think of them as collaborative partners.

Figure 11-1 shows an end-to-end view of Web application security, showing how the different technologies interact and play their individual roles.

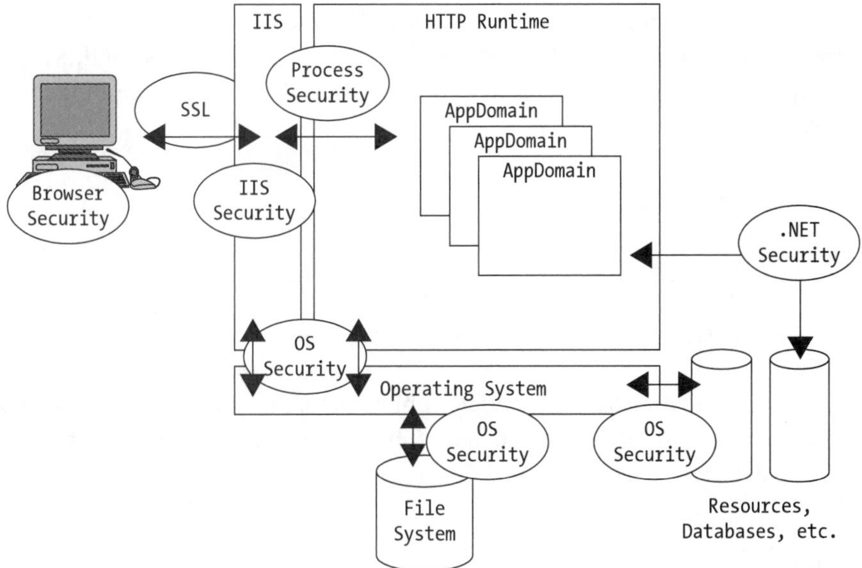

Figure 11-1. ASP.NET security model

From Figure 11-1 you can see that there are many interactions between the different technologies. We'll tackle these from front to back; in other words, we'll start with the browser request and make our way through the application to conclude with resource-based security.

Browser Security

You might be a bit puzzled at the idea of browser security. After all, the browser is out of our control both in terms of its technical capabilities and its configuration. How can we apply browser security when we have no influence over how the browser will be configured? As you'll see in this chapter, while you don't have direct control over the browser, you can exert a significant influence on it by carefully defining the content that you render.

However, you also need to be aware of the security restrictions that may have been applied to the users' browsers or their connection to the Internet. For example, many organizations configure browsers to prevent download of certain types of content, and they use firewalls and proxy servers that inhibit features such as IIS Integrated Security. In addition, there's no guarantee that the user's browser supports these features at all. For example, as we'll see in the Securing the Web Server section, popular browsers like Netscape Navigator and Opera don't support IIS Integrated Security; if you want them to have access to your application, you'll need to choose a different authentication technique.

Subsequent sections in this chapter deal with the specifics of handling logins, authorizing access to secure pages, and more; but, across all of these techniques, there exist some common browser-based concerns, including the following:

- Cookies
- ViewState
- Bookmarking

Each of these topics is a potential problem area, depending on the design of your application. You really should at least be aware of these risks, even if you make the decision to ignore them.

Cookies

Cookies are chunks of data that are transferred between a client and a Web server when requests and responses are issued (see Chapter 12). Cookies are initially generated by the Web application and sent to the client, but the client will pass the cookie back to the Web server with each request it makes. When you write code to create a cookie, you can choose whether it is *persistent* (and so is written to the client's local storage by the browser) or *transient* (in which case it is kept purely in memory). Transient cookies are often referred to as *temporary cookies* or *session cookies.*

Cookies are a potential risk because they can be stored on the client PC and interrogated by curious users. Of course, if your code is using cookies merely as a convenience, and you are not storing sensitive information in the cookie, then this vulnerability is not a problem. Therefore, the problem with cookies is best tackled at the design phase, by ensuring that they are restricted to storing public knowledge information only.

If you must store sensitive information in a cookie, then you should do two things:

1. Ensure that SSL is implemented on the Web server and make sure that all network transmissions are encrypted. We'll see more on this topic in the Implementing Secure Transmission section later in this chapter.

2. Apply your own encryption to the data within the cookie. This is especially important for persistent cookies because the data within a cookie can be read by opening the cookie file in a suitable editor—such as Notepad.

NOTE *.NET supports some powerful encryption technologies, but they require careful planning and implementation if they are to work well. In particular, you need to give careful thought to the choice of encryption algorithm and to the management of the cryptographic keys. It's beyond the scope of this book for us to start diving into the depths of .NET cryptography (and some of it really is deep). If you want to imple ment your own encryption, we'd suggest you start with the .NET documentation and the worked examples, and expand from there.*

ViewState

ViewState is another concern, because it too can be read by viewing the source of a Web page from the browser. At first glance, however, you may think that ViewState is already encrypted. For example, Figure 11-2 shows the ViewState value for a simple page.

Cookies[1].aspx

```
<!DOCTYPE HTML PUBLIC "-//W3C//DTD HTML 4.0 Transitional//EN">
<HTML>
    <HEAD>
        <title>Cookies</title>
        <meta name="GENERATOR" content="Microsoft Visual Studio.NET 7.0">
        <meta name="CODE_LANGUAGE" content="Visual Basic 7.0">
        <meta name="vs_defaultClientScript" content="JavaScript">
        <meta name="vs_targetSchema" content="http://schemas.microsoft.com/intellisense/ie5">
    </HEAD>
    <body MS_POSITIONING="GridLayout">
        <form name="Form1" method="post" action="Cookies.aspx" id="Form1">
<input type="hidden" name="__VIEWSTATE" value="dDwyMDYOMjQ3MDE1Ozs+oUZz14FNkOIM+4mEVtM6nuuDKT8=" />

            <input name="txtNewValue" type="text" value="Test" id="txtNewValue" style="Z-INDEX: 101;
            <input type="submit" name="btnStoreInCookie" value="Store In Cookie" id="btnStoreInCooki
            <input name="txtCurrentValue" type="text" value="Test" id="txtCurrentValue" style="Z-INI
            <input type="submit" name="btnEncrypted" value="Button" id="btnEncrypted" style="Z-INDE>
        </form>
    </body>
</HTML>
```

Figure 11-2. Standard ViewState

The content of the ViewState appears unreadable, but is in fact only encoded using a simple base 64 scheme that ensures that valid text characters are passed to the browser. ASP.NET performs this encoding to allow your application to store any form of data—numeric, string, or binary—in this simple text-based mechanism. Without the encoding, the ViewState could render to characters that would not be recognized by the browser, which in turn would cause the content of ViewState to be lost.

This encoding is usually sufficient to deter inquisitive users, but it's far too weak to prevent a determined intruder from reading the content. If you really want to lock down ViewState, then you need to encrypt it. You control the encoding and encryption of ViewState by entering attributes into Web.config; you can use three possible values for this:

```
<machineKey validation="SHA1" />
<machineKey validation="MD5" />
<machineKey validation="3DES" />
```

The `SHA1` value is the default setting; it causes the ViewState to be encoded, and a hash code—generated using the SHA1 algorithm—is applied to allow ASP.NET to detect tampering. The `MD5` setting still causes ViewState to be base 64 encoded, but this time the hash code is generated with the stronger MD5 algorithm. The `3DES` setting causes the ViewState to be encrypted, and is the toughest of all to crack.

So why not always use `3DES`? The reason is performance. Encryption algorithms are slow; the stronger the encryption, the slower they are. If you arbitrarily apply `3DES` to the ViewState in every Web Form, then you will really slow the application. But, if we apply this attribute in the Web.config file, how can we make it page specific—after all, Web.config is applied application-wide, right? Well, it's time we owned up to another partial mistruth in the earlier chapters. Web.config *is* application-wide by default, but you can define optional `<location>` sections that control specific files or directories. For example, to apply `3DES` only to SecurePage.aspx, you would define the following:

```
<configuration>
    <location path="SecurePage.aspx">
        <system.web>
            <machineKey validation="3DES" />
        </system.web>
    </location>

    <system.web>
        .
        .    Rest of Web.config here
```

Also, remember that you can place additional Web.config files into subdirectories within your application, and they will apply their settings to all content within that subdirectory. In this case, you would place the pages to which you wanted to apply 3DES into a separate subdirectory, then create a Web.config file in the same directory with the following content:

```
<?xml version="1.0" encoding="utf-8"?>
<configuration>
    <system.web>
        <machineKey validation="3DES" />
    </system.web>
</configuration>
```

The subdirectory version of Web.config does not need to reproduce all of the normal Web.config attributes and values because they will all be inherited from the parent directory's file. Instead, you need only enter the specific attributes you wish to override.

Bookmarking

If you've built multipage Web applications before, you're probably aware of the threat posed by bookmarks. Yes, these are the same bookmarks (or Favorites entries) that we all use to identify our favorite sites and pages, but for Web application developers they can be an unwanted nuisance.

The problem lies in the way that bookmarks could be used to short-cut carefully planned navigation paths through an application. For example, while browsing through an online purchasing application, a user bookmarks the "Confirm Your Order" page. The next day, they return to the site using only the bookmark and skip all of the product selection pages; if they were to try and submit a malformed order created this way, it could potentially cause errors within the application. No doubt you will have code in the order submission routines that ensures the order is well formed and that all relevant details are correct; but, the point is that the user should not have been able to go straight to this page, but instead should have been redirected to the application start point.

A similar problem exists when deep linking occurs. A *deep link* is a hyperlink (usually from another site) that targets a page that ordinarily would be accessible only by following a predefined path. For example, a deep link could point to a product list page in your application, but any users that navigate directly to it could bypass prior steps—such as authentication and authorization.

TIP *If you use the ASP.NET Forms or Passport Authentication techniques discussed below, the user will always be redirected to the Login page when they start to access the application, irrespective of the page they have tried to visit. They will not be able to view any other pages until they are authenticated. However, once they have successfully logged on, you still need to ensure that they follow your planned navigation path.*

In addition to implementing an authentication scheme, there are two further solutions you may choose to adopt to help you control subsequent navigation:

- Hide the real page addresses and so restrict which pages can be bookmarked. This is sometimes referred to as *concealed navigation.*
- Track navigation through the application and only allow access to each page if the user has already visited specific prerequisite pages. This is often referred to as a *ticketing scheme.*

Concealed Navigation

The principle behind concealed navigation is to prevent the user from knowing which page they are actually viewing. Many Web applications use Framesets for this purpose (we'll look at Frameset support in Chapter 12), but you'll find that a simpler solution is to perform all navigation using `Server.Transfer`, rather than `Response.Redirect` or client-side hyperlinks.

For example, the Web Form shown in Figure 11-3 contains two buttons—one which performs navigation using `Response.Redirect` and the other which uses `Server.Transfer`.

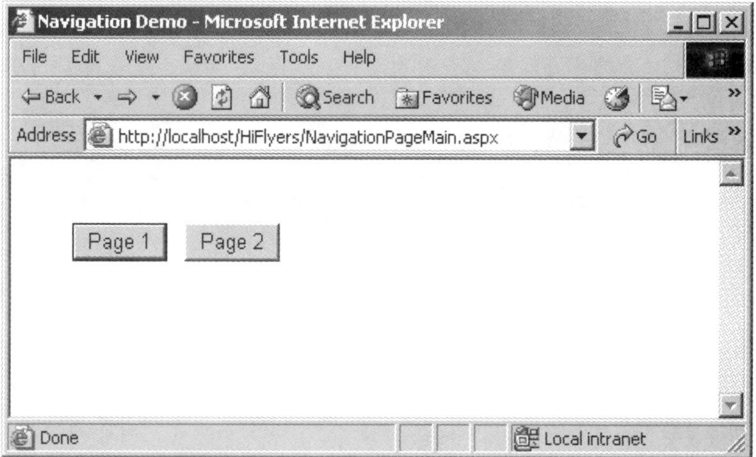

Figure 11-3. Main navigation page

The **Page 1** button uses `Response.Redirect` to perform navigation to a page named NavigationPage1.aspx. When this button is clicked, the browser displays the page as shown in Figure 11-4. Notice that the page URL is shown in the address bar.

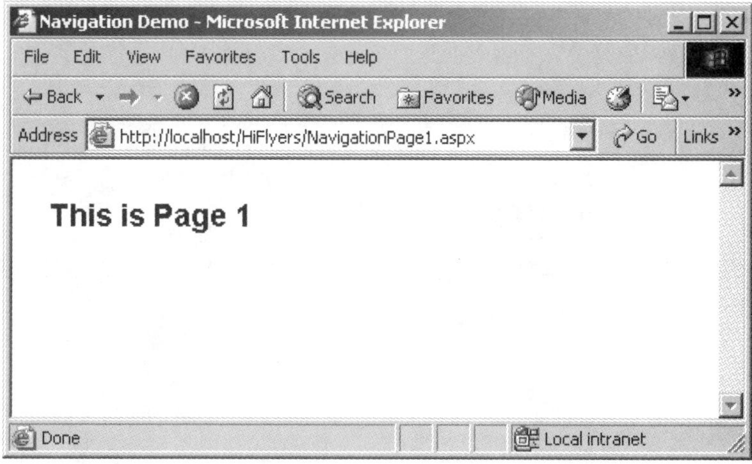

Figure 11-4. Navigating to NavigationPage1.aspx

However, the **Page 2** button on the main Web Form uses `Server.Transfer` to perform its navigation (this time to NavigationPage2.aspx). When the Page 2 button is clicked, the browser retains the original page URL in the address bar, as shown in Figure 11-5.

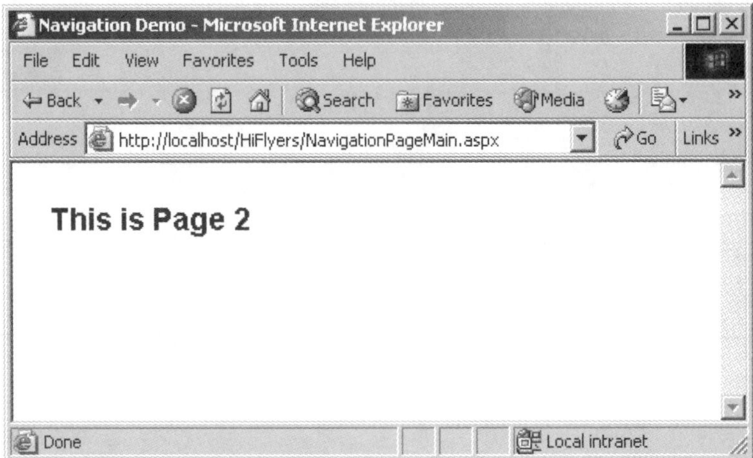

Figure 11-5. Concealed navigation

If we try to set a bookmark or add a Favorites entry to the current page (what we're seeing as Page 2), the stored reference points to NavigationPageMain.aspx—as shown in Figure 11-6.

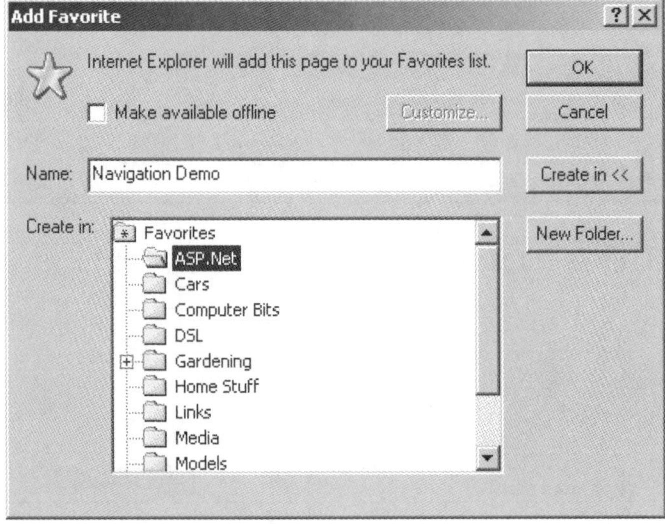

Figure 11-6. Bookmarking the concealed page

If the user subsequently tries to navigate to the bookmarked page, they are taken to the recorded URL: NavigationPageMain.aspx. While this approach is not foolproof, it is sufficient to deter casual intruders and will help reduce the number of users who navigate in error to a non-initial page.

TIP *Ensure that you set the page titles of your concealed pages to appropriate entries. In our example, we have set the titles of all three pages to* ***Navigation Demo****.*

Ticketing Schemes

Concealed navigation can be bypassed if the user either knows or guesses the name of the page being displayed. It is also ineffective when you need to perform client-side navigation—such as using hyperlinks or script. A more robust alternative is to use a ticketing scheme, where each page has a set of prerequisites that the user must meet before the page will be displayed.

A simple way to implement a ticketing scheme is to define a structure containing an element for each prerequisite, then set and read the element values in the pages that the user visits. For example, assume that HiFlyers wants a multi-page booking process where the user must select a date, instructor, and aircraft on three distinct pages. Clearly, we need to ensure that these tasks have been completed before we can accept their booking, so a ticketing scheme is required.

We would begin by defining a `Structure` that represents the `Ticket`:

```
Public Structure Ticket
    Public HasLoggedIn As Boolean
    Public HasSelectedAircraft As Boolean
    Public HasSelectedInstructor As Boolean
    Public HasSelectedDate As Boolean
End Structure
```

When the user begins the process of making a booking, we would create a `Ticket` object and persist it to some form of state. For example, the following code could be placed into the Login.aspx form:

```
Dim NavTicket As New Ticket()
Session("NavTicket") = NavTicket
```

In this example we are using Session state, but as you'll see in Chapters 12 and 13, there are a number of issues you should first consider before you decide which state-management technique to use. As the user completes each prerequisite page (for example, once they have selected an instructor) the corresponding element of the Ticket is set to `True`:

```
Private Sub btnSelectInstructor_Click(ByVal sender As System.Object, _
                ByVal e As System.EventArgs) Handles btnPlaceOrder.Click
    If IsNothing(Session("NavTicket")) Then
        Server.Transfer("Login.aspx")
    Else
        'Perform validation and ensure an instructor is selected

        'If OK, flag the ticket element
        Dim NavTicket As Ticket = CType(Session("NavTicket"), Ticket)
        NavTicket.HasSelectedInstructor = True
    End If
End Sub
```

Similar code would be present in the pages that allow selection of the aircraft and date. Finally, in the MakeBooking.aspx page, we can test each of the elements and only allow the booking to proceed if they have all been set:

```
Private Sub Page_Load(ByVal sender As System.Object, _
                ByVal e As System.EventArgs) Handles MyBase.Load
    If IsNothing(Session("NavTicket")) Then
        Server.Transfer("Login.aspx")
    Else
        Dim NavTicket As Ticket = CType(Session("NavTicket"), Ticket)

        If Not NavTicket.HasLoggedIn Then
            Server.Transfer("Login.aspx")
        ElseIf Not NavTicket.HasSelectedAircraft Then
            Server.Transfer("SelectAircraft.aspx")
        ElseIf Not NavTicket.HasSelectedInstructor Then
            Server.Transfer("SelectInstructor.aspx")
        ElseIf Not NavTicket.HasSelectedDate Then
            Server.Transfer("SelectDate.aspx")
        Else
            'Rest of code here to make the booking
        End If
    End If
End Sub
```

You can vary the implementation of the ticketing scheme to suit your application, although the principle will be the same. For example, you may choose to place the Ticket attributes into ViewState or the querystring, or perhaps implement the Ticket as a simple value that indicates only what page was last visited.

Implementing Secure Transmission

When a Web application is accessed over a network, the request and response data is passed using a protocol called HTTP (HyperText Transfer Protocol). The request data includes any information entered by the user into a form, some of which may represent sensitive details (such as credit card or account numbers, passwords, etc.). HTTP is a standardized part of the TCP/IP suite, and was only ever intended for passing non-secure data in clear text form (see Appendix A). An intruder with the right tools and knowledge (plus access to the network) would be able to intercept, read, and modify packets of data that are passed between the client and the server. This *packet snooping* is usually completely invisible to the client and server systems, and such attacks often go undetected and unresolved. When faced with a problem such as this, the solution is one of prevention, rather than cure.

You can prevent packet snooping by securing the data during transmission; SSL is the simplest way to do this. SSL acts in conjunction with HTTP by encrypting the data before it is transmitted, and then, by decrypting it when it is received. Clearly, both the client and the server need to know that they are supposed to use SSL; therefore, both must be configured appropriately.

Client-side Configuration

Assuming that the browser supports SSL (and that it's enabled), client-side configuration is easy. You use SSL by declaring HTTPS, rather than HTTP, as the protocol in the URL. For example, to access a secure page on the HiFlyers site, you could use the following URL:

```
https://www.hiflyers.org/securearea/default.aspx
```

As a developer, you also need to ensure that HTTPS is specified in any URLs that you use within your application for requests that need to be encrypted. These include:

- Hyperlinks
- Client-side script
- `Response.Redirect` and `Server.Transfer` statements
- Declarative redirection (such as URLs entered into .config files)

Remember, you only need to use HTTPS for a page you want to access over SSL. Some pages may support secure and non-secure access (as we'll see when we look at server-side configuration below); in this case, you can choose either HTTP or HTTPS.

NOTE *Any form of encryption will degrade performance; the use of SSL is no exception. This impact occurs at the server (encryption and decryption time), at the client (encryption and decryption time), and in transmission times (encrypted data is usually larger). It's impossible to give figures for the impact that SSL will have on your servers because it depends on many different factors. However, you can be sure there will be a* noticeable *slowdown, so use SSL selectively for those sites and pages that need it.*

Server-side Configuration

The server is configured to use SSL by installing a Server Certificate against the Web site. You can then specify that particular files or folders are to be accessed only with the HTTPS protocol. The first step is to obtain a suitable certificate. You can either purchase a certificate from a known and trusted Certification Agency (CA), or you can create your own certificate if you install and configure Microsoft Certificate Services. Let's explore the differences between these two approaches:

- If you obtain your certificate from a trusted CA, they will perform a number of checks to ensure that you are who you claim to be, and that there would be no risk from you having a certificate. The name of the CA (such as VeriSign Inc.) will be displayed as a part of the certificate to any users who view it. The principle is that users will trust VeriSign to perform the necessary checks; because you have been issued with a certificate from them, users can be reassured that you are legitimate.

- Private certificates are really intended for use with internal sites and applications, although they can be used on public-access sites. Because you issue and manage the certificate yourself, there are no requirements for performing any checks; so, the user is given no additional assurance regarding the legitimacy of your site.

It's important to realize that these are not two different types of certificate; they are just two different ways to obtain a certificate. There *will* be a difference in the certificate details, since the name of the issuing CA will be clearly displayed for all to see. Users are more likely to trust a certificate from a well-known company than from an obscure one. However, irrespective of the way the certificate is obtained, once installed, it will always provide support for SSL and other certificate-based services.

Installing a Certificate

We won't go into all the details of how you obtain certificates, because they will vary according to your geographic location, business type, certificate requirements, and so on. However, the process is started through the IIS property dialogs (the following applies to IIS 5.0; the precise steps may be different on other versions):

1. Start **Internet Services Manager** and right-click on the site that you want to secure. This can either be the Default Web Site or an alternative that you have created. In our example, the site is called Secure Site.

2. From the Context menu that is displayed, select **Properties,** then select the **Directory Security** tab in the Site Properties dialog.

3. Click the **Server Certificate** button, then work through the wizard selecting **Create a new certificate** when prompted. You will need to provide information such as the site name, organizational name, e-mail details, etc.

The wizard will typically produce a small text file (usually named certreq.txt), which is sent to a CA. There are numerous CAs offering certificates, but one of the most widely recognized is VeriSign Inc. (`www.verisign.com`). The CA processes the request and returns the certificate, usually in the form of a separate file.

Once you have received the certificate file, you can return to the IIS property dialogs to install it.

1. Run through steps 1 and 2 above. Ensure that you are working with the same site that you chose previously—certificates are site specific.

2. Click the **Server Certificate** button to run the wizard. The wizard recognizes that you have issued a certificate request, and prompts you to **Process the pending request and install the certificate**. Choose this option and work through the wizard until the certificate is installed.

3. At this point, if you view the **Directory Security** tab on the Site Properties dialog, you will see that the **View Certificate . . .** and **Edit . . .** buttons in the **Secure Communications** frame are enabled.

Configuring SSL

SSL support is configured both at the site level and at the individual file and directory level. Once you've installed a certificate, you can configure site-wide SSL support by displaying the **Site Properties** dialog and clicking the **Edit . . .** button in the **Secure Communications** frame on the **Directory Security** tab. This will display the dialog shown in Figure 11-7.

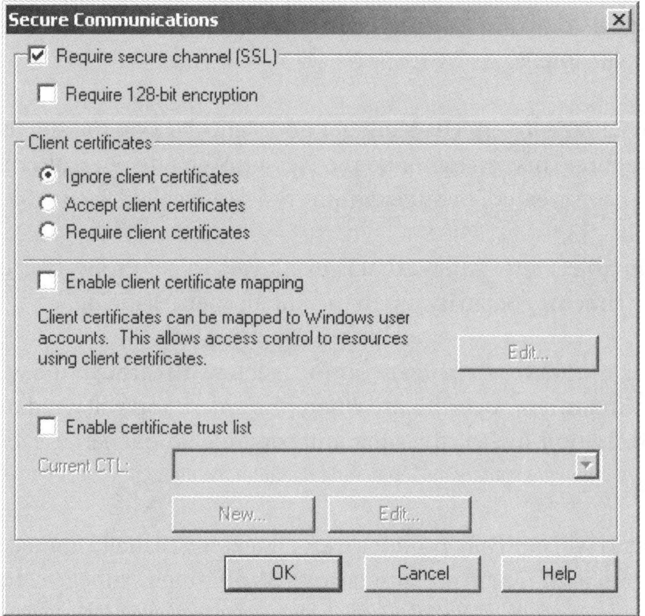

Figure 11-7. Secure Communications dialog for the site

We're interested in the main option: **Require secure channel (SSL)**. If this is selected, clients will have to use HTTPS in order to access *any* of the content in the entire site; if it is not selected, you can configure individual files and directories to require SSL access. As we mentioned earlier, it is not always appropriate to protect the entire site with SSL due to performance problems.

Similar dialogs can be displayed for individual directories and files within the site. For example, within our Secure Site, we have a virtual directory named

SecureDemo. Its Properties dialog also has a Directory Security tab with an Edit button, and this leads to the dialog shown in Figure 11-8.

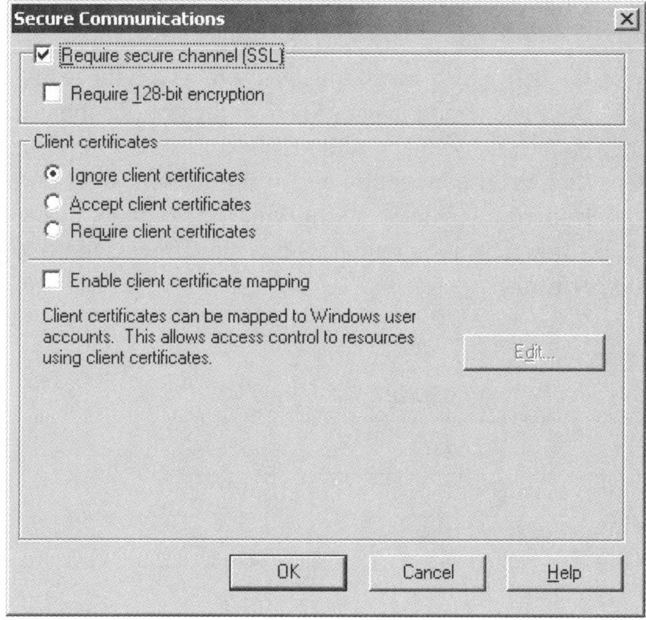

Figure 11-8. Secure Communications dialog for the SecureDemo directory

There is little difference between the site and directory level security settings. In fact, if you display the properties for a file within the site, you will see that it has a File Security tab with an Edit button that leads to the same dialog; although, this time the settings will be applied to the selected file only.

You will need to work through your application's directories and files, deciding what needs to be secure and what does not. The most common approach is to apply SSL to the Login form and any other form where non-public data is entered (such as credit card numbers, banking information, etc.). SSL is not generally applied to the remaining forms, so there is less of an impact on performance.

CAUTION *Installing and configuring SSL in a real-world environment is not a trivial task and requires knowledge and expertise in configuring servers. You'll also find there are limitations in using SSL on servers that have multiple sites or shared IP addresses. We'd recommend you leave this side of things to network and server support teams.*

Securing the Web Server

Our next stage requires that we secure the Web server against unauthorized access and abuse. IIS provides a number of different mechanisms for this, each of which can be independently enabled and controlled according to your preferences. However, the IIS security mechanisms interact with those in ASP.NET; so, the choices that you make at this stage will affect the options that you later have.

The interaction between IIS and ASP.NET becomes very important when we deal with topics such as authentication and authorization, since both technologies are ultimately involved in determining whether a request succeeds or fails. Figure 11-9 shows how a browser request is typically processed through the checks that IIS performs.

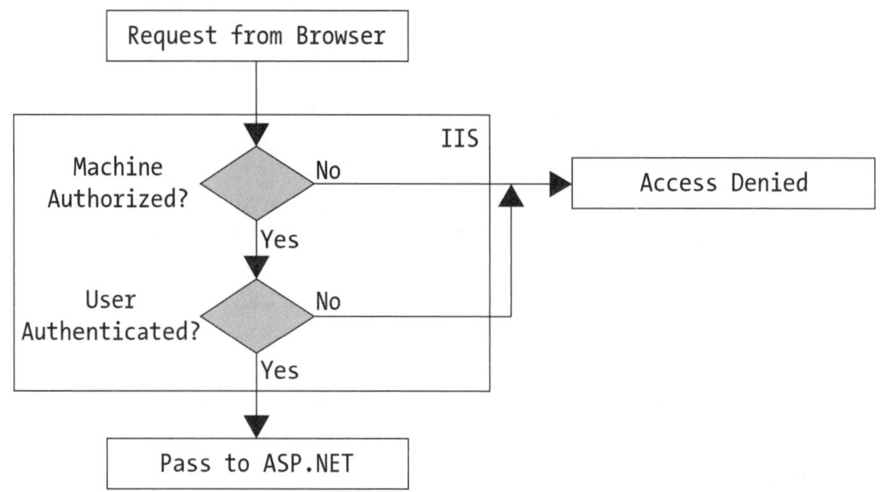

Figure 11-9. IIS security processes

If the request is successfully validated through IIS, it then checks the file extension against the table of ISAPI mappings (see Chapter 10). If the requested extension is mapped to ASP.NET, IIS passes the request to the HTTP Runtime to perform further checks. IIS maintains the identity of the request as it passes it on, and this identity will depend on the authentication method used in IIS (see IIS User Authentication below). The identity will either be the user's Windows identity or the default identity that IIS uses for Anonymous access (normally `IUSR_<Machine_Name>`).

When the HTTP Runtime receives the request, it processes it as discussed in Chapter 10, starting with the pipeline of HTTP Modules. We'll look at the detail of what happens during the ASP.NET checks in later sections; but, in principle, ASP.NET first authenticates the identity of the request (allowing for *imperson-*

ation of other identities), then it checks the authorization for that identity, and finally, it allows the operating system to check the NTFS permissions for the identity. If all of these are passed, the request is processed. Figure 11-10 summarizes the interactions.

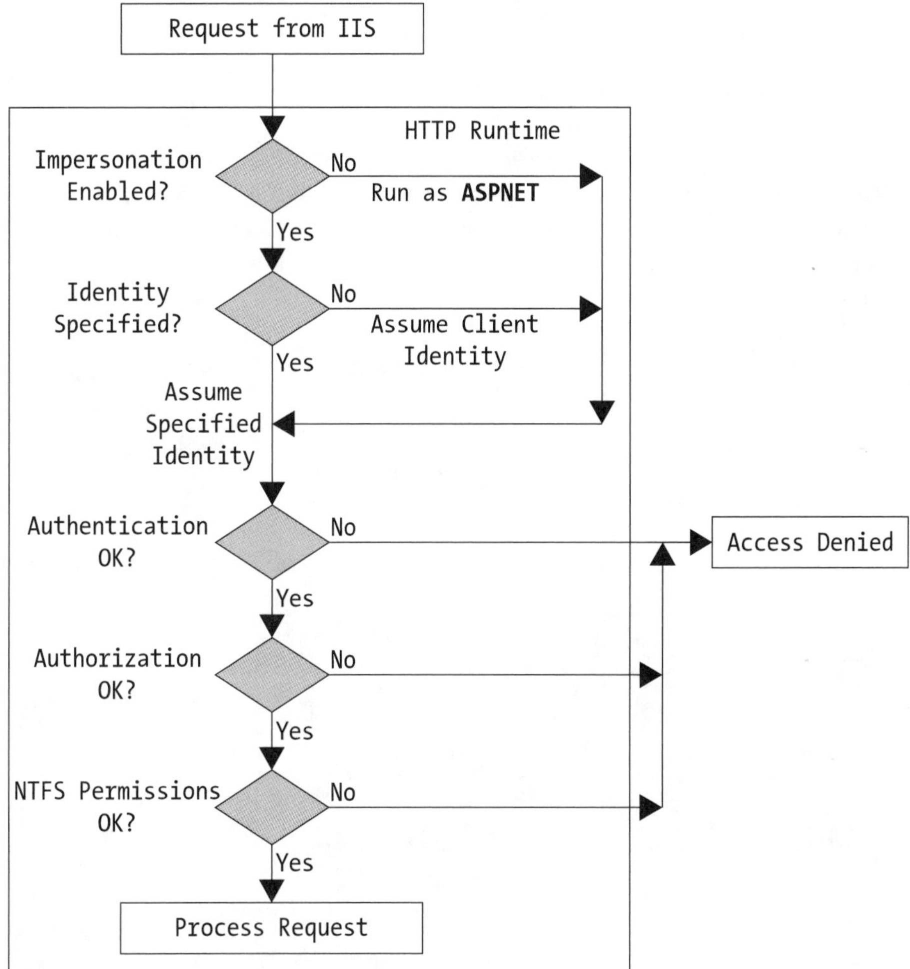

Figure 11-10. ASP.NET security processes

Clearly a lot happens through these processes, and in terms of ASP.NET authentication, even Figure 11-10 is a simplification. However, we've found that if you work logically through these stages, then you'll understand them more readily than if you try to examine them out of sequence.

Let's begin at the top then, and look at how IIS performs the initial checks.

IIS Security

IIS supports great flexibility within its security subsystems, allowing administrators and developers to apply a number of different security models according to their precise needs. Security checks can be performed against the machine or the user (or both), and can be enforced at the site, directory, or file level.

IIS Machine Authorization

Even before authenticating the user, IIS can perform authorization checks on the IP address or domain of the client machine. By default, these checks are disabled, but you can change the settings through the **Directory Security** tab in the **Properties** dialog for the directory or file. Figure 11-11 shows the dialog boxes that provide these options

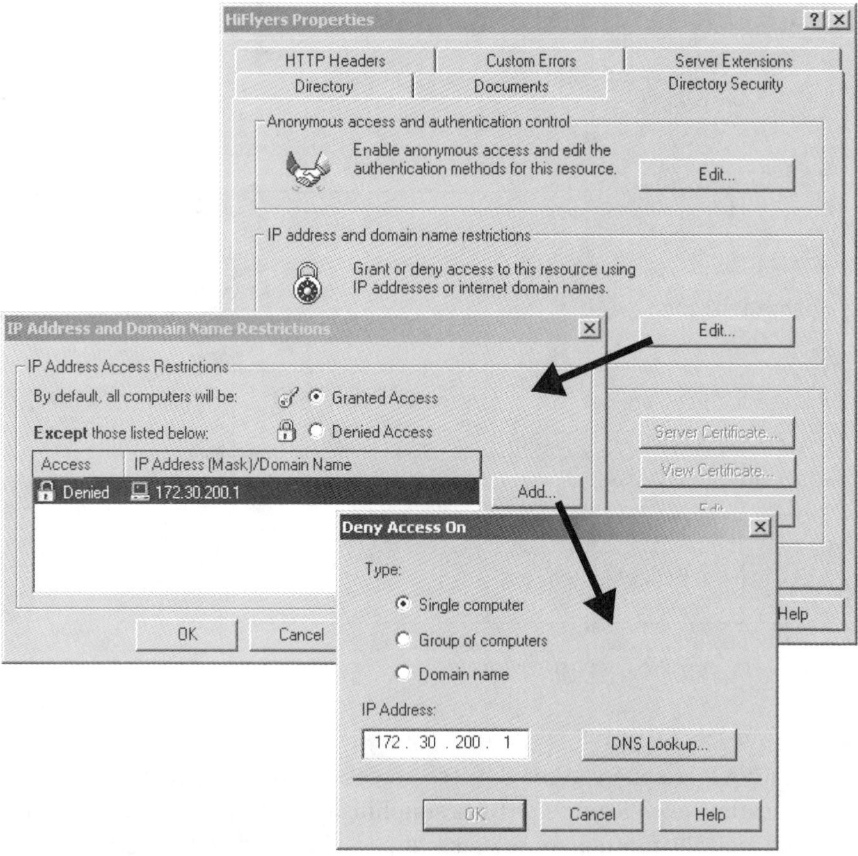

Figure 11-11. IP address and domain authorization

These are the least relevant settings for developers, and would normally be configured by the Web server administrator once the application was deployed to a live environment. However, they provide an easy way to make sure that an internal Web site is only used by internal users.

IIS User Authentication

Remember our earlier definition of authentication—it's all about knowing who the user really is. IIS can perform authentication checks in a number of different ways, all but one of which are configured through the **Authentication Methods** dialog shown in Figure 11-12. As with the machine authorization dialogs, these settings are accessed via the Security tab on the File Properties or Directory Properties dialogs within Internet Services Manager.

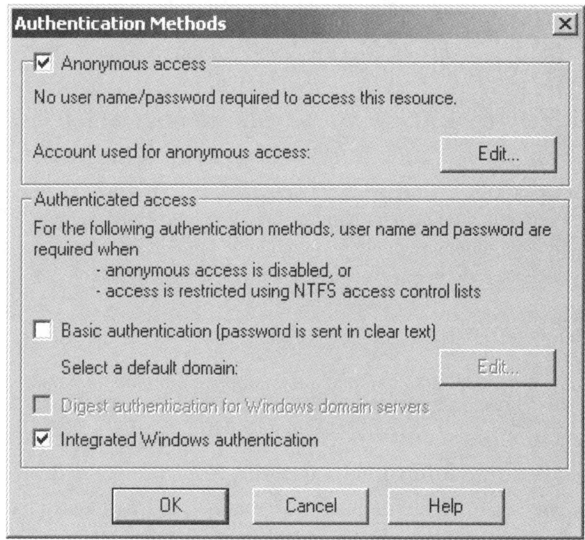

Figure 11-12. User authentication methods

The four different methods can be selected in any combination. IIS usually tries Anonymous access first, but will revert to the authenticated access methods if the user tries to access a resource secured with NTFS file permissions.

IIS can also apply the use of client certificates as another user authentication method. This approach is technically more demanding (both on the client and server systems), and typically requires a greater amount of manual configuration to establish the required settings. Nonetheless, client certificates are potentially the most secure technology for authenticating users and are being more widely implemented every day.

Anonymous Access

Anonymous access allows any user to have access to the resource and requires no username or password. In order to process the request, IIS must adopt an identity to use for authorization checks; by default, this is the `IUSR_<Machine name>` account that was created when IIS was installed. You can manually change this by clicking the **Edit...** button within the **Anonymous access** frame.

Anonymous access works with all browsers and platforms, and is unaffected by intermediate servers such as proxies or gateways. Anonymous access is ideal if you want to control authentication completely from within ASP.NET, such as when using the Forms Authentication scheme discussed later.

NOTE *Be aware that the* `IUSR_<Machine name>` *account is local, and so may cause problems if you try and access a secured resource on a remote server using this identity. It's particularly a problem if IIS is configured to automatically control the password of the anonymous account. You can overcome these problems using impersonation, as discussed below.*

Basic Authentication

Basic Authentication requires that users are verified by checking their username and password against the security accounts defined for the server machine or domain. When a user first attempts to access a resource secured with Basic Authentication, the server returns an HTTP response indicating that authentication details are required. The browser will display a login dialog to allow the user to enter the details, and then sends them back to the server with a duplicate of the original request. The information that the user enters is base 64 encoded before transmission, but because this encoding is so weak, the information is clearly readable to anyone with access to low-level network tools. However, if you apply SSL to a site that uses Basic Authentication, the credentials will be SSL-encrypted along with the rest of the request, making the site much more secure.

Basic Authentication works with most browsers and is unaffected by intermediate servers such as proxies or gateways. To use Basic Authentication, you must ensure that each user has the username and password for a valid account on one of the domains or servers on your network. Set the name of this domain or server by clicking the **Edit . . .** button within the **Authenticated access** frame. Basic Authentication works well for an application with a small set of known users who need access from a variety of client platforms, browsers, or locations.

NOTE *When accessing a site that uses Basic Authentication, the browser will pass the credentials in every request, so SSL is essential to protect the privacy of these details.*

Digest Authentication

Digest Authentication sends a *digest* or *hash* over the network instead of the password. This is a challenge-response scheme in which the client encrypts the digest using the user-entered password, and the server encrypts the digest using the stored password. The client passes the encrypted digest to the server, which compares it to the one generated from the stored password; if they are the same, then the passwords must have been the same, and the user is authenticated.

Digest Authentication works only with Microsoft Internet Explorer 5.0 and later, but it is unaffected by intermediate proxy servers, gateways, and firewalls. User accounts must already exist in a Windows 2000 Server configured to support Digest, and so the scheme works well for small intranet-type applications with a small, known group of users.

Although Digest is more secure than Basic Authentication (because it doesn't pass a clear-text password), it's still not perfect; so, it is recommended that you use SSL on Web sites that use Digest Authentication.

Integrated Windows Authentication

Integrated Windows Authentication is an ASP.NET scheme that makes use of either NT LAN Manager (NTLM) or Kerberos Authentication; it uses a negotiation process between the client and server to determine which will be used. Both NTLM and Kerberos are challenge-response schemes similar to Digest, but they are both able to use a more secure hashing algorithm. This makes Integrated Windows Authentication much more secure than Basic Authentication, and slightly more secure than Digest.

Integrated Windows Authentication requires that users are running Windows with Internet Explorer version 2.0 or later, and once again requires that they have existing Windows domain accounts. It does *not* work through proxy servers or firewalls unless PPTP (Point to Point Tunneling Protocol) is also used; so,

Integrated Windows Authentication is best suited to intranet environments within a single site.

Client Certificate Authentication

Client certificate Authentication uses a completely different approach; it authenticates users based on the presence of a recognized certificate in the request issued by the browser. You can configure IIS so that certificates are required or optional:

- **If required,** users without a certificate will be denied access. For users with certificates, you can require that they use Basic, Digest, or Windows Integrated Authentication to identify themselves, or you can map their certificates to Windows user accounts.
- **If optional,** users presenting certificates can be authenticated as above, while those without certificates will be required to authenticate via Basic, Digest, or Windows Integrated Authentication.

Client certificate support is configured in the Secure Communications dialog for the site, shown in Figure 11-13. This is the same dialog used to configure SSL support and previously shown in Figure 11-7.

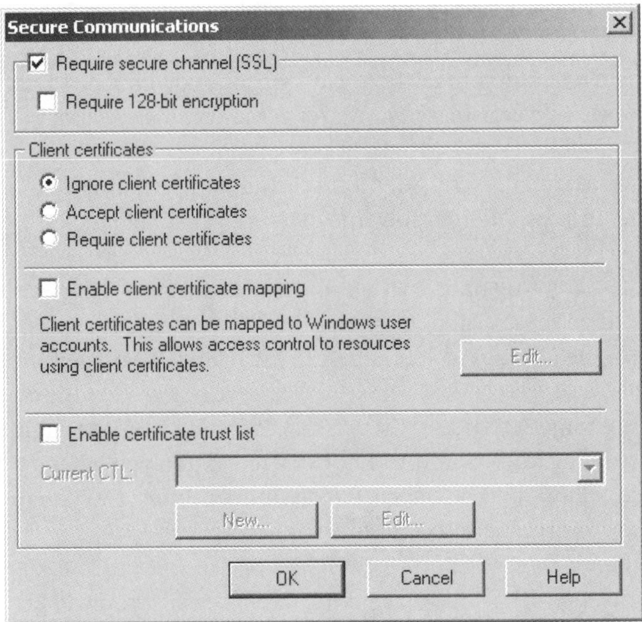

Figure 11-13. Secure Communications dialog for the site

The **Client certificates** frame allows you to define whether certificates are ignored, accepted, or required. If accepted or required, you can then establish certificate mappings and a certificate trust list. Certificate mappings allow you to specify an association between specific client certificates and nominated Windows user accounts. This can be on a one-to-one basis or a many-to-one basis (many certificates map to a single account) and will be used to authenticate clients that present certificates. Certificate trust lists (CTLs) are lists of certificates or certification agencies that your site will trust. If this feature is enabled, each client certificate is checked against the CTL to determine whether the request is accepted.

NOTE *You cannot use Client certificate Authentication unless you have installed a valid server certificate and enabled the secure communication features. Also, client certificates need to be obtained for each user, and browsers need to be configured to present certificates as a part of the server request.*

Choosing an Authentication Model

With a choice of five different authentication models, which one is best? To answer this, you must consider your target audience. In particular, are they initially unknown public users or are they known individuals with existing domain accounts? You also need to consider their technical environment, including what browser they have and whether they make use of proxy servers.

- If you are targeting unknown public users, your only choice will be Anonymous access; all of the other methods require that a valid account exists on the domain or server before the user can gain access.

- If you are targeting users with existing accounts, can you guarantee that they are using Microsoft Internet Explorer? If not, you'll have to use Basic Authentication (because Digest and Windows Integrated are both IE-specific), or drop back to Anonymous access.

- If your users work with proxy servers and firewalls, you will be unable to use Windows Integrated Authentication, so the most secure scheme will be Digest. Once again, you can drop back to either Anonymous access or Basic Authentication if preferred.

- The only time you can use Windows Integrated Authentication is in a LAN-type intranet environment. Every user must have direct access to the Web server and they must be already recognized by domain-level user accounts. Also, every user must be running Internet Explorer.

- Client certificate Authentication can be used in addition to any of the above or as a stand-alone authentication technique. There is limited browser support for client certificates and a greater need for client-side and server-side configuration; but, for known audiences that already have certificates (or will obtain them), Client certificate Authentication is potentially the most secure scheme.

However, as we will see in the ASP.NET Authentication section later in this chapter, you can also apply tight security of your own design through ASP.NET, or you can implement Microsoft Passport to authenticate users against an independent source. Both of these mechanisms assume that IIS is set to use Anonymous access so that it passes *all* requests through, rather than performing its own checking. For public access applications this really is the best approach, although special consideration then needs to be given to securing static content, such as .htm and .gif files—a point which we'll address later.

IIS Process Isolation

The final point worth noting about IIS is that it supports process isolation; so, a Web Application running within ASP.NET is quite separate from the IIS process itself. This concept was introduced in Chapter 10, where we highlighted the benefits to be gained in terms of robustness and reliability.

Isolating processes in this way also has security benefits; process isolation makes it far more difficult for intruders to gain control. This is a default feature in the operation of ASP.NET and needs no further configuration or adjustment.

ASP.NET Impersonation

After IIS has authenticated the user and determined it will pass the request to the HTTP Runtime, we need to decide what identity will be used by ASP.NET to process the request. By default, ASP.NET will run under the guise of a specific named account (called ASPNET) and will access all resources using this identity. This is a safe option as a default, but you may encounter problems because the ASPNET account has a very limited set of privileges. For example, ASPNET will not automatically be granted access to SQL Server databases using integrated security, nor will it have access to certain operating system resources, such as performance counters.

To overcome these limitations, you can configure ASP.NET to use a different identity for processing requests. The identity can be chosen on a machine-wide basis, it can be set per application, or you can have ASP.NET use the credentials of the user issuing the request. When ASP.NET assumes a different identity in this way, it's called *impersonation*. As well as using impersonation to permit access to resources, it can also be advantageous when working with audited resources (such as databases), which can log all activity against the account that was used.

To set the identity on a machine-wide basis, edit the `<processModel>` section of Machine.config. The `userName` and `password` attributes define the account credentials, where `userName` can be `SYSTEM`, `machine`, or a named user account. `SYSTEM` causes ASP.NET to use the local system account, which has almost unlimited privileges; `machine` is the default, and causes ASP.NET to assume the ASPNET account identity. For example, the following extract shows the settings required for executing ASP.NET using a user account named "DOT_NET_USER":

```
<processModel
    userName="DOT_NET_USER"
    password="secret"
```

Note that there will be other settings in the `<processModel>` section that have not been shown in this example.

At an application level, impersonation can be controlled declaratively or programmatically. *Declarative* control simply requires that you add entries to the Web.config file to establish the type of impersonation you want to implement; *programmatic* control requires that you make a number of API calls from your code to establish the required identity.

Declarative Impersonation

Declarative Impersonation is the simplest technique and relies on an `<identity>` element being defined in Web.config. You can use three possible settings:

```
<identity impersonate="false" />
<identity impersonate="true" />
<identity impersonate="true" name="domain\user" password="password" />
```

The first of these—`impersonate="false"`—turns off impersonation. This is the default setting and causes the Web Application to use the standard ASPNET user account. As discussed above, this may have serious implications if your code tries to access secured resources, such as databases or message queues.

The `impersonate="true"` setting causes ASP.NET to adopt the identity of the user making the request. Exactly what this identity is will depend on the authentication scheme used by IIS. For example, if IIS uses Anonymous access, the identity will be the `IUSR_<Machine Name>` account; whereas, if one of the other methods is used, then the identity will be that of the logged on user. Having adopted an identify in this way, all subsequent activity during the processing of the request will be performed using the adopted account.

If you want to specify an account, then you can use the third syntax—where impersonation is enabled, but an additional username and password are specified. Notice that the username *must* be qualified with the domain name (or server name for a local account), and also that the password is stored in Web.config in clear text format.

Programmatic Impersonation

Declarative impersonation is very much "all or nothing;" it is applied to the entire request processing cycle rather than just one part of it. If you want a finer degree of control, then you can implement programmatic impersonation at any point in your code.

To use programmatic impersonation, your code will need to call three API functions:

- `LogonUser`
- `ImpersonateLoggedOnUser`
- `RevertToSelf`

`LogonUser` is called first and is passed a valid username and password as parameters. If the logon is successful, the function returns a token, which you apply to the other two functions. `ImpersonateLoggedOnUser` takes the token and switches the identity of the current thread to the account specified by the token. Any further tasks performed by the thread are associated with the impersonated identity. To conclude, you can either destroy the thread or call `RevertToSelf` to return the thread to its original identity.

CAUTION *These are API calls into the Advapi32.dll library. They are not managed by .NET, so any failures when making these calls could have disastrous consequences for the application. Ensure that you check and double-check your code if you wish to use this technique.*

ASP.NET Authentication

We've already discussed the authentication model offered by IIS and looked at the methods it uses; while they're quite well-suited to intranets, they're not really appropriate for the Internet. Like us, you've probably reached the conclusion that the only workable solution for public access sites is to implement Anonymous access and let IIS pass all requests to the application.

In this respect there's no real change from the way that classic ASP applications are secured. But, classic ASP developers have to go one stage further—they still have to build their own authentication system that *does* work for public access sites. Fortunately, in the world of ASP.NET, you'll find that all of this is done for you.

ASP.NET actually provides four different authentication models that you can use; the first of these simply performs no authentication at all and accepts every request from IIS. The other three perform different types of verification services and are generally known as *authentication providers*.

Disabling ASP.NET Authentication

If you want to perform no authentication checks in ASP.NET, but simply accept every request that IIS passes through, you can disable authentication by editing the `<authentication>` element in Web.config to read as follows:

```
<authentication mode="None" />
```

Using Windows Authentication

The *Windows Authentication provider* is designed to be used in conjunction with either Basic, Digest, or Windows Integrated Authentication from IIS. It validates users against a Windows security database. It would typically be used when you wanted an authentication scheme for an intranet-type Web application, but didn't want to invest time and effort in defining your own. Also, Windows Authentication is useful when you want to make use of impersonation because it retains user account details passed across from IIS. Note that Windows Authentication *can* be used with IIS Anonymous access, but it will simply verify that the anonymous IIS account is valid.

To enable Windows Authentication, make the following entry in Web.config (note that this is the default configuration for ASP.NET):

```
<authentication mode="Windows" />
```

After you've enabled Windows Authentication, you can apply other security schemes, such as impersonation and authorization. We've already covered impersonation, so won't repeat it here, but it is worth taking an advance look at authorization because it will govern what files and resources the user can access. (Don't worry, we'll return to a more thorough discussion of authorization techniques in the next section.)

As you might expect by now, authorization is controlled by declarations added to the Web.config file. The settings are contained with the `<authorization>` element and consist of `<allow>` or `<deny>` elements that, respectively, permit or prohibit access. For example:

```
<authorization>
    <deny users="?" /> <!- Deny anonymous users ->
    <deny users="Mydomain\baduser, Mydomain\baduser2" />
    <allow users="*" /> <!- Allow all users ->
</authorization>
```

The <authorization> section is checked in sequence, stopping when a match is found for the user's credentials. In this example, the first <deny> element blocks all anonymous attempts, then the second <deny> element blocks two specific named user accounts. Finally, all other user accounts are allowed. Don't think of the ? and * values as being wildcards—the ? only matches the anonymous user, and the * always matches all users.

Notice that the named user accounts are shown in full notation: `Domain\UserName`. If the application is being tested on a server that is not a member of a domain (i.e., it's a member of a workgroup), you should substitute the domain name with the machine name. For example:

```
<authorization>
    <deny users="?" /> <!— Deny anonymous users —>
    <deny users="MyServer\Guest" />
    <allow users="*" /> <!— Allow all users —>
</authorization>
```

The authorization scheme we've defined in this example is application-wide; although, as we'll see in the ASP.NET Authorization section below, you can control permissions at a variety of different levels. You'll also see how to apply permissions by group memberships rather than for individual users.

Using Passport Authentication

The Windows Authentication provider is very much targeted at intranet applications because it relies on users having valid domain accounts. It is convenient, however, since it requires very little work on your part to implement it.

Passport Authentication provides a similar service for Internet applications, giving you an almost ready-to-use authentication model that you can integrate with relative ease. Passport Authentication uses the well-publicized Microsoft Passport service to perform authentication. It works on the principle that users establish a single, central set of credentials that can be used to authenticate on any Passport-compliant site.

Passport Authentication uses a ticketing scheme, where the ticket is provided by the central Passport service once the user has logged on. The Passport Authentication provider simply checks to see whether each request contains a valid ticket; if not, it redirects the request to the central Passport login facility. If login is successful, a ticket is added to the request and Passport redirects the request back to the original URL.

Currently, the ticket takes the form of a transient cookie that is held by the browser and passed to the Web server with each request. The content of the cookie is encrypted using a triple-DES algorithm (tough enough to keep the military happy) and SSL is used during the login process itself. Passport is a constantly evolving service, so by the time you read this it may have changed once again.

Before you can implement Passport Authentication for your application, you must first visit `www.passport.com` to download, install, and configure the Passport SDK. You may have to pay a fee to obtain the SDK, although at the time of writing it was free of charge. Similarly, you may incur ongoing charges to make use of Passport Authentication, or it may continue to be provided for free. These are decisions that will be made by Microsoft; we urge you to visit the Passport Web site to check the current technical, contractual, and financial requirements before you commit to implementing this authentication scheme.

Using Forms Authentication

The most exciting authentication model provided by ASP.NET is *Forms Authentication* because it delivers many of the benefits of an integrated authentication scheme, but still gives you the flexibility and control to determine exactly how users are verified. More importantly though, Forms Authentication is not dependent on verifying users against a Windows security database, but allows you to define your own list of users and their credentials. This can take any form from a SQL Database to an XML document.

Forms Authentication uses a similar ticketing scheme to Passport; but, whereas the Passport provider always redirects the browser to a centralized Passport login, Forms Authentication allows you to define how and where the checks are performed. You would normally do this through a customized Login form, but with Forms Authentication you get to choose what credentials are used and how they are verified. Having checked the user's details, your code drops a special Forms Authentication cookie to the user's browser, which is then detected in subsequent requests.

This approach is really attractive because it doesn't rely on any specific client-side features or functionality; it works with any cookie-enabled browser or operating system, and the authentication form can be completely designed and created as required. The one thing you do need to ensure is that the Login form is protected by SSL, otherwise all verification details entered by the user will be sent in clear text.

Enabling Forms Authentication

Enable Forms Authentication by editing Web.config and setting the `<authentication>` element to a value of **Forms**. In addition, you must also create a `<forms>` element that defines the name and location of the Login form that will perform the verification. For example:

```
<authentication mode="Forms" >
    <forms loginUrl = "logon.aspx" />
</authentication>
```

Further attributes can be specified for the `<forms>` element, including the form name. This will set the name used to identify the authentication cookie, and is important if you have several Web applications on the same server that all use Forms Authentication. If all applications share the same cookie name, users who log into one application will automatically be logged into all others; if they each have a unique cookie name, users will be prompted to login separately to each application.

The next step is to ensure that Anonymous access is permitted from IIS (other authentication schemes should be disabled). Make sure that the anonymous user is denied access to the application by placing a `<deny>` element in the `<authorization>` section:

```
<authorization>
    <deny users="?" />
</authorization>
```

You might be a little confused by this—we've permitted Anonymous access to IIS, but blocked it in ASP.NET. What actually happens is that IIS passes all requests to ASP.NET using Anonymous access, but ASP.NET then uses its own mechanism to control access from that point on. As far as IIS is concerned, the request was processed successfully—after all, ASP.NET didn't reject it. ASP.NET manages subsequent authentication by checking for the authentication cookie. If the cookie is passed from the browser, the request is accepted and passed on for authorization checking. If no cookie is passed by the browser (or it's invalid or has expired), then ASP.NET redirects the request to the Web Form previously specified in the `loginUrl` attribute.

Creating a Logon Form

Your next task is to build the Logon form that will perform validation of the user's credentials. For most purposes, this will require that the user enters details such as a username and a password that can be checked against a list, usually from a database. Cast your mind back to Chapter 1 and you'll remember that we built a very basic Logon.aspx form consisting of two TextBoxes, a Button, and some static HTML. Figure 11-14 shows how this appeared.

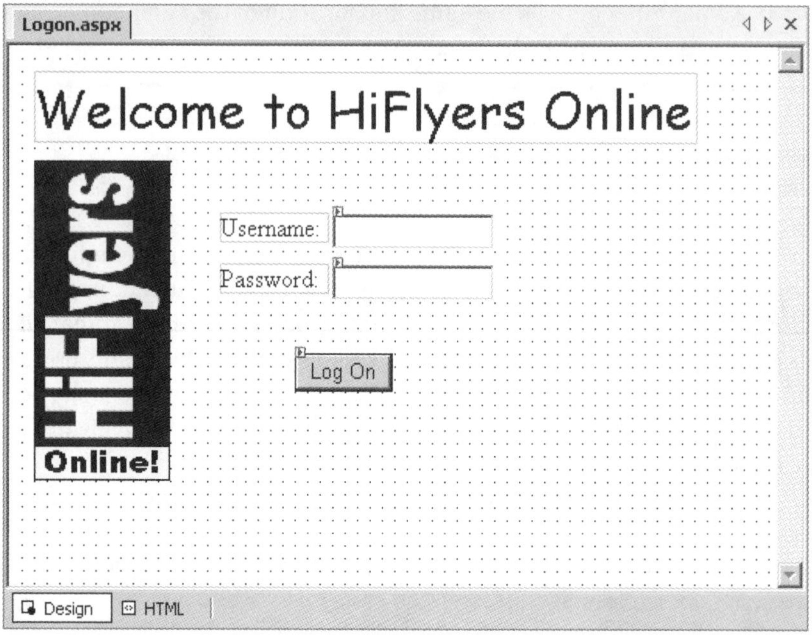

Figure 11-14. Application Logon form

We now need to code the **Log On** button to perform the check against the entered details. To start, we'll add an `Imports` statement to the top of the code-behind module:

```
Imports System.Web.Security
```

This namespace contains the FormsAuthentication class that we need to use to indicate that the verification was successful. The code to perform the check is placed in the `btnLogon_Click` event handler:

```
Private Sub btnLogon_Click(ByVal sender As System.Object, _
                ByVal e As System.EventArgs) Handles btnLogon.Click
    If txtUsername.Text = "user" And txtPassword.Text = "password" Then
        FormsAuthentication.RedirectFromLoginPage(txtUsername.Text, False)
    Else
        txtPassword.Text = String.Empty
    End If
End Sub
```

We've purposely kept the verification check simple so that you can concentrate on the authentication methods. All we're doing is checking the name and password against static entries; if they match, we'll accept that the user is valid. In a real-world application you are most likely to perform a check against database entries using a DataReader, DataSet, Command, or whatever technique is appropriate. However, if the user is authenticated, you still need to indicate to ASP.NET that the request should be accepted, and you do this by calling the `RedirectFromLoginPage` method on the FormsAuthentication class. The `RedirectFromLoginPage` method performs two tasks:

- It creates the authentication ticket (as a cookie) and adds it to the HTTP response that is sent to the client browser. This cookie contains only the cookie name and the user name; it does not contain any of the other authentication credentials.
- It redirects to the original page that the user requested when first accessing the application. The original URL was automatically appended to the querystring when ASP.NET redirected the unauthenticated request to the login page. All that the `RedirectFromLoginPage` method does is to read this value and perform another redirection.

Notice that the `RedirectFromLoginPage` method takes two parameters. The first is the name of the user, so that individual cookies can be maintained for different users if the computer is shared. The second parameter is a boolean value that indicates whether the cookie should be permanent; if you pass a value of `True`, the cookie will be made permanent and the user will not have to authenticate against the application in the future. This is often used to provide a "Remember Me" type feature.

The FormsAuthentication class supports several other methods for managing the authentication process, including the following:

- **SignOut** removes the authentication ticket from the browser cookie, and so ends the authenticated session. If the user tries to navigate to another page in the application they will be redirected to the Login page again.
- **GetAuthCookie** simply creates a cookie representing the authentication ticket. It does not attach it to the response, nor does it perform the redirect.
- **SetAuthCookie** creates the cookie and attaches it to the response, but does not perform the redirection.
- **GetRedirectUrl** returns the full URL of the page originally requested.

The last three methods allow you to exert greater control over the authentication process by manually managing both the creation of the cookie and the redirection. Of course, if you don't want to do this, just call `RedirectFromLoginPage` to perform both tasks in one go.

Testing the Security

Having completed the Logon.aspx file and made the changes to Web.config, you're ready to test the security. Build the project to make sure everything is up-to-date, then right-click **Default.aspx** and choose **View in Browser**. The Forms Authentication provider identifies that we are not currently authenticated and redirects to the Logon.aspx page, as shown in Figure 11-15.

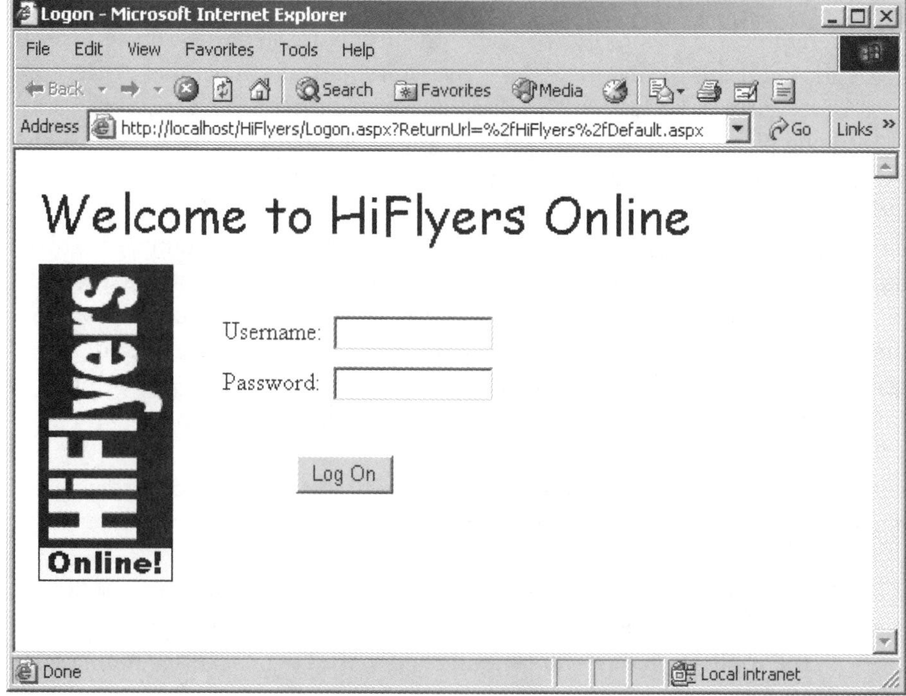

Figure 11-15. Logon form in action

Look at the address bar and you'll see that the original URL has been appended to the querystring for the current page. The `FormsAuthentication` class uses this information to perform its redirection if authentication is successful.

If we provide valid credentials and click the **Log On** button, then we are taken to the page that we originally requested. If we continue to navigate through the application using the same browser window, the authentication remains in force and we will not be prompted to login again.

Where the scheme really starts to shine is when we close the browser and then subsequently return to the application. For example:

1. Having logged in, navigate to **Page1.aspx**.

2. Set a Bookmark on the page or add it as a Favorites entry.

3. Close the browser.

4. Open the browser, then try navigating to the bookmarked page.

If you've followed these steps, you should've been taken to the Logon.aspx page, rather than to Page1.aspx. This is because the authentication cookie that we are creating is transient, so it is cleared when the browser is closed. When you tried to access Page1.aspx after reopening the browser, the Forms Authentication module checked the request and found no valid authentication cookie, so it triggered the authentication process all over again.

We've now implemented a powerful authentication mechanism, which automatically detects authenticated and unauthenticated requests and handles them appropriately. It also takes care of remembering the original requested URL and redirects to it after a successful login. Finally, if you implement SSL along with Forms Authentication, it really is secure; while no security measures can be 100 percent effective, this approach comes pretty close.

ASP.NET Authorization

The authentication techniques discussed in the previous section allow you to identify *who* the user is, but authorization techniques are required to determine *what* they can do. Authorization can be implemented declaratively (through Web.config) or programmatically at runtime. *Declarative authorization* is the simplest to apply and can be readily modified by administrators. *Programmatic authorization* tends to be more granular, giving you more specific control over which features can be accessed.

Declarative Authorization

The `<authorization>` section of Web.config is used to define the list of users or groups that are permitted or denied access. These assignments can be application-wide or location-specific. The ASP.NET authorization terminology is a little different from that used within Windows; the term "users" retains its standard meaning, but instead of referring to "groups," ASP.NET uses the term "roles."

When using Windows Authentication, "groups" and "roles" are equivalent; however, if you're using Forms Authentication, then "roles" takes on a slightly different meaning.

Authorization and Windows Authentication

The authorization entries differ slightly depending on the authentication provider you use. For example, when using Windows Authentication, the user and group names must match those defined in the user account database for the domain. Within the `<allow>` and `<deny>` elements, the user and group names need to be prefixed with a domain name. For example:

```
<authorization>
    <deny users="?" />
    <deny users="domain/badguy" />
    <deny roles="domain/guests" />
    <allow roles="domain/powerusers" />
    <allow roles="domain/administrators" />
    <deny users="*" />
</authorization>
```

This section blocks the anonymous user, as well as a specific named user (**BadGuy**). It blocks all members of the **Guests** group, then allows members of the **PowerUsers** and **Administrators** groups. Finally, all other users are denied access. The sequence is important in this section because it is traversed top to bottom until a match is found. For example, if a user was a member of Guests and PowerUsers (odd, but possible), then they would be denied access because Guests occurs first in the sequence.

Authorization and Forms Authentication

If you're using Forms Authentication, you might question the need for further authorization checks. After all, if we've authenticated the user, then surely we want them to have access to the application. This all-or-nothing approach is fine for simple applications where you're only denying access to the anonymous user; however, as your applications grow and become more sophisticated, there's a strong chance that you'll have some features that are accessible to all users, while others are more restricted. It's at this point that you need to consider authorizing individual users' requests for specific files; you would use location-specific authorization (see the next section) to do this. Before we get into the details of location-specific settings though, let's start at the beginning and look at establishing application-wide authorization.

One of the first things you'll realize is that authorization settings are different when Forms Authentication is used, since there is no concept of a domain. Therefore, you only need to specify the user or group name. For example:

```
<authorization>
    <deny users="?" />
    <deny users="guest" />
    <allow users="administrator" />
    <allow roles="powerusers" />
    <deny users="*" />
</authorization>
```

In this example, we blocked the anonymous user and a named **Guest** user, but then allowed a named **Administrator** user and a group called **PowerUsers**. But where do the concepts of named users and groups fit with Forms Authentication? After all, we are providing our own verification, rather than using anything the operating system provides.

Usernames are quite simply the names that you pass to the `RedirectFromLoginPage` method when the authentication succeeds. ASP.NET automatically checks the username in the Web.config file to determine their permissions.

Groups are a little trickier. When using Windows Authentication, we have a ready-made definition of a group based on the Groups used in Windows Security. However, in Forms Authentication we are deliberately not using any built-in security scheme, but we haven't yet established any form of group membership or even any form of group structure. The solution is to add some code to one of the event handlers in Global.asax—the `AuthenticateRequest` event. This event is raised when the authentication provider attempts to authenticate a user; it's raised even if the authentication fails. We must add code to the handler that establishes group membership at runtime. For example:

```
Sub Application_AuthenticateRequest(ByVal sender As Object, ByVal e As EventArgs)
    'Is the user currently authenticated?
    If IsNothing(HttpContext.Current.User) Then
        'No they're not - Do nothing since the authentication
        'provider will prevent further access
    ElseIf HttpContext.Current.User.Identity.AuthenticationType = "Forms" Then
        'The user was authenticated via the Forms provider

        'Record the current identity
        Dim idCur As System.Web.Security.FormsIdentity
```

```
            idCur = HttpContext.Current.User.Identity

            'Assign the user to the relevant Roles (groups)
            Dim strRoles() As String
            Select Case LCase(idCur.Name)
                Case "user"
                    ReDim strRoles(0)
                    strRoles(0) = "powerusers"
                Case "guest"
                    ReDim strRoles(1)
                    strRoles(0) = "users"
                    strRoles(1) = "guests"
                Case "administrator"
                    ReDim strRoles(1)
                    strRoles(0) = "users"
                    strRoles(1) = "administrators"
                Case Else
                    ReDim strRoles(0)
                    strRoles(0) = "guests"
            End Select

            'Assign a new principal to the current user, using these roles
            HttpContext.Current.User = New _
                    System.Security.Principal.GenericPrincipal(idCur, strRoles)
        End If
    End Sub
```

This routine first checks to see whether the user was authenticated by testing the User object. If the user is valid, the routine then uses Forms Authentication to ensure that they were authenticated before moving on. It then records their current identity, using an instance of a FormsIdentity class, which represents all of the information that we would know about a user authenticated in this way. We then manually create an array of strings, each of which represents a group name. The names are completely arbitrary, but they should match the Roles that you defined in Web.config. In a real application, this group membership would probably be read from a database or other information store.

The routine concludes by replacing the original User object with a new one derived from GenericPrincipal. When the new user is created, we pass the original Identity (so that we retain the authenticated security settings), as well as the array of group names. ASP.NET now considers the user to be a member of the specified groups.

The reason we need to add this functionality is that the Forms Authentication module is intentionally simple; it's only intended to authenticate users and provide them with a user ID. If you want to support group structures and membership, you need to provide your own code to do it.

TIP *For convenience, we've created the groups when the request is authenticated. In practice, we would recommend that you create groups when the application starts (by adding the code to the* `Application_Start` *event) and then use the* `AuthenticateRequest` *event to simply assign users to the relevant groups.*

Location-Specific Authorization

Any of the settings in Web.config can be made location-specific in two ways:

- Defining a `<Location>` element containing the specific settings
- Creating a new Web.config in a subdirectory

We introduced both of these techniques when we discussed ViewState security earlier in the chapter. You'll find that you can also apply the same techniques to authorization. For example, the following extract from Web.config would allow public access to all files in a Web application except AdminsOnly.aspx, which is restricted to members of the Administrators group:

```
<?xml version="1.0" encoding="utf-8"?>
<configuration>
    <location path="AdminsOnly.aspx">
        <system.web>
            <authorization>
                <deny users="?"/>
                <allow roles="domain\Administrators"/>
                <deny users="*"/>
            </authorization>
        </system.web>
    </location>

    <system.web>
        <authentication mode="Forms">
            <forms loginUrl="Logon.aspx" />
        </authentication>
```

```
            <allow users="*"/> <!- Allow all users ->
        </authorization>
        .
        . Rest of Web.config
    </system.web>
</configuration>
```

Notice that even though Forms Authentication is enabled for the application, it has no effect for most pages because we have *not* denied access to the anonymous user. Only when a request for AdminsOnly.aspx is made will the user be prompted to Login.

Programmatic Authorization

Declarative authorization works well for many scenarios and requirements, but it is likely that you will need a finer degree of control in some cases. For example, we can use declarative security to prevent access to a specific Web Form, but it makes sense to hide any buttons or links from unauthorized users to prevent them even knowing about the page. To do this, we need *programmatic authorization.*

Programmatic authorization requires that you know who the user is and what their permissions are. You may be tempted to create your own database of users, groups, and permissions and perform customized lookups against the data whenever you need to check authorization. However, we've found that our previously outlined approach for assigning users to groups when they are authenticated works very well. This code is associated with an application-level event and so cannot be skipped or bypassed; it also allows access to the declarative security features in Web.config.

The only questions remain:

- How do I know who the user is?
- How can I find what groups they're a member of?

Fortunately, ASP.NET makes it very easy for us to answer both of these questions.

Identity

The individual details for the current user are exposed through a User object, which, in turn, is exposed as a property of the Page.Context object. If you want to determine the username, just reference the following from within a Web Form's class:

```
Me.Context.User.Identity.Name
```

You can also shorten this to just

```
User.Identity.Name
```

If you wanted to perform a check to see whether the current user was named Administrator, you could use the following:

```
If User.Identity.Name = "Adminstrator" Then
    'Administrator-specific code here
End If
```

Group Membership

The User object also allows us to determine group membership through its `IsInRole` method. This takes the name of the group as a parameter and returns a boolean result. For example:

```
If User.IsInRole("administrators") Then
    btnAdminOptions.Visible = True
Else
    btnAdminOptions.Visible = False
End If
```

By performing checks at the group and individual levels, you will be able to implement a flexible and adaptable security system that not only protects the application from misuse and unauthorized access, but also shows the users only those features to which they should have access.

Securing Static Content

So far, we've dealt almost exclusively with securing active content—files that are processed through the HTTP Runtime. If we want to apply the same security model to static files—such as .htm and .gif files—then you need to make some additional changes.

Fortunately these changes are extremely simple. Just tell IIS to pass requests for these file types through the ASP.NET; you can do this through the Application Configuration dialog as follows:

1. Launch **Internet Services Manager** and locate the virtual directory containing the application. In our example, this will be **HiFlyers**.

2. Right-click the entry in the folder tree and select **Properties**.

3. Switch to the **Directory** tab and click the **Configuration** button.

4. The **Application Configuration** dialog is displayed (see Figure 11-16) showing the current application mappings.

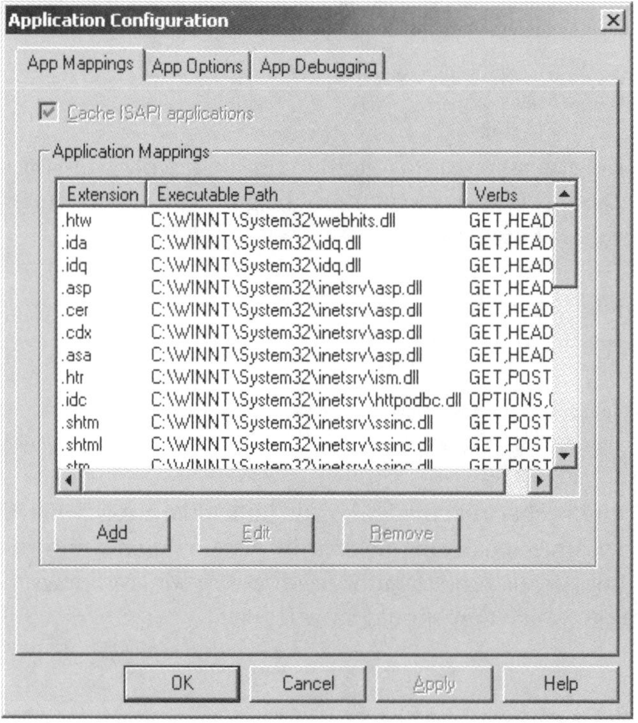

Figure 11-16. Application Configuration dialog

5. Click the **Add** button to create a new mapping. You'll need to provide details for the Executable that will process the requests. This should be the aspnet_isapi.dll, and its full path will be similar to the following:

```
C:\WINNT\Microsoft.NET\Framework\v1.0.3705\aspnet_isapi.dll
```

TIP *You can copy the executable from one of the other ASP.NET entries by clicking the* ***Edit*** *button to display the current settings.*

6. You must also specify the extension and the verbs that will be processed. Figure 11-17 shows how the completed dialog will appear.

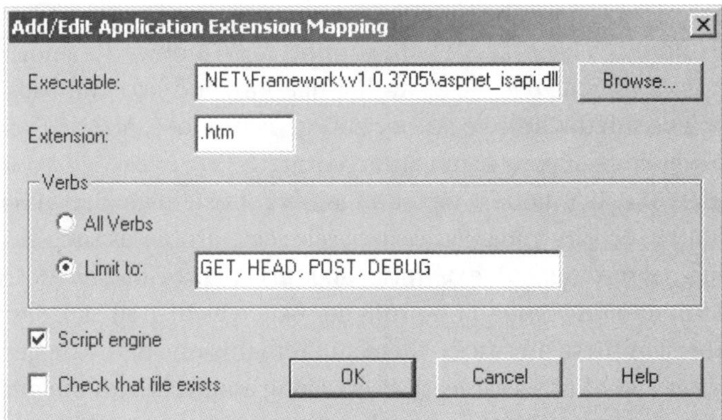

Figure 11-17. Adding an Application Mapping

If you now add a standard .htm file to the HiFlyers application and browse it, you should be redirected to the Logon page as the request is passed through ASP.NET. If you change the file extension to .html and repeat the exercise, you won't be prompted to log on because the request is still processed by IIS. To truly secure static content, you'll also need to map a number of extensions in this way, including the following:

- .htm
- .html
- .gif

- .jpg
- .jpeg
- .js
- .css

Of course, each additional file type that ASP.NET must process adds to its workload; fortunately, static files are not as "heavyweight" as .aspx files. Instead, all of these additional file types will be handled by the System.Web.StaticFileHandler HTTP Handler, since neither Web.config nor Machine.config. contain explicit handler declarations.

Summary

ASP.NET supports some powerful security features that are a major improvement over those offered by classic ASP. With support for Windows, Passport, and Forms Authentication, you can choose an authentication model to fit most situations. When coupled with the flexible authorization techniques, ASP.NET allows you to exert whatever control your application requires.

However, ASP.NET alone is not sufficiently robust; instead, you need to take a broad view of security and ensure that you tackle problems such as encryption, file snooping, and so on. Some of these facilities are provided by ASP.NET, while others are inherent in companion products—such as IIS and SQL Server.

Despite all of these advances, there still remains one of the biggest threats to security—one ASP.NET is unable to do anything about. It's not the packet sniffer, nor the super computers that can crack encryption in record time—it's the humble Post-it note. Look at any user's desktop and chances are you'll find at least one carefully positioned Post-it note containing a password and, in most cases, details of the resource its protecting. Until there's a change in attitude among the user community, security threats will always be that little bit more difficult to deal with.

CHAPTER 12

Designing Web Applications

Introducing Application Structure and Design

Understanding Global.asax

Centralizing Error Management

Controlling Navigation

Using Framesets

Using Form, QueryString, and Cookies

Managing State

Ouput Caching

WE'VE COVERED A LOT of ground in this book so far, and we've addressed many detailed topics from Web Forms and Web controls through to architecture and security. All of this material is useful stuff—it's nuts-and-bolts programming that you'll be using day in and day out. However, in addition to this, chances are you'll have other responsibilities too, and sooner or later one of these will be application design. That's what this chapter is all about—how to pull together the different concepts, strategies, and techniques we've covered so far to create a complete application.

If you've been involved in application design before, you'll know it's not a trivial topic, and you're probably wondering how we plan to cover it in a single chapter. To be honest, we're not, or rather, we won't try and cover *everything* related to design. Instead we'll start with an overview of the requirements for Web application structure and design, then move on to some practical design topics such as structured error handling, navigation, interacting with the user, and managing state. We've mentioned many of these topics in earlier chapters, but as you'll see, this chapter provides the details.

Introducing Application Structure and Design

So far, we've said relatively little about how to structure Web Applications. In truth, there has been enough to do, concentrating on making sense of the way that ASP.NET works. However, for all but the simplest systems, the design and structure of Web Applications is as important as the design and structure of any other application, and we'll spend a significant amount of time in this chapter and in Chapter 13 focusing on these issues.

To provide some context for this topic, it's worth spending a moment reflecting on what has been learned about traditional (that is, non-Web) applications over recent years. For much of the 1990s, many developers worked on traditional client/server systems, which these days are often referred to as *two-tier* or even *fat* client systems because much of the processing involved in these systems takes place on client computers. Figure 12-1 illustrates this type of design.

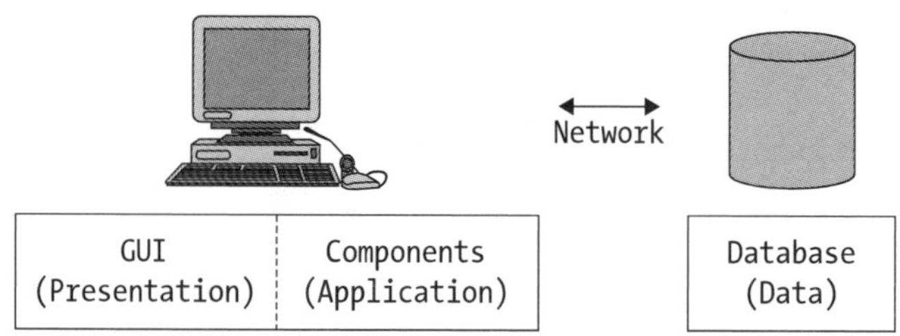

Figure 12-1. Traditional client/server system

It's clear from Figure 12-1 that the client program performs all the user interface and business (or application) functionality, while the database simply serves the results of SQL statements. This design works well for relatively small systems (up to a few dozen users), but it starts to perform badly and becomes difficult to manage as the number of users increases.

One improvement to this design is to make greater use of database stored procedures. Stored procedures shift some of the application functionality to the server, thereby making the client "thinner." Using stored procedures in place of raw SQL is a good way to improve application performance and manageability, but it doesn't go far enough for an enterprise-scale system. Instead, enterprise systems typically adopt a three-tiered approach (or become *n-tiered* as more tiers are introduced to manage the complexity of a system).

Figure 12-2 shows a classic three-tier system, where client programs contain only GUI processing logic and simple input validation code. All the real work takes place on a shared *application server,* which talks to the database (preferably via stored procedures) to read and update data. In the days before .NET, this *middle-tier* application server typically used products such as COM+ or Microsoft Transaction Server (MTS) to make the middle-tier programmer's life easier.

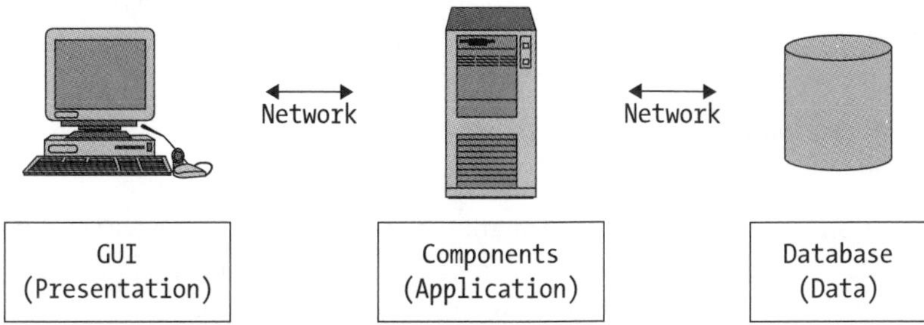

Figure 12-2. Three-tier system design

That's the history lesson over—what does this mean for ASP.NET programmers? Well, Web developers typically get very smug at this stage and point out that they're already using a three-tier design because the Web server is the middle tier and the browser is the GUI presentation layer, so by definition their programs are enterprise-scale programs. Admittedly there is some truth in this claim, but we'd like to take a more radical view.

When you write a desktop program, the fiddly code you create to read and write data in text boxes and list boxes is without a doubt user interface (or presentation) code. No one would claim otherwise. But if this is the case for desktop programs, then surely most of the code in an .aspx.vb file (which is largely concerned with processing Web controls) is also user interface code? Okay, it runs on the server, but functionally speaking, it is GUI programming. With this point in mind, which of Figures 12-1 and 12-2 is most like the simple Web Application designs we've been working with so far?

This question turns out to be harder to answer than it first appears. There's no doubt that the browser does some presentation work—it renders HTML on the screen, handles some input details, and maybe even executes some client-side script. But it is just as fair to say that the code in the .aspx.vb file is also doing user interface processing as well. The truth is that the task of handling the GUI aspects of an ASP.NET Web Application is *split* between the browser and the .aspx.vb code. Figure 12-3 illustrates this architecture.

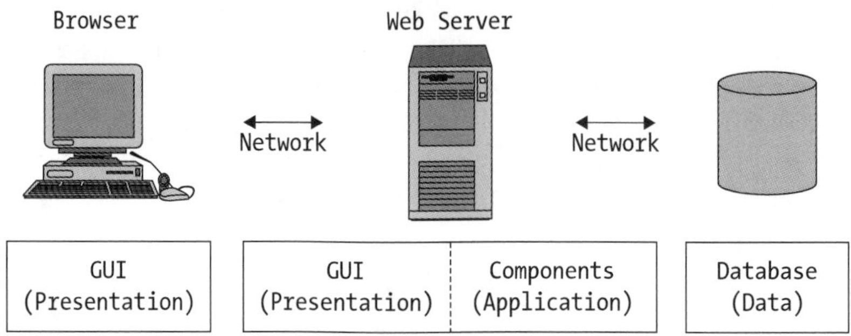

Figure 12-3. A simple Web Application

Our point is this: If you ignore the role of the browser in Figure 12-3, what you have left is the traditional client/server design you saw back in Figure 12-1. All the code that runs on the Web server can be viewed as a *fat client*.

We want to stress that there's nothing wrong with this architecture—at least for small- to medium-sized applications. However, you'll get a cleaner design if you separate out the application functionality from the GUI functionality (which is the code that processes Web controls) and place it in separate components. To create a truly enterprise-scale system design, you might even consider placing

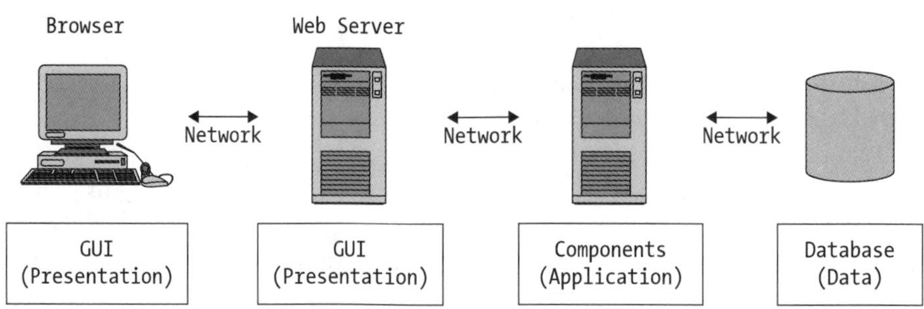

Figure 12-4. Enterprise Web Application

the application logic on a separate server from the presentation logic, by making use of Web Services (see Chapter 14) or .NET Remoting, as shown in Figure 12-4.

For the largest applications, this type of design provides the greatest flexibility for all the reasons that n-tier design offers over client/server design in traditional applications. The key point to remember is that the code you write to process Web controls is actually "client code" as far as the rest of your system is concerned. The fact that GUI processing is actually shared between the browser and your .aspx pages shouldn't affect how you design components or partition application logic between components and stored procedures.

To conclude this section, let's identify some of the core guidelines for ASP.NET Web Application design:

- **Scalability**: Identify the scale of the application. If you're building a department-level application, then you can afford to keep the overall architecture simple. There may be good reason for adopting a component-based design, but there's little need for load-balancing and other sophistications. However, if the application will be enterprise level or public facing, you'd be well advised to consider scalability as a core requirement from the outset. Chapter 13 deals with scalability in detail.

- **Performance**: Be aware of the performance that your application will offer. Users are generally intolerant of slow applications of any type, and Web applications are no exception. You must consider performance from the start of the project, as it's nearly impossible to optimize an application that's constrained by poor design. If your target audience will be working with slow link communications (for example, mobile, analog, or ISDN dialup connections), you should pay special attention to the amount of data passed between the server and the client. ViewState plays a big role in this respect, so make sure it's enabled only if needed.

- **Consistency**: Be consistent in your design. You can achieve code-based consistency through naming conventions, standard class structures, the use of interfaces, and so on. You also need to be consistent for the user, and you can achieve this by building repeated user interface features into Web User Controls or Web Custom Controls, by having standard navigation commands and techniques, and by applying cascading style sheets (CSS) to maintain a common style.

- **Code separation**: We would strongly advise you to adopt the Visual Studio .NET approach of separating code from content. Don't be tempted to place all your code into the .aspx file in classic ASP style; it's a move you'll regret when it comes to debugging and maintenance.

- **Maintaining state**: Take care with state management techniques. For scalable applications it's important to apply tight control to state management, and in particular the use of Session state is not recommended at all. We discuss state management in detail later in this chapter, and it's further addressed in Chapter 13 from the specific viewpoint of achieving scalability.

- **Security**: If you plan to secure the application in some way, determine security levels and requirements at the start of the project. It's difficult to "bolt on" security features to an existing application.

- **Client-side processing**: Consider offloading processing and state management to the client. You can use client-side script and DHTML to build a more responsive application, while client-side state management reduces the load on the server.

We could continue this list a lot further, but we'll stop here. The rest of this chapter builds on these topics and addresses the new ideas in some detail. As you read through the following sections, keep in mind that all of the techniques are possibilities rather than out-and-out recommendations. Depending on the type, scale, and target-audience of your application, you'll want to apply some, but probably not all, of what follows.

Understanding Global.asax

We've mentioned Global.asax several times in preceding chapters, but now it's time to take a more thorough look at it and see just what role it plays. Global.asax is optional, although by default Visual Studio .NET will create an empty file for you in each new Web Application. The file can take the form of a single .asax file, or it can be comprised of an .asax file with a corresponding .asax.vb code-behind module. As with all Web Application components, Visual Studio .NET uses a separate code-behind module, so it's this structure we'll discuss here. If Global.asax is present, it must reside in the application's virtual root directory, although its code can be compiled into the application's .dll.

As with other Web Application components, Global.asax is compiled at runtime into a class. Its base class is System.Web.HttpApplication, which is specified using an `Inherits` statement at the top of the class definition. The main purpose of Global.asax is to enable you to handle application-level events, such as those raised by the HttpApplication instance that's processing the current request or by any of the HTTP Modules in the pipeline. Chapter 10 introduced these events, and Chapter 11 showed an example that used the `AuthenticateRequest` event. For completeness, we'll summarize the events again, beginning with the events raised at the start of the page-processing cycle:

- BeginRequest
- AuthenticateRequest
- AuthorizeRequest
- ResolveRequestCache

- AcquireRequestState
- PreRequestHandlerExecute

When the processing of the page content is complete, there are a number of further events that could be raised:

- PostRequestHandlerExecute
- ReleaseRequestState
- UpdateRequestCache
- EndRequest

Finally, there are three non-deterministic events that may be raised at any stage of the page-processing cycle:

- Error
- PreSendRequestContent
- PreSendRequestHeaders

Synchronous Application Events

You can provide a handler for any of these events using the standard `Handles` clause suffixed to the procedure definition. If you do this, the event handler will be called synchronously—that is, the executing thread will wait for the event handler to complete before continuing. If you're new to multithreaded programming, then you will probably find this the easiest model to use. For example:

```
Private Sub MyAuthenticateRequestHandler(ByVal sender As Object, _
                ByVal e As System.EventArgs) Handles MyBase.AuthenticateRequest
    ' Code here
End Sub
```

You can also handle the same events using the notation `Application_<event name>` for the procedure name. Once again, if coded this way, the event handler will be called synchronously. For example, the following procedure will handle the `AuthenticateRequest` event:

```
Sub Application_AuthenticateRequest(ByVal sender As Object, ByVal e As EventArgs)
    ' Code here
End Sub
```

If you use both methods to create two separate handlers for the same event in Global.asax, ASP.NET calls each in turn. However, the order is non-deterministic, so you can't predict which handler will be called first.

TIP *You can also handle events from the HttpApplication class asynchronously so that the executing thread is not blocked by your code. If you want to explore this aspect of event handling further, we recommend you first become familiar with the issues surrounding multithreaded pro gramming. A recommended read to get started is* Moving to VB .NET: Strategies, Concepts, and Code *by Dan Appleman (Apress, 2001). However, be warned that multithreaded code is much more difficult to test and debug and that for many tasks there's little to be gained from the added complexity.*

Application_Start and Application_End

Two special application-level events that can be handled in Global.asax are `Application_Start` and `Application_End`. These are not "regular" events exposed by the HttpApplication class, but instead have been retained from classic ASP without being mapped to a class.

The syntax for these events is simple:

```
Sub Application_Start(ByVal sender As Object, ByVal e As EventArgs)
    ' Fires when the application is started
End Sub

Sub Application_End(ByVal sender As Object, ByVal e As EventArgs)
    ' Fires when the application ends
End Sub
```

The `Application_Start` event is raised when the first HttpApplication object is instantiated in the application. This will be triggered by the application receiving its first request from a client browser. The `Application_End` event is raised when the last user session for the application terminates. You'll see more about sessions later in this chapter.

Don't confuse the `Application_Start` and the `BeginRequest` events; `Application_Start` occurs only once in the lifetime of the entire application, whereas `BeginRequest` occurs at the start of every request received by the application. Similarly, `EndRequest` occurs once for each request, whereas `Application_End` occurs only once.

NOTE *You can't access many intrinsic objects and features during the* `Application_Start` *event, as they'll not yet have been initialized. For example, attempting to refer to* `Session`, `Request`, *or* `Response` *will cause an error. You can reliably access the* `Application` *and* `Cache` *objects, however.*

Typically, the `Application_Start` event will be used for initializing application-wide settings, resources, and data, and `Application_End` will be used to release those same objects. For example, you may want to keep track of the number of users currently in the application, and you could easily do that with an Application variable initialized in the `Application_Start` event:

```
Sub Application_Start(ByVal sender As Object, ByVal e As EventArgs)
    Application("NumUsers") = 0
End Sub
```

We'll return to the topic of Application variables later in this chapter and discuss them more fully.

Session_Start and Session_End

Just as there are application-level handlers for the start and end points in the application's lifecycle, you can also create session-level handlers. The concept of a session should be familiar to most readers; it begins when a client browser sends its first request to the Web server, and it ends when the Web server has received no requests during a predefined time, known as the *timeout period.*

To code the handlers for the session events, you would use the following definitions:

```
Sub Session_Start(ByVal sender As Object, ByVal e As EventArgs)
    ' Fires when the session is started
End Sub
```

```
Sub Session_End(ByVal sender As Object, ByVal e As EventArgs)
    ' Fires when the session ends
End Sub
```

You'll most likely use session handlers for initializing Session state values, although as discussed later, you need to be careful about using Session state in larger applications. You may also want to access Application state values as well. For example, to manage the user counter established previously in Application state, you could use the following:

```
Sub Session_Start(ByVal sender As Object, ByVal e As EventArgs)
    Application.Lock()
    Application("NumUsers") += 1
    Application.UnLock()
End Sub

Sub Session_End(ByVal sender As Object, ByVal e As EventArgs)
    Application.Lock()
    Application("NumUsers") -= 1
    Application.UnLock()
End Sub
```

Notice that you had to `Lock` and `Unlock` the `Application` object during these events. This is required because the Application object is not thread-safe and could potentially be accessed simultaneously by two separate threads in these code blocks. You'll examine this more fully in the "Managing State" section later.

HTTP Module-Generated Events

The `Session_Start` and `Session_End` event handlers are actually examples of how you can handle another category of events: HTTP Module events. The `Start` and `End` events are raised by the Session state HTTP Module (System.Web.SessionState.SessionStateModule) and are handled using the `<ModuleName>_<EventName>` syntax. The ModuleName is determined by the `name` attribute defined in the <httpModules> element of Machine.config. For example, in the following extract you can see the names for the HTTP Modules defined as `Session`, `WindowsAuthentication`, and `FormsAuthentication`:

```
<add
    name="Session"
    type="System.Web.SessionState.SessionStateModule" />
<add
```

```
    name="WindowsAuthentication"
    type="System.Web.Security.WindowsAuthenticationModule" />
<add
    name="FormsAuthentication"
    type="System.Web.Security.FormsAuthenticationModule" />
```

Event handlers for the corresponding modules will be named `Session_<EventName>`, `WindowsAuthentication_<EventName>`, and `FormsAuthentication_<EventName>`.

You can determine what events are raised by each HTTP Module by examining the definition of the class using the Object Browser. Table 12-1 lists the events raised by the standard HTTP Modules.

Table 12-1. HTTP Module Events

MODULE	EVENTS
OutputCache	None. Callbacks used instead. See the "Output Caching" section later.
Session	`Start`, `End`.
WindowsAuthentication	`OnAuthenticate`.
FormsAuthentication	`OnAuthenticate`.
PassportAuthentication	`OnAuthenticate`.
UrlAuthorization	None.
FileAuthorization	None.

Object Tag Declarations

As well as event handling, you can also use Global.asax to declare application-wide, session-wide, or request-wide objects. You do this by adding tags into the .asax file (not the code-behind module). The syntax for these tags will be one of the following:

```
<object id="id" runat="server" scope="scope" class="Class Name">
<object id="id" runat="server" scope="scope" progid="COM ProgID"/>
<object id="id" runat="server" scope="scope" classid="COM ClassID"/>
```

The first definition uses the `class` attribute to create an instance of a .NET class. The second and third forms will create an instance of a COM object, using either its human-readable ProgID (such as `ADODB.Recordset`) or its less meaningful but more accurate ClassID (such as {00000535-0000-0010-8000-00AA006D2EA4}).

The scope attribute defines the scope and lifetime of the object. Possible values are pipeline to specify that the object is available only to the current HTTP request, session to specify that the object will be maintained in Session state, and application to specify that the object will be maintained in Application state. The default is pipeline, which is also probably the most often required setting. See the "Managing State" section for a further discussion on state issues.

For example, you'll often create utility classes to perform support tasks such as error logging, auditing, and so on. You can create an instance of one of these classes using an object tag in Global.asax so that the object is always available. If you wanted to declare an application-scope instance of a class called ErrorManager, you would enter the following object tag into Global.asax:

```
<object id="ErrLog" runat="Server"
                scope="Application" class="HiFlyers.ErrorManager"/>
```

You can then refer to this object through the StaticObjects collection of the Application object, so to call a method named LogError you would use the following statement:

```
Application.StaticObjects("errlog").LogError( . . . )
```

This code relies on late binding, so it assumes that Option Strict hasn't been turned on. If Option Strict has been enabled, you'll need to perform type conversion as follows:

```
CType(Application.StaticObjects("errlog"), ErrorManager).LogError( . . . )
```

So, what benefit do you get from using an object tag declaration? The main advantage is that the object is not only declared, but it's instantiated just before it's first used. This saves you from having to manually instantiate the object in the Application_Start event, and it also means that resources are only consumed once the object has actually been used. However, this *lazy creation* scheme comes at a penalty: performance. The Web Application must check before each reference to the object to determine whether it has been instantiated; this process is similar to that performed by classic VB applications when objects variables were declared As New.

Global.asax at Runtime

As mentioned at the start of this section, the Global.asax file is not required. If it's not found in the root directory for the application (even if it exists elsewhere), ASP.NET assumes there are no application or session event handlers defined.

If the file is present, then ASP.NET will automatically track any changes or modifications made to it. When it detects a change (for example, you edit Global.asax or copy in a new .dll for the application), it waits for all current requests to complete, raises the `Application_OnEnd` event, and then terminates the application. It then restarts the application and recompiles Global.asax, and then raises the `Application_OnStart` and `Session_OnStart` events when the next request is received. This process is generally quick and should introduce no perceptible delay or downtime to the user. However, any state in the Application or Cache objects is lost, as is any Session state held in process.

Centralizing Error Management

One of the weakest design aspects of classic ASP is its almost complete lack of support for error management. Developers have the choice of using `On Error Resume Next` within their code or creating and using Custom Errors through IIS, but neither approach is ideal.

Along with many other facets of Web development, ASP.NET has completely changed the way you manage errors within Web Applications. You now have the choice to handle errors at the procedure, page, or application level, and you can define custom error pages on a page-specific or application-wide basis.

When an error occurs, the framework will allow the most local error handling routine to deal with it. For example, if an error occurs within a `Try . . . Catch` block in code, the `Catch` statement will be invoked to deal with the exception. If an unhandled exception occurs in code, the page-level error handler will be invoked, or if none exists, the error will be passed to the application-level handler. Figure 12-5 shows this error management hierarchy.

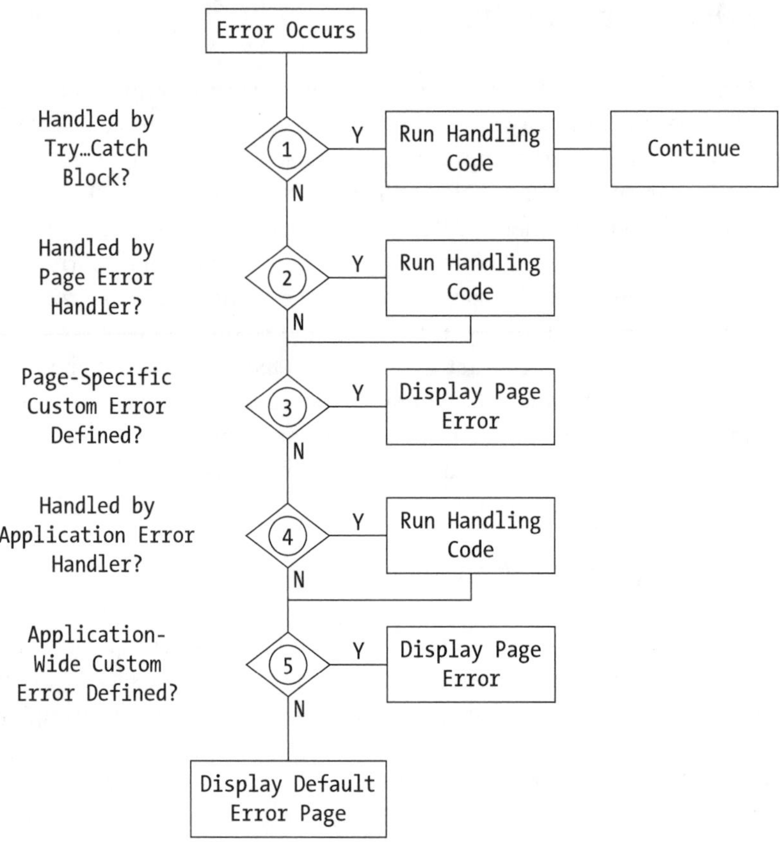

Figure 12-5. Error management process

Notice that if the error is trapped by a procedure-level `Try . . . Catch` block, then no further error handling code or features are checked. However, if no such handler is present then the error could be raised to *both* the page-level and application-level handlers. You'll look at each of these handlers and see how this behavior can be controlled.

Procedure Level

You can implement procedure-level error management using the structured exception handling features built into the VB .NET language. You do this by wrapping a Try . . . Catch block around a section of code to catch any exceptions that are raised. For example:

```
Private Sub btnCalc_Click(ByVal sender As System.Object, _
                ByVal e As System.EventArgs) Handles btnCalc.Click
    Try
        Dim intVal As Integer = Integer.Parse(txtEnter.Text)
        Dim intCalc As Integer = 10 / intVal

        lblDisplay.Text = "Result is " + intCalc.ToString
    Catch Exc As System.FormatException
        lblDisplay.Text = "Invalid numeric format"
    Catch Exc As System.OverflowException
        lblDisplay.Text = "Overflow - Number is too large"
    Catch Exc As Exception
        lblDisplay.Text = "Couldn't Calculate"
    End Try
End Sub
```

You can see that you're able to catch different types of exception, and each of the Catch blocks will be checked in turn until a class that matches the current exception is found. The final Catch block uses the base Exception class, so it'll respond to any exceptions that have not been matched previously.

Exception handling in .NET Web Applications is the same as in any other application type, so we won't go into any more detail at this point. For a review of exception handling and other core VB .NET language features, refer to Appendix C.

Page Level

You can manage errors at the page level by handling the Error event of the System.Web.UI.Page class. Within the handler, you probably want to obtain details of the error that occurred, and this information can be obtained by calling Server.GetLastError() to return the most recent exception. For example:

```
Private Sub Page_Error(ByVal sender As Object, _
                ByVal e As System.EventArgs) Handles MyBase.Error
    Dim excLast As Exception = Server.GetLastError()
```

```
    With excLast
        ' Do something with the exception
        Trace.Write(.Message)
    End With

    Server.ClearError()
End Sub
```

This routine first sets `excLast` to the most recent exception and then performs some form of processing using the details of the exception. You may want to log the details to the `Trace` (see Chapter 10), or you may want to write them to a database, text file, or event log. You may also be able to output details of the error to the browser using `Response.Write`, but this is not guaranteed because the `Error` event is non-deterministic. This simply means you don't know when it will occur; if it occurs after the page has been rendered, you'll be unable to send additional content to the browser with `Response.Write`.

Notice the final `Server.ClearError()` statement. Unless you call this method the error remains "live" and will propagate to the third stage of the error handling process in Figure 12-5. If you want to display a custom error page, then you should *not* call this method.

TIP *Page-level error handling is particularly important when you're using binding expressions in Web Forms. Because the actual binding expressions are not contained in event procedures, you can't use* `Try . . . Catch` *blocks to manage any exceptions; instead, errors generated from binding expressions are passed directly to the* `Error` *event of the Page class.*

Application Level

Before you look at custom error pages, let's briefly cover the application-level event handler as it shares a lot in common with the page-level event handler discussed previously. You can manage errors at the application level by providing a handler for the `Error` event in Global.asax. You'll once again need to call `Server.GetLastError()` to retrieve the details of the exception, but there's an added requirement at this level.

The exception returned by `Server.GetLastError()` will be of type HttpUnhandledException. This represents the exception that occurred because the original exception remained unhandled, so to get the details of the original exception you need to refer to the `InnerException` property. For example:

```
Sub Application_Error(ByVal sender As Object, ByVal e As EventArgs)
    Dim excUnhandled As Exception = Server.GetLastError()
    Dim excLast As Exception = excUnhandled.InnerException

    With excLast
        ' Do something with the exception
        Context.Trace.Warn(.Message)
    End With
End Sub
```

Also notice that because this event is in Global.asax, you need to refer to `Context.Trace` rather than just `Trace`. The same is *not* true for other intrinsic objects, all of which can be referenced directly by name—for example, `Server.GetLastError()`.

TIP *We would recommend you define an application-level error handler for all of your Web Applications because it gives you the opportunity to perform "last-chance" error management. We also recommend you log all application-level errors somewhere (event logs are a good choice) so that there's a permanent record of what has gone wrong.*

The following code shows how the `Application_Error` event could record error details to the Application event log:

```
Sub Application_Error(ByVal sender As Object, ByVal e As EventArgs)
    Application("ErrorString") += "Application_Error,"
    Dim excUnhandled As Exception = Server.GetLastError()
    Dim excLast As Exception = excUnhandled.InnerException

    Dim Message As String = _
            "URL: http://localhost/" & Request.Path & ControlChars.CrLf & _
            "MESSAGE:  " & excLast.Message & ControlChars.CrLf & _
            "STACK TRACE: " & excLast.StackTrace

    ' If necessary, create the event log
    Dim LogName As String = "Application"
    If (Not Diagnostics.EventLog.SourceExists(LogName)) Then
        Diagnostics.EventLog.CreateEventSource(LogName, LogName)
    End If
```

```
    ' Insert the details into the log
    Dim Log As New Diagnostics.EventLog()
    Log.Source = LogName
    Log.WriteEntry(Message, Diagnostics.EventLogEntryType.Error)
End Sub
```

Creating Custom Error Pages

As well as handling errors in code, you can also configure ASP.NET to display a custom error page if an unhandled exception occurs. You can apply configuration settings per page or per application, and in the case of application-wide settings you can configure different pages to be display for specific HTTP error codes.

Enabling Page-Specific Error Pages

Each Web Form supports a property called `errorPage`, which can be set to the name and location of the page you want to be displayed if an unhandled exception occurs. The error page can be any file type, but you'll probably want to use another Web Form or a plain HTML page.

If you set the `errorPage` property at design-time, the value you specify is entered for the `errorPage` attribute in the `Page` directive. For example, if you were to set the custom error page to be ErrorOccurred.aspx, the directive would read:

```
<%@ Page Language="vb". . . . errorPage="ErrorOccurred.aspx"%>
```

If an error occurs on the current page, and it's not handled by the first and second stages of the process shown in Figure 12-5, the browser will be redirected to the nominated custom error page and so it will be shown to the user. Figure 12-6 shows how such an error page might appear.

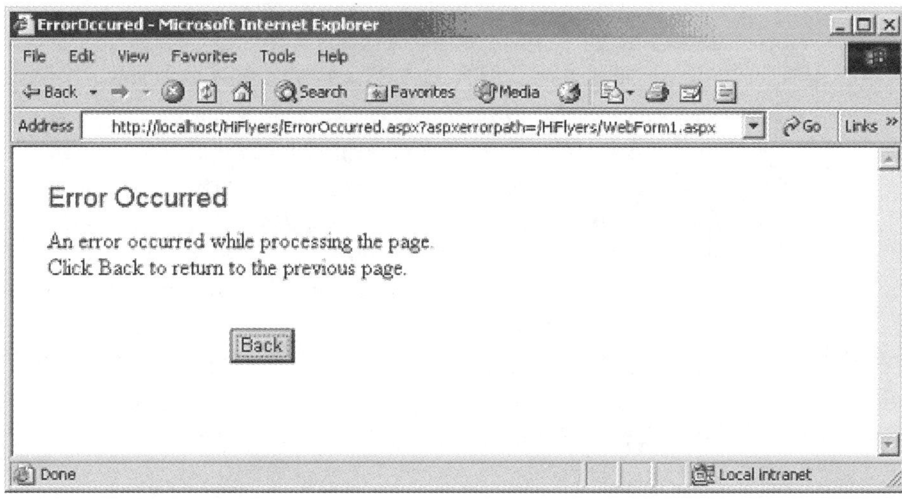

Figure 12-6. Custom error page

The ErrorOccurred.aspx page itself is extremely simple, consisting of nothing more than some static HTML and a single Web Form button. What is important is the querystring that's passed along with the page address when the redirection occurs; notice that it contains the address of the page that caused the error.

The address is typically used to allow the user to return to the problematic page and retry whatever operation caused the failure. The code to do this would be as follows:

```
Private Sub btnBack_Click(ByVal sender As System.Object, _
                ByVal e As System.EventArgs) Handles btnBack.Click
    Response.Redirect(Request.QueryString("aspxErrorPath"))
End Sub
```

Of course, you may not want the user to be able to retry the operation, or you may want to offer them other options as well. You can place whatever content and logic you want into the nominated error page to achieve this.

If you want to display additional details to the user about the cause of the error, you can retrieve the details of the exception using the same technique applied to the `Application_Error` event previously. Remember that you'll need to refer to the `InnerException` property of the exception object returned from `Server.GetLastError()`.

TIP *Although displaying detailed error messages may initially seem to be a great idea, in practice it's not something we recommend. Users rarely benefit from seeing detailed error messages from Web applications and indeed the additional information may offer unwanted assistance to hackers and intruders. Instead, we recommend you display a fairly generic non-detailed error page that tells the user that an error occurred and gives them the opportunity to retry or navigate elsewhere as appropriate.*

Enabling Custom Error Pages

If you've been trying this example already then you might have gotten different results to what you were expecting. In fact, chances are that the custom error page didn't seem to work at all, and you continued to receive detailed ASP.NET error messages. The reason for this is that when you test an ASP.NET application from a browser on the same physical machine as the Web server, the default configuration of a Web Application means that custom error pages will not be displayed. Rather, the standard, detailed, ASP.NET error messages will continue to appear. To allow custom error pages to be displayed on the local machine, you must change the `mode` attribute within the `customErrors` section of Web.config to have a value of `On`:

```
<customErrors mode="On" />
```

The default setting for this attribute is `RemoteOnly`, which sends the custom error pages to remote machines and sends detailed error messages to the local machine. You can also turn custom errors `Off`, which causes all clients to receive the standard detailed error messages when things go wrong.

CAUTION *The* `mode` *attribute is extremely important, and we recommend you set it to* `On` *to test your custom error pages, then set it back to* `RemoteOnly` *for subsequent testing and development. We recommend you don't set it to* `Off` *at all because this causes any remote workstation that generates an error to receive a detailed page of error information, including a full stack trace.*

As you'll see in the next section, `mode` is only one of the attributes that the `customErrors` section supports, and others can be used to configure support for custom errors on an application-wide basis.

TIP *Remember that if you create a page-level error handler, you should* not *call* `Server.ClearError()` *if you want ASP.NET to also display your custom error page.*

Application-Wide Error Pages

Page-specific custom errors are useful in some cases, but often what's needed is an application-wide setting to achieve the same result. This saves you from having to set the properties of multiple pages, but more importantly it ensures that you don't overlook new pages.

You configure application-wide custom error pages through the `customErrors` section of Web.config. The simplest technique is to define the `defaultRedirect` attribute. The page specified for this value will be displayed if an unhandled error occurs in a page that does not have a specific `errorPage` defined for it. For example:

```
<customErrors mode="On" defaultRedirect="ErrorOccurred.aspx"/>
```

You can also define a set of pages that will be used for specific HTTP status codes. For example:

```
<customErrors mode="On" defaultRedirect="ErrorOccurred.aspx">
  <error statusCode="500" redirect="/CallSupport.htm"/>
  <error statusCode="404" redirect="/PageNotFound.aspx"/>
  <error statusCode="403" redirect="/AccessDenied.aspx"/>
</customErrors>
```

By using a combination of these techniques you'll be able to create a robust framework for error management within your application. Application-level error handlers and custom error pages provide last-chance error handling, and individual pages and methods can override the global behavior and provide their own error management mechanisms.

Controlling Navigation

Almost every Web Application will consist of multiple Web Forms, and part of the design process is to structure those Web Forms and provide navigation features that enable the user to move easily from one to the next, albeit under your control. In some cases you'll need to exert tight control over their progress, ensuring that steps are completed in a predefined sequence, while elsewhere giving the user the choice to visit pages in any order.

ASP.NET offers a variety of features and techniques for supporting and controlling navigation, from client-side controls and scripting to server-side navigation and redirection. We've addressed some of these already, such as the ability to create custom navigation bars (Chapter 5) and using ticketing schemes (Chapter 11). However, in this section we'll bring all the different techniques together and compare the relative merits and disadvantages of each.

Default Pages

Web servers support the concept of default pages to allow users to request a resource by site or application name, rather than having to know the specific filename and extension. Each ASP.NET Web Application you create is automatically configured with a number of default pages:

- Default.htm
- Default.asp
- iisstart.asp
- Default.aspx

When IIS receives a request that includes a site or virtual directory name, but *doesn't* include a filename, it automatically searches the application's virtual root for each of these files in turn. Whichever it finds first, it processes and returns to the user as the response to their request.

Default.aspx comes last in this list, which means that if any of the other files are present in the virtual root, then the request will not be processed by ASP.NET (none of the others are mapped to the ASPNET_ISAPI.DLL filter; see Chapter 10). You may want to change the order of these default documents, or you may want to define your own default page in addition (or in place of) the current entries. You can make these changes through the Properties dialog box for the application's virtual directory:

1. Start the Internet Services Manager utility and select the virtual directory for the application.

2. Right-click to display the context menu and select **Properties**.

3. Click the **Documents** tab to display the current entries, as shown in Figure 12-7.

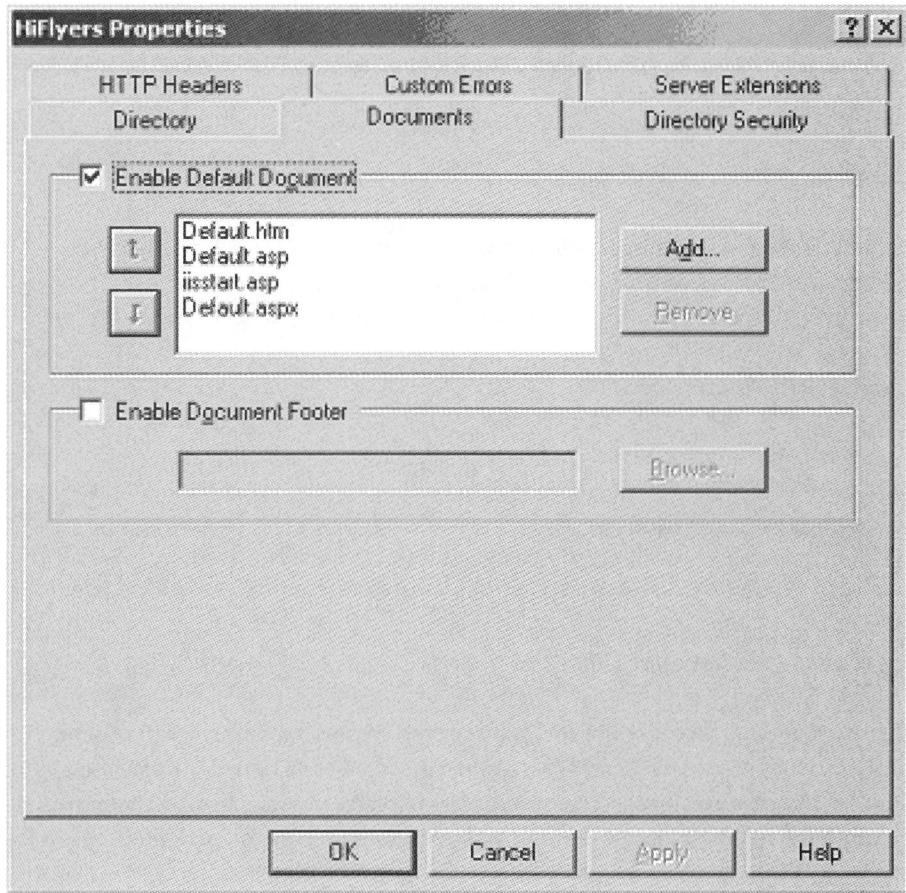

Figure 12-7. Configuring default documents

As you can see, you can add and remove entries, as well as change their order.

Default pages implemented in this way are a convenience, allowing the user to reference the server and virtual directory in the URL without having to know the page filename. However, sometimes you'll want to enforce a start page and ensure that the user visits it when they first access the application.

A simple way to enforce an initial page is to use either `Response.Redirect` or `Server.Transfer` in the `Session_OnStart` event in Global.asax:

```
Sub Session_OnStart(ByVal sender As Object, ByVal e As EventArgs)
    Response.Redirect("LatestNews.aspx")
End Sub
```

Although this guarantees that LatestNews.aspx is the first page that each user sees, it doesn't prevent them immediately moving to a different page. If you want to do this as well, we recommend you implement a ticketing scheme, as discussed later in this chapter and in Chapter 11.

Control-Based Navigation

As you've seen in Chapters 3 and 4, ASP.NET supports many different HTML Controls and Web Controls, some of which you can use to allow the user to navigate through the application. You can broadly divide them into three categories:

- Client-side navigation
- Direct navigation
- Indirect navigation

Client-Side Navigation

The most obvious member of this group is the HyperLink control, but other controls and techniques such as HTML image maps, Mobile Link controls, and PhoneCall controls support client-side behavior. All of these controls operate without the need for an additional postback to the Web Form; instead they issue a request directly to the resource they're targeting. Of course, a server round-trip is still required to process this request, but it won't be an ASP.NET postback.

Another significant thing about these controls is that once they've been rendered to the browser, you no longer have any influence over them. If you render a page containing a HyperLink to another site, your application will receive no notification if the user follows the link until their session times out. This is particularly relevant for large-scale applications where management of active sessions is a key concern, but it's also important for sites that carry advertising; if you provide a simple hyperlink to an advertiser's site from their advert, you'll have no way of measuring how many times people click through, and no easy way of billing the advertiser or providing them with statistics.

The other technique for enabling client-side navigation is to use a client-side script. This may well be the best option if you choose to add a frameset to your application. You'll see more on framesets later.

Direct Navigation

Direct navigation includes those controls that the user would *expect* to perform navigation, such as Command Buttons, Image Buttons, and Link Buttons. All of these perform a postback and allow you to write server-side code in the event handler that uses `Response.Redirect` or `Server.Transfer`.

You'll probably use direct navigation controls more than any other technique because they're obvious to the user and controllable for the developer. However, in some environments (such as when using dialup communications), the additional server round-trips required can cause poor performance.

Indirect Navigation

Indirect navigation encompasses other techniques, particularly where the user perhaps does not expect navigation to take place. For example, by setting the `AutoPostback` property of a control to True you can cause a postback to occur when the control is changed, and in the server event for the control you can once again use `Response.Redirect` or `Server.Transfer`.

The problem of indirect navigation is that it's often unexpected, and users can find the application difficult to use if it keeps posting back every time they make a change. As a rule we suggest you minimize the amount of indirect navigation that you perform.

Custom Navigation Controls

Throughout a project you're likely to find repeat requirements for things such as navigation bars, fly-out menus, hover buttons, and so on. Historically, client-side technologies such as JavaScript, Java applets, and ActiveX controls have been the chosen solutions, but these always placed particular demands on the client machine and so limited the application's reach.

With ASP.NET's support for Web User Controls and Web Custom Controls, you have an ideal server-side platform for building this type of functionality into reusable components. Chapter 5 covers the detail of how to do this, but from a design perspective the important thing is to identify at an early stage in the project just what the requirements will be. Creating Web Controls is something that can easily be allocated to an individual (or group of individuals) within the design team, but it's essential that a clear blueprint for the control exists so that everyone can refer to it.

When you're planning and building Web Controls, you should think of them as components and apply the design methodologies and disciplines you would apply to any form of component creation.

Code-Based Navigation

ASP.NET provides you with methods on two objects that support code-based navigation: `Response.Redirect` and `Server.Transfer`. Chapter 2 discusses these two techniques, and you've seen plenty of examples of their use throughout the subsequent chapters.

The following sections briefly review the methods and also highlight other useful features exposed from these classes.

Response Object

The Response object is an instance of an HttpResponse class, and its primary role is to allow your code to interact with the response that will be sent to the browser.

`Response.Redirect` is the main navigation method, and it operates by sending an HTTP Redirect header to the browser. This causes the browser to issue another request for the redirected page, resulting in two server hits to perform the navigation. For intrasite navigation within a large application this is not ideal as it places a greater load on the Web server, so you may prefer to use `Server.Transfer` instead. However, `Response.Redirect` *can* be used to navigate to external sites and URLs, whereas `Server.Transfer` is limited to local files only.

In addition to `Redirect`, the HttpResponse class exposes a number of other methods that may be useful during the page creation process. Table 12-2 summarizes them.

Table 12-2. Key Methods of the HttpResponse Class

METHOD	DESCRIPTION
AppendHeader	Creates an HTTP Header and adds it to the output stream sent to the browser.
ApplyAppPathModifier	Inserts the current Session ID into an absolute URL so that it's compatible with an application using cookieless sessions. See "Managing State" later in this chapter for more information on cookieless sessions.
BinaryWrite	Writes binary data to the output stream sent to the browser.
Clear, ClearContent	Clears all content from the output stream sent to the browser.
ClearHeaders	Clears all headers from the output stream sent to the browser.
End	Sends the current output stream to the browser, terminates processing of the request, and raises the `Application_EndRequest` event to signify that the process is complete.
Flush	Sends the current output stream to the browser, but allows processing to continue.
Write	Writes information into the output stream sent to the browser.
WriteFile	Writes the content of a file into the output stream sent to the browser.

Server Object

The Server object is an instance of the HttpServerUtility class, and its primary role is to provide supporting methods that your code can call while processing a request.

`Server.Transfer` is the main navigation method discussed so far. Unlike `Response.Redirect`, the `Transfer` method operates entirely server-side and performs a transparent redirection, so the client browser does not know it has been redirected. This requires only a single server hit, but it can be used only for pages within the current application.

The HttpServerUtility class supports a number of other methods, some of which are relevant to the topic of navigation. Table 12-3 summarizes them.

Table 12-3. Key Methods of the HttpServerUtility Class

METHOD	DESCRIPTION
Execute	Allows another page to be executed and its results retrieved and merged into the current page.
UrlDecode	Converts a string from the notation used within a URL into plain text.
UrlEncode	Converts a string from plain text into the notation required for a URL.
UrlPathEncode	Converts only the path portion of a string into the notation required for a URL. The query string portion remains in plain text.

Framesets

Framesets are familiar mechanisms for controlling navigation, as they allow separation of the visual page into different sections or frames. ASP.NET offers no special support for framesets, although Visual Studio .NET does include an integrated frameset editor.

You can create a frameset as a regular HTML file or as a Web Form, although the default in Visual Studio .NET is to use HTML. The only difference between a frameset page and a non-frameset page is the tags that they contain; they are both provided by the server in response to a request, and they are both rendered to the browser in HTML.

The problem with framesets is that they make it difficult for you to maintain control of the individual pages, especially when you want actions in one of the frames to affect one or more of the others. For example, a common use of framesets is to separate a page into a top-level menu, a submenu, and a detail area. Figure 12-8 shows an example of a classic ASP Web application that is structured in this way.

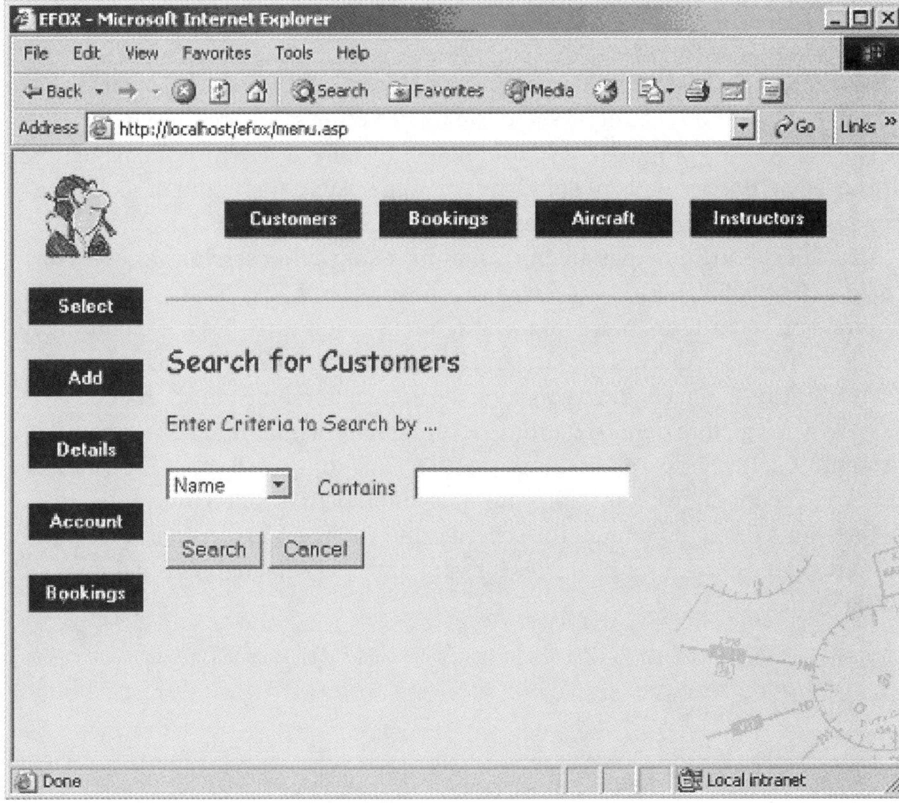

Figure 12-8. Main frameset page for a Web application

The Customers, Bookings, Aircraft, and Instructors buttons are in one frame, the Select, Add, Details, Account, and Bookings buttons are in another, and the central part of the page is a third frame. Ideally, when the user clicks one of the buttons in the top frame, you'd like the buttons on the left to change to show the appropriate submenu commands, and the content of the central frame should change to show a suitable default page. Unfortunately, framesets only provide support for changing the content of one frame at a time; any further coordinated changes must be managed with client-side script. This same problem exists with ASP.NET framesets because it's inherent in the way that framesets operate.

We'll discuss framesets in more detail in the "Using Framesets" section, including a possible solution to this problem that doesn't involve client-side script.

Ticketing Schemes

The concept of a ticketing scheme was introduced in Chapter 11 as a part of our broad discussion on security-related topics. Ticketing schemes give you a degree of control over the progress that a user makes through a series of Web pages and are based on the principle of detecting when the user visits an out of sequence page and redirecting them as necessary.

Most ticketing schemes are implemented using either session variables or cookies. If scalability is a prime concern, cookies should be chosen; if server-side control and security are more important, then session variables are preferred. As you'll see when we discuss cookies and Session variables later in this chapter, there's little difference in how you code the application for each approach.

We won't go into detail regarding ticketing schemes in this chapter as they were thoroughly discussed in Chapter 11. The one thing we'll say at this point is that you need to thoroughly plan your navigation path through the application before you try and implement the scheme, and you need to consider not only what happens as the user navigates forward, but also what happens if they navigate backward.

Using Framesets

An HTML frameset displays multiple, independent, scrollable regions called *frames* within the Web browser window, and each frame in the frameset displays a separate HTML document or Web Form. You can set properties for each frame to define whether it can scroll its content and whether the frame can be resized.

Visual Studio .NET provides frameset building features, but it's important to realize that they're all client-side features. ASP.NET itself provides no special support for frames or framesets, but on the other hand it doesn't prevent you from using them either. For example, to add a new frameset to a project:

1. Select **Project ➢ Add HTML Page**.

2. Select the **Frameset** template and provide a name for the new file.

3. In the **Select a Frameset Template** dialog box (shown in Figure 12-9) select the layout that most closely matches your requirements.

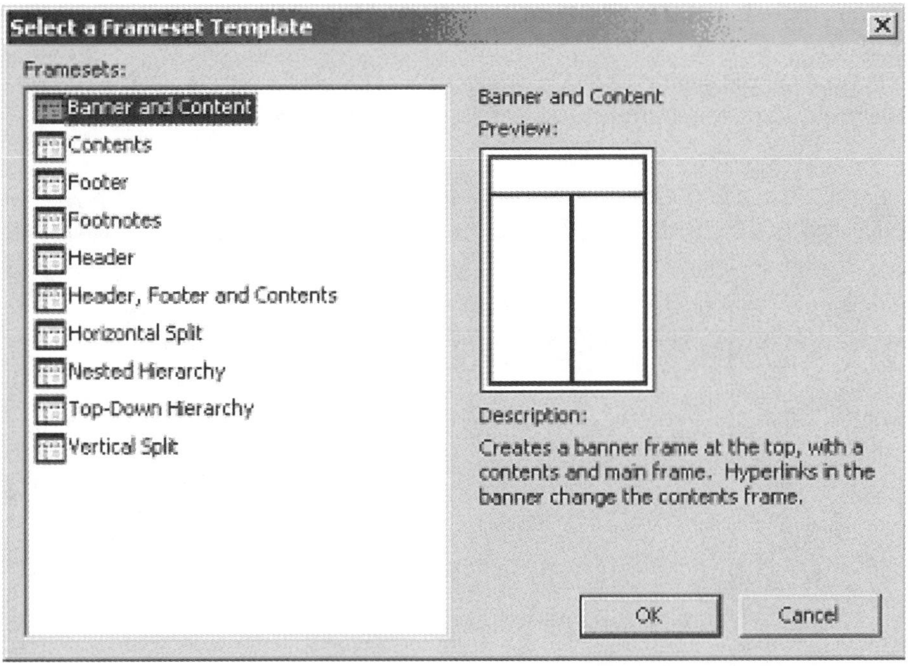

Figure 12-9. *Creating a new frameset*

The designer for the frameset page will display the frame outlines and allow you to set property values for the entire page or for each individual frame. One of the first things you'll want to do is to define the page that will be displayed in each frame. To do this, right-click in the frame and select **Set Page For Frame** from the context menu. Alternatively, set the `src` property from the Properties window. You can also change the height and width of any frame, and add and remove frames as required.

If you switch to HTML view for the frameset page, you'll see that Visual Studio .NET has conveniently added some comments for you into the body of the page. We recommend that once you've viewed these comments, you should delete them as there's a chance that on older browsers (okay, very old browsers) they will be displayed. There's no technical reason for this, it just looks unprofessional!

Navigating with Framesets

When working with pages in a frameset you'll find that any form of navigation (including hyperlinks, postbacks, and redirections) affects only the current frame. If you want navigation to affect other frames (for example, clicking a button in one frame causes a different page to be displayed in another), then you'll need to make use of the target attribute than can be applied to HyperLinks or to the page itself.

For example, Figure 12-10 shows a frameset created from the Nested Hierarchy template. Currently there are no pages defined for the frames.

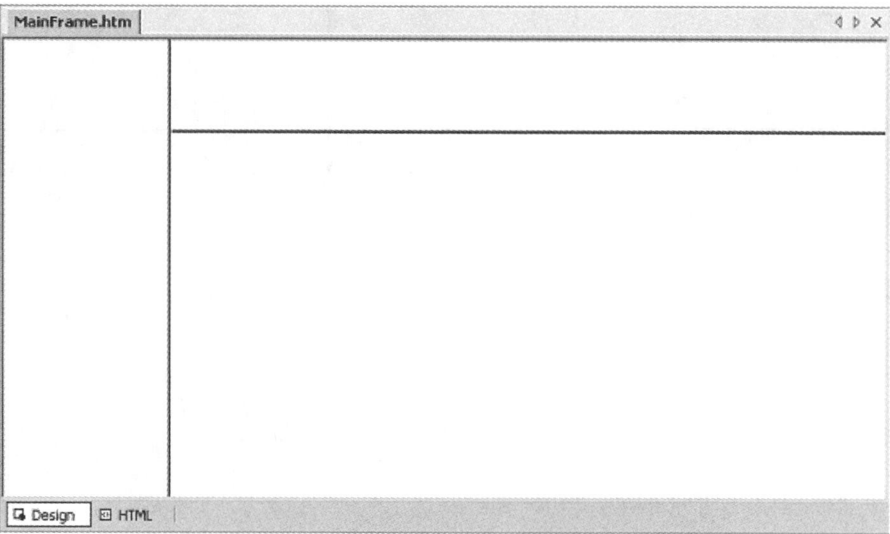

Figure 12-10. Nested hierarchy frameset

The HTML definition of this frameset is as follows:

```
<frameset cols="15%,*" border="0" frameSpacing="0" frameBorder="0">
    <frame name="left" src="" scrolling="no" noresize>
    <frameset rows="20%,*">
        <frame name="rtop">
        <frame name="rbottom" src="">
    </frameset>
</frameset>
```

You can see that each frame has been named **left**, **rtop**, or **rbottom**. It's these names that would be applied to the target attribute of any HyperLink control that was intended to display its page in a specific frame.

For this example, you'll create a Web Form called MenuLeft.aspx that will be displayed in the leftmost frame. This Web Form has its pageLayout set to FlowLayout, and it simply contains three HyperLink controls. The HTML for MenuLeft.aspx is as follows (note that meta tags have been removed for clarity):

```
<%@ Page Language="vb" Codebehind="MenuLeft.aspx.vb"
                Inherits="HiFlyers.MenuLeft"%>
<!DOCTYPE HTML PUBLIC "-//W3C//DTD HTML 4.0 Transitional//EN">
<HTML>
  <HEAD>
    <title>MenuLeft</title>
  </HEAD>
  <body>
    <form id="Form1" method="post" runat="server">
      <P><asp:HyperLink id="HyperLink1" runat="server">Option 1
                </asp:HyperLink></P>
      <P><asp:HyperLink id="HyperLink2" runat="server">Option 2
                </asp:HyperLink></P>
      <P><asp:HyperLink id="HyperLink3" runat="server">Option 3
                </asp:HyperLink></P>
    </form>
  </body>
</HTML>
```

Each HyperLink would need to have its `NavigateUrl` property set to the name of the corresponding page, but this alone would cause the specified page to appear in the left frame. If you wanted the page to appear in the top frame, you would define `Target` attribute for the HyperLink as follows:

```
<asp:HyperLink id="HyperLink1" runat="server" Target="rtop"> . . .
</asp:HyperLink>
```

Of course you'd need to define this attribute for all three controls, and although this would not be a problem with just three HyperLinks, it becomes more of a concern if your page contained 10 or 15 or even more. Also, how could you handle the situation in which HyperLinks were created dynamically, perhaps from a DataGrid control? Clearly, setting individual `Target` attributes for individual controls will work in some cases, but not all.

A preferred technique is to set the default target frame for the page; you can do this by defining a `<base . . . >` element in the `<head>` section of the page. For example:

```
<HEAD>
    <base target="rtop">
    <title>MenuLeft</title>
</HEAD>
```

With this definition in the page, all hyperlinks without a specific `target` attribute will affect the **rtop** frame rather than the current one. In fact, this same element also controls how redirections and other page navigation techniques are handled, and so solves most of the navigation problems.

In addition to using specific frame names for the `Target` attribute, the following special values may also be used:

- **_blank** causes a new browser window to be opened to display the specified page.
- **_parent** displays the specified page in the parent of the current frameset.
- **_self** displays the page in the current frame.
- **_top** replaces the content of the current browser window with the specified page.

Alternatives to Framesets

Framesets are a legacy feature that have been included to maintain backward compatibility with existing applications and to provide a quick and easy way for developers to build a Web interface that's separated into distinct areas. However, they do tend to cause problems for developers because they effectively allow distinct pages to be displayed together, even though all of the navigation and postback features that browsers offer are targeted at individual frames only. Quite simply, this means that if a postback occurs for one frame in the frameset, you have no easy way of referring to or controlling any of the other frames.

An alternative approach is available in ASP.NET, although it's rather different and not always suitable. The approach is to construct a regular Web Form using Panel controls in place of frames and to define Web User Controls instead of the regular Web Forms and HTML pages that would be displayed within the frames. At runtime your code can create instances of the required Web User Controls and load them into the Panels, and because the entire interface is constructed using only one Web Form, you have complete control over its behavior.

This approach requires a lot more planning than using framesets and requires that most of the functionality is built in the form of .ascx files rather than .aspx files. However, as you saw in Chapter 5, there are relatively few differences between these technologies, so you should find no real barriers to using this technique in your applications.

Using Form, QueryString, and Cookies

The Form, QueryString, and Cookies collections allow your code to interact with the client browser and, through it, with the user. All three are exposed as collection properties of the `Request` object, with their values represented as key/value pair combinations:

- `Form()` represents information passed from a form on a Web page that has an action of `Post`. Form data is often known as *post data* for this reason.

- `QueryString()` represents information passed from a form on a Web page with an action of `Get`, as well as parameters appended to the address in the URL requested from the server by a client.

- `Cookies()` represents information passed from the client to the server in the form of a `Cookie:` HTTP header. Cookies are application specific, and once they exist for an application, client browsers will pass them in each and every request they make to that application.

In a classic ASP application it was common to find that a high proportion of the code dealt with retrieving data from the Form, QueryString, and Cookies collections, but in ASP.NET much of this is taken care of by the HTTP Runtime and mapped to a more convenient (and efficient) format. For example, if you add a TextBox named txtUserName to a Web Form, you can retrieve its content by referring to `txtUserName.Text`. In classic ASP you would have had to explicitly reference `Request.Form("txtUserName")` and use similar code for all the other controls on the form.

So does this mean that you can forget about `Request.Form()` altogether? Probably not, because it's still useful to be able to use `Request.Form()` to pass information between pages. Similarly, `Request.QueryString()` gives you a simple way to pass parameters between pages, and `Request.Cookies()` allows you to retrieve persistent values from the client browser. So, even though the importance of these three collections is downplayed in ASP.NET, don't ignore them completely.

Using the Form() Collection

The Web Form architecture is based on the principle that you'll make use of postbacks to read Web Form content and process it, and you'll only navigate to another Web Form once you've finished with the current one. You'll find this is the case for the great majority of the Web Forms that you create, but there will always be exceptions. A simple example is where you need to capture data using a Web Form in one application, but perhaps want to pass that data to a page in a legacy application for processing. You could code the first application to present the form, capture the data in a postback, and then perhaps do a redirection to the processing application, but this would be wasteful; it would be far more efficient to simply specify the URL of the processing form for the `action` attribute of the data capture form.

For example, a standard Web Form contains an HTML `<form>` element as follows:

```
<form id="Form1" method="post" runat="server">
    .
    .
</form>
```

When the Web Form is compiled and executed, it automatically inserts an `action` attribute with the current page name as the value, causing the postback. For example, if the previous `<form>` definition were contained in Page1.aspx, at runtime the element would be rendered as this:

```
<form name="Form1" method="post" action="Page1.aspx" id="Form1">
```

If you want override this behavior and cause the form to be submitted to a different page for processing, then you need to specify the appropriate URL for the `action` attribute, but you must also remove the `runat="Server"` attribute; otherwise ASP.NET replaces your setting for `action` with the postback reference. For example, the previous `<form>` element could be modified to read:

```
<form id="Form1" method="post" action="ProcessingPage.aspx">
```

Within ProcessingPage.aspx you can now refer to the `Request.Form()` collection to read the values entered by the user into the controls on the form. For example, if the form contained a Text Box called txtSalary, you could read its content with this:

```
Dim intSalary As Integer = Integer.Parse(Request.Form("txtSalary"))
```

NOTE *If you use this technique and decide not to use the postback approach for handling the content of a Web Form, you'll find you can't handle any control-related server events, nor can you retrieve any properties of the controls other than their values.*

Postback handling of Web Forms is what ASP.NET is all about, and it's a powerful and flexible model for processing Web requests. We don't advise you to abandon this model for most of your application requirements, but the `Form()` collection does offer an alternative for those rare times when it's needed.

Passing Data in the QueryString

It is unlikely you'll need to use the `Form()` collection when working with ASP.NET because the postback model does seem to work well for most requirements. However, the `QueryString()` collection is quite different and is much more likely to be needed when creating medium to large-scale Web Applications.

Querystring is the term given to the data that is suffixed to the filename part of the URL when a request is issued. The querystring is separated from the filename using a ? character and can be made up of multiple key/value pairs separated by & characters. For example:

```
http://Localhost/MyApp/CheckBalance.aspx?AccountID=452&UserID=91
```

In this example the querystring contains two entries. The first is called `AccountID` and has a value of `452`, and the second is called `UserID` and has a value of `91`. Within the code for CheckBalance.aspx you could read these values as follows:

```
Private m_intAccountID As Integer
Private m_intUserID as Integer
Private Sub Page_Load(ByVal sender As System.Object, _
                ByVal e As System.EventArgs) Handles MyBase.Load
    m_intAccountID = Integer.Parse(Request.QueryString("AccountID"))
    m_intUserID = Integer.Parse(Request.QueryString("UserID"))
End Sub
```

This technique is important because it provides a convenient way to pass information between pages when performing a `Response.Redirect` or `Server.Transfer`. In fact, it's not only convenient, it's also efficient and scalable because there's no demand on server resources and no dependency on server state.

Reading the data from the querystring is quite straightforward, assuming you know the names of the querystring parameters. When you want to generate querystring data, you need to be aware of the fact that it must be suitably encoded for passing with a URL, and you can do this with the `Server.UrlEncode` method. For example, the code that generated the previous query string could be written as follows:

```
Private m_intAccID As Integer
Private m_intUserID as Integer
.
.
Private Sub btnDoIt_Click(. . . . )
    Dim strQueryString As String
    strQueryString = "AccountID=" & Server.UrlEncode(m_intAccID.ToString) & "&"
    strQueryString &= "UserID=" & Server.UrlEncode(m_intUserID.ToString)

    Response.Redirect("http://Localhost/MyApp/CheckBalance.aspx?" &
strQueryString)
End Sub
```

In this example, the `Server.UrlEncode` has actually made no difference because simple number formats don't need any special conversion. However, if you passed a text value containing spaces or punctuation, the `UrlEncode` method would ensure that these were translated into a URL-friendly notation.

NOTE *You* don't *need to perform a corresponding* `Server.UrlDecode` *to read the converted query string values. They are automatically decoded when they're made available through the* `QueryString()` *collection.*

Reading and Writing Cookies

Although it's certainly useful to be able to pass data in the querystring, this technique does suffer a significant limitation; the data passed is request-specific and is not available to subsequent requests unless it's passed with each and every one. One of the simplest solutions to this problem is to place the data into client-side cookies rather than passing it via the querystring.

Over the past few years, there has been a lot of inaccurate information relating to cookies, with the result that many users have great concerns over Web applications that make use of them. Users think that cookies are somehow being used to spy on them, or they're being used to collect private information from the user's computer.

These are unfounded fears; a cookie is no more than a simple chunk of text data sent from a Web server and usually stored in memory by the browser or written to the file store of the client machine. Each cookie is associated with a specific Web site or Web application, and whenever the browser makes a request against the Web application it passes the content of the cookie as a part of the HTTP Request. Similarly, when the Web server generates the response for the browser, it can send new cookie values along with the visible content.

TIP *Not all browsers support cookies, and those that do may have been configured to disable cookie support. If you can't guarantee that users will access your application with a cookie-enabled browser, then it may simply be impractical for you to use cookies. Alternatively, use cookies within your application, but place a warning on the start page of the application to tell users they're required to have cookies enabled.*

Cookies are made accessible from both the `Request` and the `Response` objects. To read cookie values you use `Request.Cookies()`, which takes the form of a collection of HttpCookie objects, referenced by name. For example, to retrieve a cookie value named `PreferredAircraftID` you could use the following code:

```
intAircraftID = Request.Cookies("PreferredAircraftID").Value
```

To write a value back for a cookie you need to use `Response.Cookies()`. For example:

```
Response.Cookies("PreferredAircraftID").Value = intAircraftID
```

Notice that this code refers to the value property. As you'll see in a moment, cookies are somewhat more sophisticated than the simple key/value pairs used for the Form and QueryString collections.

Persistent Cookies

By default cookies are transient, and they're held in memory by the client browser until the browser is closed. Such cookies are often known as *temporary cookies* or *session cookies*, and they work well when you need to hold data in the client only while the application is running. However, you may want to make cookies persistent so that they're written to the file store in the client machine and can be retrieved the next time the user visits your Web application, even though it could be some time in the future.

You make cookies persistent by setting their `Expires` property to a valid date/time in the future. For example, to make the PreferredAircraftID cookie persistent you could use the following:

```
With Response.Cookies("PreferredAircraftID")
    .Value = intAircraftID
    .Expires = New Date(2010, 12, 31)
End With
```

This creates a cookie and assigns a value from a variable just as before, but it then sets the expiry date for the cookie to be December 31, 2010. This will cause the browser to store the cookie so that it can subsequently be retrieved whenever the user visits your application.

Managing State

State management is a core concept in the development of Web applications, as opposed to Web sites. *State* refers to the data (including values, text, dates, objects, and so on) that needs to be preserved while the application is running and the users are navigating from page to page.

In a desktop environment, state is maintained within the client by way of module-level, class-level, or global variables, as well as local data stores such as files and databases. ASP.NET has features that are largely equivalent to these, but they come at a price and must be used with care.

To understand state management it's important to identify the levels at which state needs to be preserved:

- Page state, which is maintained across postbacks to a single page by a single user
- Cookie state, which is maintained in the client browser across multiple postbacks to different pages
- Session state, which is unique to each user of an application but preserved throughout their use of the application
- Application state, which is shared between all users of an application
- Cache state, which has application scope but variable lifetime

Page State

Page state is maintained in ASP.NET by way of the ViewState feature discussed in Chapter 3. ViewState performs two roles; it automatically stores the property values for the controls on the Web Form, and it also allows you to store your own state values across postbacks.

Data can be written and read from ViewState using the standard syntax for referencing items in a key/value pair collection. For example:

```
ViewState("Keyname") = strMyData
strMyData = ViewState("Keyname")
```

When considering whether to use ViewState, bear the following in mind:

- ViewState is intended for use in a postback scenario; it will not work for passing data between different pages.
- ViewState is passed between the client and server with every request and response, so excessive amounts of ViewState data will degrade performance.
- ViewState can only be used to store simple data types and instances of objects that are serializable.
- ViewState places minimal load on the Web server, so is well suited to use in scalable applications.

Remember that ViewState can seriously affect performance, so we recommend you consider disabling it for any controls that do not expressly require it. You can do this by setting each control's `EnableViewState` property to False. For a comprehensive coverage of ViewState, refer to Chapter 3.

Cookie State

Cookie state was discussed in the previous section, and you saw how it allowed state to be maintained across multiple requests and even multiple sessions. Cookies can be made permanent or temporary and are referenced in code as a collection of HttpCookie objects.

When considering whether to use Cookie state, bear the following in mind:

- Not all browsers will support cookies, either because they don't support the feature or because the user has disabled it.
- Certain nationalities and regions may have limits on the use of cookies. If you're targeting a particular geographic or political area with your

application, we suggest you check the legal position before you go ahead and use cookies.

- Cookies are passed from the client to the server with every request, so excessively large cookies will degrade performance.
- Cookies are not secure and should not be used for storing sensitive data.
- Cookies can only be used to store simple data types and instances of objects that are serializable.
- Cookie state works well for passing data between different pages in an application, and even for retaining data between different sessions.
- Cookies place minimal load on the Web server, so they're well suited to use in scalable applications.

Session State

Cookies provide a basic mechanism for storing per-user state during a working session, but because they're stored on the client machine they must be passed to the server with every request. This naturally introduces the possible performance problems mentioned earlier, but it also means that only specific data types can be placed into cookie state. For many applications this won't be a problem, but for others it could prove to be a major stumbling block.

To overcome the limitations of cookie state, ASP.NET provides a Session state facility that operates server-side. It's extremely powerful and is capable of storing as much or as little data as you decide. Session state is automatically managed on a per-user basis, and data held in Session state is automatically released when the session ends. Sounds good? Well it is—it's just that Session state really ought to come with the following health warning.

CAUTION *Inappropriate use of Session state is a real problem for medium- and large-scale applications. Session state consumes server resources for each user session, and if you store too much data in Session variables (or there are too many concurrent sessions), then resource usage becomes critical. It's quite possible that the application will become unacceptably slow, run inconsistently, or simply crash out. If you're aiming to create a scalable application, you really should read the discussion of Session state in Chapter 13 before you even consider using it.*

After reading that warning you might be thinking about skipping straight to the next section, but we really wouldn't recommend that because Session state has so much to offer Web developers. We're not saying that you shouldn't use Session state at all, but we suggest you fully consider the implications in terms of scalability, server performance, server resource usage, and so on.

If you do choose to make use of Session state, you'll probably want to store semi-transient data that is collected (or calculated) from one page but is required by others. A good example would be the content of the user's shopping cart in an online purchasing application, where products are selected and quantities entered through a sequence of pages and the details retained for final processing on a checkout page. Session state would ensure that each users' shopping cart is unique, as well as allowing the contents to be discarded if the user left the site before checking out.

Reading and Writing Session State

Session state is maintained through the Session object, which is derived from the HttpSessionState class. State is stored and managed as a key/value pair collection, using standard syntax for reading and writing entries:

```
Session("UserLogonName") = txtUserName.Text
cmAddBooking.Parameters(0).Value = Session("UserLogonName")
```

Most data types and classes can be successfully placed into Session state, including simple types such as numbers, strings, and dates through to more complex types such as DataSets, arrays, and so on.

Session Lifetime

Session state is maintained for each user session. A session starts when a user makes the first request for a file within the application, but it could end for a variety of reasons:

- Sessions time out after a period of inactivity. The default TimeOut is 20 minutes, but you can change this by assigning a value (in minutes) to `Session.TimeOut` or setting the `timeout` attribute of the `<sessionState>` element in Web.config.
- If your code calls `Session.Abandon`, the session is immediately terminated. If the user issues another request against the application, then a new session will be started.
- If the Web Application is restarted, all sessions in the application are terminated. This will happen if there are any changes made to Machine.config, Web.config, or Global.asax, and it may also occur if there is a fatal error, crash, or other problem in the Application's AppDomain.
- If the Web Server is stopped, restarted, or crashes, every session in each application will be terminated. This may happen accidentally, an administrator may restart it, or it may be done automatically by ASP.NET if it believes there's a problem with the ASP.NET worker process.

Note that *inactivity* is measured from the time at which the last request is completed, and therefore a session will time out even if the user's browser is still open. Also, if the user closes the browser, it doesn't automatically end the session. All that happens is that the timeout period continues to tick until it expires, and the session ends. Many developers question the wisdom of this last feature, but because of the connectionless nature of HTTP, it would be difficult for it to work any other way.

Configuring Session State

Session state is configured through the `<sessionState>` element in Web.config. By default, this element will appear as follows:

```
<sessionState
        mode="InProc"
        stateConnectionString="tcpip=127.0.0.1:42424"
        sqlConnectionString="data source=127.0.0.1;user id=sa;password="
```

```
cookieless="false"
timeout="20"/>
```

The mode attribute defines how Session state is managed by ASP.NET.

- The default is InProc, which causes ASP.NET to maintain state information in memory within the ASP.NET process. For small applications this will probably be fine, but for larger systems you'll probably want to choose one of the other options.

- Setting mode to Off prevents ASP.NET from maintaining any Session state for the application, and any attempts to refer to the Session() collection will generate errors.

- StateServer causes ASP.NET to store Session state in a separate process from ASP.NET itself. Furthermore, this process can be hosted on a remote machine. The benefit of this is that by moving state out of the ASP.NET worker process (especially if you move it to another machine) you're able to reduce the load on the Web server and so perhaps enhance performance.

- SQLServer takes the StateServer idea one stage further, by storing all Session state information in a nominated SQL Server database. The advantage of this is robustness; in the event of a critical failure, the SQL server database guarantees point-in-time recovery so you'll be able to restore Session state to a known good condition.

The cookieless attribute defines how sessions will be tracked. If set to false (the default) then ASP.NET will track sessions using a cookie that is sent to each user's browser. If cookieless is set to true then ASP.NET inserts the Session ID into the URL of the page when the response is generated, and subsequently tracks the Session ID across subsequent requests. You'll see more on this behavior in the "Tracking Sessions" section.

The timeout attribute defines how many minutes of inactivity must elapse before a user's session will be terminated.

In this chapter we'll limit our discussion to the use of InProc Session state, although all of the code for reading and writing Session state remains unchanged irrespective of where and how the data is actually stored. Chapter 13 returns to this topic and takes a comprehensive look at using the StateServer and SQLServer options and shows how they can be applied to Web Farm installations. The stateConnectionString and sqlConnectionString attributes are included as a part of that discussion.

Tracking Sessions

ASP.NET allocates a Session ID to each user session that is created and then subsequently uses the ID to track all activity and state data for the session. The ID needs to be held by the client browser, but it also needs to be transferred reliably with each request that the browser makes to the server. ASP.NET achieves this in one of two ways, covered in the following two sections.

Cookies

Cookies are the default mechanism that ASP.NET uses to track sessions. When a browser first makes a connection to a server, ASP.NET will add a transient cookie to the browser response that contains the Session ID it allocated. You won't see this cookie on disk because it's temporary and thus held just in memory within the browser process.

The problem with this approach is that not all browsers will support cookies, and without cookie support there will be no Session state. To overcome this you can configure session tracking to be cookieless.

Cookieless

When using cookieless session tracking, ASP.NET writes the Session ID into the URL of each page that it returns to the browser. Figure 12-11 shows how this may appear.

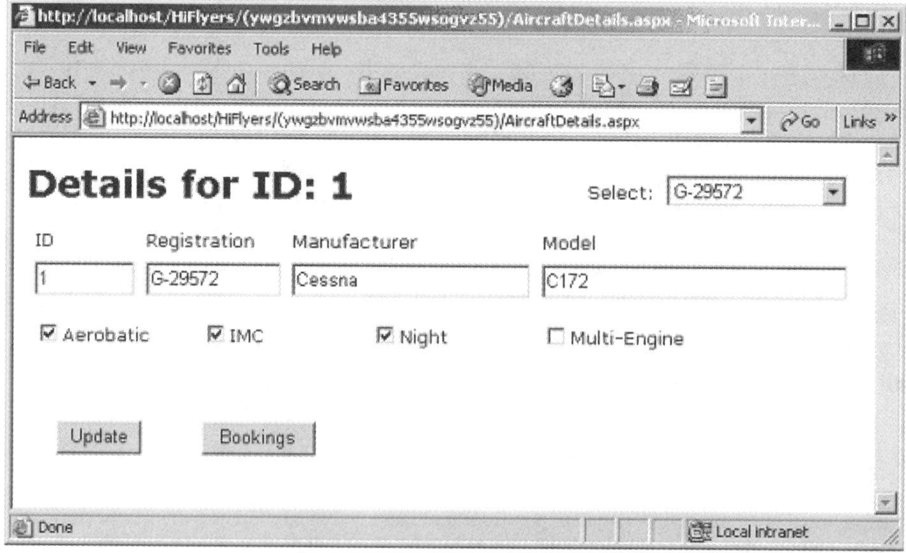

Figure 12-11. Cookieless session tracking

Notice that the Session ID has not been written at the end of the URL, but in fact just after the virtual directory name. This allows all relative URLs used for navigation (both server-side and client-side) to continue working with no changes.

TIP *If you use only relative paths in hyperlinks, redirections, and other URLs, you'll be able to switch your application between cookie and cookieless modes without having to change any code. All you need to do is change the value of the* `cookieless` *attribute in Web.config.*

If you want to create absolute URLs for navigation, then you need to ensure that they'll contain the Session ID used with cookieless sessions. You do this by calling the `Response.ApplyAppPathModifier` method, passing it the relative URL of the file; it will return an absolute URL including the Session ID in the right place. For example, you could use the following to create an absolute URL for the AircraftAvailability.aspx file:

```
HyperLink1.NavigateUrl =
                  Response.ApplyAppPathModifier("AircraftAvailability.aspx")
```

At runtime, HyperLink1 will be rendered with a Session ID in its `href` attribute, similar to the following:

```
<a href="/HiFlyers/(w4tenpfth52aolrbvpkiri55)/AircraftAvailability.aspx" . . . >
```

If cookie support is once more enabled by editing Web.config, the same code will now render the `href` of HyperLink1 as follows:

```
<a href="/HiFlyers/AircraftAvailability.aspx" . . . >
```

As you can see, the Session ID has been removed and a regular, absolute URL rendered for the hyperlink. Once again, you can see that the application can be switched between cookie and cookieless modes without requiring any code changes.

Designing for Session State

Session state is an expensive resource, and it needs to be used with care and restraint. In most applications this restraint is best applied at the design phase so that problems are prevented at an early stage rather than bug-fixed later. Among the key concerns are the following:

- Be aware of the size of data held per user in Session state. For example, if you store a 1MB DataSet in every session, you can easily consume 100MB, 200MB, or more of memory.

- Set an appropriate value for the `Timeout` of the session. Some applications work well with a short timeout of perhaps five minutes, and others require a longer duration. You may need to conduct usability tests to determine the ideal time.

- Try to manage sessions by encouraging users to click a logout button (or similar) when they've finished in the application. In this button you can call `Session.Abandon` to free all Session state content. You probably need to give users a good reason for clicking the button; otherwise they'll simply close the browser and you'll have to wait for the timeout to occur.

- Avoid using Session state to store objects built on the Single-Threaded Apartment (STA) model. Such objects have *thread affinity* and can be executed only by the thread on which they were created. This can easily lead to locks, blocks, and cross-thread marshalling.

These are only a few of the challenges you'll face if you use Session state. Chapter 13 returns to this topic and examines the particular concerns of using Session state in a scalable application.

Using Session State

When considering whether to use Session state, bear the following in mind:

- Session state depends on Session ID tracking. If you can't guarantee that user's browsers will support cookies for this task, you must enable cookieless Session state and ensure that Session IDs are specified in all URLs.

- Session state can have an enormous impact on scalability, so for large Web applications we recommend using ViewState, passing data in the QueryString, or using cookies.

- Session state places a greater loading on the Web server and can cause poor performance and reliability problems in extreme cases.

- Session state is secure, because it is held entirely server-side.
- You can store almost any type or data in Session state.
- Session state has little impact on transmission speed and volume, so it works well when users are connecting over slow links.

Application State

Application state is maintained through the Application object, which is derived from the HttpApplicationState class. Application state is stored and managed as a key/value pair collection, using standard syntax for reading and writing values.

Application state is maintained for the lifetime of the application. This begins with the first request to any page or resource in the application and ends when any of the following occur:

- The last user session ends.
- The Web server is stopped, restarted or crashes.
- The Global.asax, Web.config, or Machine.config files are modified.

Application state is shared by all users, so any changes made will be seen by all subsequent client requests. Typically, you'll use Application state for simple values, settings, and objects common to all users. Examples include DataSets containing lookup tables and other static database information, connection strings, activity counters to measure concurrent usage, objects representing utility classes, and much more. Application state does not have the same impact on resource usage and scalability that Session state does because there's only ever one copy of each Application state value per process; it doesn't change according to the number of concurrent users.

Concurrent Access

Application state is *not* thread-safe, so there's a possibility of it being corrupted if two threads try and access the state values simultaneously. ASP.NET applies no automatic locking or synchronization mechanism of its own, so you have to take responsibility for managing concurrent access to state date.

The Application object exposes two methods used for this: Lock and Unlock. `Application.Lock` is called just before you want to access a value in Application state, and `Application.Unlock` should be called once you're finished. For example:

```
Application.Lock
Application("KeyName") = Value
Application.Unlock
```

If the `Unlock` method is omitted, the Application object remains locked until the request is completed or it times out. Either way, it will block other threads that try and access the Application object until the lock is released.

You must use `Lock` and `Unlock` when writing or changing simple values in Application state, or when referencing (including reading) an object which is not free-threaded in Application state. Because of the possible corruption that could be caused if two threads access the same data, it pays to play safe and always use `Application.Lock/Unlock` when working with objects.

Using Application State

When considering whether to use Application state, bear the following in mind:

- Application state is not Web farm or Web garden friendly. Each server, and each processor within a server, maintains its own unique copy of state data. Changes made to the state data used by one server or process will not automatically be replicated to the others.

- Application state is not persistent and will always be held within the ASP.NET worker process.

- Application state is not thread-safe, so you need to ensure that you call the `Lock` and `Unlock` methods to control concurrent access.

- If an application restarts for any reason, all Application state is lost.

- Application state is shared between all users, so it has much less of an impact on scalability and performance than Session state.

- Application state is maintained server-side and has no impact on transmission speed or volume.

TIP *Although all Application state is lost if the application terminates or restarts, you can easily add your own code to persist Application state values to permanent storage and then read them back again after the application is restarted. To do this, you would add code to the* `Application_End` *event in Global.asax to store the current Application state values, perhaps in a database, XML document, or even a binary file. In the* `Application_Start` *event you'd add corresponding code to read from storage and create the Application state values once again.*

Cache State

Cache state is a new facility in ASP.NET. In some ways it's similar to Application state, in that Cache state is shared by all users of the application and it persists across multiple requests. However, here the similarity ends because values within Cache state are held dynamically; subject to the conditions and criteria that you define, items can be removed from the Cache to free up resources and so enhance performance.

The content of Cache state can be any object or value, including DataSets retrieved from a database, arrays of details read from disk, simple string or numeric values entered by the user into a form, and so on. This type of caching is nothing new—we've already discussed the Application and Session objects that offer basic storage—but the Cache provides the degree of control necessary to make this technique work with enterprise Web applications.

The items within the Cache class are exposed as a key/value pair object, much the same as Session and Application. Objects are stored and retrieved in the Cache using standard notation, such as:

```
Cache("MyItem") = objMyDataSet
DataGrid1.DataSource = Cache("MyItem").Tables("Categories")
```

However, the Cache class also provides additional functionality that's specifically designed to manage the storage of transient data, including file, time and key-based dependencies, expiration of underused items, and support for callback routines that can manage the removal of items from the cache.

Designing for the Cache

If you know that you want to take advantage of caching within your code, you need to consider its implications as a part of the detailed design phase. In particular, any code that expects to retrieve data from the Cache must ensure it checks that the item exists before it attempts to use it. This is because, unlike the Application and Session objects, items can be removed from the Cache object if they expire or are underused. Even if an entry was added to the Cache by a previous page, there's no guarantee it will be there for subsequent requests.

For example, in the HiFlyers application it's a fair bet that the list of aircraft operated by the school will remain largely static, although there may be periodic updates if new aircraft are added to or removed from the fleet. The unchanging nature of this information makes it a good candidate for caching, and the easiest way is to provide access to the data through a simple function; we'll call this GetAircraftList(). The function performs two tasks:

- If the data already exists, the function simply reads the DataSet from the Cache and returns it to the calling code.

- If the data doesn't already exist, the function creates the DataSet, places it into the cache, and then returns it.

The code required to do this is as follows:

```
Public Function GetAircraftList() As DataSet
    If IsNothing(Cache("AircraftListData")) Then
        Dim strCon As String = "Data Source=(local);" & _
                "Initial Catalog=HiFlyer;Integrated Security=SSPI"
        Dim strSQL As String = "SELECT Registration, Manuf + ' ' + Model " & _
                "AS Details, AircraftID FROM Aircraft ORDER BY " & _
                "Manuf + ' ' + Model, Registration"

        Dim da As New SqlClient.SqlDataAdapter(strSQL, strCon)
        Dim dsAircraft As New DataSet()

        da.Fill(dsAircraft, "List")
        Cache("AircraftListData") = dsAircraft
    End If

    Return CType(Cache("AircraftListData"), DataSet)
End Function
```

Your routines now call `GetAircraftList()` to obtain the data and are completely masked from the fact that the data may be cached. If the application is terminated and restarted, the first request to call `GetAircraftList()` will once again create the dataset and add it to the cache.

Of course, if the item were never expired there would be no need to perform the check, but that misses the whole point of this intelligent mechanism. By allowing items to be expired, ASP.NET is able to make more efficient use of server resources and so promote a more scalable and efficient architecture. So, how can the developer control the expiration policies?

Cache Dependencies

Dependencies allow you to define rules used by the Cache to expire a particular item based on changes to files, changes to other Cache keys, or at a fixed or relative point in time.

File-Based Dependency

A file-based dependency produces a rule that causes a Cached item to be invalidated when specific named file(s) on disk change. This could be used when the data had been read from the disk into an object but needed to be kept up-to-date with any changes in the underlying file.

For example, HiFlyers want to allow their students to pay their fees in a number of different currencies, rather than just U.S. dollars. The application needs to keep track of exchange rates so that all charges are correctly calculated, but the rates change on a daily basis. Rather than manage this facility through the database, the HiFlyers server downloads an XML document from the Internet at the start of each working day and uses its content in the application.

To keep performance high you can't afford to read the file from disk each time you need an exchange rate, so it makes sense to cache the information using a DataSet. A simple function to do this is as follows:

```
Public Function GetExchangeRates() As DataSet
    If IsNothing(Cache("ExchangeRateData")) Then
        Dim dsRates As New DataSet()

        ' Fill dataset from the Exchange Rates file
        dsRates.ReadXml(Server.MapPath("ExchRates.xml"))
```

```
        ' Insert into the cache
        Cache("ExchangeRateData") = dsRates
    End If

    Return CType(Cache("ExchangeRateData"), DataSet)
End Function
```

However, you need to ensure that the DataSet is expired whenever a new version of the XML document is downloaded by the server. You can do this by creating a CacheDependency object and specifying it when you add the data to the cache:

```
Public Function GetExchangeRates() As DataSet
    If IsNothing(Cache("ExchangeRateData")) Then
        Dim dsRates As New DataSet()
        Dim dpnFile As New
                Caching.CacheDependency(Server.MapPath("ExchRates.xml"))

        ' Fill dataset from the Exchange Rates file
        dsRates.ReadXml(Server.MapPath("ExchRates.xml"))

        ' Insert into the cache
        Cache.Insert("ExchangeRateData", dsRates, dpnFile)
    End If

    Return CType(Cache("ExchangeRateData"), DataSet)
End Function
```

When the CacheDependency is created, it's passed a fully qualified filename that it subsequently monitors for changes. When the dataset is added to the cache, notice that it's now necessary to use `Cache.Insert`, passing the keyname, value, and dependency. Any time the exchange rate file is modified or overwritten, the cached data will be expired and so re-created the next time the function is called.

Although this example has shown a dependency based on a single file, it's also possible to pass an array of files to the constructor and have the dependency invalidate the cached object when any of them change.

Key-Based Dependency

A key-based dependency invalidates a Cache item when another Cache item changes, effectively creating a hierarchy of dependencies within the Cache. The use of key-based dependencies allows you to ensure that related items are invalidated when the item they depend on is updated or modified.

For example, the HiFlyers application maintains a price list for over-the-counter sales in the club shop. This price list is dependent on the exchange rates in force for that day, so it needs to be regenerated whenever the exchange rates are modified. You can use a key-based dependency to express this relationship:

```
Public Function GetPriceList() As DataSet
    If IsNothing(Cache("PriceListData")) Then
        Dim strCon As String = ". . . . "
        Dim strSQL As String = ". . . . "
        Dim da As New SqlClient.SqlDataAdapter(strSQL, strCon)
        Dim dsPrices As New DataSet()

        'Generate the key dependency
        Dim astrKeys() As String = {"ExchangeRateData"}
        Dim dpnKey As New Caching.CacheDependency(Nothing, astrKeys)

        'Fill the DataSet
        da.Fill(dsPrices, "List")
        Cache("PriceListData") = dsPrices

        ' Insert into the cache
        Cache.Insert("PriceListData", dsPrices, dpnKey)
    End If

    Return CType(Cache("PriceListData"), DataSet)
End Function
```

When creating the `CacheDependency` object in this example, the filename is passed as `Nothing` and the key of the associated Cache item (“`ExchangeRateData`") is passed as the second parameter. Notice that the `keyname` is actually passed in an array, as you can define multiple keys if required. Whenever the value of the ExchangeRateData Cache item changes (such as when the dataset is closed or rebuilt) then the PriceListData Cache item is automatically invalidated.

Time-Based Dependency

A time-based dependency causes an item to expire at a specified point in time. As with the other dependency types, the dependency rules are defined when the item is added to the Cache with the `Insert()` method. Time-based dependencies can be defined in two ways:

- **Absolute**: Sets an absolute time for the item to expire. For example, current time + 20 minutes.
- **Sliding**: Sets a countdown time for the item to expire. Each time the item is accessed (read or written) the time is reset to its initial value. If the countdown completes, the item is expired.

The syntax of the overloaded Insert method that defines these dependencies is as follows:

```
Public Sub Insert( _
    ByVal key As String, _
    ByVal value As Object, _
    ByVal dependencies As CacheDependency, _
    ByVal absoluteExpiration As DateTime, _
    ByVal slidingExpiration As TimeSpan)
```

Values for key, value, and dependencies can be specified as before, but additionally the absoluteExpiration and slidingExpiration parameters can be used. For example, to insert an item into the Cache and set it to expire at an absolute time, in this case in 10 minutes, the following could be used:

```
Cache.Insert("WeatherData", dstWeather, Nothing, _
             Now.AddMinutes(10), Cache.NoSlidingExpiration)
```

Note that a value must be passed for the dependencies parameter, even if there are none. In this case the parameter is passed as Nothing.

To implement sliding expiration with a duration of 1 minute, the following could be used:

```
Cache.Insert("WeatherData", dstWeather, Nothing, _
             Cache.NoAbsoluteExpiration, TimeSpan.FromMinutes(1))
```

In this case the cached item will be expired if it is not accessed at all in a 60-second period.

Cache Priorities

There is one further overload of the Insert method, which allows Cache items to be allocated a priority so that lower priority items can be removed from the cache before higher priority ones. The syntax for this method call is as follows:

```
Public Sub Insert( _
   ByVal key As String, _
   ByVal value As Object, _
   ByVal dependencies As CacheDependency, _
   ByVal absoluteExpiration As DateTime, _
   ByVal slidingExpiration As TimeSpan, _
   ByVal priority As CacheItemPriority, _
   ByVal onRemoveCallback As CacheItemRemovedCallback)
```

The first five parameters are the same as those discussed earlier. The remaining two are as follows:

- **Priority** indicates the relative cost of the object compared to other items in the cache. This value must be taken from the CacheItemPriority enumeration. Items with a lower cost are removed from the cache before objects with a higher cost.

- **onRemoveCallback** specifies a delegate method or function that will be called when an object is removed from the cache. This can be used to notify applications when their objects have been deleted from the cache.

ASP.NET removes items from the Cache when the Web server begins to run low on memory. This is a completely automatic process and can occur at any time. By using the `Priority` parameter, you can fine-tune the behavior of the cache and specify which items should remain in the cache (by giving them a higher priority) and which ones should be removed. Table 12-4 shows the values for the Priority parameter.

Table 12-4. CacheItemPriority Enumeration Members

MEMBER NAME	DESCRIPTION
NotRemovable	Any cache item with this priority level will not be deleted from the cache when the server frees memory, but will wait to be expired by its file, key, or time dependency.
High	Cache items with this priority level are the least likely to be deleted from the cache when the server frees memory.
AboveNormal	Cache items with this priority level are less likely to be deleted as the server frees memory than those assigned a Normal priority.
Normal	Cache items with Normal priority may be deleted from the cache as the server frees memory, but only after those items with Low or BelowNormal priority.
BelowNormal	Cache items with this priority level are more likely to be deleted from the cache than items assigned a Normal priority.
Low	Cache items with this priority level are the most likely to be deleted from the cache.

The default priority for a cached item is Normal.

TIP *Remember that these priorities only apply when the server needs to remove Cache items to free server memory; when an item expires because of its file, key, or time dependencies, the priority value has no effect.*

Cache Callbacks

As well as being able to set priorities to control which items are removed, you can also have the Cache class notify your code when an item is expired for any reason. To do this, you pass a *delegate* to a callback object to the `onRemoveCallback` parameter. A delegate is best thought of as a pointer to a method, although it has to be a method with the correct signature. In the case of the `onRemoveCallback` delegate, the method must be declared as follows:

```
Public Shared Sub MethodName(ByVal key As String, ByVal value As Object, _
                 ByVal reason As CacheItemRemovedReason)
                 'Code here
End Sub
```

The `MethodName` can be any valid procedure name; the signature dictates only the parameter data types and sequence. To create a delegate for this method, you can use the `AddressOf` operator. For example, if the method was named `RemovedCallback`, then the call to `Cache.Insert` will be as follows:

```
Cache.Insert("CacheKeyName", CacheObject, Nothing, _
        Cache.NoAbsoluteExpiration, TimeSpan.FromSeconds(15), _
        CacheItemPriority.Default, AddressOf RemovedCallback)
```

When the `CacheKeyName` item is removed from the cache (for any reason), ASP.NET will call the `RemovedCallback` method. It will pass the name of the item being removed, the data for the item being removed, and the reason the item was removed. The reason will be one of the following values:

- **DependencyChanged** indicates that the item was removed because one of its file or key dependencies changed.
- **Expired** indicates that the item's time dependency expired.
- **Removed** indicates that the item was removed by calling `Cache.Remove` or that another item was inserted with the same key.
- **Underused** indicates that the item was removed because the server needed to free memory.

You may find it useful to record details about cache removals so that you can fine-tune the settings. For example, if you identify that important items are removed because they're *underused,* then you may want to revise their priorities and maybe suggest that more memory is added to the server.

When and What to Cache?

Though the caching facilities in .NET are easy to use, knowing when to use them may prove a different matter. As a general guide, the best items to cache have the following characteristics:

- Relatively static and unchanging.
- When they do change, the trigger for the change should be clearly identified.
- Expensive to create and destroy.

- Inexpensive to maintain once created.
- Regularly referenced.

So, the most likely candidates are small amounts of data that change infrequently but are used regularly throughout the application. This may well apply to objects such as DataSets for lookup and static entities.

It's also worthwhile using time-based expiry on such items, probably using a sliding expiration time so that frequently accessed items remain in the cache, but those that are less regularly used get removed to free up resources. You may choose to place items in Cache state with no time limit, in preference to using Application state; after all, the Cache has the advantage of being thread-safe and requires no manual `Lock`/`Unlock` methods. If you set priority values for these items then you'll be able to easily control which items remain in cache and which are evicted if the server needs to free memory.

Caching Dynamic Data

To conclude the discussion of caching, let's consider one final idea: Is it practical or beneficial to cache regularly changing data? Your immediate response will be something like, "No, I can't do that because I need to see the latest values." But hear us out—you might just be able to make a real difference to application performance with this technique.

Consider the situation in which you have some data that is changed occasionally (maybe once every five seconds) but is read frequently (maybe 30 requests a second). This is fairly typical of enterprise applications that support hundreds of concurrent users. Although we'd all like to guarantee our data is always 100 percent up-to-date, in practice it's difficult to do so because there are all sorts of delays introduced by factors outside of your control, not least of which is the Internet itself. In most cases, you could probably say that the data the user sees in their browser is at best two seconds out-of-date, and at worst 10 seconds or more. Now, here's the crunch: Could you justify introducing an additional one-second lag into the currency of that information? If so, you might want to cache that data using an absolute timeout of one second.

What effect will that have? Think about it—the data is cached for one second, so all the attempts to read it within that period can be serviced from the cache without hitting the database at all. That means you're now doing one database read per second rather than 30, and if you're dealing with data from an expensive source (such as a query with a five-table join, sorting, and filtering) then you've made a big reduction on the load you place on your database server. Do this across your application and you can make a big difference to its performance.

Comparing Cache State with Application State

Caching and Application state share much in common. They both have application-wide scope and are accessible to all users, they're both transient and will be reset if the application restarts, and they both suffer from being Web farm unfriendly. However, there are also two key differences in their implementation:

- Cache entries are transient and will normally have an expiration time or dependency that causes them to be invalidated. Application state values persist for the duration of the application.
- Cache entries are equipped with an automatic locking mechanism to prevent unwanted concurrent access. Concurrent access to Application state values must be managed by the developer.

In many other ways the two are similar, and it may well be primarily a design decision as to which is best in any given scenario.

Output Caching

The state management techniques we've covered are extremely important, and through the use of Cache and Application state you're able to minimize the amount of processing performed to generate a response for an inbound request. However, there will still be *some* processing required, no matter how trivial; you could optimize performance still further if you could eliminate this all together.

If you examine a typical Web application you may be surprised just how much of its supposedly dynamic content is actually the same across several requests, but without some form of cache to store and manage this repeated content it would have to be re-created each time. Classic ASP developers have developed different ways of providing a caching mechanism, but as with many other features, ASP.NET now provides one as a part of the framework. This caching feature is known as the *Output Cache* and is quite distinct from the Cache class discussed previously. Its implementation is quite different too, whereas the Cache class was access programmatically, the Output Cache is usually managed declaratively, by way of directives in the .aspx files.

Using the Output Cache

Chapter 10 introduced the Output Cache HTTP Module during the discussion of page processing. The Output Cache allows you to store rendered page output in server memory and return it in response to subsequent client requests. This avoids the need to regenerate content each time. This caching feature is intelligent because it can maintain distinct copies of each page based on the entire set of parameters passed with a request, as well as maintaining browser-specific versions.

Of course, it's not always appropriate to cache the output, and even when it is, it will have to be controlled in some way. ASP.NET provides this level of control through `OutputCache` directives and through the HttpCachePolicy class.

@ OutputCache Directive

You add the `@ OutputCache` directive to a Web Form Page or Web User Control to manage its output caching behavior. The syntax of the directive is:

```
<%@ OutputCache
        Duration="NumberOfSeconds"
        Location="Any | Client | Downstream | Server | None"
        VaryByControl="controlname"
        VaryByCustom="browser | customstring"
        VaryByHeader="headers"
        VaryByParam="parameternames" %>
```

The `Duration` and `VaryByParam` attributes are required, and the others are optional. Table 12-5 discusses each.

Table 12-5. `@ OutputCache` *Attributes*

ATTRIBUTE	DESCRIPTION
Duration	Duration specifies how long the page will be maintained in the cache and is measured in seconds. If a request is received for a cached page after the duration has expired, the page will be reprocessed to service the request and then placed in the cache once more. Note that duration is measured from the point at which the page is first cached, rather than being a sliding timeframe that is reset each time the page is read from the cache.
Location	Location determines where the cached page can be held. Possible values are Client, Downstream, Server, Any, and None. Client allows the page to be cached on the browser client where the request originated. Downstream locates it on a server downstream from the Web server that processed the request, such as a proxy server. Server locates the cached page on the Web server where the request was processed. Any is the default and allows the cached content to be stored on any capable device. If you want to disable caching, set the location to None.

(continued)

Table 12-5. `@ OutputCache` *Attributes (continued)*

ATTRIBUTE	DESCRIPTION
VaryByCustom	This attribute can be set to Browser to cause different versions of the page to be cached for different browser names and major version numbers. It can also be a custom string, in which case you must add code to the Global.asax file to override the HttpApplication.GetVaryByCustomString method. The custom string is passed to this method as a parameter.
VaryByHeader	The value for this attribute is a semicolon-separated list of HTTP headers that cause the cache to retain a different version of the requested document for each specified header. This attribute is not supported for OutputCache directives in user controls, only Web Form pages.
VaryByParam	The value for this attribute can be set to None, an asterisk (*) or a semicolon-separated list of strings used to vary the output cache. If set to None, the output cache will maintain a single cached image of each page irrespective of any querystring or POST parameter values that are passed. If set to *, the output cache will maintain distinct cached images of the page for each combination of different query string or POST parameter values. If you use a semicolon-separated list of strings, the output cache matches these against the query string or POST parameter values and maintains a separate cached image for each. Any query string or parameter values that are not listed are ignored. This is an important attribute, and in many cases will be set to *.
VaryByControl	The value for this attribute is a semicolon-separated list of strings used to manage the output cache according to fully qualified names of properties on a user control. This attribute is not supported for OutputCache directives in Web Form pages, only user controls.

Content-Specific Caching

If your application contains static, unchanging pages, you'll be able to use the `@ OutputCache` directive in its simplest form. All you need to specify are the `Duration` and `VaryByParam` attributes, but because the page really is unchanging you can set VaryByParam to none. For example, the following directive could be added to a static page to maintain a single image in the cache for 10 seconds:

```
<%@ OutputCache Duration="10" VaryByParam="none" %>
```

However, many of your pages will be postback pages that contain HTML forms and controls, or they may read parameters from the querystring when the page is loaded. In these cases you won't be able to use VaryByParam="none". Instead, you must ensure that the cache maintains a different image of the page for each combination of parameters.

For example, Figure 12-12 shows a page in the HiFlyers Web Application that allows the user to check availability of an aircraft for a given range of dates.

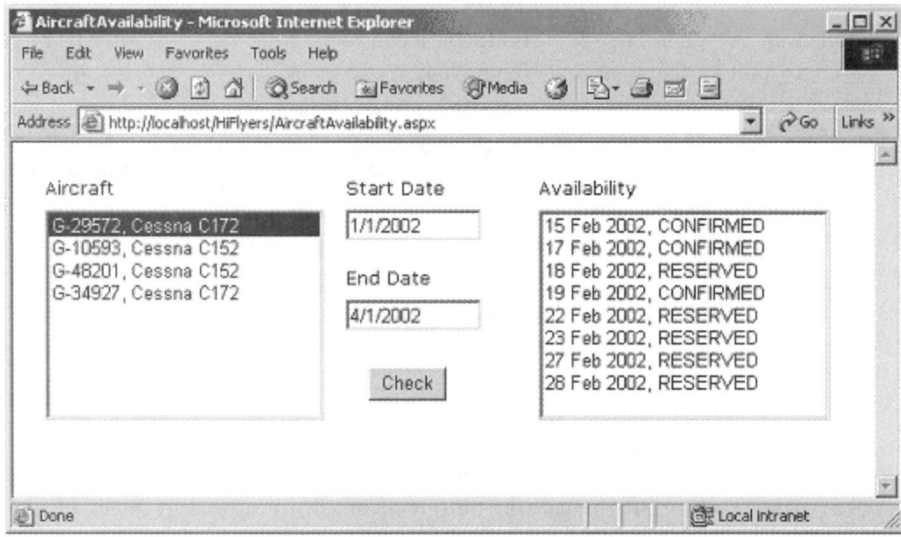

Figure 12-12. Check availability page

As you can see, there are five active controls on the page: two ListBoxes, two TextBoxes, and a Button. When the user clicks **Check** to cause a postback, the browser passes the content of each control in the Post Data part of the request, and it's these values that the OutputCache HTTPModule sees as parameters. However, if you simply set VaryByParam="none" then the parameters will be ignored and the page requests will be processed as follows:

1. When the first request is processed, the page content is rendered to the browser and also stored in the cache. Because the cached image was

generated from an initial request, the Aircraft list, Start Date, and End Date will be blank and there will be no availability listed.

2. The user subsequently completes the form and clicks the **Check** button to cause a postback. However, because a cached version of the page exists, it's returned to the browser and the postback request is never processed. Therefore the page will appear to reset itself and the user will be shown the original image once again.

Further postbacks are handled in the same way, until the cached image of the page expires. Clearly this behavior is not acceptable, so you need to modify the behavior of the cache so that it maintains different cached images dependent on the parameters.

Your first instinct is probably to set `VaryByParam="*"`, and so cause the cache to maintain a separate image for every possible combination of parameters. This solution will deliver the expected page images to the browser, but there's a hidden factor that means it could be a wasteful approach. We mentioned previously that the page contains five separate controls, but this isn't quite true; by now you should realize that there is also the hidden ViewState control, and this would be treated as a parameter as well. Therefore if you set `VaryByParam="*"`, you could end up storing many more different cached images than you need.

A better solution is to explicitly define which parameters you want to check when managing the cache. In this example, this will be the aircraft ListBox and the two TextBoxes, so the OutputCache directive should be defined with `VaryByParam="lstAircraft;txtStartDate;txtEndDate"`. Notice that you're using the control names as parameters, because these are the names passed in the Post Data. With this directive, the page is now cached efficiently using only the parameters that matter.

TIP *To prove that caching is enabled and working as expected, add a label called* `lblRenderedTime` *to your page and then add* `lblRenderedTime.Text = Now.ToShortTimeString` *to the* `Page_Load` *event handler. If the page request is processed by executing the Web Form, then the label is updated to show the current time, and if the page is served from the cache, then the label will show the time when the page was originally generated.*

HttpCachePolicy Class

The HttpCachePolicy class contains members for setting cache-specific HTTP headers and for controlling the ASP.NET page output cache. It provides for finer control than the OutputCache directive, but it requires more planning and coding.

The class is accessed through the `Response.Cache` property and could be used as follows:

```
Response.Cache.SetExpires(Now.AddSeconds(10))
Response.Cache.SetCacheability(HttpCacheability.Public)
```

This is equivalent to the following:

```
<%@ OutputCache Duration="10" Location="any" %>
```

If you need programmatic control, perhaps to vary the time a page is held in the cache according to the load on the Web server, then you may find the HTTPCachePolicy class approach to be more flexible than the OutputCache directive.

Fragment Caching

The previous techniques allow entire pages to be cached, but in some cases this may not be feasible. Instead it may be useful to be able to cache parts of pages, and you can do this by creating a Web User Control representing the cacheable content.

When creating the control, you can add an `@ OutputCache` directive to the control's .ascx file to define cache behavior, duration, and any other attributes. You'll probably want to use the `VaryByControl` attribute because this allows you to maintain different renderings of the page for different property values. `VaryByControl` works in a similar way to the `VaryByParam` attribute discussed previously.

When ASP.NET instantiates and processes the control during the page processing cycle, it will note the OutputCache directive and check the cache to see if a suitable cached image of the control is present. If so, it uses the existing image at the point the Render method would normally be called and incorporates it into the rest of the page.

Summary

Although the architecture of ASP.NET is radically different to that of classic ASP, in many ways the design process and requirements are similar. ASP.NET has not offered any major advances in terms of application navigation and control, but instead relies on the same code-based techniques as classic ASP and supports the same client-side features such as hyperlinks, forms, and framesets.

There have been big improvements in some areas, though; the entire event-handling model of ASP.NET means that technical design of Web Applications will be radically different, and facilities such as centralized error management and enhanced state management features make life a lot easier for developers.

However, where the true strength of ASP.NET starts to show is when you look at building large, scalable Web Applications that must support thousands of concurrent users and will run on multiserver Web farms. To most classic ASP developers this is a nightmare scenario, but to those with ASP.NET skills it has suddenly become a whole lot more achievable.

CHAPTER 13

Achieving Scalability

Who Needs Scalability

Let's Go (Round) Tripping

Load Balancing and State Management

Enterprise Services

Who Needs Scalability

DURING THE DEVELOPMENT PHASE of a Web project, you are typically the only user of the functionality you are creating. You'll concentrate on writing nice-looking, bug-free Web Forms that present accurate data. It's easy to forget that once your Web project goes live, your code will typically be subject to a wide range of other stresses, created by the number of users using the system and by how important your application is to the organization that has paid for it.

In this chapter, we'll cover three important "go-live" issues that must be addressed at the planning and design stages of your project—you can't build them in later. The first of these is *performance*, which is the one go-live issue that is easy to address during development. Performance really has to do with how quickly each individual operation takes when actioned by a single user.

The larger the number of users a Web application has, the less important performance becomes. This may sound contradictory, but pay attention to the specific definition of performance we just gave. The performance of individual operations becomes less important for heavily used systems because the interaction between the concurrent operations actioned by many users at the same time becomes an increasingly dominant factor in determining how well your application stands up. It's common for systems that perform well with two or three concurrent users to hardly work at all with twenty or thirty; this is because the system wasn't designed to share those resources needed by many users at the same time. As we will discuss further below, an application that doesn't need to be redesigned to cope with increasing demand is called a scalable application. In a scalable system, doubling the hardware should double the system capacity. *Scalability* is the second issue and is the main focus of this chapter.

The third issue we will address is *availability,* which is important for both large and small Web sites. If it's important that your site keeps running (because it is taking orders from customers 24 hours a day for example), you probably want to take steps so that your system can withstand a single failure—such as a server crashing or a hard disk failing. Availability is a measure of how well your application can withstand such unexpected problems.

It's important to get all of these individual issues into perspective. The way some people go on about scalability, you could be excused for thinking that it was a topic invented by consultants and Microsoft technical authors to keep themselves in work. Whatever anyone else says, it's important to realize that it is neither necessary nor appropriate to design scalability into every Web application.

Scalability costs. Building scalable software is more complex and time-consuming than building non-scalable software. Unfortunately, you have to decide to make the extra effort to write scalable software during the design stage of your project. It's hard to bolt scalability on to an existing system; you have to decide upfront whether it's worth the extra effort.

As we said above, scalability is *not* the same as performance. It is worth repeating the following: Many applications that zip along with 2 or 3 users are unusable with 20 or 30 users, regardless of how many boxes you throw at them. The root cause of scalability problems almost always has to do with the way programs manage shared resources. CPU time and memory are examples of shared resources, but so are more specific things such as database connections and record locks. It's all too easy to design systems that share resources perfectly well with a small number of users, but fall apart as the user count increases.

Imagine that you have written a Web application with built-in dependencies, meaning that every request must be processed by the same physical Web server. For example, this might be the case if your application relied heavily on frequently changing information stored in Application state. Sooner or later, as the number of users increases, your application will reach a point where no single Web server can handle the demand. A cheap and effective solution to this problem is to introduce a second Web server (or a third, etc.) so that demand can be split between multiple servers. However, because Application state is stored in memory on a single Web server, as soon as you introduce multiple servers, Application state no longer represents the entire application. You will need to redesign your application to store this state somewhere that will be accessible by all your Web servers, which, at best, will require numerous code changes, and, at worst, might mean redesigning large sections of your application and recoding them from scratch. If you had started with a scalable design in the first place, moving to multiple servers would require nothing more than a few configuration changes.

One of the main scalability-related design issues surrounds the use of Session state. Imagine (again) that you have written an application for all of the insurance brokers in your regional office that allows them to manipulate information while selecting the best insurance product for a customer who may be on the phone to the broker. It takes 20 seconds or so to read the insurance data related to an individual customer from the database, so you store it in Session state while the broker is trying out several "what-if" scenarios with the customer. Your application is a big hit, because once the data is loaded, trying out new scenarios is very fast because all the necessary data is held in memory. There are usually 10 brokers using the system at any one time (with a maximum of 25) and a customer is typically on the phone for around five minutes. Your boss asked you if it makes sense holding all that data in memory, but you pointed out (rather sarcastically) that the cost of 25 MB of RAM is a tiny fraction of the cost of one of his business lunches. Of course, you've forgotten that Session state is kept around for twenty minutes by default (and the brokers complain if you reduce it), so your peak load is closer to 100 MB—but it has never been a real issue.

It becomes a real issue the moment head office decides that the application should be made available to all 20 regional offices from a central Web Farm. It's decided that at least four servers will be needed to carry the load. Your network people explain to you that they will be using Network Load Balancing (NLB), which allows any one of a group of servers to pick up a request sent to a single URL—with the least busy server taking the next message. Unfortunately, this means that consecutive requests from the same broker are not guaranteed to be picked up by the same server. In other words, your carefully cached Session data for a particular broker may be on server #1, but the next request may go to server #3, which doesn't have the cached data for that broker. When you designed your application, you never thought about what would happen if you needed to spread the load across multiple servers using NLB—it just never seemed an issue. This is another example of a system that wasn't designed for scalability. The need for using multiple servers isn't the only scalability issue, and, in this case, your network guys may be able to come up with a solution, but not without taking some of the shine off your shoes.

There are different ways of responding to these two stories. One is to get very worried and to resolve not to write a single line of ASP.NET until you completely understand scalability and all of its implications. Another is to dismiss them as a load of tosh—if the business suddenly wants more users, they'll just have to pay for some rework. Neither of these responses is appropriate. Every Web developer should be aware of scalability issues, but there are relatively few Web applications where you'll need to worry about them too much.

If that last sentence sounds scandalously dismissive, then consider the following lesson that can be learnt from the dot-com fiasco of a few years back. Let's say GadgetsRUs is a mail-order company selling household gadgets. They make a reasonable profit, but they never had a Web-based ordering system. Back in

1998, there were people who actually thought that all you needed to do to go into competition with GadgetsRUs was to think up a slinky domain name and write a Web-based sales order processing program with groovy graphics. Never mind that it costs 1 million dollars to write the system, while GadgetsRUs has invested 100 times that amount in warehousing, marketing, distribution, inventory control, staff, and all of the other things that a real business needs. There really were people who thought that the most important component of an Internet-based retail organization was its Web site (hopefully, there are now somewhat fewer). Our point is this: If your business can only process and fulfill one hundred orders a day, there is no point building a Web site to handle one hundred thousand orders a day. Quite frankly, the cost and difficulty of scaling up the business to that size (assuming it is at all possible) will make anything quite so inconsequential as a computer program into a non-issue. So, if you are building a Web site for your local farm co-operative, don't go overboard on scalability—they can only grow so many vegetables in one year.

At the other end of the scale, if you decide you can sell hot stock tips for ten cents each over the Internet, you had better take scalability very seriously. Not only will you need an awful lot of customers before you make any profit, but you're not constrained by the limitations of selling a physical product. So, in this case, your Web site pretty much *is* the business. And, if your site falls over because it can't handle ten thousand hits a day, you can be sure that someone else's (scalable) site will be happy and prepared to take your place.

Let's Go (Round) Tripping

At its simplest level, a user's interaction with a Web site can be described as a series of round-trips. In pure HTML based applications, each page is static, so a trip to the server is needed to get any new information. Round-trips have a direct impact on performance, but they also have an effect on scalability.

For Web sites with a small number of users, there is usually no more than one round-trip being processed at a time. Compare this to a traditional client/server system where each user often keeps the client program open all day (or at least for a lengthy period of time) and it's common for each client program to hold a database connection open up until the moment that it's closed. Therefore, in scalability terms, a 100-user system needs a database server capable of serving 100 concurrent connections. However, on a totally stateless Web application, a user is only a user while they are waiting for a new page to be sent to them (in other words, during a round-trip). Therefore, it might well be rare for a 100-user system to ever result in more than a handful of concurrent users.

For many Web sites, the chances are that the server will be spending most of its time idle. In such cases, you are more likely to be concerned about performance rather than scalability. Minimizing round-trips will improve performance because the user will be able to do more without having to wait for a server response. Minimizing round-trips also improves scalability, because if there are fewer round-trips, there are fewer opportunities for resource contention (contention will only occur when the server is processing multiple user requests simultaneously).

A good design will minimize the number of round-trips required to complete a task and will minimize the amount of information sent to the user on each round-trip. The trick is to achieve this aim without users feeling short-changed. There's no doubt that users get quickly fed up with sites that take a long time to respond, so they are themselves often pretty positive about a low-overhead site. Let's take a look at some simple design approaches that can be used to keep round-trips under control.

Minimizing the number of round-trips:

- **Wherever possible, capture user input using one form, instead of several.** If you only have half a dozen bits of input to capture, it is usually possible to capture all of this information in one go. Be prepared to relax some of the user interface design ideals that you would apply on desktop applications.

- **Use validation controls with EnableClientScript set to True.** You may be tempted to design your own validation features rather than use the ones provided by ASP.NET. However, having the ability to exploit client-side validation on up-level browsers is very useful. Not only will users find the system more responsive, but you will noticeably reduce the need for round-trips.

- **Put more content in each page and make use of scrolling.** Adding text to a form does not necessarily increase its size dramatically. Desktop developers tend to forget that Web pages are scrollable. It is common to return a page that contains more text that can fit onto the screen. In the first page full of text, you can include hyperlinks to locations in the 'off-screen' text. When users click on these hyperlinks they get to see more information without needing additional round-trips.

- **Leave AutoPostback set to False.** Using AutoPostback on a Listbox, for example, will allow you to give feedback to users in response to each selection they make. This will look good and make the Web application behave more like a desktop application, but only at the cost of additional round-trips. Where scalability is an issue, try to avoid using AutoPostback.

- **Apply security tests early.** Make authorization the first step in any series of tasks that require it, then have your application display only the appropriate features and functions. If you allow users to make requests before checking their authorization, then subsequently deny access to the data they wanted (once you know who they are), they will get annoyed. They will also make unnecessary round-trips, placing unnecessary load on your system.

- **Use client-side processing.** Use client-side script to offload processing from the server. In some cases you may need to send raw data to the client; XML techniques work well in these cases. Remember that you may need to cater for all browsers though, so use the HTTPCapabilities object we discussed earlier to identify client support for scripting. Fall back to server-side processing if you need to, minimizing the amount of information sent to the user on each round-trip.

- **Every user knows that images kill Web site responsiveness.** Sadly, every Web designer seems to think that their images are so stunning that users will delight in waiting five extra seconds to download them. While we don't want to be labeled as killjoys, there is no point spending hours fine-tuning your software if your graphic designers insist on littering your pages with large image files. Most highly scalable Web sites use images very judiciously. It is extremely important to pay attention to details such as the size and resolution of image files. Good designers can create attractive interface designs without needing huge files.

- **Disable ViewState on all controls where it isn't needed.** This is particularly true for complex bound controls which can store frightening quantities of data in ViewState.

Remember also that ASP.NET Tracing is a great way to get a handle on the amount of data being sent to a user in response to a request (see Chapter 10 for more details). Tracing will also give you valuable timing information. Consider using Tracing as a matter of course to help fine-tune frequently used pages.

Keeping Round-Trips Short

It's important to spend time minimizing the number of round-trips and the volume of data sent to clients. Arguably, it is even more important to try to minimize the time spent processing round-trips. This is important from a pure performance perspective, but it is even more important for scalability.

If you are an experienced programmer, you will know many of the general techniques that can be applied to make programs more efficient. For dealing with VB .NET specifically, your best bet is to get a good book on how the .NET

Common Language Runtime works. For example, you will learn that exceptions in .NET are actually rather slow, so you should try to write code that only goes into Catch blocks in exceptional circumstances. Where performance is critical, it is much faster to test for a condition than to rely on structured error handling to patch things up for you.

Our focus in this section is not so much on how to make your code run faster, but to investigate design techniques that remove the need to execute code at all. There are two primary techniques here, both of which can have a profoundly beneficial effect on scalability:

- **Caching.** With caching, you are trying to avoid repeating work that you have done already. We've already discussed how to use Page Caching in Chapter 12; in Chapter 10 we saw the extent to which caching short-circuits the standard ASP.NET processing cycle. Page Caching is a very effective tool in busy Web sites. You can also cache objects and data using ASP.NET's state management facilities. We will be discussing these more in the next section.

- **Deferred processing.** Deferred processing means taking bits of code that don't actually need to be executed during round-trip processing and performing them later—and preferably on a different computer from the Web server. We will investigate a Microsoft product called Message Queue that makes deferred processing relatively easy.

The more shared resources you access while processing a page request, the more you increase the chances of contention with other requests wanting to use the same resources. The longer you hold onto those resources, the higher the chance you will prevent other requests from running. As soon as a battle for shared resources develops, applications start getting slower (as anyone who has ever sat in a traffic queue will understand). Faster cars are no more helpful in a traffic queue than faster processors are in resolving resource contention issues. In both cases, you are staring at a scalability problem resulting from a design that was never intended to support quite so much traffic.

Traditionally, one of the biggest causes of resource contention has concerned database locks. You need to lock database records while you are making changes to them in order to ensure the integrity of the changes you are making. This is particularly important if the changes involve multiple operations. The problem is that if you lock a record and keep it locked for any length of time, there is every chance that you will prevent another user's request from running if that user needs access to the same record. The result will be a locking contention which forces the code processing the other user's request to pause a while and retry. Worse still, your request and the other user's request might block each other, leading to the notorious problem of deadlock. Locking contentions and deadlocks are major causes of scalability problems, because they rarely occur when there are just a few concurrent users (and so don't get picked up in testing), but can have devastating consequences as the user base grows.

As you may recall from Chapter 7, ADO.NET has gone a long way toward eliminating most of the sources of locking problems that were so easy to create when using classic ADO. Nonetheless, there are times when it is essential to keep records locked while you are doing something else; and, as we saw in Chapter 7, transactions can be used to lock records and permit controlled rollbacks.

The trick with round-trip processing in general and transaction processing in particular is keeping the time they take to process to an absolute minimum. Performance tuning can only go so far and suffers from the law of diminishing returns. You can often look at a chunk of code and make it 20 percent faster; but, once you've done that, the next 20 percent is much more difficult, and the one after that, is more than likely impossible. However, one technique can often be applied: *deferred processing.* Essentially, this means identifying time-consuming processing tasks and moving them off-line.

Let's take as an example the process of confirming a booking at HiFlyer's. Assume that whenever a booking is confirmed, we give members the option of receiving a confirmation by e-mail. The total process looks something like Figure 13-1:

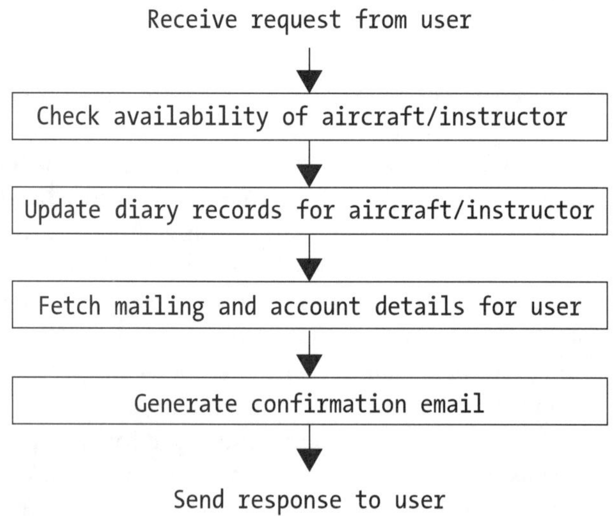

Figure 13-1. One possible booking confirmation process

Users don't always trust a Web page that tells them that their booking is confirmed. Somehow an e-mail seems a little more reliable and is certainly easier to store for later referral. You might also want to use an e-mail to include additional information, such as the member's current credit balance, or reminders of upcoming events or special offers. You might even choose to send them a more formal letter with their address at the top and so on. However, you don't need to generate this e-mail while you are processing the user's request. By deferring this task, you can respond to the user more quickly and increase scalability by reducing the processing and transaction time of the operation.

The neatest thing is that Microsoft has put a great deal of effort into developing a product that makes this type of processing deferral easy. While not many people get around to using Microsoft Message Queue (sometimes referred to as MSMQ), it is a powerful, free, and easy-to-use product that is ideal for addressing a number of scalability issues.

Using Microsoft Message Queue

We're not going to go into all the ins and outs of Microsoft Message Queue in this book; however, we will show you how easy it is to integrate Message Queue into an ASP.NET Application. If you are completely new to Message Queue, then you can tell if you have it installed on a Windows 2000 computer by looking in the Computer Management Console, which is one of the Administrative Tools available from the Control Panel, as Figure 13-2 shows.

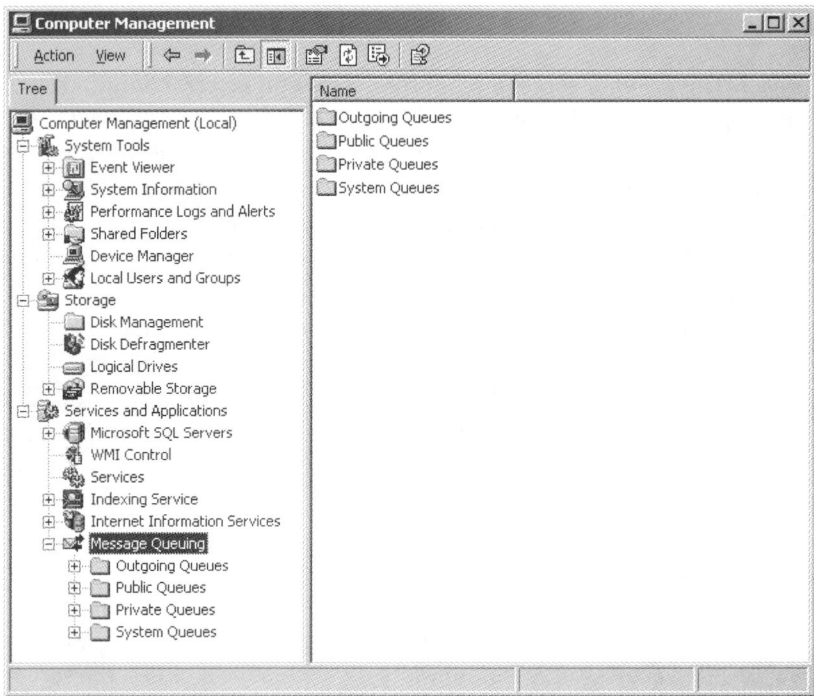

Figure 13-2. The Computer Management Console

If Message Queuing is listed as one of the Services and Applications displayed by the Console, then you already have it installed (if not, install it using the **Add/Remove Windows Components** button on the **Add/Remove Programs** applet also available from the Control Panel). Before going any further, we ought to say what Message Queue is. Ultimately, it is a product that allows you to create and use queues, and read and write messages to and from a queue. A message can contain anything you like—a string, a number, a DataSet, or a .NET object. Message Queue will look after a message until its recipient is ready to process it. If you want to send a message to a queue on another computer, your local Message Queue manager will handle that for you. And, if the network connection to the other computer is not available, your local Message Queue manager will hold the message for you and send it to the other computer when it becomes available. In this sense, Message Queue is an example of 'store-and-forward' technology. If you are thinking that it sounds rather like e-mail, you're thinking along the right lines. The difference is that Message Queue is designed to allow applications to send messages to each other, whereas e-mail is designed for communication between humans. Message Queue is also more efficient and reliable than e-mail.

Now that you know what Message Queue is, it's worth saying a few words about why you might want to use it. Here are three key reasons:

- **Deferred Processing.** Rather than perform some work as part of an on-line process, send a message that another program can read to perform the work later.

- **Availability.** If your server environment relies on several computers working together (e.g., a Web server, a database server, and an application server), then if any one of those servers is unavailable, the entire application may stop working. This kind of situation can rapidly reduce the overall *availability* of your application (the percentage of time it is up and running), which is very important in 24/7 environments. You can often use the store-and-forward capability of Message Queue to improve availability. If you write a message to a queue to be processed on a remote server, the message will be processed almost instantaneously while the remote server is running. However, if the remote server is down, Message Queue will continue to receive your messages. If you don't actually need a reply from the remote server, your application can keep running even if one of its main components is not functioning.

- **Peak Load Management.** Peak Load Management is a special case of availability. Let's say a server can handle 10 requests a second. If your application waits for the server to respond, you will experience an almost trivial sub-second delay. But now let's say that, at peak times, the server

> might receive bursts of activity of 20 requests a second. It can't keep up, and therefore your delay will build up alarmingly—you might even crash the server. However, if you communicate with the server via Message Queue, Message Queue will always take your input and return immediately, so that your code never has to wait. Under normal processing, the server will pick up the message and process it straight away. But at peak load, it will simply take messages from the queue as fast as it can, allowing Message Queue to buffer the excess demand.

As you can probably imagine, Message Queue works best when the flow of information is one-way. It is possible to coordinate two-way exchanges (so that you can get return values for example), but we aren't intending to address this aspect of Message Queue operation.

For our purposes, we are going to make use of deferred processing. To reduce the time it takes to process the round-trip, we'll take out the code that looks up the user's details and builds the e-mail content, and then place it in a different program—possibly running on a different computer—that can execute at a later time. To do this, we need to create a queue where Message Queue can hold its messages. You can create different types of queues depending on how your network is configured. For development purposes, the easiest type of queue to use is a private queue on your development computer (being private doesn't mean that it can't be accessed from a different computer). You can create an appropriate queue by right-clicking on **Private Queues** in the Computer Management Console (see Figure 13-2) and creating a new private queue called ConfirmBooking.

The easiest way to start using the queue is to drag a MessageQueue object onto a Web Form from the Component tab in the Toolbox. You can see that we've done this in Figure 13-3, where we've renamed the MessageQueue object to `mq`. Once the `mq` object has been created, use the Property Box to set its `Path` property to `.\Private$\ConfirmBooking` (you have to type in the name of private queues) and its `Formatter` property to `XmlMessageFormatter` (we'll see what this does shortly).

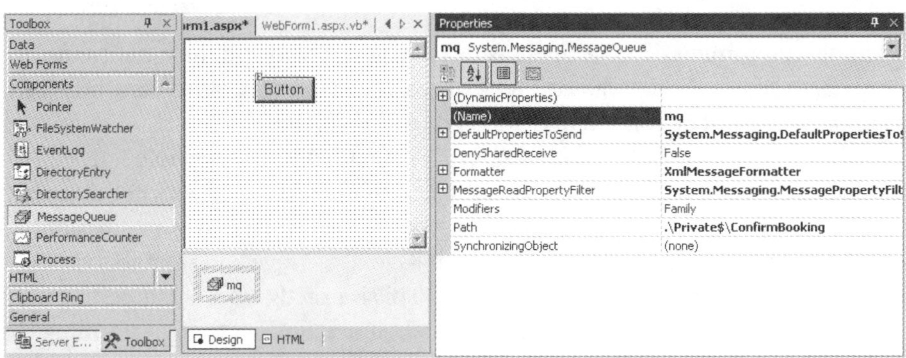

Figure 13-3. Creating a Message Queue object

You can include just about anything in a Message Queue message; many people simply insert strings into their messages. A more structured approach, however, is to place a .NET object in a message. For example, you can create a class that holds all the information required to perform the deferred processing. Here's the definition of a class that holds a MemberID and IDs for an Aircraft and Instructor diary entry:

```
Public Class Booking
    Public MemberID As Integer
    Public AircraftDiaryID As Integer
    Public InstructorDiaryID As Integer
End Class
```

Now let's look at some code that uses the Message Queue. Assume that a member has chosen the date, aircraft, and instructor they need for a lesson and has pressed a button to make a booking. The code to process their request might look like this:

```
Dim bk As New Booking()
' DO ESSENTIAL ROUND TRIP PROCESSING HERE
bk.MemberID = 22
bk.AircraftDiaryID = 1033
bk.InstructorDiaryID = 798
mq.Send(bk)
```

The essential round-trip processing includes checking the availability of the aircraft and instructor, checking the member's credit details, and inserting new records into the database to represent the new booking. This work will involve reading data from at least three tables and updating the database as part of a transaction. The remaining work is to generate the e-mail. At the very least, this involves reading data from one table to get the member's physical address and e-mail address; it might involve checking another table to see if the member needs any reminders, and at least one more table to retrieve the text for the e-mail. In addition, the content of the e-mail needs to be assembled and the e-mail software needs to be called. It may even be necessary to interact with Microsoft Word to generate a Word document and attach it to the e-mail.

The point about all this additional work is that it doesn't need to be performed as part of the round-trip. Even if you sent the e-mail immediately, it could easily take half an hour for the user to receive it. Therefore it makes much more sense to place the minimum necessary details in a message and send this message to Message Queue for processing later. This is exactly what is happening in the code above. Sending this message is much, much quicker than performing all the additional work required to read the additional table and actually construct the e-mail.

When you pass an object (such as a Booking object) to the `Send` method of a MessageQueue object such as `mq`, `mq` will convert the object into a stream of data that can be stored in the message body. Exactly how the object is converted depends on the setting of `mq`'s `Formatter` property. You may remember that we set this property to `XmlMessageFormatter`, and therefore the Booking object will be converted into an XML stream before it is stored in Message Queue. Once a message has been sent, you can actually look in Message Queue using the Computer Management tool, and take a peek at the content of the message. Figure 13-4 shows you what it looks like.

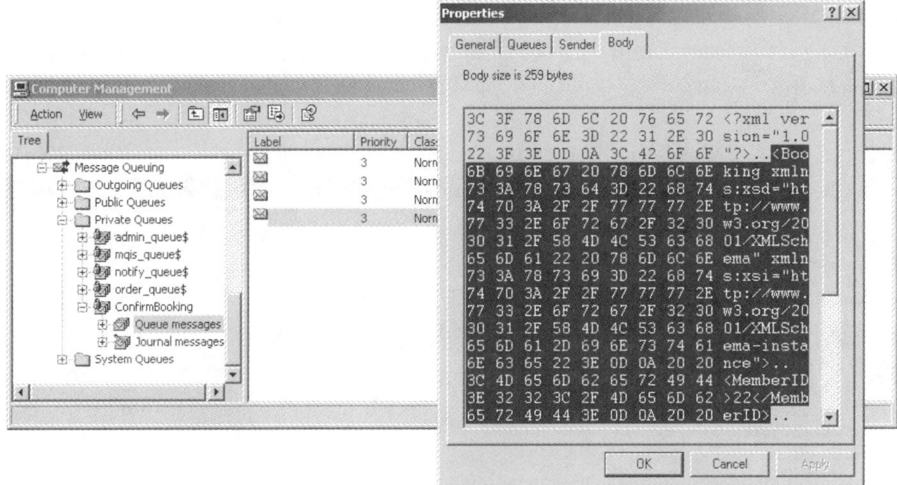

Figure 13-4. Peeking at the content of a message

While this isn't exactly pretty, if you look down the right-hand side of the Properties box, you can make out part of a Booking object and its `MemberID` property (whose value is 22) converted into XML.

Of course, once a message is in a queue, you need another program to read the queue and make use of the message. Typically, this program will be on a different computer to take processing load away from the Web server. For demonstration purposes, we will build a VB .NET Windows Application (called MessageReceiver) to read messages from the queue. In fact, you can use any type of application you like (given the ease with which you can write Windows Services in VB .NET and the suitability of a Windows Service for programs that are not user-driven, a Windows Service would ultimately be the best choice in many cases).

Figure 13-5 shows the Design View of our Message Receiver. Note that it has a MessageQueue object called `mq` (remember this is a different application from the Web Application, so this `mq` is not the same object as the one we saw earlier). Note that the `Path` and `Formatter` have been set as before, but note also that the `TargetTypeNames` property (exposed by expanding the `Formatter` property) has been set to include the string `MessageReceiver.Booking, MessageReceiver`. When you call the `Receive` method on `mq`, the content of the message will be converted into an object. The `TargetTypeNames` property tells `mq` which type of object the message content should be converted to. As you will see in the code sample below, we have added a class called Booking to the MessageReceiver project with exactly the same properties as the Booking class in the Web Application. The full name of this class (including its .NET Namespace) is `MessageReceiver.Booking`, and it resides in an assembly (the .NET name for a program or component) called MessageReceiver. The `TargetTypeName` must specify the full class name and its assembly name, separated by a comma, which results in the rather long string we met a moment ago.

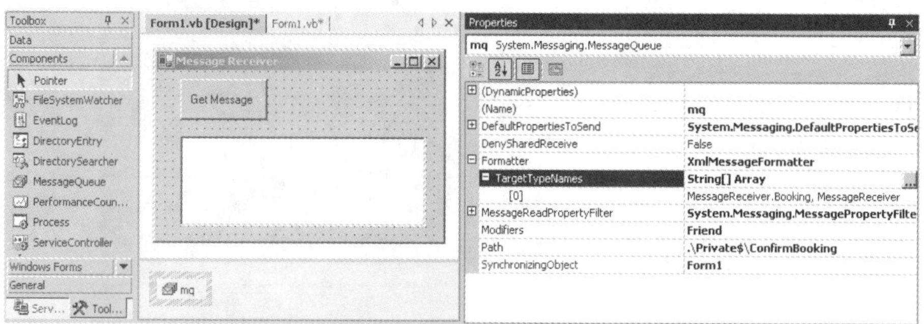

Figure 13-5. The Message Receiver

Once you've added the Booking class to your MessageReceiver project, the following code can be used to read one message and display its contents:

```
Try
    Dim wait As New TimeSpan(0)
    Dim bk As Booking = CType(mq.Receive(wait).Body, Booking)
    TextBox1.Text = "MemberID = " + _
        bk.MemberID.ToString + ControlChars.CrLf
    TextBox1.Text += "AircraftDiaryID = " + _
        bk.AircraftDiaryID.ToString + ControlChars.CrLf
    TextBox1.Text += "InstructorDiaryID = " + _
        bk.InstructorDiaryID.ToString + ControlChars.CrLf
```

```
Catch exc As Exception
    TextBox1.Text = "No Message Waiting"
End Try
```

The key element here is the call to the Receive method. Note that it takes a TimeSpan as an argument (initialized to zero), which means that the Receive method will wait zero time for a message to appear in the queue. In other words, if there is no message, it raises an exception. As long as there is a message present, the CType function will convert the message content into a Booking object that can then be processed.

This code serves to demonstrate the Message Queue principle, but in practice you need to make two changes. First, use the information contained in the Booking object to read the required data from the database and generate the e-mail. Second, place the Receive operation in a loop. You want the loop to behave efficiently when there are no messages to process, so don't choose to write code that loops around frantically when no messages are present. Fortunately, if you call Receive with no arguments, it will block until a message arrives, which turns out to be efficient and convenient behavior in a program that is essentially running as a background task or service.

There is far more to Message Queue than we have seen here; however, it has been worth spending a few pages looking at it for a number of reasons. One is that it is an excellent and under-used tool for handling many of the scalability and availability issues faced by Web sites intended to handle very high throughput. Another reason is that using Message Queue to offload on-line processing clearly requires more effort than simply handling the processing directly. You have to set up the queue and create and administer a Message Receiver. For Web sites with low loading, using Message Queue is actually less efficient than coding the e-mail generation directly into round-trip processing code. It is typically not appropriate to use Message Queue unless you anticipate scalability or availability issues. Message Queue therefore serves as a good example of our point that designing for very large throughput is not always the right thing to do. Scalability costs.

Load Balancing and State Management

The old saying 'throw hardware at it' has never been more appropriate. Installing more hardware is significantly cheaper than having some clever clogs consultant in for a day to analyze your application and tell you how to tune it. That's not to say that it doesn't make sense to design and code carefully, it's just an economic fact that hardware is getting cheaper while developers are getting more expensive (both of which, in our opinion, are virtuous trends!).

Of course, you have to buy the right hardware. If your current Web server isn't up to the job, it's easy to think that the solution is to go out and get a bigger, more powerful box. This approach is often described as 'scaling up.' There are two problems with scaling up.

Once you reach a level where prices aren't kept low by high-volume sales and fierce competition, twice the power often costs a good deal more than twice the price. Eventually, you run out of options—you can only fit so much RAM and CPU power into one box before it starts to smoke. It's often cheaper and more practical to buy four standard computers than one souped-up computer.

The other problem with buying a bigger box is that it still represents one single point of failure. If one computer out of four goes wrong, the other three may still be able to take the load while the fourth is being fixed. Remember our discussion of availability in the last section? To achieve really high availability, you should typically try to eradicate single points of failure wherever possible. Introducing multiple servers into the front-line is one of the best techniques for doing so.

Load Balancing

Load balancing is the task of spreading the processing load between multiple computers. We looked at one load-balancing technique in the last section: You can use Message Queue to move processing away from the front-line Web server and reduce its loading by increasing the load on a less busy or less critical server. In this section, we will take a broader look at load balancing and describe what programmers need to know about some of the more popular and successful techniques. For developers, one of the biggest implications of load balancing is the issues it raises concerning state management. Put simply, state management becomes a significant design task in its own right as soon as you decide to load-balance your application—and load balancing is pretty much essential for high-scalability, high-availability applications.

These days, when people talk about load balancing, they usually mean setting up a number of identical servers to spread the load created by a large number of concurrent users. This approach is often called 'scaling out.' As mentioned before, a group of servers configured this way may be called a Web Farm or a cluster. All the users use exactly the same URL when navigating to the site, but each request is handed out to the least-busy server at that time. Because HTTP is a stateless protocol, each request is treated on its own merit, making sure that the best server is used each time. If one server goes down, the load is automatically spread across the remaining servers until the faulty one becomes available again.

The process described above is known as Network Load Balancing (NLB). Figure 13-6 shows you how it works.

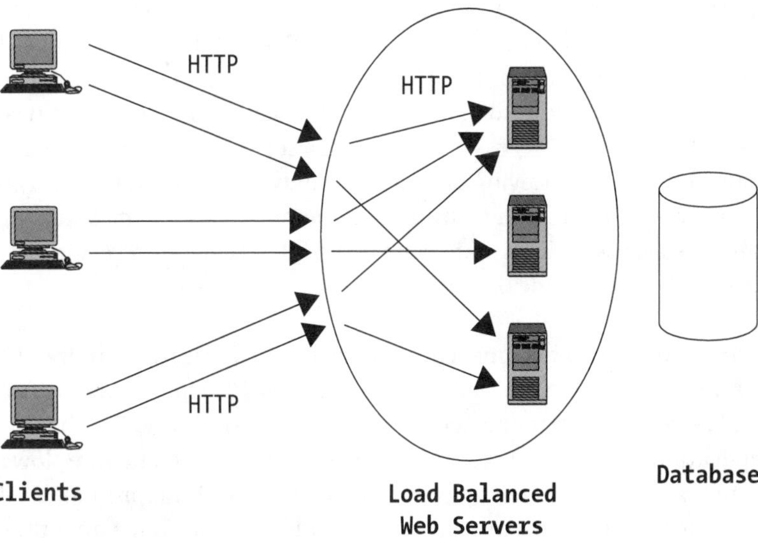

Figure 13-6. Network Load Balancing

The various means by which NLB is implemented form a fascinating subject in their own right. For very high performance, you can buy hardware solutions that receive incoming requests and farm them out appropriately. Windows 2000 Advanced Server ships with a software implementation of NLB that also gives high performance and doesn't have a single point of failure. Rather than passing through a single gateway, each server 'knows' which one should take the next request, so the best one will always get it. Fascinating indeed, but as a developer you will typically let the network guys figure out how best to set up NLB. You might not even need to worry about making sure that all the servers are set up correctly (and identically) because there are products such as Microsoft Application Center that will sort this out for you. Your job is to make sure that your application works correctly on a Web Farm.

So what kind of things should you be thinking about?

- **Each request from the same user may be handled by a different server.** There is therefore no point storing user-specific information (for example, Session state) in memory on one of the front-line servers because it won't be available to other servers. We'll discuss some solutions to this problem shortly.

- **Be very careful using Application or Cache state in a Web Farm because both Application and Cache state store information in local memory.** If you have information that doesn't change, or only rarely changes, it's easy to make sure that each Web server loads the same data. Loading non-volatile information into Application or Cache state is relatively straightforward; however, you need to be much more careful about data that changes frequently because of the difficulty of synchronizing each server. Your only real solution is to store such information on a different computer where all the Web servers can access it (such as on a separate database server). The issue here is that retrieving data across a network from a database is many times slower than reading it from local memory. This means that code that runs fine accessing local state can become dead slow when calling across a network for the same data.

- **Your database can become a bottleneck because it is much more difficult to replicate than Web servers.** Notice in Figure 13-6 that while the front-line Web servers are replicated, the database server is not. Database replication features work reasonably well for static data, but are slow and complex for data that changes a lot—such as data about product availability, customer accounts, or reservations and bookings. Consequently, while "scaling out" works well for Web servers, it can't be used to address scalability issues that result from heavy database loading. Database scalability is not the same issue as database availability, and it is quite common to use *clustering* as a technique to eliminate the database as a single point of failure. When a cluster is created, multiple physical servers maintain a single database using data storage that each server can access. If one server fails, another server can keep the application running until the failed server is repaired. When the data storage itself is implemented as a redundant disk array (for example, using RAID 5 technology), the combination of clustered servers and redundant disks results in a system that can survive many common types of failure and offer very high availability.

- **You need to ensure that you don't hard-code any references to the physical Web server into your application.** This is because each server in a Web Farm will have a different name (of course, you wouldn't do this anyway, would you?). Be particularly careful about filenames, database connection strings, and the like.

Application Partitioning

Another way to spread the load on front-line servers is to move some of the processing to a second set of servers. Many application designers choose a design approach where their front-line servers only perform user interface-related processing, passing all heavy work to a "business tier." The task of splitting functionality into presentation components and business components is called *application partitioning.* This design approach helps keep the front-line servers very lightweight (see Chapter 13). Figure 13-7 shows what this can look like.

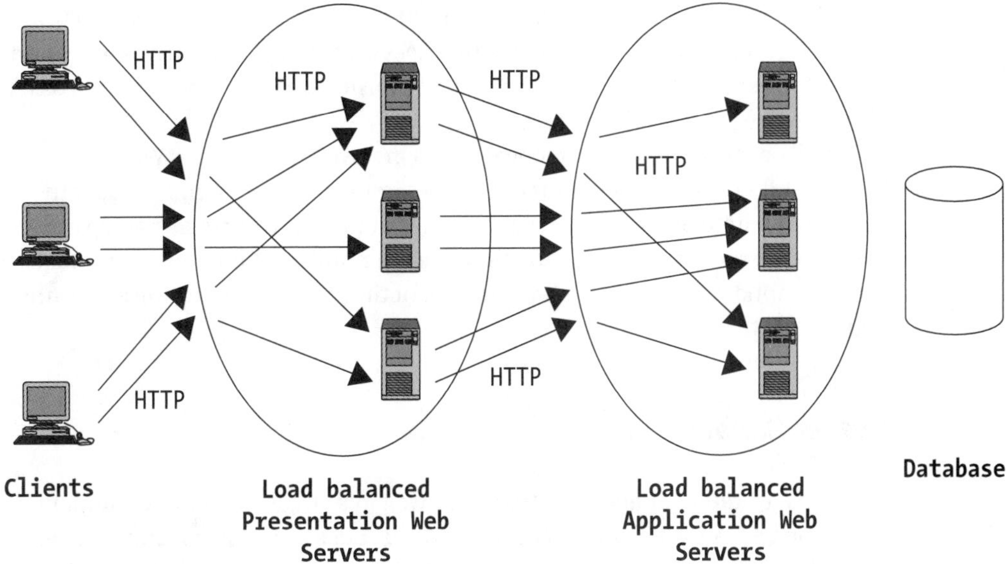

Figure 13-7. Application partitioning

In most of the examples in this book, the functionality of the Web site is coded right inside the event handlers of a Web Form. This approach works fine for small applications, but it gives no real opportunity to structure your code or reuse common bits of functionality. The object-oriented features of VB .NET make it easy to design systems where all the real business functionality is implemented as a set of objects. The code in each Web Form processes and validates user input, makes calls to the business objects to do the heavy work, and then formats the output that gets sent back to the user's browser.

There are many good reasons to follow this design model and plenty of systems design books will go through the reasons in detail. One good reason is that you can take those business objects and install them on a separate server, often called an Application Server. While a front-line server is waiting for an Application Server to return, the front-line server's CPU can be handling the presentation work for a different user. The net result is a more responsive and manageable system.

You may be wondering about how the front line ('Presentation') servers call objects that run on a different server. In the bad old days before .NET, DCOM was the most common approach for making remote object calls. DCOM has a justified reputation for being difficult to configure and it doesn't work with efficient load-balancing technologies such as NLB. .NET provides two techniques for accessing remote objects, both of which are more satisfying than DCOM. The first is the subject of Chapter 14: Web Services. The second is .NET Remoting, which in many ways is similar to Web Services, but a little more sophisticated (and therefore harder to use). Both techniques work with NLB; so, when a front-line server makes a method call on a business object, the least busy Application server will service the call, ensuring that the business-tier servers are used as efficiently as the presentation-tier servers.

We'll cover some of the practical issues involved in designing Web Services in Chapter 14. From a design point of view, it's important to remember that any call across a network takes a certain amount of time. If you are designing objects to be used remotely, you need to minimize the number of method calls it takes to get a job done, otherwise you'll waste a lot of time to-ing and fro-ing across the network.

State Management

Solutions to state management that work well in a single-server environment often don't work well in a Web Farm. This is because the simplest and most efficient way to store state is to hold it in the local memory of the Web server. In a Web Farm, each server has its own local memory. Storing data about a user in the memory of one server is not going to help much when that user's next request is handled by a different server in the Web Farm because the original state simply isn't available on the current server.

If performance isn't an issue, you might be tempted to store *all* your state in a relational database such as SQLServer. While not all data is suitable for storage in a database, most data is. A decent database server provides a safe and effective place to store data, with security, transaction control, logging, guaranteed consistency, and multi-threaded access management all thrown in.

The main reason for considering any other way of storing state is speed (another acceptable reason is convenience). This is not to say that there is anything inherently bad or slow about databases—it's just that you need to reflect on the two maxims of high performance systems design:

- About the slowest thing you can ever do with data is to save it to disk.
- The other slowest thing you can do with data is to pass it between processes or computers.

You always suffer from the second maxim when communicating with a relational database server; it can also be difficult to avoid maxim number one. Accessing data held in local memory is much, much faster than requesting it from across a network. For these and other reasons, ASP.NET provides a range of memory-based state management mechanisms (Application, Session, Cache, and View state).

We've discussed all these state management features in some detail in earlier chapters. Our purpose here is simply to readdress them when scalability is a concern, and in particular, when you are designing for Web Farm usage.

Of all the state management systems, ViewState is the most scalable because it stores state in the client's browser and not on a server. Almost by definition, each new user adds a new computer to the system; and so, by storing state on the user's own computer, ViewState completely satisfies our definition of scalability. Used carefully, ViewState should be considered a key tool when designing scalable systems.

Both Application and Cache state do more or less the same thing: They allow you to hold data in memory that is shared between all users of an application on the same server. Because data is held in memory, Application and Cache state are blisteringly fast. You can improve the performance and scalability of an application very significantly by holding suitable data in Application or Cache state, instead of reading it from a database. For example, by holding lookup data in a DataSet, you have all the sorting and filtering capability you are likely to need without ever needing to trouble your database for it. Because the quantity of data you are holding is generally independent of the number of users, you can fairly accurately calculate the amount of RAM needed on each server—a sudden peak in the number of concurrent users is unlikely to add extra stress.

The main problem with Application and Cache state arises when you need to design for Web Farms. Whereas on a single server, you can treat Application and Cache state as a read/write mechanism, they both effectively become read-only mechanisms in a Web Farm. The reason for this is that a change made to Application or Cache state on one server won't be made to the same Application or Cache variables on other servers, so you won't have consistent data on each server. The consequences will be very confusing indeed. Of course, you may well be able to think up ways of overcoming this, but more than likely you will decide that volatile data is best stored either in a database shared by all servers in the Web Farm or under the control of a single Web Service (one that is not load balanced itself).

For non-volatile data, however, Application and Cache state remain extremely effective mechanisms. You just need to remember that the cost of loading data into Application and Cache state will be duplicated across each server in your Web Farm.

Of the two mechanisms, Cache state provides more options for scalability management. Using Cache state, you can attach sliding time dependencies to all the data you add into Cache (Chapter 12). This allows you to intelligently manage the trade-off between performance and memory loading.

There is no real benefit to caching data that isn't used very much. Sliding time dependencies will ensure that data not accessed with a specified frequency is automatically unloaded, reducing the demand on your Web application's memory. Cache state is also able to detect when you are getting low on memory and will selectively release data from Cache to free up required space. You can specify priorities on cached data to control the order in which data is released.

We've left Session state until last because it is the most interesting of the ASP.NET state options. As you will already know, Session state allows you to simulate a user session in the otherwise stateless world of HTTP. It usually operates by sending a unique Session cookie to each client when the client starts a new session. The client includes the Session cookie in each subsequent request, allowing ASP.NET to recognize the request as part of an existing session. All you, as a developer, need to do to store data on a 'per user' basis is to read and write data to a Session variable. Session state is therefore unlike Application and Cache state; it is not shared, but is instead unique to each user.

Session state's ease of use as a means of storing per user data has made it a very popular mechanism (and it will be familiar to anyone who has dabbled in classic ASP). Unfortunately, Session state has been the cause of many arguments amongst classic ASP developers. Despite its ease of use, it raises some significant performance and scalability issues. It's worth reviewing these issues before looking at the improvements offered by ASP.NET:

- **Because Session state duplicates variables for each user, it can generate significant memory loads during peak demand times.** When you have a small number of users, there is no real harm storing large amounts of data in Session state. However, if you ever anticipate more than a handful of concurrent users, you should avoid storing large chunks of data in Session state.

- **The default timeout on Session state is twenty minutes.** Therefore, you can easily be holding Session state for several times the number of "active" concurrent users because Session state stays in memory long after the user for which it was created has disappeared. Making the timeout period much less than this means that a user's Session data can get lost if they take a few minutes out to get hold of some data or grab a coffee. Some sites have been successful at encouraging users to explicitly log off (by hitting a Quit button) when they have finished with a site. This allows you to drop their Session state early. It certainly helps, but you can't rely solely on this technique.

- **Managing Session IDs places extra load on the Web server.** While the load is small, it is worth pointing out that the very biggest Web sites generally avoid using Session state at all.

- **Many developers decided it was a good idea to store objects written in VB 6.0 in Session state.** For even a slightly busy site, this is a bad idea. The reason is that Web sites need to be multi-threaded. When a new request comes through, a thread is selected from a pool of available threads to process the request. Using multiple threads allows requests from different users to be processed at the same time, massively improving the responsiveness and throughput of the site. The problem is that VB 6.0 objects, once created, can only be used by the thread that created them. If a VB 6.0 object is stored in Session state, ASP is forced to use the specific thread that created the object each time a new request is received from the same user. This restriction messes up the algorithm that manages threads efficiently, putting the whole site on go-slow.

- **In classic ASP, Session state is always stored in local memory on a Web server, making it inappropriate for using in Web Farms.** One of the biggest scalability problems faced by classic ASP applications has been their dependence on Session state. Many sites basically had to be rebuilt from scratch in order to work on a Web Farm.

So much for the situation in classic ASP; in ASP.NET, things are somewhat better. The first three problems haven't changed; they are just fundamental issues that you can't do much about, apart from design to avoid or minimize their effects (for example, it is worth switching Session state off if you don't actually use it). In the .NET world, the fourth problem goes away; VB .NET objects are free-threaded and can therefore be run on any thread.

One of the biggest changes in ASP.NET concerns the last issue in the list. Session state is now no longer restricted to being stored in local memory; and therefore, ASP.NET offers a partial solution to Session state management for Web Farms. Note that we said "partial." The new features in ASP.NET are very impressive, but they are not a miracle cure. Let's explore what they can do before discussing their limitations.

ASP.NET allows you to choose where Session state is stored, without needing to change your code. You always code in exactly the same way we discussed in Chapter 12, but by modifying Web.config, you can radically change the system plumbing used to support Session state. Take a look at the following Web.config element:

```
<sessionState
        mode="InProc"
        stateConnectionString="tcpip=ermine:42424"
        sqlConnectionString="data source=ermine;Integrated Security=SSPI;"
/>
```

When the mode attribute is `InProc`, the other attributes are ignored. InProc is the default setting and is the fastest option to choose for a single Web server site. It stores Session state inside the ASP.NET worker process; in other words, it uses local memory for your Session state.

If you change the mode to `StateServer`, then all your Session state data will be stored in a separate process. This process is a specially written Windows Service, designed to store Session state. One benefit of storing Session state outside of the ASP.NET worker process is that if ASP.NET crashes or restarts, Session state is preserved. This can be very useful if you need to change Web.config on a live system. Changing Web.config forces ASP.NET to restart your application, which would normally mean all Session state would be lost. However, if the Session state is safely stored in a separate process, it will survive a restart. This is an immediate improvement in availability.

However, there is a rather more important benefit of using the State Server, which offers further gains in availability, as well as a major scalability advantage. If you look at the Web.config segment shown above, you will see that there is a `stateConnectionString`. This tells ASP.NET where to find the State Service. The string includes a port number and a machine name, which means that you can store Session state on any server that has the State Service running. The implications for a Web Farm are that all front-line Web servers can access Session state from a shared, centralized location. Each time a user makes a new request, you have no idea which front-line server will process that request. But you do know that the server will be able to extract the Session cookie from the request, and use it to access a shared Session State Service. Suddenly, Session state works in a Web Farm scenario!

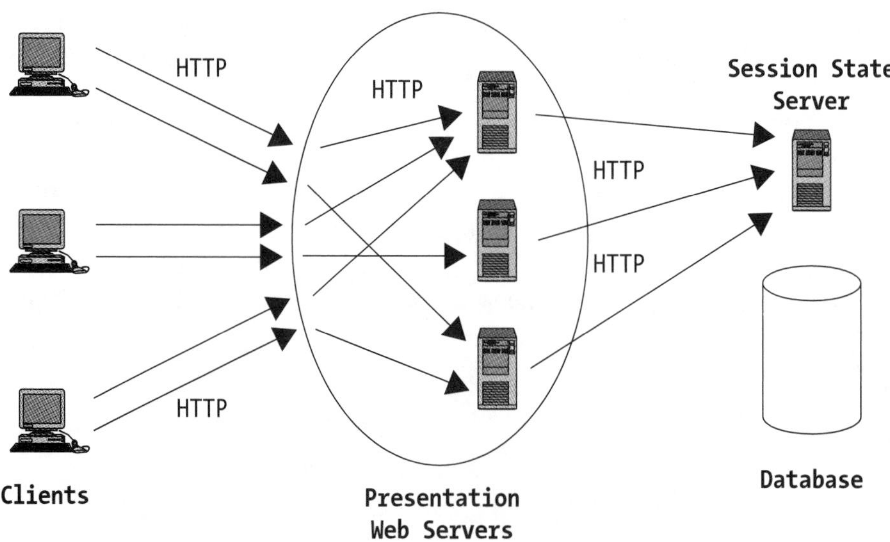

Figure 13-8. Using a shared Session State Service

Figure 13-8 shows how this can look. Before using the State Service, make sure that it is installed and running. To do this, open the **Administrative Tools** applet on the Control Panel and launch the **Services Console Application** (see Figure 13-9). If you have the full (premium) version of ASP.NET installed, you will see the ASP.NET State Service listed in console window. The status column tells you if the service is running (if it isn't, start it!). From then on, you can start using it just like 'normal' Session state.

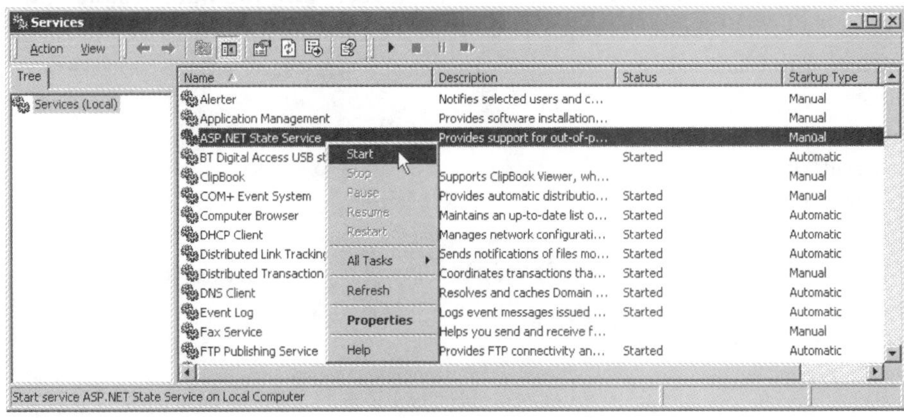

Figure 13-9. Using a shared Session State Service

As an alternative to running the State Service, you can also store Session state in SQLServer. Once again, no code changes are required; just change Web.config to use `SQLServer` as the mode attribute for Session State and provide a valid `SqlConnectionString`, such as the one shown above in the Web.config section. You also need to configure SQLServer to be able to store Session state. To do this, run an SQL script that ships with .NET, called InstallSqlState.sql. This script will set up a new database called ASPState, which contains a set of stored procedures that will automatically store Session state data in temporary tables. Because Session data is stored in temporary tables in SQLServer, it won't survive a database restart and is, therefore, no more permanent than using the Session State Service. It's possible to modify the scripts in InstallSqlState.sql to make the tables permanent if you need to. The performance characteristics of using SQLServer or the State Service are roughly similar.

Either of these approaches (using SQLServer or the Session State Service) makes it possible to scale from a single Web server to a Web Farm without needing to make code changes. However, you do need to be aware that although your code doesn't need to change, accessing data across a network is not the same as accessing it in local memory. If you design round-trip processing that reads and/or writes to or from Session state many times for each round-trip, then code that works nicely with `InProc` Session state could run many times slower when a network call is required each time you access a Session variable.

Fortunately, you can use a simple design pattern to minimize the effect of moving Session state over the network. The solution is to store all Session state data in a single object, instead of using separate Session variables. This solution works because it ensures that only two network calls are required per round-trip—one at the beginning to retrieve the object from Session state, and one to write the object back into Session state once all the round-trip processing is complete. Let's look at an example: Assume that for each user, you want to store three bits of data (their name, memberID, and a value). You might choose to write code such as this:

```
Session("Name") = "Ruth Archer"
Session("ID") = 10074
Session("Value") = 16
```

This code will store data in Session state which you can retrieve later:

```
x = Session("Name")
y = Session("ID")
z = Session("Value")
```

Reading and writing each of these values will require a total of six network calls when using SQLServer or the State Service on a shared server.

For a more efficient alternative, begin by defining the following class, which contains a property for each bit of data you want to store in Session state:

```
<Serializable()> Public Class UserInfo
    Public Name As String
    Public ID As Integer
    Public Value As Integer
End Class
```

Note that this class has been decorated with the `Serializable` attribute. This is an instruction to tell .NET that objects of this class can be turned into a stream of data (in other words, serialized). In .NET, only serializable objects can be passed across a network. Once you have defined a class such as UserInfo, you can write the following code to store all three values in Session state with a single network call:

```
Dim obj As New UserInfo()
obj.Name = "Ruth Archer"
obj.ID = 10074
```

```
obj.Value = 16
Session("obj") = obj    'makes a network call
```

The code to retrieve the object from Session state is equally straightforward:

```
obj = Session("obj")    'makes a network call
x = obj.Name
y = obj.ID
z = obj.Value
```

Because using the object reduced the number of network calls required to access Session state, this code is about three times faster than the code that used individual Session variables. The more different bits of data you need to store, the more performance gain you can expect to get by using an object. What's more, the object approach works out faster when using `InProc` Session state as well.

ASP.NET's new Session state management features are very impressive—but they can't perform miracles. Fortunately, by adopting a design approach that minimizes network calls, moving from `InProc` Session state to shared state in the State Service or in SQLServer need not have a seriously damaging effect on system performance.

Enterprise Services

Windows NT had Microsoft Transaction Server (MTS), Windows 2000 introduced COM+, and .NET uses Enterprise Services. Essentially, these are all the same thing, although COM+ and Enterprise Services provide more bells and whistles than MTS.

All three of these services are designed to make it easier to build highly scalable systems. For classic ASP applications or DCOM-based 'n-tier' systems, it was pretty much essential to use MTS or COM+ for any medium to large application (in fact, many classic ASP developers have used MTS or COM+ without ever knowing it). You might therefore think that Enterprise Services is a 'must-know' topic when thinking about scalability for ASP.NET Web Applications. It may then come as a surprise (and possibly a relief) that you really don't need to use Enterprise Services for all but some very specific purposes. If you are now considering skipping the rest of this section, please read the following three 'must-know' pieces of information about Enterprise Services before doing so:

- **In version 1 of .NET, Enterprise Services contains nothing that COM+ doesn't provide.** The reason for this is simple: Enterprise Services is actually just a wrapper around COM+ to make it accessible from .NET. Microsoft's product development ran out of time to implement native

Enterprise Services for .NET, so they simply created a .NET wrapper around existing tried-and-tested functionality. There's nothing wrong with Enterprise Services, and, in time, we may well see the dependency on COM+ removed—but right now, there is nothing new there either.

- **COM+ and MTS provide many valuable services, but many of these services aren't needed in .NET.** This is largely because .NET does the same things but in a different way.

- **The main reason for using Enterprise Services from ASP.NET is to perform distributed transactions.** A distributed transaction is a single transaction that involves two or more databases, or maybe a single transaction that makes use of SQLServer *and* Microsoft Message Queue. If you need distributed transactions, then you most likely need to use Enterprise Services; otherwise, you can safely leave them alone.

We are going to spend a little time justifying the second point from this list before moving on to see how to use Enterprise Services for controlling a distributed transaction. Here's a selection of things that COM+ (and therefore Enterprise Services) can do for you, with an explanation of why you probably wouldn't do things this way in an ASP.NET Application:

- IIS provides an Application Protection option via the properties page for each virtual directory. Because IIS security is breachable, it can be dangerous to run classic ASP applications inside the process space of IIS. The Application Protection option allows you to force IIS to run your Web Application in a separate process. What actually happens on Windows 2000 is that IIS asks COM+ to set up a COM+ Server Application in which to run the Web Application on its behalf (on NT, IIS asks MTS to set up a Server Package, which is just a different name for the same thing). This useful service provided by COM+ isn't necessary in ASP.NET Applications. This is partly because the ASP.NET worker process (also known as the HTTP Runtime) runs in a separate process from IIS anyway; and partly because each ASP.NET Web Application runs in its own Application Domain. .NET's Common Language Runtime guarantees the security of Application Domains, so there is no need for each Web Application to run in a separate process.

- COM+ automatically ensures that connection pooling works properly when using classic ADO database programming. Connection pooling works properly with ADO.NET anyway, so COM+ doesn't have much to add.

- COM+ does some pretty clever things to manage thread pools. So does ASP.NET.

- COM+ made role-based security programming possible in classic ASP programming. Role-based security is built into .NET and ASP.NET (See Chapter 11).

- COM+ provided *Queued Components* as a way of making Microsoft Message Queue programming easier. As we have already seen in the chapter, Visual Studio .NET, coupled with .NET's serialization technology, takes a lot of the pain out of using Message Queue.

- COM+ supports *Just In Time Activation* to exploit the scalability benefits of stateless programming. The objects created by ASP.NET Web Forms are stateless anyway, and as you will see in Chapter 14, Web Services are also stateless objects. You don't need Just In Time Activation in ASP.NET.

- COM+ provides export capabilities to make it easier to set up Applications on remote servers. This was necessary because of the difficulties surrounding the Registry which make configuration of COM+ applications a pain. .NET deployment is much easier, with no registry entries to worry about, so the need for such tools more or less disappears.

- Both MTS and COM+ provide some handy graphical tools for system configuration. There are no similar tools for Enterprise Services.

Enterprise Services provides a whole set of objects and interfaces to do all the things that COM+ does via .NET code. However, in most cases, you simply don't need to do these things because .NET has its own baked-in solution. There is, however, one major feature of COM+ and MTS for which there is no simple .NET alternative—COM+'s distributed transaction capabilities. We'll spend the remainder of the chapter looking at how Enterprise Services supports these.

Distributed Transactions

Imagine for one crazy moment that the software team that built the HiFlyers Web site has decided to launch a business hosting Web sites for small airfields all around the world. In this one huge application, they will hold the data for each of their airfield clients on the same tables. Worried that eventually they may start overloading their database, they decide to have two separate database servers—one for aircraft data and one for instructor data.

Convinced that this design approach will really work, the team needs to address what happens when a member books a training session, which requires booking both an aircraft and an instructor. This will require performing an update on two different databases. Now, clearly this update should be done as a transaction; otherwise, you might end up booking an instructor, but not booking an aircraft. The problem is that, in this case, you can't use an ADO.NET Transaction object, because Transaction objects are tied to a single database connection. You need to perform a distributed transaction involving two different databases, which ADO.NET can't do by itself. This is where Enterprise Services gets useful.

While this may sound like an unlikely design, it represents a very real situation faced by many organizations developing e-commerce sites. In order to safely make an e-commerce sale, you may well need to be sure that updates are made to two separate databases—a product inventory database and a customer accounts database. In the past, your business may have got by with these databases being separate and being run by the two departments that built them. But your e-commerce requirement means that you need a distributed transaction, involving both databases.

Take a look at the following piece of code that will turn a reserved booking for an aircraft and an instructor into a confirmed booking:

```
cdAircraft.Parameters("@ID").Value = 16
cdAircraft.Parameters("@Status").Value = "CONFIRMED"

cdInstructor.Parameters("@ID").Value = 7
cdInstructor.Parameters("@Status").Value = "CONFIRMED"

cnAircraft.Open()
cdAircraft.ExecuteNonQuery()
cnAircraft.Close()

cnInstructor.Open()
cdInstructor.ExecuteNonQuery()
cnInstructor.Close()
```

This code uses two different Connection objects (`cnAircraft` and `cnInstructor`) for the two different databases in the new design. There is no ADO.NET syntax that allows the two updates carried out in this code to be part of the same transaction. ADO.NET transactions are always tied to a single connection.

Enterprise Services removes this restriction. Enterprise Services (via COM+) uses a product called the Distributed Transaction Coordinator (abbreviated to DTC, but not to be confused with Design Time Controls) to take control of a transaction. The DTC can work with any number of different databases (and Microsoft Message Queue as well) to control a single transaction involving changes on all those databases. The only requirement is that the databases are configured to understand the way the DTC controls transactions. SQLServer works with the DTC out of the box. Most other major databases can be configured to do so with a little effort.

The simplest way to use Enterprise Services with ASP.NET is to make the whole Web Form transactional. This isn't necessarily the most efficient way because it means that Enterprise Services will start a transaction for every round-trip (even if a transaction isn't needed), but it will be adequate to explore the principles involved. If you want to go deeper, it is worthwhile exploring how to use Enterprise Services with Web Services or .NET classes, as these offer more scope for control of the transaction process.

In order to make a Web Form transactional you need to edit the .aspx page to add the `Transaction` attribute (in bold in the following code) to the Page directive. Here's what it should look like:

```
<%@ Page Language="vb"
AutoEventWireup="false"
Codebehind="WebForm1.aspx.vb"
Inherits="DistTx.WebForm1"
Transaction="Required" %>
```

There are various different values that can be applied to the Transaction attribute. If you want to create a transactional Web Form, use either `Required` or `RequiresNew` (they have the same effect in a Web Form).

The `Transaction` attribute declares that you want the Web Form to be transactional. This means that each round-trip will generate a new transaction. In your code, you can use the ContextUtil object to vote on whether you want the transaction to commit or rollback. When multiple objects get the chance to vote on the transaction's outcome, the voting rules can get quite subtle; but as long as there is only one vote, it is all very simple. To use ContextUtil, you need to set a reference to System.EnterpriseServices.dll and then import the System.EnterpriseServices namespace. Once you have done this, you can modify the code as so:

```
Try
    cdAircraft.Parameters("@ID").Value = 16
    cdAircraft.Parameters("@Status").Value = "CONFIRMED"

    cdInstructor.Parameters("@ID").Value = 7
    cdInstructor.Parameters("@Status").Value = "CONFIRMED"
```

```
        cnAircraft.Open()
        cdAircraft.ExecuteNonQuery()
        cnAircraft.Close()

        cnInstructor.Open()
        cdInstructor.ExecuteNonQuery()
        cnInstructor.Close()
        ContextUtil.SetComplete()
    Catch
        ContextUtil.SetAbort()
    End Try
```

When the page first loads in response to a user request, Enterprise Services will start a new transaction. Any database that is accessed while the request is being processed will be enlisted in the transaction by the DTC. Without needing to use any transaction objects in code, both of the updates will be executed as part of the DTC's transaction. If the code runs through without any problems, calling `SetComplete` tells the DTC to commit. The DTC then coordinates with both databases to commit the transaction. If an error occurs in the code, the `SetAbort` method is called in the Catch block. This tells the DTC that the transaction must be aborted. Both databases will be forced to rollback, even if their own update was problem-free. The DTC makes sure that distributed transactions appear to behave just as single database transactions behave.

If you know you are only ever going to use a single database, then you wouldn't use Enterprise Services to control transactions—it's faster to use an ADO.NET transaction object. If you need to use two or more databases, but don't need to do distributed transactions, then there is no need to use Enterprise Services either. However, if you want the ability to perform a transaction involving two or more databases, or a database and Microsoft Message Queue, then Enterprise Services is the most sensible way to do this from within a .NET application.

Summary

Only a few chapters ago, ASP.NET seemed pretty straightforward. Since then we've layered in a better understanding of the architecture of ASP.NET, introduced some important real-world design topics, and then marched head-on into scalability issues. Sadly, the real truth is that building the biggest, busiest Web sites requires going significantly deeper than we have gone here.

One of the most difficult aspects of designing a Web application is to decide how much scalability you can realistically allow for. Scalability costs and it doesn't make commercial sense to build in expensive capability that will never be needed. If you are moving to ASP.NET from being a desktop or client/server developer, it is unlikely that you will immediately take on the responsibility for a massive Web application. For 90 percent of the Web sites that will ever be built, most of the techniques covered in this chapter can be ignored. If anything, ASP.NET will result in a much larger number of small- to medium-sized Web sites, simply because it makes Web site development a far more attractive option.

However, the folks at Microsoft know that they will never be taken seriously unless ASP.NET is suitable for highly scalable, 'enterprise' type Web applications. It's not surprising that they have created and integrated some very powerful technology into ASP.NET to make such systems possible. ASP.NET really can deliver highly scalable, high availability systems—especially in conjunction with other back-office products in Microsoft's arsenal. In this chapter we have introduced some of these tools and techniques; your mission is to decide whether to use them.

CHAPTER 14

Web Services

What Are Web Services?

For the past ten years or so, there has been something very unfair about the world of computers. Although the Internet has made it possible for people (equipped with a browser) to interact with just about any type of computer, anywhere in the world with great ease and convenience, the same can't be said of program-to-program communication. If you want to write a program that requests information from another program on a different computer, you generally have to start getting very technical, very quickly.

First, you need to decide how the two programs will make contact with each other. What information does the client program need to locate the remote computer and the correct process running on that computer? Does the server program need to be running or will it automatically start up when a client needs it? Then you need to decide what networking protocol the client and server will use to communicate—it had better be one that both computers can understand! Next you need to decide how a request will be formatted, and what format each data type will take (how many bytes for an integer, how to terminate strings, and what about more complex data such as objects?). You then need to worry about what happens if one of the computers goes down or the network fails. If a client fails, does the server need to know so that it can tidy up loose ends? And we haven't even started talking about error handling or security. Choosing technologies that have a good chance of working on a range of different platforms has been a major challenge for developers wanting to create distributed systems.

Microsoft's own technology for doing this, DCOM (Distributed Component Object Model) is actually one of the easiest, but it's still beset with problems:

- DCOM is complicated to develop and difficult to deploy and configure. DCOM applications make heavy use of the Windows Registry and require each client to store a large set of identical Registry settings in order to be able to contact the server.

- DCOM is not very scalable. DCOM uses a sophisticated model to allow servers to tidy up when clients crash that requires constant network traffic between each client and the server to persuade the server that the clients are still up and running. Once the number of clients gets beyond a few hundred, the cost of all this sophistication gets too much, and there's nothing that advanced server technology such as Microsoft Transaction Server (MTS) or COM+ can do to remove this overhead.

- Using DCOM between different organizations is problematic because firewall administrators don't generally like the idea of opening up new ports for binary data exchange. Even if you get this sorted out, you get stuck as soon as you want to talk between a Unix box and a PC, for example.

It would be a brave person who claimed that DCOM (or even similar offerings such as CORBA or Java RMI) was a truly universal solution.

Yet at the same time, HTTP and HTML have solved all these problems for human access to remote servers. You can of course write computer programs that process HTML, and many organizations have been doing this successfully for years as a way of exploiting the Internet for remote program-to-program communication. It's a clever way of treating HTML as raw data that can be retrieved and processed by a program instead of displayed in a browser. The problem with this approach is that HTML is a presentation language, and it's not really suited to the task of exchanging data between programs.

There's one technology we've already discussed that is ideal for exchanging data between programs, and that technology is XML. XML is text-based and yet highly structured. Surely you could write a Web Application that returns XML instead of HTML? A client program could simulate calling a method by making an HTTP request and receive an XML document containing the return values of the method call. This, in a nutshell, is what Web Services are all about. A Web Service is a component that runs on a Web server and can be accessed across the Internet using standard Web protocols. The Web has more than proven itself as a technology capable of exchanging structured information in a scalable, cross-platform, and location-independent fashion. Applying the "Web approach" to components removes all of the obstacles that have bedeviled remote-method calling in the past. Web Services provide a whole new way of using the Internet and exploiting the massive investment that has already been made in communications infrastructure for the Web. If you believe that the Internet has already changed the world in profoundly deep and meaningful ways, you ain't seen nothing yet.

Just as ASP.NET hides much of the dreary HTTP and HTML processing required for Web Applications, it does much the same task for Web Services. Figure 14-1 shows you how this works. A client program wants to call a method on an object that is implemented as a Web Service on a remote Web server. Using .NET's client tools for Web Services, all the client programmer needs to do is to make a method call on an object passing in the required arguments (in this case, y and z) using exactly the same programming syntax they would use when calling a local object. .NET will convert this method call into an XML document and send it using an HTTP request to the Web server. ASP.NET will receive this call, unpack the XML document, and execute some code to process the arguments and generate a return value. ASP.NET will then convert the return values into XML and return them as the response to the client's HTTP request. Once back in the client, the .NET client tools will extract the return value from the XML document and assign it to the target variable (in this case, x) in exactly the same way as a local method call would.

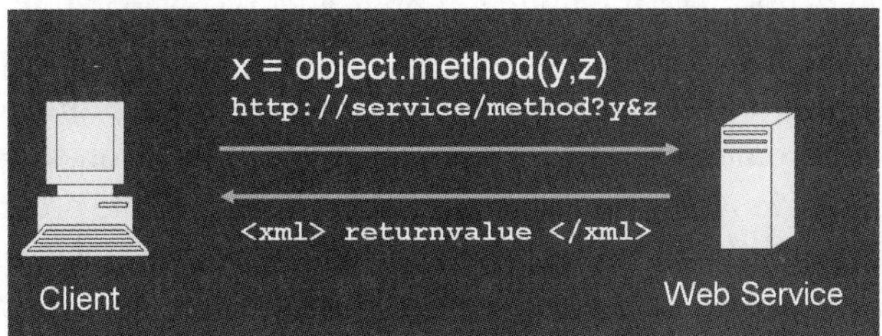

Figure 14-1. Calling a Web Service

It's crucial to remember that Web Services are a cross-platform technology. The same Web Service could be called from a completely different platform, and it would return the same XML document in response to the same method call. The Web Service client tools for use in a Unix client will not look the same as the .NET ones, but they'll work with the same inputs and outputs and provide a similar capability. Similarly, the .NET client tools can be used to talk to any properly defined Web Service, not just one created using .NET. It usually takes a moment for the importance of all this to sink in.

It's easy to see why Microsoft sees Web Services (or XML Web Services as Microsoft sometimes calls them) as more or less solving the cross-platform interoperability problem. Just about any computer can process HTTP requests and process XML—their main virtue is their incredible simplicity. However, don't see Web Services as purely a "Microsoft thing." All the major vendors are singing from the same hymn sheet.

The implications are huge. Calling a Web Service is like calling any other component—except that you don't care what language it's written in, what platform it runs on, or where in the world it lives. If you're on the Internet and have access rights to that Web Service, you can call it. Period.

To achieve full interoperability, Web Services require some additional standards over and above HTTP and XML. For example, to hide all the details of how Web Services work, Web Service tools need to know exactly how the name of a method and the value of its arguments should be represented in XML. It's also important to know what data types are supported by Web Services and how they should be represented in XML. A number of new standards have been developed and widely accepted for Web Services—these include Simple Object Access Protocol (SOAP) and Web Service Definition language (WSDL). New ones are under development to extend the capability of Web Service technology without losing the benefits of standardization and interoperability.

Creating Web Services and Web Service Clients

Let's get down to business and build a simple .NET Web Service, and see how to use it. Like many airfields, small and large, HiFlyers has its own meteorological black box that spits out basic weather information—temperature, wind speed and direction, barometric pressure, general outlook, and so on. A data feed plugged into our Web server makes this information available programmatically. You could display this weather information on a Web page. However, a more interesting thing to do with it is to make this information available as a Web Service. That way, other developers can call this Web Service and build the information it provides into their own front ends or Web Applications—they're not forced to receive this information as part of an HTML document. For example, the mobile application developed in Chapter 6 could get its data from this Web Service.

You're going to go through three stages to see how Web Services work in practice:

1. Build a Web Service.
2. Test the Web Service.
3. Develop a Windows client program for the Web Service.

Building a Web Service

The first step is to use Visual Studio .NET to create an ASP.NET Web Service project. Call it Weather and create it on your local Web server. To begin with, you'll code just two methods in the Web Service (Web Service methods are called *Web Methods*) one for temperature and one for outlook. You enter code in the code window just as you would for Web Applications, and the entire code for this Web Service (ignoring the designer-generated code) is simply this:

```
Imports System.Web.Services

<WebService(Namespace := "http://tempuri.org/")> _
Public Class Service1
    Inherits System.Web.Services.WebService

    'return a random Celsius temperature
    <WebMethod()> Public Function Temperature() As Integer
        Temperature = (New Random()).Next(-10, 30)
    End Function

    'return a random outlook
    <WebMethod()> Public Function Outlook() As String
        Dim values() As String = {"Sun", "Cloud", "Snow", "Rain"}
        Dim random = (New Random()).Next(0, 4)
        Outlook = values(random)
    End Function

End Class
```

Several things are going on here, but for now, just focus on the two Web Methods, `Temperature` and `Outlook`. Interfacing to meteorological data recorders is not a selling point of this book, so the two Web Methods simply return random data. Of course, you could use any VB .NET code here, and typically, Web Services interact with databases or other server-based data stores.

The Web Methods are standard bits of code, with the exception of the `<WebMethod()>` attribute that prefixes each method signature. The `WebMethod` attribute is simply an instruction to ASP.NET to treat this method as a Web Method. This means that it will be callable over the Internet and that its return values will be automatically converted into XML documents.

Having coded the two Web Methods, the Web Service is now ready to use. Your next task is to test it. Before doing so, it's worth addressing some of the things that ASP.NET and Visual Studio have done in the background to make building a Web Service so easy. You'll be able to draw on your knowledge of ASP.NET architecture learnt in earlier chapters to make sense of what follows.

An HTTP request needs a URL, and ASP.NET Web Services are all created to use URLs with an .asmx extension. Visual Studio .NET automatically generates an .asmx file when you create a Web Service project, so you don't need to do too much with the file (so long as you remember to distribute it), but it does help to know what it contains. Fortunately, the .asmx file generated by ASP.NET is always simple. The file generated for the Weather Web Service (called service1.asmx) contains the following:

```
<%@ WebService Language="vb" Codebehind="Service1.asmx.vb"
    Class="Weather.Service1" %>
```

The actual code that implements the Web Service (the VB code shown previously) is contained in a class called Weather.Service1 in a file called service1.asmx.vb, although Visual Studio .NET automatically compiles the code to a DLL that resides in the \bin subdirectory of the IIS virtual directory created to hold the Web Services files.

Hopefully, this structure will sound familiar to you. It's exactly the same as the structure used for ASP.NET Web Applications. There's a navigable file containing an ASP.NET directive (in this case the `@WebService` directive), which references code compiled into a .NET assembly. In fact, if you want to know the processing architecture for ASP.NET Web Services, it's precisely that discussed for Web Applications in Chapter 10. Because Web Services have an .asmx extension instead of an .aspx extension, the HTTP request will be routed to a different HTTP Handler, based on the configuration information stored in machine.config. The HTTP Handler for Web Services knows about Web Methods in just the same way that the HTTP Handler for Web Forms knows about Web Controls. There's no other difference between a Web Application and a Web Service, meaning that you can apply practically all the techniques you've learned for state management, caching, deployment, and security to Web Services.

Testing a Web Service

Web Services generated using ASP.NET have a built-in test facility that enables a Web Service to be tested without needing to build a client program with which to test it. This is a useful feature, especially during development. All you need to do is to type the URL for the Web Service into the address line of a browser, and ASP.NET will generate a test page (known as the Service Help page) that you can use to test the Web Service. Alternatively, running a Web Service project from within Visual Studio will also display the test page. Figure 14-2 shows the test page for the Weather Web Service.

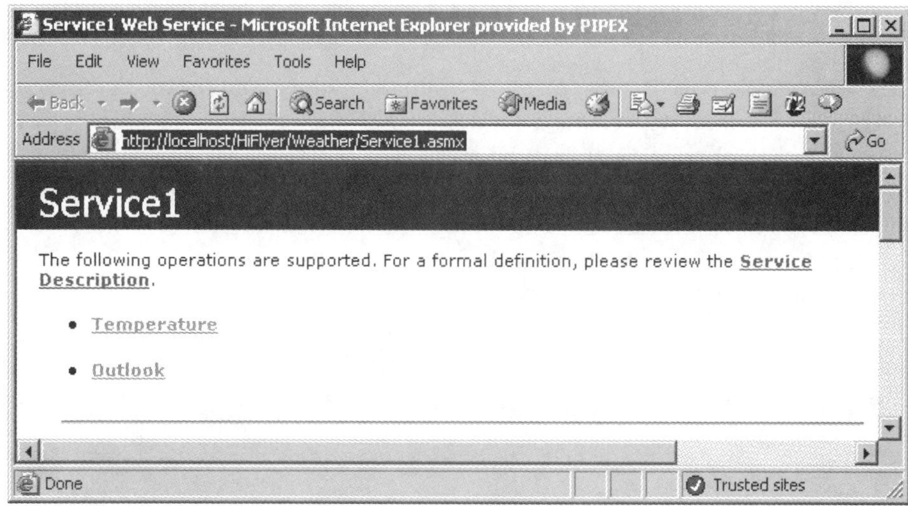

Figure 14-2. The Service Help page

As you can see, the Service Help page displays the name of the Weather Web Service and lists the two methods currently implemented by it. Better still, by clicking on one of the method names, you can call the method and see what it returns. If you have the Web Service project loaded into Visual Studio .NET, you can even set break points in your code, in which case you can use the Service Help page as a means of testing and stepping through the your code. Figure 14-3 shows the result of calling the `Outlook` method through the Service Help page.

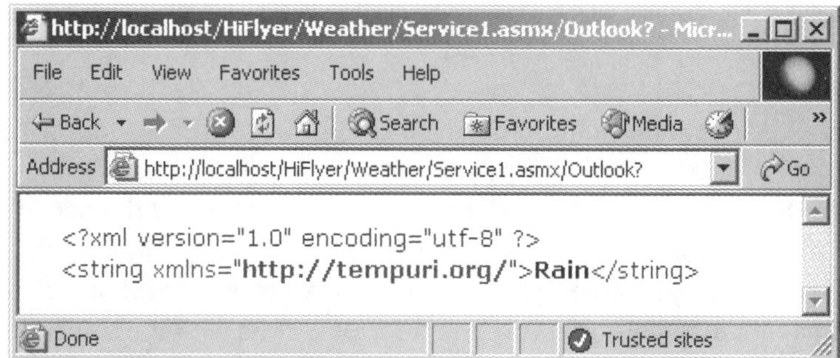

Figure 14-3. Web Service return data

Here you can see that an XML document has been returned to Internet Explorer, containing the result of calling the `Outlook` Web Method.

Building a Web Service Client

The Service Help page is convenient for testing, but it's not how a Web Service is intended to be used. We'll create a Windows Application using Visual Studio .NET to act as a client for our Weather Web Service, and see how a desktop application can be Web-enabled without users even knowing that they're using the Internet. Figure 14-4 shows you what this client program looks like. Pressing the Get Weather button will call the Web Service and display the results, along with an appropriate picture.

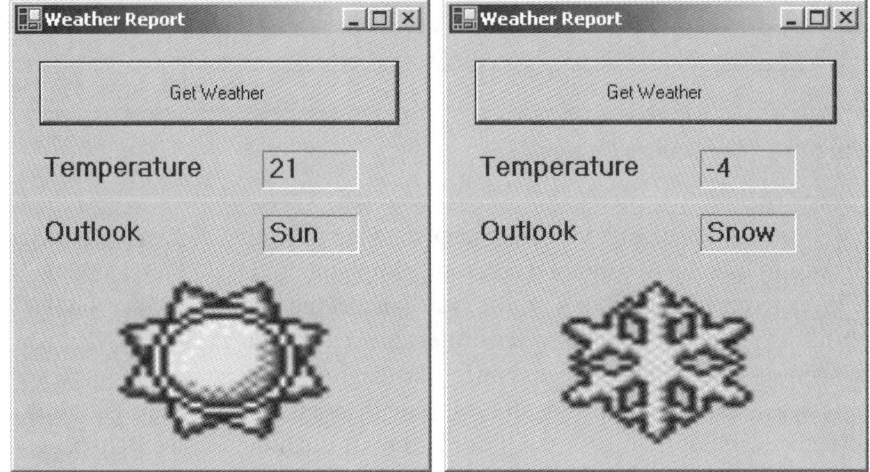

Figure 14-4. The Weather client

A Web Service client program needs to know how to access the Web Service, so at the very least, the client program needs the URL that leads to the .asmx file for the Web Service. More than this, though, you want to avoid the need to worry about XML processing wherever possible. When you're programming the client program, you want to be able to treat the Web Service like a local object. .NET ships with a tool that will generate code for a local class with the same methods as the Web Methods exposed by the Web Service. Whenever you call one of these methods on an instance of the local class, this local object generates an HTTP request to the actual Web Service and processes the response on your behalf. This local object is called a *Web Service proxy object*, and you can create the proxy object using the Add Web Reference dialog box.

To create the proxy object, .NET needs to know more than just the URL for the Web Service, it needs to get hold of a description of the Web Service that defines its methods and their arguments and return values. There's a standard way of creating such a description, using a language called Web Services Description Language (WSDL). You'll learn a little bit more about WSDL in the next section, but for now, it's enough to know that ASP.NET can automatically generate a WSDL definition (or WSDL *contract*) from the Web Service class you write. By appending the ?WSDL querystring onto the URL for the Web Service, you can ask ASP.NET to return the WSDL contract for that Web Service (see Figure 14-5). The Add Web Reference dialog box uses the WSDL contract to generate the proxy object that hides away all the grungy details of working with a Web Service.

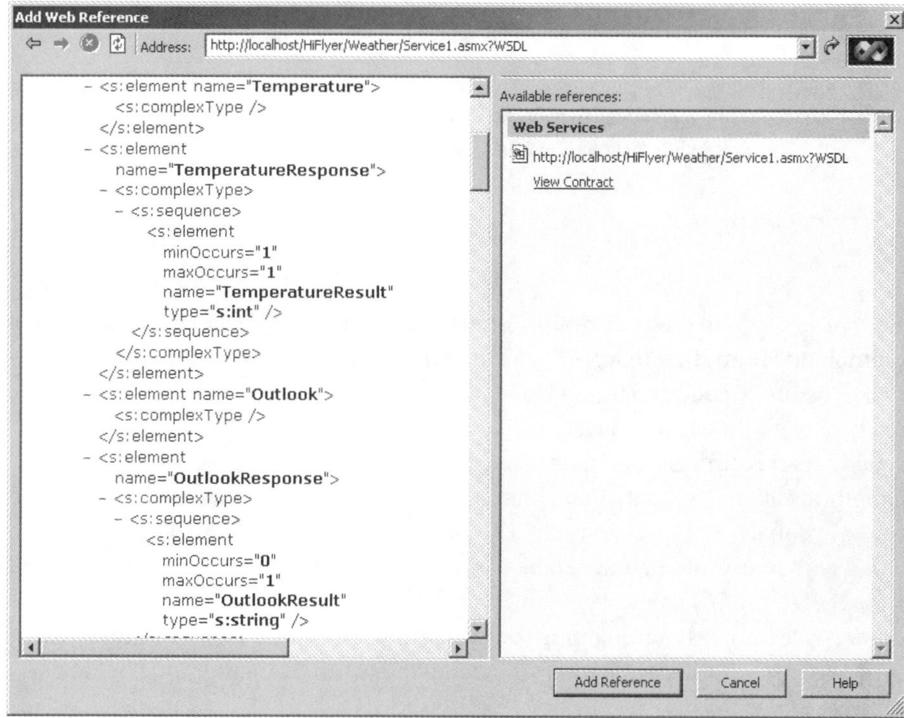

Figure 14-5. The Add Web Reference dialog box

Figure 14-5 shows the Add Web Reference dialog box available from the Project menu in Visual Studio .NET. The address bar shows the URL for the WSDL contract for the Weather Web Service. In the left-hand pane you can see part of the WSDL contract itself. It's an XML document, and you can see the `Temperature` and `Outlook` methods and the data types of the results they return. Clicking the **Add Reference** button generates the VB .NET code for the proxy object's class and adds this code to your project. You don't need to look at this code much, but it may help to see just part of it:

```
Namespace localhost

 'attributes removed
 Public Class Service1
     Inherits System.Web.Services.Protocols.SoapHttpClientProtocol

     Public Sub New()
         MyBase.New
         Me.Url = "http://localhost/HiFlyer/Weather/Service1.asmx"
     End Sub

     'attributes removed
     Public Function Temperature() As Integer
         Dim results() As Object = Me.Invoke("Temperature", New Object(-1) {})
         Return CType(results(0),Integer)
     End Function
. . . .
```

We've suppressed some of the details (including a long list of client-side Web Method attributes that tell .NET how to handle this class and its methods) to make the proxy code generated by Visual Studio .NET a bit more readable. All you really need to note is that a class called `Service1` has been generated in a namespace called `localhost`, and that it has a method called `Temperature` (it also has a method called Outlook). Also of interest is the constructor (`Sub New`) that sets the `Url` property of this class to the URL for the Web Service. The `Url` property, along with many others that can be useful when using a Web Service, is inherited from System.Web.Services.Protocols.SoapHttpClientProtocol. Note that the namespace name is nothing more than a name. It has nothing to do with where Web Service requests are sent to, which depends entirely on the value of the `URL` property.

Now that you've created a Web Reference, you can use a proxy object whenever you want to connect to the Web Service and call a method. Assuming you have anonymous access enabled on your Web Server (see Chapter 11 for more details), the following code is all you need:

```
Private Sub btnWeather_Click( . . . ) Handles btnWeather.Click

    Dim outlook As String
    Dim img As Bitmap

    Dim pxy As New localhost.Service1()
```

```
    lblTemp.Text = pxy.Temperature.ToString
    outlook = pxy.Outlook
    lblOutlook.Text = outlook

    img = New Bitmap("..\" + outlook + ".ico")
    pcbOutlook.Image = CType(img, Image)
End Sub
```

This code creates pxy as an instance of your local Web Service proxy class (which was added to your project by the Add Web Reference dialog box). It then calls the Temperature method and the Outlook method and displays the values returned. The return values of the Outlook method (such as sun, rain and so on) happen to match the filenames of a set of "elements" icons that ship with Visual Studio .NET (sun.ico, rain.ico, and so on), which we've used here to add a graphical touch to the client program. At no point does this client code know or care about Web Services, HTTP, or XML. It simply calls methods on the proxy object to get the information it needs, while the proxy object handles all the work of talking to the Web Service.

It's possible that this simple Web Service client brings back some memories of the first Web Application you looked at in Chapter 1. Back then you managed to generate some HTML output without actually needing to write any HTML. Here, you've made an HTTP request for an XML document, but the entire exchange is hidden behind a façade of object-oriented programming made possible by the proxy object. The truth is that if you intend on becoming a Web Services expert, then some knowledge of XML and WSDL is necessary, just as some knowledge of HTML is required to be an ASP.NET Web Application expert. Nevertheless, you can go a long way without needing this expertise, and even when you have it, you don't have to use it all the time. It's vital to realize that this Web Service is as reachable as any Web site. Any developer, anywhere in the world, can access information from your Web Server with a few lines of code and integrate that information into their own application. The combination of Web Service standards and .NET technology make distributed computing not only easier, but more powerful and with greater reach than ever before.

We'll say a bit more about Web Service security later in the chapter, but you might be interested in what to do with this current example if you have anonymous access disabled because the client program described will fail if IIS is required to authenticate the HTTP requests that the client program makes. The short and simple answer is that the Web Service proxy object has a Credentials property to which you can assign the credentials of a known user, in the form of a user id, password, and (optional) domain name. To use this property, add the following code after the pxy variable is created, but before the first call to the Web Service via one of the proxy's methods:

```
pxy.Credentials = New System.Net.NetworkCredential ("GoodGuy", "secret")
```

As long as IIS can authenticate GoodGuy as a known user with a secret password (using either Windows integrated or basic authentication), then access will be allowed.

Learning Web Service Standards

Most developers find standards pretty boring. Whether you fall into this camp, you need to recognize the important of standards when using Web Services. If you want to exploit the many benefits that Web Services provide, it's necessary to push the pain barrier and learn at least the basics of Web Service standards.

Web Services derive their ability to exploit the Internet for remote method calling from their roots in HTTP and XML, and these are without a doubt the most important standards in the Web Services world. However, as you saw earlier, there are some other Web Service standards already established, as well as some emerging ones likely to become equally important. In this section, you'll take a look at some of these.

SOAP

The most widely known "new" standard associated with Web Services is Simple Object Access Protocol (SOAP). SOAP is now firmly established as the standard protocol used to exchange data between a client and a server during a Web Method call. All that SOAP does is to provide a standard way of using XML to send a method request to a server, and to return a method response to a client. It simply adds a precise definition of how the method request and response are formatted. To explore SOAP it'll help to have a method that takes arguments, and so, for the benefit of users who prefer Fahrenheit to Celsius, we've added a new Web method to the Weather service:

```
<WebMethod()> Public Function TempForC(ByVal Fahrenheit As Boolean) As Integer
    Dim temp As Integer = (New Random()).Next(-10, 30)
    'convert the Fahrenheit if requested
    If Fahrenheit Then temp = (temp * 1.8) + 32
    Return temp
End Function
```

When you call this method, the .NET client tools for Web Services need to convert a message call such as this:

```
temp = pxy.TempForC(True)
```

into an XML message that can be carried in the body of an HTTP request to the Web Service's server. SOAP actually allows a certain amount of flexibility in how the message is formatted, but the message created by .NET for the previous Web Method looks like this:

```
<?xml version="1.0" encoding="utf-8"?>
<soap:Envelope xmlns:xsi="http://www.w3.org/2001/XMLSchema-instance"
        xmlns:xsd= "http://www.w3.org/2001/XMLSchema"
        xmlns:soap="http://schemas.xmlsoap.org/soap/envelope/">
    <soap:Body>
        <TempForC xmlns="http://tempuri.org/">
            <Fahrenheit>true</Fahrenheit>
        </TempForC>
    </soap:Body>
</soap:Envelope>
```

This is simply a formalized XML encoding of the message call, which shows quite nicely the standard structure of a SOAP message. Every SOAP message has a root element called an Envelope that must contain a SOAP Body. In this example, the SOAP Body contains the name of the method and also the name and value of each argument (there's only one argument here—`Fahrenheit`). All of the information needed to process this message call is contained in this SOAP message.

In addition to a SOAP Body, a SOAP Envelope may contain a SOAP Header. SOAP Headers are optional, but when they're present, they appear before the SOAP Body. SOAP Headers allow you to send additional information that isn't part of the method call itself, but may be necessary to process it. A good example is security information that can be included in the SOAP message as a SOAP Header. A Web Service could inspect the SOAP Header to decide whether to process the call based on any security credentials the SOAP Header contains. Many of the newest standards for Web Services are concerned with standardizing the use of the SOAP Header for things such as security, transaction processing, and attachments.

When you call the `TempForC` method in code, the SOAP message is what actually gets sent to the Web Server where the Web Service resides. On the server, ASP.NET will unpack the SOAP message (more precisely, the HTTP Handler for Web Services will do this) and work out which method to call in your Web Service code. Whatever value the Web Server code returns will be packed up into another SOAP message, which is sent back to the client program. Let's say the current temperature is 68 degrees Fahrenheit. The SOAP message returned in the HTTP response would look like this:

```
<?xml version="1.0" encoding="utf-8"?>
<soap:Envelope xmlns:xsi="http://www.w3.org/2001/XMLSchema-instance"
        xmlns:xsd="http://www.w3.org/2001/XMLSchema"
        xmlns:soap="http://schemas.xmlsoap.org/soap/envelope/">
    <soap:Body>
        <TempForCResponse xmlns="http://tempuri.org/">
            <TempForCResult>68</TempForCResult>
        </TempForCResponse>
    </soap:Body>
</soap:Envelope>
```

Once again, you can see the standard structure of a SOAP message, based around an Envelope and a Body. In the client, .NET will extract the value 68 from this XML document and return it from the TempForC method. Therefore, after this line of client code:

```
temp = pxy.TempForC(True)
```

temp will have the value of 68.

It's important to know at least the basics of a SOAP message exchange because when things don't work as planned, you can often debug Web Service problems by looking at the raw SOAP. We've covered the minimum SOAP information that every Web Service developer needs in this section. If you want to become a SOAP expert, or you want to understand more about Web Service interoperability, the next step is to read the SOAP specification, available at http://www.w3.org.

You may have noticed that the XML displayed in Figure 14-3 is a lot simpler than the SOAP response that we've just discussed. ASP.NET actually allows a number of different ways of interacting with Web Services, and although SOAP is the most popular and most powerful, there are simpler protocols that are more convenient when the client developer doesn't have a good SOAP tool such as the Add Web References dialog box. Also, SOAP doesn't work well when testing a Web Service using the Service Help page, so the Service Help page also used a simpler Web Service protocol based on an HTTP-GET request, as shown previously in Figure 14-3.

The fact that SOAP is more sophisticated than the HTTP-GET protocol means that SOAP has many advantages over the more primitive HTTP-GET mechanism:

- SOAP can handle more complex data types and provide better error handling.

- SOAP makes it possible to pass arguments by reference as well as by value, providing developers with a full range of method calling features.
- SOAP Headers provide a powerful extensibility mechanism, which will become increasingly important as SOAP matures.
- SOAP is an industry standard with wide cross-platform support.

When the extra complexity of SOAP is hidden behind a SOAP toolkit (such as that used by .NET), SOAP is the best way to go.

WSDL

SOAP adds the necessary standards to ensure that Web Method requests and responses are transmitted using a recognized structure. However, SOAP doesn't do anything to help a client program find out what methods are supported by a Web Service—SOAP is essentially a runtime tool rather than a design-time tool. Furthermore, SOAP allows Web Service developers some flexibility in how they return data types or even how data is formatted within a SOAP Body (the SOAP specification outlines some specific choices that Web Service developers can choose between). To be able to work out what Web Methods a Web Service provides, and which SOAP-compliant techniques a Web Service uses, a client program needs a description that tells it about the Web Service. This is particularly important from the point of view of interoperability. The Microsoft SOAP tools use different SOAP options from other vendor's tools, and therefore the method format expected by an ASP.NET Web Service (as discussed previously) may be subtly different from that expected by a Web Service constructed using other toolkits such as Apache or SOAPLite. Good SOAP client software should be able to cope with any SOAP-compliant Web Service but needs information with which to do so.

These needs are met by Web Service Description Language (WSDL), which provides an XML-based structure for describing the inputs and outputs of a Web Service in a formal way. If you're familiar with COM's Type Libraries and IDL (or just the information that VB 6.0 provides through its Object Browser), then it's easy to understand WSDL because it's just a Web-friendly alternative to these existing ways of describing how to interact with a software component. It's important that you know what WSDL is (it's the Web Service description that Web Service client tools use to generate proxy objects). It's less important (at least initially) to be able to read it, so we'll give just the lightest introduction to WSDL next.

Like SOAP, WSDL is capable of describing more than just Web Methods, so the structure of a WSDL document is more flexible, abstract, and complex than is strictly needed for most Web Services. The Service Description link on the Web Service Help page that ASP.NET automatically generates (Figure 14-2) allows you to inspect the WSDL contract for a Web Service. The Service Help page also contains links to the WSDL specification, although be warned that this is less easy to read than the SOAP specification.

You don't have to spend too long looking at WSDL to be thankful that ASP.NET generates it for you, and although some hardy developers have taken to writing their own WSDL contracts, most of you will be happy to let the tools do it for you. However, there are some aspects of the WSDL that is generated by default by ASP.NET that really ought to be changed—even for a simple Web Service, and ASP.NET has thoughtfully made it easy to change these by allowing you to modify attributes associated with your Web Methods and Web Service class.

You're going to explore some ways in which you can modify the WSDL contract. One of these modifications (the one concerning the Web Services XML namespace) is particularly important, so it'll be worth picking out at least that detail from the description that follows.

Below are the last few lines of the WSDL contract for the Weather Web Service. It shows the definition of a *binding* for an operation called `Outlook` (in other words, the `Outlook` method) and some definitions that apply to the Web Service as a whole such as its name (`Service1`) and location. We've configured our Web Service so that it only supports the SOAP protocol, and therefore our WSDL looks simpler than it otherwise would:

```
 ...
  <operation name="Outlook">
    <soap:operation soapAction="http://tempuri.org/Outlook" style="document" />
    <input><soap:body use="literal" /></input>
    <output><soap:body use="literal" /></output>
  </operation>
</binding>
<service name="Service1">
  <port name="Service1Soap" binding="s0:Service1Soap">
    <soap:address location="http://localhost/HiFlyer/Weather/Service1.asmx" />
  </port>
</service>
```

Let's see how (and why) you might modify this WSDL contract. If you remember, the class definition for the Web Service contains the following code:

```
<WebService(Namespace := "http://tempuri.org/")> _
Public Class Service1
 ...
```

Here you can see that the class name is Service1. You can also see that the class definition is prefixed by the WebService attribute, which specifies that the Namespace for this Web Service is `http://tempuri.org`. The namespace appears in several places in the WSDL contract, including the `soap:operation` element of the `Outlook` operation in the WSDL section shown previously. To distinguish your Web Services from anyone else's that might happen to have the same name, it's important to provide a unique XML namespace for your Web Service. In fact, the Service Help page displays an unsightly warning if you don't change the XML namespace, partly as an incentive to change it.

As you may recall from Chapter 9 an XML namespace is not the same thing as a .NET namespace, but it performs the same task—to uniquely identify the names you use for things. ASP.NET assigns the namespace `http://tempuri.org` to all your Web Services by default, but unfortunately it's rather indiscriminate—it uses the same namespace for everyone else's Web Services too. You therefore need to change this namespace, and it's conventional to use your domain name (or that of your organization) to guarantee uniqueness. Here, then, is the modified WebService attribute specifying a unique namespace (with a few other options thrown in for good measure):

```
<WebService(Namespace:="http://apress.com/hiflyers/", _
    Description:="A Weather reporting Web Service", _
    Name:="AirfieldWeather")> _
Public Class Service1
 . . .
```

In addition to specifying an XML namespace, we've also used the WebService attribute to provide a description of the Web Service, and changed the name of the service to be different from the class name. Let's see what this does to the WSDL:

```
  <operation name="Outlook">
    <soap:operation soapAction="http://apress.com/hiflyers/Outlook"
      style="document" />
    <input><soap:body use="literal" /></input>
    <output><soap:body use="literal" /></output>
  </operation>
</binding>
<service name="AirfieldWeather">
  <documentation>A Weather reporting Web Service</documentation>
  <port name="AirfieldWeatherSoap" binding="s0:AirfieldWeatherSoap">
    <soap:address location="http://localhost/HiFlyer/Weather/Service1.asmx" />
  </port>
</service>
</definitions>
```

You should be able to spot that the service name has changed and some documentation has appeared and, more importantly, that the new XML namespace is reflected in the `Outlook` operation element. We trust that you can appreciate the importance of changing the XML namespace for the Web Service, but you may be wondering who gets to see the description you added. One answer is that it appears in the Service Help page. Figure 14-6 shows what this now looks like.

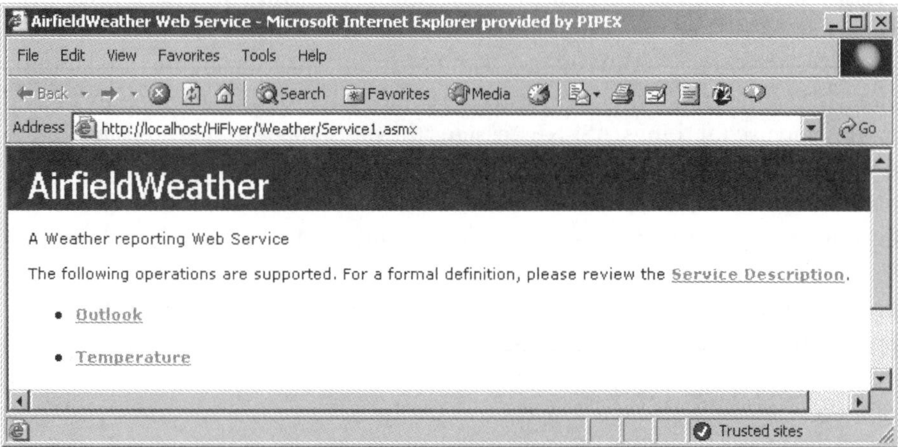

Figure 14-6. The Service Help page showing WSDL modifications

Therefore, by changing the WSDL, you can also customize the Service Help page and add documentation to it, which will be of help to anyone choosing to use your Web Service.

Any changes you make to the WSDL are also picked up by the Add Web Reference dialog box when it generates a proxy class, so (for example) if you regenerated the proxy class, the proxy class name will now be AirfieldWeather instead of Service1.

You can make similar changes to the WSDL for each Web Method by adding descriptions or specifying alternative method names via arguments to the WebMethod attribute, much as you've just done for the WebService attribute. Once again, these changes are not only reflected in the WSDL, but also affect the Service Help page and the generated proxy code.

UDDI and Other Standards

SOAP makes Web Services work at runtime, and WSDL provides the design-time description of how to work with a particular Web Service, which allows proxy classes to be generated, saving you the bother of working directly with XML documents when all you want to do is to call a method. However, before you start looking at a Web Service, a potential user needs to know that it exists and where to look for it.

Arguably, one of the major factors leading to the immense popularity of the Internet has been Web search engines, which have taken a great deal of the guesswork out of Net surfing. You can apply the same logic to Web Services and provide a centralized location that potential users can use to locate and explore available Web Services. At a simple level, this is exactly what Universal Description, Discovery, and Integration (UDDI) does. UDDI is essentially a standard for creating a searchable repository of Web Services. Microsoft, IBM, and Hewlett-Packard have already established UDDI catalogs, and other companies have pledged to set up UDDI catalogs. UDDI catalogs are intended to share repository information, allowing a Web Service provider to register their Web Service with one catalog and have its information made available through all the others.

At first thought, the idea of being able to search for a Web Service and "just start using it" sounds exactly like a Web Service equivalent of Yahoo or Google. However, the reality is that using someone else's Web Service is not the same casual encounter as visiting a Web site. For one thing, you actually need to invest time in writing code to use a Web Service, so you'll want to be sure the one you select is worth the effort. It's also much more likely there will be commercial or security issues to address before using many Web Services than is typically the case for Web sites. Consequently, the comparison between UDDI and search engines should not be taken too literally.

UDDI is a great way of cataloging and using Web Services, but both the Web Service provider and the potential user of the Web Service will need to invest far more time in using UDDI than the casual Web surfer. Nevertheless, accessing UDDI is actually pretty simple for Visual Studio .NET users, as the Add Web Reference dialog box contains a link to Microsoft's UDDI catalog, which you can use to search for Web Services by business name and retrieve WSDL contracts. Once you have a WSDL contract you can generate a proxy class for a Web Service and (security issues aside) start using it. In time, you should be able to search for Web Services by a range of different categories using UDDI. At the time of writing however, the number of properly configured UDDI entries is relatively small.

The world of Web Services is new, and although SOAP and WSDL are now pretty well-established, other standards are needed before the full vision of Web Services is achieved. For example, because there are no security standards for Web Services, each secured Web Service currently does its own thing. You can expect the Web Service providers to supply documentation about how to access their services, but each different Web Service you use may have a different approach to security. A similar story applies to other topics, such as transaction handling between Web Services. A great deal of activity is currently under way in the standards world, and surprisingly, the different vendors are working together far more effectively than is usual for the computer industry.

Unsurprisingly, Microsoft is playing a major role in this activity, under the banner of its Global XML Web Services Architecture (GXA) initiative. GXA contains a set of related proposals including WS-Security, WS-Routing, and WS-Inspection.

You can start using Web Services today and derive a great deal of benefit from the combined capabilities of HTTP, XML, SOAP, and WSDL (and to some extent, UDDI). Right now, you'll need to develop your own solutions to those areas where existing standards don't apply. Given the high level of investment in Web Services by the major IT vendors, it's reasonable to hope that a flurry of additional standards will emerge to fill the gaps.

Using Web Services

Right now, most Web Applications are accessed via browsers. Browsers offer relatively limited client-side capability and do little to exploit the power of desktop computers. One of the constant topics throughout this book has been the design trade-offs that result from using a thin-client mechanism such as a browser. (As thin clients go, you may be of the opinion that Internet Explorer is rather on the thick size. However, this is rather like saying that a 5KB program is huge because you need to install an operating system before you can run it. What makes an application *thin-client* is the amount of application-specific code that needs to be placed on a typical computer before it can run. In the case of ASP.NET Web Applications, the user needs only download a tiny quantity of HTML to use the application, which can be thrown away after use).

An increasing number of Web-based applications use the Internet to deliver data but provide installable front-end applications so that they can deliver a better user interface than a browser is capable of doing. We predict that Web Services will accelerate this trend because they simplify and standardize the process of delivering raw data over the Internet for use by sophisticated front-end programs. Furthermore, .NET technology makes it easy to download and run Windows applications with minimum installation fuss and trustworthy security protection.

Many organizations have turned to browser-based applications simply because of the difficulty of deploying and maintaining COM-based VB 6.0 programs on hundreds of desktops. However clever you are with browser-based technology, it's always easier to build a great user interface using desktop technology. To get close to competing with a Windows program, a Web Application must abandon a pure HTML approach and make significant use of client-side code and features such as dynamic HTML (DHTML). If you've decided to use DHTML, you have pretty much decided to target only Windows users with an up-to-date version of Internet Explorer. Therefore, you could argue that you might as well give your users a Windows application as their front end—especially if .NET allows you to download that application, ready-to-run, across the Internet anyway—because it's much easier to build classy user interfaces using Windows Forms than using Web Forms. The combination of an easily downloaded, highly interactive Windows application that gets data from the Internet by calling Web Services provides a powerful challenge to the dominance of browser-based applications.

So, have you reached almost the end of this book, only to be told that everything you've learned so far will soon be replaced by powerful Windows front ends calling Web Services to get their data? Are we saying that browser-based applications are passé? Worry not—and bear the following points in mind:

- People love the Internet and the freedom it gives them, and they'll equate this with browsers for a long time to come. The browsing mindset is different from the application user mindset. No one wants to install programs (however small or simple) and learn their user interfaces if they only intend to use them occasionally. Web Services with rich clients won't compete for users who are browsing, but they might put the brakes on the trend for complex HTML applications such as e-mail clients or workplace applications that users may use for several hours a day.

- As we write, the .NET Common Language Runtime is not built into desktop operating systems and won't be an assumed feature of desktops for some time to come. Although Web Services can be called easily from any platform, most Windows client programs currently require complex installation (based on COM and the Registry) and create sharing and security problems that make users wary about downloading applications casually. Until the idea of downloadable applications becomes readily acceptable, browser-based Web Applications will continue to be the norm.

- Web Services will never capture the public imagination like browsers do. The reason is simple; Web Services are not aimed at the general public.

- Web Services can't carry advertising, and they can't be used to sell products unless a client program is created for them. You must either be able to charge for the data that Web Services provide, or a Web Service must be an essential part of some other product or service. Web-enabled rich clients (such as Spinner.com's Internet music service) can carry advertising, and advertising may well become a common feature of free-to-use, downloadable Windows applications that make use of the Internet.

In short, browser-based applications are here to stay. However, if you're building a complex application intended to be used regularly and for significant periods of time by its users, you should think carefully about whether a Windows client/Web Service combination is going to be a better bet than a browser-based Web Application.

So far, you've seen how to use a Windows Application as a client for Web Services. There are many other types of application that are potential Web Service clients, and although the process of connecting to and using a Web Service is much the same in each case, it's worth reviewing the different ways in which Web Services are being put to use:

- **Windows Applications**: As you've already seen, Web Service–enabled rich clients provide an alternative to browser-based applications. Such clients are not limited to .NET clients. As you'll see below, it's easy to write VB 6.0 programs that call Web Services.

- **Web Applications**: Chapter 13 introduced the idea of using Web Services to offload processing demand from a front-line Web server. It's easy to call a Web Service from an ASP.NET Application, and doing so can be a useful way of load balancing and resource sharing. However, there are other reasons why a Web Application might want to call a Web Service. Imagine a Web site for private pilots across the country that allows pilots to check weather conditions at any airfield from a single Web page (this would be useful to a pilot planning a trip between several airfields). If each airfield has its own weather Web Service, then a centralized site can use the Internet to retrieve real-time weather information from any airfield and integrate it into a consolidated Web page. This is a much better proposition for the pilot than being forced to link to each different site and hunt around for its weather information. In general, Web Services make it extremely easy to deliver real-time information to a highly dispersed user base. The potential that Web Services provide for connecting different systems together is hard to overestimate.

- **Up-level browsers**: Many browsers allow some degree of client-side processing. One reasonably common client-side approach is to include XML *data islands* inside an HTML page. Client-side scripts are able to manipulate this XML that has been downloaded with the page, giving users limited scope for manipulating data without needing a trip back to the server. Web Services provide another source of XML that can be manipulated client-side. When a user selects an option that requires more data, you would typically post back to the server to build a new page. This can be expensive if the volume of data required is small compared to the size of the whole page. An alternative is to call a Web Service from some client-side script, retrieve some data, and update the user's page using DHTML without needing to completely rebuild the whole page. We'll show an example of this approach later in this section.

- **Hand-held, and mobile devices:** Web Services are ideal for wireless communication devices, especially those that have restricted bandwidth, because downloading raw data is faster than downloading a whole load of presentational information too.

- **Embedded applications:** Ultimately, the greatest potential for Web Services may be in embedded devices that use the Internet (and especially wireless IP) for communication. From traffic-alert systems built into motor vehicles to domestic devices connected into the much-hyped home network, it's getting increasing simpler and cheaper to make everyday objects smarter by sharing information—and Web Services, through their raw simplicity, are an ideal technology for making this happen.

In short, anytime a program wants to access the information or use the processing power of another computer, Web Services are likely to be useful. And that's an awful lot of times.

A Visual Basic 6.0 Web Service Client

Forget about .NET just for a while and imagine you want to write a VB 6.0 client program to call a Web Service. It could be any Web Service for which a WSDL contract is available, but we'll use the Weather Web Service described previously. It's *very* simple to build a VB 6.0 client for a simple Web Service, although it does get more complicated for Web Services that return complex data types or use more advanced Web Service capabilities.

To call Web Services from VB 6.0, you first need to download and install the Microsoft SOAP Toolkit for Visual Studio 6.0. You should use version 2 of the toolkit, and get the latest service pack release if possible. Once you've installed the Toolkit, you can reference it from a Visual Basic 6.0 project, by looking for Microsoft SOAP Type Library in the References dialog box.

Unlike .NET, the SOAP Toolkit reads WSDL at runtime rather than design-time. This means that you don't get the support of a custom proxy object when programming with a Web Service. Instead, you use a generic proxy object. This works perfectly well, but you don't benefit from AutoComplete (IntelliSense) prompting you with method names and argument lists as you do with the .NET proxy.

After referencing the SOAP Type Library, you can create a generic proxy object of type SoapClient as shown in the following code. Before using the proxy object, you need to initialize it by passing the URL of the Web Service's WSDL contract to its `mssoapinit` method. You can then start calling Web Methods! Here's the code:

```
'VB6 Code !!
Dim pxy As New SoapClient
Dim sOutlook As String
pxy.mssoapinit "http://localhost/HiFlyer/Weather/Service1.asmx?WSDL"

sOutlook = pxy.Outlook
MsgBox sOutlook
```

With .NET still being new, there are many organizations that are unwilling to deploy the Common Language Runtime to each desktop. However, setting up a small number of Web Servers hosting ASP.NET and some Web Services is much less scary. Consequently, the idea of continuing to use VB 6.0 to create desktop applications that call a Web Service to retrieve data and perform business processing is very attractive. Absolutely no .NET technology needs to be installed on a computer for it to be able to call Web Services. It's therefore possible to build new applications that exploit .NET technology without needing to deploy .NET and without being forced to develop a browser-based front end. VB 6.0 programs calling Web Services via the Microsoft SOAP Toolkit work very well.

A DHTML Web Service Client

Another interesting type of client for a Web Service is Internet Explorer. This idea may sound strange because Web Services return raw data as XML, not presentation information as HTML. But the key point is that the Web page must contain client-side script to be able to work with a Web Service. The client-side script can be used to call a Web Service, get back some data, and update the current page *without* the overhead of rebuilding the entire page.

Internet Explorer–based applications can make use of DHTML to allow client-side script to manipulate the browser content without rebuilding the page. To see where the DHTML/Web Service combination can be beneficial, take a look at Figure 14-7.

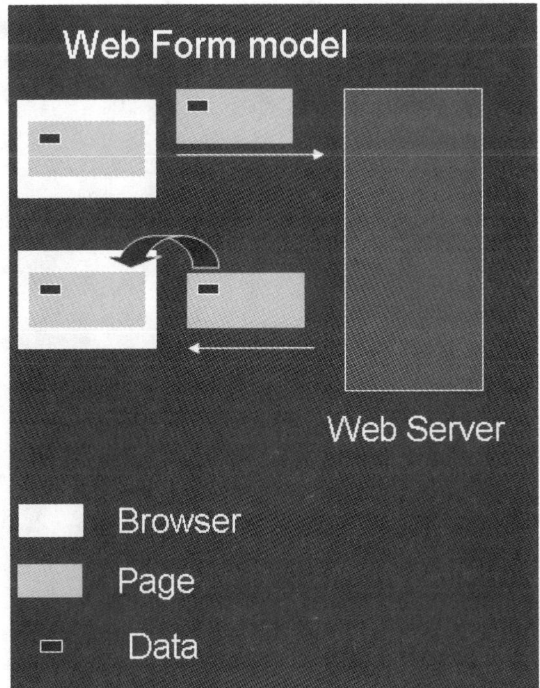

Figure 14-7. A Conventional Web Form refresh

This is the more conventional way to refresh a Web page. Imagine that the user clicks a button that will update a single piece of data (shown as Data in Figure 14-7) on a large Web page (shown as Page in Figure 14-7). To do this, a page request must be submitted to the Web server, which must rebuild the entire page and then send the new page containing the single change the user wanted back to the client. A very large sledgehammer is being swung here to crack a very small nut.

Now image you have a Web Service that has a Web Method capable of returning just that single piece of data. Figure 14-8 shows how this looks.

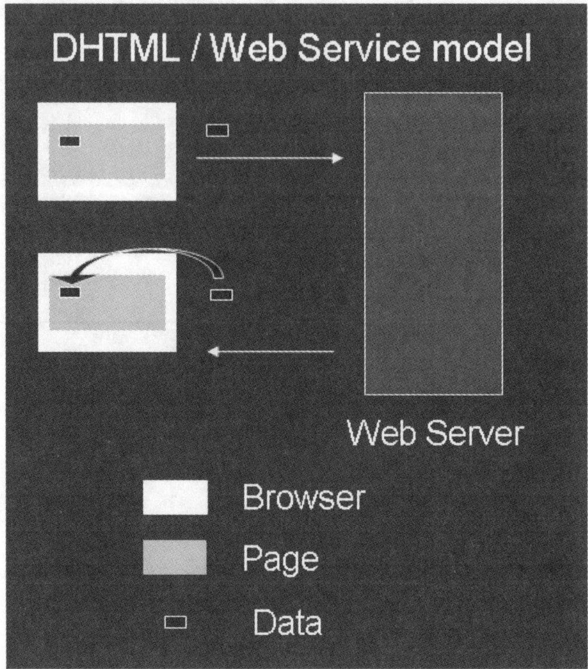

Figure 14-8. DHTML/Web Service refresh

In this case, the amount of data exchanged across the network, and the amount or processing that the Web server is required to do, is substantially reduced. All that is needed is an easy way to call a Web Service from a browser and make use of its results.

To make DHTML programming easier, Internet Explorer (version 5.0 onwards) supports the use of *behaviors*. A behavior is like a component or object that adds prebuilt functionality to a Web page. Unlike normal components, behaviors are pure source-code components (typically written in JavaScript) that can be downloaded from a Web site at runtime and attached to an HTML element, giving the HTML element additional functionality that can then be exploited by client-side script. Microsoft provides a behavior for calling Web Services, which is called `WebService.htc`. This file needs to be placed in the same directory on your Web server as the Web page that wants to use it. `WebService.htc` is accessible from several locations on MSDN. At the time of writing, you can download it from `http://msdn.microsoft.com/downloads/samples/internet/`.

To see how to call a Web Service from a Web page, take a look at Figure 14-9, which shows a simple HTML page called temperature.html that resides in the same virtual directory as the Weather Web Service. Pressing the button calls the `TempForC` Web Method on our Weather Web Service and then updates the page with the latest temperature. Note that the page has an .html extension—it's not even processed by the ASP.NET HTTP Runtime.

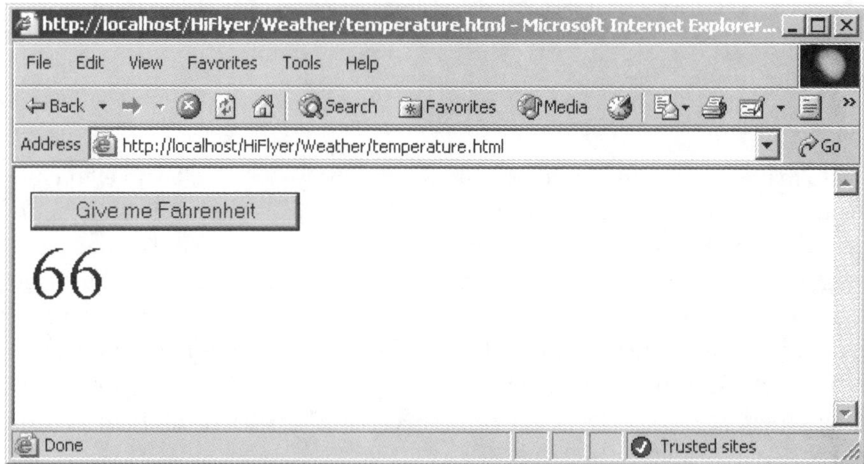

Figure 14-9. Calling a Web Service from Internet Explorer

You'll now want to see the code for this page. The functions in the script section of the code shown next are part of the page—they're not the code that is contained within the WebService Behavior, which is quite substantial:

```
<html>
  <script language="JavaScript">
    function init()
    {
      //initialize the behavior with the WSDL
      service.useService("Service1.asmx?WSDL","MyService");
    }

    function callTheWebService()
    {
      // specify the callback function, the Web Method name, and any arguments
      service.MyService.callService(serviceCallback,"TempForC", true);
    }

    function serviceCallback(result)
    {
     Temp.innerText = result.value;
    }
  </script>
```

```
  <body onload="init()">
    <div id="service" style="BEHAVIOR:url(webservice.htc)">
    <input type="button" value="Give me Fahrenheit" id="B1"
           onclick="callTheWebService()">
    <div id="Temp" style="FONT-SIZE: xx-large; ">
  </body>
</html>
```

To make sense of this code, look first at the `<body> . . . </body>` element. The first element it contains is a `<div>` element called `"service"`. This element exists only so that the WebService behavior can be attached to it. The behavior can actually be attached to any element—we've chosen to use a `<div>` as its recipient, and a `style` attribute is used here to load the behavior from the Web server. You'll see how the behavior works shortly. The next element is a button. This has an `"onclick"` attribute that references a function called `"callTheWebService()"`. Finally, there's another `<div>` element, called `"Temp"`. We'll use this to display the data returned by the Web Service.

Next, notice that the opening `<body>` tag specifies that a function called `"init()"` should be run when the page is loaded. If you look in the script section of the page, you'll see that the `"init()"` function calls the `useService` method on the `"service" <div>` element. The `useService` method was created by the WebService behavior and allows the page to use a Web Service specified by a WSDL contract, which in this case is `Service1.asmx?WSDL` (it isn't necessary to specify the full URL to the WSDL contract because the .html file and the .asmx file are in the same directory). Consequently, once the page has been loaded, it's ready to call the Weather Web Service.

When a user clicks the button, the `"callTheWebService()"` function is called. This function calls the `TempForC` Web Method on the specified Web Service, passing it the argument `true` (meaning that a Fahrenheit temperature will be returned). However, note that `"callTheWebService()"` doesn't process the result of the method—it simply calls it. The reason for this is that (by default) the WebService behavior calls Web Methods asynchronously so that the user doesn't have to wait for the results to be returned (if you look closely at the proxy code generated for .NET Web Service clients, you'll see that they too have the ability to call Web Services asynchronously).

When the Web Service returns, a function called `serviceCallback()` will be called (the name of this callback function was passed as the first argument to the `service.MyService.callService`), and it's this function that displays the temperature by setting the `innerText` property of the `<div>` element called `"Temp"`.

In this particular example, the Web page is so small that the benefits of calling a Web Service are limited. But with larger pages, this approach can deliver substantial benefits to any application targeted at Internet Explorer 5.0 browsers.

You've now seen three different types of client, based on .NET, VB/COM, and browser technologies. This is one of the key benefits of Web Services—they allow you to write reusable code that can be called from virtually anywhere.

Designing Web Services

Throughout this book, we've covered Web Application design issues by exploring in detail the characteristics of the Internet (especially HTTP and HTML) and the architecture of ASP.NET. From a design perspective, a Web Service is just a programmable version of a Web page—the mechanism for calling a Web Method is identical to the mechanism for requesting a Web page, with the exception that XML is returned instead of HTML.

Consequently, most of the design techniques needed for Web Services are the same as those we've already discussed, and we won't be reproducing detailed information about state management, security, round-trips, and scalability that has already gone before. Instead, we'll address Web Service specifics. There are two additional guiding principles that need particular attention when designing Web Services:

- **Always remember that a Web Service may look like an object, but it's really a Web site with a programmatic interface.** You can't design a Web Service using object-oriented principles; instead you must apply the design thinking of a Web site designer (without, of course, caring about graphics, fonts, and browser capabilities).

- **A Web Service does not have a user interface and is typically not called from a browser.** This means that certain things that ASP.NET Web Application developers take for granted aren't applicable (or at least aren't as easy) when creating Web Services. One example concerns security. As you saw in Chapter 11, Forms security is a convenient way of handling security for public Web Applications. Unfortunately, Forms security assumes that the user is looking at a form in a browser. This assumption doesn't work for Web Services and therefore this otherwise excellent security mechanism can't be used. Another example is Session state management. Most Web browsers automatically manage the transient cookies required to make Session state work. A typical Web Service client does not have built-in cookie management. You can use Session state with Web Services, but (as you'll see) it requires a bit of extra effort on the part of the client programmer.

Web Service Characteristics

You can't design a Web Service without knowing the key characteristics of a Web Service. Just as you would never design a Web Form that round-trips on each mouse move, so there are certain invariable characteristics of Web Services that must be acknowledged in any sane design.

Web Services Form Part of a Distributed System

When designing a Web Service, you need to remember that the Web Service is only ever part of another system. Designing a Web Service is in many ways similar to designing a class library—your customer is another developer, not an end user. Therefore, you often don't know exactly what use will be made of your Web Service, and you need to design it so that you don't restrict the flexibility of what can be done with it. Although there are exceptions to this rule, you should try and avoid assuming the order in which methods are called. Wherever possible, you should allow other developers to use your Web Service "their way" and make sure you avoid building order dependencies into your code that force them to call your Web Methods in a particular order.

You should make sure you use .NET's structured error handling in every Web Method. This will make sure that any error details returned to clients present only the error information you want clients to see.

You should also make sure your Web Service is properly documented and that the documentation is available over the Internet. There's no point offering the flexibility of Internet access to your Web Service if a potential user needs to phone up to request paper documentation. Ideally, you should provide links from the Service Help page (via the Description arguments of the WebService and WebMethod attributes) to your documentation. This is easy to do because you can assign a string containing HTML to the Description arguments. For example, imagine you have an HTML document called details.htm that contains detailed documentation on the Weather Web Service. To make use of this document, you could modify the Web Service class as follows:

```
<WebService(Namespace:="http://apress.com/hiflyers/", _
Description:=Service1.ServiceDescription, _
Name:="AirfieldWeather")> _
Public Class Service1
    Inherits System.Web.Services.WebService

    Public Const ServiceDescription As String = _
      "A <b> Weather</b> reporting Web Service. " + _
      "Click here for <a href=""details.htm"">more</a>"
```

To avoid making the WebService attribute definition hopelessly long, we've created a public constant (called `ServiceDescription`) as part of the class definition and used this constant as the value for the `Description` argument to the WebService attribute. Note that we've used bold font for `Weather` and made `more` into a hyperlink. The user can click on this hyperlink to see detailed documentation. Figure 14-10 shows what the Service Help page now looks like.

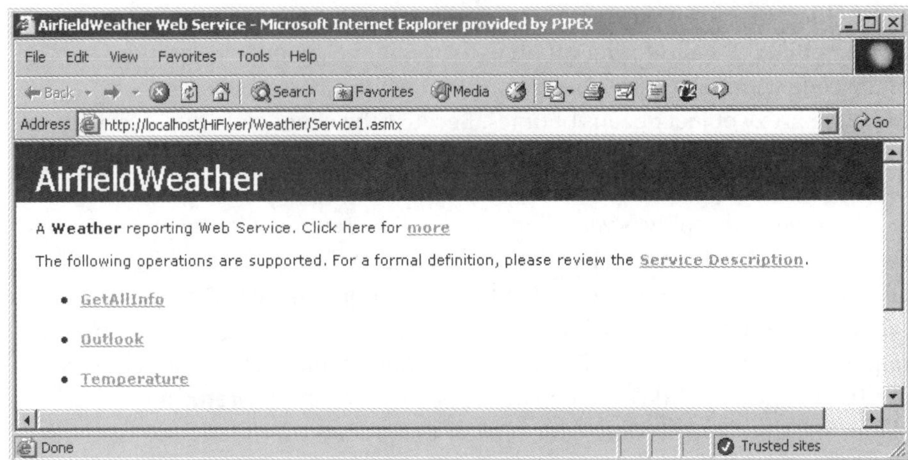

Figure 14-10. The Service Help page showing a link to detailed documentation

Web Service Objects Are Stateless

Your Web Service objects behave just like the Page objects now familiar from ASP.NET Web Applications. In other words, ASP.NET creates a new object for each Web Method request and discards the object once the request is processed. This is the why Web Service objects have methods, but not properties. Properties don't make sense on stateless objects because properties are by definition a state mechanism. You therefore face exactly the same challenges that Web Application designers face concerning state management and have access to exactly the same solutions—Application, Cache, and Session state are fully available to Web Service designers. ViewState (of course) can't be used with Web Services because they have nothing to view and don't make use of HTML.

It's easy to confuse the lifetime of Web Service objects with the lifetime of proxy objects. For example, here is some client code that calls the Weather Web Service (note that the class name is now AirfieldWeather following the change to the WebService attribute made while discussing WSDL):

```
Dim pxy As New localhost.AirfieldWeather ()
lblTemp.Text = pxy.Temperature.ToString
outlook = pxy.Outlook
```

Consider this code from the point of view of the client program developer. The first line of code creates a new proxy object (an instance of the proxy class). The next two lines of code make method calls on this proxy object. The client really has created one local object and called two methods on the same object. In fact, it's quite common and perfectly reasonable to declare a proxy object as a class-level variable (that is, in the general declarations section of the code window), create the proxy object when a Form loads, and use the same proxy object dozens of times. Because the client code interacts with the same proxy object each time, it's easy for the client developer to imagine that they're interacting with the same server object each time.

However, the reality is very different. The `Dim` statement in the previous code creates a new local proxy object, but it does not involve the Web Service itself at all—all that is happening here is that the client program creates a local object. When the client calls the second line of code, the proxy object makes an HTTP request to the server. ASP.NET creates an instance of our Web Service class, calls the `Temperature` method and then destroys the object before returning to the client. The third line of client code repeats the process for the `Outlook` method, resulting in a second Web Service object being created and destroyed on the Web server.

There's clearly a difference between what is really happening and the client programmer's perception of what is happening, and it's your job as a Web Service developer to prevent the client programmer from making errors based on this perception. The easiest way to do this is to make each Web Method stateless (or at least make it give the appearance of being stateless). Design each method so that the client programmer provides all the arguments needed for that method, regardless of what methods they may or may not have called before. This doesn't mean you shouldn't use state in the Web Service. But it does mean you should use state for performance reasons, rather than to provide the user with a complex state model. Sooner or later, you won't be able to maintain the façade that the user is calling the same object each time. It's much better to be open and honest up front and design the methods for your Web Service as though the Web Service has no memory so that the client programmer treats it as a stateless object—even if it does actually use state management internally.

Web Method Calls Are Expensive

Web Methods may look harmless but you know that in reality, they always involve an HTTP round-trip to the server. Round-trips for Web pages are expensive, and round-trips for Web Methods are no different—they operate in an almost identical fashion—and are therefore expensive too.

From a design perspective, this means you should design a Web Service so that the client need only call a small number of methods to get their work done and to make each method do as much work as possible. As you've seen with Web Forms and scalability, although it makes sense to limit the amount of data exchanged on each round-trip to only that which is necessary, it's much more important to limit the overall number of round-trips because each one has a considerable processing overhead regardless of the amount of data exchanged.

Let's say you have several pieces of weather information that your Web Service can provide. You might design a set of methods such as this:

```
<WebMethod()> Public Function Temperature() As Integer
<WebMethod()> Public Function Outlook() As String
<WebMethod()> Public Function WindSpeed() As Double
<WebMethod()> Public Function WindDirection() As String
```

The problem with this type of design is that a client program wanting all four pieces of information will need to call four methods and therefore make four separate round-trips. To improve efficiency, you should provide another method that returns all four pieces of information at the same time. There are two ways you can do this. One is to return an object from a Web Method that contains all four pieces of information. The other is to use a method that takes four arguments. Let's look at each of these approaches in turn.

To return an object from a Web Method, you need to either return an instance of an existing class or create a new class specifically for the purpose. An ADO.NET DataSet is one example of a flexible type of object that can be returned from a Web Service. Using a DataSet is an attractive idea, as you'll see shortly. However, because our data needs are simple and specific, we'll create our own class in this instance. Here's its definition:

```
Public Class WeatherInfo
    Public Temperature As Integer
    Public Outlook As String
    Public WindSpeed As Double
    Public WindDirection As String
End Class
```

After you've added this class definition to your Web Service project, you can then add a method such as this to your Web Service class:

```
<WebMethod()> Public Function GetAllInfo() As WeatherInfo
    Dim info As New WeatherInfo()
```

```
    Dim outlookValues() As String = {"Sun", "Cloud", "Snow", "Rain"}
    Dim dirValues() As String = {"N", "E", "S", "W", "NE", "EE", "SW", "NW"}
    Dim random As Integer
    info.Temperature = (New Random()).Next(-10, 30)
    random = (New Random()).Next(0, 4)
    info.Outlook = outlookValues(random)
    info.WindSpeed = (New Random()).Next(80)
    random = (New Random()).Next(0, 8)
    info.WindDirection = dirValues(random)
    Return info
End Function
```

This code will return an instance of WeatherInfo to the client program. Before our existing client program can use the new method, the proxy class in the client project will need to be regenerated, which can be easily done by choosing the **Update Web Reference** menu item available when right-clicking on a specific Web Reference in the Solution Explorer for the client project.

Here's the new code for the WeatherClient application, making use of the `GetAllInfo` WebMethod:

```
Dim img As Bitmap

Dim pxy As New localhost.AirfieldWeather()
Dim info As localhost.WeatherInfo
info = pxy.GetAllInfo

lblTemp.Text = info.Temperature.ToString
lblOutlook.Text = info.Outlook
lblWindSpeed.Text = info.WindSpeed.ToString
lblWindDirection.Text = info.WindDirection

img = New Bitmap("..\" + info.Outlook + ".ico")
pcbOutlook.Image = CType(img, Image)
```

The client program creates a variable of type WeatherInfo and assigns it the results of calling `GetAllInfo`. This action creates a local copy of the WeatherInfo object returned by the `GetAllInfo` Web Method in the client program. Because it gets a local copy of the object, the client can access the properties of this object without needing any further round-trips. As a result, this code is actually more efficient than the original client code because only one round-trip is required (see Figure 14-11).

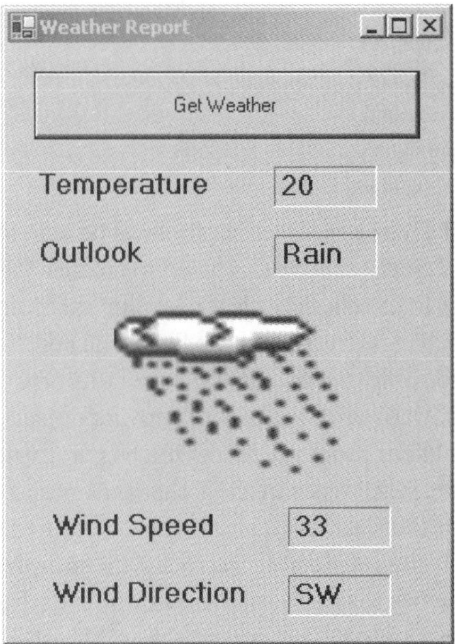

Figure 14-11. The Weather Client with wind information

You may be wondering how it was possible for the client program to declare a variable of a type defined in the Web Service project, especially as the WeatherInfo class isn't even part of the Web Service class. You can find the answer to that by looking at the WSDL contract for the Web Service. The SOAP specification defines a range of standard data types (integers, strings, booleans, and so on) and also allows custom types to be created, which are called *complex types* (even if they're pretty simple). If you add a Web Method that returns a data type that is not a standard SOAP data type, ASP.NET generates a complex type definition for the type if it can) and adds that type definition into the WSDL contract for the Web Service. Some objects, such as an ADO.NET DataReader, can't be converted into an XML format for inclusion in a SOAP message, and you'll get a runtime error if you try and return one from a Web Method.

In the WSDL contract for the Weather Web Service, the type definition for the WeatherInfo class looks like this:

```
<s:complexType name="WeatherInfo">
    <s:sequence>
        <s:element minOccurs="1" maxOccurs="1"
            name="Temperature" type="s:int" />
        <s:element minOccurs="0" maxOccurs="1"
            name="Outlook" type="s:string" />
        <s:element minOccurs="1" maxOccurs="1"
```

```
            name="WindSpeed" type="s:double" />
        <s:element minOccurs="0" maxOccurs="1"
            name="WindDirection" type="s:string" />
    </s:sequence>
</s:complexType>
```

By reading the WSDL file, a SOAP client tool will be able to learn about this complex type. The .NET SOAP client tools (used to create a Web Reference) generate the code for a new class in the client project based on this complex type specification, and then add that class into the same file as the code for the proxy class. Client programs are then able to create instances of this new class just like any other local class, and .NET will look after the task of copying objects of this class between the Web server and the client program. All of which is pretty neat and makes programming with complex SOAP types in .NET clients easy and efficient.

Not all SOAP client tools are as clever as those supplied with .NET, and therefore, although all SOAP clients are able to work with complex types, some require a fair amount of extra work to use them. One example of this is the Microsoft SOAP Toolkit for Visual Studio 6.0. It works brilliantly with simple types, and even with arrays of simple types, but it doesn't provide automatic support for complex types, leaving the client developer to write fiddly mapping code that maps the XML form of a complex type contained in a SOAP response method onto a local class. For this reason, if you know a lot of your Web Service clients are going to be using the Microsoft SOAP Toolkit (or some other SOAP toolkit with similar restrictions), you might choose a different way to return multiple values in a single method call, instead of returning a complex type.

Take a look at the following WebMethod that takes four arguments, one for each piece of required information:

```
<WebMethod()> Public Sub GetWeather( _
        ByRef Temperature As Integer, _
        ByRef Outlook As String, _
        ByRef WindSpeed As Double, _
        ByRef WindDirection As String)
    Dim info As New WeatherInfo()
    Dim outlookValues() As String = {"Sun", "Cloud", "Snow", "Rain"}
    Dim dirValues() As String = {"N", "E", "S", "W", "NE", "EE", "SW", "NW"}
    Dim random As Integer
    Temperature = (New Random()).Next(-10, 30)
    random = (New Random()).Next(0, 4)
    Outlook = outlookValues(random)
    WindSpeed = (New Random()).Next(80)
    random = (New Random()).Next(0, 8)
```

```
    WindDirection = dirValues(random)
End Sub
```

The crucial thing about this method is that its arguments are passed *by reference*. Usually, .NET arguments are passed by value, meaning that the value of the arguments can be changed in the method without affecting the original variables that were passed as arguments by the caller. Passing by value is usually appropriate for Web Services because it means that arguments are only passed in one direction—they're part of the HTTP request, but they're not passed back in the HTTP response.

When you pass arguments by reference, any changes made in the method are seen as changes to the original variables when the method returns. For Web Services, this means that the values of each argument must be included in the HTTP response as well as the request so that the client program gets to see any changes that are made to the arguments by the Web Service. Normally, you wouldn't choose to write a Web Service like this, but pass-by-reference makes complete sense when you want to return more than one piece of data from a single Web Method. A method created as a `Function` can only have one return value, but methods can have any number of arguments. Therefore, a `Sub` that has no return value but has its arguments defined as `ByRef` arguments can actually return several pieces of information in a single round-trip.

This approach is far more efficient than calling several Web Methods where one will do, and although it's not as elegant as returning an object from a Web Method, it's a convenient approach for clients that can't process complex SOAP types easily.

We'll round this discussion off by looking at some VB 6.0 client code that calls the `GetWeather` Web Method:

```
'VB6 Code !!
Dim pxy As New SoapClient
Dim lTemperature As Long
Dim sOutlook As String
Dim dWindSpeed As Double
Dim sWindDirection As String

pxy.mssoapinit "http://localhost/HiFlyer/Weather/Service1.asmx?WSDL"
pxy.GetWeather lTemperature, sOutlook, dWindSpeed, sWindDirection

'populate some VB6 Label controls
lblTemperature.Caption = lTemperature
lblOutlook.Caption = sOutlook
lblWindSpeed.Caption = dWindSpeed
lblWindDirection.Caption = sWindDirection
```

Web Service performance is greatly enhanced by minimizing round-trips. Using complex types and passing multiple arguments by reference are invaluable techniques for achieving this aim. Another useful technique is to use arrays. SOAP allows arrays to be returned by Web Services, so long as they're single dimension arrays. It's possible (and easy) to create Web Services that return arrays of complex objects, and in doing so, it's possible to design efficient Web Methods for clients capable of handling such return values.

Exposing Web Services Can Be Dangerous

You should be just as diligent about malicious attacks when developing a Web Service as when developing a Web Application. Good security is extremely important, but it's only a starting point. Without careful coding, it's easy to give bad guys a back door into your system or return information to otherwise innocent users that get them asking questions.

If you're building a Web Service for public consumption, then absolutely anyone can take a crack at breaking your security. Many security issues are the responsibility of systems administrators rather than developers, and it pays to work with your admin people to get security right. However, administration is mostly about making sure that only authorized users get access to your code. Bugs or weakness in your code can lead to a wide range of security holes that are entirely your responsibility. Client programmers simply won't use your Web Service unless they think it's trustworthy. When writing secure code, there are two standard rules you should always apply:

1. Assume every user is a malicious user, until you have proven otherwise. Make sure you apply your desired security tests to every Web Method, and be aware that valid logon credentials can fall into the wrong hands, so program defensively even after a user has been authenticated.

2. Always be in control of what information you return to users. For example, if you allow an ADO.NET error message to get back to a user, you're revealing information about how your system is organized (and maybe even the name of tables in your database) that a hacker might find helpful. You should wrap .NET-structured error handling around all the code in every Web Method so that you remain in complete control of the error messages generated by your code.

Working with Databases

Chapter 7 explored ADO.NET, and the two data access models it provides, based on DataSets and DataReaders. We explained that the role of DataSets in Web Applications was typically rather limited because DataSets are only really useful when they can be stored somewhere and used multiple times, and by and large Web Applications should tend to avoid storing data, particularly data that needs to be stored for each different user (such as Session state).

One important difference when designing Web Services as opposed to designing Web Applications is that you can typically rely on your client program to store state information far more readily than you can when the client is a browser. This fact gives you more options when aiming to achieve scalability with Web Services because state stored at the client never creates a scalability problem.

In particular, DataSets become valuable in Web Service design. A Web Service can return a DataSet to a client and let the client work with the data while the Web Service holds no state. This is an extremely scalable design. Furthermore, the batch-oriented, two-stage update model used by DataSets is ideal for use in an application based on Web Services. The Web Service can return a DataSet to a client. The client can make multiple changes to the DataSet and then return the whole DataSet structure to the Web Service, which can validate the changes and generate the necessary SQL updates. It's almost as though DataSets were designed for use with Web Services.

You can choose between two different ways of designing Web Services that access databases:

- One option is to rely entirely on DataReaders to read data and Command objects to perform updates. We covered how to use these in some depth in Chapter 7, and there's nothing special to add concerning their use in Web Services. When using this approach, users of your Web Service will have no idea you're using ADO.NET. You'll simply use DataReaders to read data from a database and return the results as strings, integers, custom types, arrays, or whatever suits your design. Similarly, you'll update the database by assigning argument values supplied by client programs to the parameters of Command objects and then executing SQL or stored procedure updates.

- The other option is to design your Web Service around the use of DataSets. This is a different approach from the previous option but is just as valid. It's particularly useful if you want to return multiple rows of data (or even multiple tables of data) because they can all be returned as part of a single DataSet. Of course you'll need to be aware of the volume of data you're returning. It doesn't make sense to write a Web Method that is likely to return 20,000 rows. It really doesn't. Ever.

To see how the DataSet approach can be put to work in a Web Service, we'll develop a simple Web Service called WSMembers that allows a user to update the contents of the Members table in the HiFlyers database.

Even though Web Services don't have any visual interface themselves, it's still possible to use the visual programming approach when building Web Services. Data components can be dragged from the Toolbox onto the Web Service designer, as shown in Figure 14-12. Here you can see that a DataAdapter called `da` has been created based on an SQL query selecting all the data from the Members table.

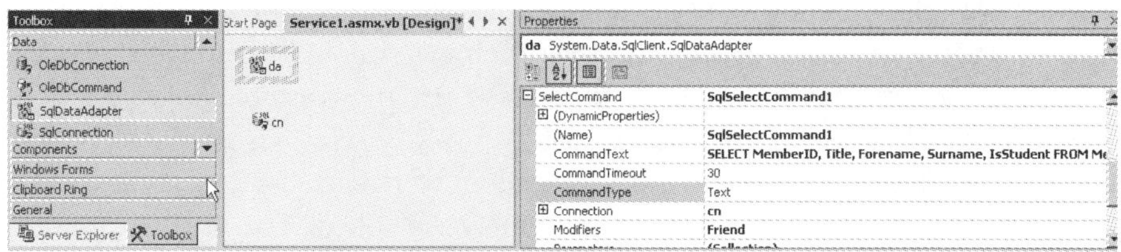

Figure 14-12. Visual data programming with Web Services

The coding for the Web Service is amazingly simple, although you'll need to bear in mind the security issue discussed in Appendix D when accessing SQL Server from ASP.NET using integrated security. Assuming you don't intend to validate the data before performing any updates, and assuming you're happy to ignore the data integrity issues that can arise when performing batch updates with DataSets (see Appendix F), this Web Service need only consist of two methods, each with minimal code:

```
<WebMethod()> Public Function getMembers() As DataSet
    Dim ds As New DataSet()
    da.Fill(ds)
    Return ds
End Function

<WebMethod()> Public Function updateMembers(ByVal ds As DataSet)
    da.Update(ds)
End Function
```

The `getMembers` method will return a DataSet to a client program. While the user has the data, there's no state tied up on the Web server. When the user has made their changes, they'll pass the DataSet containing any changes back to the Web Service as an argument to `updateMembers`. In this very simple code, the Web Service merely calls `Update` on the DataAdapter. As explained in Appendix F, this will trawl through the DataSet looking for any changes and will generate and execute any SQL statements required to write the changes back to the database.

The client program is hardly any more complicated. Figure 14-13 shows a Windows Application that has a DataGrid control and a button on it and has a Web Reference to the WSMembers Web Service.

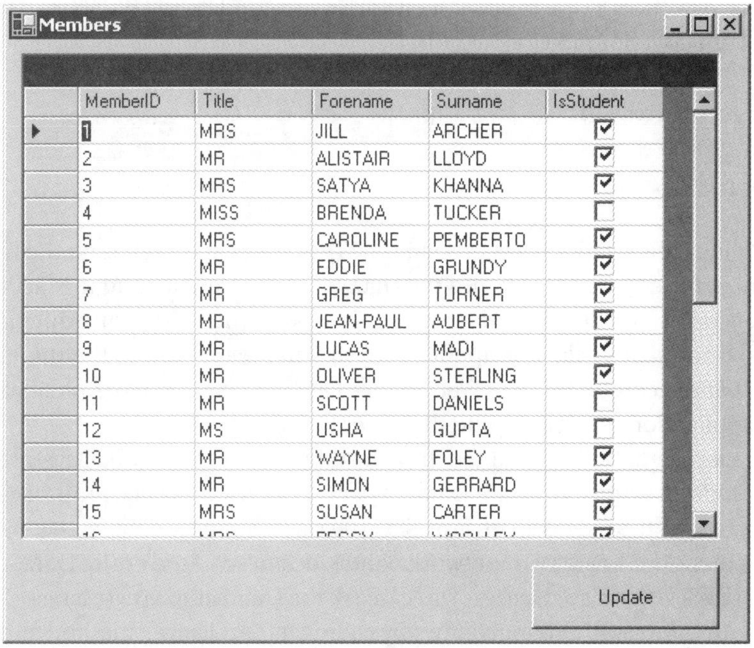

Figure 14-13. A Windows Application displaying a DataSet returned by a Web Service

The code required to create this display is as follows:

```
Dim ds As DataSet
Dim pxy As localhost.Service1

Private Sub Form1_Load( . . . ) Handles MyBase.Load
    pxy = New localhost.Service1()
    pxy.Credentials = New System.Net.NetworkCredential("GoodGuy", "secret")
    ds = pxy.getMembers
    DataGrid1.DataSource = ds.Tables(0)
End Sub
```

This code creates a Web Service proxy, sets the required security credentials (yours will, we hope, be different from these) and then calls the `getMembers` method. The Web Service will create a DataSet that will be converted to XML and returned inside a SOAP response to the client program, which will recreate the DataSet object and bind it to a DataGrid. The client can now operate on the DataSet as it chooses, using the DataGrid as a powerful editing tool.

Once the user is happy with the changes they've made, they can press the Update button. This will send the entire DataSet back to the Web Service (by calling the `updateMembers` method), which will in turn update the database. Here's the first cut code for the Update button:

```
Private Sub Button1_Click( . . . ) Handles Button1.Click
    pxy.updateMembers(ds)
End Sub
```

Coding can't be much easier than this. This application relies on the huge amount of functionality built into the DataSet and DataGrid, and the fact that DataSets work so well with Web Services. Of course, there are many things that need to be done to make this application work in the real world, but there's no doubt that the combination of Web Services and DataSets make sophisticated n-tier applications easier to build than ever before.

There is actually one final touch we'll add to this application. Currently, the client program sends the entire DataSet back to the Web Service for processing. In many cases, the user will retrieve, say, 100 rows, but only change, say, four or five. It's therefore wasteful of network bandwidth to send the entire DataSet back to the Web Server. In such cases, you can ask the DataSet to create a new DataSet object containing only changed rows by calling its `GetChanges` method and then send this much smaller DataSet back to the Web Server for update processing. Here's the updated version of this code containing this extra level of performance-enhancing sophistication:

```
Private Sub Button1_Click( . . . ) Handles Button1.Click
    pxy.updateMembers(ds.GetChanges)
End Sub
```

We've discussed two different approaches to database programming with Web Services (the DataReader/Command object approach and the DataSet approach). Deciding which to use is an important and multifaceted design decision. It's obvious that the DataSet approach is extremely attractive. However, please bear in mind our conclusions concerning the DataSet update model, discussed in Appendix F. DataSets are extremely powerful, but the update model in particular is hard to learn, and you shouldn't believe anyone who says you don't need to learn much about DataSets before you start using them—that way, madness lies.

You should also bear in mind that .NET is the only client environment that understands DataSets. This fact does not mean that DataSet-based Web Services can't be used from other types of client. When a client that doesn't understand DataSets calls `getMembers`, they'll simply see the returned data as an XML document with an accompanying XML schema to make sense of it. But they won't have the full power of DataSets at their disposal. You should only return DataSets from Web Services when you expect most clients to be using .NET technology.

State Management

Virtually everything we've covered in Chapters 12 and 13 concerning state management for Web Applications applies to Web Services. Both Application and Cache state work in exactly the same way when writing Web Services, with the single exception that you must access Cache state via the Context object, which is not necessary when writing an ASP.NET Web Application. Therefore, this is how you'd place a DataSet in Cache state when writing a Web Service:

```
Dim ds As DataSet
Context.Cache("Data") = ds
```

Although Application and Cache state knowledge learnt from Web Applications can be directly applied to Web Services, the same can't be said for Session state. To use Session state with Web Services, some small changes are required in the Web Service and also in Web Service clients. Consider the following extremely simple WebMethod:

```
<WebMethod()> Public Function HelloWorld() As String
    Session("Greeting") += "Hello"
    Return Session("Greeting")
End Function
```

You've probably worked out that every time you call this method, it should return a slightly longer greeting, by concatenating the string "Hello" on to the greeting each time. However, you can see what actually happens when you test this Web Method from the Service Help page in Figure 14-14.

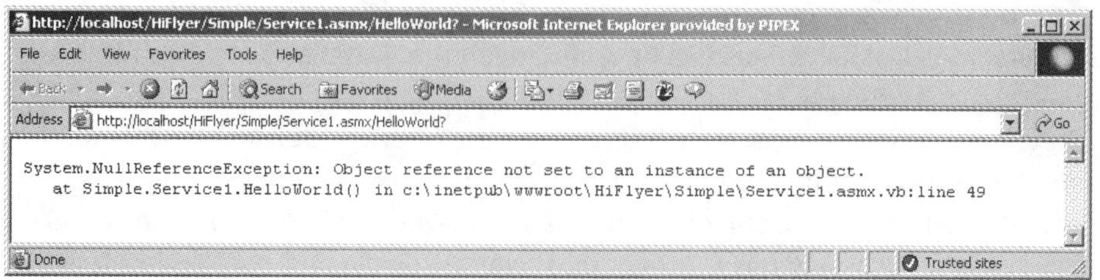

Figure 14-14. When Session State is not enabled

This error occurs because Session state is not enabled automatically for Web Services (although you wouldn't know this from the rather unhelpful error message). To enable Session state, you need to modify the `WebMethod` attribute for each Web Method that uses it to set the `enableSession` argument to true:

```
<WebMethod(enableSession:=True)> Public Function HelloWorld() As String
    Session("Greeting") += "Hello"
    Return Session("Greeting")
End Function
```

Having made this change, the Service Help page yields the output shown in Figure 14-15 after several calls.

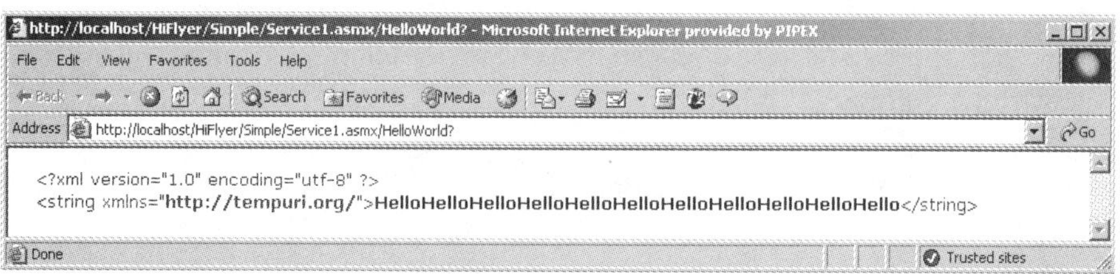

Figure 14-15. When Session State is enabled

This result is far more satisfactory, and you would be forgiven for feeling you have now done all that's necessary to make Session state work. In one sense you have, but you'll get a nasty surprise when building a Windows Application client for this Web Service. Assuming you've created a client and added a Web Reference to the simple Web Service, you might think all you need to call the Web Service is some code such as this:

```
Private Sub Button1_Click( . . . ) Handles Button1.Click
    Dim pxy As New localhost.Service1()
    MessageBox.Show(pxy.HelloWorld)
End Sub
```

Unfortunately, however, many times you press this button, the MessageBox will always display exactly the same content—a single and rather lonely "Hello." In other words, if any data is being built up in Session state, you aren't seeing anything for it. To understand why this is the case, you'll need to cast your mind back to the discussion of how cookie-based sessions work in Chapter 12. Assuming you're using cookies for state management, ASP.NET writes a Session ID into a cookie stored in the Header of the HTTP response. The browser then adds that cookie into each future request it makes to the same server, allowing the server to recognize a previous caller and maintain a session. This kind of cookie management is built into most browsers, but it's not something that Windows Applications are typically expected to do. Consequently, calls to the HelloWorld Web Method made by clicking the button will generate an HTTP request that contains no session cookie, and so ASP.NET will treat each request as coming from a completely new client program. To put things right, you need to add cookie management into your client code.

This isn't actually as frightening as it sounds because Web Service proxy classes inherit some basic cookie functionality. You have to make sure that you reuse the same proxy object each time you call a Web Method where you intend to benefit from Session state, and you also have to enable cookie management by creating a CookieContainer object. Here's how it's done:

```
Private pxy As localhost.Service1

Private Sub Form1_Load( . . . ) Handles MyBase.Load
    pxy = New localhost.Service1()
    pxy.CookieContainer = New System.Net.CookieContainer()
End Sub

Private Sub Button1_Click( . . . ) Handles Button1.Click
    MessageBox.Show(pxy.HelloWorld)
End Sub
```

The Web Service proxy object is declared as a class-level variable, and is initialized in the Form_Load event handler, at which time a CookieContainer object is created and assigned to the proxy object's CookieContainer property. Once this is done, cookie management will be handled automatically, although you can write lower-level cookie management code if you want.

As you can see, handling Session cookies using a .NET proxy is not exactly hard, and it delivers all the benefits (and disadvantages) of using Session state in Web Applications. One concern is that there's no formal way of telling client developers that your Web Service requires cookies to be handled to make them work. There is no provision in WSDL to specify this, and you'll need to make sure your Web Service documentation clearly states this requirement.

Web Service Security

To a certain extent, Web Service security is similar to Web Application security, and everything we covered in Chapter 11 concerning the use of IIS and ASP.NET security features is relevant background material for discussing Web Service security. We'll address the task of securing Web Services from two different perspectives: local intranet-based Web Services and public Internet-based Web Services.

Intranet-Based Web Service Security

When developing Web Sites for intranet purposes, the combination of IIS and ASP.NET security works well for Web Services, and it's simple to disable anonymous access and enable integrated security for IIS (as discussed in Chapter 11), and then use Windows security within ASP.NET to control access to your Web Service.

Once you've secured your Web Service, you quickly find that (just as you saw with Session state) browsers actually do more for you than you sometimes think. When making an HTTP request, Internet Explorer will automatically supply the credentials of the logged on user when requested to do so. Therefore, you'll probably be able to test your secured Web Service using the Service Help page because the browser will supply the required credentials. Most Web Service clients, including Windows Forms applications, aren't so clever. Fortunately, Web Service proxy classes inherit some built-in security functionality (just as you saw with Session state) to make life easy for client developers. Each proxy object exposes a `Credentials` property, which can store either an individual set of security credentials or a cache of different sets of credentials as may be required by different Web Services.

There are two main ways of providing credentials. You can choose to provide a specific user ID and password (and optionally domain name), which can be captured from the application user, or you can use the credentials of the logged on user. You saw the first of these approaches earlier in the chapter and will reproduce it here only for convenience:

```
pxy.Credentials = New System.Net.NetworkCredential ("GoodGuy", "secret")
```

To remove the need for users to type in their credentials, you can also pick up the credentials of the logged on user as follows:

```
pxy.Credentials = System.Net.CredentialCache.DefaultCredentials
```

In both cases, the proxy object will supply the credentials to IIS according to the IIS authentication method in force. What this means is that if IIS is using basic authentication, then the user's credentials will be passed in clear text, although if Integrated Windows security is used, the credentials will be authenticated securely.

If your organization has the infrastructure in place to use more sophisticated authentication techniques such as the use of client certificates, these can be used with Web Service proxies as well.

Public Internet Web Service Security

Windows Integrated security provides safe and convenient authentication for intranet-based applications, but it can't be used for public Web sites, because it doesn't work with firewalls and assumes that the client is running on a Windows PC in the same domain as the Web server where the Web Service is running (or at least on a domain trusted by the Web Server's domain). Neither of these restrictions is suitable for public internet-based Web Services, and therefore different authentication schemes must be used instead.

In the Web Applications world, ASP.NET Forms security provides a clever and convenient way to create authentication schemes that work for public Internet applications, but this approach won't work for Web Services because it assumes that the client is a browser.

The most common approach currently in use for Web Service security is to use basic authentication over Secure Sockets Layer (SSL). You can easily program basic authentication using the `Credentials` property, and it functions through firewalls. So long as you're able to supply each user with a user ID and password matching a domain account known to the Web Service, both IIS and ASP.NET Windows security can be used. By using SSL, the user ID and password will be encrypted before being passed across the Internet, thus avoiding the danger of sending credentials as clear text.

It isn't always convenient to use Windows accounts to authenticate users, especially if you're planning a Web Service with a large user base. In such cases, you may want to hold user credentials in a database and implement your own flexible security mechanism. It's also possible that you're less interested in security and more interested in tracking which users are using which parts of your service. In either of these cases, the issue arises of how the user's credentials should be provided. You could of course include arguments to each method to allow clients to provide a user ID and password, but this would be cumbersome and unpopular.

A better solution is to exploit SOAP Headers. If you recall, SOAP Headers are an optional part of a SOAP Envelope that can be included before the SOAP Body. By using SOAP Headers, a client can add additional information to each method call without interfering with the main purpose of the method. What's more, once the client program has set the Header contents via the Web Service proxy, the proxy will ensure that the correct SOAP Headers get sent with each method call. SOAP Headers therefore provide a great way to add a user ID and password to each method call without cluttering up the client code.

We'll take a look at how to use SOAP Headers as part of our Weather Web Service. Even if you don't intend using SOAP Headers for security purposes, you may see applications for SOAP Headers for other purposes. The coding approach will seem a little strange at first, but it works out to be perfectly convenient. Start by adding the following Imports statement at the top of the code window of the Weather Web Service class:

```
Imports System.Web.Services.Protocols
```

The next step is to define a class that inherits from a generic SOAP Header class called SOAPHeader that lives in the System.Web.Services.Protocols namespace:

```
Public Class ClientID
    Inherits SoapHeader

    Public Username As String
    Public Password As String

    Public Sub Authorize()
        If Username <> "GoodGuy" Or Password <> "secret" Then
            ' throw an error unless user is authorized
            Throw New SoapHeaderException _
                ("Invalid User", SoapException.ClientFaultCode)
        End If
    End Sub
End Class
```

The public properties of this class (`Username` and `Password`) will become elements that clients will need to supply in the header of the SOAP messages they send. The `Authorize` subroutine won't have any effect on the SOAP Header itself (only the properties affect the header) but will prove to be a convenient location to contain our authorization code. In this case, the authorization test is extremely simple. In a real Web Service, it might check a database to see if this user should be allowed to continue. Note that if the authorization test fails, a SOAP exception is raised, which will be propagated back to the client as a standard SOAP error.

The next step is to add a public property to the Web Service class whose type is ClientID (our custom SOAP Header class defined previously):

```
Public Check As ClientID
```

The final (and most bizarre) step is to specify how this header should be used for each Web Method. Here is a modified version of the `Temperature` Web Method, which now makes use of this SOAP Header:

```
<SoapHeader("Check"), WebMethod()> _
Public Function Temperature() As Integer
    Check.Authorize()
    Temperature = (New Random()).Next(-10, 30)
End Function
```

The first thing to notice about this code is the `SoapHeader` attribute that has been added before the WebMethod attribute. This attribute tells ASP.NET to look at the data type of the `Check` property, to find out what SOAP Header information is required. ASP.NET will look at the ClientID class (which inherits from the generic SOAPHeader class) and note that a Username and Password are required (because the class has these as public properties). ASP.NET will then check the incoming SOAP message to see if the SOAP Header contains the required elements, and if it does, it will assign the appropriate values to the `Username` and `Password` properties of a ClientID object that it will assign to the `Check` property of the Web Service (if you feel the need to read that again relax, it means you're normal). Therefore, when the `Temperature` WebMethod calls the `Authorize` method on `Check`, the object assigned to the `Check` property will run its authorization code, checking the properties assigned by ASP.NET. If authorization fails, the SOAP error will be thrown and passed back to the client.

To be secure, you need to apply the same approach (adding the `SoapHeader` attribute and calling the `Authorize` method) in each and every Web Method in the Web Service. Once that's done, you've added custom SOAP Header security to your Web Service.

You get some clues to what these changes actually do by taking a look at the WSDL contract generated by ASP.NET after changing the code as described. Firstly, a new complex type has been defined in the WSDL:

```
<s:element name="ClientID" type="s0:ClientID" />
<s:complexType name="ClientID">
    <s:sequence>
      <s:element minOccurs="0" maxOccurs="1" name="Username" type="s:string" />
      <s:element minOccurs="0" maxOccurs="1" name="Password" type="s:string" />
    </s:sequence>
</s:complexType>
```

This addition to the WSDL will tell client programs that a type called ClientID with two properties exists. More interesting is the how the WSDL for the `Temperature` Web Method has been changed (some detail has been suppressed for clarity):

```
<operation name="Temperature">
    <soap:operation soapAction="http://apress.com/hiflyers/Temperature" . . . />
        <input>
            <soap:body use="literal" />
            <soap:header d5p1:required="true" . . . part="ClientID" . . . />
        </input>
        <output><soap:body use="literal" /></output>
</operation>
```

This shows that the input to the Web Method now requires a SOAP Header, as defined by a type called ClientID.

If you now try and run a client program that doesn't know about the need for these SOAP Headers, ASP.NET will return the following error message:

```
Server did not find required ClientID SOAP header in the message.
```

proving that the requirement for the SOAP Header has been properly enforced.

To make sure that the client knows about the SOAP Header, you need to refresh the Web Reference to the Weather Web Service. When you generate the proxy class code, .NET will create a new local class called ClientID based on the information it found in the WSDL contract, and it will also add a new property to your proxy class (called `ClientIDValue`) whose data type is ClientID. After the line of code where you create the proxy object, you can add the following code:

```
pxy.ClientIDValue = New localhost.ClientID()
pxy.ClientIDValue.Username = "GoodGuy"
pxy.ClientIDValue.Password = "secret"
```

This will create an instance of the local ClientID class and assign it to the (newly created) `ClientIDValue` property of the proxy object. You can then set the `Username` and `Password` properties on this object. All subsequent calls to the Web Service using this proxy will have the required SOAP Header added automatically, thus meeting the conditions specified in the WSDL fragment we saw above.

To put this into context, once the `ClientIDValue` property has been initialized, calling the `Temperature` method will result in the following SOAP being sent in the HTTP request:

```
<?xml version="1.0" encoding="utf-8"?>
<soap:Envelope . . . >
    <soap:Header>
        <ClientID xmlns="http://apress.com/hiflyers/">
            <Username>GoodGuy</Username>
            <Password>secret</Password>
        </ClientID>
    </soap:Header>
    <soap:Body>
        <Temperature xmlns="http://apress.com/hiflyers/" />
    </soap:Body>
</soap:Envelope>
```

You can clearly see that a SOAP Header element has been added to the SOAP Envelope along with the SOAP Body, and this will ensure that the Web Service gets the information it needs to validate the user.

Be aware that the SOAP Header (like the rest of the SOAP Envelope) is transmitted across the Internet as clear text. If you want to be genuinely secure, you need to use SSL for the entire Web Service. SSL is easy to set up, but of course it does slow down the HTTP exchange between client and server if the entire content of every message needs to be encrypted. There are some standards under development for Web Services where only the SOAP Header needs to be encrypted, but no such standards exist as we write.

Setting up SOAP Headers on the server involved a certain amount of effort, but supplying the header information in the client was extremely easy. This should make you feel good as a Web Service developer. Good component writers (and a Web Service is just a component that is called across the Internet) are always prepared to invest time to make components that are easy for users to use, even if doing so involves a fair bit of server-side complexity.

Summary

Most of the attention that ASP.NET (and even the whole .NET platform) has received has centered on its ability to create browser-based, HTML Web Applications. This is absolutely how it should be, given the importance of the Web and the really great functionality that ASP.NET provides.

However, it's interesting to note that in high-level presentations, Microsoft itself focuses more strongly on Web Services rather than Web Applications. ASP.NET Web Applications are a better way of doing something that you already know about and without a doubt will encourage many developers who've never quite had the time for classic ASP to apply their programming skills to the development of Web Applications.

In contrast, Web Services are something rather more novel. Right now, most programmers are happy with the idea of calling code libraries to draw graphics on a screen or maybe add two dates together. In other words, the code libraries you call are (with the exception of database access libraries such as ADO.NET or classic ADO) generally limited to things that can be done right there on your local computer. If the massive hype and (more importantly) investment concerning Web Service technology by all major vendors is anything to go by, Web Services will make our current view of code libraries look like flat-earth thinking. Using Web Services, you can access code libraries anywhere. As we said at the beginning of this chapter, allowing programs to communicate over the Internet via Web Services will, if anything, have a greater impact on the world than the Web already has had so far.

It's fitting, therefore, that the final chapter addresses Web Services. You've seen that ASP.NET provides almost identical infrastructure to support both Web Applications and Web Services. Both use exactly the same Internet technology and require the same Web site mentality for issues as diverse as state management, security, and scalability. Web Applications are in the limelight now, but this doesn't mean that Web Services can be ignored. Like Bill Gates himself, we predict that the importance of Web Services will grow and grow.

APPENDIX A

Web and ASP Basics

Understanding HTML

Understanding HTTP

Using IIS

Using ASP

ONE OF THE MOST EXCITING THINGS about ASP.NET is that it allows developers who have never created any Web pages before to apply their existing development skills to Web development. The purpose of this appendix is to explain the basic terms and techniques of Web development for those developers who until now have only ever been users of the Internet or have been insulated from the coding detail by using products such as Microsoft FrontPage or Macromedia Dreamweaver.

So, if you're basically comfortable with HTML, if you have a clear idea of how a Web server fundamentally works, or if you've spent more than a few days using Active Server Pages (ASP) to create Web content in the pre-.NET world, you don't need to read this appendix. However, if any of these topics are new to you, you should read these next few pages before delving into the main text of the book, which makes certain assumptions about Web basics, all of which we'll address here.

Everyone knows how to use the Internet. You type an address into the address line of a browser or maybe click a hyperlink on an existing page. You wait slightly longer than you really want, and then the page you requested displays in your browser. Figure A-1 shows this basic model.

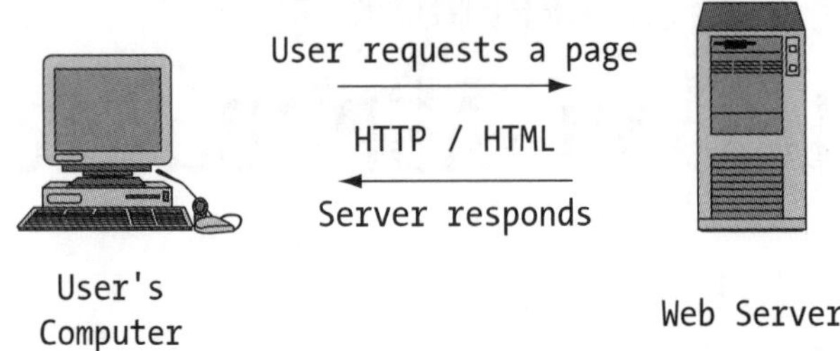

Figure A-1. How the Web works

To be able to write programs for the Internet (that is, programs that construct the pages that Web servers send to browsers when a user requests them), you need to know some things about exactly how the page you asked for gets displayed in your browser. Actually, two things are going on here that you need to understand. The first is how your browser displays the page. The second is how the page gets to your browser in the first place. To display a page, the browser needs to understand a markup language called HyperText Markup Language (HTML). To be able to get hold of the page, the browser needs to use a communication protocol called HyperText Transfer Protocol (HTTP) when talking to the Web server.

Understanding HTML

HTML is a markup, or layout, language designed for use on the Web. It describes how a page of information should be displayed by a browser. The browser is responsible for reading HTML and generating specific graphic instructions suitable for the computer and operating system on which it's running.

HTML itself doesn't care about any specific type of computer, operating system, or browser. It simply contains instructions for browsers to use to create a display.

Here's an example of a simple HTML file (created in Notepad and saved to `c:\simple.htm`):

```
<html>
    <head>
        <title>A Simple Browser Page</title>
    </head>
    <body>
        Here's some text
    </body>
</html>
```

Just before seeing what this looks like in a browser, examine the structure and content of this HTML document. The document begins with an opening `<html>` tag and finishes with a closing `</html>` tag. Together, opening and closing tags define an *element*. Elements can contain other elements, as well as having their own content. Everything inside the `html` element is treated by the browser as potential page content to be displayed. Within the `<html>` tags are further tags defining the head and body of the page. Within the body is some plain text. As you'll see, HTML defines a wide range of other tags that can be used within the body for specific effects.

Figure A-2 shows what this HTML looks like in two different browsers (Microsoft Internet Explorer 6.0 and Opera 6.01). In each case, the display is created simply by typing `c:\simple.htm` into the address line and pressing Enter.

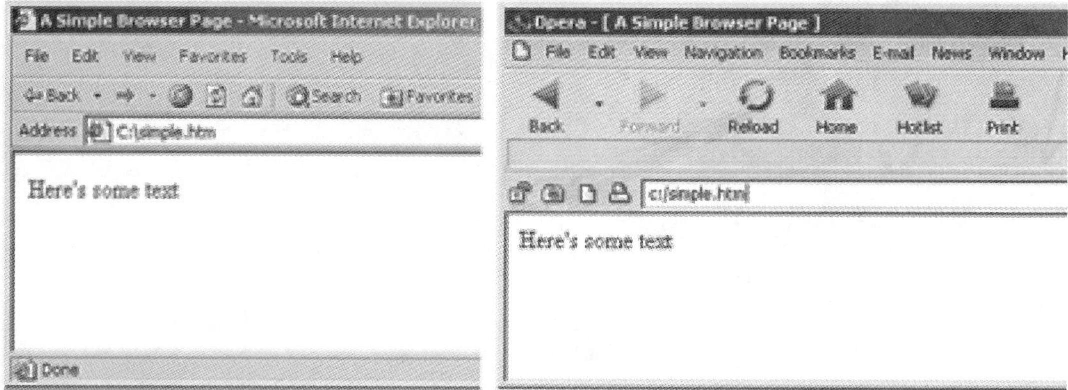

Figure A-2. Using Internet Explorer (left) and Opera (right)

Note that the tags themselves don't get displayed, only their content. Tags give information to the browser about how to display the data they contain. Note also that the title actually gets displayed in the browser's caption bar, rather than directly within the page. There are some slight differences in how the two browsers handle the HTML (for example, the title is displayed differently), but what you see in each case is fundamentally the same.

In the next example, the simple page has been slightly enhanced:

```
<html>
    <head>
        <title>A Simple Browser Page</title>
    </head>
    <body>
       Here's some text <br>
        <font size="7" color="Red">Here's some BIG RED text</font>
```

```
    </body>
</html>
```

In this example, a simple element called `<br>` has been added to create a line break between two pieces of text (note that this tag doesn't have a corresponding closing tag because it doesn't contain any text). The next line uses the slightly more complex font element, which has a closing and opening tag: `<font> . . . </font>`. The text between the tags is displayed according to *attributes* that specify the font size and color. Figure A-3 shows how this looks in a browser. Attributes and their values appear within the opening tag of an element. For example, the `size` attribute in the opening tag of the `font` element has a value of `"7"`.

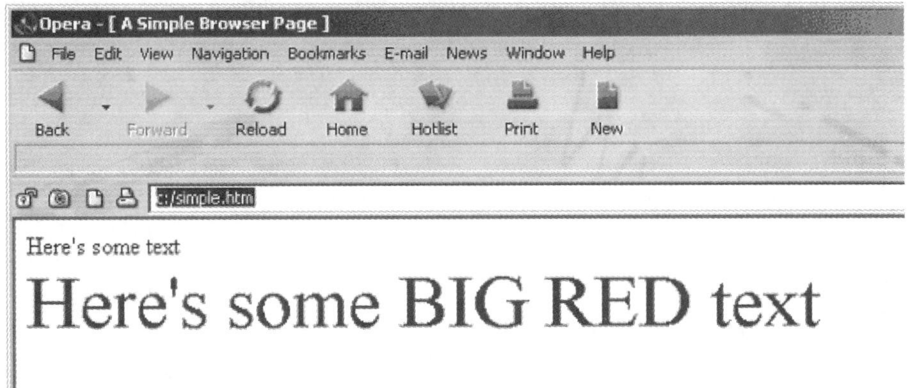

Figure A-3. Using elements and attributes for layout effects

We'll add one more touch of sophistication to the page by including a table and an image. Figure A-4 shows what this looks like.

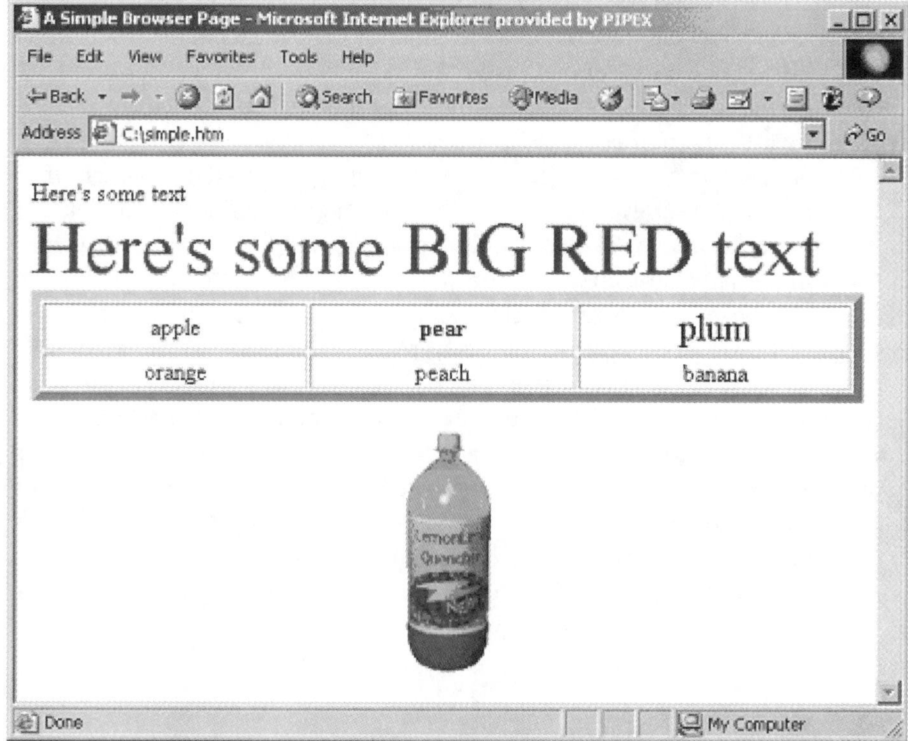

Figure A-4. Using tables and images

To add the table and the soda bottle image, insert the following HTML into the body of the document:

```
<table border="6"  width="100%">
    <tr>
        <td width="33%" align="center">apple</td>
        <td width="33%" align="center"><b>pear</b></td>
        <td width="34%" align="center"><font size="5">plum</font></td>
    </tr>
    <tr>
        <td width="33%" align="center">orange</td>
        <td width="33%" align="center">peach</td>
        <td width="34%" align="center">banana</td>
    </tr>
</table>
<p align="center">
    <img border="0" src="soda4.gif" width="60" height="160">
</p>
```

Here you can see the HTML syntax for creating a table, using table tags (<table>), table row tags (<tr>) and table data tags (<td>). Each table row element contains three table data elements, resulting in a table with three columns of data. You can also see the use of attributes to control the appearance of the table—its width and border size.

The last section of this HTML displays an image, presented in a paragraph (<p>) whose contents are centered. Note that the <img> tag has an `src` attribute that identifies the image's filename. Because no path is specified, this image file must be in the same directory as `simple.htm`.

You've seen enough to get a basic idea of what HTML looks like and how it's displayed by browsers. Of course there is a great deal more to HTML, and there are plenty of HTML books and resources that go into amazing detail on the subject. You've probably also worked out that writing complex HTML pages in Notepad is unlikely to be a rewarding task. Many Web page authors use graphical tools such as FrontPage or Dreamweaver to generate HTML. Visual Studio .NET also contains an HTML designer.

So far, you've seen only static layout in our Web page. HTML also enables you to interact with a Web page, and perhaps the most common ways to interact with Web pages is via hyperlinks and forms.

Interacting with a Web Page

Figure A-5 shows a simple page called `welcome.htm` that contains a hyperlink to `simple.htm`.

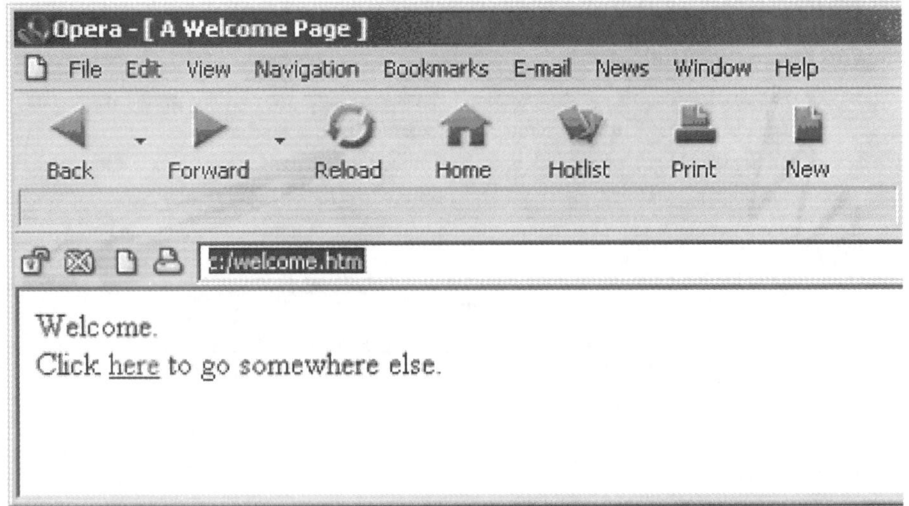

Figure A-5. Hyperlinking

The HTML for this page is as follows:

```
<html>
    <head>
        <title>A Welcome Page</title>
    </head>
    <body>
        Welcome.<br>
        Click
        <a href="simple.htm">here</a>
        to go somewhere else.
    </body>
</html>
```

The hyperlink functionality is provided by the anchor element (`<a href="simple.htm">here</a>`). This specifies that when the text contained in the anchor element is clicked, the browser should request the page specified by the `href` attribute. In this case, the `href` refers to a local file in the same directory as the current page, but the `href` can equally be a fully qualified HTTP-based Uniform Resource Locator (URL), such as `"http://www.mydomain.com/simple.htm"`. A hyperlink can also link to a named location within the same document, in which case the user gets the experience of hyperlinking without the delay of a round-trip back to the server.

HTML forms provide a more flexible kind of user input. This is where the Web page presents control elements (such as text boxes, check boxes, list boxes and buttons) that you can use to interact with the page and send information to the server. You can see an example in Figure A-6.

Figure A-6. An HTML form

The extra HTML that creates this form is as follows:

```
Or enter your email address and click 'Done'<br>
<form method="POST" action="http://ermine/processwelcome.asp">
    <input type="text" name="T1" size="20"><br>
    <input type="checkbox" name="C1" value="ON" checked>Please sell my email
    address to all and sundry<br>
    <input type="submit" value="Done" name="Button1"> <br>
</form>
```

Here you can see three HTML control elements contained with `<form> . . . </form>` tags. Note that the Done button is an `input` element of type `submit`. When this button is clicked, the form will be submitted to the Web page identified in the `action` attribute of the `form` element that contains the button. In this case, the form will be submitted to an ASP page called `processwelcome.asp`. By submitting the form, any settings made by the user to the controls in the form will be sent to the target location, which will be able to read the settings and thereby process the user's input. You'll see how an ASP page might process this input later in this appendix. Note that each element in the form has a name.

These names can be treated like variable names by code that processes the form, allowing the values typed into individual page controls to be identified.

One final thing to notice is the form's `method` attribute, which can either be `GET` or `POST`. The choice refers to how the values that the user has entered into the form get sent to the server. When you use GET, the values entered by the user are appended onto the URL in the form of a querystring:

```
http://ermine/processwelcome.asp?T1=billg@microsoft.com&C1=ON&Button1=Done
```

When you use POST, the same data is sent, but it's embedded inside the HTTP message sent to the server.

Interacting with Animation and Scripts

Even with hyperlinks and forms, HTML is a fairly static medium. The roots of the Web may be in hyperlinking between different pages of information, but the current usage of the Web is rather different, with more and more applications being made available on the Internet with increasing complexity. To try and make Web pages more dynamic, developers frequently use more than just HTML to build a Web page. One common practice is to include client-side script in a Web page. This is code that can be downloaded as a part of an HTML document, but rather than just being displayed it's intended to be executed on the user's computer by the browser. Other non-HTML Web page content such as animation and audio is also common, and downloadable applets written in Java (or even using .NET languages) can be used to pep up a Web application.

These additional features make the Web far more interesting, but they don't come without certain problems. A huge amount of effort has been invested in standardizing HTML, and yet there are differences between even the major browsers that can catch developers out. Cross-browser incompatibilities become amplified in areas where there's not so much standardization effort. For example, Internet Explorer allows client-side script code to modify the HTML inside the browser so that the user's page can be updated without needing to go back to the Web server to request a new page. Unfortunately, script code that works on one browser may not work on another (in particular, script code written in VBScript will only work with Internet Explorer. You won't see VBScript used anywhere in .NET applications). The more fancy features you add into Web pages, the less the chance your site will work with a decent range of browsers. This doesn't mean you shouldn't use these features. Many Web developers take the view that there are enough Internet Explorer users who can use their site, so they don't worry so much about users who have other browsers. You just need to be aware of the trade-offs involved in Web development.

Understanding HTTP

As you've seen, you can open a local HTML file simply by typing its file path into the address line. However, this isn't how things work on the Internet (and therefore should not be used as a means of testing Web Applications). Instead, Web pages move around the Internet using a protocol called HyperText Transfer Protocol (HTTP). HTTP itself makes use of a lower-level protocol called Transmission Control Protocol/Internet Protocol (TCP/IP).

We don't want to start getting into too much networking detail, but it's worth saying a word or two about TCP/IP; after all, the IP bit stands for Internet Protocol—or put another way, IP is how the Internet works.

For two computers on the Internet to communicate, they each need a unique IP address. This means that when you're browsing, both your computer and each Web site you visit must be represented by an IP address. An example of an IP address is this:

```
150.215.13.19
```

Web servers tend to have *static* IP addresses so that they can always be found at the same address. Many end user computers are assigned *dynamic* IP addresses by their corporate network or an Internet Service Provider (ISP).

When your computer requests a Web page from a Web server, your computer sends one or more packets of information (which together represent your request) to your local Internet gateway. Each packet will contain the IP address of the Web server you want to contact, as well as your own IP address. The packets you send will be passed between various servers until they reach their intended destination. As far as IP is concerned, each packet is completely separate from any other packet and it's quite likely that the different packets of information that make up your request will travel to their destination via different routes because the Internet servers between your computer and the target Web site may make different routing decisions for each packet. This means that the packets of data could arrive at their destination in any order. It's also possible that one or more packets might get lost or corrupted. It's the job of TCP to make sure that all the data needed to reconstruct your request on the target computer is present and in the right order. TCP software on your computer puts sequence and checksum information into the IP packets that it sends so that TCP software on the target computer can reassemble the packets correctly and rerequest any that go missing or arrive corrupted. In other words, TCP makes sure your message reaches the server containing the same information that it contained when it left your computer.

When the Web server has processed your request, it sends the response (for example, an HTML document) back over the Internet, targeted at your IP address, as a series of IP packets. IP makes sure that the response packets find their way to your computer, and TCP makes sure you receive a complete message with no missing or corrupt packets.

TCP is a higher-level protocol than IP because it *uses* IP (which only cares about packets of data) to achieve a more specific aim (a properly delivered message). HTTP is at a yet higher level because it uses TCP/IP to achieve a yet more specific aim—delivering documents in response to requests for documents. HTTP basically defines how a browser and a Web server should behave when a user requests a document. You can type IP addresses into the address line of a browser if you want, but it's not the usual way of getting to a Web site. IP addresses don't exactly trip off the tongue. Instead we tend to use Uniform Resource Locators (URLs) such as this:

```
http://www.apress.com/about/about.html
```

The `http` part of this URL specifies the protocol being used to access the Internet. The next part (`www.apress.com`) contains the domain name used to access a specific Web server. The Internet uses a service called the Domain Name Service (DNS) to translate domain names into IP addresses so that humans can work with friendly names while computers and networks can work more efficiently with IP addresses.

The remaining part of the URL tells the Web server the path of the requested file. When the user navigates to that URL, Apress's Web server will simply look for a file called `/about/about.html` and return it across the Internet (using HTTP, TCP, and IP) to the user that requested it.

We've covered the basic mechanics of how HTTP works, but more important are some of the implications for developers interested in building Web sites. These include the following:

- **Round-trips**: Every time a user requests a new page, that page request must be sent across the Internet to a Web server, and the Web server's response must be sent back across the Internet to the user's browser. This process is known as a *round-trip*, and it's not surprising that each round-trip can take time to process. Now, if your Web server is on your own private network, getting data back from it is going to be much faster than a request that must pass through a whole series of gateways and routers before it reaches its destination. Nevertheless, round-trips always take time, and Web developers must always be thinking about how many round-trips their Web application actually needs.

- **Statelessness**: HTTP is a stateless protocol. This means that each HTTP request is treated by the Web server as a separate request. If the same browser issues two identical requests in quick succession, the Web server will have completely forgotten about the first request when it gets round to processing the second. This statelessness gives Web application developers a bit of a problem. When users use desktop applications, they get used to the fact that the application remembers things that they did a few moments, or even a few hours before (after all, what are global variables for?). Web applications aren't like this—or perhaps more correctly, you have to work much harder as a developer to make your Web application remember things. Dealing properly with the stateless nature of HTTP will take up several chunks of this book.

- **Security**: Both HTTP and HTML are based on text. An HTTP request and the HTML returned by Web servers are easily readable by any reasonably computer-literate person. Couple this information with the fact that the Internet exists in the public domain, and you might start to see a problem. IP is a truly marvelous thing, but it means that your HTTP traffic could pass through any number of servers, gateways, and routers as it moves between browser, Web server, and back, and there are plenty of opportunities for bad guys to read or tamper with your HTTP messages. Still keen on typing your credit card details into an HTML form? Fortunately, there are secure ways to use HTTP, as you'll see in Chapter 11, and given the amount of sensitive and private information moving around on the Internet, it's just as well. You cannot underestimate the importance of good security when programming the Web.

- **Scalability**: IP makes a Web server accessible from any computer, anywhere in the world. There are an awful lot of computers out there, and if each one of them started sending HTTP requests to your server at the same time, it would almost certainly get swamped and die of shock. This is unlikely, but processing one million hits a day is not uncommon for a really popular Web site. Processing one million requests, and storing even a few kilobytes of data for each one (even only temporarily) is not easy. It certainly isn't what your typical desktop application ever needs to do. As a Web developer, you need a clear idea of how many requests your application is going to need to process and how many concurrent users you are going to need to support. If you anticipate heavy demand, you need to design your site so that it doesn't need to be redesigned as it gets more popular. In other words, it needs to be *scalable*.

Using IIS

A Web server is a program that runs on a computer and listens for Web requests. From our perspective, it responds to HTTP requests targeted at a given domain name or IP address. When a Web server receives a proper HTTP request, its job is to return a proper HTTP response. A Web server really is a program (in other words, software). However, it's quite common to point at a lump of hardware and say, "that's our Web server." It's just a short-hand way of saying, "that's the computer where our Web server runs."

There are many different Web servers, but they all do pretty much the same thing, as defined by a set of standards created and maintained by the World Wide Web Consortium (W3C). The most common Web servers are Apache, which typically runs on Unix servers, and Microsoft's Internet Information Server (IIS), which runs exclusively on Windows servers. At the time of writing, ASP.NET requires IIS, so we'll focus exclusively on IIS (the design of ASP.NET is such that it could be integrated with other Web servers in the future).

At its most basic, when IIS receives an HTTP request, it simply looks for the requested file and returns it. Say, for example, you wanted to use HTTP to retrieve `simple.htm` from your local machine. If you use `localhost` instead of a domain name or computer name, your browser will talk to the Web server running on your computer (regardless of what the computer is called) and ask it to process the request. Therefore, you might type the following into the browser's address line to retrieve this page:

```
http://localhost/simple.htm
```

IIS does not view files in the same way that they're organized on the hard disk of the computer where it runs. Instead, IIS sees files organized according to its own *virtual* file space, made up of a set of *virtual directories*. The *virtual root* of this file space is typically a real directory called `c:\inetpub\wwwroot`. Therefore, in order for IIS to be able to find the `simple.htm` file in response to the `http://localhost/simple.htm` request, the file must be copied into this virtual root, along with any related files, such as `soda4.gif`.

It doesn't make sense to keep every file needed by a Web site in the same virtual root directory, and subdirectories can be used to organize files. For example, `c:\inetpub\wwwroot` has a subdirectory called `images` that is a handy place to keep image files. Given that `simple.htm` actually makes use of an image file (`soda4.gif`), you can place this image file into `c:\inetpub\wwwroot\images`. You would also need to modify the `src` attribute in the `<img>` tag so that the browser can pick this file up from its new location. This is what the modified section of the HTML looks like:

```
<img border="0" src="images\soda4.gif" width="60" height="160">
```

Creating subdirectories to hold associated files is a good way to organize all the files for a given Web application, but it's quite common to have many different Web applications on the same Web server. It's good practice to create a new virtual directory for each Web application because each one can then be administered separately, assigned different security characteristics, and so on. A virtual subdirectory of IIS's root directory need not be an actual subdirectory of `c:\inetpub\wwwroot`. It can actually be any directory anywhere in your file system. This is what we mean when we say that IIS sees files organized according to its own scheme of things. In order to explore this concept, it's time to introduce the primary tool used to manage IIS, the Internet Service Manager, which is accessible from the Administrative Tools applet in the Control Panel. Figure A-7 shows you how it's organized.

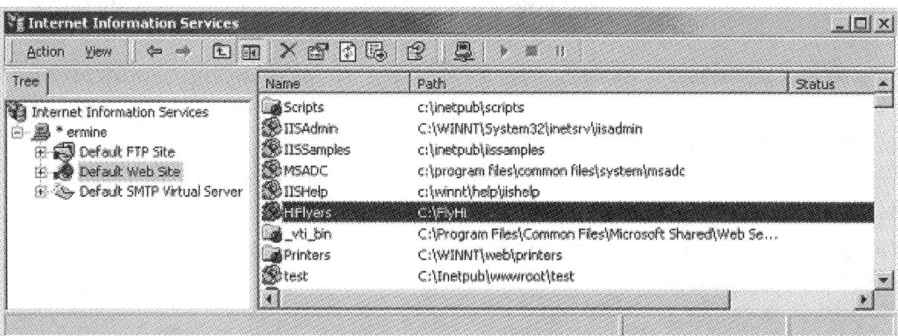

Figure A-7. Internet Services Manager

The right hand side of the Figure A-7 lists some of the virtual directories on our test computer. Notice that there is a virtual directory called HiFlyers whose path is `c:\FlyHi`. This is clearly not a real subdirectory of `c:\inetpub\wwwroot`; nevertheless the URL to access a file called simple.htm stored in the real directory `c:\FlyHi` is this:

```
http://localhost/HiFlyers/simple.htm
```

The mapping relationship between the virtual directory and the real file system on the Web server is maintained by IIS and created and edited using Internet Services Manager.

You can create new virtual directories using Internet Services Manager by right-clicking on **Default Web Site** or on an existing virtual directory. However, if you use Visual Studio .NET to create ASP.NET Web Applications or Web Services, it will create virtual directories for you. Nevertheless, you still need to use Internet Services Manager from time to time because there are certain administrative tasks that can't be performed through ASP.NET or Visual Studio .NET.

These days, Web sites do a great deal more than simply return files picked up from a hard disk. When a user interacts with a dynamic Web site (such as any database-driven or e-commerce site) instead of reading a file from disk, a file is generated for that user, on the fly, at the time of the request.

IIS can be configured to look out for files with a particular file extension, and instead of reading these files from disk, IIS passes them on to another program or a code library to retrieve. As you'll learn in Chapter 10, this is how ASP.NET works: All requests from files with a particular extension are passed directly from IIS to ASP.NET.

Other dynamic Web content services work in much the same way. One example is classic ASP, the primary means by which Web sites were developed in the pre-.NET days. Any file with an `.asp` extension is passed to the ASP code library. Rather than just return a file from disk, the ASP code library will read the file and execute any code that it contains before returning it. By placing code in the file, an ASP programmer can generate dynamic Web content.

Once you start creating several pages with dynamic content, and start linking them together so that one page calls another, it's easy to give users the impression they're working with an application. However, the definition of a Web application is rather different from the definition of a more traditional desktop application that's launched by running an EXE file. In Web terms, an application is deemed to be a virtual directory, all the files it contains (both static and dynamic) and all the virtual directory's subdirectories and their contents. Web applications can get large, and when there are many pages with dynamic content, such as ASP pages, very sophisticated applications can be created.

If you've never used classic ASP before, relax—with ASP.NET you'll never need to. You might still find it useful to know how it works—if only so you can appreciate just how much better ASP.NET is. Therefore we'll finish this chapter with a short tutorial on classic ASP.

Using ASP

Classic Active Server Pages (ASP) achieved two notable things. Firstly, it made it easier to develop dynamic Web sites than had previously been possible, and it has therefore made its own positive contribution to the development of the Internet. Secondly, it turned otherwise sober and professional programmers into mad hackers, intent on writing impenetrable spaghetti code that executes at a snail's pace because of its reliance on interpreted, weakly typed and late-bound code written in languages such as VBScript. It's possible to write good ASP-based systems, but ASP does not make it easy (ASP.NET, as the main part of this book explains, is a completely different story).

The basic mechanics of ASP are actually clever and elegant. You can turn any HTML page into an ASP page simply by giving it an `.asp` file extension. So let's start exploring ASP with a simple HTML file (created in Notepad and saved to `c:\inetpub\wwwroot\simple.asp`):

```
<html>
    <head>
        <title>A Simple Browser Page</title>
    </head>
    <body>
        Here's some text
    </body>
</html>
```

Apart from the file extension, this is the same as the `simple.htm` file from earlier in this appendix, and it will behave in exactly the same way. To make it more interesting, you can add some server-side script:

```
<html>
    <head>
        <title>A Simple Browser Page</title>
    </head>
    <body>
        Here's some text
         <% Response.Write (" at " + CStr(Now)) %>
    </body>
</html>
```

The difference is the VBScript code contained within the `<% . . . %>` tags:

```
         <% Response.Write (" at " + CStr(Now)) %>
```

These tags tell ASP that this is some server-side code that must be executed on the Web server and integrated into the page before it's returned to the user. This script uses the ASP Response object (which is responsible for building the response to an HTTP request) to write some text into the page. The text results from executing the VBScript `Now` function, which returns the date and time, and converting it into a string. The actual HTML generated on the server and returned to the user looks like this:

```
<html>
    <head>
        <title>A Simple Browser Page</title>
    </head>
    <body>
        Here's some text
 at 2/22/2002 4:19:45 PM
    </body>
</html>
```

Figure A-8 shows what this file looks like in a browser.

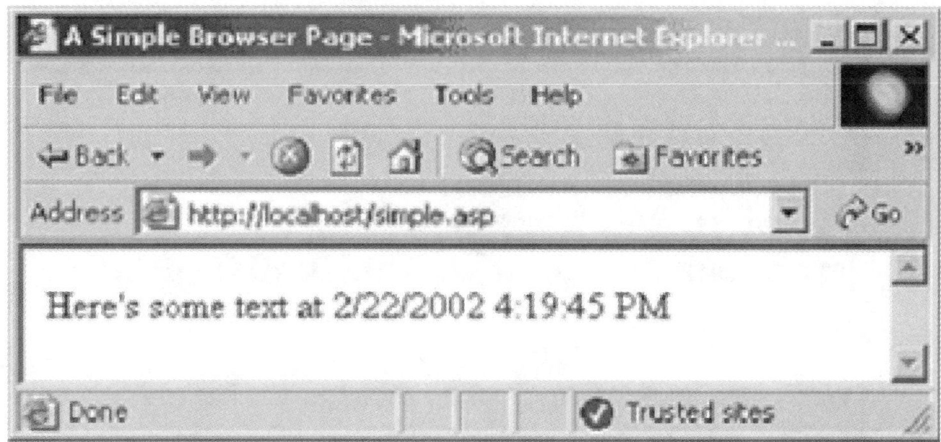

Figure A-8. Basic ASP output

As you can see, the server-side script has been executed and the results woven into the page returned to the user. Each time this page is requested, the content returned to the user will be different, according to the script (and the time of day). This alone makes ASP different from a standard HTML file. To understand more about how ASP code works, take a look at this next example:

```
<html>
    <head>
        <title>A Simple Browser Page</title>
    </head>
    <body>
     <% For count = 1 to 6 %>
        <font size=" <% Response.Write (count) %>" >
        <BR> Here's some text
        <% Response.Write (" at " + CStr(Now)) %>
        </font>
     <% Next %>
    </body>
</html>
```

Figure A-9 shows what the page looks like in the browser:

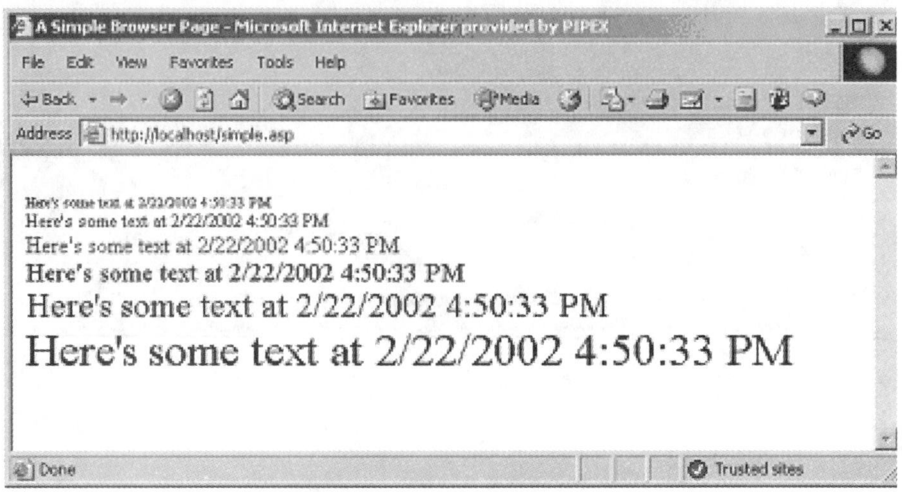

Figure A-9. Slightly less basic ASP output

Once you've worked out how the script code generated this output, you'll probably realize why so many people got excited about ASP. What you can see here is a `For . . . Next` loop embedded in the page, actually controlling the way the page is created, so that all the plain HTML (that is, the stuff outside the script tags) is actually processed according to the script's programming logic. Add to this the fact that ASP code can call classic ADO (or any other COM-based objects) to do database and other backend work, and it's easy to see how ASP opened up the world of Web programming.

To complete this basic introduction to ASP, recall the welcome.htm page we created earlier. It contained an HTML form defined as follows:

```
<form method="POST" action="http://ermine/processwelcome.asp">
    <input type="text" name="T1" size="20"><br>
    <input type="checkbox" name="C1" value="ON" checked>Please sell my email
    address to all and sundry<br>
    <input type="submit" value="Done" name="Button1"> <br>
</form>
```

Clicking the **Done** button in this form will post a request to the URL specified in the `action` attribute of the form element. The settings on each control on the form will be included in the request. You can pick these settings up in ASP by interrogating the Request object. Let's see the ASP code for `processwelcome.asp` that could be used to process this request:

```
<html>
    <head>
        <title>Welcome Response</title>
    </head>
    <body>
        Thank you
        <% Response.Write (Request.Form("T1")) %><br>
        <% If Request.Form("C1") = "ON" then %>
            We have sold your email address to all and sundry.
        <% else %>
            Your email address is safe with us.
        <% end if %>
    </body>
</html>
```

This code uses the Request object to read the text that the user has typed into the form into the input box called "`T1`" and writing it back to the user using the Response object. A more elaborate ASP page might save the user's e-mail address to a database for future spamming abuse. The code then reads "`C1`" (the Checkbox) to decide what to do with the user's email.

Figure A-10 shows the kind of output this ASP page might generate.

Figure A-10. Using ASP to process user input

There is a great deal more to ASP than we've covered here, but you've seen enough to understand how it works in principle.

ASP looks simple enough, but if you think for a moment about what's missing, you start to realize how hard it can be to write complex ASP applications. For one thing, there's no concept of controls or events in classic ASP. Imagine writing a graphical desktop program using purely procedural code! Tools such as Visual

Basic revolutionized desktop development by introducing an event-driven, object-based development model and opening up Windows development to millions of programmers almost overnight.

Moving from Visual Basic to ASP was a shock for many developers. It's no accident that ASP.NET brings the concepts of controls and events to Web development, and the improvement in productivity that these changes bring will revolutionize Web development just as they revolutionized desktop development.

Summary

In this appendix you've taken a quick look at Web basics, and you've received the background information that's assumed in other parts of the book. In doing so you've explored HTML, HTTP, IIS, and the basic mode of operation of the Web.

You've also seen how classic ASP works. There's no doubt it's an elegant concept that has proven to be liberating for Web developers. One of the problems of ASP is that the very feature that makes it look so clever in simple pages (the weaving together of HTML and server-side script) becomes its undoing in more realistically complex pages, where the intermingling of script and HTML results in obscure code that's difficult to manage and maintain and that's slow to execute. Fortunately, thanks to ASP.NET, that's all history.

APPENDIX B

The What and Why of .NET

The .NET Vision

The .NET Framework

THIS IS A BOOK ABOUT ASP.NET; however, it isn't possible to understand ASP.NET without knowing something of the broader framework to which it belongs—a framework Microsoft simply calls .NET. You should know that ASP.NET relies entirely on the .NET Framework. It doesn't work without it.

Make no mistake, .NET is the biggest thing ever to hit the Microsoft programming community. Bigger than COM, bigger than XML, bigger than ASP, bigger than Visual Basic, bigger than the Win32 API—because it either replaces or fundamentally changes the way we use all of these things, plus many more. The purpose of this, and the remaining appendices, is to provide the minimum background to .NET required to effectively use ASP.NET.

From Microsoft's viewpoint, .NET is both reactive and proactive. .NET is reactive in the sense that Microsoft had to invent it in order to survive. Microsoft's existing suite of development technologies simply can't compete in the development world unfolding now and over the next few years. .NET is proactive in the sense that Microsoft has been bold, investing huge sums of money in creating a brand new development platform. This innovative move by Microsoft has included consulting leading academics and taking huge risks. The result is a startlingly radical and cohesive new product of huge consequence to all who develop using Microsoft technology. Don't get into thinking we are being starry-eyed here. We are still talking about the same old Microsoft with the same old strengths and weaknesses. We are just trying to explain the effort Microsoft needed to expend in order to retain its leading position by creating .NET.

Most developers we know have responded to .NET with a mixture of excitement and anxiety. The excitement is easy to understand. We shouldn't even be developers if we don't find new technology at least mildly interesting—especially if it potentially removes some of the hassle the old stuff always generated and allows us to do brand new things. Also, with a bit of luck, it means we can spend some time attending courses or building pilot systems we never have to deliver, instead of redrafting some dull documentation or fixing some other guy's bugs.

New technology also has its downsides. It means there is new stuff to learn. It means that some developers will feel that all this new technology doesn't add much to what they do today. In this case, it would be tempting to say to those developers that they probably don't need to learn .NET just now—horses for courses and all that. But we don't feel we can say that to all but a few developers. Let's face it; if Microsoft has had to replace its technology in order to survive, this probably says something about *our* skill sets. Just as relatively few people now build green screen mainframe systems, it's beginning to look as though fewer and fewer people will be building the kind of client/server systems that millions of developers are building today using tools like Visual Basic and SQLServer. This is simply because our paymasters—the business people and administrators who run the organizations we work for—are starting to see that there are better ways for us to spend our time. They are seeing what other organizations are doing with the Internet or with mobile hand-held devices, and they want us to be doing the same—or better. That's what .NET is all about.

The .NET Vision

Microsoft has never been a business to be scared of 'the vision thing' and there is a very clear set of aspirations behind .NET. These can be summarized as follows:

- Software is a service you connect to, rather than a product you install.
- Applications communicate using open protocols over global, broadband networks.
- The desktop computer is becoming less important.
- No one gets religious about programming languages.

It's worth looking at each of these aspirations in turn.

Software is a service you connect to, rather than a product you install . . .

If you are already building Web-based applications, the chances are you'll know exactly what this means. If you are currently a Visual Basic desktop developer in the process of moving to Web development, we'd ask you to sit back and think about the applications you write. You probably build beautiful applications. When you think you have finished, you start thinking about how you are going to install your application on the users' computers. You start thinking of excuses for calling in sick.

The way we currently deploy desktop applications is actually crazy (and no, that's not too strong a word). There are so many things we need to think about: What DLLs and OCXs do I need to install? How do I make sure I don't overwrite components installed by someone else? What version of data access software do I rely on? Does the installation require administrator privileges? Who is going to install this on everyone's computer? In fact, we can only think of one thing that is more crazy—deploying maintenance fixes!

Compare this to how you start using a Web-based system: You navigate to the URL. And how do you start using a Web-based system after a maintenance upgrade? You navigate to the URL. No installs, no patches—you just start using it.

Right now, Microsoft makes nearly all its income selling shrink-wrapped or pre-installed software (mostly Windows and Office). Installing shrink-wrap products is rapidly being seen as an outdated and cumbersome way to start using software. Microsoft knows it has to change quickly, and its vision is that software should be viewed as a service you connect to (via a URL), rather than a product you install.

The commercial and administrative benefits of supplying and using software this way are huge—it's something we should all start doing as soon as possible.

Does this mean that all software will soon be based on HTML running in a browser? Well, even though this is a book about ASP.NET, we have to say that this is unlikely to be the case. The fact is that, while many business applications developed today could function just as well via HTML, there are many others that couldn't. No matter how wonderful ASP.NET is (and it is wonderful), it can't exploit the full power of a rich windowing system.

Not all software has a user interface. So, in the Web world, not all Web applications should deliver HTML because HTML is only for user interfaces. This is where Web Services come in. Web Services are an important part of ASP.NET. They use a great deal of ASP.NET functionality; yet, instead of returning HTML over the Internet to a browser, Web Services return raw data over the Internet in the form of XML to any program that wants raw data.

A rich GUI application can use a Web Service to get data from anywhere in the world in much the same way that it might also get data from a nearby database server. While this sounds good, you may be thinking that the rich GUI is going to have all the deployment problems that rich GUI programs currently have, and therefore, won't really be in the spirit of 'software is a service you connect to.'

There are several ways to answer this question, but here's just one. Rich client applications developed using .NET technology have much simpler installation requirements than (for example) VB 6.0, which is based on COM technology. So long as the .NET Framework has been installed on a user's computer, .NET makes it easy to download applications directly from a Web server. To keep the download small, you can leave most of the functionality for an application on the Web server and allow the downloaded client program to access it by calling a Web Service.

It turns out that .NET comes with a great deal of specific support for developing "mobile" code designed for downloading, including tightly integrated security functionality for this specific scenario. However, it's not the business of this book to go into details on such issues. It is enough to say that .NET really does provide support for "software is a service you connect to," and ASP.NET is a key part of that capability.

Applications communicate using open protocols over global, broadband networks . . .

There are two key points about this ambition. The first concerns a concept Microsoft frequently refers to as "reach." Applications with high reach are highly accessible to users regardless of their geographical or technological location.

In practice, this means that your application can be reached from any client that can use HTTP to access the Internet. HTTP is implemented on just about every computing platform, and the World Wide Web ensures that users can access your Web server from almost anywhere on earth. HTTP is used to carry text messages, and while the HTTP payload can be just about anything, two text-based standards are ubiquitous: HTML output for consumption by human users (via a browser) and XML output for consumption by other programs.

If your application delivers sensible HTML or XML output in response to an HTTP request, it has high reach. ASP.NET has been created to meet this need.

The second point about this ambition concerns the idea of global, broadband networks. For many people, the Internet is currently too slow and too unreliable to truly deliver the type of high-class application that will provide a similar user experience to desktop applications. A significant cause of current Internet problems is the absence of sufficient communications infrastructure required to keep it running quickly and smoothly.

Right now, your response to the paragraph above will depend to some degree on where you happen to live and work. Most buyers of this book will live in the United States, and you may well have good broadband access into your offices and maybe even into your homes. The authors of this book, however, live in a technical backwater known as southern England, where broadband is only really enjoyed by workers in the offices of large companies or at home by IT professionals living in high population areas. Everyone else is on dial-up or ISDN. And even we are better provided for than many others around the world.

The reality is that broadband business-to-consumer communication is a minority sport at present; reliance on it diminishes your access to global consumer markets. What does this mean for ASP.NET? It comes back to the vision thing again. Even if broadband Internet access seems just a pipe-dream to you right now, you can still build ASP.NET applications for your local area networks that will dramatically reduce the cost of software development, delivery, and maintenance on that network. Or, you can build ASP.NET applications for public consumption that are no more pedestrian than any other Web application and are significantly easier to build than traditional ASP programs.

Whatever your current situation, there are few people skeptical enough not to believe that it is only a matter of time before the broadband vision becomes a reality for the majority of the people we'd like to be using our applications.

The desktop computer is becoming less important . . .

I'm sitting at a desk surrounded by desktop computers and it seems mad to suggest that such devices are in decline. But it's true. There are people driving cars with more on-board computers than my local library has PCs, and none of those on-board computers have 17-inch monitors. They are controlling and monitoring the engine, calculating fuel economy, supporting automatic braking systems, and using positioning systems to avoid traffic jams—and they are increasingly capable of making HTTP requests.

This last point should get your mind whirring. Maybe you can make a fortune by providing a Web Service that directs a driver to the cheapest filling station in the neighborhood for a one cent fee. Or a simple Web page that displays flight or train arrival times to a user on the move.

There's plenty of this kind of crystal ball gazing in print at the moment, so we don't really want to add to it any more than we have already. But we do want to emphasize that you shouldn't be putting too much effort into writing systems that have a great deal of business functionality wrapped up into a single user interface. The chances are that at some time in the future you'll need to ditch the interface, but keep the functionality.

.NET takes this vision on board, and ASP.NET is a very good way of preparing yourself for it.

No one gets religious about programming languages . . .

This is one part of the .NET vision that is specifically Microsoft's. .NET's biggest competitor is Java and the whole support infrastructure that surrounds it. It's possible that you're reading this book while trying to decide whether to go the Java route or the .NET route. We are providing a great deal of information about .NET and ASP.NET in this book, but we aren't answering this question. We don't believe any author can provide an answer. The reality is that both platforms work; both have had many brilliant brains working on them and both are targeted at solving roughly the same set of problems. Whichever you or your organization chooses is a personal or political choice.

Microsoft takes the view that the Java platform has one big weakness: You have to use Java. There isn't anything especially wrong with Java, quite the reverse. But Java isn't going to be everyone's favorite language, and because (like VB or C++) it's a general purpose language, it might very clearly be the wrong language for specialist requirements where languages like Perl or Caml might be better. .NET allows you to write in many different languages. Microsoft itself emphasizes two languages for .NET: Visual Basic .NET and the all new shiny C# language. There's more about languages in Appendix C, but you should know that Visual Basic .NET and C# are virtually identical in their power and performance. The only substantial difference between them is their syntax.

There's a lot of activity currently going on outside of Microsoft by people writing compilers for many different languages for use with the .NET Framework. The chances are good that someone is producing a .NET version of the language you love best.

Different .NET languages can interoperate far more closely than has generally been possible before. For example, you have probably heard that Visual Basic .NET supports inheritance, but you might not be aware that Visual Basic .NET code can be inherited by C# code, which can in turn be inherited by COBOL code. You might also not have known that you can compile VB .NET code and C# into the same DLL. You'll learn more about how all these things are possible in Appendix E.

The multilanguage capability of .NET is important to Microsoft because it provides a clear differentiation between .NET and the Java community. You will make your own decision as to whether it is important to you.

The .NET Framework

We have described some of the thinking that led to Microsoft creating .NET, as well as some of the benefits .NET delivers. The remainder of Appendix B will take a look at some of the components that make up .NET.

Figure B-1 is a commonly used diagram to describe the .NET Framework. It's a useful starting point for understanding the basic elements that form the framework.

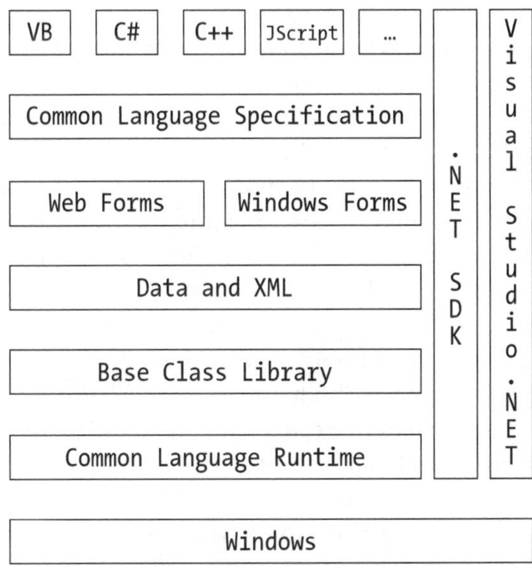

Figure B-1. The .NET Framework and Visual Studio .NET

Note first of all, that everything sits on Windows. There are versions of .NET currently under development for non-Microsoft platforms. At the time of writing, it's not possible to say very much about these.

The next rung on the stack is an element called the *Common Language Runtime* (CLR). This is the core functionality that makes .NET what it is; it's impossible to overstate how important it is to have an understanding of how the CLR works. Appendix E covers the very basics needed to get started.

You're probably a Visual Basic developer and aware that Visual Basic has always required a runtime environment to make it work. These days, most languages provide some kind of runtime library. The CLR is a runtime library not unlike the Visual Basic runtime library except for two major differences:

- **The CLR is a standard runtime for all .NET languages, not just one language.** More precisely, it runs the code generated by .NET language compilers; so, in reality, it doesn't even care about the difference between Visual Basic .NET and C#. The CLR ensures that all .NET languages receive a standard set of runtime services.

- **The CLR provides a far wider range of services than the Visual Basic runtime.** Here's one single example: When a VB 6.0 program wants to use a class implemented in a COM Server (or ActiveX DLL)—such as the ADO object library—it relies on the COM runtime library to locate and load the DLL and create the required object. .NET is not based on COM, so it doesn't use the COM library to locate DLLs. Instead, all of the functionality required to locate and load libraries is built into the CLR.

Moving to the top of the diagram, you'll see beneath the different .NET languages a layer called the *Common Language Specification* (CLS). This is primarily of interest to compiler writers, as it defines a set of rules that all .NET languages must comply with. What makes the CLS of interest to application developers is that it demonstrates that nearly all the .NET functionality lies beneath this layer and is, therefore, completely language neutral.

Between the CLS and the CLR, the diagram shows a very large set of classes, organized into four broad groupings. .NET ships with literally thousands of different classes, which supply prebuilt functionality for use in any .NET program. The good news is that you don't need to know all these classes to consider yourself a proficient .NET developer; although, there are several dozen you should become familiar with fairly quickly.

At the bottom is a group called the *Base Class Library.* This is a set of system-level classes covering everything from input/output (files and streams) to threading. It also includes a set of "collection classes." In VB 6.0 or VBScript, you may know of the Collection and Dictionary classes. Instead of just two collection-like classes, .NET provides a dozen or more different classes providing different capabilities on the theme of collections. We mention this to give you some insight into the power (and complexity) of the functionality available to you off the shelf with .NET.

Next up the ladder is a group of *Data* and *XML classes.* These are both likely to be amazingly important to you. The Data classes constitute what is known as ADO.NET, the .NET replacement for the ADO used in VB 6.0 programs (from now on known as classic ADO). Appendix D provides an introduction to ADO.NET, which you may want to read before taking on the Working with Databases chapter in the main text. For now, it's enough to say that while ADO.NET does similar things to classic ADO, it does them in rather different ways (for example, there is no Recordset object in ADO.NET).

The XML classes are just as important because XML has an important role to play in Web applications; .NET also relies on XML in many different ways. We don't provide a primer on XML in this book (although Chapter 9, Working with XML, eases you in gently), but there are many good sources on XML available—try *XML Programming: Web Applications and Web Services With JSP and ASP,* by Alexander Nakhimovsky and Tom Myers (Apress).

The next layer up includes *Web Forms* and *Windows Forms.* We don't have much to say about Windows Forms in this book, but Web Forms are the major focus of several chapters. Web Forms includes a huge set of classes to simplify the development of Web-based applications.

Figure B-1 also shows the .NET *Software Developer's Kit* (SDK). This is a set of tools that can be used to build .NET programs. It includes command-line compilers for Visual Basic .NET and C#, as well as many other utilities that generate .NET source or components or perform configuration tasks. In fact, you can build .NET applications without needing Visual Studio .NET at all—all you require is Notepad and the .NET SDK.

The chances are, though, that you will want to use Visual Studio .NET. It's a big improvement on previous versions of Visual Studio and proves that, if nothing else, Microsoft deserves its reputation for creating the best developer tools.

We aren't going to make a big deal about Visual Studio in this book, although we will be showing you how best to use it to perform specific tasks in relevant chapters.

Assemblies and Namespaces

Although this is a very high level appendix, there are two bits of .NET jargon worth introducing even at this level.

In very loose terms, .NET uses the word *assembly* where you might currently use the word component. In other words, a compiled DLL containing some classes you want to use is called an assembly in .NET. An assembly actually is rather more than just a compiled DLL. In fact, all .NET code must be in an assembly before it will be processed by the CLR (and all .NET code must be processed by the CLR).

You may be surprised to learn that everything you use in .NET is an object, and all the code you write must belong to a class. If you're a VB 6.0 programmer, you may be more used to writing code in Forms; if you're an ASP programmer, you'll be used to coding Pages. Well, in .NET, Forms and Pages are simply special types of class, which come with their own designers that allow you to build up their appearance graphically.

However, object-orientation in .NET goes much deeper than that. Even a number is an object—albeit a very efficient one—in .NET. Now, it so happens that all objects have certain methods in common (this is because .NET uses inheritance, and all classes inherit from a "root" class called *Object*. The Object class has a set of public methods, which are inherited by every .NET class). These methods include a method called `ToString` that allows any object to represent itself as a string. Therefore, the following is legal (although not very sensible) Visual Basic .NET code:

```
Dim s As String
s = 42.ToString
```

Now that we know that everything in .NET is an object, we can define an assembly as a set of one or more classes compiled into a single, self-describing unit. Usually, an assembly is compiled as either a single EXE or DLL, although there are exceptions to this rule. For example, ASP.NET knows how to build an assembly from source code. This means that you can place a source file directly into a Web Application, and ASP.NET will turn it into an assembly and run it as compiled code without you needing to run a compiler yourself.

One of the great things about assemblies is that, in addition to containing code, they carry around enough information about themselves to be fully self-describing (in other words, they store their own metadata). This removes the need to hold information about an assembly in the Registry. In fact, .NET programs have no need to use the Registry at all, which is extremely handy when you come to install or uninstall assemblies.

When building ASP.NET applications with Visual Studio .NET, Visual Studio .NET will make sure that all your code gets compiled into an assembly in the form of a DLL. Your assembly will almost certainly rely on other assemblies (such as the ADO.NET or XML libraries in the .NET Framework). You will access these other assemblies by setting references to them—a process very similar to setting a reference to a COM server in VB 6.0.

So, we have seen that every class has a physical location within an assembly. For example, these classes:

- DataSet
- DataTable
- XmlDataDocument

all reside within the same physical DLL, which happens to be called *System.Data.DLL*, while these classes:

- XmlDocument
- XmlNode
- XmlReader

all reside in a physical file called *System.Xml.DLL*.

In addition to having a physical location, all .NET classes also have a logical location based on the concept of *namespace*. Namespaces are a way of organizing names so that they don't clash or get lost in the sea of thousands of class names. For example, both Windows Forms and Web Forms provide a class called Button. A Windows Forms Button represents a Win32 Button, while a Web Form Button represents an HTML Button. It's possible to have two classes with the same name because each name lives in a different namespace.

Web Forms define a namespace called *System.Web.UI.WebControls* that contains (in a "naming" sense) a whole lot of useful controls—such as Button, ListBox, Label, etc. The long-hand way to create a Web Forms Button variable is:

```
Dim myWebButton As System.Web.UI.WebControls.Button
```

It's easy to see that this will never get confused with a Windows Forms Button. But at the same time, it's a whole lot of typing every time you need a Button variable. Visual Basic .NET provides a sensible short-cut mechanism to avoid all this typing. At the top of any file of Visual Basic .NET code, we can include the following:

```
Imports System.Web.UI.WebControls
```

The `Imports` statement tells the Visual Basic .NET compiler that when we say

```
Dim myWebButton As Button
```

We mean the Web Forms Button, and not any other Button that may be hanging around.

It's very easy to assume that an `Imports` statement is the same as setting a reference—easy, but wrong. To use a class in an external assembly, you *must* set a reference to it (this is easily done using the Visual Studio Add Reference dialog). If you want to avoid typing out the class's fully qualified name, you can use an `Imports` statement; it's never *necessary* to use `Imports` statements, they are merely a handy short-cut.

One of the reasons that it's so easy to get confused between assemblies and namespaces is that .NET frequently uses the same name for related assemblies and namespaces. For example, these classes:

- XmlDocument
- XmlNode
- XmlReader

all belong to a namespace called *System.Xml.* You'll remember from earlier that these classes also physically reside in an assembly located in the System.Xml.DLL file. It's tempting to assume that, in practice, there's a one-to-one correspondence between a namespace and an assembly (even when you know that they are conceptually different).

As a rule of thumb this might even work for you most of the time, but be warned that it isn't always the case. Remember the class XmlDataDocument?

It belongs in the System.Xml namespace along with the other Xml classes, but for entirely plausible implementation reasons, it resides physically in System.Data.DLL. In other words, you may set a reference to System.Xml.DLL, but not gain access to all the classes in the System.Xml namespace. You can only make sense of why this is if you have a clear understanding of the difference between namespaces and assembly references.

Assemblies and namespaces are important concepts in .NET; this example has been introduced so early in an attempt to illustrate the difference between these two concepts without causing too much confusion. We hope it has worked!

Summary

This appendix has explained some of the reasons why Microsoft has invested so heavily in .NET, along with the kind of systems .NET helps you build. We've seen that .NET embraces a vision about what kind of computing world we are entering into.

We have also looked at the major components of .NET and, in particular, started to look at the very vital role played by the CLR in all .NET programs.

Finally, we have explored assemblies and namespaces. These are two of the major concepts used in .NET to help organize code, and they appear relentlessly in all .NET documentation.

APPENDIX C

The Visual Basic .NET Language

Introducing Language Constructs

Learning about Data Types

Understanding Error Handling

Using Classes

Exploring Inheritance

WHETHER YOU'RE COMING TO Visual Basic (VB) .NET from Visual Basic 6.0 or VBScript, don't feel you can march straight into VB .NET without some readjustment—it isn't like that.

Granted, a lot of VB .NET code will look familiar to you—possibly even identical to code you already know. But many other features of Visual Basic .NET are entirely new and possibly alien. And some features you may have relied upon in the past are no longer there.

More importantly, there are aspects of VB .NET that look as though they make sense to you (the syntax is familiar), but in fact what really happens is not what you expect. We're going to take you quickly through many of the aspects of VB .NET that you would want us to in an appendix such as this (data types, language constructs, inheritance, and so on), but before doing so, take a look at the following piece of code and apply your existing Visual Basic 6.0 or VBScript knowledge to it:

```
Dim obj As New MyClass 'line 1
obj.doSomething 'line 2
obj = Nothing 'line 3
```

Syntactically, the first thing that will hit you is that there is no `Set` keyword in the third line. Okay, so there's no `Set` keyword in VB .NET. It's not required or even available. That will remove the tedious bugs that occur when you leave it out by mistake, but otherwise this piece of code is no big deal.

However, there are two far more important differences that a .NET programmer needs to know about. Let's deal with the less important one first. Assuming the previous code was Visual Basic 6.0 code, ask yourself whether a MyClass object is created in the first or second line. You get good marks if your answer is the second line. The `As New` statement in VB 6.0 doesn't actually create objects. Instead, it causes the VB 6.0 compiler to insert code before *every* reference to `obj`, which will create a new instance of MyClass when `obj` happens not to be referring an existing object. Many VB 6.0 developers regard this as an unethical way for a compiler to behave and therefore studiously avoid using `As New`.

In VB .NET, the compiler treats an `As New` statement in the way you'd like. In other words, the VB .NET code creates a MyClass object on the first line.

The second difference between VB 6.0 and VB .NET occurs on the third line. Assuming the `doSomething` method doesn't create any further object references, a programmer looking at VB 6.0 code would be correct to believe that immediately after this third line, the object created in this code sample will have been destroyed, and any code in its `Terminate` event will have been executed.

This is not what happens in VB .NET, however. In VB .NET, dereferenced objects simply stay in memory. Because nothing happens to them, object creation and dereferencing in VB .NET is much more efficient than in VB 6.0. More efficiency is obviously good, but you've probably already spotted the snag. Although this scheme of leaving objects in memory is efficient, something needs to be done to prevent your program from running out of memory, which a long-running ASP.NET application will surely otherwise do. What stops this from happening is a process called *garbage collection*. Garbage collection is a function that the common language runtime (CLR) performs when object memory is full. We'll spare you the details, but garbage collection basically removes any unwanted objects from memory to free up a nice, big block of memory for new objects. For programmers from a C++ background, garbage collection is a major new feature of .NET. Previously, they had to tidy up unwanted objects manually, and this being a difficult task, they could easily make mistakes. As VB programmers, we're used to having objects destroyed when they're dereferenced because the VB runtime has always done this for us.

Garbage collection is still important to us, though, because it affects the *timing* of object destruction. We can no longer rely on objects being destroyed as soon as we release them. Instead, in VB .NET, objects might not be destroyed for minutes or even hours after we've kissed them good-bye. Does this matter? Often it doesn't, but if your objects hold some important external resource (such as an open file handle or a database connection), it can matter a lot.

After this admittedly esoteric discussion, you're probably keen to get talking about code.

Introducing Language Constructs

If you're primarily an ASP programmer, you should know that .NET doesn't support VBScript, and there isn't really a need for it in the .NET scheme of things. ASP.NET will automatically compile fully blown VB .NET source code when it finds it, and therefore VB .NET code is just as convenient as VBScript, while also being safer and more efficient.

Most of the language constructs you know from VB 6.0 or VBScript have survived unscathed into VB .NET, so you can carry on writing For Loops, Select statements, and declaring Subs and Functions much as you've done in the past. One notable exception is that the untrendy `While . . . Wend` construct has gone and is replaced with the shiny, all-new `While . . . End While` construct instead.

Although there are many new language features of interest, two in particular are essential background knowledge when reading VB .NET code.

The first of these concerns how events raised by controls are handled. Controls and events aren't just for desktop developers in .NET because server controls are one of the major new features in ASP.NET. It so happens that the way you write code for controls and events in .NET follows exactly the same model whether you're working with desktop Windows controls or ASP.NET server controls. Here's an event handler for a button click:

```
Private Sub DoSomething( _
        ByVal sender As System.Object, _
        ByVal e As System.EventArgs) Handles Button1.Click
    Button1.Text = "Clicked"
End Sub
```

This could be a button on a Windows Form or a button on an ASP.NET Web Form—the code is identical in both cases. First, notice the `Handles` keyword. Next, observe that this event handler is *not* called `Button1_Click`. It could be, but it really doesn't matter. This is because the `Handles` statement performs the task of wiring up an event (`Button1.Click`) to an event handler, instead of relying on the event handler name as in VB 6.0. The `Handles` statement is not only a more elegant way of associating events with event handlers, it's also more powerful because it enables you to associate several events with the same handler.

You may also have noticed that this event handler has two arguments. You'll find that all event handlers in VB .NET have two arguments. The first argument identifies the control that raised the event (in this case, Button1), and the second argument gives you access to any information associated with the event. (In the case of a button click, there's no associated information. The button has been clicked, and that's all the information you need.)

The second piece of essential background knowledge concerns attributes. Attributes are a way of extending the description of a method (among other things) beyond the usual information such as its name, arguments, and return type. Consider the following example that applies to Web Services:

```
<WebMethod()> Public Function getnumber() As Integer
    'VB.NET functions can now use the Return keyword
    Return 42
End Function
```

This method could hardly be simpler, except that the method's signature has a strange prefix inside pointy brackets. This prefix is an attribute (which happens to be called WebMethod), and it extends the information available about the `getnumber` method. In this case, the `WebMethod` attribute tells ASP.NET that `getnumber` can be invoked using an HTTP request. ASP.NET will take whatever value `getnumber` returns and safely package it up into an XML document so that it can be added into an HTTP response.

You'll hear plenty about the `WebMethod` attribute in Chapter 14 because it's an essential part of writing a Web Service. For now, it's enough to remember that this weird syntax can be used to give additional meaning to methods, properties, classes, and even whole assemblies (*assemblies*, you may remember from Appendix B, are the .NET name for compiled programs and components). You'll see this syntax appearing often in VB .NET code. .NET itself defines hundreds of attributes for specific tasks, and if you like, you can even create your own.

Learning about Data Types

As you'll have already gathered, everything in .NET is an object, and every object belongs to a class. Some authors prefer the word *type* to *class*, but either way, they're talking about the same thing. We'll be using the terms interchangeably.

.NET types (or classes) split into two major categories: value types and reference types. Value types represent simple, frequently used objects such as integers and booleans, for which performance is absolutely critical. Reference types look and feel more like regular objects and include everything from ASP.NET Page objects and ADO.NET database connection objects to comparatively simple objects such as File or Collection objects.

The most important difference between value types and reference types is how they're stored in memory. Two major parts of an application's memory are the stack and the heap. The stack is used to support procedure calls (function and subroutine calls). Every time a new procedure is called, a new *stack-frame* is added to the stack to hold the procedure's local variables and arguments. If one procedure calls another procedure, a new frame is added to the stack. When a procedure returns, its stack-frame is taken off the stack.

Value types are stored entirely on the stack, and reference types are stored in heap memory. The heap is a global memory area available to all procedures. A local variable of a value type such as integer will hold the value of the integer within its own stack-frame. For a reference type, the object lives in the heap and only the location of the object is held on the stack. You can see how this works in Figure C-1.

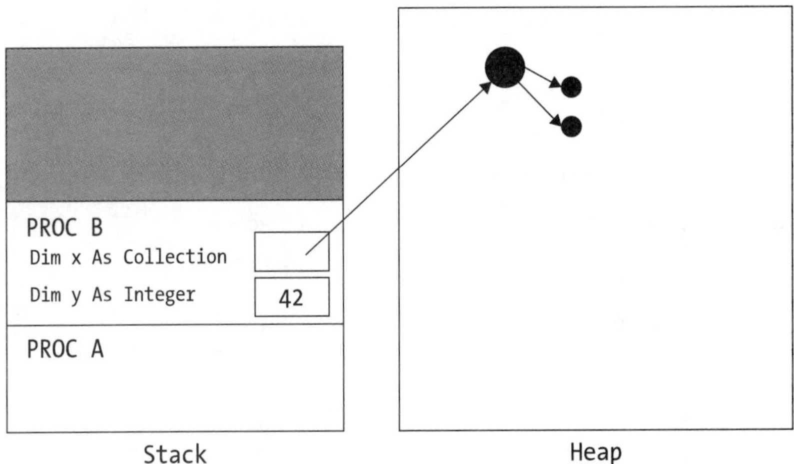

Figure C-1. The role of the stack and the heap

Here, procedure A has called procedure B, which takes up the next position on the stack. Procedure B has two local variables, x and y, both of which have been given values by code that the figure doesn't show. Variable y is a value type, and its value (42) is held on the stack. Variable x is a reference type, and the stack holds only a pointer to where the object actually exists in the heap. It's easy to see how you might have two variables referencing the same reference type, whereas each value type variable will always have its own memory for its value.

When a procedure returns and its stack-frame is removed, all its local variables are removed, too. This means that value types will be completely destroyed, but reference types will still remain in the heap after the variables that reference them have been destroyed. The heap will eventually fill up with objects that are no longer wanted. That's why we need garbage collection.

In .NET, value types provide a full range of numeric types. There's nothing especially dramatic about these, but you should know that a VB .NET Integer is a 4-byte integer, whereas a VB 6.0 Integer is a 2-byte integer. The VB .NET Integer can therefore hold the same range of numbers that a Long can hold in VB 6.0. On

32-bit operating systems, 4 bytes is the most sensible and efficient size for an Integer, and we should simply see this change as a bonus.

Table C-1 summarizes the main value types in .NET. It shows the conversion functions you can use to convert one type to another, and it also shows the .NET name for each type. What we call an *Integer* in VB .NET is called an *int* in C#, and is actually known as *System.Int32* in the language-neutral world of the CLR. It can be handy to know these .NET names at times.

Table C-1. .NET Value Types

VB NAME	.NET NAME	BYTES	CONVERSION FUNCTION
Boolean	System.Boolean	4	CBool
Byte	System.Byte	1	CByte
Char	System.Char	2	CChar
Date	System.DateTime	8	CDate
Decimal	System.Decimal	12	CDec
Double	System.Double	8	CDbl
Integer	System.Int32	4	CInt
Long	System.Int64	8	CLng
Short	System.Int16	2	CShort
Single	System.Single	4	CSng

Notice that String isn't in this list. In the pre-.NET world, there was a great deal of difference between a VB 6.0 string and a C++ string. This difference meant that C++ programmers had to go to enormous lengths to make their components accessible to VB. All .NET languages use exactly the same type of string (and every other data type as well), making language interoperation much more efficient and straightforward. You'll be pleased to learn that you can process .NET strings in much the same way as you used strings in VB 6.0 (unless you frequently use fixed-length strings, which .NET doesn't provide), although the functionality provided by the Base Class libraries requires you to learn some new string manipulation functions. Interestingly, .NET strings are reference types rather than value types (which is why there's no String entry in Table C-1), so in many ways strings behave more like objects in .NET than you might expect.

There's no Variant data type in VB .NET. Having said that, you can still make use of Variant-style functionality if you like it (by and large, we don't). This capability relies on two facts. The first (as Appendix B mentioned) is that every .NET object inherits from a built-in class called Object, which means that a variable defined `As Object` can hold any .NET object. The second fact is that VB .NET enables you to decide whether you want to make use of .NET's strict type checking via a new setting known as `Option Strict`.

To understand `Option Strict`, take a look at the following code:

```
Dim s As String = "Hello"
Dim obj As Object
obj = s
' convert s to upper case and write the result to a Web page
Response.Write(s.ToUpper)
Response.Write(obj.ToUpper)
```

This code may work, or it may not. If it doesn't, it will fail to compile because of an error on the last line. First, let's consider what happens when `Option Strict` is `On` (in which case the code will fail to compile). We create and initialize a string, and assign the string to a variable of type Object. The `obj` variable can hold any .NET object, and so the assignment works. The next line calls the `ToUpper` method on `s`. The compiler knows that `s` is a string, and it knows that strings have a `ToUpper` method, so it's happy with this line of code. However, the compiler also knows that objects of type Object don't have a method called `ToUpper`, so it will complain about the last line of code and fail to compile. This is strict type checking at work, and it helps you write less buggy code. It's therefore a good thing.

If you switch to `Option Strict Off`, the compiler won't bother checking method names for variables of type Object. Instead, it will insert some additional code that enables the check to be performed at runtime. At runtime, this additional code examines the type of whatever object is currently referenced by `obj` (which could be any .NET type) to see if the object supports the named method. If the method exists, the additional code will call the method. Otherwise it will raise a runtime error (this is a technique known as *late binding*). Although late binding is flexible, it's also slow and is more likely to result in buggy code. It's therefore a bad thing. Although there are times when it is excusable, and there are times when we use it because it can make code easier to read when we have more important points to make, we don't encourage working with `Option Strict Off`.

Unfortunately, when using Visual Studio .NET, `Option Strict` is `Off` by default. You need to go into the Project Properties dialog box to switch it on or insert `Option Strict On` at the top of each code file. `Option Strict` has other effects too, generally aimed at drawing your attention to potentially dangerous type conversions. You may want to read up on this in the online help.

Understanding Error Handling

One of the worst things about VB 6.0 is its error handling. There's only one thing worse than only being able to handle errors using On Error Goto and On Error Resume Next statements, and that's VBScript where you can't even use On Error Goto.

If you don't agree, you'll be pleased to know that these loathsome constructs are still supported by VB .NET. However, the saner reader will be interested to know that VB .NET supports structured exception handling. Out with Goto and out with error numbers. In with Try . . . Catch blocks and Exception classes. Here's a quick introduction:

```
Try
    Dim num As Integer = CInt(TextBox1.Text)
    num = 100 \ num
    Response.Write(num)
Catch ex As DivideByZeroException

    'return the error message from the DivideByZeroException class
    Response.Write(ex.Message)
Catch ex As Exception
    Response.Write("Something terrible happened")
Finally
    Response.Write("<BR>thanks for asking")
End Try
```

If you expect your code may throw errors (which is always a sensible thing to expect), you can place the code in a Try block as shown previously. In this code, you're assigning the content of an ASP.NET TextBox to an integer and then attempting to divide this value into 100. If the user types **0** into the TextBox, you don't need us to tell you what will happen.

Instead of using error numbers, .NET uses an exception class for each type of error or exception that can occur. Every exception class provides a Message method that usually returns a surprisingly meaningful error message. Using a class to represent an error is much better than using a number because a class can have additional properties and methods associated with it to help handle the error that it represents.

If all goes well, the previous code writes the result of the integer division to a Web page. If an exception occurs, the CLR will examine the type (or class) of the exception. It will then compare this class to the class named in the first Catch block it finds. If the class matches, then the code in that Catch block will be executed. If not, the next Catch block (if there is one) will be tried and so on. The Exception class (which you can see in the second Catch block) will match any type of exception, so if the user types a non-numeric string into the TextBox instead of a number, the second `Catch` block will pick up this particular error.

A `Try` block can also contain a `Finally` block, although it's optional. The code in a `Finally` block always executes, so whatever the user types, your Web page will be consistently polite.

Using Classes

You are bound to know that VB .NET supports inheritance. In this section, we want to address some of the other changes to building classes in VB .NET (we'll discuss inheritance in the next section). The following code shows a simple class and demonstrates some of the basic syntactical differences between VB 6.0 and VB .NET:

```
Public Class SimpleClass

    Public DataMember As String
    Private PropVal As Integer

    Public Property Prop() As Integer
        Get
            Prop = PropVal
        End Get
        Set (ByVal Value As Integer)
            PropVal = Value
        End Set
    End Property

    Public Function Method(ByVal Param As Integer) As Integer
        Param = Param + 1
        Return Param
    End Function
End Class
```

You can see that this class begins with a class name and ends with `End Class`. VB 6.0 classes don't need this syntax because each VB 6.0 class is stored in a separate .cls file. In VB .NET, you can store as many classes as you like in a single .vb file, which means you need proper delimiters to tell you when one class starts and another ends. If you are familiar with property procedures, you'll also be able to see from the previous code that VB .NET uses a new and more intuitive syntax for this construct.

One valuable new feature in VB .NET is called *overloading*. Overloading enables you to create two methods with the same name. That may sound a bit odd because how do you know which method you're calling? The answer is that overloaded methods must have different argument lists—a different number of arguments or arguments with different data types. You can then use this distinction to determine which actual method a user of your object is calling, according to the arguments they supply.

It's one thing to see how this might work, but it's another to see why it might be useful. Imagine you want to provide a method that returns details about a customer. You might write a `GetCustomer` method that takes a customer ID as an integer argument and looks up the data in the database. Maybe your user has the customer's name, but not the ID. You can provide another `GetCustomer` method that takes a string argument. You can check your database to see if the string contains a unique customer name, and if it does, you can return the same customer data that your first `GetCustomer` method returns. Overloading simply allows you to offer users different ways to do the same thing—a service endorsed by the fact that they can use the same method name in both cases.

One especially nice thing about overloading is that you can use it with object constructors. Constructors are the code that runs when an object is created, and they replace the `Initialize` event in VB 6.0. In VB .NET, the default constructor is a procedure called `Sub New()`, but because of overloading, you can have multiple constructors with different argument lists, all called `Sub New`. Essentially, this means you can choose to pass arguments to objects at the time that you create them if they have been written with multiple constructors. This is convenient, and you'll see this feature used a great deal in the .NET Base Class libraries. You can (of course) also use this technique for classes you write yourself. Here's an example:

```
Public Class Life
    Private Answer As Integer
    Sub New()
        Answer = 42
    End Sub
    Sub New(ByVal OtherAnswer As Integer)
        Answer = OtherAnswer
    End Sub
    Public Function GetAnswer() As Integer
        Return Answer
    End Function
End Class
```

This handy little class will answer the ultimate question about Life, the Universe and Everything. You could use it to build an ASP.NET Web page with the following code:

```
Dim lf As New Life()
Response.Write("The answer to the ultimate question is :")
Response.Write(lf.GetAnswer)
```

which will write this:

```
The answer to the ultimate question is :42
```

to a Web page.

VB .NET classes don't have an `Initialize` event; instead they have a `Sub New` routine known as a *constructor*. In the Life class however, the constructor has been overloaded so that there are two versions of `Sub New`. You can exploit this by writing the following Web page that answers the ultimate question after allowing for inflation:

```
' supply and argument when creating the object

Dim lf As New Life(51)
Response.Write("The answer to the ultimate question is :")
Response.Write(lf.GetAnswer)
```

which generates this:

```
The answer to the ultimate question is :51
```

The difference is that you can pass in a value to the object at the time it's created, rather than being stuck with its own default initialization scheme.

There's one final thing about classes that we can't ignore. Most of the time, when you are designing a class, the properties and methods you create apply to individual instances of the class. Sometimes, however, you want to create functionality that applies to the class as a whole, instead of individual instances of the class. A good example is the Integer class. Let's say you've got a long (called `LongValue`) that you want to convert to an integer. This is only going to be safe if the long is small enough to fit into the integer. The following code makes sure this is safe:

```
Dim LongValue As Long = 1000000
Dim IntValue As Integer
If LongValue <= Integer.MaxValue Then
    IntValue = CType(LongValue, Integer)
End If
```

This code introduces the CType function, which is a generic way to convert one type into another, and is especially useful when Option Strict is On. However, the most relevant thing in this code sample is Integer.MaxValue. This property contains the maximum value that can be contained in an integer and is perfect for the test you want to perform. MaxValue is a property of the Integer *class* rather than any particular integer, and it really does make most sense for this property to belong to the Integer class as a whole because it has the same value for all integers. In VB .NET, properties and methods that belong to a class rather than an instance are called *shared* members (in C# they're called *static members*). You'll see shared members being used a lot in the Base Class libraries. You can create your own ones using the Shared keyword in VB .NET.

Exploring Inheritance

Inheritance is an amazingly powerful feature that happens not to be appropriate for many business applications. Inheritance can be very, very useful when you are creating complex class libraries for other people to use, but a relatively small percentage of developers actually spend a lot of their time doing this. As a general guide to any reader who is new to both .NET and the idea of inheritance, we'd say that it's more important to spend time learning about ASP.NET in particular and .NET in general, than it is to invest a lot of time learning how to design and implement inheritance hierarchies.

At the same time, you'll spend a lot of your time using features of .NET heavily based on inheritance (after all, the Base Class libraries are a complex set of classes written for other people to use), so it's essential to grasp the concept of inheritance at an early stage.

Inheritance enables one class to reuse and extend the functionality of another class. Ironically (given what we said a moment ago), a good way to investigate inheritance is to explore a business scenario where it might actually be sensible to use it. Assume you have written a set of class libraries for use in a payroll system. You may have a class called Employee, defined something like this:

```
Public Class Employee
    Public Name As String
    Public EmployeeNumber As Integer
    Public TaxCode As String
    Public AnnualSalary As Decimal

    Public Overridable Function GetMonthlyGross() As Decimal
        'complex stuff here
    End Function
```

```
    Public Function GetMonthlyDeductions() As Decimal
        'very complex stuff here
    End Function

    Public Function GetMonthlyNet() As Decimal
        Return Me.GetMonthlyGross - Me.GetMonthlyDeductions
    End Function
End Class
```

You can probably imagine how you can use a class such as this in a payroll system. `GetMonthlyGross` contains some code that works out how much a given employee should be paid this month, before any deductions for tax and so on. `GetMonthlyDeductions` contains some really complex code for working out the deductions, and `GetMonthlyNet` simply deducts this amount from the gross to return how much the employee actually sees in their bank account.

In fact, the only aspect of this code that may be new to you is the `Overridable` keyword. You'll see what this is for shortly.

Now assume your system is running smoothly (we can all dream, can't we?), but you need to add some functionality to allow for employees who get paid on a commission basis (such as sales staff). You could of course write a new class from scratch for these employees, but this is a situation where inheritance might help out.

To find out, you can apply the following test for inheritance: Is the new class simply a specialization of an existing class? If the answer is a clear yes, then inheritance may be appropriate. Let's assume that it is, and take a look at what the code for a CommissionEmployee class might look like:

```
Public Class CommissionEmployee
    Inherits Employee
    Public QualifyingSales As Decimal
    Public CommissionRate As Decimal

    Public Overrides Function GetMonthlyGross() As Decimal
        'do more complex stuff here
    End Function
End Class
```

You can see that CommissionEmployee inherits from Employee, which has a number of implications. Firstly, any instance of CommissionEmployee will have six properties—the four inherited from Employee, plus the two defined specifically for CommissionEmployee. This is a classic example of how what's often called a *derived* class (CommissionEmployee) reuses and extends the functionality of its *base* class (Employee).

Secondly, any instance of CommissionEmployee will have three methods. If you call the `GetMonthlyDeductions` method on an instance of Commission Employee, it will simply run the code that it inherits from its base class. This is what you might expect it to do—after all, tax is tax, and we like to think that the same tax rules apply to everyone. However, CommissionEmployee provides its *own* implementation of `GetMonthlyGross`, which will take into account the commission aspects of the relevant remuneration. This is only possible because the base class used the `Overridable` keyword when defining `GetMonthlyGross`. In other words, the base class must grant permission to a derived class before the derived class can override any of its methods. The derived class uses the `Overrides` keyword to show that it is overriding its inherited `GetMonthlyGross` method with its own code.

The following code that uses an instance of CommissionEmployee might clear this up:

```
Dim emp As New CommissionEmployee()
Response.Write(emp.GetMonthlyDeductions)
Response.Write(emp.GetMonthlyGross)
```

The second line of code will run the `GetMonthlyDeductions` that `emp` inherits from Employee, and the third line of code will run the `GetMonthlyGross` that is implemented in the CommissionEmployee class.

It's clear that the amount of code needed to write CommissionEmployee is much less than would be needed if inheritance was not used. This makes inheritance sound attractive, but simple examples such as this one are dangerous unless they carry appropriate health warnings.

What you've seen here is an example of the *concept* of inheritance, but nothing like the information needed even to begin to understand the real complexity of designing inheritance-based systems. To borrow a phrase from tourist guides describing the rougher areas of major cities, know where you're going before you venture into inheritance—and leave your wallet at home!

Summary

In this appendix you've taken a brief look at the Visual Basic .NET language. You've seen that .NET data types are divided between value types and reference types and learned that strings are actually reference types.

VB .NET continues to support the `On Error . . .` style of error handling but also provides the more powerful structured error handling, based on `Try . . . Catch` blocks.

Classes are important in VB .NET, and they exhibit some powerful new functionality, such as overloading and shared members. You have also seen that classes can make use of inheritance, which, although undeniably powerful, should not be seen as an easy, quick-fix technique likely to benefit most business applications.

APPENDIX D

An Overview of ADO.NET

ASP.NET and SQLServer Security

Before ADO.NET

Exploring ADO.NET

Using .NET Data Providers

The DataSet Object Model

DATA ACCESS IS A CRITICAL FEATURE of nearly all Web sites that provide anything more than just static pages. Most organizations prefer the performance and security provided by a leading relational database engine to store their data; they typically choose a product such as SQLServer, Oracle, or Sybase for this purpose. Most Windows developers currently use ActiveX Data Objects (now called classic ADO) to interact with such products. In the .NET world, ADO.NET is the natural replacement for classic ADO, and is the obvious choice for all database access requirements.

These days, however, there is considerably more to data access than relational databases. XML is playing an increasingly significant role in data access and management, so no data access story would be complete without at least touching on XML. The big relational database vendors are aware of the importance of XML and are increasingly building XML functionality into their products—supporting not just SQL, but also XPath queries. If you are completely new to ADO.NET, it may surprise you to know that ADO.NET is just as good at processing XML data as it is at processing the results of SQL. Of course, the .NET Base Class Libraries contain full support for XML through a set of generic XML processing classes; but, in many cases, ADO.NET will actually prove a more convenient means for processing XML than a conventional XML DOM (Document Object Model) approach. If you're a die-hard database programmer, then ADO.NET might just provide you with a kick-start into the XML world.

This book contains two whole chapters (Chapters 7 and 8) dedicated to using ADO.NET in ASP.NET applications. Chapter 7 assumes a basic understanding of the main components of ADO.NET; Chapter 8 builds on Chapter 7 to discuss ASP.NET data binding. So, the purpose of this appendix is to present the basics that Chapters 7 and 8 assume in a form that is accessible to readers who are completely new to .NET data access.

ASP.NET and SQLServer Security

Before saying anything else, we need to explain a feature of ASP.NET security that could stop you from using SQLServer unless you know about it. This feature was introduced very late in the production cycle of ASP.NET, and was not present in any of the beta versions. SQLServer supports two security modes: *standard* and *integrated.*

Standard security is when you supply a user ID and a password as part of your database connection string. For example:

```
"Data Source=(local);Initial Catalog=HiFlyer;User ID=sa;Password=secret;"
```

Standard security will work just as you expect it to with ASP.NET.

Integrated security doesn't make use of user details passed in a connection string. Instead, SQLServer joins forces with Windows security to validate the account that is trying to connect. An integrated security connection string looks like this:

```
"Data Source=(local);Initial Catalog=HiFlyer;Integrated Security=SSPI;"
```

If you prefer using SQLServer's integrated security, you need to be aware that (by default) ASP.NET code is executed using a special user account called ASP.NET, which is created when you install ASP.NET. Allowing you to control the account used to execute ASP.NET code is an important security benefit of ASP.NET. SQLServer will not know about this account, however, so you'll need to take some steps to make ASP.NET data access code work with integrated security. We'll cover ASP.NET security in depth in Chapter 11; our objective here is simply to provide some pointers for addressing this issue when starting out.

To make integrated security work with ASP.NET, you basically have two main options. One is to configure SQLServer security so that it knows about the ASP.NET account and grants it the necessary privileges to log on to the database and access the required database resources. You will need to use SQLServer administrative tools to do this.

An alternative approach is to ask ASP.NET to impersonate the user when running code on behalf of that user. This approach can be convenient during development because, assuming that you have access to SQLServer, ASP.NET will use your account details (in other words, it will impersonate you) when logging on to SQLServer, instead of using the ASPNET account details (to which SQLServer may deny access). To use impersonation this way, you must perform two tasks. First, you need to use Internet Service Manager to disable anonymous access to your ASP.NET Application (if you're not sure how to do this, refer to Chapter 11). The second task is to modify the `Web.config` file generated by Visual Studio .NET when you create a Web Application. Change this file so that the top four lines appear as follows:

```
<?xml version="1.0" encoding="utf-8" ?>
<configuration>
    <system.web>
        <identity impersonate="true" />
```

Once you have inserted the XML element that enables impersonation, ASP.NET will use the authenticated user's account details when accessing SQLServer.

You shouldn't assume that using impersonation is the correct approach to take for your application in production simply because it can be convenient during development. Making Web applications secure is a complex process and there are many factors to consider—as Chapter 11 explains. If you use integrated security to access SQLServer, you should think very carefully about how to configure its use before deploying any applications.

Before ADO.NET

Not so long ago, processing relational data was fairly straightforward, and using data in a read-only fashion typically involved the following four steps:

1. Open a database connection.
2. Execute a SQL statement.
3. Do something interesting with the results.
4. Close the connection.

The task of opening and closing connections typically slows things down a bit, so developers of client/server applications often keep a database connection open and repeat steps 2 and 3 before closing the connection at the end of a session.

Updating a database is always slightly more complicated than read-only processing. In classic ADO, it typically involves either changing fields on a Recordset object (which then magically get sent to the database when an `Update` method is called), explicitly constructing SQL update statements, or calling stored procedures. The updating task is further complicated because allowances have to be made for other users who may be reading or updating data at the same time; therefore, various types of locks or even transactions are required to safeguard valuable data.

Unfortunately, this picture of data access is too simplistic for use in Web-based applications where the concept of a user session is not appropriate when applied to data access, and the number of concurrent users may, at times, be too high to consider creating one connection for each user. While there are many issues raised by these observations, there are two in particular that we should focus on now.

The Need for Disconnected Data

Early data access technology only worked while you held open a live database connection. This fact resulted in the following problems:

- **Databases need to allocate resources for each open connection.** The longer connections are kept open, the more server resources are tied up—even if those connections are not being heavily used. Servers can literally run out of connections.

- **Not all databases are equal.** Some databases (even some expensive ones) simply do not provide the kind of functionality that developers expect of data access technology.

- **Connections are not portable.** A database connection can only exist in the program (or more specifically, the process) in which it is created. As a result, data that is dependent on an open connection cannot be copied between programs or written to files without being converted into another form. Because the popularity of distributed applications (which includes most Web applications) has grown, the need to move data flexibly and efficiently between different programs has become increasingly important.

- **Databases are cursor-based.** A SQL query actually creates a set of results; the programmer is usually required to move a cursor to get access to one result (that is, one row of data) at a time. This form of data access is limited and inflexible when compared to the arrays or collections that developers typically use to access other types of data.

Classic ADO solves the first three of these problems by providing two very different types of Recordset. By default, ADO uses what are known as *server-side Recordsets*. Server-side Recordsets rely on the database itself to keep track of the current record. By setting the `CursorLocation` property of a RecordSet to `adUseClient`, the Recordset suddenly starts behaving very differently (this is known as a *client-side Recordset*). All operations (except for updates) performed on a client-side Recordset are handled by the Recordset itself, with no intervention from the database. Changes made to the fields in the Recordset are translated by the Recordset into SQL statements and sent to the database for processing. Client-side Recordsets can even be disconnected entirely from the database, resulting in *disconnected Recordsets*. Disconnected Recordsets are portable—they are easy to pass between programs or save to file. And of course, once they are disconnected, there is no longer any drain on the database, enhancing the overall scalability of the system. Changes made to disconnected Recordsets are stored inside the Recordset, so that they can all be sent as a batch to a database whenever the Recordset is reconnected to its database.

Even though the internal workings of a client-side Recordset are very different from the standard server-side Recordset (where the data is managed by the server rather than by ADO), the programming model (methods and properties) used in either case is virtually identical. With hindsight, the decision to use the same programming model for both client- and server-side Recordsets has proven to be a mistake. This is partly because it obscured the important differences between these two models from most developers, who are often simply unaware that the difference exists. Also, it prevented the client-side Recordset from addressing the fourth of the problems listed above. Because databases are cursor-based, classic ADO is forced to use a cursor when selecting individual records—even for client-side Recordsets—leaving developers with a clumsy cursor-based model for processing a powerful in-memory data structure.

Nevertheless, classic ADO's ability to create and disconnect client-side Recordsets has been a very powerful extension to the data programmer's armory; the success of this technique has had a profound effect on ADO.NET.

The Need for Connection Pooling

By using client-side, disconnected data processing techniques, the need for large numbers of database connections is dramatically reduced. You can open a connection, create a Recordset, and then immediately drop the connection before going on to use the Recordset, so that each connection is only needed for a very short period of time. While it is undoubtedly good to reduce the number of connections needed at any one time, the downside of working this way is that you are forever creating and destroying database connections, which can be very expensive.

This performance problem is readily addressed by *connection pooling*. When connection pooling is used, a database connection is not destroyed when it is released by a program. Instead, it is held in a connection pool for a fixed period of time. Whenever another connection is needed, a connection is taken from the connection pool if possible, rather than creating a completely new connection. A connection from the pool can only be used if it *exactly* matches the requirements for the newly requested connection, thus ensuring that the pooled connection cannot be used to get around any security restrictions.

Generally speaking, a pool of just a few connections can serve the needs of many dozens of users. By getting a connection from a pool, instead of always creating a fresh connection, the process of opening and closing connections becomes fast, which encourages developers to release connections frequently and thereby keep the number of simultaneous connections to a minimum. Connection pooling makes it easier to create high performance, highly scalable data access applications.

In classic ADO, the rules were unclear about when connection pooling was being used and what type of programming was required to use it, which led to situations where developers were tempted not to trust connection pooling. In ADO.NET, however, connection pooling is always on by default; so, except for one or two very specific situations (discussed in Chapter 7), it can never hurt to release database connections as soon as possible.

Exploring ADO.NET

So much for history, let's take a look at what ADO.NET has to offer. Figure D-1 shows the type of objects ADO.NET programmers deal with:

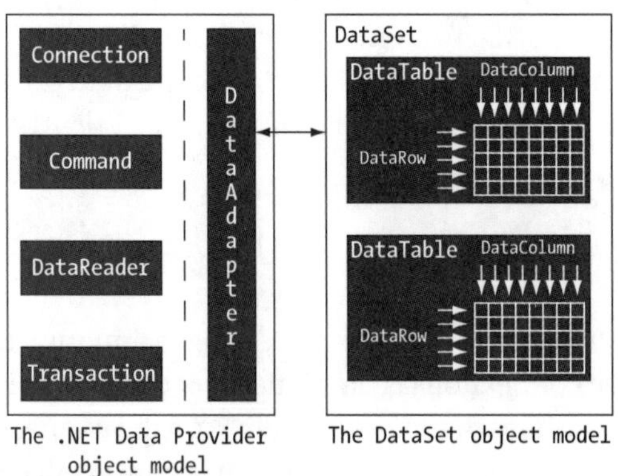

Figure D-1. The ADO.NET object model

The first thing you will notice is that ADO.NET provides not one, but two, object models. The distinction is important for a number of reasons, as we will see.

.NET Data Providers

A .NET Data Provider is a set of objects used to communicate with a specific data source. In fact, Microsoft has developed not one, but four, .NET Data Providers. These are:

- The SQL Data Provider
- The OleDb Data Provider
- The Odbc Data Provider
- The Oracle Data Provider

In addition to these Microsoft-created providers, other organizations are in the process of developing many more.

Those of you who are familiar with the way ODBC or OLEDB work may well be thinking that these Data Providers are the .NET equivalent of the ODBC drivers and OLEDB Providers that you've been using for years. In one sense, you would be right; but in another important sense, there is a difference.

For example, when you work with ADO (and therefore use OLEDB Providers), you always use the same ADO objects regardless of which Provider you use. This is because classic ADO objects exist as a layer on top of the OLEDB Provider, so that programmers never work directly with the Provider. However, in .NET, you do work directly with the Data Provider, cutting out the middle man, which means you use different objects depending on the Data Provider you have selected. In other words, you use a SqlConnection object when working with the SQL Data Provider and an OleDbConnection object when working with the OleDb Data Provider. This seems strange at first, although you soon get to realize that whichever Data Provider you are using, they all work in the same way—it's just the name of the classes that differ.

The SQL Provider and the OleDb Provider are the ones that ship as part of Visual Studio .NET; the Odbc Provider can be downloaded from Microsoft's Web site and the Oracle Provider was rumored to be close to release at the time of writing. The SQL Provider is the one to use when working with SQLServer version 7.0 or later. The OleDb Provider can be used with existing OLEDB Providers and therefore allows you to exploit existing data access software. However, a word of warning is due here. Firstly, the SQL Provider is considerably more efficient than the OleDb Provider when working with SQLServer 7.0 or later, and so should be used in preference. Secondly, the OleDb Provider is actually noticeably less efficient than the Odbc Provider. Therefore, even though ODBC is older technology than OLEDB, and even though the OleDb Provider is the one that ships with

.NET, it's worthwhile downloading the Odbc Provider if you have a reliable ODBC driver available.

DataSets

.NET Data Providers are intimately involved in interacting with a specific type of data source. The DataSet object model is the exact opposite. It has no involvement at all with data sources and is concerned only with disconnected data. It is the direct descendent of the classic ADO client-side, disconnected Recordset. Despite looking rather different, DataSets and classic ADO disconnected Recordsets are actually very similar in terms of functionality. It can't be denied that the ADO.NET approach is slicker and more finely honed, but if you already know the ADO Recordset inside-out, you won't find too many surprises when learning about DataSets. Because DataSets are always disconnected, you actually need a separate means for getting data into and out of them. Take another look at Figure D-1 and you will see that the .NET Data Provider object model includes a DataAdapter. All .NET Data Providers provide a DataAdapter object, whose sole function is to move data in and out of DataSets. They help to keep DataSets completely independent of any data source.

At this point, you may be thinking that ADO.NET does not look much like classic ADO; and you may even be thinking that it seems a bit of cheek to use the name ADO.NET, which seems to imply some kind of evolution from one to the other. Before getting on your high horse, we'd ask you to think about it the following way.

You may recall from earlier that we described how the classic ADO RecordSet actually provides two very different sets of functionality, accessible through exactly the same objects. We also said that it appears to have been a mistake to provide a single programming model to use two very different sets of functionality. It is because ADO.NET has corrected this mistake that it looks so very different on the surface. Take another look at Figure D-1 and concentrate on the .NET Data Provider object model. Ignore the DataAdapter, and consider the DataReader as a replacement for the RecordSet. We'd hope that you'd agree that it doesn't look that different from the classic ADO you probably know and love.

The DataSet object model is just what you get when you take a rational look at how best to expose the client-side, disconnected functionality of classic ADO RecordSets. One of the reasons that many developers never really exploited this functionality in classic ADO is that it was just plain hard to see where it was. In ADO.NET, the programming model for using disconnected data has been redesigned to be far more transparent in the hope that people will now actually use it.

Using .NET Data Providers

The following code shows the three main objects in the SQL Data Provider in action:

```
Const CONN_STRING As String = _
     "Data Source=(local);Initial Catalog=HiFlyer;User ID=sa;"
Const SQL_STRING As String = "select Registration, Manuf, Model from Aircraft"
Dim cn As New SqlConnection(CONN_STRING)
Dim cd As New SqlCommand(SQL_STRING, cn)
Dim dr As SqlDataReader
cn.Open()
dr = cd.ExecuteReader()
While dr.Read()
Response.Write _
     (dr("Registration").ToString + ":" + _
    dr("Manuf").ToString + ":" + _
    dr("Model").ToString + "<BR>")
End While
dr.Close()
cn.Close()
```

All of these objects live inside a .NET namespace called System.Data.SqlClient; therefore, in order for this code to work, the following statement needs to be inserted at the top of its code file:

```
Imports System.Data.SqlClient
```

The code makes use of the HiFlyers database, which is the sample database being used throughout this book. The book's Introduction explains how to set up the database under SQLServer. Once you have set the database up, the code can be inserted into the `Page_Load` event handler of an ASP.NET Web Application (you will learn how to do this in Chapter 1). It produces the output shown in Figure D-2.

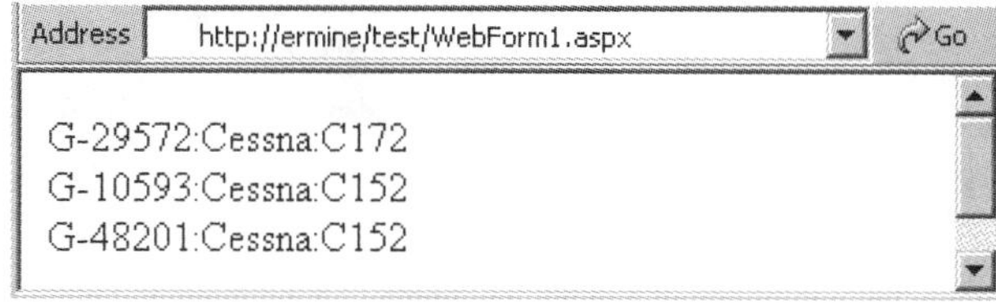

Figure D-2. Output from a simple DataReader program

Before explaining what's going on in this code, take a look at the sample below that performs exactly the same task using the OleDb Data Provider:

```
Imports System.Data.OleDb
 . . .
Const CONN_STRING As String = _
    "Provider=SQLOLEDB;Data Source=(local);Initial Catalog=HiFlyer;User ID=sa;"
Const SQL_STRING As String = "select Registration, Manuf, Model from Aircraft"
Dim cn As New OleDbConnection(CONN_STRING)
Dim cd As New OleDbCommand(SQL_STRING, cn)
Dim dr As OleDbDataReader
cn.Open()
dr = cd.ExecuteReader()
While dr.Read()
    Response.Write _
        (dr("Registration").ToString + ":" + _
         dr("Manuf").ToString + ":" + _
         dr("Model").ToString + "<BR>")
End While
dr.Close()
cn.Close()
```

Note that this code is almost identical to the SQL Provider code. The only differences are the namespace, the prefixes of the class names, and the connection string. The OleDb connection string requires a Provider name to identify which OLEDB Provider to use; the SQL connection string always uses SQLServer and does not use an OLEDB Provider—it talks directly to SQLServer.

The description that follows applies equally to either of the above code samples. The code starts by opening a connection using a connection string. It then executes a command using a Command object, which returns a DataReader object. You can think of the DataReader as a forward-only, read-only equivalent of a classic ADO RecordSet. The DataReader is used to process the results, which are processed in the `While . . . End While` loop.

If you're a classic ADO programmer, you may be wondering what has happened to the `MoveNext` statement inside the loop. Forgetting the `MoveNext` statement in classic ADO code has trapped just about every ADO programmer we know—doing so results in an infinite loop. This isn't the case in ADO.NET.

This is because the ADO.NET DataReader is perfectly honed for its task. Each time the `Read` method is called, it does one of two things: If another row exists in the resultset, it reads that row and returns `True`; if no more data exists, it simply returns `False`. There is never any need to explicitly move onto the next row because the `Read` method takes care of it. It's worth noting that when using a DataReader, you need to call `Read` to access the first row; whereas, in classic ADO, a RecordSet object automatically contains the first row when it is opened.

You will find this change convenient when writing a loop to process a DataReader; however, you will find it less convenient when executing a command that returns a single row, because you will need to call `Read` before you can get at any data.

Inside the processing loop you will see that the code uses a fairly familiar syntax for accessing each column of data:

```
dr("Registration").ToString
```

By using the column name, you can directly access the data value for the current row. Because the data in question could be of virtually any data type, ADO.NET defines the data type returned by this syntax as "Object". You may remember from Appendix C that every type in .NET inherits from Object, so this is a wise choice. However, whenever `Option Strict` is `On` (which should be most of the time), you'll need to convert the data to a string before you can concatenate it into an output string. Conveniently, the Object data type supports the `ToString` method (which is inherited by every .NET object), which makes it easy to convert data into a string representation.

Although the syntax shown above is the most convenient way to access data from a DataReader, it's not the most efficient. When performance is critical, a more direct syntax is provided that uses the position of the column in the resultset, and a data type specific access method. Here's what the loop looks like using this more efficient syntax:

```
Const REG_COL As Integer = 0
Const MANUF_COL As Integer = 1
Const MODEL_COL As Integer = 2
While dr.Read()
    Response.Write _
        (dr.GetString(REG_COL) + ":" + _
         dr.GetString(MANUF_COL) + ":" + _
         dr.GetString(MODEL_COL) + "<BR>")
End While
```

In this case, we have defined constants to make the code more readable. In this example, all the columns are defined as strings (varchars in SQLServer terminology) in the database, so the `GetString` method has been used. If you study the DataReader documentation, you will see that a large number of similar methods exist for other common database data types (e.g., `GetBoolean`).

This very simple piece of ADO.NET code finishes with these two lines:

```
dr.Close()
cn.Close()
```

Don't consider these lines as an afterthought—they are absolutely essential in ADO.NET. As you learned in Appendix C, .NET doesn't actually destroy objects just because you have released them. Instead, it waits (sometimes for a long time) until it needs to free memory before running a process called "garbage collection," which then destroys any unwanted objects. One consequence of this approach to object management is that if you don't call `Close` on database Connection objects, those connections can be tied up for a long time without actually being usable (the objects stay alive until the garbage collector runs, even though you can't access them). It is therefore imperative to call `Close` on any Connection object that you open. This will ensure that the physical connection to the database is returned to the connection pool so that it can be reused immediately.

So far, we have taken an initial look at reading data using ADO.NET. In the ASP.NET world, the ability to read data is enhanced massively by the data binding functionality that allows attractive and flexible user interfaces to be created using DataReaders; this topic is discussed in detail in Chapter 8.

Before moving on to looking at the DataSet object model, it's likely that you may be wondering how updates are performed when working with DataReaders. The answer to this question is that updates must be performed using Command objects. .NET Data Providers don't have any support for "in-place" editing, where you assign a value to a column for a specific row and call an `Update` method. Instead, you need to write SQL `INSERT`, `UPDATE`, and `DELETE` commands, or use stored procedures, in order to write changes back to your database.

This revelation sometimes comes as a shock to developers when they first meet ADO.NET. The truth is, however, that many of the approaches to data management that worked perfectly well for client/server systems with classic ADO simply aren't that safe to use in Web-based applications—in-place editing is one such approach. For one thing, in-place editing requires that connections are kept open while editing takes place (which we now know to be an evil practice). For another thing, in-place editing typically only makes sense with fully scrollable cursors, supporting `MoveNext`, `MoveFirst`, `MovePrevious`, and such operations. These operations are acceptable when using disconnected data, but typically place a monstrous strain on the database when working in a connected fashion. For this reason, DataReaders are not fully scrollable; they only support moving forward one row at a time by calling the `Read` method.

To restrict the opportunity to write inefficient and unscalable code, .NET Data Providers don't allow you to perform updates through any means other than executing commands. While this is a draconian policy, it's worth noting that developers of the largest Web sites tended to use classic ADO in exactly this fashion anyway—creating read-only, forward-only Recordsets, and performing all updates through Command objects, typically calling stored procedures. In this sense, ADO.NET is simply encouraging you to use best practice as demanded by popular Web applications.

The DataSet Object Model

DataSets make it easy to work with disconnected data. In fact, the best way to think of a DataSet is as an object that can hold and store multiple in-memory tables of data, where each table is typically the result of executing a single SQL command or stored procedure.

Newcomers to ADO.NET often seem to pick up on the fact that ADO.NET contains a DataSet object as a "replacement" for a classic ADO RecordSet, and are liable to conclude that they will spend most of their time working with DataSet objects when using ADO.NET. In fact, this is unlikely to be the case. While the DataSet is a powerful and useful new object, it actually depends a great deal on the other objects in the DataSet object model (such as DataTables and DataRows); developers will typically spend more time working directly with these objects than working with DataSet objects themselves. So, the first point we want to make in this section is to be aware of the distinction between the DataSet class and the DataSet object model (a collection of classes including DataSet, often used together). Refer back to Figure D-1 to see this relationship.

The second key point about the DataSet object model is that you will typically only use it for data that you want to keep hanging around in memory for some period of time. For data that you intend to read once and throw away, it's more efficient to use DataReaders and Command objects from the .NET Data Provider object model. Now, if you think a little about how the Web works, you will realize that the standard model for producing a dynamic Web page is:

1. Receive the requested URL.
2. Create some objects (including data objects) and run some code to process the request.
3. Create the HTML to send to the user.
4. Throw away the objects created in step 2.
5. Send the HTML to the user.

It is clear from this sequence that most of the data objects you create in Web-based applications are very short-lived indeed. Given that the DataSet object model is of little value in short-lived scenarios, you will probably spend far more time working with DataReaders and Command objects than you will with DataSets and their kin. In fact, it is fair to say that virtually all uses of DataSets in ASP.NET applications fall into three scenarios:

- **When you want to cache data to support multiple users or between requests from a single user.** ASP.NET has some sophisticated support for caching data as a way of improving performance. Caching is never straightforward, and while it can be an extremely useful technique, it should always be used with great care. Chapter 12 discusses ASP.NET caching in some detail and explains how DataSets can play a valuable role in a caching strategy (because cached objects can be long-lived).

- **When you are building an ASP.NET Web Service and want to return structured data to a Web Service client.** DataSets can easily be passed between a client and a Web server in the form of XML, and so have an important role to play in many Web Service designs. Web Services are discussed in Chapter 14.

- **When you want to exploit the XML features of a DataSet.** If your Web application is based on pure HTML, the scope for using XML is quite limited (in fact, it is limited to XML processing within the Web server).

Programming with DataTable Objects

A good way to start understanding more about the DataSet object model is to start by looking at the DataTable object. A DataTable is an always-disconnected object representing the results of a single database query. Because it's always disconnected, you can't actually load data directly into a DataTable from a data source. Instead, you can use a DataAdapter object (which lives inside a .NET Data Provider) to load data into a DataTable. Here's an example that creates a DataTable containing all the students contained in the Members table of the HiFlyers database:

```
Const CONN_STRING As String = _
    "Data Source=(local);Initial Catalog=HiFlyer;User ID=sa;"
Const SQL_STRING As String = "select * from Member where IsStudent = 1"
Dim da As New SqlDataAdapter(SQL_STRING, CONN_STRING)
Dim dt As New DataTable()
da.Fill(dt)
```

The first `Dim` statement here creates a SqlDataAdapter object and assigns a SQL command string and a connection string to it, while the next line creates a new DataTable object. All of the real work takes place on the last line. Calling the `Fill` method on a DataAdapter causes it to open a database connection (using the supplied connection string) and execute the command contained in the command string. The DataAdapter then creates a DataRow object for each row in the resultset and inserts the DataRow object into a collection of DataRow objects maintained by the DataTable object called `dt`. Finally, the `Fill` method closes the database connection and releases it back to the connection pool.

That's an awful lot of work to do in a single method call; the impressive thing about it is that it wraps up the entire philosophy of disconnected data in one stroke. There is no need to open or close connections or DataReaders because the DataAdapter handles all of this for you automatically (although there are times when you will want to take control of how the connections are used by the DataAdapter, such as when processing transactions).

Of course, once you have data in a DataTable, you need to do something with it. The following code loops through all the rows in the DataTable and generates some basic Web output for them:

```
Dim dr As DataRow
For Each dr In dt.Rows
    Response.Write(dr("ForeName").ToString + ":" + _
                   dr("Surname").ToString + "<BR>")
Next
```

This code will write the names of all the selected members to a Web page. It does nothing that couldn't be done with the DataReader and is less efficient (because we must first load data into the DataTable and then process the DataTable to generate the output, instead of writing data from a DataReader directly to the Web page).

Clearly, you are unlikely to use a DataTable in this scenario. Let's say, however, that we want to allow users to repeatedly extract different sets of flying club members based on the first letter of their surname, for example. It may be expensive to go to the database each time a user wants a list of members, so we decide to cache the DataTable so that it is accessible to all users without needing to hit the database. ASP.NET has a special Cache object that can be used to hold long-lived data in memory:

```
  Cache("Members") = dt
```

As you can see, Cache is easy to use. There are actually some major assumptions I'm making in this Appendix about whether it's appropriate to use Cache like this (all will be revealed in Chapters 12 and 13), but for now let's assume that the above line of code meets our needs—it stores the DataTable in Web server memory, so reading it will be faster than going back to the database.

In order to extract just the members whose surnames begin with a certain letter, we can exploit another feature of the DataTable: its `Select` method. This method allows us to apply a filter criterion, by which we can extract from the

DataTable just those rows that meet the filter criterion. Actually, the `Select` method also allows us to sort the rows; the entire filtering and sorting process is carried out by ADO.NET, without needing to touch the database. For example, the following code will filter out all the DataRows whose surname begins with the letter 'A':

```
Dim drs() As DataRow
drs = dt.Select("Surname like 'A%'")
```

It's worth doing a double-take on this code in order to see what the `Select` method returns. It actually returns an *array* of DataRow objects for which the `drs` variable has been appropriately declared. This feature will strike you as odd if you come from a classic ADO background, but you'll soon get used to processing an array of objects like this. The array approach also helps to emphasize another aspect of using the DataSet object model. It has no concept of a cursor or a current row. Instead, we have random access to an array or collection of data—which is actually a much more convenient way to work with data than the constant cursor-positioning required in classic ADO (in other words, there are no `MoveNext`, `MovePrevious`, or similar methods on a DataTable, you simply access whichever row you are interested in by its index).

Assembling these various pieces of information, we can now see code that retrieves a DataTable from Cache, selects an array of DataRow objects, and loops over them to build an output Web page. The code shown below does this with the help of an ASP.NET TextBox in which the user can type the initial letters of the members they are interested in:

```
Dim drs() As DataRow
Dim dt As DataTable
Dim i As Integer
dt = CType(Cache("Members"), DataTable)
drs = dt.Select("Surname like '" + TextBox1.Text + "%'")
For i = 0 To drs.Length - 1
    Response.Write(drs(i)("ForeName").ToString + ":" + _
                   drs(i)("Surname").ToString + "<BR>")
Next
```

This code uses the `CType` function to ensure that the data held in Cache is indeed a DataTable before assigning it to the `dt` variable. It then selects an array of DataRows that have the matching surnames, and performs a standard array loop to generate the output. Figure D-3 shows the output, which includes the TextBox used by the user to specify the starting letters.

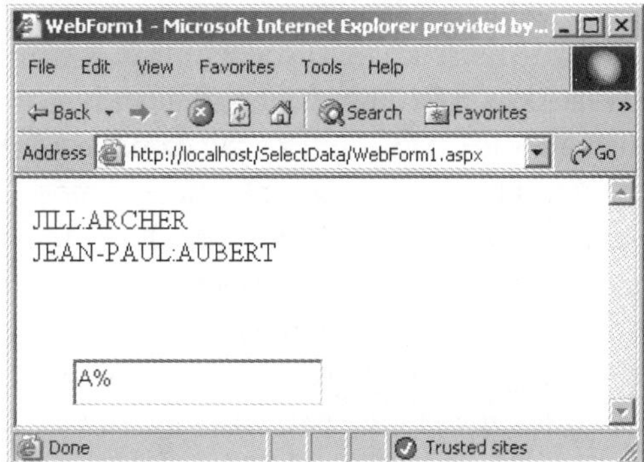

Figure D-3. Selecting rows using a DataTable Select

Programming with DataSet Objects

We have seen how to use DataTable and DataRow objects. Let's conclude this Appendix by looking specifically at the DataSet object. You can use a single DataSet to hold multiple DataTable objects. Figure D-4 shows how this can work:

The DataAdapter's `Fill` method can accept either a DataTable or a DataSet. When used with a DataSet, it actually creates a DataTable and inserts it into the DataSet with a specified name. For example, the code below uses two DataAdapters to create the structure shown in Figure D-4:

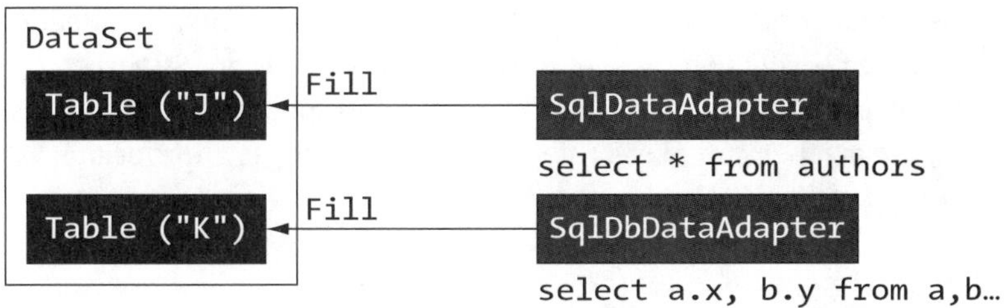

Figure D-4. Filling a DataSet with multiple DataTables

```
Dim ds As New DataSet()
da1.Fill(ds, "J")
da2.Fill(ds, "K")
```

Using a DataSet object allows a group of two or more DataTables to be treated as single unit. It's easy to extract the individual DataTables from within the DataSet, but at the same time it can be convenient to handle the DataSet as one object. Furthermore, ADO.NET allows you to create relationships between the DataTables within a DataSet, which can make navigating between DataTables much easier. We won't be discussing this aspect of DataSets in great detail because it's generally used in "rich client" scenarios, rather than in HTML-based applications (but you can find an example of this approach in Chapter 7).

The DataSet object model provides a sophisticated model for updating data. In reality, however, in those occasions where you're likely to use DataSets in ASP.NET applications, they will typically be used as read-only structures. As we will see, you are more likely to perform database updates by working directly with Command objects. For this reason, we won't be discussing DataSet updates in this Appendix, but we will return to the issue in Appendix F, which is designed to be read after Chapter 7.

Summary

This chapter has taken a first look at data access in the .NET world. It's impossible to understand ADO.NET without understanding the problems it has been designed to solve; to do this, we explored the distinction between connected and disconnected data. This distinction is expressed very clearly in the difference between the .NET Data Provider object model and the DataSet object model.

While at first sight it looks like DataSets and DataTables should be the objects of choice when writing ASP.NET applications, it actually turns out that in most cases, the data objects used in ASP.NET applications are typically very short-lived. Disconnected data objects (such as DataSets and DataTables) are only really of use when long-lived data objects are needed; therefore, DataReaders and Command objects will meet most of the data access needs of ASP.NET.

Nevertheless, disconnected objects are useful in specific circumstances, and we have seen how they can play a role when data caching is appropriate.

APPENDIX E

The Common Language Runtime

Managing Memory in .NET

Understanding Intermediate Language and Metadata

Locating Assemblies

THE OBJECTIVE OF THIS APPENDIX is to provide just enough information about how .NET's common language runtime (CLR) works, so that you're able to understand why certain development, administration, and deployment tasks need a fresh approach in the .NET world. The CLR is a bold and sophisticated processing engine and to do it real justice would require a whole book.

The CLR executes every line of VB .NET code for you. In this respect it's no different from the VB Runtime engine used by earlier versions of Visual Basic. However, there are two key things to know about the CLR:

- It's common to all .NET languages, and it processes the code generated by all .NET compilers in exactly the same way. VB .NET code is no less efficient than C# code and can do all the things that C# code can do.

- It does many more things than the VB Runtime used by VB 6.0. It also does some things differently from the VB Runtime, which can profoundly affect the code you write.

Because VB .NET code is no longer processed by its own runtime engine, some commentators claim it's no longer really Visual Basic. We don't give a hoot about this argument. VB .NET looks a lot like VB 6.0 and, generally speaking, is the correct way for existing VB developers to move into the world of .NET. However, you can't ignore some of the key aspects of how the CLR works.

Code executed by the CLR is called *managed code* because the CLR is able to provide certain system services (if required) for each line of code it executes to make sure the code doesn't do anything dangerous. The end result should be safer and more efficient code, with fewer bugs and runtime configuration problems.

Amongst the things that the CLR does for you is to make sure you never perform an illegal operation on an object (this is known as *type safety*). The VB 6.0 runtime does a reasonably good job of doing this, but it wasn't able to protect your code when calling Win32 API functions, for example. The CLR provides complete protection to all .NET languages, even when making calls to *unmanaged* code such as COM objects or API functions. It's able to do this because it knows about every method call you make.

Because the CLR is watching you (or at least, watching what your code does) Big-Brother fashion, it's able to apply tight security to your code. In a world where software is more mobile than ever before (such as code downloaded over the Internet) it's vital to be able to control the permissions that one piece of code has when calling another. Security is hard-wired into the guts of how the CLR works, and .NET promises to address many of the security holes that currently bedevil software and its users. We'll be discussing security as it applies to ASP.NET in Chapter 11. All we'll say for now on this topic is that if you're the type of programmer who has traditionally considered security as someone else's problem, think again. If you've written a piece of code that has access to any secret or sensitive information, and you make that code accessible to a Web Application or a Web Service, the only thing that gets between proper and improper use of that code is how you've secured it.

So, you've seen that the CLR can guarantee the type safety and security of VB .NET code. We want to discuss two other CLR services in more detail because they apply to everything you do in the .NET world. This first of these is how the CLR manages memory.

Managing Memory in .NET

Appendix C introduced the idea of garbage collection—the task that .NET performs to remove unwanted objects from memory when memory gets full. You saw that in VB 6.0, as soon as the last reference to an object is released, the object is immediately destroyed by the VB 6.0 runtime. You also saw that in .NET, things work very differently and the object may not be destroyed for some time after the object is released. We'll now expand upon this process and also explore its consequences in a bit more depth.

You can use Figures E-1, E-2, and E-3 to help understand how garbage collection works. For each step you can see a number of objects (obj 1, obj 2 and obj 3), each taking up space in the available object memory (known as the Heap).

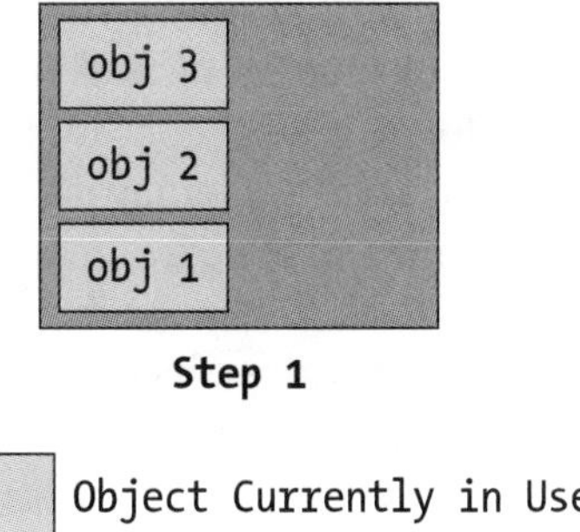

Figure E-1. Garbage collection: step 1

Just before step 1, obj 1 and obj 2 were the only objects that existed in memory. In step 1, when obj 3 is created, obj 3 is simply allocated the next available free space in memory (see Figure E-1).

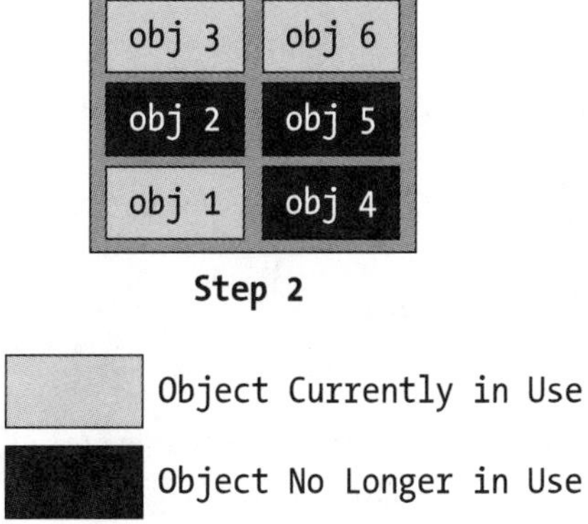

Figure E-2. Garbage collection: step 2

Between step 1 and step 2, obj 4 and obj 5 have been added, and obj 2, obj 4, and obj 5 have been released. It's quite usual in .NET to create an object and release it immediately, and therefore we're describing a common scenario. For example, strings are created on the heap in .NET, so if you create two strings and then concatenate them to create a new one, the two original strings are created and almost immediately released.

Just before Step 2, obj 6 is created, which takes up the last remaining space in the heap (as shown in Figure E-2). Now, obj 2, obj 4, and obj 5 have already been released by the program. However, the CLR doesn't do anything to memory when an object is released, it just leaves it in there. This policy leads to a problem that occurs when the program attempts to create obj 7. There's no room in the heap to create obj 7, so at this point, the CLR runs the garbage collector. The garbage collector walks through memory, looking for "unreachable" objects. Unreachable objects are those that can no longer be used because there are no programmatic references to them. The garbage collector removes unreachable objects and then rearranges all the objects that remain in the heap to create a large block of free memory for new objects (an operation called *defragmentation*). At the same time, it adjusts every reference to those existing objects that have been moved during defragmentation, to ensure that these references remain correct after the objects have been moved. Once this process is completed, it's now possible to create obj 7 and allow the program to continue running (Figure E-3).

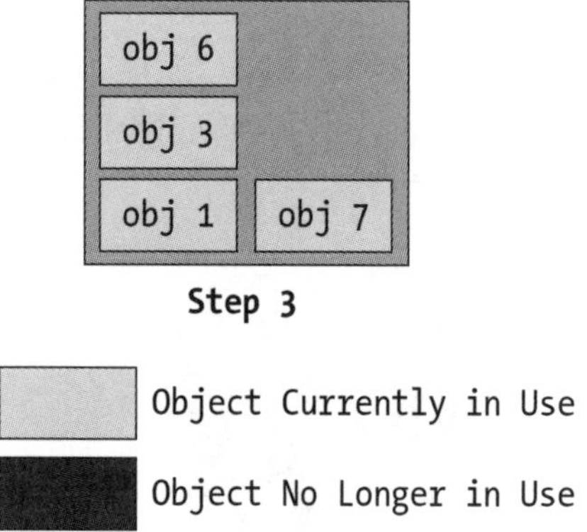

Figure E-3. Garbage collection: step 3

The garbage collection process just described is completely hidden from developers. The only thing you might notice is a slight delay while the garbage collector is running.

Of course we've massively simplified what really goes on but have provided almost enough information for you to understand what's happening. Garbage collection sounds complicated, and it sounds like it makes the execution of your programs more difficult to control. It so happens that there are many good reasons why .NET uses garbage collection. You may want to research it in more depth (and we would encourage you to do so), but for our purposes, we simply ask you to trust us that, on balance, it's a good thing.

A key question concerning garbage collection is: Can anything bad happen because objects are left in memory for what may be a long period of time after they're released? The answer to this is (as usual): It depends. If an object that has been left on the heap until the garbage collector runs contains only .NET data, then no harm can come of leaving it there. However, if the object is using some resource that the CLR can't directly manage, then serious problems can result.

Imagine you release an ADO.NET Connection object without closing it first. This object will live on the heap until the garbage collector runs, which may not be for minutes or even hours. While it lives there, it can't be used, and yet the physical connection to the database that it holds remains open, so it can't be returned to a connection pool. Each time your piece of code is executed the problem will get worse, until pretty soon, the database runs out of connections. The same kind of thing can happen (only worse) with resources such as file handles.

What all this means is that any .NET object that holds resources that exist outside the managed world of the CLR needs to be handled carefully before they're released. For objects such as ADO.NET Connections or DataReaders, this means calling the `Close` method before releasing the object. For many other .NET objects this means calling some other "cleanup" code before releasing the object, and by convention, .NET encourages object implementers to provide a method called `Dispose` for this purpose. `Dispose` is *not* called automatically by the CLR; if a `Dispose` method exists, the program that created the object is responsible for calling `Dispose` before releasing the object. Interestingly, the ADO.NET Connection object supplies both a `Close` method (old convention) and a `Dispose` method (new convention), and both do exactly the same thing (so you can call either). Should every object have a `Dispose` method? No, only those objects that hold onto system resources that exist outside of the CLR's control need a `Dispose` method.

It's possible to force garbage collection to occur when you want it by programmatically asking the CLR to run the garbage collector. In general, this isn't recommended—certainly not on an object-by-object basis. It's a bit like putting the dishwasher on just to clean a butter knife.

In looking around .NET you may have noticed that each object has a `Finalize` method, which looks temptingly like the `Terminate` event provided on all VB 6.0 objects that is often used to write cleanup code. Please don't take the Oscar Wilde approach here (a man who can resist anything but temptation). The `Finalize` method is called by the CLR during the garbage collection process, just before the object is actually destroyed. You have no control when this will be, so generally speaking you shouldn't rely on the `Finalize` method to clean up objects in a predictable way. Worse still, adding a `Finalize` method to an object seriously slows down the garbage collection process. There are correct ways of using `Finalize`, but in all honestly it's better to create objects that don't depend on `Finalize` being called, unless you're prepared to investigate the issue in some detail.

The good news is that in most ASP.NET applications, you're unlikely to write many objects yourself for which Finalization or even a `Dispose` method is needed. But you must remember to call `Dispose` (or `Close`) on any object that uses physical resources outside of .NET.

In summary, .NET manages object lifetime using garbage collection, rather than the reference counting approach using by VB 6.0 and COM. This means that objects don't actually get destroyed when you release them, and you need to worry about objects that make use of system resources other than the heap memory used by the CLR to hold .NET objects. Worrying simply means making sure that you call `Close` or `Dispose` on objects that provide these methods before you actually release them. If you write your own objects that hold system resources, you'll need to think about providing your own `Dispose` method.

Understanding Intermediate Language and Metadata

VB 6.0 produces compiled code, but VBScript is always interpreted. As a programmer, you probably know this means VBScript code executes much more slowly than compiled VB 6.0 code. .NET takes a different approach. When you *compile* a .NET program (for example, using the Build menu in Visual Studio .NET) rather than generate fully compiled binary code, the compiler generates what is known as Intermediate Language (IL).

IL is a bit like assembly language, except that it isn't targeted at any particular processor. Instead, it easily maps onto the binary instruction set of most standard processors. In fact, the claim you often hear about .NET supporting many different languages (a claim we made in Appendix B) is actually a bit of a cheat because .NET only really supports one language—IL. It just so happens that all .NET compilers generate IL, making it easy for components to interoperate, regardless of what language they were originally written in.

.NET compilers also have another responsibility. As well as being required to generate IL, .NET compilers are required to generate *metadata*. Metadata is simply a description of what the compiled program does. You may recall that when VB .NET code is compiled, the compiler generates an *assembly* that contains the code for the classes defined within a VB .NET project. We can now say more formally that each assembly contains both IL code for each class and also metadata for the entire assembly. There are actually two types of metadata produced. First, there's metadata about each class—the names of its methods and their arguments and so on. Second, there's metadata about the assembly as a whole, which contains the name of the assembly, its version number, and information about its dependencies (the other assemblies that need to be loaded for the current assembly to work). This second type of metadata is called the assembly's *manifest*.

To bring these ideas to life, let's create a VB .NET Class Library application called SmallLibrary. SmallLibrary will contain a single class, defined as follows:

```
Public Class SmallClass
    Public Function SayHello() As String
        Return "Hello Mum"
    End Function
End Class
```

When this trivial project is compiled, it'll create an assembly called SmallLibrary. This assembly will be contained in a file called SmallLibrary.dll. We can actually look inside this .dll by running a program called ILDASM.EXE, which is supplied as part of the .NET Framework. After starting ILDASM, you can use it to open SmallLibrary.dll. Figure E-4 shows you what the ILDASM display looks like.

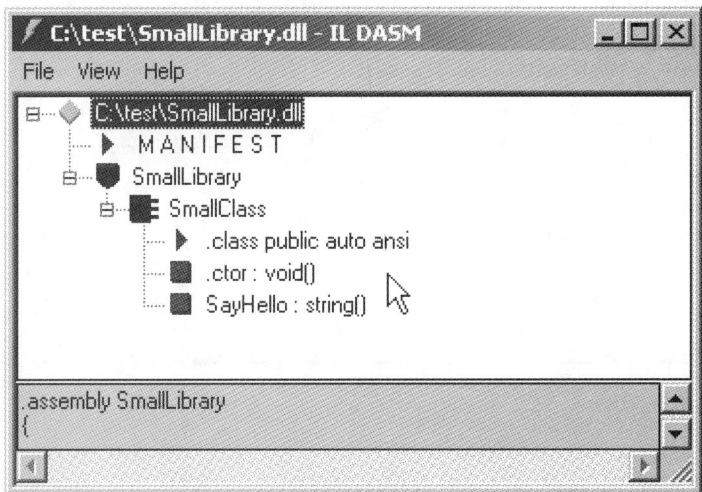

Figure E-4. Using ILDASM to display metadata

What you're seeing here is the metadata for SmallLibrary.dll in a graphical form. Specifically, you can see that this assembly contains a class called SmallClass, with a method called `SayHello` that returns a string. This is actually all you need to know to call this method successfully. You can also see that ILDASM allows you to access the manifest for this assembly.

By double-clicking on the `SayHello` method, you can display the IL code generated by the VB .NET compiler (see Figure E-5).

```
SmallClass::SayHello : string()
.method public instance string  SayHello() cil managed
{
  // Code size       11 (0xb)
  .maxstack  1
  .locals init ([0] string SayHello)
  IL_0000:  nop
  IL_0001:  ldstr      "Hello Mum"
  IL_0006:  stloc.0
  IL_0007:  br.s       IL_0009
  IL_0009:  ldloc.0
  IL_000a:  ret
} // end of method SmallClass::SayHello
```

Figure E-5. IL code

Don't feel you need to understand IL—that's a job for compiler writers. However, you can see enough to tell that this code does something with a string containing `Hello Mum`.

Now that you know what a *compiled* .NET program contains, take a look at Figure E-6, which shows the whole managed execution process.

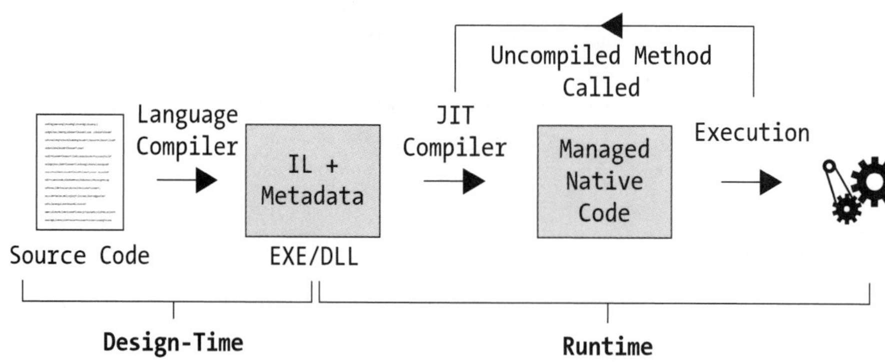

Figure E-6. The .NET managed execution process

At design-time, you compile your source code, which will produce an .exe or .dll file containing IL instructions and metadata (an assembly). When this file is loaded (by ASP.NET, for example), the CLR generates a pointer in memory to the

IL code for each method in each class contained in the assembly. The first time any method in the assembly is called, the CLR compiles the IL code for that method into binary instructions. It then stores this binary in memory and executes the binary code. The next time the same method is called, the CLR directly executes the binary. When another method is called, the CLR compiles its IL into binary code and then executes the method in the same manner. In other words, every time your assembly is loaded, the code for each method goes through a compilation step the first time it's called, after which it runs as fully compiled binary code. For most Web Applications, each method will be called hundreds or thousands of times, so the initial compilation cost is soon lost.

This process of compiling IL to binary only when it is needed is called *Just In Time compilation* (or JIT compilation).

When you create ASP.NET Applications using Visual Studio .NET, Visual Studio always compiles your code into a .dll file and the code runs exactly as described. However, it's also possible to place raw source files of VB .NET code onto your Web server and run these files as ASP.NET Web pages. In this situation, one further step is taken in addition to the process just described. ASP.NET runs the appropriate language compiler to generate an assembly using the code contained in the source file. That assembly (containing metadata and IL) then feeds into the managed execution process, as shown in Figure E-6.

It's important to know about IL and metadata, especially once you get into debugging and configuration. Tools such as ILDASM can help you find out what's really happening in a program, and you can't really make sense of how .NET applications fit together without having a good understanding of metadata and what it can do for you. It also helps to understand how managed execution works, although the main impact you'll see of the JIT process is that code runs a bit more slowly the first time it executes. Of course, if you've worked before with Java, none of this will be completely new to you.

Locating Assemblies

Shout out loud now if you love the Registry. The chances are that even if you're reading this in a public place, we won't be accused of disturbing the peace because every developer knows that the Windows Registry actually stinks. And yet every existing VB or classic ASP program relies on the Registry to help locate components used within an application. Every time you use the `CreateObject` function, or access components in VB 6.0 by setting a reference using the Add Reference or Add Component dialog boxes, your code relies on the Registry to locate the object you need.

The use of a machine-wide Registry to locate objects seemed like a good idea not that many years ago, but once you start installing many different programs on the same computer, there's a grave danger that they will overwrite each other's

Registry entries when others try to install different components that happen to have the same name, or more likely, different (and subtly incompatible) versions of the same component. You're almost bound to be familiar with the DLL Hell problems that result from the way COM uses the Registry and handles versioning issues. You might also be aware of the problems that the Registry raises for Web hosting companies. When applications created by different companies are all hosted on the same Web server, it becomes difficult to control security and robustness when all those applications rely on a central Registry to work.

It's therefore a good thing that .NET does not use the Registry when one assembly needs to locate and load another, but this fact raises the question: How does the CLR locate assemblies? It turns out there are two main techniques, based on two different types of assembly: private assemblies and shared assemblies.

Using Private Assemblies

Unless you go out of your way, all of the assemblies you generate in .NET will be private assemblies. As you'll see shortly, you need to take positive steps to create a shared assembly.

Unlike COM objects, which are available to all applications on the machine where the COM object is registered, .NET private assemblies are private to a single application. More specifically, a private assembly can only be called from an application if the assembly's .dll file exists either in the same directory as the application or in one of the application's subdirectories. This means you can have two assemblies with exactly the same name, containing identically named classes, but if they're stored in the file space of two different applications, they'll never interfere with each other.

When using Visual Studio .NET to create an ASP.NET Web Application, Visual Studio .NET places most of the files for the application in a directory that it creates for you on the Web server. These files include the .aspx pages that contain a Web page's graphical layout, and the .config files that specify how the Web Application has been configured (these files are explained in great detail in the main part of the book). However, all the application's code is compiled into a .dll and placed in the \bin subdirectory of the Application directory. ASP.NET is configured to look for private assemblies in a Web Application's \bin subdirectory, so Visual Studio .NET automatically creates a \bin directory and places private assemblies in it so they can be accessed. Should you choose to create ASP.NET Web Applications without using Visual Studio .NET, you need to be sure to configure the Web Application so that assemblies are stored within a \bin subdirectory.

By locating assemblies based on a Web Application's file space, rather than a global registry, .NET provides much greater isolation between applications and dramatically reduces the scope for DLL Hell. This is particularly good news for

Web hosts (and their customers) because by combining private assemblies with some of .NET's tight security features, it's now much easier to offer secure but flexible hosting of applications written by different organizations on the same Web server.

Using Shared Assemblies

Private assemblies are useful in many circumstances, but they're not a good idea for assemblies intended to be shared by many applications. ADO.NET is a good example. If System.Data.DLL (the file that contains ADO.NET) needed to be copied into the private file space of each application that used it, there would rapidly be a proliferation of copies of the same .dll, making upgrades a real headache.

For this reason, if you have an assembly that you know is going to be used by several applications, or maybe dozens of applications on the same computer, it makes sense to turn it into a shared assembly.

A private assembly has a simple text name, such as SmallLibrary. To create a shared assembly, you need to give an assembly a *strong name*. A strong name includes not only a simple text name but also some other elements. The most important of these are the following:

- **A formal identity**: To make sure your SmallLibrary assembly can be distinguished from anyone else's SmallLibrary assembly, you can attach an identity key to all your assemblies (or all your organization's assemblies) that make your assemblies uniquely identifiable as belonging to you (or your organization). .NET actually uses public/private key technology to create an identity for an assembly, and at the same time, it creates a digital signature for the assembly to make sure no one is able to tamper with it (for example, by replacing code that returns a friendly message with code that formats your hard disk).

- **A specific version**: A strong name contains a specific version number that can be set to change automatically each time an assembly is compiled. When a client program stores information about its dependencies (which you may remember is stored in its manifest), it also stores the precise version of each dependency it uses. As a result, a client program can be configured so that it always uses the version of an assembly that it knows it works with, ignoring any newer version that may contain unexpected bugs.

Strong names are actually quite easy to create, but we encourage you to read up on some of the details before launching straight in. Once you've created a strong name for an assembly, that assembly becomes a shared assembly, and it's possible to access the assembly from an application without needing to place it in the application's own file space (as required for private assemblies). In particular, shared assemblies can be placed in the *global assembly cache*. The global assembly cache (GAC) is a special location where the CLR will always look for shared assemblies before looking anywhere else.

You'll usually find the global assembly cache physically located at `C:\WINNT\Assembly`. At first glance, it sounds just like a new .NET location for the shared DLLs that often reside in `C:\WINNT\System32`, but there are important differences. If version 1 of xyz.dll is already installed in the GAC, and another application installs version 2 of xyz into the GAC, both versions will continue to exist there side by side. The same is true for two DLLs called xyz that have different identities (public keys) as part of their strong name. When a client program tries to load an assembly with a strong name, the CLR will look in the GAC for an assembly with exactly the same strong name, making sure the client gets the assembly it needs and not some other one that happens to have the same simple text name.

As with every topic discussed in these appendices, there's considerably more in the detail of how shared assemblies work than there is space to discuss in a book that's really about ASP.NET. Most of the assemblies you create will probably be private assemblies, but it's important to know what shared assemblies can do and the problems they solve.

Summary

You've seen that VB .NET code is managed code, executed for you by the CLR. The CLR provides a range of services, including type safety, security, memory management using garbage collection, and Just In Time compilation. We've also explored the main differences between private and shared assemblies and how the CLR locates them (which it does without using the Registry).

If you've read these four .NET appendices, you haven't learnt enough to be a .NET expert, but you certainly have enough background knowledge to start working with ASP.NET.

APPENDIX F

Updating DataSets

Writing Changes to a DataTable

Updating a Database One Row at a Time

Batch Updating a Database

UNLIKE THE FIRST FIVE APPENDICES, this one is intended to be read after reading material in the main text, rather than before. Specifically, this appendix picks up where Chapter 7 leaves off on the topic of DataSet updates.

With DataSets, you can either update the database one row at a time, or you can cache changes to a whole batch of rows in a DataSet, and then submit all these changes to your database in a single operation. Each approach has its strengths and weaknesses. We will explore both, but whichever approach you use, it's vital to understand that DataSet updating is a two-stage process: First you update the DataSet, and then you send changes in the DataSet to the database using a DataAdapter (Figure F-1). You must explicitly perform each of these steps before any changes will take place on your database.

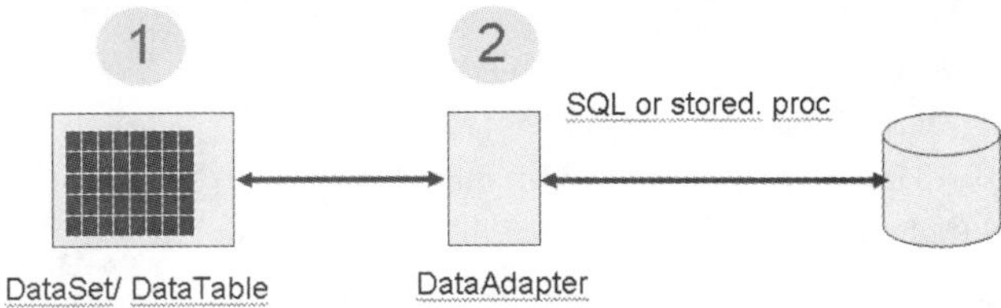

Figure F-1. Updating with DataSets is a two-stage process

In order to explore DataSet updating, we will extend the Bookings browser developed in Chapter 7 with some specific update capability. First, we will allow users to convert a reserved booking into a confirmed booking; then, we will allow bookings to be deleted. We will also briefly discuss the task of adding bookings. To make life slightly more simple, we will remove the sorting and filtering functionality developed in Chapter 7. The reason for this is that it will allow us to map the index of the row selected in the ListBox directly to a DataRow in the bookings DataTable. We have already discussed the task of identifying the correct DataRow in a DataTable; therefore, the extra layer of complexity that sorting and filtering add will only get in the way of understanding DataSet updating.

Please also bear in mind that in order to use DataSets for updating, you need ready access to a DataSet. In the case of ASP.NET Web Applications, this typically means storing the DataSet in Session state, which is not always something you will want to do.

We'll explore the process of turning reserved bookings into confirmed bookings via a DataSet that contains a DataTable of bookings made for a specific member of HiFlyers.

Writing Changes to a DataTable

The first stage of DataSet updating—the task of writing changes to a DataTable—is actually very easy. It largely concerns identifying the correct column in the correct row and assigning a new value. Here's the code that does this for a button that confirms a booking:

```
Dim ds As DataSet = CType(Session("Data"), DataSet)
Dim dt As DataTable = ds.Tables("Bookings")
'assume no filtering or sorting
Dim Row As Integer = lstBookings.SelectedIndex
Dim dr As DataRow = dt.Rows(Row)
'change the data here
dr("Status") = "CONFIRMED"
'call the Apply button code to re-build the list
btnApply_Click(Nothing, Nothing)
```

This is very simple stuff. Basically, once we have identified the correct DataRow, we assign `CONFIRMED` to its `Status` column—and that's it. It's worth pointing out that certain important things happen behind the scenes in the DataTable when you update a DataRow like this. First, each DataRow has an internal state tracking its history. When a DataTable is filled using a DataAdapter, each DataRow's state is set to "unchanged". Whenever a DataRow is modified, its state is set to "modified". Just as important, the DataRow remembers the original version of each value, as well as the current value based on any changes you make in your code. We'll get to see why this background work is so vital a little later.

The key thing to remember here is that changes made by this code are only stored in the DataTable; we have not yet done anything to send changes back to the database where it can be permanently stored.

The code required to delete a DataRow from a DataTable is equally straightforward:

```
Dim ds As DataSet = CType(Session("Data"), DataSet)
Dim dt As DataTable = ds.Tables("Bookings")
'assume no filtering or sorting
Dim Row As Integer = lstBookings.SelectedIndex
Dim dr As DataRow = dt.Rows(Row)
'delete the row here
dr.Delete()
'call the Apply button code to re-build the list
btnApply_Click(Nothing, Nothing)
```

After deleting a DataRow like this, you will no longer see it when looping through the DataTable. The DataRow is actually still there, but its state has been set to "deleted". The DataTable keeps track of a DataRow that has been deleted so that it can send an appropriate delete instruction to a database.

While we won't be developing a user interface to insert new rows, it's worth seeing how to do it, especially because it is just as straightforward as modifying or deleting a row. For example:

```
Dim ds As DataSet = CType(Session("Data"), DataSet)
Dim dt As DataTable = ds.Tables("Bookings")
'create a new DataRow
Dim dr As DataRow = dt.NewRow()
'add column values here
'..
'..
'then add the row into the DataTable
dt.Rows.Add(dr)
```

Here, we have called the `NewRow` method on the DataTable object to create a new DataRow object with all the correct columns in it. We then assign values to the columns in the new DataRow object before adding it into the DataTable using the `Add` method. The new row will have a row state of "added".

Admittedly, DataTables provide quite a bit more functionality for data manipulation than we have covered here; but, most of this additional functionality is aimed at using DataSets and DataTables in desktop applications, and is not generally very useful in Web Applications. If you want to know more, seek out a good ADO.NET book (such as *ADO.NET and ADO Examples and Best Practices For VB Programmers, Second Edition* by William Vaughn (APress)).

Updating a Database One Row at a Time

You must use a DataAdapter to transfer changes made in a DataTable into database updates. Typically, you will use the same DataAdapter that you used to create the DataTable in the first place. A DataAdapter has a handy method called `Update` that will do this work for you.

Most of the code examples you'll see concerning DataSets and updating describe only how to process multiple changes at a single stroke (often called 'batch' updating). We'll see how this is done shortly, but first we are going to explore how to perform updates for one DataRow at a time. There are two reasons for this. First, it will allow you to understand how DataSet updating works in a relatively simple scenario before going onto the conceptually more difficult task of batch updating. Secondly, you'll see that, in many ASP.NET Web Applications, the "row at a time" approach is often more useful. Batch updating is undoubtedly useful in rich client scenarios because it can deliver significant performance gains, but it is much less useful when the client does not have direct access to the DataSet. This is typically the case in Web applications and consequently there are no major performance gains to be had from batch updating. Nevertheless, for completeness, we'll discuss batch updates later in the appendix, and you'll see one situation in which they are very useful.

One way of performing updates using a DataAdapter is by passing it an array of DataRows that contains changes. In our case, we only want to update one DataRow at a time (for now), so our array will contain only one DataRow. Remind yourself of the functionality behind the Confirm button. Currently, this button only saves data into a DataTable; it doesn't write any changes back to the database. To go one step further, we would need to add the following code:

```
'create an array containing one DataRow
Dim drs() As DataRow = {dr}
da.Update(drs)
```

This code uses the unusual, but convenient, VB .NET syntax that makes use of braces ({}) to simplify the construction of an array. Once our DataRow is snugly tucked into an array, we can pass it to the DataAdapter's `Update` function. Easy. There is only one problem here—this code won't work. Instead, it will return the following error:

```
Update requires a valid UpdateCommand when passed
a DataRow collection with modified rows.
```

The problem here is that the DataRow doesn't know how to perform the update. In order to send changes back to the database, a DataAdapter relies on three properties called `UpdateCommand`, `DeleteCommand`, and `InsertCommand`. Each of these needs to hold a Command object containing the SQL needed to perform (in turn) an update, delete, or insert. When you call the DataAdapter's `Update` method, it simply looks at the row state for the relevant DataRow (now you can see why we had that discussion about row state earlier) and uses it to determine whether to use the `UpdateCommand`, `DeleteCommand`, or `InsertCommand` to send the changes to the database. In other words, the process of sending DataRow changes back to a database relies on identifying and executing the correct SQL for the task—and we haven't yet created the necessary SQL.

Not so long ago we said that, when using DataSets, you could send changes back to your database without needing to write the SQL yourself. That much is true, but you need to tell ADO.NET to generate the SQL for you, and you still have decisions to make about how and when the SQL should be generated.

The first decision you face is when the SQL is generated. You can either ask ADO.NET to generate the SQL for you at runtime or you can use Visual Studio .NET to generate the SQL (or stored procedures) at design-time. Let's look at the runtime approach first.

.NET Data Providers include a class called a CommandBuilder. You can use a CommandBuilder to generate the required SQL for updates, inserts, and deletes so that you don't need to do it yourself. Here's the same code, with the addition of a CommandBuilder:

```
'create a CommandBuilder
Dim cb As New SqlClient.SqlCommandBuilder(da)
'create an array containing one DataRow
Dim drs() As DataRow = {dr}
da.Update(drs)
```

I can almost hear you saying, Is that it? One line of code? Can we get on with it then? Well, it *is* only one line of code, and it *does* work, but there *are* catches. First, there is a performance catch. When you use a CommandBuilder it asks the database to return the information required for constructing the update, delete, and insert commands correctly. In other words, using a CommandBuilder involves a runtime cost of an extra hit on the database. The second catch is that you have very little control over exactly what SQL the CommandBuilder generates. There are other catches too, which we will return to later.

You can eliminate the performance overhead of an extra database hit and gain extra control over the SQL by asking Visual Studio .NET to generate the SQL for you at design-time. Cast your mind back to how we created the da DataAdapter in Chapter 7, and in particular, our use of the so-called "Advanced" SQL generation options we saw in Figure 7-16. At that time, we only wanted a read-only

DataTable so we unchecked all of the options on this 'Advanced' dialog. Now, however, we want to perform updates using the da DataAdapter; by choosing the correct option on the Advanced dialog we can get the correct SQL and Command objects written into our code at design-time, rather than using the CommandBuilder at runtime. All we need to do is to check the first checkbox in this dialog—the one called (reasonably enough) "Generate Insert, Update and Delete Statements."

Choosing this option will add quite a lot of extra code into the collapsed section of your code window. Specifically, it will create three Command objects—one for inserts, one for updates, and one for deletes—and assign these Command objects to the appropriate properties of the DataAdapter.

Take a look at the code that Visual Studio .NET generates just for the delete operation. We've pulled it together into a single lump of code and removed some of the namespace detail to make it easier to read:

```
Me.SqlDeleteCommand1 = New SqlCommand()
Me.da.DeleteCommand = Me.SqlDeleteCommand1
Me.SqlDeleteCommand1.CommandText = "DELETE FROM AircraftDiary" & _
        " WHERE (AircraftDiaryID = @Original_AircraftDiaryID)"
Me.SqlDeleteCommand1.Connection = Me.cn
Me.SqlDeleteCommand1.Parameters.Add( _
        New SqlParameter("@Original_AircraftDiaryID", SqlDbType.Int, 4, _
        ParameterDirection.Input, False, CType(0, Byte), CType(0, Byte), _
        "AircraftDiaryID", DataRowVersion.Original, Nothing))
```

This code creates a new Command object, assigns some SQL to its CommandText property, and assigns the whole Command object to the DeleteCommand property of da. It also adds a parameter into the Parameters collection of the Command object so that we can provide the primary key of the row we want to delete.

Take a close look at the last line of code listed here. The first two arguments on the last line specify data-binding information that takes data from a DataRow and writes it into one of the Command object's Parameters (and vice-versa). So far, whenever we've used parameter objects, we've had to provide the values for them in code that we write. This binding information removes this need. Here's what happens.

When Update is called on the DataAdapter, it inspects the array of DataRows it has been given, looking for any rows whose row state is anything other than "unmodified" (at present, we are only passing it an array containing one DataRow, so it doesn't have far to look). If the DataAdapter finds a DataRow whose row state is "deleted," the DataAdapter calls its DeleteCommand. The DeleteCommand uses the DataRow to locate the required parameter values automatically; the "AircraftDiaryID" argument in the code above specifies that the parameter value should be taken from the AircraftDiaryID column of the current

DataRow. Do you remember that a DataRow remembers both the current and original values for any changed data? The `DataRowVersion.Original` argument tells the DataAdapter to use the original value rather than the new one (in other words, if the primary key has been changed by mistake, the change will be ignored).

Deletes are fairly easy. The code generated for the update operation is more complex. (for one thing, it will require a parameter for each column). Here is a cut-down view of the code that the DataAdapter wizard generates for you (we know this is getting pretty grungy, but you need to see this, if only once):

```
Me.SqlUpdateCommand1.CommandText = "UPDATE AircraftDiary " & _
    " SET AircraftID = @AircraftID, DiaryDate = @DiaryDate, " & _
    "Status = @Status WHERE (AircraftDiaryID = @Original_AircraftDiaryID)"
Me.SqlUpdateCommand1.Connection = Me.cn
Me.SqlUpdateCommand1.Parameters.Add(New SqlParameter("@AircraftID", _
     SqlDbType.Int, 4, "AircraftID"))
Me.SqlUpdateCommand1.Parameters.Add(New SqlParameter("@DiaryDate",  _
    SqlDbType.DateTime, 8, "DiaryDate"))
Me.SqlUpdateCommand1.Parameters.Add(New SqlClient.SqlParameter("@Status", _
    SqlDbType.VarChar, 11, "Status"))
Me.SqlUpdateCommand1.Parameters.Add(New _
     SqlClient.SqlParameter("@Original_AircraftDiaryID", SqlDbType.Int, _
    4, ParameterDirection.Input, False, CType(0, Byte), CType(0, Byte), _
     "AircraftDiaryID", DataRowVersion.Original, Nothing))
```

You can see that the SQL takes four parameters and that four Parameter objects have been auto-generated. Note that while the last parameter (the one in the `WHERE` clause) uses the original value from the DataRow, the other parameters (the ones in the `SET` clause) use the current value from the DataRow. This way, the code ensures that the changes made to the DataRow are written back into the correct row in the database via the primary key for the relevant database table.

We can now remove the CommandBuilder code from the Confirm button because all the required Command objects are constructed in code generated at design-time by the DataAdapter wizard.

Let's summarize what we've seen so far. When you call `Update` on a DataAdapter, you can pass it an array of DataRows. We've passed an array containing just one DataRow. The DataAdapter will look at the status of this DataRow to determine which Command object to use for the update. Having selected the correct Command object, it binds the Command object to the DataRow and then performs the update. Once the DataAdapter has been set up with the correct Command objects, the process of updating any single DataRow is easy. Simply pass the correct DataRow to the `Update` method—the DataAdapter takes care of everything else.

There are still some potential problems with this code. It may be that since we built the DataTable, another user has been in and changed the live data in the database. For example, after we read a particular booking, another user may have changed the date for that booking (because the aircraft needs to be serviced, and service requirements are allowed to override reserved bookings). We are completely unaware of this change, and the danger exists that we confirm a booking for a date that is no longer available. This is the "concurrency violation" problem, and it applies to virtually all multi-user Web applications that use databases. If we want to ensure that we don't overwrite important changes, we need to adopt an approach that rejects our updates if the database record we are about to update has changed since we last read it.

Visual Studio .NET has an elegant and efficient solution to this problem. If you check the "Use Optimistic Concurrency" option on the Advanced SQL Options dialog, Visual Studio will generate a more complex SQL statement that only updates the database if the data has not been changed since you created your DataTable (and raises an error if the data has been changed by another user). We're not going to show you what this SQL looks like. You can easily try it yourself by setting the appropriate option; we have given you all of the necessary information to figure out how it works. What you'll see is that the optimistic concurrency approach adds extra checks to the `WHERE` clause for update and delete operations, so that the SQL will only locate the required database record if it still contains the same data that it had when the DataRow was created. We did a very similar thing manually in Chapter 7.

If concurrency violation is not a worry for you (and in some application designs it isn't), then you shouldn't check the "Use Optimistic Concurrency" option. While Visual Studio's solution *is* elegant and efficient, it adds complexity to your code and requires sending bigger SQL statements to your database; so, you should only use it if you need it (although unless you are absolutely sure you don't need it, the chances are that you do need it).

There's one other option that the Advanced SQL options provide, called 'Refresh the DataSet'. If you select this option, even more complex code and SQL is generated, which will slow down your program even further. This option will execute a `SELECT` statement for the current row after executing the `UPDATE`, `DELETE`, or `INSERT`, which will reread the data from the database. It's quite likely that you won't need to do this. This option is only necessary if the act of changing the database runs code in the database that makes further changes to the current row. This might be the case if you use database triggers. It will also be the case for inserts to tables with auto-increment primary keys. In all other cases, this extra complexity is entirely unwanted.

Unfortunately, the default action of the DataAdapter wizard—selecting all of these three options—makes your program run more slowly than it might need to. If you need the functionality that these options provide, then be sure to use them—they do a good job. But, if you don't need the functionality, switch these options off.

It's also worth noting that all of the examples I've shown you are based on dynamic SQL. We all know that stored procedures are more efficient than dynamic SQL; you can also have useful business logic built into stored procedures. Take another look at the DataAdapter wizard and you'll see that it has options for generating stored procedures for the insert, update, and delete Command objects, or for allowing you to hook up your own stored procedures. This is one of the really nice things about the ADO.NET approach—you can take as much control as you want. Taking control can be essential. For example, if you choose to build DataTables based on `JOIN` queries (rather than selecting data from only one table), then you can't use the features we've been describing that generate the SQL for you. Instead, you would have to hand code the insert, update, and delete Command objects yourself.

Batch Updating a Database

We've looked in some depth at how to update a database once a single DataRow has been changed. In many cases, this is a sensible approach to updating when working with DataTables and DataSets because many applications are designed to allow users to update data one row at a time. In such cases, it makes great sense to write these changes back to the database as they happen.

In other circumstances, either the user makes changes to multiple rows before posting back to the Web Application, or you have a need to store up several row modifications and process them as a single operation. In these cases, it can make sense to use the 'batch' updating capability of DataAdapters.

We'll explore this by changing the `SelectionMode` property of our Listbox control from Single to Multiple. This way, a user might select several bookings and then press the Confirm or Delete button. We can then process all of these changes as a single operation.

The code to do this is surprisingly simple:

```
Dim ds As DataSet = CType(Session("Data"), DataSet)
Dim dt As DataTable = ds.Tables("Bookings")
Dim dr As DataRow
Dim i As Integer
'assume no filtering or sorting
For i = 0 To lstBookings.Items.Count - 1
    If lstBookings.Items(i).Selected Then
        dr = dt.Rows(i)
        'change the data here
        dr("Status") = "CONFIRMED"
    End If
Next
```

```
'call the Apply button code to re-build the list
btnGetBookings_Click(Nothing, Nothing)
    'update the database
da.Update(dt)
```

The first part of this code gets a reference to the DataTable stored in Session state. The middle section loops through the Listbox identifying selected bookings and updating the corresponding row in the DataTable. The last line of code calls `Update` on our DataAdapter as before, but this time passes the entire DataTable to the DataAdapter. In this case, the DataAdapter will loop through all the DataRows in the DataTable, looking for DataRows whose state is anything but 'unmodified'. For each such DataRow, the DataAdapter selects the correct Command object, binds it to the DataRow, and executes the Command. Figure F-2 shows the general process.

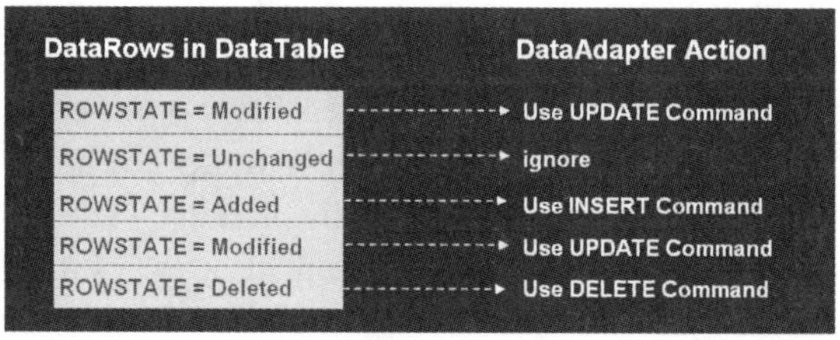

DataRows in DataTable	DataAdapter Action
ROWSTATE = Modified	Use UPDATE Command
ROWSTATE = Unchanged	ignore
ROWSTATE = Added	Use INSERT Command
ROWSTATE = Modified	Use UPDATE Command
ROWSTATE = Deleted	Use DELETE Command

Figure F-2. Batch updating with a DataAdapter

For readers familiar with batch updating in classic ADO, the ADO.NET model is very similar to what you already know.

One challenge with the batch updating model is that you need to decide what action to take when something goes wrong. Any one of the SQL statements could fail, leaving you in a situation where some updates have been successful while others have failed or aborted. This is particularly likely to happen when using optimistic concurrency because an error will be generated if any of the records being updated has been changed by another user. There are many ways to control this situation, and ADO.NET provides some very sophisticated options to choose between. The problem with most of them is that they demand very intricate programming.

One solution that is perfectly safe and easy to program is to wrap up the entire update process in a transaction. This way, if any update operation fails, you can roll back the whole transaction, leaving you in control and your database intact. You may recall from Chapter 7 that we discussed how to implement transactions using ADO.NET. We can reuse that learning to apply transactional control to the batch update process. In order to do this, we need to take control of the Connection object used by the DataAdapter. For the following example, assume that the optimistic concurrency option has been enabled, so that we might get errors if another user has modified our data. Here's the code for a transactional update:

```
Dim tx As SqlClient.SqlTransaction
Try
    cn.Open()
    tx = cn.BeginTransaction
    da.UpdateCommand.Transaction = tx
    da.DeleteCommand.Transaction = tx
    da.InsertCommand.Transaction = tx
    da.Update(dt)
    tx.Commit()
Catch
    tx.Rollback()
    lblError.Text = "Update(s) failed because " & _
                           "another user has been updating this data"
    lblError.Visible = True
Finally
    cn.Close()
    btnGetBookings_Click(Nothing, Nothing)
End Try
```

This code relies on the fact that `cn` is the Connection object used by all the Command objects associated with `da`. Having opened `cn`, a transaction object can be created, which must then be attached to all of the Command objects that will be used in the transaction (for the purpose of this operation, it is strictly only necessary to include the `UpdateCommand` in the transaction, but we've shown you what is needed in the more general case). Having set up the transaction, we then call `Update`. Normally, the `Update` method (like the `Fill` method) will open its connection, do its stuff, and then close the connection. However, if we call `Update` when the connection is already open, it will leave the connection open after the operation. This is important, because it allows us to control how the transaction should behave before the connection is closed.

If the `Update` succeeds, we commit the transaction and move on to the `Finally` block, which closes the connection and then reloads the data. If an error occurs (for example, due to a concurrency violation) we rollback the transaction and generate an error before moving into the `Finally` block.

Although the code we have shown you works, we have only really covered the basics of working with the DataSet object model. It would take another fifty pages to give the topic a thorough treatment, by which time we would have written an ADO.NET book and not an ASP.NET book. This should get you thinking. We've been able to cover pretty much all you need to know about working with .NET

Data Providers to write efficient and sophisticated applications, yet our treatment of the DataSet object model has only really been introductory. If you want to use DataSets to their full potential, be prepared to invest significantly more time after reading this chapter.

Summary

There are two ways to view DataSet updating. One is that it is very simple, because the tools do everything automatically. The problem with this approach is that it provides no way to deal with what happens when things go wrong, and it will typically end up with code that is far less efficient than it could be.

That said, it is true that when things work, the ADO.NET model makes life pretty easy. Our view is that you need to learn in detail how DataSet updating actually works (and we've given enough information in this appendix to do so). You can then let the tools do most of the donkey work for you, safe in the knowledge that you understand what they are doing for you, and how to take control of the process should you need to.

Index